GOD'S OTHER CHILDREN

God's Other Children

Protestant Nonconformists and
the Emergence of Denominational
Churches in Ireland, 1660-1700

RICHARD L. GREAVES

STANFORD UNIVERSITY PRESS

STANFORD, CALIFORNIA

Recipient of the Albert C. Outler Prize in
Ecumenical Church History, American
Society of Church History

Stanford University Press
Stanford, California
©1997 by the Board of Trustees of the
Leland Stanford Junior University

Printed in the United States of America

CIP data appear at the end of the book

Stanford University Press publications are
distributed exclusively by Stanford
University Press within the United States,
Canada, Mexico, and Central America;
they are distributed exclusively by
Cambridge University Press throughout
the rest of the world.

To
Stephany and Michael

Preface

In recent years a number of historians have contributed significant studies of Protestant religious developments in late seventeenth-century Ireland. Among them are Sean Connolly's *Religion, Law, and Power: The Making of Protestant Ireland 1660–1760* and Phil Kilroy's *Protestant Dissent and Controversy in Ireland 1660–1714*. Important too are Kenneth Carroll's studies of Irish Quakers, the work of Raymond Gillespie and John Neville on Irish Presbyterians, Marilyn Westerkamp's investigation of Scots-Irish piety, Helen Hatton's study of charitable giving by Irish Friends, Peter Brooke's sweeping survey of Ulster Presbyterians from 1610 to 1970, Audrey Lockhart's examination of Quaker emigration from Ireland to North America, and James McGuire's studies of the Convention and the restoration Church of Ireland. The present book, intended as a modest contribution to this field, grows out of my long-standing interest in the Puritan and nonconformist traditions in England and Scotland, and more recently my trilogy on British radicals in the period 1660 to 1689.

Of the religious groups studied in this book—the Scottish and English Presbyterians, the Congregationalists, the Baptists, and the Friends—only the Scottish Presbyterians had established themselves prior to the mid-century upheavals. The Congregationalists and Baptists arrived in the train of the English armies dispatched to quell the Irish rebellion. Neither group established firm roots outside the military and civilian republicans, and both therefore found themselves without an effective base after 1660. So too did the English Presbyterians. The Congregationalists and Baptists survived, but barely. In contrast, the Friends, whose work in Ireland commenced in 1654, crisscrossed the island in their search for converts and thus established a much stronger foundation on which to build in the later decades of the century. In addition to examining the internal history of these groups in the period from the restoration to the eve of the penal laws in the early eighteenth century, I have explored the relationship between the civil authorities and the established church on the one hand and the nonconformists on the other. The treatment of the latter theme in the first three chapters of this book is a much expanded outgrowth of a paper I read in April 1993 at a conference entitled "Principle and Pragmatism: Towards a History of the Church of Ireland." Sponsored by the Department of History at University College, Dublin, its organizers were Alan Ford, James McGuire, and Kenneth Milne.

Dates are given in the old style (which was ten days behind the new style used on the Continent); however, I have taken the year to commence on 1 January rather than 25 March, and I have used the traditional names of months and days when discussing the Friends. Quotations preserve the original spelling and capitalization, and the punctuation has been altered only when necessary to facilitate understanding. Contractions and abbreviations have been spelled out. I have not reproduced the often erratic italicization of the original materials. As a guide for the spelling of place names I have used *Census of Ireland: General Alphabetical Index to the Townlands and Towns, Parishes, and Baronies of Ireland* (Dublin: Alexander Thom, 1861).

For access to manuscripts and other rare materials I am indebted to the fine staffs at the following libraries and archives: Trinity College, Dublin; National Library of Ireland, Dublin; National Archives of Ireland, Dublin; Representative Church Body Library, Dublin (Raymond Refaussé and Heather Smith); Historical Library of the Society of Friends in Ireland, Dublin (Mary Shackleton); Marsh's Library, Dublin; Dublin Municipal Library, Pearse Street; Armagh Public Library (the Very Rev. Herbert Cassidy); Public Record Office of Northern Ireland, Belfast (D. M. Neill); Gamble Library, Union Theological College, Belfast (Doreen E. McDowell); Presbyterian Historical Society of Ireland, Belfast (Robert H. Bonar); Linen Hall Library, Belfast; Religious Society of Friends, Ulster Quarterly Meeting, Lisburn (George Stephenson); Irish Baptist Historical Society, Belfast (Dr. Joshua Thompson); Edinburgh University Library (John V. Howard); National Library of Scotland, Edinburgh; Scottish Record Office, Edinburgh; Bodleian Library, Oxford; Nottingham University Library (Dorothy B. Johnston); Public

Record Office, London; British Library, London; Library of the Society of Friends, London (Malcolm Thomas, Rosamund Cummings); Dr. Williams's Library, London; Haverford College Library (Elisabeth Potts Brown); Henry E. Huntington Library, San Marino, California (Mary L. Robertson).

I would like to express my gratitude to the American Society of Church History, which awarded this work the Albert C. Outler Prize in Ecumenical Church History.

I owe special thanks to the following people: William F. Bewley, Kenneth Carroll, Alan Ford, Ian Green, Eileen Groth, Paul Hardacre, Kevin Herlihy, James McGuire, Geoffrey F. Nuttall, Phil Kilroy, and Robert Zaller. Raymond Gillespie and Ted L. Underwood read early drafts of this work and offered much valuable criticism, as did Alan Ford, who read the manuscript in a more polished version. It is also a pleasure to thank my wonderful editors, Norris Pope and John Feneron. My wife Judith has been an invaluable research assistant and a perceptive critic. For their unceasing encouragement I am grateful as well to my daughters, Sherry Elizabeth and Stephany Lynn, and to my mother. This book is dedicated to Stephany and Michael, who were married in October 1995, with best wishes for a fulfilling, happy marriage.

This book also commemorates the victims of sectarian violence in Ireland in the hope that the forces of religion, working together in a spirit of ecumenicity, can effect a reconciliation that will provide a lasting foundation for peace and justice throughout the island.

R.L.G.

Contents

GOD'S OTHER CHILDREN

Introduction: Roots of Irish Nonconformity

THE 1640S AND 1650S were pivotal in the religious history of Ireland. After a century-long struggle to establish and extend a base on the island, the Church of Ireland suffered a severe blow at the hands of a revolutionary regime unsympathetic to its claims of religious monopoly. In Ulster the Scottish Presbyterians, their roots already planted, used these decades to develop an organizational structure and extend their popular base so effectively that they would withstand all subsequent attempts to enforce their conformity to the reestablished episcopalian state church. The English Presbyterians and the radical groups—the Independents (Congregationalists), Baptists, and Friends—seized the opportunity provided by a moderately tolerant regime to make forays in search of converts, though their success was largely limited to English men and women who had taken up residence in the island or had assignments there on a relatively short-term basis as administrators, officers, and soldiers. Efforts to convert the Gaelic Irish to any variety of Protestantism met with scant success. Indeed, the Protestants devoted more energy to internecine liturgical, theological, and polity disputes than to missionary endeavors. Nor were the Independents and Baptists effective in establishing a vigorous base outside the army, so that when the republican regime collapsed and command of the army reverted to royalists in 1660 the Independents and Baptists saw most of their support evaporate. Among the radicals, only the Quakers had been successful in establishing a reasonably effective base outside military circles, but numerically they remained small and, like other Protestants, minimally effective in winning converts among the Gaelic Irish.

After the restoration only the Scottish Presbyterians and the Friends were capable of sustaining a substantive challenge to the restored Church of Ireland, but the other groups continued to exist.

Of Sects and Denominational Churches

This book will argue that in the four decades following the restoration of the monarchy in 1660, the Friends and the Scottish Presbyterians in Ireland underwent an evolutionary process that by the turn of the century had transposed them into rudimentary denominations (or denominational churches). Despite beginning from strikingly different origins, the two groups had many common characteristics by 1700, the result largely of a shared experience of recurring persecution. This persecution, it will also be argued, was primarily the result of security considerations on the part of the government and ecclesiastical and ideological concerns on the part of leading Church of Ireland clerics. Unlike most prominent episcopalian clergymen the government was often inclined to adopt a relatively tolerant position with respect to the nonconformists. The clergy must therefore bear the brunt of the responsibility for espousing and defending a persecutorial policy.

At the outset of the restoration period the Scottish Presbyterians and the Quakers in Ireland were fundamentally dissimilar. In sociological terms the Scottish Presbyterians embraced a vision of and a program for a national church that would displace the episcopalian state church, whereas the Quakers were a sect—an ideological movement and "a self-consciously and deliberately separated religious minority" intent on maintaining and propagating distinctive tenets. The earliest Friends manifested characteristics of two of the basic sectarian types identified by the sociologist Bryan Wilson, namely the thaumaturgical, because of their profound emphasis on the experiential workings of the indwelling Spirit, and the revolutionary, because of their hostility to the contemporaneous social order and their belief in rapid conversion. After the restoration the Quakers slowly changed, retaining their thaumaturgical traits but damping their revolutionary fervor. Still, they were a long way from becoming an introversionist sect in the eighteenth century, as described by Wilson, when, he avers, they withdrew from the world to emphasize personal holiness and became indifferent to social reform.[1] As we shall see, however, during the last decades of the seventeenth century they began enforcing stricter standards of behavior, dress, and home furnishings that highlighted their separation from certain aspects of traditional society.

The Irish Quakers' unmistakable attempt to preserve their distinctive identity was in fact a deliberate effort to retain what sociologists would call their sectarian status in the face of their evolution into a denominational church. The Friends' virtually obsessive behavior with respect to simple dress and home furnishings was a rearguard action—a protest against what Armand Mauss and Philip Barlow have described as the "transition from high tension to low tension with the host society." In one important respect the Irish Quakers deviated from the typical pattern depicted by Mauss and Barlow, according to which new sects "typically begin in a state of high tension with their host societies and culture; that is, they promote ideologies, requirements, and life-styles among their members that are noticeably different from those of the surrounding normative environments."[2] The Friends accentuated their differences in the late seventeenth century in reaction to their emergence as an institutional church and their growing acceptance—socially and economically but not theologically or ecclesiologically—by other groups in Ireland.

Under the largely common experience of persecution in the late seventeenth century the Quakers and the Scottish Presbyterians essentially became protodenominations (or denominational churches) even while continuing to manifest certain sectarian attributes. For the Scottish Presbyterians this entailed the practical recognition of their inability to impose their ecclesiastical program on the Church of Ireland and their consequent acceptance, however grudgingly, of *de facto* sectarian status in the 1660s. They became a sect in the sense that they were "a separated body of believers" that protested against the clerical authority of the Church of Ireland and to a limited degree against the Stuart regime that enforced it. Like the Quakers, the Scottish Presbyterians were a voluntary body that accepted members according to clearly articulated criteria, maintained a strong sense of self-identity, laid claim to be the defenders and propagators of supernatural truths, and demanded allegiance to themselves as opposed to competing religious groups.[3] Taken collectively, these are sectarian traits, and all were present among both Scottish Presbyterians and Friends in restoration Ireland, yet alongside these characteristics there developed others that increasingly altered the nature of both groups.

The contention of this book that Scottish Presbyterians and Friends in Ireland evolved into protodenominations by 1700 obviously depends in part on how "denomination" is defined.[4] Some sociologists see the distinction between sect and denominational church fundamentally in terms of degrees of zealousness or eschatological outlook, with the sect likely to espouse an adventist eschatology and a revolutionary fervor (unless it has retreated to quietism as a result of its disillusion with the world). Such interpreters depict denominations as moderate in their perspective and less confrontational in their relationship with the world.[5] Other specialists frame their interpretation in institutional terms. The church historian David Thompson, for example, posits that denominations typically have one or more of the following attributes: common origins, a common founder, a common theology or program, and a common adherence to certain institutions.[6] Both of these approaches are too narrow and do not sufficiently demarcate a sect from a denominational church.

A more satisfactory understanding of sect and denomination has been propounded by Bryan Wilson, who sees the distinction largely in terms of degree. "Denominationalism [entails] the loosening rigour; the loss of the sense of dissent and protest; the reduction of distance from other Christians; and the muting of claims that the sect's distinctive teachings are necessary for salvation." The process of denominationalism is impeded if sectaries believe that divine intervention in world affairs is imminent or that evil can be avoided only by withdrawal into a sanctified community, but it is enhanced by the vigorous and successful recruitment of new members, which creates the need for someone, such as professional ministers, to nurture them in the ways of their new faith. A key element in the evolution of a sect to a denominational church is thus the acquisition of a professional (paid, ordained) ministry or, in groups that reject ordained clergy on theological grounds, a body of administrators. Because groups evolving from sects into denominations repudiate religious coercion (as did the Quakers) or lack the political means to implement it (as did the Scottish Presbyterians in Ireland) they rely on "devices that were intended to induce regularity, sustain commitment, promote education, and encourage systematic endeavour." As we shall see, both the Friends and the Scottish Presbyterians in Ireland employed such devices. Wilson also contends that "an important facet of a sect's shift towards denominationalism is the steady relinquishment of the pristine rigour of its theology and ideology" as it becomes more concerned with "claiming parity of status with other denominations in a culturally pluralist tradition" than with the uniqueness of its claims to truth.[7] But the development of culturally pluralist traditions is a later historical occurrence, and we cannot therefore expect to find such a shift in outlook in late seventeenth-century Ireland. We can appropriately speak of the emergence of protodenominations by 1700 while simultaneously recognizing that denominational churches underwent additional changes, some of them substantive, as they continued to evolve in subsequent centuries. The concept of denomination is not static but fluid.

As a sect evolves into a denomination it acquires those characteristics typically associated with a church, taking the latter term in its sociological rather than its theological sense. Essentially the process of denominational evolution is one of rationalization as a religious community develops institutional means to preserve its traditions, propagate its ideals, nurture its converts, and sustain its veteran members. This organizational structure is not unitary but, as Mark Chaves has contended, dual and parallel. A denomination comprises both an institutionalized religious authority and an agency structure. The former is "a social structure that attempts to enforce its order and reach its ends by controlling the access of individuals to some desired good, where the legitimation of that control includes some supernatural component, however weak."[8] This was true of both the Scottish Presbyterians and the Friends in Ireland by 1700. The agency structure consists of organizational units that engage in specificic activities for the denomination, such as educating young people, collecting and disbursing funds to relieve the needy or ransom captives, or censoring manuscripts and then supervising their publication and distribution. Again, such organizational units were present among the Scottish Presbyterians and Quakers in Ireland by the turn of the century.

Whereas a sect is relatively open to fresh "revelations," a denominational church has a stronger, more vital sense of its past and a greater commitment to preserve its historic traditions. Consequently a sect is much more likely to be responsive to new trends or "revelations" introduced by charismatic leaders, but this is not to say that such leaders are essential to the founding or the continuation of a sect, as the early history of the Baptists demonstrates.[9] A denominational church has a more complex structure than a sect, is less easily altered in its organizational structure, and has provisions for the training and vetting of its leaders, whether formally ordained or not. Denominational churches develop a multiregional network of ministers or leaders who move between local units, fostering a greater sense of common ideals and purposes. Typically the denominational church establishes its own schools.

Although discipline is important for both sects and denominational churches, the latter have a more structured disciplinary system with which to enforce the distinctive values, tenets, and life-style which they espouse.

Moreover, denominational churches, unless state-supported, construct their own houses of worship, raising funds as necessary from areas well beyond that of a local congregation. In fact, such is a denominational church's fund-raising apparatus that it can collect money to assist needy congregations or members at home or abroad (as when Irish Friends aided their English Friends) or others in need, such as persecuted Huguenots on the continent or Europeans held in captivity by Muslims. Such systems of fund-raising were necessary for churches that either did not believe in or were excluded from the traditional system of mandatory tithing.

Finally, while both sects and denominational churches can range from authoritarian to libertine, a sect's ability to sustain its existence requires a greater degree of cohesion and the authority to maintain it, as George Fox realized when he and his supporters struggled to suppress the John Story-John Wilkinson faction. In contrast, the more established a church, the greater latitude it can tolerate owing to the complexity of its institutional structure and the strength of its historical roots. The process of rationalization thus provided a safeguard against the danger of atomization. In general, the more developed the organizational structure and historical roots, the greater the denominational church's ability to contain within itself disparate doctrinal, ethical, and behavioral strains. In the early stages of denominational development we can therefore expect to see greater attention to theological "purity," as in fact was the case with Scottish Presbyterians and Quakers in restoration Ireland.

This study will further argue that Phil Kilroy, whose study of theological controversy in late Stuart Ireland is invaluable, errs in averring that nonconformists survived because of firm leadership and the loyalties of families which originated in Ireland during the Interregnum or immigrated after 1660.[10] Although both of these factors contributed to nonconformist survival, neither would have mattered had the Scottish Presbyterians and Friends not developed effective organizational structures and a pronounced sense of their historic identity and the importance of their traditions. Indeed, the Friends had leaders such as William Edmondson and Anthony Sharp, and the Scottish Presbyterians had Patrick Adair and Thomas Gowan (among others), but the Congregationalists had Samuel Mather and Thomas Harrison, the Baptists Richard Lawrence and Jerome Sankey, and the English Presbyterians Daniel Williams and, for a time, John Howe. English Presbyterians, Congregationalists, and Baptists did not dramatically decline in Ireland because they lacked firm leaders, nor is there evidence to prove that families in these religious communities were disloyal to their convictions. This study will therefore focus primarily on structural and historical elements and the religious life that invigorated them rather than theological controversy in explaining why only two of the five nonconformist groups survived in appreciable numbers.[11]

This study will also explain why English Presbyterians, Congregationalists, and Baptists failed to survive in Ireland to any appreciable degree. Theological issues were virtually irrelevant to the question of survival. Although Kilroy avers that each group had its own "particular theology,"[12] in fact the Scottish Presbyterians, the English Presbyterians, and the Congregationalists were proponents of the Reformed tradition and disagreed on no substantive theological issue until the English Presbyterian Thomas Emlin espoused Socinian tenets, for which the Dublin presbytery expelled him in 1702. The English and Scottish Presbyterians did assert different positions with respect to their relationship with other groups, some English Presbyterians professing a willingness to worship in the episcopalian Church of Ireland and others effectively merging with the Congregationalists notwithstanding professed differences in polity. In this regard the English Presbyterians in Ireland behaved like their counterparts in England. Particular Baptists were also disciples of the Reformed tradition, but the advocacy of believers' baptism by all Baptists set them apart from other religious communities, in Ireland as elsewhere. The Friends, who rejected an ordained ministry, the sacraments, and Reformed tenets, were theologically distinctive,[13] but neither they nor any other group sustained measurable decline in Ireland as a consequence of doctrinal warfare.

The English Presbyterians, the Congregationalists, and the Baptists experienced nearly catastrophic decline in Ireland after 1660; by way of contrast, around 1715 there were 179,000 Presbyterians, 60,000 Congregationalists, 40,000 Particular Baptists, and 19,000 General Baptists in England (approximately 5.3 percent of the population).[14] In Ireland the Congregationalists (Independents), it will be argued, made the strategic mistake of allying themselves with a relatively small group of civilian republicans in the 1650s, and when the latter's political fortunes collapsed, the Congregationalists proved unable to establish a self-sufficient, deeply rooted organization that could maintain their ideals and garner significant numbers of new recruits. Much the same fate awaited the Irish Baptists, who had linked their cause in the 1650s to military radicals. The English Presbyterians in Ireland also suffered because they had allied themselves with Henry Cromwell's regime, but they might have survived more effectively had they devoted the 1660s and early 1670s to establishing a vigorous oganization. Instead their adherents drifted in opposite directions, some toward the Congregationalists, others toward the Church of Ireland, not unlike their compatriots in England, where hopes of comprehension within the established church continued in some circles throughout the period, the failed attempts of 1666–1667, 1680, and 1689 notwithstanding. In Ireland persecution—or the threat of it—was most effective in dealing with the English Presbyterians, some of whom, as in England, found limited conformity less objectionable than *de facto* independency. In contradistinction, the Scottish Presbyterians in Ireland, aided by their sense of national identity, their relatively compact geographical base, their earlier organizational work, and their socially unifying tradition of festal communions, maintained far greater cohesiveness. The unity of the Scottish Presbyterians was disrupted in Ireland only by a small but noisy group of militant Covenanters who professed the ideals of a church but in most respects manifested sectarian attributes, as did their parent group in Scotland, variously known as the Cameronians or United Societies. Apart from these militants, the Scottish Presbyterians in Ireland enjoyed greater cohesiveness than their colleagues in Scotland, where the government's indulgence policy had a very divisive impact on Presbyterians.

The Setting

Demographic patterns reflect the impact of war and revolution in seventeenth-century Ireland. The island's population had increased dramatically from 1.4 million at the end of the Elizabethan age to 2.1 million at the outbreak of revolution in 1641. Three decades later the population had declined to 1.7 million, from whence it rose to 2.17 million on the eve of the revolution of 1688. Notwithstanding the depredations of the ensuing war, the population reached 2.8 million in 1712, thus roughly doubling itself in approximately a century.[15]

Irish towns increased at an even faster rate, providing an excellent opportunity for Protestant groups to establish solid bases. In the 1640s

Dublin, despite having grown rapidly from a population that numbered a mere 5,000 in 1600, was still smaller than Edinburgh, which had between 20,000 and 30,000 residents. In the quarter century after 1660 Dublin's populace more than doubled, rising from 25,000 to perhaps as many as 60,000, making it second in size in the islands only to London. By 1685 Cork had surpassed 20,000 whereas Limerick and Waterford were still small, at 5,000 each.[16] Towns in Ulster had even fewer inhabitants. Derry doubled its population between 1659, when it had 1,052 residents, and 1685, as apparently did Belfast, which numbered 589 in 1659 and between 1,000 and 2,000 35 years later. The other towns of note in Ulster were Carrickfergus and Coleraine, where populations in 1659 were 962 and 633 respectively. Armagh and Lisburn trailed at 409 and 357.[17]

Immigration was the principal cause of the upsurge in population. An estimated 10,000 Scots emigrated to Ireland in James VI's reign and a comparable number followed in the ensuing quarter century. Immigration slowed in the 1660s owing to economic stagnation and a rather inhospitable religious climate, though a 1662 statute encouraged Protestant immigration and enticed French, Dutch, and German settlers. The pace of immigration quickened after 1670, with some 35,000 English immigrants arriving in the ensuing fifteen years, many of them to work in the woolen industry. Another wave of immigration occurred in the 1690s, when 4,000 to 5,000 Scots crossed the North Channel each year, attracted by the low cost of Irish land.[18] But between 50,000 and 100,000 people *left* Ireland in the seventeenth century, approximately three-fourths of whom were Catholics from the southern part of the island. Many of the others were probably Protestant conformists. Ulster Presbyterians and Friends began departing in significant numbers in the 1680s and 1690s, though James Froude's depiction of the "fatal emigration of Nonconformist Protestants from Ireland to New England" is overstated. By 1715 approximately 27 percent of the population was Protestant of one variety or another.[19]

When William Petty surveyed the population of Ireland in 1672 he estimated that eight-elevenths of the people (800,000) were Catholic, and that a third of the 300,000 Protestants were Scottish Presbyterians; his figure for Scottish Presbyterians, however, was greatly exaggerated. "The only parts of Ireland where the Number of Protestants exceeded the Papists," observed an anonymous author in 1690, "were the Northern Counties," in which Protestants were so numerous "that they became a Terror to their Irish Neighbours, and were for that reason believed to have been thrice as many, as they afterwards appeared to be."[20] The Catholic archbishop of Armagh, Oliver Plunkett, complained in 1679 that Presbyterians were so numerous in his area that one could travel 25 miles without finding six Catholic or conformist families. At Templepatrick, county Antrim, in the late 1660s few or none attended the parish church except the parish clerk according to a government agent. Among those alarmed by the growing numbers of Scottish Presbyterians in Ulster was Arthur Capel, earl of Essex, who, as lord lieutenant, informed the earl of Arlington in October 1673 that 80,000 to 100,000 Scotsmen were capable of bearing arms.[21] This was a greatly exaggerated figure, though it reflected the government's concern. In 1639, when English planters made up perhaps half of Ulster's Protestant population, the province was home to 10,000 adult Scottish males. Two decades later, according to Philip Robinson, 26,000 English and Scottish people lived in Ulster, as did nearly 45,000 Gaelic Irish. The heaviest Protestant concentrations were in counties Antrim (45%), Derry (45%), and Down (43%), followed by Armagh (35%), Donegal (28%), Fermanagh (25%), and Monaghan (11%). Not surprisingly, Protestant strength was greater in the towns: Coleraine (74%), Belfast (62%), Derry (54%), and Carrickfergus (51%). In contrast, Armagh was 55% Catholic. The religious consequences of these demographic developments were significant. By the end of the century the descendants of the adventurers and the Cromwellian troops had severely dwindled. The earl of Clarendon told James II and VII in 1686 that "not twenty families and no great number" of former soldiers or their descendants remained in Ireland. Karl Bottigheimer estimates that of the 35,000 soldiers the government had wanted to settle on the island, perhaps only 7,500 remained—with some 500 adventurers—by 1670. In contrast, the Ulster Scots established themselves so firmly that their politico-religious influence remained strong for more than three centuries.[22]

The ability of the English to achieve similar success was undercut by their fragmented ecclesiastical and political loyalties as well as the shifting religious allegiances of Ireland's governors, especially in the 1650s. Shortly after the Gaelic Irish revolted in October 1641, the Old English, firmly Catholic, joined them in a confederacy. Although Protestants opposed the confederates, the former were split among supporters of Charles I and adherents of the parliamentary cause. Nevertheless, apart from many Protestants in Ulster, they shared a common religious bond. This unity, grounded in the Calvinist Articles of 1615, had been temporarily disrupted by the earl of Strafford and his chaplain, John Bramhall, bishop of Derry, in the late 1630s, but Strafford's dramatic fall in 1641 enabled most Protestants to rally in support of the established church. The collapse of the royalist cause in England in the second civil war prompted royalist forces in Ireland to ally with the confederates. By that point many Irish Protestants had thrown their support to Parliament because of religious considerations; others now followed suit despite their distaste for the radical Protestantism espoused by elements of Oliver Cromwell's forces.

As in England significant alterations in the established church antedated Charles's final defeat. In Ireland the first such changes occurred in 1647 when parliamentary forces substituted the Directory of Worship for the Book of Common Prayer in Dublin. Two years later the government extended these changes to the rest of the country. Never, however, did Parliament enact an ordinance to this effect or one to abolish episcopacy in the Church of Ireland. Instead, throughout the 1650s the basis for such policies rested on instructions from London to the governors of Ireland. Apparently anticipating an act of union that would have brought the Church of Ireland into conformity with its English counterpart, the Rump contented itself with increasing the endowments of Trinity College, Dublin; dispatching six ministers to Dublin in 1650; and offering financial incentives to ministers who accepted assignments in Ireland.[23]

The government shaped religious policy in the period 1649 to 1660 primarily with reference to the competing positions of the various Protestant groups. The first of these were the adherents of the traditional Church of Ireland, who were strongly represented among the landowners and whose clerical members had to choose between the loss of their positions and participation in a nominally reformed state church deprived of its episcopal hierarchy and Book of Common Prayer. More than 65 clerics opted for the latter course and served the Cromwellian regime.[24] The second group, the radical sectaries, though divided among themselves on numerous issues of theology and polity, generally shared a conviction that the Gaelic Irish were, in Christopher Hill's words, "part of the international forces of Antichrist" whose subjugation was essential to prevent reactionary, pro-papal forces from restoring the monarchy and a persecuting episcopal establishment.[25] The zenith of sectarian influence in Ireland occurred during the administration of Charles Fleetwood (July 1652 to September 1655).

Following the establishment of the Protectorate Cromwell became concerned about Fleetwood's close relationship with the Baptists, some of whom were political radicals. Yet a Dublin observer played down Baptist discontent with the new regime:

As to the grand affaires of Ireland especially as to the anabaptist party, I am confident they are much misconceiv'd in England, truely I am apt to beleeve that uppon the change of affaires, here was discontent enough, but very little animosity, for certainly never yet any faction so well fortified by all the offices military & civill allmost in the whol nation did quitt theyr interest with more silence.

The incarceration of several radicals for alleged plotting and the publication of libels "caused such a general compliance, that should a stranger arrive here now he would never beleeve there had been any difference."[26] Taking no chances, Cromwell dispatched his son Henry to assess the political situation. Although the latter's report criticized Fleetwood's affinity with the Baptists, Oliver, eschewing a confrontation, named Fleetwood lord deputy in August 1654 and left him in charge of Ireland for another thirteen months. In the meantime Henry received an appointment to the Irish Council and command of the Irish army. When Fleetwood returned to England in September 1655, Henry was well positioned to assume the reins of power. For a year he sought a reconciliation between the competing parties, but the Baptists, most of whose support was in the army, resisted his efforts to balance military and civilian influence and pressed for Fleetwood's return. Henry finally struck back, reducing or terminating the salaries of some Baptists and transferring others to remote posts. His victory culminated in November and December 1656 when the principal Baptist officers in Ireland, William Allen, Daniel Axtell, Robert Barrow, and John Vernon, resigned their commissions.[27]

Faced with the intransigence of the sectarian radicals, Henry Cromwell initially turned to the moderate Independents led by Dr. Samuel Winter, but they became disenchanted with his rule when he courted Presbyterians and moderate episcopalians. In 1658 the Independents allied with the Baptists in opposition to Cromwell's administration. By this point he had forged alliances with the Ulster Presbyterians and the Munster-based party of Dr. Edward Worth. Through the agency of Sir John Clotworthy, in November 1655 Cromwell established a *modus vivendi* with many Ulster Presbyterians, giving some of them government salaries and an opportunity to solidify and extend their base of power in the north. The following year he attempted to establish a Scottish Presbyterian congregation in Dublin by offering the church of St. Catherine's to John Livingston, but the latter refused.[28]

In Munster, Worth, who had been dean of Cork and still enjoyed widespread support among Protestant settlers, founded an association of area clergy in 1657. Concerned initially with the ordination of ministers, Worth intended the association as the first step in establishing a national church that would impose uniformity. The association maintained ties with English Presbyterians at a time when Winter and his colleagues were linked to such prominent Independent opponents of the Protectorate in England as John Owen and Hugh Peter. Not surprisingly, Henry Cromwell found in Worth a kindred spirit as well as a political ally. Both men favored a formally ordained parochial ministry, tithes, paedobaptism, and a structured system of discipline. In the face of Winter's opposition, Worth championed the restoration of tithes at a convention of twenty ministers in Dublin in 1658. When seventeen of the other clerics supported tithes, Worth reported optimistically to Cromwell: "There is such a uniting spirit breathed forth among those presbyterians that they said with one accord they could freely close with the Congregationall Brethren on the termes humbly presented to your Excellencie by the Dublin Convention." But both sides then appealed to supporters in England, and Winter, emboldened by the encouragement of English Independents, organized his own association of ministers in Dublin and Leinster (see below). Protestantism in Ireland, never united, now presented the specter of two rival associations.[29]

During the protectorship of his brother Richard, Henry Cromwell became lord lieutenant, but the restoration of the Rump the following year led to his replacement by Edmund Ludlow in June 1659. Henry's fall opened the way for the return of political and religious radicals to power in Ireland. Having learned nothing from their earlier political mistakes and sectarian infighting, the Baptists were cool to the idea of cooperating with the Independents. Largely discredited, the radicals commanded little support. In December a cabal of ten officers seized Dublin Castle in a bloodless coup, subsequent to which they turned over power to Major-General Sir Hardress Waller. The new administration enjoyed widespread backing among Protestant landowners, including Sir Charles Coote and Roger Boyle, Lord Broghill. Two months later, in February 1660, Coote and Colonel Theophilus Jones mounted a campaign to support the return of excluded members to the English Parliament. Opposed to this plan, Waller unsuccessfully attempted to arrest Coote and then briefly seized Dublin Castle. His defeat signaled the collapse of the republican movement in Ireland. Lord Caulfield captured the radicals' mood when he wrote to Coote from Charlemont:

"Before I came down, the Anabaptist party were very high, and spake big words, being confident of a sudden change for their advantage: but now they are more dejected than ever." The council of officers and their civilian advisers ordered elections for a Convention that met in March 1660 and would, before its dissolution in May, explore an Erastian presbyterian polity akin to that favored by Worth's association. The eight clergymen appointed to advise the committee for the maintenance of ministers provide another indication of the relatively broad spectrum of religious opinion in the Convention: Among them were the Ulster Presbyterian Patrick Adair, the English Presbyterian Samuel Cox, the moderate Independent Stephen Charnock, and the episcopalian Thomas Vesey. Although the Convention included supporters of episcopacy and recognized the surviving bishops, the restoration of episcopal polity was fundamentally Charles II's decision. His return to the throne and the restoration of the traditional church marked the culmination of "that great Hurricane, that overturn'd both Church and State."[30]

Early Presbyterians in Ireland

The roots of the Presbyterian movement in Ireland reach back to the 1610s, when two Scots-Irish prelates, Robert Echlin, bishop of Down, and Andrew Knox, bishop of Raphoe, granted several Scottish clerics freedom to conduct their ministerial vocation despite having been deprived by bishops in Scotland for nonconformity. Several ministers, including Josias Welch, grandson of John Knox, came to Ireland at the invitation of James Hamilton, Lord Clandeboye, a territorial magnate in county Down. In at least two cases Bishops Echlin and Knox tailored ordination services to satisfy the presbyterian scruples of the ordinands, one of whom, John Livingston, professed that he "was from [his] infancy bred with an aversion to episcopacy and ceremonies." Another was Robert Blair, who accepted Echlin's suggestion that he be ordained as a presbyter rather than a priest in 1623. Altogether, fifteen nonconforming ministers, thirteen of whom came from Scotland, took up pastoral duties in eastern Ulster between 1613 and 1625. Properly, these men were nonconformists rather than Presbyterians, for they were not organized in presbyteries, nor, with the exception of Blair, is there evidence they espoused the church's independence from civil power.[31]

In 1624 or 1625 the Church of Ireland witnessed the commencement in Ulster of what came to be known as the Six-Mile-Water revival, the instigator of which was a powerful, intellectually suspect, and apparently neurotic preacher, James Glendinning. Appalled by Glendinning's sham intellectualism, Blair persuaded him to leave his parish at Carrickfergus for a rural church at Oldstone. Dropping his practice of citing works he had never read, Glendinning terrified his new hearers with a gospel of divine wrath. When Glendinning proved incapable of responding to his audiences' plaintive cries to show them the path to salvation, John Ridge, the minister at Antrim, organized a monthly lecture, featuring a Thursday-evening sermon followed by three or four more sermons on Friday. In addition to Blair and Ridge, the principal ministers participating in the revival, which lasted until 1631, were Clandeboye's nephew James Hamilton of Ballywalter, Robert Cunningham of Holywood, and, after his arrival at Killinchy in 1630, John Livingston. While they were gathered together for the revival, the ministers discussed their pastoral work, but these meetings were unlike presbyteries because they did not impose discipline on wayward members. Peter Brooke has depicted these men as pioneers of the "privy kirk" movement in Scotland, wherein nonconformists exercised ministerial duties, often as itinerants; preached to mammoth outdoor conventicles in defiance of the authorities; and stressed repentance and piety rather than the imposition of discipline. While there is some truth in this attribution, the Irish revival occurred under the watchful but not disapproving eye of James Ussher, archbishop of Armagh, whereas outdoor conventicles in Scotland, especially after 1660, were firmly opposed by the prelates. Not until1632, by which time the revival had spread throughout eastern Ulster as far afield as Shotts and Stewarton in western Scotland, did Irish bishops suspend the principal nonconforming clergy. Even then, Blair successfully defended them of the charge of treason before Charles I and they regained their livings.[32]

These early nonconforming ministers in Ireland are typically referred to as Presbyterians. Left to their own devices they might have erected presbyterian polity, but this they could not do, and in fact they ministered within the parameters of a tolerant episcopalian system. This toleration ceased following the appointments of William Laud as archbishop of Canterbury and Thomas Wentworth as lord deputy of Ireland in 1633. As part of his attempt to attain greater uniformity between the established churches in England and Ireland, Wentworth persuaded the Irish Convocation in 1634 to adopt the theologically broad-based Thirty-nine Articles, though Convocation did not repeal the Calvinist Irish Articles of 1615. Convocation also approved new canons in 1634; refusal to subscribe them or the Thirty-nine Articles rendered a cleric subject to legal prosecution. Despite his previous will-ingness to accommodate nonconformists, Bishop Echlin deposed Blair, Welch, and George Dunbar of Ballymena and Larne in 1634. Two years later Echlin's successor in the see of Down, Henry Leslie, deposed Liv-ingston, Cunningham, Hamilton, Ridge, Edward Bryce, and Samuel Row. The same year John Leslie, bishop of Raphoe, deprived Robert Pont of Ramelton, and in 1638 the High Commission in Dublin removed David Kennedy of Newtownards. Unaware that Cunningham had died in Scotland in 1637, the High Commission summoned him five weeks later, fined him £20 when he failed to appear, and seized his widow's estate as security.[33]

Instead of producing the desired uniformity, the repression of the 1630s exacerbated religious differences to the point of creating rival ecclesiastical organizations in the early 1640s. Differences between non-conformists and conformists were not a major issue for planters in the early decades of the century. Bishop Bramhall complained in 1634 that landlords sheltered dangerous nonconformists because they "merely wanted to plant their lands and cared for nothing else." In fact, the articles of the Ulster plantation stipulated conformity to the established church, and in areas where colonization was well advanced before the arrival of nonconformity the latter made relatively little headway. The regions most subject to nonconformist influence were those in close proximity to Scotland and those in which Scottish settlers were pre-dominant, notably counties Antrim, Down, Derry, Donegal, and Ty-rone. Bramhall complained to Laud in 1638 that his diocese was "in the midst of Scotch colonies, and two-thirds planted with them." The sig-nificance of the Scottish link was vividly manifest in 1639 when Went-worth, responding to the Scottish National Covenant of the previous year, attempted to impose the so-called Black Oath, requiring all Protes-tants over sixteen years of age to renounce the Covenant and pledge never to oppose royal commands. Those who refused were subject to fines as high as £5,000 and imprisonment, forcing some to emigrate to Scotland.[34] The latter, at least, were not subjected to danger when the Gaelic Irish rebelled in the fall of 1641.

The arrival of a Scottish army in 1642 to quash the rebellion set the stage for the establishment of formal presbyterianism in Ireland. The army's five Presbyterian chaplains organized the soldiers into congre-gations with sessions, and then, at Carrickfergus on 10 June 1642, they convened a presbytery. As word of this development spread through-out Ulster, lay people requested ministers to preach and administer the sacraments. Presbyterians established sessions at Antrim, Ballymena, Ballywalter, Bangor, Carncastle, Carrickfergus, Comber, Dervock, Donaghadee, Holywood, Killyleagh, Larne, Newtownards, Portaferry, and Templepatrick. The immediate problem was finding ministers, for by the eve of the rebellion Wentworth had driven every nonconformist clergyman in Ulster from his living. Responding to a request from the Carrickfergus presbytery, the general assembly of the Kirk of Scotland dispatched supply ministers to serve brief periods of duty until peace was restored. Among them were Blair, Livingston, and Hamilton. This system was operative until 1648, by which time resident clergymen were in place. Among the earliest were John Baird, the first moderator of the Carrickfergus presbytery, who became pastor at Derrykeighan in 1646 but also preached in Belfast, and Hugh Peebles, the presbytery's first clerk, who was installed at Dundonald and Holywood in 1645. Two of the other five chaplains, John Aird and John Scott, returned to Scotland, but the fifth, Hugh Cunningham, became the minister at Ray. Throughout this period the Scottish army assisted the Carrickfergus presbytery in deposing conformist clerics.[35]

The increasing radicalization of the revolution had a significant impact on Presbyterians in Ireland. Not only were the Scots on the losing side in the second civil war but their relationship with the ensuing republican government was severely complicated by that section of the Solemn League and Covenant in which they had sworn "to preserve and defend the King's Majesty's person and authority." One option was to renounce the Solemn League and Covenant, as Viscount Montgomery of the Great Ardes did. Another was to condemn outright the execution of Charles I, as the presbytery did in *A Necessary Representation of the Present Evils and Eminent Dangers to Religion* (1649). Late the following year the Presbyterians in Scotland split into two groups: the Resolutioners, who were loyal to Charles II as a covenanted monarch, and the Remonstrants, whose detestation of the Stuarts prompted them to cooperate with the republican regime.[36]

The introduction in 1650 of the Engagement Oath, which required the renunciation of Charles Stuart's "pretended title" and the Stuart dynasty as well as a pledge of loyalty to the commonwealth, intensified the Presbyterians' plight. All but six ministers in Ulster lost their livings; some clergymen went to prison and others fled to Scotland. In 1653 the council of war determined that recalcitrant ministers and their congregations should be transplanted to Kilkenny, Tipperary, and Waterford, but the government never implemented the plan, probably, as

Toby Barnard suggests, because of objections from prominent landowners concerned primarily with profits. The plan seems to have been less an attempt to intimidate or destroy the Presbyterians than a security measure to separate the Presbyterian communities in Scotland and Ireland, perhaps with the intent of increasing the latter's dependence on civilian authorities.[37]

During the oppressive years of the Commonwealth few Presbyterian services were held in Ulster, but they resumed in 1654 in the more moderate climate of the protectoral regime. The Presbyterians now divided the presbytery into three "meetings"; these were not initially intended to be presbyteries, for they could neither conduct trials of ministerial candidates nor ordain them. They could, however, handle disciplinary cases referred by congregations and temporarily license preachers until the presbytery convened. The three meetings were Antrim, Down, and Route (northern Antrim, northeastern Derry, and originally northeastern Donegal and northwestern Tyrone). In 1657 Presbyterians carved the Lagan (Laggan) meeting, centering on the Foyle basin in Donegal and northeastern Tyrone, out of Route, and two years later the Tyrone meeting was formed out of Down. These meetings occasionally convened together in a "general presbytery," in effect a synod.[38]

When the exiles returned from Scotland, the danger of a bitter conflict between Resolutioners and Remonstrants was substantial. This could easily have sparked a schism between Lagan and Route, whose four ministers, including Hugh Cunningham and William Semple, were Remonstrants, and the other meetings. To avert a split, delegates at Bangor in 1654 resolved to avoid disputes about the division in the Kirk of Scotland, but the tensions continued into the next century.[39]

The Irish government endeavored to establish close ties to the Remonstrants by providing them with stipends. In the spring of 1654 Cunningham, Semple, James Wallace, Thomas Drummond, and two other ministers received salaries ranging from £40 to £100. Other ministers held back, insisting on their right to receive tithes, but when Clotworthy failed to persuade the council of their case in the spring of 1655, they agreed to accept stipends owing to the poverty of their congregations, the absence of conditions attached to the salaries, and the rationalization that the money was rightfully theirs. By year's end the government had authorized fourteen ministers to receive £100 *per annum* and a fifteenth £60. The government added an additional clergyman to the civil list the following May. Their number included such prominent ministers as John Greg, Andrew McCormack, William Jacque, and Patrick Adair, each of whom would play a significant role in the restoration era.[40]

The government's attempt to conciliate the Presbyterians met with mixed reactions. On hearing that Greg had been appointed minister of the Carrickfergus church, the town's governor, the Particular Baptist Thomas Cooper, protested to Henry Cromwell that no Scottish clergyman should be allowed in Ireland unless his loyalty to the government was assured, and Cooper additionally recommended that no Scot be permitted to reside in Carrickfergus, Derry, Coleraine, or Belfast for security reasons. Belfast, in fact, had no Presbyterian minister in the 1650s, though many were in the region; the government paid stipends to two ministers in Belfast, the episcopalian Essex Digby and the Baptist William Dix. Suspicion of Presbyterians resulted at least in part because they neither discouraged royalist activity nor acknowledged a duty to support the regime.[41]

The Presbyterians' coolness toward the government did not prevent them from cooperating with it or seeking its assistance. In June 1658 John Hart appealed to Henry Cromwell on behalf of a Presbyterian congregation at Raphoe where the "prelaticall pairtie" disrupted the deacons as they collected money for the poor at the church door, assaulted the elders, and bound over the latter to the assizes for having exercised discipline. Hart also complained he was the target of opprobrium for having reported scandalous and inadequate ministers in the diocese of Derry. Hart and Semple persuaded the government to grant William Keyes a stipend of £140 *per annum* to preach at Strabane. The government also displayed some sensitivity to the needs of parishioners, as when it transferred William Jacque to Clongesh, county Longford, after its inhabitants and the neighboring parishes complained of "their deplorable condition (for some years past) through the want of the public ordinances of Jesus Christ, by the means of a godly & faithful minister."[42]

The Presbyterians benefited substantially from the improved relations with the government that commenced in 1654, for they used the ensuing years to solidify and broaden their work. The records of the Antrim meeting indicate some of the ways in which this was accomplished, perhaps the most significant of which was visitation. In October 1654 Adair, Anthony Kennedy, Thomas Hall, and two elders visited the church at Broadisland, heard Robert Cunningham preach, and then asked the members about the soundness of his doctrine, his "painefullnes in catecheising, visiting of families and sick persons, and how they were satisfied with his lyfe and conversatisoun, with his impartiallity in discipline &c." After receiving satisfactory responses, the visitors queried Cunningham about the elders' "faithfullnes and painfullnes in theire calling, their mutuall concurence in discipline, there unanimity with him, and amongst themselves." The Antrim meeting also concerned itself with ministerial supply: At Clotworthy's request it invited James Durham of Glasgow to accept the pastorate at Antrim, and at the behest of Major Hugh Montgomery it assigned David Buttle to supply Maghera on a temporary basis. When Greg informed the meeting that Livingston had returned to Ireland from Scotland, it resolved "to study all lawfull reasons" to persuade him to remain in the country. The meeting also monitored the plans of the parishioners of Drummaul, county Antrim, to construct a new meetinghouse, and wrestled with the enigma of resolving cases of probable adultery and fornication when one of the parties wanted to deny the charge under oath; it submitted the latter issue to the general presbytery for resolution.[43]

Another important facet of the Antrim meeting's work was the appointment of fast days. These were observed for a variety of reasons, including unseasonable weather, disregard for the gospel, and "the abounding of filthynes, drunkenes, and Covetousnes in the Common Multitude." In November 1657 the Antrim meeting offered an elaborate rationale for a fast: (1) the "unfruitfullnes" of most people despite the availability of gospel ordinances; (2) abuse of former fasts and failure to honor vows; (3) abundant "gross" sins, such as sexual promiscuity, inebriety, pride, malice, and swearing; (4) sabbath abuse, including the neglect of spiritual duties before and after public worship by masters of families; (5) disobedience and disrespect by children and servants, and imprudent dealing with such persons by parents and masters; (6) declining fellowship among the godly; (7) treating one's personal affairs in higher regard than those of Christ; (8) "the plague of hyrlings and men unsent of God to preach the gospel, which hath beene and may prove a snare to the people through their inadvertencie and simplicity"; and (9) hope that God would avert judgments and instead "enlarge and establish the freedome of the Gospel in the land."[44] The range of subjects suggests that Presbyterians kept watchful eyes on everything from the behavior of the godly and the profane to the state of the ministry and the activities of other religious groups.

In sum, a profoundly significant transformation occurred between 1610 and 1660. In the 1610s and 1620s nonconformists rather easily found accommodation in the Church of Ireland, but by the late 1650s the Presbyterians had established a rival ecclesiastical organization that would refuse to capitulate to demands for religious uniformity after 1660. This dramatic change transpired in part because of Wentworth and Laud's religious policies, the Scottish army's introduction of a formal presbytery in 1642, and the close links between Ireland and Scotland. But the Commonwealth government nearly eradicated formal presbyterianism in the early 1650s, and had it not been for the desire of Henry Cromwell's regime to ally with Ulster Presbyterians, the latter might not have recovered in sufficient time to pose a serious challenge to the restored Church of Ireland. Instead, by 1660 Ulster had 74 Presbyterian parishes, 69 of which were in counties Antrim, Down, Derry, Donegal, and Tyrone.[45]

Although Presbyterians, including some who were English, were concentrated in Ulster, some—mostly English—lived elsewhere in Ireland. Among the most prominent was Francis Roberts, a chaplain to Henry Cromwell and a divine who had preached a fast sermon to the English Parliament in December 1646 (later published as *A Broken Spirit*, 1647). Roberts obtained the living of St. Werburgh's, Dublin, probably in 1656. Of all the ministers in Ireland in the 1650s who were on the civil list, only the Independent Dr. Thomas Harrison received a larger stipend (£300) than Roberts's (£250). Another influential Dublin Presbyterian, Samuel Cox, had become the pastor at Athlone in 1655 before moving to St. Catherine's in the capital two years later. In the Dublin area the Westmeath native William Lecky, who had been educated at Trinity College, Dublin, became the minister at Dunboyne, county Meath, in 1655 and two years later moved to a parish in his native county. Still in the Dublin region, James Levingston assumed pastoral duties at Finglas in 1657. The Scot William Jacque moved from Aghadowey, county Derry, where he had been ordained in 1655, to Clongesh in 1659 and acquired the additional living of Rathcline, also in county Longford, the following year. Jeremy O'Quin, the pastor at Billy, Antrim, was to have moved to Athy, Queen's County (Laois) in 1654, but he was still in Billy three years later. The following year he preached in Irish in Connaught but apparently returned to Billy before his death in 1657.[46]

Other Presbyterian clergy were undoubtedly at work in Leinster, Munster, and Connaught. Some were presumably like Mr. Squire, who ministered to a Presbyterian church in Limerick in the 1650s but did not receive a stipend; his congregation worshipped in St. Peter's Cell, an old Augustinian nunnery. Other Presbyterians must have been among the more than 200 ministers about whom St. John Seymour had insufficient information to attach a denominational label. Many of them may have embraced presbyterian polity and liturgy in the 1650s and then conformed at the restoration. Such men probably composed the bulk of Worth's Cork Association. In a letter to Henry Cromwell in 1656, Justice John Cooke described Worth, Joseph Eyres, and their colleagues as "classical Presbyterian ministers," though the primary reason for their organization, as we have seen, was not the espousal of a particular ecclesiastical polity but the closure of ranks in defense of formal ordination. Presbyterians participated with Independents in Winter's Dublin and Leinster Association, the principal purpose of which was to forge unity based on common theological tenets despite divergence over polity.[47] These associations were the earliest significant instances of ecumenical activity among Protestants in Ireland.

The Arrival of the Independents

The first Independents in Ireland were probably chaplains in the army of Philip Viscount Lisle, who left England in February 1647 for his second tour of duty. Two years later, other Independents, including John Owen, accompanied Oliver Cromwell to Ireland. By the fall of 1651 Dublin had at least five Independent congregations, the oldest of which may have been that to which John Rogers began ministering in 1650 in Christ Church. His congregation attracted leading Cromwellian officers, such as the city's governor, Colonel John Hewson. No less prominent was Samuel Winter's congregation at St. Nicholas's church, where the aldermen worshipped. Other Independent congregations met at St. Michan's, where John Murcot was pastor, and St. Thomas's, the minister of which was Thomas Huggin, who in 1653 would serve as a chaplain in Hewson's regiment. John Bywater, who subsequently moved to Ulster, likewise preached in Dublin in 1651. Timothy Taylor, who was at Carrickfergus by October 1651, undoubtedly had some of the garrison's troops in his congregation. By the following year Thomas Jenner was preaching to a mixed congregation of Independents and Presbyterians in the Drogheda garrison, and he would later serve at Carlow (1658) and probably at Limerick (1656). Again in 1652, James Wood was the pastor of an Independent church at Youghal, as was Edward Wale at Waterford.[48]

The administration of Charles Fleetwood, an Independent, was conducive to the continued growth of the movement. Winter's son, Samuel junior, was at Clondalkin, county Dublin, in 1654. The following year found Edward Veal at Dunboyne, Roger Muckle at Carlow, Nathaniel Brewster at St. Andrew's in Dublin, and Stephen Charnock ministering to several of the capital's congregations (St. Patrick's and St. Kevin's in July, St. John's in September, St. Catherine's in October, and St. Werburgh's in November).[49]

Because the demand for ministers greatly exceeded the supply, Henry Cromwell's government actively recruited clergymen. The moderate Independent Thomas Goodwin acted as his agent in England, using a recruiting list that Cromwell himself provided. John Spilsbury, a member of Richard Baxter's Worcestershire Association, declined to move to Ireland because he was, explained Goodwin, "greatly engaged to a people, a Very Great people in England." Mr. Wotton, who would be ejected from a Herefordshire living at the restoration, was seemingly willing to go to Ireland; presumably he was not the Henry Wotton who had been ministering at St. Audoen's, Dublin, in December 1652. Another potential recruit would not commit until he knew where he would be assigned, having heard of "some discouragements" from ministers who had gone to Ireland. Among those who arrived in the Cromwellian period was Edward Baines, who became an assistant to Robert Chambers at St. Patrick's, Dublin, in 1656, and minister of St. John's, Dublin, two years later. Another was Jeremiah Marsden, who preached at Armagh and Carlow in 1657. Henry Cromwell's efforts won acclaim from religious centrists in England. The Independent minister George Griffith, who knew of Cromwell's achievements through Harrison, told Henry "you do Rejoyce the very souls of Many here." John Gauden, one of the most prominent preachers during the revolution, reported to Cromwell in May 1658 that "the renown of your Lordships goverment, with such piety, justice and clemency, as gives life and recovery to that state of Ireland, which was lately languishing & dying, This . . . hath made marry your Lordships admirers."[50]

A request for ministers from New England had been made to John Cotton in August 1651, and Cromwell's council renewed the invitation in March 1656. Some pastors, such as Peter Bulkeley and John Davenport, declined, but Edmund Weld went to Kinsale and was at Bandon by the fall of 1655, the same year John Millard took up duties at Passage, near Waterford. Dr. Thomas Harrison, who had ministered in Virginia and Massachusetts before returning to England, went to Ireland as one of Henry Cromwell's chaplains and in 1655 became the Sunday morning preacher at Christ Church, Dublin, with a salary of £300 *per annum*. Samuel Mather had also been in New England before returning to England, where he served as chaplain of Magdalen College, Oxford, and ministered at Leith in Scotland before accepting an appointment as preacher to the Irish council and lecturer at Christ Church, Dublin. In December 1656 he became the senior Winter's co-minister at St. Nicholas's. Mather's brother Increase left New England to preach at Magherafelt and Ballyscullion, both in county Derry, in 1657.[51]

The Independents' base in Ireland was largely limited to the English army and the circle of civilian officials and their followers who administered the country in the 1650s. Never did they effectively penetrate the old Protestant landowning class or acquire a popular base akin to that of the Ulster Presbyterians. The results might have been different had the interregnum government lasted a full generation and had the Independents avoided a disastrous split with their centrist allies in the later years of Henry Cromwell's administration. The Independents' opportunity to influence the future course of religion in Ireland increased substantially when Winter, a graduate of Emmanuel College, Cambridge, became provost of Trinity College, Dublin, in September 1651. During his tenure the fellows of Trinity included, at one time or another, Samuel Mather and Edward Veal. Cromwell wanted Charnock to accept a fellowship at Trinity, but this he could not do without resigning as fellow of New College, Oxford, which he found unacceptable.[52] Given time, Trinity might have become an influential Independent seminary to staff the Protestant churches of Ireland, at least in Leinster, Munster, and Connaught.

When Henry Cromwell came to Ireland, Winter rallied Independents to his support, in effect mortgaging their future by tying it to the success of Cromwell's administration. Winter was undoubtedly influenced by his brother-in-law, John Weaver, a member of his congregation, a parliamentary commissioner in Ireland in the early 1650s, and, as a prominent proponent of civilian authority, a political enemy of Sir Hardress Waller and John Lambert. At Winter's instigation, Cromwell became the chancellor of Trinity College in 1655, but in the ensuing years the two men drifted apart as Cromwell broadened his base of suport by seeking allies among conservative Presbyterians and moderate episcopalians such as Edward Worth. After Weaver returned to England, Winter developed a close relationship with William Steele, who had come to Ireland in September 1656 as lord chancellor. Steele and Cromwell dueled in the council, the former favoring toleration for all the godly, a policy now opposed by Cromwell. When Steele failed to block Cromwell's appointment as lord deputy in November 1657 and Worth decisively bested Winter at the Dublin Convention the following year (as discussed earlier), the Independents sustained a nearly fatal political defeat. They enjoyed a brief Indian summer in 1659, but even then they were unable to establish a stable alliance with the Baptists.[53] The Independent movement, which had come to Ireland in the train of an English army, had tied its fate to the political fortunes of a narrowly based circle of civilian republicans, whose demise in late 1659 effectively doomed the Independents' opportunity to become a major religious force in Irish history.

The Baptists in Cromwellian Ireland

Like the Independents, the Baptists came to Ireland in the army. No Baptist was more influential in Ireland in the 1650s than the Particular (Calvinist) Baptist Thomas Patient. Like some Independents he had been in New England in the 1630s, but he played an active role in London Baptist circles in the 1640s before coming to Ireland, where he was ministering by April 1650. He preached in Kilkenny and was the leader of a group of Baptists in Waterford who were initially affiliated with John Rogers's Dublin congregation before establishing their own church. Among Patient's converts was Colonel Jerome Sankey, who was not "assured of the faith of his parents to make his infant washing effectual"; he would serve as governor of Clonmel and in 1658 receive a knighthood from Henry Cromwell. Patient persuaded Richard Lawrence, governor of Waterford, and Daniel Axtell, governor of Kilkenny, to become Particular Baptists. In December 1652 he received an appointment as a preacher in Christ Church, Dublin.[54]

Among the other early Baptist leaders was Andrew Wyke, who was preaching at St. Michan's, Dublin, in the summer of 1651; at Lisburn that fall; at Dromore and Lurgan in 1654; at Donaghcloney and Tullylish, county Down in 1658; and at Magheralin the following year. Robert Clarke was advocating Particular Baptist tenets at Galway in 1652, and the following year Christopher Blackwood obtained a government appointment as preacher at Kilkenny and helped found a Particular Baptist church at Wexford. For his work the state paid him £150 *per annum*, but two years later he was no longer on the government payroll and had gone to Dublin, where by 1656 he had become an "overseer" of a Particular Baptist church. By 1653 the Baptists had churches not only in Dublin, Kilkenny, Wexford, Galway, Kerry, and Waterford but also at Bandon, Carrickfergus, Clonmel, Cork, Kinsale, and Limerick. In the ensuing years Baptists were also active in Belfast, Carlow, Enniscorthy, Belturbet (county Cavan), Maryborough (Queen's County), and Gowran (county Kilkenny). So successful were the Baptists in military circles that their ranks included twelve military governors in 1655. The government, in fact, turned to such Baptist officers as Sankey, Robert Barrow, and Henry Pretty to recruit ministers. Officers such as John Vernon and Captain Samuel Wade themselves preached; Vernon, a Particular Baptist, did so at Clonmel, Kilkenny, and Waterford.[55]

Fire destroyed the only Baptist church records known to have survived the seventeenth century—those for Cork—in 1729. Joseph Fowke, Lawrence's great-grandson, reconstructed an outline of the church's history, in part by utilizing recollections of the congregation's elder members. The founder was Major Edward Riggs, who settled near Cork in 1651, having come to Ireland as a parliamentary commissioner. Because no Baptist minister then worked in the Cork area, Riggs gathered a congregation in his home and preached to them. A local schoolmaster, Mr. Woods, assisted him. Woods eventually married an ex-nun to whom Riggs had given shelter and whom he had converted after she left her convent. Shortly after 1653 Thomas or William Lamb preached to this congregation. About the same time James Coleman, who had been preaching in Dublin, came to Cork and held services in a house in Coleman's Alley. In 1658 a Baptist congregation worshipped in St. Peter's under the leadership of John Coleman.[56]

A different perspective on Baptist activity in this period is found in a letter of 11 June 1657 from Reuben Esthorp, a government preacher in Galway, probably of Presbyterian or episcopalian persuasion, to Henry Cromwell. The Baptists in Galway, he complained, "ar now as high as if all Ireland was theirs." The wife of the governor, Colonel Thomas Sadler, had been baptized as an adult, and out of respect for her the governor was "wholly theirs." When Esthorp refused to permit the Baptists to preach in the parish church, Sadler threatened to resign his commission if Esthorp did not stop baptizing infants. The Baptist minister, Robert Clarke, whom Esthorp sarcastically called an archbishop, reportedly averred that all who did not share his views were as bad as Irish Catholics. "I know," complained Esthorp, "the state doth give much liberty unto them to tread all others under their feet & to set upp their fift[h] monarchy to rule the world." There is no evidence that

Clarke was a Fifth Monarchist, but Esthorp sensed the usefulness of such an emotive charge, and he resorted as well to hyperbole in charging that English immigrants would rather live under Turkish rule than in a Galway dominated by Baptists and Quakers.[57] Such complaints must have contributed to the hardening of Cromwell's stance toward sectaries.

If the Independents thrived and declined because of their close affiliation with civilian republicans, the Baptists experienced a like fate because their cause in Ireland was closely linked to military radicals. During the Protectorate many of them made an uneasy peace with the regime, though some, such as Vernon and Allen, were hostile. Both men went to England and at Dorchester in May 1658 unsuccessfully argued for the unification of Baptists and Fifth Monarchists. When the radicals regained control of the Irish government in June 1659, Baptists such as Axtell and Allen briefly regained their commands. For a few months the Baptists again had sympathetic ears in Dublin's halls of power. This was evident, for instance, in the government's response to a petition from the residents of Magheralin, county Down, most of whom were English settlers. The neighboring parish of Donaghcloney, where Andrew Wyke was minister, consisted mostly of "Papists & Scots, who are so bound up to their own judgments that they will not admit of any other." Because Wyke's efforts in Donaghcloney were largely wasted in their judgment, they asked that he be assigned to their parish. The government authorized Wyke to preach in Magheralin but without surrendering his other charge.[58]

The rapid collapse of the radical cause in Ireland commencing in December 1659 left the Baptists shorn of crucial political support. Without a significant base in the civilian population, only a handful of scattered congregations survived. As early as April 1655 west country Baptists in England had warned their Irish compatriots of the danger of relying on the state:

> We have to minde you of . . . your dependency of the ministry on the maintenance of the magistrate which we do not see to be according to the Gospel constitution. . . . We nowhere finde it in the Gospel, that the ministers of Christ should make use of the magistrate's power for to get a coercive maintenance for them.[59]

Dependent on the government for financial support and a narrow political-military base for their adherents, the Baptists could not survive as a significant force in Ireland when those pillars crumbled.

The First Friends in Ireland

Tradition recognizes William Edmundson, a carpenter or cabinet-maker, as the founder of the Society of Friends in Ireland. After serving with Oliver Cromwell in Scotland, he was persuaded by his brother to settle in Ireland as a trader, and he and his wife purchased a house in Antrim. While attending one of James Nayler's meetings on a business trip to England in 1653 he was convinced of "the Lord's blessed truth." The following spring Edmundson moved to Lurgan, county Armagh, and shortly thereafter he and his wife and brother began meeting twice weekly. Four others soon joined them, and thus was born the first settled meeting of Irish Friends.[60]

Throughout the rest of the seventeenth century and beyond, English Friends trekked across Ireland, initially to spread the Quaker message but increasingly to fortify Irish Friends and to share in common worship. In time, Irish Quakers made similar journeys to England, and both groups carried their gospel as far afield as North America, the European continent, and points east. The first English Quaker missionaries to Ireland—Miles Bateman, Miles Halhead, and James Lancaster among others—arrived in 1654, followed by Edward Burrough and Francis Howgill in August 1655. Burrough and Howgill had experienced a dramatic divine calling aptly compared by Hugh Barbour with that of Paul to the Macedonians. Here, first, is Burrough's account:

On the 10th day of the 4th Moneth [June] late in the Evening, The Mooveings of the Lord came upon me to goe to Dublin citty in Ireland, upon the 30th day of the 4th Moneth I Submitted . . . ; and as I was in the deepe where the Wonders of the Lord are to be seene, it came upon me to write as Followeth:

> Into Ireland thou must goe, my word for to declare—
> The Mountaines high, Nor the Rocks hard, thy hammer must not Spare.

Howgill's account reflects his mastery of visual and biblical imagery:

The word of the Lord came unto me the 7th day of the 4th moneth, about the 10th houre of the day, neere Islington, a mile off London, as I was wayting upon the Lord, Saying,

> Goe to Dublin in Ireland with my Servant Edward Burrough, I have opened a doore for you. . . . My flaming two Edged Sword into your hands I will put; Ride on, Sound an Alarme, make the Sound of my word goe foorth as Thunder, That the Heathen may feare and Tremble.[61]

The strength of Burrough's and Howgill's convictions was one of the keys to the Friends' success in Ireland.

Women were among the Quaker pioneers in Ireland. One of the most significant was Elizabeth Fletcher, daughter of Westmorland gentry; she came alone to Ireland and preached in Dublin and Cork, prompting Burrough to write to Margaret Fell expressing concern for her safety. Elizabeth Smith joined Fletcher in January 1656, and both women went to prison for preaching at St. Audeon's in Dublin. They carried the Friends' message to Munster as well. The former Bristol governess Barbara Blaugdone, who had been stabbed and incarcerated for witnessing in England, came to Ireland in 1656. After complaining in person to Henry Cromwell about his harsh treatment of Friends, she traveled to Cork and there was maliciously accused of witchcraft and imprisoned.[62] After 1660 women became increasingly important as itinerant preachers.

The Quaker thrust in the 1650s targeted the English and Scottish communities, including the garrisons; Friends enjoyed considerable success among the troops in Munster. Gathered churches of Baptists and Independents were another major target; within weeks of their arrival in Ireland, Howgill and Burrough posed 26 questions to these groups. Among the early converts were the ex-soldier and Baptist William Ames and the Irish-born Baptist John Perrot, who would subsequently incite a major schism among Friends. The message of these early Friends was direct, uncompromising, and often harsh. Almost as soon as he landed, Howgill issued a prophetic admonition to the magistrates and residents of Dublin, urging them to hear the word of the Lord and ominously concluding, "I have cleared my Conscience unto you. . . . Be you warned." To all the rulers, judges, and magistrates in Ireland Burrough proclaimed: "God hath laid it upon me to give you warneinge, which if I Doe not your blood will be upon me & if . . . yow refuse to heare & obay your blood be upon your selves, & your posterity forever." Apostates received no sympathy: Howgill denounced Thomas Royle as one who had once eaten from the tree of knowledge and dwelled in God's garden but was now "driven into the Earth, and now feedest upon dust." Prophesying to the people of Cork that the day of their visitation was at hand, Howgill reserved his harshest comments for the professional clergy, for they had allied with "the Beast, to uphold his Image, and to Resist the Lord." Misery would befall them because they "sell that for money, which is not bread, and are found walking in the way of the false prophetts of Israell; not one of you can cleare yourselves. . . . The lords Controversy is with you, you shall be as stubble."[63]

Initially, magistrates were unsure of who the Friends were or how to deal with them. The governor of Kinsale, Major Richard Hodden, adjudged them descendants of the Puritans and an extension of the ongoing process of reformation:

Consider that Reformation is begun, not finished, and the foundation & principall parte thereon spirituall, without which all outward formes are but Deceipt. And as it is written, wee looke for a new heaven and a new Earth wherein Dwells Righteousnes, And it hath been & is hoped that in this wast Lande may be Comfortable habitations for Religious English men, if therunto incouraged.

Hodden told Cromwell he had known these people both in England and in Ireland and that Cromwell would not regret rewarding their virtue. The governor of Limerick, Colonel Henry Ingoldsby, viewed Friends in a very different light, deeming them a "wild yett subtill & designeinge generation off people." Adjudging them a threat to Limerick's security, he suppressed their more visible activities but allowed them freedom to meet quietly among themselves as long as they did not attract crowds. With an eye to the garrison's well-being, he refused to permit Friends from outside Limerick to stay in the town, probably a response to the effectiveness of Quaker itinerants in winning converts among the troops. Residents who entertained visiting Friends in their homes without permission faced expulsion, and soldiers who became Quakers were subject to court martial and dismissal from the army for insubordination. The threat of such action, according to Ingoldsby, "cur'd more then a hundred off that . . . distemper they were Inclineinge to." Many more might have converted had not the penalties been so severe. Friends who abused traditional ministers or disrupted their congregations risked imprisonment or expulsion from Limerick. Ingoldsby's most vociferous critic in the town, Captain Thomas Holmes, had been cashiered from his company in the Waterford area and now used "base Languadge" against him in a letter and submitted a petition to the council criticizing him.[64]

Perrot too felt the sting of Ingoldsby's wrath. When Perrot and other Friends met at the home of Captain Robert Wilkinson in the spring of 1656, Ingoldsby had them arrested and forced them to hear a sermon in the parish church. When the minister had concluded, Perrot brazenly asked to address the congregation, whereupon he was forcibly removed from the building and incarcerated. Although subsequently banned from Limerick, he returned a week and a half later and again met for worship in Wilkinson's house. Once more he was arrested, but this time he was taken to Dublin and incarcerated.[65] From his cell in the

Four Courts' prison he wrote a fiery epistle to the lawyers and clerks throughout Ireland. God, he asserted, "beholds your loathsome Abominations, and how many of you joynes oftentimes, as one, in the Destruction of your neighbour by overthrowing his just Cause for your dishonest and unrighteous Rewards & gaine." Chiding the legal profession for scorning the innocency of sufferers, he admonished attorneys for their greed, pride, superfluity, "Chambering," and exhorbitant fees.[66]

Persecution of Friends at the national level had commenced as early as 17 December 1655 at Henry Cromwell's behest. Understandably, Burrough castigated him and his allies—"all the Trayne of perverters of the Just law of god"—for their cruelty. In the first wave of Quaker persecution Friends in the military were cashiered and Quakers in general faced incarceration and banishment. Fortunately for the Friends, by the time the government began banishing such pioneers as Howgill and Burrough in early 1656, local leaders were firmly in place; such persecution twelve months earlier might have eradicated the Quaker movement in Ireland just as it was emerging. As Burrough and Howgill awaited their banishment in prison, they drafted an epistle to the military officers and "all the honest hearted" in which they demanded the right "to be tried by the Just law of Equitie, and Righteousnesse." They had traveled to Ireland, they explained, "by vertue of a Command given unto [them] by the Eternall Spirit of the Lord" to minister the gospel of reconciliation and salvation, expecting no rewards and suffering reproach. Contrary to the charges levied against them, they professed not to have been disturbers of the peace, nor did they consider it just to have been charged under a statute framed to curtail vagabondage.[67] Their plea was in vain, but their work had been so effective that it could not be uprooted.

A crucial ingredient in the Friends' recipe for survival was their care in nurturing one another in the spiritual life. Quaker epistles to fellow Friends have a wholly different tone from the letters addressed to those beyond the movement's pale. Encouragement, praise, and exhortations to faithfulness are standard themes. Typical is Howgill's spiritual counsel in June 1656 to Friends in Cork and elsewhere:

Stand armed, having your loynes girded up by the truth. . . . Watch over one another in love, and beare one anothers burthens. . . . And take heed now when the power is striving among you, that none run out in Imaginations and act any deceite.

About the same time Howgill and Burrough promised Friends throughout Ireland: "If you wayte in the patience [of God], a little season, the strange Operation of the power of god will appeare among you . . . to the confounding of all your owne wisdom." The Quakers often copied and circulated such epistles widely, using a system that combined the intimacy of a letter with the wider distribution associated with pamphlets but without the latter's expense. When Howgill wrote from Bristol to Friends at Cork in July 1656, he asked that his letter be copied and sent to Youghal, Waterford, Kinsale, Bandon, and Dublin. The message was representative, urging unity among Friends and eschewing the tendency to judge one another. Moreover, "be not forward nor Rash, but wayte to have power over your owne Wills, & over your thoughts, that soe they may dye, & Sin & Iniquity may be put to an end in you."[68]

Exhortations to unity among Friends appear with such frequency as to suggest a widespread problem with sanctimony and censoriousness. In the absence of formal ministers and elders, all members were monitors and judges of one another's behavior, a state prone to internal divisiveness. After visiting Friends in Ireland, Humphrey Norton wrote to them while he was on a ship off the American coast: "Keepe to it [the power of the Spirit], and it will keepe you out of all divisions & strife, which Eates Even as a Canker where it comes; The Liveing god give you a sight of it, & strength & Wisedome to resist it." Watch for the good, Burrough counseled, covering one another's weaknesses rather than disclosing them, but do not emulate the many hypocritical professors of truth whose "false Imitations of Ordinances" and "Steeple-house worshipp" should be "Threshed." Let your words be few, seasoned with fear, and moderate, Thomas Loe advised Friends in the Carlow area, and "let not your wills run before the Light to Speake of truth, for thats not of it." Perhaps the greatest danger to the early Friends was not the persecution of Cromwell, Ingoldsby, and their associates but the ease with which people reputedly guided by the Spirit's leadings could speak about and act on things some of them barely grasped, and the quickness with which some Quakers condemned the words and actions of fellow believers who saw things differently.[69]

Friends everywhere struggled to find a workable balance between gospel order and spiritual freedom. For most Quakers James Nayler's entry into Bristol on a horse, though intended as a symbolic and prophetic sign, was an intolerable exercise of his freedom to espouse the Christian message, and Perrot, Norton, and William Shaw warned Friends in Cork that "the Agents of J[ames] N[ayler] would come creeping on theire Bellyes." The invective that characterized the more bitter internecine quarrels is manifest in this trio's denunciation of "Martha

[Simmonds] theire Miserable Mother." When Jane Stokes left England on a missionary journey to Ireland in November 1659, Howgill felt compelled to warn Friends that "shee is out of truth, her comeing was & is disowned, & shee can doe noe good for god, send her backe if you can gett her, cleare Truth off her, if shee will Joyne to the world or live with them let hir alone, but Freinds not to mind her." In apparent contrast, Perrot, while en route to Venice in 1659, enunciated one of the classic expressions of Quaker freedom in a letter to Friends in Ireland:

As god hath dealt unto you Soe doe you Minister unto them in the Lords house and if any is Mooved to sit in the high way to call in a stranger let him doe it, and if any is Moved to thresh a priest let him doe it, and if any is moved to thresh deceite in the Market places let him doe it, and all mind your owne Motions.

When Perrot later quarreled with George Fox over wearing hats during prayer, he discovered that practical limits governed what most Friends would accept; freedom had its bounds.[70]

While Irish Friends strove to maintain internal unity they engaged in a running battle with other Protestant religious groups, particularly the Baptists. In some cases the conflict took the form of queries posed to religious rivals, as when Howgill put 29 questions to Dublin's ministers on such issues as the origin of sin, the power of Satan, the nature of a true minister, whether true religion can be learned by natural means, and the nature of the church. The thirteenth query probed one of the most crucial issues dividing these groups: "What is your rule That you walke by & what is the ground of your Doctrin & practise whether is it the scripture yea or nay?" If the traditional minister responded affirmatively, Howgill demanded biblical evidence for paedobaptism and the treatment of the Lord's supper as a sacrament. When Robert Turner came to Lurgan in March 1657 to visit Edmunson's meeting, he brought queries from a priest. Richard Cleaton provided Turner with questions written by Fox, which Turner conveyed to a priest at Lisnagarvy, county Antrim. The priest replied to the queries and presented Turner with a new set, to which Cleaton responded in this duel for spiritual mastery.[71]

Debate was thus the order of the day. As in England it took other forms, including such printed attacks on rival sectaries as Thomas Morford's *The Baptist and Independent Churches (So Called) Set on Fire*, written at Clonmel in October 1659 and published in London the following year. The Friends also wrote epistles to Baptists, perhaps hoping for results similar to those sometimes attained when they preached in person to fellow sectaries. From Athens Perrot addressed Irish Baptists in September 1657, recounting his earlier experiences with them: "I beare a love to the Remnant of the Lord which is yet behind, mingled with your Corrupt & strange seed, whilst I was among you I was Earnest for the Lords sake, with the witnesse of his word, seeking an Entrance to provoke you unto Jelousy, but god shewed me your hearts, & for all my Love, at best yet did but cast dirt, seeking to stayne my face, but the spotts turned upon your owne garments and they were not shaken of[f] in your feasts." Perrot told the Baptists that God would make their pastors behave as wolves among the flock. Reminding Baptists that they had rejoiced when he left Ireland, he admonished them that their vain confidence led them to have "rotten hope" in the kingdom's stability. Prophesying a calamitous political future for Ireland, he asked: "Hath the winde of the Lord which blasted you (whilst I was in that nation with you) fayled since, or will it fayle to divide your kingdome, & rent & blow your body asunder?"[72]

When William Morris wrote to Irish Baptists in June 1658 he adopted a different tack, asking them to take an honest look at themselves, especially their fondness for lavish dress, a point made of Irish Baptists no less critically by Particular Baptists in western England. Appealing to the "more sober" Baptists, Morris inquired if their consciences were not troubled by all the worldly pomp and excess around them. His description of Baptist dress indicates the extent to which these radicals had embraced the trappings of higher society and thus the gulf between Baptists and Friends with respect to their separation from earthly things:

If Friends goe into the parish Temples & their find men daubed with Lace, Their hatts & their Garments hung with Ribons & paynts of divers Collours, like Antickes or Bedlams, their heads powdered like millers, their Breaches like coates, Cuffes near the Elbowes, . . . allsoe women with naked neckes & Collors about with their Armes pinnioned like fellons Condemned. . . . And if they come to your meettinges are their not such monsters as these to be found, which you call Bretheren & sisters . . . are these the Garments of the bride the Lambs wife. . . . Againe, if Friends goes into the Idol temples they find a man stands prayinge Exalted above the Rest of the Congregation (which christ forbad his disciples to doe) & is not the like to be found in your mettings.[73]

Irish Friends themselves, of course, were not free from some of these perceived abuses.

The Friends enjoyed their greatest success in Munster and Ulster, though Edmundson complained that he found in the latter "a thick dull sottish people." As in England Quaker converts were largely smallholders, artisans, and shopkeepers. The army's importance as a source of converts slowly diminished, owing, as Kenneth Carroll has suggested, to four factors: Henry Cromwell's hostility to Friends as a military and political threat; the reduction of the army from 34,000 to approximately 14,500 in 1658, partly because of financial exigencies, partly to reduce the number of Baptist and Quaker soldiers; opposition to Friends from prominent officers such as Ingoldsby; and the emergence of the peace principle in Ireland commencing in late 1656. Despite the growing conservatism of the Cromwellian years the imprisonment of Friends actually declined, from 77 in 1655 to fifteen in 1656, five in 1657, three in 1658, and one in 1659.[74] The reduction of Quaker numbers in the military apparently enabled the authorities to regard them as a nuisance rather than a security threat.

A growing willingness to tolerate the Friends did not, however, stem from a diminution of their prophetic message or provocative symbolic actions. In an undated epistle written from Rome between 1658 and 1661, Perrot warned the people of Limerick and Kilkenny: "Remember yee now the day of your visitation, wherein the voyce of the word of the lord, was sounded in your streets, & if through hardnesse yee will not confesse to the truth thereof, then may the stones of the citty walls breake forth and beare witnesse against you for loe the overturne, Overturne is already come, & the prophecy is truly fulfilled." After Robert Turner heard Winter preach in Christ Church, Dublin in January 1659, he attempted to address the congregation and was forcibly expelled, undoubtedly in part because he castigated Winter's church as "the sinnagogue of Satan where the deceivers and Robbers yet remaines unwhipped out."[75]

This sense of keen separation from Baptists and Independents gave the Friends an unmistakable sense of identity that served them well in the remaining decades of the century, their proclivity to internal friction notwithstanding. So too did their establishment of a solid base in the middling social ranks that enabled them to withstand the collapse of the interregnum regimes which very nearly swept Independents and Baptists into oblivion. Unlike Ulster Presbyterians the Quakers maintained their existence despite the lack of a geographical heartland and a strong sense of national or ethnic community. Whereas the festal communions helped to bond Scottish Presbyterians as a community, the Friends' distinctive mode of dress, speech, and worship did much to fashion their sense of communal identity. This strong sense of community helped both groups to withstand periods of persecution after 1660 and provided the basis on which they could erect effective ecclesiological structures.

CHAPTER 1

Nonconformity and the Restoration, 1660-1663

THE DOMINANT CONCERNS of the political nation in 1660 were constitutional legality, political and social stability, and security for Protestant landowners. Its religious goals comprised the reassertion of orthodoxy, the reestablishment of episcopal polity, the maintenance of a preaching ministry, and moderate toleration for nonconformists as long as they did not threaten security. Although the duke of Ormond was interested in a *modus vivendi* with nonconformists, episcopalian clerics generally opposed toleration, in part because of their experiences during the Interregnum. The Irish Parliament signaled its interest in a relatively moderate policy in May 1661 by approving two declarations on religion, the first of which endorsed episcopalian polity and the Book of Common Prayer, while the second condemned the Solemn League and Covenant. With Parliament's orthodox credentials established, its members then focused on the land question. Unsatisfied, the clergy made their desire for a harsher policy manifest in August 1662 when the lower house of Convocation pressed for the suppression of all nonconformists as well as Catholics. Three months later, the government, worried about security, ordered magistrates to suppress conventicles. Disclosures of plotting by Thomas Blood and other nonconformists in early 1663 proved the state's concern valid and led to the apprehension of at least forty nonconformist ministers. Generally, however, Ireland's lay rulers demonstrated little interest in the early 1660s in prosecuting nonconformists for religious offenses. To the extent, therefore, that dissenters engaged in activities that seemingly threatened the state, they played into the hands of the episcopalian clerics who cried out for their repression.

The Convention and the Work of Rebuilding

Following the seizure of Dublin Castle from the political radicals in December 1659 the key political figures in Ireland were the civilians Lord Broghill in Munster and Sir Charles Coote in Connaught and three military officers: Major General Sir Hardress Waller, Sir Theophilus Jones, and Colonel Thomas Cooper, a Particular Baptist who commanded the troops in Ulster. Cooper's death the same month had an incalculable impact on the events that ensued, but his demise undeniably removed the sole voice among these men who might have pushed the hardest for a reasonably broad religious settlement. Even so, religious radicals were not left without an advocate in the halls of power, for the Council of Officers appointed Colonel Richard Lawrence, a Particular Baptist, as well as Dr. Henry Jones, a future bishop, and Sir William Bury, to serve as emissaries to the Council of State in London. Although no evidence indicates they left Ireland, the intended mission was significant both because its members reflected the centrist orientation of the leaders of the December coup and because the draft instructions manifested their aims.[1]

Above all, the draft instructions revealed a concern for legality, stability, religious orthodoxy, and parliamentary rule. The seventeen articles were emphatically not a manifesto for monarchical rule and an episcopal church. To prevent the prosecution of those who had served the protectoral regime, the drafters sought an act of oblivion embracing everyone who had engaged in or obeyed the government in Ireland since 19 April 1653. They insisted as well that all laws and ordinances enacted since that date and not repealed by 22 April 1659 be made "firme and inviolable" by Parliament. No less important was a provision that all grants and dispositions of land made by the government since April 1653 be statutorily confirmed, and another demanding security of Protestant-owned estates notwithstanding the inquisitions undertaken during Strafford's rule. Security was also a consideration in calling for payment of the army's arrears.[2]

James McGuire has cogently argued that the Council of Officers was concerned with orthodoxy, as reflected in its call for a parliamentary statute to settle "godly faithfull orthodox learned and Gospell preaching" in all parts of Ireland, and to provide ministers with sufficient maintenance. The meaning of orthodoxy in this sense is ambiguous—perhaps deliberately so—for it could refer to the Calvinist tenets of the early Stuart church or to the much broader Nicene orthodoxy. Either way, the intent was not to delimit the state church to moderate episcopalians and Presbyterians, but also to embrace Independents and Particular Baptists such as Colonel Lawrence. The intent must have been the exclusion of Laudians on the one hand and General Baptists and Friends on the other. The Council of Officers was at least as interested in the church's material possessions as its theology, for it addressed the rents and other income from the lands formerly held by the crown and the episcopal establishment. These it wanted to reserve for ministerial maintenance and free schools. This would suggest that the Council in general had no plan to restore episcopal polity and the traditional parish system, though some form of reformed episcopate, shorn of its pomp, power, and wealth, might have been acceptable. The Council advocated a relatively moderate stance toward Catholics, proposing that Parliament suspend the 1656 statute aimed at Catholic recusants until it determined its own policy, and in the interim it recommended diligence in instructing people in Protestantism.[3]

A fissure in the new regime between centrists such as Coote and Broghill on the one hand and Waller on the other over the readmission of excluded members to Parliament probably rendered the mission to carry these instructions to London moot. Waller's abortive attempt to seize and control Dublin Castle on 15 February effectively played into the centrists' hands. The following day Coote and 54 officers serving in Dublin issued a declaration calling for readmission, and on 18 February Broghill and 43 officers stationed in Munster published a comparable manifesto. The declarations registered concern about the legal status of the assorted acts of the 1650s, the growth of heresy and schism, the need to restore tithes, and tax reform. Questions were raised about the fitness of ministers appointed by the governments of the 1650s, and the Dublin declaration explicitly condemned "anabaptists" as well as Quakers. The intent of both declarations was a return to a national church devoted to the espousal of orthodoxy and the suppression of heresy, but not necessarily episcopalian in polity. Although centrist in tone, these declarations probably fanned mounting popular hostility against radical preachers such as the Particular Baptist Christopher Blackwood, who was threatened with assassination, and the Fifth Monarchist John Rogers, who spent several weeks in prison when he came to Ireland to preach. No less ominous was the rumor of an imminent proclamation to expel Baptists and Friends from Ireland.[4]

Concern for legality, stability, and religious orthodoxy prompted civilian and military centrists to support the summoning of a convention.

The Convention could not have met without the support of Broghill, Coote, and William Bury, and it is virtually certain that the orientalist Dr. Dudley Loftus was the principal intermediary who brought the key parties together. The plan probably germinated in city circles where order and legal certainty were keys to economic success. Summoned by the Council of Officers, the Convention, which formally met for the first time on 2 March at the Four Courts in Dublin, comprised 137 members. They were elected from the traditional parliamentary constituencies, though typically only a single representative from each.[5]

On opening day the Convention heard the English Presbyterian Samuel Cox preach at Christ Church on Proverbs 11:14. Members of the Convention, he suggested, were physicians whose task was to heal a heartsick nation. He lost no time in dissociating himself from the interregnum regimes, whose actions he compared to the rebellion of Korah, Dathan, and Abiram against Moses and Aaron (Numbers 16). The litany of republican abuses included the discountenancing of laws, the impropriation of property, the infringement of liberties, and the silencing and banishment of godly ministers. He laid the blame not on Puritans, "the good old Non-conformists," but on sectaries who traced their roots to Jan of Leiden and the Anabaptist tradition, and who committed treason "under the vizzard of holiness." Divisions among the sectaries were the sign of the godly's deliverance, and he warned the Convention to pay no heed to the sectaries' efforts to retain power: "Ye shall no doubt have many giddy phanatick spirits fawning upon you, who will seek to unsettle your judgments, and to turn you out of the right and old way; for these croaking frogs swarm in every corner." Conscious of the relationship between England and Ireland, Cox urged his listeners to follow England's lead:

The Islands of great Brittain and Ireland are like two bottles swimming in the water, if they clash they break; or rather they are like a gallant ship and a small boat floating in the Ocean, if they dash one against the other by reason of winds and tempests, the boat is in great danger to be sunk, or split in pieces. Think not that you are able to stand alone.

The Convention's most important work, he averred, was the restoration of reformed Protestantism, the extirpation of popery, and the suppression of schismatics and separatists. The Convention must not permit the unordained to hold ministerial offices or appoint ignorant, scandalous, or theologically unsound clerics. Polity should be determined by an assembly of godly representatives from the three kingdoms, and universities and other schools must be supported. Cox's sermon constituted a blueprint for sweeping church reform.[6]

A mere six days after the Convention formally convened, it approved a statement outlining the basis for a religious settlement, in effect reiterating the key features of the Dublin and Munster declarations and thereby underscoring the influence of Broghill and Coote. But a crucial difference underscored a subtle shift in political power from the military to the Protestant gentry: Like the drafts of the earlier declarations, the Convention wanted an orthodox preaching ministry supported by tithes and an ecclesiastical structure organized by parishes. The difference was an explicit assertion that *only* this form of state church was acceptable; no accommodation would be provided for gathered congregations as favored by Baptists and many Independents, nor was mention made of toleration for such groups.[7]

The Convention left the question of polity open, though its preference was unmistakably for a presbyterian or moderately episcopalian structure along the lines once favored by James Ussher. This openness to the two systems is reflected in the Convention's two principal ecclesiastical appointments, namely the Presbyterian Samuel Cox as chaplain and the episcopalian Dudley Loftus as the apparent chairman of the committee for the maintenance of ministers. The Convention approved that committee's recommendation to appoint a committee of ministers to assist it. The advisory committee's makeup underscores the Convention's relative open-mindedness at this point with respect to church polity: The eight members included the English Presbyterian Cox, the Scottish Presbyterian Patrick Adair, the Independent Stephen Charnock, and the episcopalian Thomas Vesey.[8]

The advisory committee's initial work signaled its support for religious moderates. It drafted two lists, one of which named 160 "honest able" ministers, sixty of whom, according to Adair, were members of the Ulster presbytery. James McGuire is undoubtedly correct in suggesting that most of the 160 were already receiving state support for their ministerial work. The Convention excluded those on a second list, described as Baptists, from state maintenance and the right to preach. The first recognizable fissure between Presbyterians and episcopalians opened when the episcopalian-dominated committee for the maintenance of ministers pressured the advisory committee to recommend eight "old prelatical men" whom Adair accused of being immoral and theologically corrupt (presumably Arminians). The growing rift was evident as well in the Convention's rejection of Adair's effort to persuade it to acknowledge the Solemn League and Covenant, a proposal advanced at the urging of Ulster Presbyterians and some members of the advisory committee. The Convention's chairman, Sir James Barry, a former supporter of Strafford's, led the opposition to the proposal.[9]

The increase in support for episcopalian polity reflected the shifting views of the Protestant gentry in Ireland far more than events in England, where the restored Long Parliament endorsed the Westminster Confession and ordered copies of the Solemn League and Covenant displayed in all churches. In fact, one of Broghill's correspondents, Robert Douglas, wrote approvingly on 27 March 1660 that Parliament had hinted "that the surest settling of government will be upon the grounds of the Covenant, and according to the ends therein propounded." Broghill and two of the other three men appointed as commissioners by the English Council of State to administer Irish affairs—Clotworthy and William Bury—were still sympathetic to presbyterianism, and Broghill at this point favored religious uniformity—a Presbyterian state church— in all three kingdoms. But Broghill's primary concern was order and security, not ecclesiastical polity. On 30 March he wrote to a friend in London:

> This Nation, & the Army in it . . . is fixed to serve the Councill of state or the next Parliament in effectinge such a settlement, against all oposers whatever in order to which we have purged . . . in our . . . Phanactick Factions [of] Officers[,] Troopers & Privat foot soldiers, & fild up their vacancies, with Persons fitted for that worke.

Perhaps with Broghill's knowledge, Coote had dispatched Sir Arthur Forbes to Breda to pledge Coote's loyalty. Broghill in any case reported in his letter of 30 March that Clotworthy would go to England to consult with the Council of State and that Irish officials would follow the lead of their colleagues in England. By this point the Long Parliament had dissolved itself and the Council served as an interim government until the election of the (English) Convention. General George Monck too was in contact with Charles, undoubtedly helping to prepare the way for a restored monarchy.[10]

Broghill and his colleagues seem to have followed the advice of their friends in England, for on 11 May Francis Lord Aungier wrote to Ormond, assuring him and Charles of "the high devotion" of Coote and "his interest (who have now the effective power of Ireland)," adding that they would have "out run" England in declaring for Charles had Aungier and others in London not urged caution. Ireland, he explained, had to be kept "in reserve, to give a check to rigorous proceedings here,

in case we should find the perverseness run so high as to impose unreasonable and dishonourable terms upon his Majesty." Ireland's zeal
"was no small spur unto the slow and heavy paced Presbyters, who
therefore hastened to our wished for end, lest they should see themselves cast behind and in the rear of Ireland."[11] As in 1641, events in
Ireland forced developments in England.

English Presbyterians probably found it difficult to track the subtle shifts in Irish religious policy, but even had they succeeded they
might have expected a comprehensive religious settlement. Although
Forbes was sympathetic to presbyterianism, at Breda he almost certainly would have been exposed to the episcopalian convictions of Ormond and Sir Edward Hyde, the future earl of Clarendon. If Forbes
reported strong episcopalian persuasions at Breda to Coote, the latter's
shift to episcopalianism is readily explained. But Clotworthy and Bury
remained firm in their support for presbyterianism. The former, according to Adair, a partisan observer, attempted to travel to Breda to persuade Charles that Ireland would be inhospitable to an episcopalian
settlement, but Monck blocked him. For his part, Bury finally succeeded
in persuading his fellow commissioners to issue instructions to the advisory committee of eight ministers. The directions were in keeping
with the Convention's earlier statement of religious principles, including an orthodox ministry and parish organization. The instructions also
referred to several matters dear to the Presbyterians, especially the exclusion of ignorant and scandalous people from the Lord's supper in
accordance with the Westminster Assembly's regulations. A provision
banning the presentation of parishes to Baptists reaffirmed the earlier
hostility to sectaries, as did the insistence on formal ordination.[12]

The rightward religious trend was manifested as well when, in
April, the government recognized five surviving bishops, including
Robert Maxwell of Kilmore and John Leslie of Raphoe, granting each of
them £200 *per annum* but not restoring their episcopal authority. Subsequently Adair plausibly attributed this decision "to court the few old
bishops who were in Ireland, and who then had repaired to Dublin," to
reports about "the pulse of the court at Breda." In May, amid the celebration in Dublin surrounding the proclamation of Charles II as king,
the Convention appointed Henry Jones, Oliver Cromwell's sometime
scoutmaster-general, to preach a thanksgiving sermon in Christ Church
on the 24th. Jones, who had been consecrated to the see of Clogher in
1645 but had subsequently suppressed his ecclesiastical calling, was
once again recognized as bishop of Clogher. In his sermon to the Con-

vention he alluded to the recent controversies in the Church of Ireland in which he had been a participant: "We will know that much of the evil in the State, hath broaken in upon, and proceeded from, sad divisions and factions in the Church." He then signaled what would become the dominant clerical position on ecclesiastical unity in the ensuing decades, averring that "our happinesse in the State, will be in union in the Church," for nothing else would bring peace. Jones, who had an unmistakable talent for survival, concluded that the polity of the new church would be episcopalian. Judging from the contents of his library he would have been no less ready to embrace a Presbyterian settlement, for his collection included the Westminster Assembly's catechism, a Scottish psalter, William Perkins's treatise on the Lord's supper, Richard Sibbes's *The Bruised Reede* (1658), John Goodwin's *Innocencies Triumph* (1644), Robert Bolton's *A Discourse about the State of True Happinesse* (1611), and a work of John Knewstub's.[13]

Loftus's letter of 1 June 1660 to Ormond further charted the rising episcopalian fortunes. People of sober judgment, he claimed, could envision no change in the traditional episcopalian constitution of the established church and "delight in nothing more than the antient government by Bishops." He cautioned, however, that a few Presbyterian divines had "crept in amongst us . . . and industriously Laboure to subject us to the rules of the Covenant, & to regulate us by the Directory." Loftus attributed the Presbyterians' inability to check episcopal ascendancy to their small numbers, presumably restricting his observation to Dublin, for Presbyterian strength in Ulster was considerable. Ormond, he recommended, should preserve the bishops and the liturgy as well as appoint ministers of "gravity and learning" to benefices.[14]

Before the Convention adjourned on 27 May, it dispatched Broghill, Coote, Clotworthy, Barry, and nine others to London as commissioners. The overriding concern expressed in their instructions was constitutional legality, order, security for Protestant landowners, and indemnity for those who had served the interregnum governments. The recent trend toward episcopalianism notwithstanding, the Convention made no attempt to delimit the commissioners by committing to a particular ecclesiastical polity, for it was clearly willing to be flexible on this issue if it could obtain assurances for Protestant landowners. The commissioners had directions concerning ecclesiastical lands and finances but not church government. They discussed polity in their meeting with Charles on 18 June, at which time the king undoubtedly indicated his preference for episcopalianism, for the commissioners subsequently revised their proposals to include the following clause on church government:

That the Church of Ireland be resettled in Doctrine, Discipline and Worship, as it was in the time of your most Royall father of blessed memory, according to the Lawes then and now in force in the Kingdome ... with such Liberty to tender Consciences as your majestie in your Declaration at Breda ... hath beene gratiously pleased to Declare, and that Godly, Learned, orthodox, and ordained preaching Ministers of the Gospell be settled there as speedily as may be in a parochiall way and supported by Tythes, Gleabes and other Legall maintenance.[15]

James McGuire, the Convention's modern historian, underscores the extent to which this crucial ninth clause embodied a compromise between conformists and Presbyterians. In part he contends that the phrase "Godly, Learned, orthodox, and ordained preaching Ministers" would have been uncomfortable for most Anglicans, but the reforming element in the Churches of England and Ireland had espoused such a view since the mid-sixteenth century. Such an outlook was undoubtedly discomfiting to the sacerdotal and liturgical emphases of the Laudians, but they were no longer in the ascendant. The commissioners were embracing the Grindalian conception of the church and simultaneously endorsing the king's pledge of liberty to tender consciences. This outlook—episcopalian polity, moderate toleration, and an orthodox, preaching ministry—would prevail among most influential lay leaders of Ireland in the ensuing decades.[16]

The importance of the commissioners' mission in clearing the way for the restoration of episcopacy in Ireland should not be overemphasized, for no later than 2 June the court was assessing the status of the Irish bishops. All four archbishoprics—Armagh, Dublin, Tuam, and Cashel—were vacant, and there were only eight bishops: John Bramhall of Derry, John Leslie of Raphoe, Henry Leslie of Down and Connor, Robert Maxwell of Kilmore, William Baily of Clonfert, Griffith Williams of Ossory, Henry Jones of Clogher, and Thomas Fulwar of Ardfert. The court was undoubtedly considering candidates to fill the vacant sees as well as the deanry of St. Patrick's, Dublin, while the commissioners were in London, and probably even before their arrival. The commissioners' willingness to support episcopalian polity facilitated royal policy, and on 23 June James Sharp reported that the bishops had been nominated. Formal nominations were not made, in fact, until early August, but offers of appointment must have been extended as soon as the commissioners had indicated their acquiescence in the restoration of traditional church government.[17] Although formal consecration did not occur until January 1661, the crucial decisions concerning the restoration of the traditional Church of Ireland had been made the previous June. The resulting bench was decidedly Anglican, reflecting the views of John Bramhall and the support he enjoyed from Ormond. An anthem composed by the dean of St. Patrick's for the consecration of twelve bishops in the cathedral on 27 January captured the significance of order as the crucial reason for the return of episcopal polity:

> Angels look down, and joye to see
> Here, as above, a Monarchie;
> Angels look down, and joye to see
> Here, as above, a Hierarchie.[18]

Conformist Perspectives: The Laity

Once it was clear that official policy supported the restoration of an episcopalian state church, lay leaders and magistrates were concerned about the potential impact of dissidents on their ability to impose and maintain order. On 7 August 1660, about the time many new bishops received their letters patent, Dublin's municipal council petitioned Charles to signify his pleasure "that the forme of church government and divine worship which was used in your fathers and grandfathers dayes in this kingdome, and which is already established here by lawe, bee declared to bee practised publiquelie amongst us, to which the ministers of the gospell of Christ may conforme themselves." The concern was acute in Ulster. William Lord Caufield reported to Bramhall in October that the region abounded with "licentious" people, especially Presbyterians claiming the church's right to excommunicate monarchs. When magistrates tendered the oaths of allegiance and supremacy one Presbyterian told Caufield that "we had pulled down one Pope and set up another." The lack of clear instructions from Dublin as to how to deal with nonconformists intensified the uncertainty. Caufield attempted to suppress Presbyterian services if he deemed them a threat to the church's or the commonwealth's peace, but he fretted that his actions might be illegal.[19]

Differences of opinion among principal lay officials complicated their dealings with the nonconformists. Coote, the newly created earl of Mountrath, complained bitterly in October 1660 that his fellow commissioner, William Bury, "a grate presbeterian," obstructed the church's settlement. Broghill, elevated to the earldom of Orrery in September, supported the restoration of the traditional church, though he was clearly a moderate, as reflected in his attempt to help Richard Baxter obtain an appointment as a royal chaplain in June 1660. Orrery's sister, Lady Ranelagh, was a Presbyterian and, in the earl's words, "an honest

Sectary, and all her friends."[20] In January 1661 Orrery told Ormond most of the people of Munster were now "common prayer men," adding that he hoped shortly to see "a general conformity" throughout Ireland. To this end he encouraged nonconformists to resign their ministerial posts voluntarily. Shortly after his arrival in Munster he proclaimed to a small assembly of clergy that

> wher ther was a Division in the Church, ther would be always as a necessary consequence therof, the Like in the state; That the Church Government beinge settled in this kingdom by law, I must, & would only make that my Rule. . . . Therefore such as would not Conforme thereunto must expect noe Settlement or Publike mayntenance, & would doe well to retire by Choyce before they were Compeld unto it by Necessity.

All but two clerics complied out of a sense of duty, and those two he "Prevayled with to be gon." Consequently Munster, he promised, would be "universally obedient to the Legall & Settled Church Government."[21] Compelling lay dissidents to conform proved to be more difficult, but a month later he reported to Sir Edward Nicholas, the royal secretary, that he and his colleagues gained ground each day against "the nonconformists & Phanatticks, for we give no Indulgence to any, but Proceed according to the known Lawes of the Land." This zeal for conformity was not the outgrowth of Orrery's ecclesiastical principles but his concern for order in the crucial months in which the restored regime attempted to reassert its control over Ireland. This concern is manifest in his letter to Nicholas expressing fear that the omnipresent Edmund Ludlow, "one of the most dangerous" regicides, and Thomas Wogan, a fellow regicide, were in Ireland.[22]

By late 1661 the lords justices and other lay leaders had begun to discriminate more effectively between quiescent nonconformists and radical sectaries, collectively referred to as Anabaptists, who were considered threats to the peace. Some "Phanatticks" were mellowing, according to Orrery, but the situation in Ulster was substantially different from that in Munster. From Derry Colonel John Gorges expressed fears to Sir George Lane, Ormond's secretary, that the Presbyterians' "Generall principles in Church-Discipline are soe Diametrically opposed to what is by Law established" that the region was unstable. Although the bishops were attempting to impose uniformity "by severe Jurisdiction," including excommunication, their actions were having an effect opposite to that which was intended by creating martyrs and "Stoute Champions for the truth" and instilling contempt for the bishops and their courts. Gorges proposed that the government of the north be vested solely in English hands.[23] Unlike the rest of Ireland, Ulster would continue to pose special problems for the government.

Although Ormond was incontestably Anglican in his religious principles and hoped for "a generall conformity," his principal concern as lord deputy was the maintenance of order rather than rigid uniformity. There were limits to his patience with nonconformists, as indicated in his letter of 15 October 1662 to the bishop of London: The bishop of Derry, he pledged, "shall not want such acquaintance as I am able to furnish him with to Convince his flock, & those are Troopes & Companyes[;] hee is a reverend man, & gaines as much upon that people as any man in a Rochet can doe." In large measure Ormond's resolve to delimit nonconformity stemmed from his determination to prevent a repetition of the reputed 1641 massacre of Protestants, but this he would do, he informed Edward Worth, now bishop of Killaloe, by "prudent & just meanes." Nothing would render nonconformists so open to destruction at the hands of Catholics "as their Obstinate & unreasonable separation from those that professe the Doctrine & conforme to the discipline of Our Church." Dissenters, he told Worth, could not

Expect the cleene Countinance or the perfect confidence of the State nor can there be betwixt them & those that hartily conforme that mutuall trust & affection which is so requisite for their Common safety. Hence your Lordship may be incouraged to labour as you have begunn to Rectify the Judgement of Separatists of whome I dare say many keep off [from the Church of Ireland] more out of Stubborneness and a vitious shame to depart from what they have erroniously & unlawfully contended for then from any Reall or invincible sample of Conscience.[24]

The last sentence, with its almost arrogant dismissal of the legitimacy of nonconformist principles, reveals Ormond's inability to understand the roots of Protestant dissent.

Despite this shortcoming, Ormond was not insensitive to the need for a satisfactory *modus vivendi* with the nonconformists. In May 1663 he wrote to Forbes as the latter prepared to depart for Ulster, expressing concern about the vexation and suffering imposed on the people of that region by "the rigid & sometymes irregular execution of the lawes." Ormond insisted that he opposed excessive severity against dissenters as long as they behaved in other matters, in which case he proposed to do everything possible "to give them all fitting ease & protection consistent with my duty and the Peace of the Kingdome." Because the judges were bound by oath to enforce the laws impartially, any indulgence, he insisted, would require the approval of the Council and chief governor, to whom they should apply in an orderly manner.[25] Limited indulgence would be permitted only as long as order and security were not threatened.

Ormond recognized the significance of a peerage committed to the Church of Ireland. Worried that the dowager countess of Clanbrassill might instruct the young earl in Presbyterian tenets, Ormond made his displeasure known and threatened to impede the earl's interests, not least because Clanbrassill would eventually wield considerable influence in the north, Ireland's "most dangerous part." When the countess dutifully insisted she wanted the earl to be "a true Son of the Church" and asked Ormond's help in finding an Oxford tutor, the duke obliged, seeking the bishop of London's assistance.[26] Ormond was less willing to accord much significance to early reports that Clotworthy, now Lord Massereene, was "countenanceing an unconformable party but affecting the estimation of being their head or protector." He knew, however, that Massereene permitted a conventicle to worship in his own house and maintained an "intimate aquaintance & confidence with those that opose as farr as they dare & declaring constantly against the government of the church as established by law."[27] In fact, Massereene provided crucial support to northern Presbyterians in the ensuing decades.

As the leaders of the new regime imposed their authority in the early 1660s they began to evince a modest degree of toleration toward nonconformists so long as the latter did not threaten security. James Anthony Froude was mistaken in his assertion that after the restoration the nonconformists in Ireland "became at once the objects of an unrelenting and unscrupulous persecution."[28] Such repression as did occur was primarily based on pragmatic considerations, which hardly deserve to be described as unscrupulous. Conformity was unmistakably the ideal of the principal lay authorities, but they were cognizant of the dangers—even the impossibility—of attempting to eradicate nonconformity. Instead in these early years they began to explore the possibility of tolerating the relatively innocuous manifestations of dissent, in effect expressing a willingness to accept a religiously pluralistic society.

Conformist Perspectives: The Clergy

Whereas most key lay officials were increasingly willing to treat peaceful nonconformists with moderation, clerics of the Church of Ireland generally espoused a harsher position. Religious principles were undoubtedly the primary motivation for their stance, but conformist clergy were also influenced by bitterness stemming from their treatment in the Cromwellian era. For instance, Griffith Williams, who had been consecrated bishop of Ossory in 1641, castigated the Long Parliament as Antichrist's agent. Henry Jones distanced himself from the regime he had helped to establish by exalting the restoration as a golden age of religious reformation: "Then was the Church out of Confusion and deformity thereby returned to her former Beauty and Order, and then were the breaches in Gods House repaired, its scattered Members recalled, and fit persons sought out for supplying and filling up those Vacancies which the wickedness of those dismal times had occasioned." The seemingly convenient conversion of various ecclesiastics to the newly restored church sparked some cynicism. When Edward Worth acted moderately toward nonconformists shortly after his nomination to fill the see of Killaloe, critics spead a report that he was "cherishing & encouraging the Presbyterian party in theyr opposition against the Church."[29]

Despite the bitterness of some ecclesiastics, uncertainty existed with respect to their dealings with nonconformists in the early months of the restoration. Two cases, one involving the bishop of Waterford, George Baker, and the other the bishop of Derry, John Bramhall, indicate the modest extent to which some prelates initially sought to accommodate the Presbyterians. Shortly after Baker was consecrated in January 1661, Edward Wale requested admission to the diocese on condition that he be excused from reading the prayers in the Book of Common Prayer, claiming he was too infirm to say them and to preach in the same service. Baker tried unsuccessfully to accommodate Wale, but the latter made no further overtures to preach in the diocese "as publickly licensed, or desiring so to be."[30]

Bramhall insisted that ministers lacking episcopal ordination be reordained, but he did so without challenging their prior ministerial status or actions. As in the case of Edward Parkinson, the minister at Ardee since 1656, Bramhall contended that episcopal ordination was essential as stipulated by canon law to assure the right to collect tithes. In practice he employed a variety of tactics to deal with the Presbyterians, including theological discourse, friendly persuasion, and patience, and he succeeded in converting some of them. At Bramhall's funeral Jeremy Taylor eulogized him as a primate who "weed[ed] the fields of the Church; he treated the Adversaries sometimes sweetly, sometimes he confuted them learnedly, sometimes he rebuked them sharply."[31]

Whatever leniency Bramhall displayed toward nonconformists, he condemned their polity and tenets in scathing terms, damning their discipline as "the very quintessence of refined popery, or a greater than even Rome brought forth, inconsistent with all forms of civil Government" and dangerous because it eradicated "the sight, but not the burden of slavery." He ostensibly aimed this invective at Presbyterians in Scotland, but his readers would have had no difficulty including Ulster Presbyterians as objects of his assault. Bramhall's ire was incited above all by the Presbyterians' claim to wield authority over secular rulers, a contention he associated with the Jesuits. He warned as well of what he perceived to be the dictatorial tendencies inherent in presbyterianism; should it be established,

the common people shall have an High-Commission in every parish, and groan under the Arbitrary decrees of ignorant experienced Governours, who know no Law but their own wills. . . . If there arise a private jar between the parent and the child, or the husband and the wife, there domesticall Judges must know it, and censure it.

Bramhall was no less offended by what he deemed the hypocrisy of the Presbyterians in claiming the right to impose their religion on others but denying the lawfulness of others to enforce their own religious uniformity.[32]

Bramhall's harsh opinion of nonconformists was hardly unique in the early 1660s. Daniel Burston, a minister at Waterford, deplored the dissenters' "arrogated zeal and sanctity," not least for having extruded divinely instituted episcopacy from the church. Because the Solemn League and Covenant imposed an oath against episcopalian polity it was "a league with hell, and death" which fomented "Diabolical divisions." Zealousness and external manifestations of piety, he pointedly noted, were not infallible marks of religious truth. "Gods true Worship . . . might, and ought more temperately to be celebrated; Look we therefore all of us, who would not be deceived[,] to the straitness of the rule, not to the bendings of mens affections." The fervent worship of dissenters, Burston implied, was akin to that of Baal's worshippers in 1 Kings 18.[33] The ideological seeds to justify a harsh policy toward nonconformists were clearly present among leading conformist clerics in the dawn of the restoration period.

A number of leading ecclesiastics were optimistic about the prospects for religious uniformity. Shortly before his consecration in January 1661 Bramhall confided to Sir George Lane that nonconformists would "never be able to make any considerable, scarcely visible opposition against . . . the Orthodox Clergy." When Jeremy Taylor, bishop-elect of Down, welcomed Hugh Viscount Montgomery of the Great Ardes to

Ireland the previous October, he reported that the Presbyterians would generally submit to episcopacy and that a number of their ministers intended to conform: "I have had private notice that they will turne Nicodemus's & come to me in secret; & shortly they will be publike." A week earlier he had been received at Carrickfergus with great ceremony by civil and military officials, but the ministers suspected the delay in consecrating the bishops meant that Charles had decided against restoring episcopacy in Ireland.

> They generally say, that if they must have Bishops they are very glad they are fallen under my hand, & I doe not doubt, if God gives his blessing, & his Majesty any Countenance to me & assistance by his civil officers, I shal reduce this Diocese to good temper & a quiet & uniforme religion according to the lawes.

Taylor's optimism did not stem from any kindred spirit with the Presbyterians, whose "most ignorant" ministers he accused of preaching sedition, prevaricating, and inciting people to revolt. The principal villains, in his estimation, were James Ker of Ballymoney and Thomas Hall of Larne. The key to imposing order in the region, he advised Montgomery, was the imprisonment of two or three of these "incendiaries" and the expeditious consecration of the bishops-elect. His outlook toward the Presbyterians did not improve after some of them allegedly threatened to assassinate him in December 1660.[34]

George Wild, bishop-elect of Derry, had a better sense of how difficult it would be to keep the Presbyterians quiescent. After he had been consecrated and gone to his diocese his apprehensions were confirmed. He went to Strabane to prevent "some greate dangers which were justly feared for the notorious Conventicles in these Parts," and then turned his attention to Ballykelly and Newtown Limavady, where he was "alarum'd with high Contempts, and where I meane to throw myself . . . amidst the Thickett of those schismatiques." Peace was impossible, he told Bramhall in September 1661, "so long as those Trumpetts of sedition Cann gett the People to Heare them."[35]

From Ballykelly Wild's chaplain filed an alarmist report the same month, noting the possibility of a Presbyterian insurrection in Ulster.

> The Faction is growne very potent and very impudent. They crow extreamely, & our Party is . . . much disheartned here abouts. The Fame is that they now go armed to their Conventicles; that they talke of having another day for it; That this [restoration of episcopacy] is but one Turne among many, which will bee shortly succeeded by another; That they are providing and fixing Armes apace; & such things. . . . Not to speake now of the Pulpitt-Drumms, and mouth Granades which they beate & cast at your Lordship [Wild] and all Bishops men.

In assessing this report Wild attributed the overt hostility to "Elder Gunns" and suggested to Bramhall that a troop of horse be temporarily posted to the area to intimidate "the Fanatique Presbyterians" and boost the spirits of loyal episcopalians. Wild pledged to do everything he could to prevent the spread of seditious remonstrances among the Presbyterians, but his attempts to suppress the conventicles at Bally-kelly and Newtown Limavady succeeded only in forcing them to gather in the hills and forests.[36]

John Leslie, bishop of Clogher, and Robert Leslie, bishop of Raphoe, reinforced Wild's assessment of troubled conditions in Ulster. Although John Leslie considered his own diocese to be in decent order, he worried about the unsettling impact of fiery zealots: "My Lord," he told Bramhall, "the Irish can not, (if not induced and supported from abroade) the honest English wil not; so I apprehend the G[h]ost of the Covenant is sent . . . from hell to trouble us once more." He also observed that "al ulster is affrighted out of their wits" by reports of "most fearful and portentous visions from England." These would have stemmed from the radical publication, *Mirabilis Annus, or the Year of Prodigies and Won-ders*, the intent of which was to prophesy imminent judgment for those who persecuted the true church.[37] From Raphoe, Robert Leslie complained to Bramhall in November 1661 that nonconformist disobedience was increasing in his diocese as people who had been attending Church of Ireland services were ceasing to do so and that the Presbyterian ministers threatened to preach without licenses. Leslie not only appealed for a detachment of cavalry but also sought permission to leave his diocese until it was "in some better Order."[38]

Like Bramhall, Wild initially experimented with various methods to deal with Presbyterians, including pulpit oratory and intellectual persuasion in his consistory. By late summer 1662 he could report to Ormond that nonconforming Scots had begun to fear the government, but in January 1663 he found it necessary to begin issuing writs *de excommunicato capiendo*. "Now I see I must quiet the Scottish (Presbyterian) Nettle that by my Gentle usage hath only served to sting me; & am ready to signify to Dublin diverse Refractory and violent Non Conformists."[39] In the end, no measures could quash the hard core of Ulster Presbyterians, whose recalcitrance hardened the attitude of embattled prelates, especially in the north. Neither side was prepared to cede its claim to be the true church, nor were conformists willing to embrace a compromise to accommodate the Presbyterians in the Church of Ireland.

Nonconformist Reaction

Nonconformist responses to the restoration varied widely. As in England the interregnum regime had its defenders, though they risked punishment at the assizes if they were too vocal in expressing their opinions.[40] Modern historians have followed the early eighteenth-century Presbyterian apologist James Kirkpatrick in averring that the Presbyterians were not enemies of Charles's restoration, but his contemporary, the Anglican historian White Kennett, contended that Presbyterian ministers in Ulster were preaching against the king in the summer of 1660.[41] Much of their opposition was directed against the government's religious policy rather than the monarch himself. At year's end Presbyterian ministers in the north pledged to draw swords before they would take the oaths of supremacy and allegiance, and they denounced the Book of Common Prayer as something that had been hatched in hell. The government, they warned, would confiscate Bibles from private houses and the bishops would introduce popery. During the preceding four months, Jeremy Taylor wrote in December 1660, implacable Presbyterian clerics had preached against episcopacy and the liturgy, disparaged royal government, talked of "resisting unto bloud," and incited the people to act seditiously. Prepared to satisfy any demands he deemed reasonable, Taylor invited them to meet with him and preached among them every Sunday, yet they "covenanted" not to speak with any bishop or "endure . . . their Governement nor their persons."[42]

Not content to stop here, the Presbyterians, led by John Greg of Newtownards, John Drysdale of Portaferry, Gilbert Ramsey of Bangor, and Alexander Hutcheson of Tonaghnieve (Saintfield) mounted a daring attack on Taylor, accusing him of Socinianism, Arminianism, and the repudiation of original sin. They purchased copies of Taylor's books and, in the bishop-elect's words, "appointed a Committee of Scotch Spiders to see if they can gather or make poison out of them." In fact, they compiled extracts from his writings and conveyed them to an agent in London in the hope of persuading Charles to appoint someone else to the see of Down. "Remove me from this insupportable burden," Taylor pleaded to Ormond, "or . . . support me under it." The Ulster Scots, he claimed, were trying to disgrace him and had even threatened to murder him. Mountrath and Bury refused to intervene in his behalf on the theological charges, but the Presbyterians' attempt to block his consecration failed.[43]

In a sermon preached in late 1660, William Richardson of Killyleagh, county Down, proclaimed the Presbyterians' resolution to denounce prelacy and the Book of Common Prayer. Preaching on Ephesians 4:14, he predicted an imminent period of persecution more severe than that under Mary Tudor, warned that the government would no longer permit Bibles in private homes, and speculated that it would soon be safer to violate the sabbath than a traditional holy day. In the judgment of Mountrath and Bury, this sermon reflected adversely on royal government in matters civil as well as ecclesiastical, manifested contempt for the law, incited popular dislike of monarchical and episcopal polity as well as the Book of Common Prayer, and stirred up seditious opposition to royal authority.[44] Not all nonconformists adopted such a confrontational posture. Dissenters in Munster pledged their obedience to the government, abhorring disobedience to, plotting against, or resistance to "a settled government exercised by an undoubted lawful authority, as we own his majesty to be."[45]

Two sermons preached by Samuel Mather in Dublin on 27 and 30 September 1660 give some indication of the Congregational reaction to the restoration. Mather looked on Charles not as the incarnation of evil but as a potential Hezekiah who would reform the church, ridding it of "all the Ceremonies, and whatever other Inventions of men have been introduced into the worship of God by the Spirit of Anti-Christ, and reteined, and continued by some reforming Magistrates, who have made but incompleat and imperfect Reformations." The surplice, the sign of the cross in baptism, kneeling in the Lord's supper, bowing toward the altar or at the name of Jesus, organs and cathedral music, holy days and places, prelacy, and the Book of Common Prayer were, for Mather, relics of popery and remnants of Baal. In millenarian tones Mather told his audience that Christ's work was the purification of the church preparatory to the coming of the new Jerusalem. "Suppose Prelacy should get up again, yet it will not be able to stand, but after three dayes and a half [Rev. 11:11] . . . it will fall and perish." Christians should therefore pray that prelacy, "the Image of that Beast the Papacy," not be restored.[46]

In his sequel on the 30th, Mather launched an all-out attack on the Anglican practices identified in the first sermon before exhorting the bishops and their supporters not to revive or enforce the idolatry and superstition of the past. Reminding episcopalians that they had been tolerated in the 1650s, he urged them not to use carnal weapons "to oppress those Truths of Christ, which by dint of Spiritual Reason you cannot subdue." He was careful not to threaten to take up arms against the new regime, even if it became persecutorial, but he minced no words in pronouncing the fate that such a policy would bring: "As the Saints will pray, so the Lord himself will fight against you." "Swift destruction" awaited persecutors. "If once you super-adde the sin of Persecution to the sin of Superstition, you will be quickly ripe for final Ruine."[47]

Mather's sermons provoked the ire of the government, which had permitted him to continue preaching in Dublin only because he had accepted Charles's return. After consulting others, including Bishop Jones, Sir Theophilus Jones, William Bury, and Sir James Ware, Mountrath prohibited Mather from preaching again. Mountrath demanded his sermon notes, but Mather procrastinated, claiming they were inelig-ible. He later sent them to his brother Increase in New England, where the sermons were printed in 1670. Mather escaped further punishment, in part because the Four Courts had not been resettled by the new government and in part because he professed obedience to the civil authorities.[48]

In addition to their pulpit oratory the nonconformists mounted peti-tion drives in an attempt to influence the government's religious policy. In the summer of 1660 the Presbyterians circulated a petition asking Charles to establish presbyterian polity in the Church of Ireland; George Burdett of Limerick was to take the document to London. After Sir George Rawdon sent a party of horse to break up a Presbyterian synod at Ballymena, county Antrim, its members, reconvening in secret, dis-patched four agents to Dublin to petition the lords justices for freedom from the yoke of prelacy and to express consternation that they had been linked with Catholics and "Phanaticks" in the Council's proclama-tion against unlawful meetings. After considerable debate, the Council resolved

That Wee neither could nor would allow any Discipline to bee Exercised in Church affaires, but what was warranted and Commanded by the lawes of the Land; That they were punishable for haveing exercised any other; That Wee would not take any advantage against them for what is past, if they would Comport them selves Conformably for the tyme to Come; That if they were dispensed withall, by Pl[e]adeing a submission thereunto was against their Consciences, Papists and Phanaticks would expect the like Indulgence on the like Plea; which wee knew their owne practice as well as Judgements lead them to disallow of; That Wee tooke it very ill divers of those which had sent them had not observed the Day sett aparte for humbleing them selves for the barba-rous Murther of his late Majestie . . . ; That some of their number had preached of late seditiously, in Cryeing up the Covenant. . . . In lamenteing his Majesties breach of it, in seteing up Episcapacy as introductive to Popery; which they had not punisht in Exerciseing any of their pretended Discipline over such notorious offenders; and lastly that if they conformed themselves to the Discipline of this Church they should want no fiteing Countenance and Encouragement in carryeing on their Ministry, soe if the[y] Continued Refractory they must Expect the penaltyes the lawes did perscribe.

The Council's key theme was its unwillingness to surrender the established church's monopoly on discipline, not least because this would have permitted presbyteries to determine what actions were punishable offenses. Sovereignty could not be shared, even in the name of individual conscience, but the Council tendered an olive branch of sorts by offering to include the Presbyterians in the Church of Ireland without punishment for past infractions if they endorsed episcopalian polity.[49]

The Presbyterian delegates responded that they would comply to the extent their consciences permitted, but otherwise suffer patiently for their dissent. They unqualifiedly recognized the king's legitimate authority, disowned clergy who preached sedition, and insisted they would have punished such persons had they been permitted to exercise discipline. Many Presbyterians, they insisted, had observed the fast to commemorate Charles's execution, which they deplored, and had suffered incarceration and sequestration during the interregnum. To their inquiry as to whether sabbath services of prayer and preaching would be illegal, the justices and councillors responded moderately, prohibiting meetings that exercised "Ecclesiasticall Jurisdictions" but not those concerned exclusively with "Parochiall Dutys." The administration's goal was a workable compromise within a broad frame of conformity, and the Presbyterians "seemed much Comforted" with the assurance that they could continue to preach. "Wee dismist them," Orrery reported to Ormond, "to try what this usadge and the Admonition will produce."[50] Adair, however, saw the conference in a very different light, insisting the delegates had been treated unkindly because of the presence of bishops and other hostile persons in the Council. The "Episcopal party" in Dublin mocked them, he complained, nor did the Council grant the substance of the Presbyterians' request, clearly implying that discipline was the crux of the issue for both sides. The Council thus found itself between two competing clerical groups, neither of which found the proferred middle ground satisfactory.[51]

Petitioning continued. "The presbiterian Ministers begin to torment the Councell with their papers," wrote one of Ormond's correspondents, "to which they obtayne answers, that would discourage any people in the world for further addresses, but such reprobate fellowes, as these are." Encouragement for the Presbyterians came from Massereene and Sir Audley Mervyn, who held out hope of a royal indulgence. In September 1661 Michael Boyle, bishop of Cork, learned that Presbyterians in Ulster had prepared a remonstrance for Charles in which they professed their loyalty, recounted their suffering during the 1650s, and sought toleration. The remonstrance disingenuously claimed that Presbyterians had not endorsed the government of the "usurpers," a curious assertion in light of the number of Presbyterians whose names are recorded on the civil list. The authors concluded: "It is evident that the whole series of our Carriage from the first to this day doth hold forth our constant Loyalty, in soe far as wee beleeve the like instances can hardly be given of soe many Ministers of the Gospell together, who soe constantly, and under soe many temptation[s] & tryalls have stuck soe closely to their alleageance to his Majesty without dissimulations or waverings & professed sideing with every power which for the time prevailed Whereas wee made it still our practise to feare God and the King and not to medle with them who were given to change." Boyle urged Bramhall to investigate, arguing that toleration would be prejudicial to settling the Church of Ireland. Petitions asking Charles to honor his promise at Breda of liberty to tender consciences circulated in the dioceses of Derry and Raphoe on the eve of the Dublin plot.[52]

Presbyterians manifested disaffection with the restoration in other ways as well. Some distributed books reminding readers of Charles's avowal of the Solemn League and Covenant in Scotland in June 1650, while others refused to let conformist clergymen baptize their children. At Dromore Presbyterians "opposed & abused" a conforming minister. At Ballyrashane in 1661, after the Scottish Presbyterian minister Robert Hogsyard had twice ignored citations from ecclesiastical officials to accept episcopal ordination or resign, a troop of dragoons surrounded his church. Bearing orders to apprehend Hogsyard, an officer entered the church, alarming the congregation, but Hogsyard persuaded the officer to allow him to finish his sermon and had the congregation make room in the pews for the dragoons. The sermon done, Hogsyard descended from the pulpit, shut its door, and struck it with his Bible three times, exclaiming, "I arrest this pulpit in the name of the Lord Jesus Christ as King & Head of His Church, that neither Episcopalian, Erastian nor indulged Presbyterian should ever enter it, or address a congregation in this church until the top stone of this building is as low as the foundation."[53]

The most celebrated instance of overt nonconformist disobedience in the early 1660s occurred at Glendermott, county Derry, in November 1661. His ire raised by the seemingly endless conventicles, Bishop Wild went to an illegal service at the home of John Will, expecting "due reverence." Instead, "hot spirited" women reviled him, threatening to "pray him to distraction, & let him doe his worst, they would worship God." When members of the congregation ripped his gown the bishop "Layd them flat on thier backs." Wild subsequently had the ringleaders arrested and ordered Will to appear before him and the justices of the peace. Will came with some of his congregation, who freely admitted holding services but cited the Declaration of Breda as justification. Wild, exercising his episcopal authority "with greate clemency," as his dean, George Beaumont, claimed, bound the offenders over to the next assizes, hoping to persuade them to reform. But the garrison commander at Derry, Colonel John Gorges, was dubious, "not knowinge what a viollent Spirited people might doe in theire rage." To Sir George Lane he proposed increasing the size of the garrison and using only English officers.[54] Bramhall informed Orrery of the abusive treatment of Wild, and Will was apparently detained for several months. "Some Talke . . . as if Mr Will were to Returne Triumphantly," but Wild was optimistic, not least because some Presbyterians were making their peace with the Church of Ireland. Will himself continued to be nettlesome; though deprived in December 1661 he continued to minister, and in November 1665 the authorities finally ordered him to surrender the parsonage and garden to the dean of Derry.[55] Clearly the restoration of episcopal authority in Ireland was a complex process, replete with hostile confrontations, legal challenges, and personality clashes. Yet the prospect for modest toleration was real enough had the competing episcopalian and Presbyterian clerical camps opted for ecumenical cooperation in lieu of confrontation and mutual recrimination.

Restoring the Church of Ireland

The reimposition of episcopal government was the simplest facet of the Church of Ireland's restoration. Far more difficult was the task of enforcing the bishops' authority—a task we now know proved to be impossible. Building a vibrant episcopalian church required adequate clergy, and in this respect it made sense to seek an accommodation with the Presbyterians, easily the largest group of nonconformists and the only ones who could provide sufficient numbers of educated clergy to

help staff the restored Church of Ireland. Episcopally ordained ministers were not available in large enough numbers to fill the pulpits of
parish churches, forcing the authorities to continue paying Presbyterians and Congregationalists to perform their pastoral duties into 1661.
Among them were such noted Presbyterians as Samuel Cox, Patrick
Adair, William Jacque, John Crookshanks, and Thomas Gowan and the
Congregationalist Timothy Taylor.[56] Loftus urged Ormond to appoint as
many ministers of "gravity and learning" to benefices as he could procure, and Worth received state funds to recruit clerics in England. Even
the congregation that worshipped in the chapel of Dublin Castle had to
seek the help of ministers in the Dublin area and others who visited the
capital. Major Richard Thompson, who would die for his involvement
in the Dublin conspiracy in 1663, bemoaned the lack of preaching in the
countryside northwest of Dublin: "Wee have not heard a sermon in the
Country these tenn yeares, unless wee came to this towne [Dublin], or
to Trym, this hath been our greife." A plea for able, godly ministers
from England was incorporated in an anonymous Presbyterian remonstrance delivered to the government in October 1660. As late as February 1671 the town council at Youghal urged the mayor to protest "the
great strange neglect of preaching and reading of Divine Service in this
great Congregation of Youghall" and to request the appointment of an
able minister.[57]

Some clergymen who had held ecclesiastical appointments in the
1650s made their peace with the new regime. Among them were clerics
who on 1 January 1661 pledged to Orrery that they would serve Charles
loyally and not engage in "secrett ploteings or open resistance against a
setled goverment." One such minister was Thomas Vesey, who vowed
to Bramhall that he resolved to be "a son of the Church of England, &
never to joine with any party, that [espoused the] churlish way of Reformation . . . by the sword." The desire of some ministers ejected by the
interregnum governments to return to their livings alleviated the need
for clergy to some degree, but the evidence suggests that the churches
most affected were probably those involving substantial tithes, such as
the living of St. Peter's, Cork, now worth £100 *per annum*.[58] Incumbents
were not always prepared to leave their charges without a battle. One of
the most interesting cases occurred in February 1661 when the archdeacon of Glasgow petitioned the ecclesiastical commissioners on behalf of
Dr. Thomas Bruce, aged 74, to permit the archdeacon to officiate for
Bruce at Taughboyne, county Donegal, where Bruce was rector. The
archdeacon lived near Taughboyne, where the Scottish Presbyterian

John Hart had ministered since 1656 by government appointment with a salary of £150 *per annum*. Hart, asserted the archdeacon, had

the charge of all the churches of the North-West of Ireland, being hither recommended by Mr [George] Gillespie, the great Remonstrator in the West of Scotland, & one of his fraternity: [Hart] Takes it in derision that any should offer to dispossess him that thought & thinks himself immovable, saying flatly that he will not suffer any man to officiate in the aforesaid parish so long as he can hinder them, exhorting the people in public to stick by him & he will stick to them.

Hart reportedly not only attacked Bruce but also condemned the possibility that the parishioners would be served by a curate, which he denounced as the buying and selling of God's people. Moreover, Hart preached throughout the region on a daily basis, urging the inhabitants not to pay tithes or maintenance to Bruce. The commissioners ruled that if the bishop of Raphoe deemed the archdeacon qualified and if Bruce appointed him as his curate, Hart must step aside.[59]

The government was more concerned with providing ministers to counter the Presbyterian threat in the north than with converting the Gaelic Irish, presumably because of its historically weak record on the latter front owing to linguistic, cultural, and ethnic factors. At the duke of Albemarle's behest, Orrery recommended a conformable minister to Bramhall for an appointment in Ulster, where he would be "usefull in poynt of Intelligence, as to the Actings & designes of the seperatists." The Presbyterian problem had to be considered in dealing with pluralistic appointments. Dr. Thomas Buttolph held the livings of Drumachose cum Aghanloo, county Derry, and Ardstraw, some twenty miles away in county Tyrone; Wild supported his request to surrender one living and obtain another closer to the remaining one because "the Two New-townes" were "Factious Places, made so by grand Presbyterians," and thus required a resident clergyman. In September 1662, after Wild's dean had gone to England, the bishop sought assistance from Bramhall, noting that unless he could fill his many cures, conventicles could not be prevented. Wild made plural appointments reluctantly, for his goal was to provide as many clerics for the "Refractory Scotts" as possible; "[If I] make double-Benefices, my worke here would be left half undone." Some livings, especially that at Strabane, were especially onerous owing to Presbyterian opposition. Because the incumbent at Strabane "hath fought with Beasts," Wild complained to Bramhall in December 1662, he "deserves a Remove." Strabane was deemed "too meane" for one potential minister, Dr. James Harwood, whom Wild appointed to Leckpatrick, county Tyrone, where he and his parishioners were "Hand & Glove" by early 1663. "By this I see," Wild observed, "If wee had able ministers, we should have but few Presbyterians."[60] Whether his assessment was accurate is arguable, but it certainly suggests a popular desire for clergy who could preach effectively.

Although simplistic, Wild's last point embodied a kernel of truth, for the shortage of well-qualified clergymen posed serious problems for the restored Church of Ireland, and not just in Ulster. In January 1663, for instance, one of Sir John Percival's correspondents complained bitterly that the parishioners of Liscarroll, county Cork, were supposed to receive fortnightly visits from a Mr. Packington, who had been hired for this purpose by Orrery's chaplain, John Vesey. But Bishop Michael Boyle kept Vesey in Cork, leaving the parishioners of Shandrum as well as Liscarroll without religious services. To cite but one other example, the bishop of Clogher, John Leslie, who considered the parishioners at Clogher "the most obstinate congregation in my Diocese," was very concerned in January 1663 when the people of nearby Errigal Keerogue sought the appointment of a minister who was "a puritane ingrained." If this happened, Leslie warned Bramhall, the work of Read, the minister at Clogher, would be substantially more difficult.[61] The task of the bishops would undoubtedly have been less onerous with a greater supply of talented clergy, but this the mother church in England never provided in the seventeenth century. In both countries the episcopalian clergy paid a high price for refusing to accommodate the Presbyterians—if indeed the Scottish Presbyterians would have considered any compromise.

Judging from lay plaints the bishops themselves were not free of blame for preaching too little and too poorly. In October 1681 a complainant protested that Ireland had "too many Bishops who preached but seldom before they were Bishops and seldome since," and he urged the Commissioners for Ecclesiastical Causes to investigate because the king himself had allegedly been deceived by spurious reports of their qualifications. This and other protests were occasioned by Michael Ward, bishop of Derry from January 1680 until his death on 3 October the following year. Another layman objected to the commissioners that too many prelates read sermons, so that many artisans took notes and subsequently read them to their families, boasting they could do as much as the bishops. The new bishop of Derry, he insisted, should preach frequently, by which he meant more than merely reading a formal text. Another layman lodged a similar complaint, attacking Ezekiel

Hopkins, bishop of Raphoe (who sought a transfer to Derry and shortly thereafter received it), as one who only read sermons; "his ill exampel hath taught many of his Clergy to doe so too." Anthony Dopping, bishop of Meath, was reputedly "a very dull Preacher."[62] Sir Leoline Jenkins wrote to Ormond objecting to the possible transfer of Patrick Sheridan, bishop of Cloyne, to the see of Derry because Sheridan was notorious for his non-residency. In general, Jenkins contended, the practice of non-residency among conformist clerics was so prevalent that it was a "matter of perpetual declamation among our schismatics" in England. When Francis Marsh, bishop of Kilmore and Ardagh, was being considered for the archdiocese of Dublin, John Graham, a landowner, asked the archbishop of Canterbury to support the appointment of two resident prelates, one for Kilmore and another for Ardagh. Graham wanted them to require clergy to reside in the respective dioceses, "and then wee should have good house keeping and a good trade by reason of many people, and I would set up many Manufactures." In February 1682 Marsh received his appointment to Dublin, where most of the established clergy were young but "Constant, pious, learned preachers," but Kilmore and Ardagh remained united (except for a brief interval in 1692) until 1742, when Ardagh was jointly held with Tuam.[63]

For practical reasons the first restoration bishops had to devote substantial time in the first year or so following their appointments to economic matters. Dr. Edward Worth's survey of the diocese of Killaloe reveals the considerable effort required to identify church lands and the prevailing leases, especially because the interregnum governments had let some of the land, and in certain cases the leases were of dubious validity. Tithes and fee farms also demanded his attention. The account book of Henry Jones during his decade-long tenure in the see of Meath offers another example of fiscal concerns, though he was apparently less troubled with the problem of leases than was Worth. Jeremy Taylor's campaign to impose his authority in the diocese of Down included a legal struggle with the Congregational minister Timothy Taylor over a disputed grant of land from the interregnum regime. The bishops had anticipated some of these difficulties and petitioned the king to preserve the church's revenues. Charles had responded favorably in December 1660, but eight months later John Parker reported to Bramhall that Ormond, Bishop Gilbert Sheldon of London, and Bishop George Morley of Worcester were still fending off attempts to seize part of the Church of Ireland's patrimony.[64]

The physical devastation inflicted on the church in the 1640s severely complicated the economic problem. In 1668 Ormond and his Council complained that parish churches in most parts of the realm had not yet been repaired or rebuilt, so that in many places services had to be held in other buildings. The diocesan surveys made in the early 1690s following the war include numerous references to churches ruined half a century earlier. In some instances the spoliation is reminiscent of the dissolution of the monasteries in England: At Inishmore, county Galway, "stand[s] a castle & a chappell ruinated; possessed 1641 by the Earle of Thomond & made use of for his Deere." Because the cathedral churches of Down and Connor were "wholly ruinous" as well as inconveniently located, the king designated the church at Lisburn as the new cathedral in September 1662.[65] The physical and economic conditions of the church thus demanded a significant portion of the bishops' time and distracted them to some degree from the nonconformist challenge.

The prelates, of course, did not have to deal with the nonconformists by themselves. Ormond used his influence at court to ensure that Charles did not fulfil his promise of liberty to tender consciences by granting toleration to "Phanatiqe & disaffected persons" in Ireland. The lords justices and Council set the tone when they issued a proclamation on 21 January 1661 calling for a day of fasting and humiliation on the 30th, at which time all subjects were to attend their parish churches "to discover more and more those who have been the principal contrivers and actors in that unparalleled murder" of Charles I.[66] The importance of the parish churches as the scene of this national day of repentance and mourning was underscored by a second proclamation, issued on the 22nd, prohibiting all assemblies of Protestant nonconformists and Catholics. According to the claims of the proclamation these groups had been meeting in the hundreds and even the thousands, and in some instances appointing public fasts and days of humiliation, ordaining and inducting ministers into benefices, depriving clergy, castigating lawful magistrates, and—the crucial point—usurping "the essential rights of Soveraignty it self." The lords justices and Council directed the archbishops and bishops to compel offenders to obey and conform, ensuring with the aid of civil magistrates that no more conventicles were held. The prelates thus marched at the forefront of the campaign to curtail nonconformity, not primarily because of religious considerations but owing to the perceived threat of nonconformity to royal sovereignty.[67]

The reaction to the declaration had ramifications on both sides of the Irish Sea. Orrery hoped it would prove to Hyde that he was not sympathetic to presbyterianism as well as dampen dissent: "Because we found the Distempers & heats of such as are Disaffected to the Established legall Discipline of this Church dayly Increased, We Did Pass & Publish this . . . Proclamation; the signinge wherof will I thinke invite your Lord to beleeve me no longer, half a Presbiter, & may possibly by Fear effect, what Duty & reason could not." Orrery also hoped the proclamation would have a positive influence on England and Scotland, lending force to Ian Green's argument that the Church of Ireland's supporters helped shape ecclesiastical policy in England by their actions. Indeed, Henry Jones passed the news to Bramhall that the declaration had been well received at court and proved to be "a greate disapointment to the factious partie in England who had Laid much of their hopes on a prevailing party in the kinde among us."[68]

The interrelatedness of developments in the three kingdoms was apparent as well in parliamentary elections. After London nonconformists succeeded in March 1661 in electing four of their number (John Fowke, Captain John James, Sir William Thompson, and William Lane) to the House of Commons, they dispatched reports to their friends in Ireland and Scotland, prompting concern in government circles about "seditious designes." The same month Hyde told Orrery he hoped the new Parliament would condemn the Solemn League and Covenant and that the Irish Parliament would set a good example for England in this respect. Orrery, he advised, should persuade his associates "to pull up those bitter rootes from whence rebellion might hereafter springe," particularly the Covenant. When elections for the Irish Parliament took place later in the spring, Catholic and sectarian candidates stood in many places, but only in the borough of Tuam, which returned one of each group, did they enjoy any success.[69]

In his sermon to the Irish Parliament on 8 May, its opening day, Bishop Taylor stressed the importance of obedience, averring that religion was an imposture if it called for disobedience to any superior's command that was either in accord with God's will or not expressly contrary to it. Noting that nonconformists differed among themselves on religious issues, he contended that such disagreements had created "a great heap of disorder: they all confess that authority must be obey'd; but when you come to the Trial, none of them will do it, and they think they are not bound: but because their Opinions being contrary cannot all be right, . . . Authority is infinitely wronged and prejudiced amongst them, when all fantastick Opinions shall be accounted a sufficient reason to despise it." No one, Taylor told members of Parliament, should be permitted to disturb the peace or dishonor the government by pleading conscience, for those matters concerning the good of humanity and the peace of the realm were so plainly taught that no person could fail to know his or her duty. The nonconformists' talk of passive obedience, he claimed, was mockery, "for what man did ever say the Laws were not good, but he also said the punishment was unjust?" By falsely claiming to be persecuted, nonconformists denigrated the law. Parliament should therefore restore religious peace by forcing all persons to conform.[70]

This uncompromising tone was in keeping with Bramhall's position at this point. On 23 April, coronation day, he had preached in Dublin that nations should not "swim with blood" because of "a few innocent rites established by law." The cause of past miseries had been the inability to distinguish between "essences and abuses" in churches. Better tyranny, he told the House of Lords on 11 May, than anarchy. With nonconformists in mind, he averred that "those innovators and incendiaries who labour to pull down a settled form of government, are like a phrenetick person, who takes pains to hew down the bough whereon he himself doth stand."[71] In the eyes of Bramhall and Taylor, the issues of conscience raised by the nonconformists paled in significance to the more fundamental issue of obedience and authority. This emphasis meshed well with the lords justices' and Council's determination to reestablish royal sovereignty.

In its first month the Irish Parliament approved two major declarations on religion, the first of which recognized the church's traditional episcopalian polity and the Book of Common Prayer and required all subjects to conform thereto. The only secure way to settle the church was on its "legal and antient foundations, . . . filling all vacancies with men of signal piety, parts, and loyalty, and . . . having added so much by his Royal bounty to the patrimony of the Church." This declaration was to be read in all churches, and magistrates received instructions to punish contemners of the Book of Common Prayer. Once again Ireland's lead was recognized as Wild subsequently observed to Bramhall: "I am exceeding Glad our Irish Declaration was out, before the English Act for Uniformity."[72]

Like the first declaration, the second originated in the House of Lords, but whereas only four of the eleven peers who drafted the first declaration were bishops (Cork, Clogher, Down, and Elphin), prelates comprised three of the latter committee's five members (Down, Raphoe, and Waterford), underscoring its theological orientation. The second declaration condemned the Solemn League and Covenant as "that horrid Confederacye & Commission," "the Grand Incentive of the Rebellion in all his Majesties Dominions," and a document that was schismatic, seditious, and treasonable. Parliament ordered it burned by the common hangman or another magistrate in all cities and towns, and proclaimed that anyone who defended it by word or deed would be an enemy of the king and public peace. The Lords ordered the printing of 1,500 copies of the declaration and a search of booksellers' shops in Dublin with a view to confiscating all copies of the Solemn League and Covenant, including those bound with the Westminster Assembly's lesser catechism. Only one magistrate—Captain John Dalway, mayor of Carrickfergus—refused to burn the Covenant, for which he was compelled to kneel before the bar in the House of Lords and fined £100; he produced a certificate of compliance and had the fine remitted but still had to pay fees. In Convocation, which met concurrently with Parliament, hostility to the Covenant was no less intense. Burning copies of it may have been a satisfying symbolic gesture, but Presbyterian fidelity to the Covenant remained strong, even beyond Ulster. The bishop of Cork complained to Convocation in December 1662 that some of his clergy refused to renounce the Covenant.[73]

In the aftermath of the passage of the second declaration John Parker, bishop of Elphin, preached to both houses of Parliament in Christ Church, pleading for unity in the face of enemies at home and abroad. He seems to have had the moderate Presbyterians in mind, hoping they would suppress their reservations about episcopalian polity and the liturgy to attain unity among all who professed "the true Protestant Religion." If this was Parker's aim, his plea fell on deaf ears, for the House of Lords continued its anti-Presbyterian campaign well into the summer. In June it ordered the public burning of the Engagement and the Oaths of Association, and the following month it banned the use of the primer because it contained a prayer for the lord protector and instigated a search for copies among Dublin stationers. Some Bibles still carried title-pages with the words "Printer to his Highness the Lord Protector," and the Lords ordered that such pages be ripped out. On occasion the House of Lords even concerned itself with individual clergymen, such as the Presbyterian Thomas Boyd of Aghadowey, county Derry, who were allegedly preaching illegally.[74]

For the most part, once Parliament had passed the two principal declarations in May 1661 it concerned itself with land issues, including ecclesiastical properties. In this area the primary question was the restoration of church lands to those who had possessed them in 1641, but in June 1662 the Commons did recognize "the impoverished condition of the Ministers of this Kingdom, for want of competent means to subsist upon, occasioned through the many impropriations that are within the same." Parliament tried to solve the financial problems of the church in part by uniting some of the smaller parishes and dividing certain of the larger ones, a subject considered by the Convention as well. Although Ormond promised to do everything in his power "to preserve the true protestant Religion Established by Law," the magnitude of the land settlement was so great that the financial problems of the restored church could not be satisfactorily resolved, and for that reason too the Church of Ireland's ability to deal effectively with the nonconformist challenge was impeded.[75]

Coping with Nonconformists

In the epistle to a sermon preached at the consecration of two archbishops and ten bishops in St. Patrick's on 27 January 1661, Jeremy Taylor warned that nonconformists were "resolved to keep up a faction."[76] So they were, though none of them would have phrased his conscience-based opposition to prelacy and the Book of Common Prayer in such terms. Following his consecration on 27 January, Taylor instructed the clergy of Down and Connor to meet him at Lisnagarvy for his diocesan visitation. Under the terms of the Convention's proclamation the Presbyterians could not meet to plan a response, but the funeral of Massereene's mother in late February or early March provided the necessary opportunity. There they decided they could not, on principle, submit to episcopal jurisdiction, though they offered to meet with Taylor in private. When he demanded a written statement from the three Presbyterian delegates, they declined on the grounds that their colleagues were absent. In response to a question from Taylor the delegates affirmed their belief in *jure divino* presbyterian polity, but they insisted they had not transgressed the law because they were not exercising that form of government, an apparent admission that meetings were no longer operational. Even so, Taylor disagreed, contending "that they were now subject to another government . . . contrary to law." When Taylor asked the delegates if they would take the oath of supremacy, they responded that they could answer only for themselves, and that they would subscribe the oath only in the sense in which Archbishop Ussher had explained it. Refusing to accept any reservations, Taylor countered that he would tender the oath in its strict grammatical sense, but that only Jesuits and Presbyterians, the principal enemies to monarchy, took the oath in this manner. Lumping Presbyterians with Jesuits and alleged republicans was discomfiting for the delegates, but the bishop had no legal basis to compel them to take the oath inasmuch as they occupied neither civil nor ecclesiastical office, having not been episcopally ordained.[77]

When Taylor conducted his visitation the following day, he preached a sermon in which he made only a passing reference to the Presbyterians, criticizing them for their senseless attacks on ceremonies, prelacy, and the Book of Common Prayer. Along with the sermon he issued 83 rules for his clergy, several of which stressed the importance of unity, urging ministers to shun "doubtful Disputations" that would disturb the peace. Taylor's counsel concerning nonconformists was relatively moderate: The clergy must confer with them frequently "in the spirit of meekness," but incite no violence against them and leave them, if refractory, to face the legal consequences of their dissent. "Think no man considerable upon the point of a tender Conscience, unless he live a good life, and in all things endeavour to approve himself void of offense, both toward God and man: but if he be an humble person, modest and inquiring, apt to learn, and desirous of information; if he seeks for it in all wayes reasonable and pious, and is obedient to Laws, then . . . use him tenderly, perswade him meekly, reprove him gently, and deal mercifully with him." If, on the other hand, he separates from the Church of Ireland or gathers a congregation, he has forsaken the communion of saints.[78] Taylor clearly had hopes that his clergy could persuade at least some Presbyterians to make peace with the established church, but he also seems to have been chary of his clerics' ability to challenge the nonconformists in vigorous debate as distinct from mild-mannered persuasion.

Only two Presbyterians heard Taylor's visitation sermon, and he in turn rejected a Presbyterian proposal for a private conference. Although he consulted with a few Presbyterians individually, hoping to persuade them to conform in return for preferment, this endeavor proved fruitless. Taylor thereupon declared 36 churches vacant because their ministers lacked episcopal ordination, but he neither suspended nor excommunicated the ministers. The action was indisputably legal because the Ordinal, which the Irish Parliament had approved in 1560, mandated episcopal ordination. The wisdom of Taylor's decision is another matter, for he effectively foreclosed the possibility of further discussions despite the explicit request of the Presbyterians for another conference. The likelihood that such deliberations would have produced a workable compromise may have been slight, but the consequences of a permanent split were so great for the future of Irish Protestantism that Taylor's precipitous action renders him largely culpable for the breach. To say, as Charles Stranks does, that the break "was unavoidable if each side was to keep its self-respect" ignores the fact that on numerous occasions in the seventeenth century episcopalian and Presbyterian moderates explored a polity centered on a reformed episcopate that both sides might have been able to embrace.[79] Taylor erred by refusing to provide a context in which such discussions might have resumed.

Taylor's visitation is the best documented, thanks especially to Adair's account, but other prelates were active too. About the same time Bramhall made a northern visitation that took him through counties Armagh, Derry, and Down. Wild's visitation of Derry in April 1661 included inquiries about those who denied the royal supremacy and acknowledged subjection in ecclesiastical matters to other jurisdictions, about traducers of episcopal policy and the Book of Common Prayer, and about those who disturbed ministers during church services. When Bramhall visited Derry in August 1661, the governor of Derry city noted that it was "a very quiet visetation," though he had heard of "sufficient Discontents." A year later Wild reported to Bramhall that his visitation had given him more satisfaction "then ever I had yett," though his diocese was still replete with "Dangerous Spiritts."[80] Sixty-five Presbyterian ministers in Ireland lost their livings during Bramhall's tenure as lord primate (1661–1663). The large majority of them were in Down and Connor, followed by Raphoe and Clogher.[81]

In the early eighteenth century the Anglican apologist William Tisdall reflected that the parliamentary declaration of May 1661 reaffirming the laws on episcopal polity and the Book of Common Prayer were intended as a reminder to nonconformists, especially in light of the leniency with which the latter had been treated since the restoration. The declaration, according to Tisdall, had little impact on dissenters in the ensuing twelve months. Tisdall was only partly correct, for Presbyterians continued to minister in their churches notwithstanding their ejection until curates took possession or magistrates physically prevented access to the buildings. According to Adair this occurred within two or three months after the ejections, that is by late spring 1661. He noted only two exceptions—Robert Hamilton of Killead and James Cunningham of Antrim—both of whom received permission to continue preaching as long as they did not lecture before sermons owing to Massereene's intervention. The others, according to Adair, had to content themselves with pastoral calls in the homes of their flocks and occasional nighttime services. The Presbyterians kept up their spirits by hoping for an indulgence from the king in keeping with the spirit of his declaration at Breda, but Ormond and the bishops of London and Worcester convinced Charles that "the best way to secure the Kingdom [was] to secure the church." In August 1661 Parker informed Bramhall that the king would not grant an indulgence if it would lead to an increase in nonconformity.[82]

Some churches and ministers sought to avoid a confrontation by partial or gradual conformity. This happened at Christ Church, Dublin, where the Book of Common Prayer was reintroduced gradually. Elsewhere, Thomas Wilkinson, minister of Swords in the diocese of Dublin since 1657, hired a curate to read the Book of Common Prayer after Parliament required its use, but remained outside the church during most of the service. According to his interpretation of the nineteenth canon, "a Constant Preacher of the word" had to read the Book of Common Prayer only twice a year. Since his collation to the parish, he claimed, he had not attacked the Book or episcopalian polity, though he had hitherto propounded a course of "moderation and accomodation for reconcileing of different parties." A parishioner accused Wilkinson in Convocation of having his curate administer the Lord's supper to "Protestants in Communion with the Church of Ireland" while he tendered it "to others of a different Judgment, and in a way of administration differing from and not allowed by the Church of Ireland." Wilkinson denied the charge, insisting that he refused communion only to grossly ignorant or scandalous persons.[83] Wilkinson must have been representative of others who complied to the minimal extent possible to keep their livings.

The dioceses of Raphoe and Derry provide useful case studies to examine the early impact of attempts to reimpose the traditional Church of Ireland. Bishop Leslie observed in September 1661 that he knew of no Presbyterian conventicles in his diocese, though Presbyterians were "verie backward" in attending Anglican services, presumably, he mused, because Presbyterian clergy still lived among them. Three months later he had to admit that his "unrulie flocke continue[d] stubberne," though they did not engage in physical attacks on him as did the parishioners of Glendermott. Either the Presbyterians grew bolder or Leslie's knowledge of their activities improved, for in February 1662 he informed Bramhall that the Scottish Presbyterians John Hart and William Semple were holding conventicles at night, the former at Taughboyne and the latter at Letterkenny. Furthermore he suspected that the Scottish Presbyterians Thomas Drummond of Ramelton and Adam White of Clondavaddog were probably preaching to illegal gatherings as well. From Bramhall he sought instructions as to whether he should prosecute these ministers at the assizes or send them to Dublin. He preferred the latter course as the best way to prevent conventicles, for "so long as those persons who have so much seduced the people, are permitted to live amongst them, they will sow more tares in the night, than we shall be able to weed out in the day."[84]

Virtually from the outset of his tenure in the see of Derry, Wild confronted Presbyterians who were more vigorous in their opposition than their fellow believers in the diocese of Raphoe. When he was at Ballykelly and Newtown Limavady in late September 1661 he saw people en route to conventicles but could not discover their location. His frustration prompted him to rely less on persuasion and more on the vigorous exercise of episcopal authority, but the Presbyterians countered by moving their conventicles further into the forests and hills and posting sentries.[85]

Glendermott continued to be especially irritating despite the fact that Wild periodically sent his dean, George Beaumont, to minister there. Beaumont's presence sparked the curiosity of some Presbyterians: When he officiated at Glendermott in October the church was very full, though only some thirty people took communion, the rest moving to the lower end of the church at Beaumont's bidding; "but after, in time of Administration [they] came up to see our order, which they stayed & observed with grave silence & reverence." These were obviously people who had never attended an Anglican service. In the meantime, the local Scottish Presbyterian minister, John Will, remained defiant, holding services in his house and justifying his behavior on the grounds that he was a minister of the gospel. When Will was arrested, his supporters gathered at the pursuivant's lodging to demonstrate their support, prompting Wild to draw a parallel with the popularity enjoyed by Henry Burton in London in 1636. As Wild himself observed, the intensification of the religious struggle between the Church of Ireland and the Presbyterians in the Glendermott area actually drew more people into the arena: "I thinke their Lordships [the lords justices] have done an unexpected kindnesse to Mr Will; and indeed have Preferrd us Both, The Bishop (and his Clerke) to Greater Congregations." In early December 1661 at least 160 people were in church when the bishop presided, whereas in the past the number had never exceeded forty. Will subsequently fled to Scotland, but he seems to have returned shortly thereafter and begun to hold conventicles at night. So great was Will's popularity that Beaumont requested permission not to attend Convocation in Dublin so he could deal with the Presbyterian challenge.[86]

By January 1662 Wild seemed unable to control the dissenters. "My Presbyterian Jugglers," he complained to Bramhall, "are every day more & more improved in Hocus Pocusing." In some places they met before daylight on Sunday mornings, but elsewhere they boldly worshipped during the daytime. Although Wild could prove that some Presbyterians had attended a large conventicle at Aghadowey, county Derry, the solely Scottish grand jury at the quarter sessions on 9 January refused to present any of them. Even the magistrates of Derry city included dissenting partisans: The mayor for 1662 was an Englishman committed to the established church, but both sheriffs were Scottish merchants who entered the church only after the prayers had been read. Wild received assistance from Dr. Thomas Buttolph, who accepted the living at Urney in return for Drumachose cum Aghanloo while retaining Ardstraw. Buttolph drove the Scottish Presbyterian Thomas Fulton of Drumachose from the area, but Fulton merely relocated in the diocese of Down, where in early January 1661 he preached to a conventicle numbering at least 3,000 people. Buttolph still had to contend with Presbyterian occupants in his livings, namely William Moorcroft at Ardstraw and James Wallace at Urney—"& until they are removed I feare I shall find the people refractory." An Englishman educated at Glasgow, Moorcroft reportedly promised Buttolph he would conform or stop holding conventicles after a fortnight, but he continued to have "irregular meteings," as did Wallace, a Scottish Presbyterian who frequently baptized children in private homes. Buttolph warned that it would be prejudicial to church and state "if their contempt & impudency be not tymely restrain'd."[87]

Wild finally reported progress against the nonconformists in March 1662 owing primarily to the work of Sir Jerome Alexander, "a Resolute Anti-Presbyter Judge" who had the cooperation of a loyal bench and a supportive grand jury. The area had not seen anything like this for two decades, Wild exulted, though he expressed wonderment that Will and his supporters preferred to suffer at Alexander's hands than submit to episcopacy. The bishop obviously failed to understand the depth of the Presbyterians' convictions. In any event, one of the local gentry won special acclaim from Wild by indicting his tenants for nonconformity and conventicling. Wild accompanied Alexander on his circuit through the diocese, noting that at both Lifford and Strabane three bishops sat on the bench, an unmistakable indication of the seriousness which the authorities accorded nonconformity. Alexander's assize was moderately successful, for the Presbyterians of Derry were "much softned by the Judges most Judicious Censures," according to Wild, while those at Strabane pledged to conform on the eve of the assizes. But would the Presbyterians' seeming embrace of moderation prove fleeting? "I feare nothing," Wild wrote to Bramhall,

> but the Presbyter-Mac-Johns, who now hide out of the Way, will Returne to their Conventicles as soone as the Judge is gon hence. But I shall endeavor with my owne Court to spoyle this Interregnum, till the next half yeares Assize, when, if wee have but the second Part of Sir Jerome or such another, I doubt not but the Councell Board shall heare indifferently well of these Parts.[88]

For the bishop of Derry, the key to controlling the Presbyterians was a tough assize judge.

Praise for Alexander's work also came from Bishop Leslie of Raphoe. Leslie ordered the apprehension of Hart, Drummond, and Semple to stand trial at the assizes for holding conventicles at night and illegally baptizing children. Hart and Drummond could not be found, but Semple appeared, and after he learned how Alexander had treated Will at Derry he submitted to Leslie, promising to cease such actions. Bowing to pressure from Dublin, Leslie dismissed Semple without punishment.

> If this clemencie reclaime him . . . he is the first of his partie I have knowne so gayned. But this cours seems most pleasing to the Lords Justices and Counsell, which made me the more willinglie yeeld unto it.

On the basis of Leslie's evidence the grand jury found Hart and Drummond guilty *in absentia*, and orders for their arrest were issued. Alexander, reflected Leslie, "hath so daunted the presbyterians that I hope our Taske will be much more easie."[89]

In the meantime there were renewed pressures for an indulgence. In the spring of 1662 Catholics indicted under an Elizabethan recusancy statute petitioned the lords justices for relief. The justices ordered the judges to suspend execution of the statute until the king's pleasure was known, and shortly thereafter they issued comparable instructions concerning nonconformists in the north; the suspension of penalties applied only to recusants, not conventiclers. "Tho we would Connive at their not doeinge what they should; yet we would not connive at the doinge what they should not." Not surprisingly, the bishops protested, citing the ill effects of even this minimal gesture of toleration. Their statement, presented to the justices and councillors on 25 April, urged strict adherence to the laws and opposed toleration as inconducive to peace. Although admitting that in some cases the suspension of or dispensation from penal statutes might contribute to stability, they feared that all Catholics, Presbyterians, Independents, Baptists, and Quakers in Ireland would claim an indulgence if the government offered one to some. As long as these groups were countenanced, the prelates argued, "wee Cannot hope that the People will bee soe easily reclaymed." The justices, they proposed, should request from each bishop a list of "the most dangerous seducers in his Diocess," and then direct the judges and justices of the peace at the ensuing assizes and sessions to admonish them to conform or leave Ireland on pain of suffering the legal penalties for dissent.[90]

Responding to the bishops with a course less severe than they demanded, the justices and councillors issued a proclamation on 30 April expressing disappointment that their policy of leniency had resulted in increased nonconformity. They still hoped gentle action would be effective, hence they directed that no one be prosecuted for past violations regarding the Book of Common Prayer, church attendance, or administration of the sacraments. Effective immediately, however, they instructed the judges and justices of the peace to enforce the penal laws.[91]

The proclamation of 30 April notwithstanding, the possibility of indulging nonconformists continued to receive periodic consideration. The course of action favored by the bishops was so severe, in Orrery's judgment, that ten-elevenths of the Ulster population would be dissatisfied. Yet failure to take responsible action would leave the Church of Ireland discontented and permit "sects & heresyes" to continue unabated. Orrery succinctly expressed the enigma confronting magistrates:

If any of the sects be indulged, twilbe Partiallity not to Indulge to all; If none be favord, it may be unsafe. . . . If England, & Scotland, fall Roundly upon the Papists, & nonconformists, & we do not, Ireland wilbe the sink to receive them all; if they are fallen upon equally in the Three kingdoms, may not they all unite, to Disturbe the Peace?

As he reflected on the enigma, Orrery concluded that the religious issues should be resolved in Ireland prior to tackling the land settlement because Catholics and Presbyterians would be more compliant to an ecclesiastical settlement as long as they had hopes of favorable land arrangements.[92] Orrery's views were harmonious with the king's position, for when Ormond received his instructions in June 1662, the overriding concern was security. Although Charles favored religious uniformity, he ordered the duke to act sagely and moderately in removing "the tares and Cockles which many Years [of] War and confusion have sowed."[93]

Almost immediately Ormond found it necessary for commercial reasons to embrace a limited indulgence for Congregationalists. When "some very considerable Merchants of London" offered "to bring over thier stocks" if they could obtain an indulgence, Ormond consulted the bishops. Robert Price, bishop of Ferns, told Bramhall he had no objection if the merchants were peaceful and disturbed neither church nor state, but he opposed indulging Presbyterians because as espousers of "factious principles" they were "a restlesse generation, and noe other way to bee managed but by the coertion of Lawes."[94]

After Ormond's arrival in Ireland, Massereene, whom Adair called the Presbyterians' "constant and great friend," sought a rapprochement between them and the government. To this end he drafted a statement which he urged the Presbyterians to sign vindicating themselves from aspersions made against them to Ormond. The Presbyterians rejected the suggestion because the statement was not required by the duke, nor did they deem it safe "to please Court lords, without saying more than was right and suitable to their consciences." When Massereene told Ormond and various Councillors that Presbyterian delegates would soon come to Dublin to vindicate themselves, the Ulster Presbyterians dispatched Adair, Andrew Stewart, and William Semple. The three were in Dublin from August through October 1662. Massereene initially urged Ormond to grant an indulgence to all nonconformists, but this the duke refused to do. Massereene thereupon procured an audience with Ormond for Adair, Stewart, and Semple, who gave him a petition requesting an indulgence for the Presbyterians and pledging their loyalty.[95]

Sensitive to the fact that Presbyterians had suffered for Charles during the interregnum, Ormond pondered his options. Several days after receiving the petition he posed four queries to the Presbyterians through his secretary, Sir George Lane: On what matters did they have scruples? Who had wronged them, and how? Who had been forced from their homes? Who were the ministers for whom they petitioned? To the first query the delegates responded that they objected to reordination and the ceremonies in the Book of Common Prayer. To the second they explained that some ministers, whom they named, were threatened by penalties under civil law as well as excommunication in ecclesiastical courts. They declined to give specifics relating to the third question because they were primarily concerned with the freedom to minister, not physical possessions, but in reply to the last query they provided the duke with a list of Presbyterian clergy. Ormond had their petition and other papers read in the Council, where the bishops and others spoke in opposition while Massereene pleaded the Presbyterians' case. Ormond refused to punish the delegates, as the hardliners demanded, but he ordered Presbyterians to obey the law. They could worship as they saw fit in their own families, with occasional visitors present. Insisting that the government already granted liberty to tender consciences, Ormond contended that it countenanced "all pious and peaceable orthodox ministers of the Gospell in their severall places and callings," but neither unlawful assemblies nor "innovation, by exerting of pretended religious houses or publicque meeting places, under color of the worship or service of God." In the aftermath of the Dublin mission, according to Adair, the younger ministers "took advantage, as if the Duke had granted the brethren some great thing," thereby provoking complaints from the bishops. The older ministers, however, "lived without great molestation, performing what duty they could in their several parishes, and having their private societies one with another." The meetings, moreover, corresponded with one another.[96]

Church of Ireland clergy were dissatisfied with the limited steps taken by civil magistrates to suppress nonconformity. In August 1662 the lower house of Convocation asked the upper to propose a course to suppress Catholics, Presbyterians, Independents, Baptists, and other sectaries who reportedly met frequently in large numbers, discouraging "Orthodox" ministers and seducing the people. Indeed they did. One ecumenical group gathered in the home of Captain Thomas Jones on College Green in Dublin, where the minister was the earl of Anglesey's chaplain, the English Presbyterian Edward Bagshaw, and the congregants included Colonel Jerome Sankey and Colonel Richard Lawrence, both of whom were Particular Baptists, and alderman William Cliffe. One of Bramhall's correspondents reported that Bagshaw's conventicle had "made so great a noyse here, that I heare from Court, that they thought the Bisshops of Ireland were all asleep that they doe not represent it to his Majesty who is resolved to stand by them in suppressing all such insolencies, and to bee severe against all offenders of that nature."[97] Elsewhere, the regicide Miles Corbet's former chaplain, a Mr. Smith, "played his conventicling freaks" in Derry city but escaped before magistrates could arrest him, while nighttime conventicles continued in the diocese. Both sides received encouragement from their supporters in England, underscoring the importance attached to the religious situation in Ireland.[98]

One of Margetson's earliest actions as the newly appointed archbishop of Dublin was to prohibit Bagshaw from preaching. When the latter continued to do so in private, soldiers dispersed his congregation. On 1 September 1662 Bagshaw vigorously protested, insisting he subscribed to the Thirty-nine Articles as well as the articles of the Church of Ireland. He also noted that he was episcopally ordained and not opposed to bishops, though he objected to the mandatory imposition of *adiaphora* as an impingement on Christ's royal office. Silencing Bagshaw was a strategic error, for he, like Richard Baxter in England, was a voice of moderation and accommodation: "I have not nor ever shall decline Communion with the Church of England: It being one of the Points which I was handling, at the very Instant when I was interrupted, to Prove That Errors in Doctrine and False mixtures in Worship, are no sufficient Grounds to divide and separate from the Publicke-Assembly."[99]

More than liturgy and polity were at stake, as the deliberations in Convocation made clear in November 1662. The clergy registered their concern about "two Errors newly sprung up," the first of which denied the legality of tithing and a corresponding refusal to pay. They attributed this error to the Anabaptists, but they were probably referring to the Friends, whose numbers, unlike those of the Baptists, were rising. They associated the second error with Scottish Presbyterians in Ulster "who live for the most part upon sallary's in their owne Country and so have Consented here to the alienation of Tithes in point of fact and Comitted the Tithes into the hands of their landlords whoe do Assume them all and dispose them to their tenants together with their lands allowing the Minister who hath Actuall Care of Soules such a yearly sallary as they think meet which is the ready way to make the revenue of the Church Arbitrary at the disposition of such Landlords as have Ingrossed the tithes into their owne hands."[100] The issue was not simply monetary; with control of tithes went substantial influence over the clergy, as experience with lay impropriations had long manifested.

On 12 November 1662 the lord lieutenant and his Council issued another proclamation ordering the suppression of unlawful assemblies and citing frequent gatherings of Catholics, Presbyterians, Independents, Baptists, and Quakers in large numbers as a threat to security. A key reason for the decision to renew this ban may have been the arrest of several prominent dissidents three days earlier in a conventicle at Finglas outside Dublin. Those apprehended included "Major" John

Desborough (not to be confused with the major-general of the same name), one of Edmund Ludlow's relatives (probably his brother-in-law, Lieutenant-Colonel Nicholas Kempson), and Captain Henry Aland.[101]

Although at least some nonconformists were aware that their toleration might mean an indulgence for Catholics as well, some kept pushing for toleration. The Carte manuscripts contain a document dated April 1663 explaining why "the Petitioned Indulgence" should be granted to Ulster nonconformists. The petition appeals in part to a letter of Charles dated 26 December 1662 holding out hope of an indulgence, but most of the reasons are economic. Tolerated, the dissenters would cheerfully pay "great taxes," whereas if left prey to episcopal courts they would soon be impoverished. The financial penalties attached to excommunication would ruin entire families, nor did Ireland have enough prisons to hold all the dissenters. Moreover, if toleration were not bestowed, many nonconformists would emigrate, laying waste the property of numerous landlords. In political terms, the author(s) of the statement reminded the government of the Presbyterians' loyalty to Charles during the interregnum, argued that prosecuting so many people for matters of conscience was bad policy, and stressed that freedom from persecution would enhance the nonconformists' loyalty to the king. In short, toleration of Protestant dissenters was fiscally sound and conducive to political stability and security.[102] The argument had substantial merit, though the actions of a minority of militant extremists gave the government pause, forcing it to balance economic and security considerations.

Nonconformity and Security Concerns

The state's concern with nonconformity was a matter of security as well as religious, economic, and political considerations. This was especially the case in the early 1660s because of the difficulty in distinguishing between political dissidents and religious nonconformists. Both groups were suspected of seducing the people, and the government was obviously aware of considerable overlapping between the two. The link was explicit in Sir Theophilus Jones's call for a purge of "the most disaffected" from the army because of the trouble "fomented by that factious presbiterian spiritt raised among us." The earl of Mountrath cited his difficulty in securing Connaught for the royalists because of the number of Baptists and other "fanatics" in such places as Galway and Athlone. When the king ordered the lords justices in August 1661 to commission Major Arthur Graham to arm and train undertakers and other men in the plantations of Leinster and Ulster, the justices protested on the grounds that many thousands in the latter province had not professed obedience to the Church of Ireland and were thus a security threat. Two months later the justices and councillors ordered the justices of the peace of county Antrim to seize the horses, weapons, and ammunition of anyone believed to be ill-affected to the government, and in the same proclamation they instructed magistrates to prevent and suppress illegal assemblies.[103] In December 1661 the Irish Parliament informed the lords justices that it wanted only Protestants well-affected to the government to serve in trained bands and it ordered the seizure of the horses, arms, and ammunition of all disaffected persons. Nor did it want dissidents or Catholics to reside in any walled town—or even in Ireland—without license.[104] Parliament was perhaps paranoid, but memories of the 1640s and 1650s were powerful.

Concern about the threat of nonconformity to security was still evident during the fall and winter of 1662–1663, on the eve of the Dublin plot. In October Ormond and the Council commanded Orrery to remove dangerous persons from the garrisons in Munster. The government's dilemma was its inability to suppress both Catholics and Protestant nonconformists. As Henry Coventry explained to Clarendon, Irish towns were replete with Protestant dissidents, the countryside was peopled with Catholics, and the army was still largely comprised of men who had fought for the commonwealth. Ormond was installing officers known to be loyal, but it would be years before the army was reasonably reliable. The duke hoped he could keep disaffected Englishmen from rebelling by threatening to arm the Gaelic Irish, not by using his army. If the land settlement provoked a significant disturbance, he warned Charles in February 1663, the army was in "a very ill state" to suppress it, not least because he lacked the necessary funds. Without a reliable army, he argued, a few desperate men could start "a commotion" with unpredictable consequences.[105]

The proximity of Ulster and Scotland and the large numbers of Presbyterians in both places severely complicated security. The government did not coordinate policies in Dublin and Edinburgh to deal with the Presbyterians in the early 1660s, and only belatedly did it attempt to establish effective, direct communications between its principal agents in both realms. As a result, throughout much of the period nonconformists could cross and re-cross the North Channel to flee from magistrates and hold conventicles wherever opportunity presented itself. In an attempt to halt the movement of Presbyterian clergymen from Ireland to Scotland, the Scottish Parliament enacted a law in February 1661 requiring all persons coming from Ireland to produce a statement from a magistrate attesting to their peaceful deportment, but the statute proved to be ineffective. The following month the king ordered the lords justices and Council to apprehend "dangerous or seditious persons" arriving in Ireland from Scotland, but without curtailing all movement of people because of the importance of trade between the two countries. In September Charles instructed the sheriff of Clydesdale to arrest two ministers who had come from Ireland.[106] Orrery initially believed Ulster Presbyterians might conform if they received copies of the royal proclamation restoring episcopacy in Scotland, but by the spring of 1662 he concluded the episcopalian settlement in Scotland would drive both Presbyterians and Catholics to Ireland. The recognition that policies in one kingdom had an impact on the other made direct communications essential, and the first attempt to establish such a link was made in September 1662, though its operation was sporadic and sometimes nonexistent for years.[107]

From the government's standpoint one of the most significant threats to security was plotting. From the historian's armchair it is easy to dismiss the alleged conspiracies as the products of overheated imaginations, but Charles and his principal advisors could not afford to assume that all reports were baseless, even when the number of men who were reputedly involved was obviously exaggerated. Thus in August 1661, for instance, the king directed the lords justices to be diligent in "discovering what Plotts & designes the Papists or any other may have for the embroileing that kingdom in new disturbances."[108]

During Charles's reign only one conspiracy was sufficiently advanced in Ireland to pose a major security threat. Because I have recounted the history of that plot elsewhere, I shall only summarize it here before assessing the extent to which nonconformists were involved and the ramifications of the conspiracy for dissenters in general. Lieutenant (or Colonel as he called himself) Thomas Blood, a Presbyterian, first conceived the plot around September 1662. As in the case of the conspiracies of December 1659 and February 1660 Blood's plan centered on the seizure of Dublin Castle, the center of Irish government. His goal was not to overthrow the monarchy but to ensure the security of Protestant and English interests in Ireland; had he been able to win the support of the Ulster Presbyterians, he would have been no less committed to Scottish concerns. His principal co-conspirators were Colonel Robert Shapcote (an attorney), Majors Abel Warren and Richard Thompson, Captain Theophilus Sandford, and the merchant Thomas Boyd. The attempt on the castle was originally scheduled for early March 1663, but a soldier whom the plotters had attempted to recruit informed the authorities. Lacking sufficient evidence the government chose not to prosecute the cabal, which shortly thereafter resumed its scheming, this time scheduling an uprising for 21 April. Ormond bided his time, determined to amass the necessary evidence to convict the plotters. When Blood and his associates could not muster the necessary men in the early hours of 21 April, they postponed the uprising, but the government ordered their arrest the same morning.[109]

Although dozens of dissenting clergymen were arrested in May, June, and July 1663, most were victims of an apprehensive government that suspected widespread nonconformist involvement. The Irish-born Presbyterian minister William Lecky was intimately engaged in the plotting, and the Scottish Presbyterians John Crookshanks and Andrew McCormack knew and at least initially approved of it. McCormack allegedly recruited men in Ulster but subsequently became disenchanted with the conspirators when he learned they were considering assassination. Three others—the episcopalian Robert Chambers, author of an allegedly treasonable book, and the Congregationalists Edward Baines and Stephen Charnock—were probably participants. Other clergymen—the Scottish Presbyterians John Hart, John Greg, Andrew Stewart, and Henry Livingstone—knew of the scheming but did not report it to the authorities. The evidence for the involvement of other ministers is sketchy and inconclusive, but three Dublin congregations—two Presbyterian and one Congregationalist—allegedly knew of the conspiracy and met on the morning of 20 May to pray for God's blessing on the uprising.[110]

Lecky, Blood's brother-in-law and the fomer minister at Dunboyne, had gone with Blood in December 1662 to Ulster to seek Scottish support. They met with Greg, Stewart, and Captain James Moor of Killinchy, county Down, discussing "the usurpation of the bishops, the tyranny of their courts, the increase of Popery, and misgovernment in every affair," and encouraging the Presbyterians to join them in the proposed "design," the details of which they did not disclose. When Greg, Stewart, and Moor declined to participate, Blood and Lecky went to Lagan and Armagh, where they won the support only of McCormack, formerly the minister at Magherally in Down, and Crookshanks, who had been ejected from his church at Raphoe. Blood and Lecky made two more trips to Ulster in the spring of 1663, at which time they met with Henry Livingstone, the ejected minister of Drumbo. Livingstone sent them to Newtownards to confer with Greg, who allegedly refused Blood's request to sign a pledge of support. Hart subsequently confessed that he had discussed the plot with Blood and Lecky, and Richard Thompson, who admitted his role in the conspiracy, testified that he had corresponded with Hart about the affair. Following Hart's admission, the authorities conveyed Greg and Stewart to Dublin for interrogation. Because Stewart had been privately informed that another witness, the Scottish merchant Thomas Boyd of Dublin, had implicated him, he admitted his discussion with Blood and Lecky, but Greg, not knowing this, refused to confess.[111]

The role of Chambers and the reputed involvement of Charnock and Baines are more difficult to document. Three witnesses, including Richard Thompson, provided evidence against Chambers. James Tanner, formerly a clerk to Henry Cromwell's secretary, claimed Blood had told him Chambers was involved and that Blood had been at Chambers' house. Richard Thompson testified that Chambers told him he was afraid he would be ruined, presumably because of his involvement in the plotting, and the tailor James Milligan confessed that Blood had sent him from Antrim to Dublin to deliver a letter to Chambers, but this was in July 1663, when Blood was in hiding. All of this is second-hand or circumstantial, but Chambers admitted that Blood had discussed the plot with him, and in 1669 he accepted a pardon for treason or misprision of treason.[112]

The principal evidence against Charnock came from Tanner and Colonel Edward Vernon, whose agent, the attorney Philip Alden, was the government's chief source of information as the plotting unfolded. According to Tanner, in early April 1663 Blood showed him a letter in canting language from Charnock, who was then in England, indicating that an unnamed person (whom Tanner believed was Henry Cromwell) would soon arrive in Ireland to lead the insurrection. Shortly thereafter, Charnock came to Dublin, where he met with Blood, Major Alexander Staples, and Tanner at a house in Castle Street. Blood reportedly told them of his plan to seize the castle and of his trip to Ulster the previous December. According to Vernon, Charnock told the plotters "that they warr soe Hampered in England that they could not stir till the Eyce was broken, either in this place, or Scott Land." Charnock, then, probably knew of the conspiracy and possibly served as a link to dissidents in England. Baines, who had assisted Chambers at St. Patrick's and then served as the minister of St. John's, Dublin, was implicated by Alden, who also named Hart, Chambers, McCormack, Charnock, Lecky, and two others identified only as Cox and King. Baines's congregation was probably one of the three churches that allegedly met on 20 May to pray for the plotters.[113]

Other ministers appear fleetingly in the records. The Cox to whom Alden referred was also mentioned by Milligan; in July 1663 Blood allegedly told Milligan he intended to hide at Cox's house near Carlow. This may have been Samuel Cox. No less enigmatic was the possible role of the Presbyterian William Jacque, the ejected minister of Clongesh and now pastor of a Scottish Presbyterian congregation in Bull Alley, Dublin; this church was probably one of the three that purportedly met on 20 May. One week earlier Sir Arthur Forbes had informed Ormond that Jacque had gone to county Antrim, and that prior to his departure he had warned a confidante to expect trouble because the duke had not discovered "the botom" of the plotting "nor any of the considerabel parsones tharein ingaged." According to Major David Monro, nephew of the prominent Scottish dissident Major-General Robert Monro, Jacque had come from Dublin with a Lieutenant Shields in May 1663 to persuade the major to join them. Monro contended that as soon as Dublin Castle had been seized, Major Alexander Staples would secure Derry and Shields would attack Major Rawdon's troop. The conspirators also allegedly planned to send for Colonel Gilby Carr to command the Ulster Scots.[114]

Probable confirmation of Jacque's involvement is found in a letter dated 10 July 1663 from J. Thomson (Tomson) in Derry to William Jackson at the post office in Dublin. Jackson is almost certainly Jacque, and the communication he received conveyed the contents of two letters, presumably to Thomson, from Carr and the Edinburgh merchant John Wallace respectively. Carr's letter, which was written at Kintyre, Scotland, on 18 June, said:

Be stedfast in the faith; you have not as yet ressisted unto blood but I hear that some will and if so be that they do suffer ther blood will cry strongly before the throne of God then if they themselves were alive: we are not yet sufficiently tryed and purged otherwise our deliverance would appeare, but there cup is affilling And wilbe full before the day be long & wo unto them that shall drinke it: hitherto God did never yet permitt such men to triumph over his owne Inheritance; they are so furious that a short time reaps them for Judgement; they are blind that do not see them both fierse and confused, disordering the house of God, Ading parish to parish. . . . God grant us patience.

This is a striking illustration of the temper of militant Presbyterians. An earlier letter from Thomson, dated 27 June, had reported Carr's movements in Ulster and his return to Scotland.[115]

Because the authorities seized a copy of the plotters' declaration, which called for a religious settlement according to the Solemn League and Covenant, the Presbyterians in particular were obvious objects of suspicion. Accordingly, on 16 June the lord lieutenant and Council ordered the northern bishops and other magistrates to secure all clergy suspected of involvement in the conspiracy or believed likely to seduce the people to disobey the king's civil or ecclesiastical authority. On 29 June Ormond and his Council made a concerted effort to distinguish between dissidents and the many nonconformists who refused to engage in the conspiracy. Their proclamation of 30 April 1662, they said, had not produced the desired conformity, but they were determined once again to employ gentle means, specifically a prohibition on holding people accountable for past infractions against the Book of Common Prayer. The archbishops and bishops, they added, would follow a similar course, though this indulgence would last only until 24 December 1663 and would not extend to any minister who exhorted people not to conform. In Ulster, however, the bishops blatantly ignored the indulgence and prosecuted dissenters in their courts.[116]

The security measures employed because of the plotting affected nonconformists throughout Ireland. In the south, for example, Bishop Boyle's investigation following the initial disclosure of the plot did not turn up enough evidence to arrest anyone, but on 23 April Orrery, citing an order of the lord lieutenant and Council issued the previous October, commanded the mayor and other officials of Limerick to expel anyone who refused to conform to the Church of Ireland within two months, excepting only persons of quality and demonstrated loyalty, physicians, apothecaries, merchants engaged in sea trade, shipmakers, mariners, and anglers. Orrery issued similar instructions to the other garrisons in Munster. Most of the more than 1,000 nonconformists and Catholics in Limerick were expelled, and to offset their loss, Orrery settled eighty Dutch Protestant clothworkers in the town.[117]

The most dangerous "fanatics," in Orrery's judgment, were flocking to Cork, a judgment Boyle corroborated when he told Ormond in late May 1663 that there was "a greater resort of those kinde of people to this citty then formerly was usuall," and that they had "a secret Caball in the suburbes." Boyle thought more people would conform if Ormond released "the factious Minister" Richard Powell, formerly of Timoleague, from prison and permitted him to go England, liberating his "proselytes" from his domineering influence. The Congregationalist Zephaniah Smith, who had come to Ireland from New England to preach in the mid-1650s, was incensed when zealous magistrates arrested him at a conventicle near Clonmel on 29 May. "If he had been at Masse or at an Alehouse amongst a company of drunkards, swearers or heathens," he reportedly said, "he doth suppose that he should not have been interrupted." He was correct, but the magistrate who ordered his arrest found justification in a statement made by one of the women at Smith's conventicle: "There must be another Boute or Blowe for it, & that very suddenly."[118] In mid-1663 Protestant nonconformity—not Catholicism or debauchery—appeared to be the gravest threat to the realm.

Ulster posed a greater problem than Munster. Ormond ordered the apprehension of "all the Scotish sylenced ministers in the North who are a dangerous artillery; what I shall doe with them I know not, only I take it to bee reasonable that if they trouble mee a great deale I may trouble them a little." And so he did. In the summer of 1663 eleven ministers, including the Baptist Andrew Wyke, the Congregationalist Timothy Taylor, and the Presbyterians William Keyes, James Cunningham, and Thomas Hall, were incarcerated at Carrickfergus. Another seven—the Presbyterians Andrew Stewart, John Greg, John Drysdale, Gilbert Ramsey, Alexander Hutcheson, William Richardson, and James Gordon—found themselves imprisoned at Carlingford. The authorities were searching for an additional dozen, excluding Henry Hunter, Anthony Kennedy, Joseph Hamilton, and Michael Bruce, who were thought to have fled to Scotland. The bishop of Derry reported the arrest of four more—Robert Craghead of Donaghmore, James Wallace of Urney, John Hamilton of Donaghedy, and Robert Wilson of Strabane—in August, and Hugh Wilson and Robert Hogsyard were incarcerated.[119]

At least forty ministers went to jail, were forced into hiding, or fled Ireland in the aftermath of the plotting. The incarceration of ministers on such a scale for any length of time was clearly impractical, not least because the government lacked adequate space to detain them. At Carlingford the ministers faced confinement in a single room, which gave them, complained Viscount Conway and others, "too much opportunity to communicate their councells." The king wanted the more dangerous ones moved from prison to prison to prevent their release on writs of *habeas corpus*. The duke had a more drastic solution, proposing to free them on condition that they leave Ireland, believing they could do less damage in Scotland and England, where the problem of a contentious land settlement did not exacerbate tensions. The king, however, rejected Ormond's proposal. Viscount Alexander then re-endorsed the plan to liberate those, such as Drysdale, who would post bonds and transfer the rest to other prisons. They could not continue to reside in their accustomed places, he contended, or the people would never attend services in the Church of Ireland except to see a dignitary such as himself; "I think I must goe in procession from church to church to convert the people," he told Ormond.[120]

Although Ormond seriously proposed to send dissident clerics to Scotland and England, the Dublin plot intensified concerns about the links between Presbyterians in Ireland and Scotland, not least because of suspicion that Ulster nonconformists would not rebel without assurances of support from coreligionists in Scotland. The northern realm was also an obvious place for Irish dissidents to seek shelter, hence the king directed the Scottish Privy Council on 1 June 1663 to interrogate everyone coming from Ireland and examine the mail between the two kingdoms. Charles feared that if disaffected Presbyterian clergymen left Ireland for Scotland or England, they would not be readily recognized, making it difficult to silence them. Knowing he could not expel Presbyterian ministers apparently prompted Ormond to curtail his investigation of the conspiracy. Fifteen years later he reflected to the earl of Anglesey: "I found the design was too far spread to ravell any further into it, & that, if I should follow on the thread of the discovery as far as it might lead me, possibly I might bring on that insurrection & rebellion, which they designed, & I had rather should be prevented then punished."[121] For this reason historians will probably never be able to trace the full extent of nonconformist involvement in or prior knowledge of the Dublin conspiracy.

The Dublin conspirators had unwittingly lent substance to the government's concerns about security and in so doing had at least temporarily persuaded it to embrace a much tougher policy on dissent, as leading episcopalian clerics had been advocating. By their actions the conspirators had thus done more to alter the administration's policy than had the Church of Ireland's spokesmen. The early 1660s proved to be a lost opportunity for episcopalians and moderate nonconformists in Ireland to find a suitable means of working together to advance the many basic Protestant principles they held in common. In so doing they complicated the government's efforts to maintain peace and security and perhaps had less of a positive economic impact than would otherwise have been the case.

CHAPTER 2

In Search of a *Modus Vivendi*: Nonconformists and the Government, 1664-1685

BRAMHALL'S DEATH in June 1663 occurred as the investigation of the Dublin conspiracy was at its height, but neither Ormond nor Bramhall's successor, James Margetson, archbishop of Dublin, supported a persecutorial campaign against all nonconformists. From January 1664 through mid-1666 repeated rumors of an imminent rebellion by the Gaelic Irish focused some of the government's attention away from the nonconformists,[1] but the outbreak of the Second Dutch War in 1665 created major security concerns. These intensified when militant Covenanters rebelled in Galloway in November 1666, sparking both renewed efforts to improve communication between Dublin and Edinburgh and conflicting proposals to deal with nonconformists in Ireland. Lay leaders themselves now split, with some, such as Orrery, advocating repressive policies, and others, such as Viscount Conway, espousing liberty of conscience and economic development. Clerical leaders, however, generally continued to demand the suppression of nonconformity. Ormond's recall in 1669 led to the brief tenures of John Baron Robartes, who was sympathetic to the Presbyterians, and John Lord Berkeley of Stratton, a known favorer of Catholics. The reins of power in Ireland were in the hands of Arthur Capel, earl of Essex, from 1672 until Ormond's return five years later. Although Essex favored a policy of indulgence for nonconformists, the increasing activities of militant Covenanters challenged the government, undermined Essex's preference for tolerance, and may have contributed to the king's decision to recall him in April 1677. The government's policy toward dissenters in Ireland hardened in the final years of Charles's reign owing especially to the disclosure of the Rye House plotting. Once again, the activities of extremists adversely affected the hopes of most key lay leaders for some accommodation of dissent. Faced with a choice between toleration and security, the government, urged on by uncompromising clerical leaders, opted for security.

From the Shadows of the Dublin Conspiracy to the Outbreak of Rebellion in Scotland

The revelation of the Dublin plot confirmed the hardliners' suspicion that Protestant dissenters threatened the kingdom's stability. "The late meetings of the pretended Ministers without any pretence of imploy-ment or estates visibly to detaine them in these parts," complained Jeremy Taylor, "makes us full of confidence that as long as their Minis-ters are permitted amongst us, there shall be a perpetual seminary of schisme & discontents." Taylor was irritated that John Greg, James Gor-don, Hugh Wilson, James or Robert Cunningham, and Gilbert Ramsey were attempting to pressure those who conformed into returning to presbyterianism. None was reputedly as bad, however, as Henry Liv-ingstone, whom Taylor regarded as "the most perverse & bitter enemy we have to the [religious] Lawes." As early as 11 June 1663 Taylor urged Ormond to tender the oath of supremacy to dissenting ministers and require them to post bonds, believing this would either compel them to leave "or give a reasonable account of them as long as they stay."[2]

The most effective way to deal with dissenting clergymen continued to be a matter of debate. In early August Ormond implemented the king's order to transfer the most dangerous incarcerated ministers to different locations. He moved John Shaw, James Shaw, Timothy Taylor, Andrew Wyke, Hugh Wilson, John Drysdale, William Richardson, Gil-bert Ramsey, James Gordon, and Alexander Hutcheson from Carling-ford and Carrickfergus to prisons in Limerick, Cork, Youghal, and Waterford. Ormond apparently won Charles's acquiescence to exile some of the dissidents. One of the first was the Scottish Presbyterian James Gordon, the former minister at Comber, county Down, and the chaplain of the dowager Viscountess Montgomery; the earl of Mount-Alexander's mother prevailed with him to intervene on Gordon's be-half, allowing him to remain in Ireland without being confined to prison, though he was permitted to hold services only for Mount-Alexander's mother and members of her family. Powerful patrons enabled others to stay in the country: Robert Cunningham because of support from Lady Crawford Lindsay, the duke of Hamilton's sister; William Richardson because of help from Mount-Alexander's mother and the countess of Clanbrassill; Alexander Hutcheson owing to Lord Dungannon's assistance; James Cunningham and Robert Hamilton of Killead thanks to the intercession of Massereene and his wife; and Adair, for whom unnamed persons intruded with Ormond. Others had to leave Ireland: Thomas Hall, John Douglass, Hugh Wilson, Robert Hogsyard, John Shaw, and James Shaw for Scotland and Wyke for England. Adair implies that two ministers refused to go into exile; they were, in any event, incarcerated in distant prisons, William Keyes in Galway and John Colthart in Athlone. Other clergymen remained in hiding.[3]

Despite these rather severe steps, nonconformists found reason for hope in Margetson's indulgence, which caused Bishop Wild to fume: "Only That Faction whom no kindnesses could yett ever oblige & whose Clay-soules are only Hard'ned with the kindly Warmth of an Indulgence, beginn to hold them selves Considerable (though indeed not so) by the Favor they receive." The dissenters, remembering the declaration of Breda, expected the indulgence to be extended. Reports of conventicles continued, but not in large numbers; many Presbyterians, though unable to attend their own services, were apparently registering their protest by refusing to worship in the Church of Ireland.[4] By year's end Ormond admitted to Charles that dissenters were meeting in larger numbers than the government should connive at, but he opted not to enforce the penal laws rigorously, partly because of nonconformist unrest about the land settlement and partly because civil and ecclesiastical officials were typically more concerned with personal gain than reformation. The government also had difficulty finding adequate numbers of trustworthy magistrates. Captain Robert Manley complained to Ormond in June 1663 that many "unfit persons" had been appointed justices of the peace; most, he alleged, were Oliver's "offspring." Later that summer Conway and Taylor sent the duke two lists, one naming men known to be well-affected and able to serve on commissions of the peace, the other of current justices of the peace who should be omitted from future commissions owing to questionable loyalty. Most justices of the peace, constables, and even churchwardens in the north reportedly favored presbyterianism. From Ormond's perspective the policy of indulgence was at least in part the consequence of practical considerations that precluded the possibility of eliminating nonconformity, whether Protestant or Catholic. Indeed, Protestant nonconformists cited the *de facto* toleration necessarily accorded to the Gaelic Irish as part of their claim to enjoy similar freedom.[5]

Ormond's policy of dealing firmly with the more active Presbyterians while quietly indulging the others enjoyed some success. According to John Thompson, a Church of Ireland cleric, most Presbyterian ministers had eschewed conventicles, but their insistence on observing fasts inspired the laity to remain loyal to dissenting principles. Still, in Thompson's judgment, the actions of a minority brought "A verie Deep staine upon the whole." In January 1664 Michael Bruce, Henry Hunter, and James Campbell returned from Scotland without permission or fanfare and apparently in no mood to challenge the government; although they urged their followers to petition Ormond on their behalf, they were primarily concerned to be tried by a judge of assize rather than an ecclesiastical tribunal should they be accused of an offense. Bishop Wild observed in the spring that his efforts to bring the people of his diocese "to a peaceable conformity" were achieving some success, though Sir Richard Kennedy, judge of the northern circuit, did not share his optimism. Most residents of the Carrickfergus area, he found, were "Infected with the presbiterian Disease" and remained loyal to the Solemn League and Covenant. The policy of indulgence, in his view, had only encouraged them to remain steadfast in their convictions.[6]

Margetson's report of his triennial visitation in the summer of 1664 sheds valuable light on conditions in his archdiocese. In county Antrim some Scottish conformist clergy could not read the liturgical prayers in their proper order, whereas the ministers in county Derry were not only orthodox but capable. The Derry laity generally conformed and most of the rest—except some women—were "tractable," a tribute to Wild's work. Wild, in fact, subsequently reported to Margetson that his attempts to persuade dissidents to conform "hath produced a good effect, yet a full conformitie of that people cannot be expected" as long as the "silenced" Presbyterian ministers lived among them. This was a clever way of currying Margetson's favor while pressing for a tough policy to deal with nonconformist clerics. Moreover Wild proposed to increase the number of Englishmen in the Derry corporation, especially among the aldermen and common councillors. He was not averse to clergymen and schoolmasters of Scottish descent as long as they were loyal sons of the church.[7]

Margetson's more tolerant policy notwithstanding, some nonconformist activities made the government uneasy in 1664–1665. They included a collection of more than £500 for John Greg, at least some of which was raised in Dublin itself, though there was nothing sinister about this inasmuch as the donors' names were recorded on a long scroll. Moreover the dissenters were waiting for Parliament to meet in the apparent expectation of a statutory indulgence. Preparations were reportedly underway for a collection to enable Andrew McCormack to purchase a pardon, and McCormack himself had allegedly found a haven on one of Massereene's estates, though Conway wanted the preacher arrested. John Crookshanks, the reputed translator of George Buchanan's *De jure regni apud Scotos,* left for Scotland in the summer of 1664, but only after conferring with leading dissenters in Ulster. About the same time Hart preached to 500 conventiclers at Taughboyne, county Donegal, but the magistrates arrested him shortly thereafter for disobeying a summons to appear in the bishop of Raphoe's court; he remained incarcerated—with Semple, Drummond, and Adam White—until 1670.[8] Reports of an alleged new nonconformist plot surfaced in December 1664, and though such accounts were fairly routine,[9] they caused alarm, in part because Ulster Scots were sending agents to Dublin to sell their "stocks" as the country drifted toward war with the Dutch. Although a new law imposed a fine of £100 on a minister without episcopal ordination each time he administered the Lord's supper, the number of conventicles in Ulster rose in 1665 according to Michael Boyle, archbishop of Dublin.[10]

The war, which was officially declared in February 1665, exacerbated fears of conspiracies, reports about which mushroomed in 1665 and 1666. Within a fortnight after the declaration Orrery was fretting that Ulster Scots would join forces with militants in the rest of Ireland in an attempt to seize control, and Henry Jones, bishop of Meath, believed the "fanatics" were pleased with disturbances in the country. The government could not afford the luxury of ignoring the reports, however spurious most of them obviously were in retrospect, hence Arlington, probably acting with the king's approval, dispatched an agent to spy on suspected malcontents in June 1666. Intelligence reports gathered in England by Lord Arlington indicated that English dissidents looked to their associates in Ireland to lead the attack on the government: "He that will *England* win, with *Ireland* must begin." Blood, almost as ubiquitous as Ludlow, and Gilby Carr were believed to be en route to Ireland to launch an insurrection. A worried Arlington dispatched another spy to capture Blood; an English agent tracked him through western England and Wales before reporting that he never went to Ireland.[11]

Although some nonconformists in Ireland were scheming in 1665–1666,[12] the vast majority were not, but they were nevertheless affected by the security measures employed by the government. The determination of officials such as Arlington, Orrery, and Conway to discover what nonconformists might be plotting resulted in a much closer monitoring of their activities, especially in Ulster and Munster. Yet Ormond was frankly uncertain as to how best to prevent a nonconformist uprising and, as before, concerned that precipitous government action might provoke dissenters to take up arms. "I have not yet given any directions for secureing The cheefe Fanaticks," he told Orrery, "both because I know not well how to begin & where to end a lyst of them, and that I would not yet fright them from their contrivances till some of them might be convicted & proceeded against upon full evidence." He had learned a lesson from his ill-fated initial attempt to suppress the Dublin plotters before he had sufficient evidence to obtain convictions, and he was also confident he could quash a rebellion by either the dissenters or the Gaelic Irish if he allied with one against the other. Orrery kept pressing him to apprehend the principal dissidents, but this the lord lieutenant refused to do unless they engaged in fresh acts of defiance; past behavior was not grounds for preventive detention.[13]

The number of conventicles reportedly increased in 1666, though the rise may have been an illusion—the result of closer monitoring by the state. In Ulster the Presbyterians were purchasing weapons, but to defend themselves against an expected Gaelic Irish uprising rather than to attack the government. When the latter attempted to impose an oath of loyalty on Presbyterian clergy, some of them resolved to meet in Ulster with a view to petitioning Ormond for time to consider an appropriate reply, but nothing seems to have come of this. Nor did the passage of an Act of Uniformity in the spring of 1666 provoke much response among the nonconformists, probably because it essentially reinforced an Elizabethan statute; schoolmasters, however, now had to be licensed by a Protestant bishop and take the oath of supremacy.[14]

The outbreak of the Galloway rebellion in November 1666 forced the authorities to deal with a possible nonconformist uprising in Ireland. On 20 November, one day after news of the revolt reached London, Charles ordered Ormond to be alert, but only as the king realized the magnitude of the rebellion in the ensuing days did he instruct the duke to take substantive precautions, including the stationing of ships in the North Channel to intercept correspondence between the Scottish rebels and dissidents in Ireland. The involvement of Crookshanks and McCormack, both of whom would die in the battle at Rullion Green, heightened suspicion that militant Presbyterians in Ireland were on the verge of rebelling.[15] Following their defeat, some insurgents fled to Ireland, prompting Charles to send Ormond instructions for their apprehension. Convinced that as many disaffected people were in Ireland as in Scotland, the duke stepped up his monitoring of Presbyterian activity and ordered the arrest of two unnamed Presbyterian clergymen who had come from Scotland and were allegedly preaching sedition to large crowds. Ormond asked Jeremy Taylor for a list of exiled ministers who had gone to Scotland and subsequently returned as well as the names of landlords and others who approved payments from their tenants to these clerics. Finally, he ordered the arrest of the Scottish Presbyterian minister Andrew Kennedy of Templepatrick.[16]

The rebellion exacerbated a security problem that was already worsening on the eve of the uprising. Dungannon informed Ormond in October that he was having trouble with the militia, especially in Donegal, because Presbyterians refused to take the required oath though they were willing to serve. Orrery did not have this problem in Munster, where he had enough reliable Protestant volunteers for a militia of 2,000 horse and 3,000 foot—sufficient, he believed, to suppress English fanatics or discontented Gaelic Irish. Nevertheless the rebellion unnerved Orrery to some extent and he was obviously relieved when he received Ormond's command to apprehend dangerous persons in his province. Only in Ulster did the militia continue to pose a problem after the Galloway rebellion.[17]

The insurrection intensified the government's concern with the relationship between Presbyterians on both sides of the North Channel. In the years leading up to the rebellion Presbyterian clergy had gone from Ireland to Scotland and there preached against episcopacy. The most notorious of these had been Crookshanks and Michael Bruce. Suspicion in official Scottish circles, both civil and ecclesiastic, of what Archbishop Alexander Burnet called "ane intercourse between the scots in the north of Ireland and our own male-contents in the west" was rife. To monitor these ties Burnet began to correspond with Wild in the spring of 1665. This proved to be inadequate because the official post between Dublin and Edinburgh had fallen into disuse; Charles finally ordered its resumption in June 1667, but it was still not operating the following January.[18] No measures could completely cut off the movement of Covenanting ministers between Ireland and Scotland. Scottish magistrates finally arrested the elusive Bruce near Stirling in June 1668 and formally sentenced him to exile in Tangier, but the government allowed him to return to Ireland, where he settled at Killinchy, county Down, in the spring of 1670.[19] In the years after the Galloway rebellion, reports of

Irish conventicles reached Scotland, where they inspired Covenanters to continue holding illegal services—another reminder of the intimate ties between the two realms and further evidence of why the administrations of both countries were preoccupied with security.[20]

The Aftermath of the Galloway Rebellion: Ramifications for Ireland

The Galloway rebellion sparked a debate among civil and ecclesiastical leaders in Ireland over the treatment of dissenters. For the most part Orrery's reaction to the uprising involved military improvements, but he also wanted to secure those most likely to incite an insurrection, especially in Ulster. Bishop Jeremy Taylor espoused a tougher line: Convinced that the Galloway uprising was "either borne in Ireland or put to nurse here," he used it to justify his argument that indulging Irish Presbyterians was ill-conceived.[21] In his first year as bishop of Derry, Robert Mossom also urged firm action against the dissenters, beginning with Hart, Semple, White, and Drummond, whom he wanted transferred from Lifford prison to a distant place because they seduced the people at Lifford and Strabane "under the pretence of being prisoners of the Lord." He further urged the arrest of "factious" preachers from Scotland who, "like wild Bores hunted out of a Forrest . . . throw their fome of seditious doctrine amongst the people," and to this end he requested two or three blank warrants for his agents to use "privately," thereby avoiding public blame for the resulting arrests. In addition, he asked that arrested persons be required to post bond never again to come to Derry or anywhere else the lord lieutenant thought appropriate. He also recommended apprehending some of the "chief" residents of county Derry who attended conventicles and compelling them to post bonds to cease such activity.[22]

In contrast, Viscount Conway, urging greater emphasis on trade and manufacturing and less on "that beggerly trade of transporting of Cattle," contended for liberty of conscience. His specific concern at this point was luring Huguenots and Dutch Protestants to Ireland, but he also had in mind the advantages of toleration for all Protestants:

If you think this [growth of trade and manufacturing] can be effected without liberty of conscience you are mistaken, tis the want of that hath lost it heare, for [the dissenters] are the sober part of the people, that follow their businesse diligently, and doe not drink, such men will thrive, and if the Bishops keep up their Courts, which yeeld them little profit, and still may be kept up as to matters of vertue, and good life, but not to conformity of worship, if they will loose the Kingdome and their owne revenues upon this point, they will repent it when it is too late.[23]

A conformist alderman named Smith issued a substantive proposal for freedom of conscience about this time. He argued on behalf of those who had come to Ireland seeking exemption from prosecution in civil and ecclesiastical courts for recusancy. Smith proposed that Charles grant toleration to each congregation that sued for it, using letters patent or issuing an indulgence under the great seal, thereby ensuring that dissenters were no less dependent on the crown than conformists. Nonconformists, Smith proposed, would periodically demonstrate both their doctrinal orthodoxy as defined by the relevant principles in the Thirty-nine Articles and their "blameless" lives. Dissenters would accept the king's authority in all civil matters and over all persons of ecclesiastical estate, and their congregations would be subject to state-appointed commissioners empowered to punish disorderly conduct. Moreover nonconformists would hold their services either in parish churches or in other approved places. Smith recommended that no one be admitted to a dissenting congregation until she or he had first attempted "to gett satisfaction in such scruples & Doubts as discourage him in respect to the Publick establishment, And hath Conferred with the Minister of the parish where hee Inhabiteth of whome if hee receave not satisfaction, yet to bring a Certificate (if hee can obtayne it) that he hath had Conferrance with him to such a purpose." Dissenters could not hold their services at the same time as those of parish churches, especially in the countryside, and they must pay tithes and rates to the Church of Ireland "freely & without Molestation, and bear all parish offices or [pay a] fine according to the ordinary rate, if not free to it." Finally, nonconformists would subscribe to the oaths of allegiance and supremacy as well as permit parish ministers and other interested parties to observe and report on their doctrine and order.[24] Smith was clearly anxious to reduce the tensions resulting from nonconformity, but dissenters would have found these conditions overbearing.

Another version of this proposal included a provision for a register in each province to record the names of all dissenters over age 16, their places of residence, and their social rank. Prior to registration each person would subscribe to the oath of allegiance and pay a stipulated fee: 7s. for a servant or laborer, 20s. for a yeoman, £3 for a gentleman, £7 for an esquire, and £20 for everyone of higher rank. Each person's registration would be valid for seven years and then had to be renewed.

Each dissenter would receive proof of registration in the form of a certificate for which a servant would pay 1s. and everyone else 5s.[25] Thus the immediate impact on Ireland of the Galloway rebellion was a desire on the part of some civil officials to implement a policy of toleration, partly for security reasons, partly because dissenters, including Huguenots and Dutch Protestants, were needed for economic growth.

Prominent clerics in the Church of Ireland continued to take a hard line against dissenters. In his consecration sermon for Ambrose Jones, bishop of Kildare, in June 1667, Bishop Henry Jones of Meath defended episcopacy and hierarchy in the church, warning that the state could not survive if the Church of Ireland were toppled. "Our Church Levellers," he thundered, "in such their Schisme teare and rend the seamless garments of the Church, and as a generation of Vipers eat out, and through the bowels of their Mother; disturbing Church unity and peace, drawing into factions, and filling all with confusions." In the epistle to the published version, Jones accused Calvinists of overturning the foundations of civil and ecclesiastical government.[26] Such views reflected the general dichotomy between lay proponents of toleration and ecclesiastical hardliners.

The hardliners' hostility to dissent notwithstanding, the government could not realistically suppress Presbyterians in Ulster any more than it could eradicate Catholicism among the Gaelic Irish. The diocese of Derry provides a useful case study. The physical condition of the churches was deplorable, with only one church in the area controlled by the London Companies' plantation in decent repair and properly outfitted for worship. According to Bishop Mossom, services were often held in cabins or alehouses and ministers were seldom resident owing to a lack of manses and insufficient funds to rent accommodations. Twenty-six ministers, eighteen of whom held two or three livings, had to serve 47 parishes. In Mossom's judgment, more than religion was at stake, for Derry city, "the very Centre of the Scotch party" in Ulster and western Scotland, was strategically located and an obvious target of a Dutch invasion. Although Dungannon believed the garrison itself was secure, the Privy Council ordered the demolition of the citadel in August 1667 as a security measure. The sympathy of some magistrates toward Presbyterians compounded the government's difficulties. The garrison commander, Colonel Gorges, complained in December 1667 that the new recorder, John Wilson, ingratiated himself with those who "would gladly attempt any designe or make use of any Instrument to roote us all out."[27]

Ecclesiastical courts were ineffective in curbing religious dissent. When Wild died in December 1665 a mere 68 men and no women stood excommunicate for recusancy or nonconformity including some whose children had been baptized by unlicensed ministers; eighteen men, eleven with distinctive Gaelic Irish surnames, for not paying church rates or tithes; and one for plowing on Christmas day and "reviling and contemning the government Ecclesiasticall." The small numbers do not reflect widespread conformity, for a year and a half later Mossom admitted that conventicles had been held in the past with impunity: "The awe of my personall presence in these parts, with the great opinion of your Grace's Countenance in your noble zeale . . . for the Churches welfare, hath putt some restraint upon the Insolence of the Conventiclers, Who now steale their meetings, rather then (as formerly) vaunt & avow them."[28]

Vigorous reliance on church courts to punish dissenters met with resistance. In the diocese of Down and Connor Presbyterians in Carrickfergus and elsewhere in county Antrim ignored summons to the ecclesiastical tribunals on the grounds that "the Case will be altered shortly," referring to an expected indulgence. Some of this boldness stemmed from Massereene's support of Presbyterians. Pressured by Massereene, Bishop Roger Boyle chided his surrogate in early 1668 for zealously prosecuting dissenters. Massereene had attempted to enlist the earl of Donegall's support in this campaign, and he also had the backing of a Templepatrick gentleman named Upton.[29]

When Massereene and Upton complained of "the great injuries and oppressions used by the Ecclesiasticall Courtes" against their tenants, an investigation ensued, the results of which indicate the extent of dissent in county Antrim. According to the court's officers, for nearly two years no one in Antrim town had been prosecuted for nonconformity, "though the fortyth man goes not to service & sermons," and no more than a dozen persons conformed. In Templepatrick only the minister and parish clerk went to church. In the four or five adjacent parishes no one conformed or worshipped in the Church of Ireland, and not one in forty had his children baptized by conformist clergy. Moreover, fewer than three persons summoned by the court in the previous year had appeared despite frequent citations. Of more than £100 in fines levied on residents of Templepatrick parish, they paid a mere 40s. in the previous eighteen months. For most of the preceding two years "there was not one person denounced by order of Courte till of late when the people runne headlong after their owne Inventions and speake openly that the courte could not proceed against them, refuseing over the whole County to give the leaste obedience to the Courte, and utterly falleing from the church." Such fees as were paid in the town and parish of Antrim in the preceding eighteen months amounted to less than £5 and were tendered by Massereene, presumably for his tenants.[30] As in the see of Derry, the ecclesiastical courts were ineffectual in curbing dissent, nor, for all intents and purposes, did they seriously try.

Encouraged by the relatively tolerant policy of the magistrates and the ineffectiveness of the church courts, the nonconformists held their conventicles with greater boldness and probably increased frequency in the late 1660s. This was true even in Dublin, where the principal ministers were the Congregationalists Edward Baines, Samuel Mather, and Timothy Taylor, and the English Presbyterians Daniel Rolls and Samuel Cox. These men worked closely together, sometimes preaching in pairs to the same conventicles. Worshippers gathered in homes, a malthouse, and apparently out of doors; Baines preached "over against" St. Patrick's. Their boldness—especially that of Baines—perturbed Ormond, and the king finally ordered the Irish government to make an example of him. Prior to his departure for England Baines preached his farewell sermon in September 1668 on the theme "That although God did for some time afflict his chosen people, yet it would not be long, he would visit them againe in his mercy, & that there redemtion drew neere, & he bid them expect it." Yet nothing substantive was done to suppress the conventicles in the capital for fear dissenters would protest that Catholics were tolerated. Indeed, in June 1669 Margetson complained that conventicles in the capital were increasing.[31]

The problem was far more serious in Ulster, partly because Covenanting ministers were arriving from Scotland. In some cases they came with the government's knowledge, though often not. One of the former was James Shaw, whom authorities permitted to return from exile on condition that he not come within three miles of his former parish of Carnmoney. Others, including John Shaw and probably Semple, preached to conventicles, holding out hope of imminent indulgence. As more and more clergymen arrived from Scotland, Dungannon observed, people who had been attending the Church of Ireland left to attend conventicles in houses and barns; "the orthodox cleargie have now very emptie churches to preach in."[32]

The authorities were chiefly concerned with the ministers' renewed attempts to persuade people to subscribe to the Covenant. Adair, Keyes, Gowan, and Hall were active in this effort in county Antrim in the late summer and fall of 1668. In a nighttime service in a Carncastle barn they exhorted people from such places as Coleraine, Belfast, Carrickfergus, and Antrim "to stand to the Covenant, and not to yeild to the Government, assureing them that God would fight their quarrell." Some nighttime services, according to Bishop Roger Boyle, were "very greate & universall meetings." Increased numbers of conventicles in Ulster did not trouble Ormond, but the revival of "the old Covenant or . . . any other Ingagement" did, especially if those responsible were not expeditiously brought to justice, for "they will conclude that either they are fear'd or that those who have power & reason to restraine them are stupidly negligent and miraculously infatuated for their deliverance." He directed the lord chancellor to investigate, and even if the latter found that conventiclers were not taking the Covenant he was to warn them that their liberty stemmed from the government's compassion for their "misguided Judgements," not fear of their power. In Ormond's mind, subscribing to the Covenant was the intermediate step between holding conventicles and openly rebelling.[33] Indeed, a radical Presbyterian document seized by the government in late 1669 (though composed a year or more earlier) protested that evil counsellors were seducing Charles, that the government was confiscating Protestant estates and giving them to Catholics, that Ormond was in league with papist murderers, and that evil was being planned against Protestant dissenters. The author or authors promised, like Jonathan, to stand up for their rights, called on Protestants in all three kingdoms to support them, and demanded liberty of conscience for Protestants, fidelity to the Solemn League and Covenant, payment of army arrears, the restoration of confiscated lands held in 1659, and the restoration of the liberties of corporations.[34]

Charles's firm endorsement of the policy of arresting Covenanting preachers did not satisfy leading clerics. The lord chancellor, Michael Boyle, archbishop of Dublin, complained that Dungannon had made insufficient progress apprehending those who preached the Covenant in Ulster. The mild-mannered Margetson lost his patience: "How sad the consequences of this libertie may prove," he lamented to Ormond as he reflected on the fact that nearly every Ulster parish had a dissenting meetinghouse and that presbyteries had been organized, elders elected, and salaries given to ministers, most of whom had been banished from or sent by Presbyterians in Scotland. Margetson pressed Charles to command Irish magistrates to enforce the penal laws, reducing the people to obedience and attendance in their parish churches, thereby liberating them from the necessity of maintaining two clergymen in each parish and "the falsely soe called minister secured from abusing them any longer."[35] Thus the Presbyterians' fidelity to the Covenant was the key factor that persuaded prominent lay leaders in Ireland to rethink the policy of *de facto* toleration.

Interlude: The Robartes and Berkeley Years

In February 1669 Charles informed his committee for foreign affairs that he intended to remove Ormond as lord lieutenant. In his place the king appointed John Baron Robartes, who had helped draft an abortive declaration of indulgence in 1662 and who was subsequently involved in the English House of Lords with an unsuccessful bill to grant the monarch authority to dispense with the penal laws. Given the fact that Charles made the change in the lord lieutenancy at a time when Covenanter activity was sharply increasing, he cannot have intended to placate all Presbyterians. An eye to French policy may have been involved, as James McGuire suggests, but if so, Ormond's recall must have been an added touch, for overtures to France predated it. Another factor was the intensifying rivalry between the energetic Orrery and Ormond, whose mediocre administrative abilities frustrated the earl. When Orrery went to England to complain in mid-1668, Ormond followed without royal approval. In part, Ormond lost his Irish post because of this incident, but the key to his recall is not to be found in France or England but in Scotland, where royal policy was designed to drive a wedge between moderate and Covenanting Presbyterians. This too was Charles's goal in Ireland, especially after the Covenanters became a serious problem.[36]

Robartes's task was to effect such a breach, though his instructions do not indicate a fundamental change in royal policy. Charles commanded him "to bring the severall dissenting parties within that our Kingdome to a Conformity to the Religion & Worship established by law," but to do this "soe farre as you may without endangering a disturbance of the quiet of the Kingdome." Difficulties in administering this policy were to be reported to the king.[37] During his tenure Robartes, though personally conforming to the Church of Ireland, demonstrated considerable tolerance of Presbyterians in Dublin and Ulster. When Archbishop Michael Boyle pressed him to repress nonconformists, Robartes refused on the grounds that he had no commission to do so as long as they were peaceful and were not Catholics. His closure of the Dublin theaters and his criticism of Boyle for his excessive expenditures won plaudits from the Presbyterians; Robartes was, opined Adair, "no enemy to godly people." In Ulster the Presbyterians were sufficiently encouraged not only to continue their pastoral work but also to license new preachers and recommend them to congregations without ministers.[38]

Robartes's leniency provoked criticism from unhappy conformists. In August 1669 Sir Nicholas Armorer complained from Dublin to Joseph Williamson that the "fanatics" were now very numerous "to the great scandal of all good men, and ground their impudence upon the encouragement given them from your side." He warned Williamson that the government would rue liberty to tender consciences. When Charles subsequently received a report on Catholics and Protestant dissenters from Robartes, he urged his lord lieutenant to be more cautious, making certain to secure the realm and "distinguishing your favour of indulgence so as the more moderate may partake most of it." Charles soon decided that Robartes too should be recalled, possibly, as Ronald Hutton suggests, because Robartes was "a martinet bereft of tact or courtesy," though more significant was the hostility he provoked among some conformists because of his leniency toward Presbyterians.[39]

That hostility is reflected in several conformist sermons preached about this time. At Christ Church, Dublin, in January 1670 Ezekiel Hopkins pointedly stressed the importance of submitting to a lawful government, adding that disobedience to a magistrate reflected contempt for God. Although he acknowledged that obedience to a sinful or an unlawful command was wrong, so was active resistance. The nonconformists, in his judgment, had carried their scruples too far: "This Generation . . . have been so hot, and fiery about little circumstances, and thought the debate of a Rite, or the mode of Discipline, cause enough, to warrant arms, and blood, and the ruins of Kingdoms." A month later Joseph Teate made a similar accusation in a sermon at St. Canice's, Kilkenny. Referring especially to the sectaries but probably to Presbyterians as well, he ridiculed their "Pretences of strictness, and a Tender Conscience," castigated them as traitors who "fill Kingdoms with Seditions," and mocked them as "incontinent in all Excesses, and fierce in all Errors, with a Rage reaching up to heaven."[40]

In early 1670 the king appointed John Lord Berkeley of Stratton, a known sympathizer of Catholics, to succeed Robartes. In making this choice Charles undoubtedly had an eye on France, but again the change of governors did not entail a shift in the king's basic policy. Charles commanded Berkeley "to settle such good order in the church that

Almighty God may be better served in the true established religion than now he is, and the people by that means reduced from their errors in religion." This was to be done with a view to moderating the zeal of those who disturbed church and state.[41]

The government's failure to implement a tougher policy to deal with dissenters remained a source of frustration among some prelates. A manifest example of this was the attempt by the bishop of Raphoe, Robert Leslie, to persuade Bishop Roger Boyle of Down and Connor "to play the man in his dioceses" by cracking down on nonconformists. Leslie, says Adair, "had persecuted but four" Presbyterian ministers— Hart, Drummond, Semple, and Adam White—each of whom had been incarcerated in 1664 on a writ *de excommunicato capiendo*. Robartes and Sir Arthur Forbes had unsuccessfully intervened on their behalf. Responding to Leslie, Boyle summoned twelve Scottish Presbyterian ministers in county Down to his court with the intention of excommunicating them. The twelve were John Drysdale, John Greg, Andrew Stewart, Gilbert Ramsey, William Richardson, James Gordon, Henry Livingstone, Alexander Hutcheson, Hugh Wilson, William Reid, Michael Bruce, and Gilbert Kennedy. None of them received the initial summons, Adair claimed, and all were declared contumacious and summoned a second time. After consultation they sent Drysdale and Hutchinson to urge Boyle to act moderately, but the laity denounced them as rebels and seducers of the people. Drysdale then went to Dublin to seek Berkeley's assistance.[42]

In the meantime Forbes, apprised of the situation, conferred with Berkeley, who referred him to Margetson. In conjunction with Lord Chancellor Michael Boyle, Margetson pressured Bishop Roger Boyle to postpone action until Margetson came to the diocese on his triennial visitation in August 1670. All this had been done before Drysdale could see Margetson, at which time the archbishop asked only if the clergymen had exercised the powers of ordination and ecclesiastical discipline. This, Drysdale assured him, they had not, though, as Adair later admitted, "the brethren were but upon a way to it." Greg, Ramsay, and Richardson died before the matter was resolved, but Margetson, determined to demonstrate his authority over Bishop Boyle, opted not to prosecute the others. He admonished Hart, Drummond, Semple, and White to demonstrate their loyalty by subscribing the oath of supremacy, but when they refused he left them in prison. Not until Charles intervened did they obtain their freedom in October 1670.[43]

Between deaths and incarceration the Ulster Presbyterians found themselves short of ministers. In addition to Greg, Ramsey, and Richardson, three other clerics died—Thomas Crawford, James Cunningham, and Thomas Peebles. Shortly after Richardson's funeral the Presbyterians decided "to enter on trial" three young men—John Cunningham, William Leggat, and George Montgomery—preparatory to licensing them to preach. They also appointed a fast for 16 August 1670 "to deal with God for the continuance of their liberty" and prevent "the fury of the bishops." Additional clergy came from Scotland to meet the need for ministers, some of whom, such as Alexander Peden and James Renwick, were militant Covenanters. One of the most dangerous of these, according to Margetson, was Archibald Hamilton of Benburb, county Tyrone, "who compasseth sea and land to disaffect the people." In the Carrickfergus area William Keyes and six Scottish preachers had a massive outdoor communion service in late May or early June 1670 that attracted between 3,000 and 4,000 people, many of them recently arrived from Scotland. Such evidence suggests that the demographic changes occurring among Presbyterian clergy in Ireland resulted in an increase in the relative numbers and influence of Covenanters.[44]

Berkeley's tenure as lord lieutenant was no less important because of the government's more tolerant policy toward Catholics. In February 1672 the king directed Berkeley to issue a general license to all subjects, including Catholics, to purchase houses and lands in the cities and towns and to restore Catholics who had the right to be freemen to their privileges and freedoms, including the right to trade freely. Such open favor, coupled with the king's decision to reconsider the land settlement, provoked considerable concern among Irish Protestants. An anonymous protest in 1672 complained about the proclamation "for a Generall Tollerration, whereby the Roman Catholicks sett up there publike Masse houses in all the Corporations in the Kingdome severall being in Dubline; And Monnestrys being Errected in severall parts of the Kingdome, each order being in there respective habitts." The protestors also objected to the appointment of Catholics as justices of the peace, exempt from the usual oaths; the restoration of Catholics to the corporations; the disbanding of six troops of horse and twelve companies of foot, all mostly Protestant; and the reopening of the land settlement.[45]

In the spring of 1672 Charles decided to replace Berkeley, in part because of his handling of the Catholics. Ignoring his instructions Berkeley had favored the "orthodox" faction among the Catholics led by Oliver Plunket, archbishop of Armagh, and Peter Talbot, archbishop of Dublin, instead of the Remonstrants. This enabled Ormond to condemn

Berkeley before the king. Berkeley also fell afoul of Orrery, whose military command he had unsuccessfully endeavored to terminate, but the earl was also opposed to Berkeley's leniency toward Catholics, a policy that was in fact Charles's, for Berkeley and the Privy Council in Dublin had opposed both the appointment of Catholic justices of the peace and the admission of Catholics to the corporate towns. In contrast, the earl of Essex, whom Charles appointed to succeed Berkeley, supported the king's Catholic policy and thus was an obvious candidate for the lord lieutenancy; he was, moreover, avowedly Protestant.[46]

Essex and the Nonconformists:
The Quest for Compromise

Essex's instructions manifested essential continuity with those of his predecessors. Religious uniformity remained the ideal, but attaining it would pose many difficulties, hence Charles instructed him to proceed cautiously. This time the king also requested an assessment of religious conditions in Ireland to use as the basis for additional instructions. After his arrival in Ireland Essex commenced the requisite investigation, the results of which seem not to have survived. During his five years as lord lieutenant Essex pursued a moderate policy toward dissenters in keeping with the spirit of his orders, and he even eschewed the employment of strong measures against Covenanters, apparently for fear of provoking a militant response. Indeed, Orrery stressed to Essex at the outset of his administration that thousands of discontented people who had lost their estates might rebel, especially during wartime.[47]

   Derry's bishop, Robert Mossom, moved quickly to persuade Essex to take firm action against the Presbyterians. Stressing the strategic importance of Derry city and its garrison, he accused the Presbyterians of holding frequent services near the town and constructing a large meetinghouse within the city walls a mere two or three doors from Mossom's mansion. They met in such large numbers, the bishop averred, that no magistrate dared to act, and the conventicles outside the city attracted as many as 2,000 people. Mossom also found the dissenters offensive because they disparaged the Church of Ireland and its clergy as popish. Essex forwarded his complaint to the court along with his own proposal that Charles issue a declaration of indulgence for Ireland, offering licenses to some dissenters and prohibiting the rest from holding services. Charles responded by asking Essex to suggest a solution to the problem of Derry, apparently rejecting a declaration of indulgence.[48]

Mossom's efforts to proscribe conventicles persuaded some Presbyterians to desist, but others, led by the merchant John Campsie, continued to meet and enlisted the services of the minister William Hampton. When the bishop dispersed their service in the Presbyterian meetinghouse on 1 September with the assistance of the mayor, the sheriff, and their officers, the conventiclers returned less than an hour later, some of them carrying stones in their coats. With soldiers stationed near the meetinghouse, Mossom addressed the Presbyterians for thirty minutes, exhorting them to join conformists in their worship in return for exemption from prosecution. After the conventiclers refused, a riot erupted when the major's men arrested Hampton and were subjected to a barrage of stones and wooden stools. In suppressing the riot the soldiers inflicted serious head wounds on three or four conventiclers. Mossom exhorted Charles, Arlington, and Essex to act, recalling that illegal assemblies, riots, and "scandalouse Libells" had been forerunners of the civil war. Arresting the conventiclers was not feasible, he averred, because he lacked sufficient troops to quash "the tumult which the women would have raised." He requested more troops or, failing that, permission to retreat to Dublin or England.[49]

Essex responded by prohibiting conventicles in Derry city or any other garrison, but he was still resolved to issue licenses to peaceful dissenters as long as they worshipped in designated places. In October Charles directed him to strengthen the Derry garrison and caution the Presbyterians not to assemble "in Numbers of soe much offence." When Campsie and two other leading Covenanters in Derry city pledged in writing that Presbyterians would no longer hold services in their meetinghouse unless this could be done without offending Charles and Essex, Mossom agreed to stop prosecuting them if the lord lieutenant approved and if they ceased using their meetinghouse. Essex was willing to permit the Presbyterians to meet outside Derry's walls as long as their sermons did not attack the government, and he advised Mossom to be moderate: "The greater tenderness that is used towards them, the better."[50] The Lagan presbytery deemed this a victory and thanked God "for putting a stop to the Bishops designe against them."[51] It also dispatched William Semple to Dublin the same month, apparently to assess Essex's position toward nonconformists, but it expressly warned him to agree to nothing "in relation to publike affairs of common concernement" without the meeting's advice. Probably as a result of Semple's mission the general committee employed Sir Robert Hamilton as an agent for persecuted dissenters the following spring.[52]

While the controversy at Derry was being resolved, Forbes, who had been appointed marshal of the army in Ireland in August 1670, persuaded Charles to provide a grant of £600 *per annum* to moderate Presbyterian ministers in Ulster. In mid-October 1672 Forbes invited Adair, Semple, Hutcheson, and Archibald Hamilton to Dublin, where he informed them of the king's offer. Charles originally hoped to provide £1,200 from hitherto unallocated Irish revenue, but only half this amount was available. When Forbes asked the four clerics for advice on how best to distribute the funds, they proposed that every minister who had been in Ireland in 1660 should receive an equal share, with money as well for widows and orphans of ministers who had died in the interim. Forbes arranged for the first quarter's payment and suggested that the four ministers send letters of appreciation to Lauderdale and Sir Robert Moray, each of whom had spoken in their behalf, as well as the king. They did so and transmitted the letters through Forbes. One of Lauderdale's correspondents, Sir Robert Hamilton, described these clerics as "verie sensible of their obligationes to Your Grace, And verie readie to expresse theire dutie & allegiance to His Majestie on all occasiones; . . . they are of Considerable number in this kingdome, & Able to doe His Majestie good service when call'd to it if they be prudently managed; And I believe Sir Arthur has as great influence on them, And studies as much to ingadge them to His Majesties service as Any Man cann." Charles provided the grant only irregularly and not at all in the late years of his reign. The funds made moderate ministers less dependent on the laity at a time when the latter were inclined to give financial support to itinerant militants from Scotland.[53]

The continuing arrival of militant ministers in Ireland was very much on Essex's mind. He complained to Arlington on 8 October that nearly all the seditious preachers banned from Scotland had crossed the North Channel, "and these are the men who are most followed by the multitude." Because of the militants' activity, he remarked, coastal areas were populated by factious, turbulent people whereas Ulster's inland counties, though largely Scottish, were inhabited by "very conformable good People." To keep abreast of the situation he wanted a resumption of regular contact between Dublin and Edinburgh. When Lauderdale went to London later in the month, Arlington promised Essex he would obtain a list of proscribed persons from Lauderdale to enable Essex to "prevent the Contagion they may bring of their doctrine into Ireland."[54]

Essex found a partial ally on the episcopal bench in the person of Thomas Hacket, bishop of Down and Connor, perhaps owing to the influence of Massereene, who attempted to forge close ties with Hacket about the time of the latter's consecration in September 1672. Hacket distinguished between moderates and "mad, factious" Remonstrants who preached "the peoples libertyes," distributed seditious books printed in the Netherlands, deprived conformist clergy of their fees by performing parochial duties such as marriage, and incited physical assaults on conformists. Encouraged because "all the principall men" repudiated the Remonstrants, he held out hope that he could obtain "a faire Treaty" with the moderates by employing some "to decoy in the Rest." Unlike Essex, Hacket opposed a formal indulgence on the grounds that it would encourage militants to demand comparable freedom. Until recently, he claimed, dissenters in his diocese had conformed, but the indulgence of two (unnamed) women "opened the present gap by giving countenance to others." The better course, he contended, was to encourage uniformity, though he did so in moderation and won Essex's praise two years later.[55]

Other Church of Ireland clerics maintained the now traditional firm stance toward nonconformists. On the twenty-fourth anniversary of Charles I's execution Benjamin Parry, preaching before Essex in Christ Church, Dublin, mercilessly castigated Protestant dissenters, associating sectaries with regicides and denouncing them as mad and deaf to the voice of reason and religion. He mocked them as well, pointedly urging the lord lieutenant to enforce the penal laws:

And if it shall be further urged, that even amongst Christians, as Sectaries and others (if they may be called Christians that are out of the Church) there are some so stout, that no penalties almost can force them to recant or renounce their errours . . . : we must say first, That they are few for the number, and fewer for their worth. Secondly, That the obstinacy of bad men in a bad cause, as it doth not justifie their crimes, so neither doth it disparage the piety and virtue of good men in a good [cause].

Levelling churches and toppling crowns—accusations commonly hurled at Presbyterians as well as Congregationalists and Baptists—were, opined Parry sarcastically, the saints' privilege. He went on to warn that "we are ready to repeat our sins [which led to rebellion and regicide], . . . willing and forward to warm our hands with new fires . . . and consume the Church with fresh combustions," as reflected by the growth of "wildfire-doctrine and religious nonsense."[56]

In an epistle to Bramhall's works published in 1676, the bishop of Limerick, John Vesey, launched a sustained attack against Protestant dissenters, whom he considered well-meaning but misled people whose "boggling at a shadow of Popery . . . in their imaginations" had "open'd a door to let in the substance" of Catholicism. The nonconformists' drumbeat of criticism against the ceremonies and practices of the Anglican communion as "Popish trumperie, and rags of the Whore" ironically persuaded most people, who saw "no superstition in an habit or a gesture," to have a higher regard of Catholicism and consider it to be "no such Bug-bear." Some people, Vesey argued, favored a return to Catholicism as a means of terminating the internecine disputes that plagued Protestantism, and the Presbyterians in particular furthered the Catholic cause by inculcating disputes among Protestants over discipline. Vesey also underscored the similarity between Presbyterian and Catholic views on the right of resistance:

It is too well known how directly our Dissenters serve the interest of the Roman Court, in propagating the same doctrines about Civil Government, and the duty of Subjects to their Princes, how loosly they tye the Yoke of Obedience on the necks of the people, and exempt the Clergie in many cases from the authoritie of the Magistrate, and take on them to censure not his actions onely, but his decrees, and his Person, and make him as accountable to the Acts of their Assemblies, as the Pope to his Bulls and Breve's.

The hardliners' hostility to Essex's indulgent treatment of most dissenters was manifest in Vesey's accusation that the latter's "unsatisfyable humors, and seditious practices" often compelled magistrates "to use Religion for a game of state Policy," treating some people kindly despite disagreements with their faith and worship in order to "ballance Interests and make one poison an antidot to another." Indulgence was thus the policy of compromising the truth and a surrender to the politics of faction: "The Non-conformity of this present Age, is the most absurd of anye, and a plain demonstration, that the World is not govern'd, so much as is pretended, by Religion and reason, but that Interest, and Lust, and Faction have too great an influence over most men."[57]

Despite the continuing expression of such views by clerical hardliners, Essex and other prominent civil leaders remained committed to a policy of moderation. In 1673 he refused to permit Sir George Rawdon to punish a Presbyterian minister who was holding large conventicles in the Lisburn area, and he asked Ezekiel Hopkins, bishop of Raphoe, not to be "too forward to begin any prosecution against these Nonconformists." Conway too continued to espouse moderation, partly because his wife was a nonconformist and partly because the *regium donum* was having a calming effect on some Presbyterians.[58]

By 1675 Orrery had returned to the moderate stance he had espoused in the early 1660s. In late May 1675 he went to London, where he conferred with Richard Baxter and John Owen, "perswading 'em to continue no longer in their non Conformity; representing to them how ill they would be able to answer for rendering themselves useless by their scrupling of indifferent Things, and for making a Division in the Church by keeping up a Separate Party: urging 'em to tell him, if there was any thing in itself Sinful in Conformity; which, if there was not, they were exceedingly to blame in keeping off: if there was he desir'd 'em to instance in it." Orrery also urged the bishops to deal moderately with dissenters in order to reunite them with the established church. He also argued that dissenters should be allowed to hold their own services as long as they did not attack the government, for it was "a hard Thing that men sho'd be debar'd from Preaching Christ, Repantance and a holy Life, for scrupling an indifferent Thing." At Orrery's request, Baxter drafted a statement setting forth nonconformist tenets, but the critique of this document by George Morley, bishop of Winchester, convinced Baxter that conformist professions of interest in accommodation were "deceitful snares."[59] Although Orrery's efforts failed, they provide another example of the desire of key civil leaders in Ireland to find a *modus vivendi* with Protestant dissenters.

In response to complaints from Ulster Presbyterians in the fall of 1673 that dissenters were being excommunicated to the detriment of trade and the peace of the realm, Essex personally investigated the case of a peddler named Martin whose case the Presbyterians had made a *cause célèbre*. The lord lieutenant's goal was "to prescribe some way how these matters might be accommodated to their satisfaction, & with the support of the Church Government." He found that Martin had not been excommunicated for nonconformity but for contempt after ignoring a citation to appear in an episcopal court on a charge of fornication. Essex concluded that no dissenters had been prosecuted simply for nonconformity, for they were permitted to meet on Sundays as long as they did so in "convenient places" and did not "affront the publick worship established." Martin's case stemmed from the nonconformists' refusal both to wed in the Church of Ireland and to explain the basis on which they married to judges in ecclesiastical courts, whose jurisdiction they denied. Essex was willing to tolerate dissenting marriages, but only if nonconformists explained "what way & in what manner they marry."[60]

Essex's desire to accommodate nonconformists was based in part on security considerations. As he indicated to Arlington in October 1673, their numbers had dramatically increased and they were now very powerful. Dealing with them, he averred, required prudence, especially in the context of the Third Dutch War. Yet a mere six months earlier he had downplayed the danger because Ulster Presbyterians had "no man of eminent popularitie to head them." Of the two most likely leaders in Essex's estimation, Forbes was loyal to the regime and Essex recommended that the government "oblige" Lord Mount-Alexander, the earl of Mount-Alexander's son, perhaps the only person in Ulster "capable of raising their Interest to any great height." Essex did not concur with those in the English House of Commons who believed it was safe to permit Protestant dissenters, unlike Catholics, to bear arms, for the Ulster Scots, he contended, would support Covenanters in Scotland if the latter rebelled. Rather than risk this, he preferred to rely on a professional army instead of a militia that incorporated Ulster Scots. Although Charles dispatched additional troops early in 1674, delays in paying the army made Essex question their reliability. Moreover, when troops were sent to Ulster because of unrest in Scotland, the local population did not welcome them.[61]

Essex was especially concerned with religious conditions in Scotland, which he attempted to monitor with the aid of Forbes and Arlington. Communications between Presbyterians in Ireland and Scotland may have been better than those between the king's agents in Dublin and Edinburgh. Indeed, in October 1674 Essex requested that a post be established between Carrickfergus and Edinburgh to ensure that Forbes could obtain information rapidly about events in Scotland. Despite the buildup of troops and renewed efforts to improve communications, the flow of preachers between the two countries apparently increased during Essex's administration; he referred to it in August 1674 as "a perpetuall going to & fro between the Two Countrys of those preaching fellows." Although Essex and Forbes sought better intelligence concerning dissident activities in Scotland, in part by dispatching their own agents, the Covenanters too improved their lines of communication, prompting Essex to strengthen the garrisons in Derry, Charlemont, and Carrickfergus.[62]

The activities of Covenanting ministers in county Derry in the summer of 1676 alarmed both Essex and the committee for foreign affairs at Whitehall. The latter resolved to proceed against the Covenanters "as high as by Law can be, to the utmost extremity, Ecclesiastically and Civilly," and Essex wanted to make examples of the preachers who were urging people to subscribe to the Covenant.[63] Thomas Otway, bishop of Killala, accused two of these ministers, Robert Hendry and

Samuel Halliday, of "debauch[ing] the people in their Religion & Loyalty" and likened them to Jesuits undertaking missions. Otway had Hendry arrested, but released him on £100 bond despite the fact that Hendry was carrying documents attacking episcopacy, the Book of Common Prayer, and reportedly even the king as well as justifying the right of subjects to resist rulers. The statement on resistance set forth ten reasons, eight of which cited biblical examples, to justify this position. Those who opposed "the fury & blind rage of princes" did not resist God but the devil, the abuser of "the sword & Authority of God." Moreover, the bond between prince and people is reciprocal, hence a prince is bound to keep his promises to his subjects or "be bridled." The author(s) used 2 Kings 9:7 to prove the right of subjects "to Execute Gods Judgments against the King or upon him." Both the idolater and the murderer must die.[64]

The imprecision of Essex's *de facto* indulgence policy is apparent in Otway's admission that he did not know the extent of the toleration allowed to dissenters, though he felt confident it did not extend to those who undermined loyalty to the government. The defiance of Hendry and Halliday inflamed feelings. After his release on bond Hendry told his followers he would not only go to the assizes when ordered but also preach there, and Halliday claimed the right to preach wherever he wished and threatened to go to Dublin and preach in Essex's ear. Convinced that Hendry and Halliday were "little folks," Otway wanted Essex to muzzle "the Grandees" who had commissioned them. The bishop also complained about the two preachers to Archbishop Boyle, who vented his displeasure to Ormond: "It sticks mightily with me how . . . [the Presbyterians] can be credited in anything they promise for his Majesty's safety and advantage, since, by the articles of their beloved Covenant . . . they are engaged by a religious vow to advance their Covenant by all the industry they can."[65] One of Essex's agents arrested Hendry in late February 1677 and conveyed him to Dublin under guard. Halliday, who had been installed as minister at Raphoe in December 1676, resigned the following June and became the pastor at Longfield (Drumquin) and Drumragh, county Tyrone, later the same year.[66]

Charles terminated Essex's tenure as lord lieutenant in the spring of 1677 largely because of the machinations of his political enemies, including the earl of Ranelagh, who worked hand in glove with the earl of Danby to divert Irish funds to the English treasury. Irate because of the deleterious impact of this practice on his ability to pay the Irish army,

Essex investigated Ranelagh's activities. Conway, Essex's erstwhile ally, had established ties with Ranelagh and was the choice of Lauderdale, Danby, and Ranelagh to succeed Essex as the *de facto* governor of Ireland, though the title of lord lieutenant would be bestowed on the duke of Monmouth. This did not suit James, duke of York, who saw Monmouth as a potential rival to succeed Charles, and in the end the king restored Ormond to the lord lieutenancy.[67]

Ormond and the Decline of Indulgence

Ormond's instructions did not mention nonconformists, but he was clearly dismayed by what he learned of them after his arrival in Ireland in the summer of 1677. "Thay are much increased, spread, & imboldned beyond what they were about 8 or 9 yeares since," and they were meeting by the thousands, according to the prelates in the north, for communion services. Convinced that Essex's tolerant policy had lured many of the Scottish immigrants to Ireland, Ormond weighed his options. To enforce the penal laws against Protestant dissenters alone would incite protests, but to execute them against both nonconformists and Catholics would overcrowd the prisons, drive people from their homes and jobs, and enervate the economy. Yet to tolerate dissenters would encourage them to surmise that the government feared them, thereby emboldening them to grow in numbers and defiance. He advised Charles to let them meet as long as they did not renew the Covenant or exercise ecclesiastical jurisdiction. Violators should be severely punished, and as a cautionary measure Ormond recommended that the army be placed in a state of preparedness.[68] Ormond's reluctant decision to continue indulging moderate dissenters was a setback to Archbishop Boyle, who had condemned accommodation in May and urged the government to adopt "a more rough proceeding" with conventiclers. Because Scotland was so near at hand, "they will never want discontented factionists to enflame them."[69]

Throughout 1677 tension mounted in Scotland because of field conventicles, the construction of Presbyterian meetinghouses on some of the commons, physical threats to conforming clergy, and apparent preparations for an uprising. Wary authorities in Ireland monitored these developments, not least because some Covenanters continued to seek refuge in Ireland.[70] In September the king directed Ormond to dispatch troops to Ulster under the command of Forbes, now Viscount Granard. They would serve from November 1677 to March 1678, by which point the Highland Host had intimidated western Scotland.[71] Renewed efforts were made to improve communications between Dublin and Edinburgh, this time on a twice weekly basis, but the results were still unsatisfactory. Despite a viable postal service Ormond complained to Coventry as late as June 1678 that a settled correspondence between officials still did not exist.[72]

Communications between the two capitals were nevertheless better, in part because of the earl of Mount-Alexander's visit to Scotland, and they revealed portents of the rebellion that would erupt in Scotland in 1679.[73] Such reports contributed to concern about the intentions of Ulster Scots. If the Covenanters rebelled in Scotland, Sir George Rawdon warned, Ireland's "dance will be after their pype." In his judgment the indulgence policy was responsible for unrest in both countries, but he believed the harsh treatment meted out to the disaffected in western Scotland would intimidate the Ulster Scots.[74] Rawdon's opposition to the indulgence policy did not sway Ormond, who was convinced the nonconformists and Catholics balanced each other, making it impossible for either to rebel "for fear [one] should make use of the other to suppress and chastise the first disturbers." He also distinguished between English and Scottish dissenters in Ireland: The former were unlikely to rebel, in his estimation, because they were geographically scattered, economically prosperous, engaged in trade, and diverse in their religious views, whereas Ulster Scots were "more heady, more united in opinion, more compact in habitation and neighbourhood, more ready to abandon their wretched residences, and for all these reasons more apt to be inflamed."[75]

Rawdon and Granard became entangled in a bizarre development that commenced shortly after the Presbyterian minister Thomas Douglas arrived in Ireland around the beginning of December 1677. Ejected as rector of St. Olave's, London, at the restoration, Douglas subsequently became embroiled in a scandal, left England, and eventually settled at Padua, where he earned a medical degree. Returning to London he practiced medicine until he fell into debt and relocated to Ireland. In 1677 he and John Welsh preached to large conventicles in Scotland, for which he was outlawed. Seeking refuge in Ireland, he was arrested at Larne and taken to Belfast, where Colonel Roderick Mansell, one of Granard's officers with ties to Essex, interrogated him. "After spending some heavy sighs and groans with him," Mansell reported to the earl of Arran, "and promising unto him kindness and friendship, and that he should be provided for in this kingdom, provided he would disclose what was truth to his knowledge of the designs now on foot in Scotland," he eventually claimed that the Covenanters intended to revolt in Scotland, that they were renewing the Covenant, and that they were raising money to purchase weapons. Douglas identified those involved, including Welsh, Donald Cargill, Alexander Hamilton, William Cunningham (the earl of Argyll's chaplain), and "a very eminent statesman, of whom he says they are assured of, and two more of the greatest peers of the kingdom."[76]

At first Rawdon seemed to believe Douglas's account of an imminent rebellion in Scotland, though he soon condemned him as "a notorious disembler." Two officers dispatched to Scotland by Granard to investigate reported that "somewhat" of Douglas's story was true, but Scottish magistrates could find no weapons in the places Douglas named. Granard thereupon denounced him as "a mountebank and almost as great a knave as his prompter Mansel," and Ormond castigated Douglas as "a notorious cheat, and so esteemed by those of all sides." Douglas, it seems, had told Mansell that Granard and Lauderdale secretly supported "the Fanatic party" in Scotland and that Granard provided funds to Presbyterian ministers. When Mansell repeated the allegations, Douglas denied being the source and an irate Granard had Mansell cashiered by the council of war.[77] Douglas or Mansell apparently knew something about the *regium donum* but erroneously concluded that two of its principal architects, Granard and Lauderdale, had surreptitious ties to militant Covenanters as well as Presbyterian moderates.

Mansell soon returned to England and subsequently became embroiled in the overheated atmosphere of charges and countercharges that followed the initial disclosure of a supposed popish plot in August 1678.[78] For a time, allegations of this plot distracted attention from the Ulster problem and forced the Ormond administration to concentrate more intensely on security measures. Concern was greatest in Munster, "from whence the terror is diffused through the whole Kingdom, to the greatest disheartening of the English and encouragement of the disaffected Irish." The lord lieutenant temporarily considered the Gaelic Irish to be the greatest threat to security, but by year's end he worried that nonconformists would again try to assassinate him, as Thomas Blood and his cohorts had attempted to do in London in December 1670.[79]

As part of the security precautions following the revelation of the alleged plot, the court instructed Ormond to maintain surveillance over the North Channel. Clearly Westminster was concerned that militant

Covenanters would take advantage of the government's preoccupation with the Catholics to strike. Earlier in the year Scottish authorities had run into opposition as they attempted to compel heritors to subscribe to bonds holding them accountable for their tenants' behavior. Scottish officials were concerned as well that tenants would flee the country for Ireland or the English borders, and Ormond told Arran in June that he could not send troops to Scotland because disaffected families as well as Covenanting ministers were immigrating from Scotland. Manifesting Covenanter defiance, Welsh excommunicated all the heritors in western Scotland who subscribed to the bond, and his followers took up arms against royalist troops. As the investigation of the Popish plot occupied center stage in the minds of most of his subjects, Charles worried that Welsh and his colleagues would escape to Ireland.[80]

Whether Welsh found temporary refuge in Ireland is impossible to say, though the government received reports in the spring of 1679 that he did. More significant is the fact that large numbers of Presbyterians from Scotland, some of substance, found refuge in Ulster, where they sparked fears that they might be conspiring against the governments of both realms. They wrote and published anonymous tracts critical of the authorities and even established schools that one critic described as "nurseries where a kind of philosophie and tongues are taught."[81] As in Scotland, Presbyterians, some of them bearing arms, were attending massive outdoor conventicles where ministers told them that if the magistrates did not punish sin, they had a "dutie to supply that defect."[82]

Although Ormond had yearned for "a large access of English and Protestants" in March 1679 as the best means to secure Ireland from a Gaelic Irish rebellion, the immigration of Scottish Covenanters was not what he had in mind. The assassination of James Sharp, archbishop of St. Andrews, in May 1679 inaugurated a new crisis in Scotland, prompting the English Privy Council both to renew its orders of September 1678 to guard the routes from Scotland and to instruct Ormond to prohibit dangerous conventicles and the shipment of weapons to dissidents.[83]

The outbreak of the Bothwell Bridge rebellion in Scotland in May 1679 again required the dispatch of troops to northern Ireland with the possibility that some would be shipped to Scotland. The latter prospect was risky, for Ormond, the earl of Orrery, and Archbishop Boyle feared the Ulster Scots might revolt in support of their coreligionists in Scotland. The rebellion altered the flow of preachers to Ireland, for now it was the conformists who fled Scotland. Loyalists in Ireland feared that Ulster Presbyterians would support the insurrectionists, possibly by shipping them weapons. According to the dean of Derry, the town's Presbyterians thought the rebels had acted hastily "with the Covenant, since it was comeing about of itselfe," but Ormond seems not to have detected this sense of disapproval. He told Sir Robert Southwell that "the brethren in all parts of this kingdom especially in the North were growing very bold & ready to come in to bear a part, if those of Scotland had had success."[84]

The rebels' defeat by English and Scottish forces obviated the need for Granard's troops, who limited themselves to the apprehension of rebels seeking refuge in Ireland.[85] With the exception of "some very few inconsiderable" nonconformists, as Ormond and his council described them, Ireland remained loyal. Archbishop Boyle nevertheless urged Ormond to suppress the Presbyterians, whom he accused of following "the methods and ways for discipline of their brethren the Jesuits." With the king's concurrence, Ormond saw no reason to adopt severe measures except against those who had solicited subscriptions to the Covenant or exercised ecclesiastical jurisdiction. "There is not yett any publique notice to be taken of armed Conventiclers," he told Rawdon, but he wanted to know if they were carrying weapons more than previously, in which case "it is no good signe of their quiett inclinations, for their feare of the Papists cannot reasonably be more now that the Militia is better armd, & in better order then it was."[86]

J. C. Beckett has correctly attributed the quiescence of Ulster Scots during the rebellion to the Irish government's policy of moderation, though indulgence had not prevented rebellion in Scotland owing largely to the harsh repression inflicted on the southwest by the Highland Host. Ormond had recognized the benefits of a modest indulgence in the aftermath of the uprising, prompting him to defend the justice and prudence of discriminating between peaceful nonconformist ministers and those who were "turbulent & troublesome." This could only be done, he informed Sir William Stewart,

by suffering the one sort to live & Exercise their calling without disturbance, & to remove the other from burdening & misleading the people, & this is the Method I am informed his Majestie purposes to hold with his discenting Subjects in Scotland & may properly be observed here, tho it may be also observed that such an Indulgence here requires greater returnes of duty & thankfulnesse, for that here no Law or Sanction of the Prince ever abolisht Episcopacy or Establisht Presbitery or the Covenant as is pretended in Scotland with some Colour.

He made it clear that he had expected the moderate clergy to distinguish themselves from the militants by submitting an address to Granard. Their initial effort proved to be "too loos to be binding" and thus unsatisfactory, "for where it shall come short of giveing intire Satisfaction in those points it intends to disowne, it amounts to little lesse then an approbation of the Doctrine charged upon them."[87]

The statement to which Ormond objected had been subscribed on 25 June 1679 by fifteen Presbyterian clergymen, including Michael Bruce, Archibald Hamilton, Alexander Ferguson, Alexander Hutcheson, James Gordon of Comber, George Waugh, Archibald Young, and William Leggat (Legate). Although they unequivocally professed their loyalty to the government and reminded Ormond of their suffering during the interregnum on behalf of the royalist cause, they neither renounced the Covenant nor their belief that magistrates were accountable to God through the church. Referring to their sufferings on behalf of Charles in the 1650s, they professed themselves "oblidged from the same unalterable principles of Conscience and Loyalty, to declare the stedfastness of our resolutions to continue in the same Loyalty and due obedience to his Majesties Authority, from which if we should resile, we might be accounted most undutifull to God, and ingrate to our most gracious Soveraign."[88] For Ormond this appeal to the 1650s did not eradicate the memories of Presbyterian opposition to the crown in the decade 1638–1648, and he wanted Hart, Halliday, Rule, John Rowatt, "& all of that Kind" to leave Ireland or face more severity than he wished to impose.[89]

In July Stewart urged the Presbyterians to compose a new declaration disowning the rebellion in Scotland and the principles on which it was based. Preparation of another statement was delayed until 17 September because ministers acting in a private capacity had no authority to draft one. Submitted to Granard, the new statement carried the names of eight ministers: Hart, Rule, Trail, Craghead, John Hampton, William Hampton, William Liston, and James Alexander. The declaration was not the collective work of the Ulster Presbyterians (in effect, a general assembly) because of the great distances that separated them, explained the authors. After professing their loyalty to Charles, they pledged "to obey his lawfull commands, & wherein we cannot in conscience, actively obey his Majesties Lawes, yet peaceably to submit to his Majesties undoubted Authority over us, exhorting the people among whom we labour to beware of all seditious disturbances." Adair and others presented a similar statement to Granard, who thought the declarations might be "a leding carde to others of thate prinsipale ate laste to bi sensibel of thair deuti."[90]

Further testimony to the success of Ireland's moderate policy came from Robert Rule, who had been exiled from Scotland in 1672 and now gave Stewart a statement deploring the oppression of Covenanters in Scotland while denouncing their rebellion against legal authority. "I know none of our perswasion in [Ireland]," he insisted, "who are for such courses (neither have they any temptation thereunto from the lenitie & Indulgence of the Majesstrate aloweing us the free exercise of our religion & worship)." Presbyterians in Ireland were split, however, over subscription to the oath of supremacy. In September 1679 Charles directed Ormond not to be overly severe in dealing with "so great a multitude" of Presbyterians unless they engaged in overt acts of rebellion, including "sitting upon the covenant or publicly avowing a separate jurisdiction."[91]

Like Rule, James Gordon of Comber denounced militancy. In a letter written to his daughter Jean in Scotland in 1680 he discussed various problems and suggested remedies. To counter those who espoused the Stuarts' overthrow and the establishment of a commonwealth he wanted people to view Charles II and his successors as bastions against not only the pope and Catholic states but also republicans and Fifth Monarchists. Arguing that bishops had been responsible to a large degree for Charles I's overthrow, he denounced the prelates of northern Ireland and their clerics as "the great and hard bone of contention which this Kingdome finds most hard of digestion." Gordon recommended that Charles II convene a European synod of orthodox divines to settle church government; doctrine, he thought, would not pose problems because of the shared tenets of moderate episcopalians and Presbyterians. Another grievance in his estimation was the importation of radical literature such as *Jus Populi Vindicatum* from the Netherlands. To refute the spread of such radical tenets Gordon proposed that everyone entering the ministry and possibly the civil service be required to subscribe to a statement embracing sound political principles. Gordon and Rule are good examples of the moderation characteristic of mainline Presbyterians.[92]

The wisdom of the government's moderate policy rested not only on the impossibility of coercing substantial numbers of Ulster Scots to conform but also on the fact that many local magistrates continued to sympathize with dissenters or were themselves nonconformists. Mount-Alexander complained bitterly of justices of the peace who went to conventicles more frequently than services in the Church of Ireland and refused to take the stipulated oaths. When Hugh Campbell, a staunch Presbyterian, received an order to search for Archbishop Sharp's assassins, he sent it to the Presbyterian minister of Donaghadee, county Down, who passed it to dissidents in Scotland. Reflecting on the decade following the Bothwell Bridge rebellion more than twenty years later, William Tisdall was impressed not only by the substantial growth of dissenters in Ireland but also by the construction of meetinghouses and the exercise of ecclesiastical discipline with the magistrates' conniv- ance.[93] Indulgence was not simply a policy of choice; circumstances dictated it, at least for quiescent dissenters.

The line between tolerable and intolerable activity was difficult for both sides to demarcate, particularly in an atmosphere periodically poi- soned by suspicion and recrimination. The continued movement of Presbyterian clergymen between Ireland and Scotland troubled some observers and contributed to fears that another insurrection was being planned. Reacting to such concerns, Sir Hans Hamilton summoned Adair, Hutcheson, Archibald Hamilton, and John Abernethy in July 1680 to answer charges of suspected disloyalty. The four denounced the "absurd and rebellious papers [of militant Scottish Covenanters] tende- ing (to their power) to the subversion of the King and his goverment and the fundamentall lawes of these nations." The papers in question, which had been obtained the previous month when a party of horse guards unsuccessfully attempted to apprehend Donald Cargill at Queensferry in Scotland, espoused a "new Covenant" calling for the church's libera- tion from the tyranny of prelacy and Erastianism and the restoration of the church's and the people's "civill rights & liberties." Magistrates on both sides of the North Channel were understandably concerned, but Adair and his colleagues repudiated such tenets "both as rebellious against our Lawfull Soveraigne and highlie sinefull against God."[94]

The Presbyterians repeatedly tested the limits of tolerable activity. Since resuming his post in 1677 Ormond had allowed existing con- gregations to meet while opposing the founding of new churches or the construction of meetinghouses. This did not dissuade Adair and Hutch- eson from urging Rawdon to permit Presbyterians at Lisburn to build a meetinghouse and employ a Scottish preacher; when he declined, they petitioned Ormond. After Presbyterians constructed a "capacious" church near the Council Chamber in Dublin, the English Privy Council warned Ormond in April 1681 that he could not tolerate "such a novelty as carries along with it not only a breach of the laws but a contempt of his Majesty's authority." Although reluctant to act until he had ob- served how Dubliners responded to the new church, he had the minis- ter, William Jacque, arrested not only for preaching illegally but also for permitting another minister to espouse the Covenant from his pulpit.

Jacque defiantly preached to some of his congregants the following Sunday from his prison cell.[95]

Presbyterian fasts also tried the government's patience. In early February 1681 the Lagan presbytery convened at St. Johnston in county Donegal to schedule a public fast. The ministers included Hart, Trail, Craghead, Rule, Liston, James Alexander, Robert Campbell, and "many more" in counties Derry, Tyrone, and Fermanagh. Each received "his briefe of the causes & motives [i.e., breach of the covenant] & intimated the same to their respective flocks." Although the English Privy Council had instructed Ormond to suppress such observances because they encroached on royal authority, he was initially reluctant to prosecute. According to Captain John Nisbet, an informer, "the day & motives [of the fast] were generall thorowout all this country & punctually observed with most ardent earnestnes so that I cannot think lesse then six or seven thousand in this barony of Rapho . . . did joyne to the observance of the day with preaching, fasting & abstinence from their ordinary occasions." Yet four of the ministers themselves subsequently insisted the number was at most in the hundreds.[96] After the fast Bishop John Leslie commissioned a group of local gentry to conduct an investigation, subsequent to which Trail, Hart, Campbell, and Alexander went to prison. Although Ormond was irritated because the Presbyterians attributed "the indulgence more to the feare then the good nature of the Government," his inclination was "not to Mollest men of peaceable spirits" as long as he could be tolerant and still perform his duties.[97]

For their part the Presbyterians endeavored to find a *modus vivendi* without surrendering their principal convictions. To this end they assured the government of their loyalty, as when Adair, Alexander, Ferguson, and Hutcheson sent a supplication to the king on behalf of the Presbyterian clergy of northern Ireland in which they insisted they were innocent of all disloyal practices and requested an opportunity to respond to any accusations to the contrary. Trail went so far as to seek state approval for an oath that Presbyterian soldiers could take in lieu of the oath of supremacy. This was Trail's proposed substitute:

I A:B: doe promise & swear that I shall bear faith & true Allegiance to the King. That I renounce the popes & all forraign Jurisdiction. And I acknowledge the Kings Majesty to be the onely Supream Governour of this & all his Majesties other Dominions, and all persons therein.

As one of Bishop Leslie's correspondents sagely observed, this oath omitted "the most materiall points," namely the monarch's status as the only supreme governor in matters spiritual as well as temporal.[98]

About the same time the leading Church of Ireland proponent of accommodation with the Presbyterians, Edward Wetenhall, bishop of Cork, issued a plea for Protestant union in *The Protestant Peace-Maker*, to which Baxter and others wrote a postscript. On the one hand Wetenhall professed to find some good in all Protestant groups: fervent prayer, the indefatigable performance of spiritual duties, diligence in the instruction and governance of families, and strict observance of the sabbath among Presbyterians and Congregationalists; plain dress, simple living, respect for oaths, and honest speech among Quakers. For this reason he advised his readers not to condemn entire religious groups. On the other hand, he told dissenters he could find no legitimate reason for them to separate from the established church "which neither urges nor receives any Article of Faith, but what must be confessed pure; which worships God by no Office more or less than what is of his own institution, and the forms thereof not dissonant to his word; whose Government . . . is truly Apostolical; and in fine, where Discipline . . . suffers few or none to be as bad as they would, and encourages all to be as good as they can." He chided nonconformists for their ostentatious display of separation, which he thought scandalized weaker members of all Christian communions, but he was also realistic in assessing the barriers to Protestant unity posed by the often substantial differences between dissenting groups. To meet the conditions of one sect would hardly satisfy the demands of the others, nor could the Church of Ireland accept the abolition of its liturgy, episcopacy, and the principle of religious uniformity without being guilty of schism. To achieve religious peace he urged everyone to practice self-denial "with a peculiar eye and regard to Accommodation," and he asked "the soberest of the Dissenters" to determine which elements of the established church they could accept.[99] Although few nonconformists would have found these principles an adequate basis for unity, Wetenhall's attitude toward dissenters was more positive than that of most Church of Ireland clerics.

Samuel Fowley, chaplain to the archbishop of Dublin, espoused the now traditional hard line against nonconformists in sermons for the consecration of the bishops of Kildare, Kilmore, and Killala at Christ Church, Dublin, in February 1682, and at St. Patrick's for the visitation of Francis Marsh, archbishop of Dublin, in April of the same year. Before his audience at Christ Church he sharply distinguished between the prelates of the established church, who rendered due obedience to the king, and the Presbyterians, whose consistories claimed spiritual jurisdiction over princes, including the power to excommunicate them, and Congregationalists, who "do exempt their Congregations from all Spiritual Subjection to the Civil Powers."[100] At St. Patrick's he spoke derisively of nonconformists as persons of weak understanding, disorderly principles, impractical "Notions," minimal learning, and charitableness. Some of their leaders were crafty and seditious, others honest but mistaken. "Let us not, under pretence of Zeal against Popery, countenance or support a Faction; or out of a Project of an Impossible Union, put People in the head to desire that all Ecclesiasticall Laws be taken away." He reminded his hearers that dissenters espoused the same principles as had those who wielded power so harshly in the 1640s and 1650s, and compromise was thus inadvisable. "Let us not betray the most Pure and most Reformed Church in Christendome," he argued in his assault on accommodation, "to humor and court a perverse stiff-necked Generation, who will not be wrought upon by any Condescentions."[101]

While some Protestants in Ireland were calling for unity in the face of a seemingly mounting Catholic threat,[102] the conformist Robert Ware republished John Nalson's *Foxes and Firebrands* (1682), a tendentious attempt to link Catholics and nonconformists. In *The Hunting of the Romish Fox, and the Quenching of Sectarian Fire-Brands* (1683) he printed extracts from the works of Thomas Cranmer, Matthew Parker, George Abbot, William Laud, James Ussher, and Sir Henry Sidney to make the same point. Catholics, he contended, operate in the guise of nonconformists, espousing greater purity and a more thorough reformation in their conventicles in an attempt to advance the secular goals of the Roman court. "When the Jesuits in the dress of Nonconformists have canted the people into an abhorrence of the Church of England, and withdrawn her Subjects from that just Devoir, in which they stood bound to her sacred Canons; when they have infused a thousand religious Phrensies into 'em and procur'd a Toleration for all the zealous Madnesses of the Rabble; the many ignorant and unstable will not be able to oppose the Introduction of their new Form." Toleration was thus an insidious Catholic plot, and the pedigree of the "mungrel" Presbyterians was traceable to a Jesuit and "a Republican Factionist."[103] With those who espoused such tenets there could be no hope of religious accommodation.

Growing suspicion of the dissidents' intentions in the early 1680s reinforced the proclivities of those who opposed indulgence. An informer in January 1681 accused assorted dissidents in counties Wexford and Waterford of plotting and contended that the Waterford leaders, some of whom had once boasted they would "wash their hands in the Stuarts Blood," were communicating with Presbyterians and "Fanaticks" in Ulster. As in England, stories circulated of a Presbyterian conspiracy—a reaction to the alleged Popish plot. According to Southwell, the nonconformists were dissatisfied with Ormond: "Having no fortunes, [they] desire a new scramble, and so are impatient at all things that obstruct it," whereas conformists remain loyal to the duke. In the face of this growing dissatisfaction among dissenters, Dublin's municipal council sent an address to the king in April 1682 pledging to defend him and the established church against all threats and associations, whether Catholic or fanatic.[104]

After receiving reports of nonconformist disaffection in Ulster, Archbishop Boyle ordered Captain George Philips, the governor of Derry city, to investigate. "Many mutinous and petulant discourses, and plain menaces of resisting it unto blood," he learned, stemmed from fears that the government intended to repress conventicles as it was already doing in England. Philips sought the assistance of a minister recently suspended by the Presbyterians, and from him learned that throughout Ulster the Presbyterian clergy reportedly taught that the godly could legally take up arms to defend the reformation and that their meetings were collecting money to purchase weapons on the continent. The former charge reflected traditional Presbyterian political tenets, and the latter accusation was both plausible given the fears of another Catholic uprising and something the government already suspected. Philips's informer also alleged that a Presbyterian general assembly met regularly and maintained contact with allies in London and the Netherlands. He was probably referring to meetings of the presbyteries, and communications with Presbyterians in other countries, especially Scotland and England, were hardly new. The prime conduit for the correspondence, the informer claimed, was Robert Trail in Ulster and his brother William in London, which may have been true. He also claimed, probably truthfully, that ministers recently banished from Scotland were "the most eminent at their meetings," and he identified two of them as David Houston, who was in the Dublin area, and "Dorat," probably John Darroch, who had been deprived at Kilcalmonell and Kilberry, Argylshire, and was now in county Antrim.[105]

The ex-Presbyterian minister who provided Philips with this information was the eccentric James Gordon, a Banffshire native who had been ordained by the bishop of Moray. (This Gordon is to be distinguished from James Gordon of Comber.) Although engaged to another woman, he had run off with the laird of Carnborough's daughter to Ireland, where Robert Mossom, bishop of Derry, permitted him to preach at Glendermott in 1668. After Gordon did public penance and married the laird's daughter in Scotland, he obtained a living near Aberdeen and there became the father of four or five children before running off with his housekeeper, for which he was deposed. Following a stint in the highlands as a farmer and assorted adventures, he went to Boveagh, county Derry, where he became a Presbyterian and held services in a meetinghouse. The presbytery of Coleraine learned of his past and expelled him, whereupon Gordon turned informer, providing his services to Ezekiel Hopkins, bishop of Derry. Ormond himself approved the arrangement in December 1682 but asked Hopkins to make special efforts to verify Gordon's trustworthiness. The information Hopkins gleaned from Gordon was substantially the same as that told to Philips the following month, though William Keyes of Dublin was named along with the Trail brothers as principal figures in the Presbyterian communications network. So too was Robert Ferguson in London, who at this point was deeply enmeshed in the Rye House plotting, but Gordon seemingly knew nothing of that. Gordon also provided Hopkins with more detail about the reputed arms shipments, claiming the weapons would be conveyed in three vessels with false decks covered with ballast in their holds.[106]

Gordon fell out of favor with Hopkins when he boasted he could preach freely despite his refusal to conform, and Ormond too soon distrusted him as "a rascal" who tailored his reports to obtain profit. "Yet if there must be conventicles," the duke told Arran, "it is better a man of his immorality should be their guide than a more faultless man, so that he ought to be connived at, and a little money cast away upon him." In mid-January 1683 Archbishop Boyle sent Hopkins £20 to pay Gordon and instructed Hopkins to overlook Gordon's conventicle preaching as long as Ormond wanted to use him as an informer. Although the duke had no confidence in Gordon's information, Arran continued to employ him in the early months of 1683, even calling him to Dublin for secret consultations in mid-February. The same year Gordon was installed as minister at Glendermott, though he conformed the following year.[107]

Although Gordon probably had no knowledge of the Rye House conspiracies, he was aware that dissidents in Ireland had links to like-minded persons in London whose circle included Robert Ferguson. The latter was a pivotal figure with ties to both groups of conspirators—Monmouth and other proponents of a general uprising to block James's accession on the one hand and a band of extremists centering around the attorney Robert West whose assassination schemes included the notorious plot to ambush the royal brothers at the Rye House in Hertfordshire as they returned from Newmarket.[108] Evidence for the involvement of Irish dissidents in these schemes is extremely thin. One of West's confederates, the barrister Nathaniel Wade, allegedly sent messengers to militants in Ireland and Scotland in the spring of 1683 to determine if they would support an insurrection,[109] and Captain Thomas Walcott, a Baptist who had served in Ireland under Edmund Ludlow in the 1650s and had since been in and out of trouble for reputed plotting, was involved in the proposed assassination schemes.[110] Colonel Henry Owen, brother of the prominent Congregationalist minister John Owen, may have been a party to the planned uprising and was arrested in June 1683 as he was preparing to leave Minehead for Ireland.[111] The next month magistrates in Devon apprehended Thomas Slape (alias John Sealy) of Taunton as he too was travelling to Ireland; in his possession were fragments of a treasonable Scottish declaration, possibly intended for militant Ulster Presbyterians.[112]

Gauging the extent of probable support for a popular uprising on Monmouth's behalf in Ireland is virtually impossible, although the evidence suggests that any participation would have been minimal. Assize records would give some indication of the extent of popular hostility toward the government but almost none have survived. Three men were bound over at the Clonmel Assizes in April 1683 for allegedly having made hostile comments about Charles and James. John Lane reportedly said it was "base and unlawfull for his Majestie that he did not exile the Duke of York out of his Dominions for feare he should breede any Disturbance among the Nacion," while Henry Shrimpton purportedly insisted Monmouth would succeed Charles or there would be no monarchy at all. Charles, Shrimpton averred, "was as unjust a King as ever was and . . . never performed any promise that he gave." When Monmouth returned to royal favor after privately confessing his role in the plotting to the king, dissidents in Ireland were delighted.[113] The most substantive indictment of royal policies is found in a lengthy statement written by Edward Richardson, a merchant at Skibbereen, county Cork, who traced popular unrest to such factors as Charles's fondness for James and suppression of Monmouth, the prorogation of Parliament, the king's doubts about "all the circumstances" of the Popish plot, the delay of the trial of Danby and other lords, Charles's "Female extravagancies," and the government's inability to protect merchant vessels from Turkish attacks. The conformist minister Hugh Pughe, formerly a dissenter, accused William Jacque, the Tipperary schoolmaster

John Price, and several men in the Dublin area of propounding similar sentiments, including indictments of Charles for shedding blood, inebriety, Catholicism, and profanity; of James for treason, uncleanness, and the fire of London; and of Ormond for Catholicism, treason, and cheating the king and realm of Ireland.[114]

Ormond was in London when news of the Rye House plotting broke, but Arran, his deputy, promptly tightened security. He ordered officers to repair to their commands and dispatched two troops of horse to Strabane, "that being the place inhabited by people much of the same stampe with those concerned in that detestable plott." He also sent agents to Ulster to discover if the plot had been "universal," stationed troops in key ports to investigate suspicious persons travelling between Scotland and Ireland, prohibited the sale of weapons without written authorization, and ordered the apprehension of all conventicle preachers.[115]

The stepped-up security measures were especially formulated with the Protestant dissenters in mind. Conventicles came under renewed scrutiny. Mountjoy observed nothing unusual in the conduct of Ulster Presbyterians, who had been holding large conventicles (a thousand periodically met outside the walls of Carrickfergus, Rawdon noted) as well as complaining about the treatment of Covenanters in Scotland and considering emigration to Carolina to avoid persecution. Deeming large conventicles imprudent and knavish, Arran promised to incarcerate their ministers, but he was initially cautious, knowing the army was ill-prepared.[116] He was also uncertain of the loyalty of Granard, whom Walcott had implicated in the conspiracy,[117] and Massereene, who, though a privy councillor, attended a conventicle in the house of his mother, the dowager Lady Massereene, and maintained close relations with Presbyterians.[118] More than a year earlier, in May 1682, Arran had pressed his father to urge Charles to strip Massereene of his offices because he frequented dangerous conventicles. After the Rye House disclosures Massereene met with Arran in Dublin, promising the lord deputy he would encourage his mother to cease holding conventicles in her home and pledging to be "a good Churchman." In August 1683 a grand jury presented Massereene for not submitting a certificate indicating he had received the Lord's supper according to the Book of Common Prayer as required by proclamations issued by Ormond and Arran. Massereene not only conformed but also demanded that dissenting clergy in Antrim provide recognizances for their good behavior and instructed moderate Presbyterians to persuade their brethren not to

convene "bold" conventicles. Because Charles did not remove Massereene from the Council, Arran could not oust him from the commission of the peace inasmuch as a councillor served as a justice of the
peace *ex officio* throughout Ireland.[119]

Arran also had problems with lesser magistrates who were dissenters or who were sympathetic to them. In July 1683 the Irish Council
ordered judges on circuit to determine which justices of the peace were
conventiclers with a view to purging them, but the Council deemed it
unnecessary to impose a new oath in addition to those of allegiance
and supremacy on justices of the peace and militia officers. Rawdon
expressed concern about whom he could employ to arrest dissenting
clergy and repress conventicles because many constables and residents
of Down, Antrim, and probably Armagh were nonconformists; though
some militia officers would assist, their counterparts in the army would
not help without direct orders from their commanders. In a similar vein
the bishop of Raphoe complained that many of the militia in county
Donegal had refused the oath of supremacy, but more encouraging
news came from Captain Philips, who claimed in August that few justices of the peace or militia officers in county Derry and the contiguous
areas attended conventicles. He boasted of success in suppressing illegal services, as did Archbishop Boyle, who averred that he knew of only
one justice of the peace, the Particular Baptist Richard Lawrence, who
refused to conform. The same month Arran instructed the lord chancellor to remove some justices from the commission of the peace, "tho no
frequenters of Conventicles," simply because they were suspected.[120]

The prosecution of dissent posed substantive legal questions, even
for hard-liners such as Rawdon. According to the Act of Uniformity two
justices had to commit offending preachers, and this they could do only
if they had a certificate from the ordinary specifying the offenses allegedly committed in violation of the statute. Legal doubts arose if a
certificate had been procured from an ordinary's deputy or chancellor
in his absence, and the justices themselves could be fined if they arrested ministers without the requisite certificates. Moreover, a large
assembly was unlawful only if magistrates could demonstrate that the
intent of its gathering was illegal. Rawdon requested advice concerning
both the conditions stipulated in a recognizance and the form of a *mit-
timus* to commit those who refused to post bond, an indication that
accused clerics were posing substantive legal challenges.[121] A year earlier, in July 1682, Archbishop Boyle had cited Sir Robert Reynolds's
opinion that conventicles could be suppressed simply because the king
commanded it, but Ormond objected, insisting "wee must goe no fur-

ther then Law will carry Us." Attorneys in Ireland, he reflected, did not believe Irish penal laws could be employed against Protestant dissenters because they had been enacted with Catholics in mind. Admittedly, Protestant nonconformists might be prosecuted under the statutes dealing with illegal assembly and rioting, but he opposed "the stretching of penall laws beyond their originall intention by subsequent construction since it cannot be foreseen whome such precedents may hurt."[122]

Ormond's reticence to prosecute dissenters melted in the heat of the Rye House disclosures. He was incredulous when the early confessions ignored Ireland, especially because of the number of dissenters concentrated in Ulster, the number dispersed elsewhere in the kingdom, and the communications between nonconformists in all three realms. As allegations about Irish involvement surfaced he exhorted Arran to act, insisting he had sufficient authority to disarm all conventiclers. The more Ormond learned about the revelations, the more he pressed Arran to intensify his suppression of dissenters. In securing the country against overindulged fanatics, he wrote on 31 July, "it is better to exceede in suspition then confidence since wee have many more instances of such as stick or return to their old principles then of such as forsake them otherwyse then to prevent inconvenience or to Capacitate them for imployment." The political climate in England was at least partly responsible for Ormond's new-found firmness, for he instructed the earl of Longford to remind Arran that the royal court should not perceive him as being asleep in Ireland.[123]

Ormond pressed his views on Mountjoy as well. The nonconformists habitually claimed to suffer persecution, he argued, "if they had not liberty to persecute others, even those that come nearest to their principles," a comment that reflected his growing embitteredness. Mountjoy's inability to implicate Ulster Scots in the conspiracies did not surprise Ormond; rather than risk secret correspondence, he conjectured, the plotters had planned to launch their insurrection in London in the expectation that compatriots "in all the corners of the three kingdoms" would follow their lead. He warned Arran that dissenters in Ireland would break their promise not to hold public conventicles, at which time "any further trouble that shall bee given them will bee the more justified." To Mountjoy he feigned surprise at the change in the Presbyterians' attitude, for he had no faith in their sincerity or professed disapprobation of the plotting.[124] Dissenters in Ireland were undoubtedly fortunate that the disclosure of the Rye House plotting occurred while Ormond was in England.

Cognizant of the gravity of the situation, many Irish nonconformists ceased to meet or convened privately, and magistrates rarely had trouble suppressing conventicles of any consequence. By mid-August 1683 Arran could report to his father that many dissenters were attending services in the Church of Ireland and their ministers had posted bonds that would be forfeited if nonconformists met in large numbers. Those who refused to attend the Church of Ireland faced fines of 12d. per Sunday. The Quakers refused to conform, but Arran and Ormond rightly deemed them no threat, though the latter reminded his son that "all sortes of dissenters Joyne in Rebellion against the King & Church," a correct assessment of the ecumenical range of the Rye House plotters' religious views.[125] Nonconformists in Cork were another exception, in part because Viscount Shannon, Bishop Wetenhall, and the mayor only reluctantly agreed to suppress conventicles. Even then, they resolved to turn a blind eye to the Friends, many of whom were prominent traders as well as peaceful residents. One of the most visible and obstinant cases of resistance occurred in Dublin, where William Jacque attracted even larger numbers of worshippers in the summer of 1683 than the period before the revelation of the plotting, probably because other congregations ceased to meet. Jacque stepped up the frequency of his services. On Arran's instructions the mayor arrested Jacque, but he soon obtained his release on bail and returned to his pulpit. Summoned before the Council by Arran, Jacque insisted he had broken no law, whereupon Arran freed him after warning him not to hold another conventicle. Arran was prepared to incarcerate Jacque in Dublin Castle if he disobeyed, but Jacque seems to have learned his lesson. Arran preferred a moderate course, requiring dissenting clergy to provide recognizances for good behavior rather than imprisoning them, though he was not convinced this would permanently convert many nonconformists.[126]

In contrast, John Vesey, archbishop of Tuam, reiterated the traditional harsh line against dissenters in a sermon preached on 16 September 1683 at Clonmel for the Tipperary assizes. Against the backdrop of the Rye House disclosures Vesey stressed the duty of Christian obedience, comparing those who resisted the government on religious pretenses to Muslims. "To contrive the Death of a Prince, or the Subversion of a Government, for the sake of some Differences in Religion, is not only unchristian but inhumane." He chided Presbyterians and Catholics for using Scripture to justify treason, insisting that divine law prohibited Christians from rebelling even when persecuted. If primitive Christians believed themselves bound to obey heathen governors, then different opinions in religion could not justify rebellion by contemporary believers against their prince. Like conservative writers before him he likened rebellion to witchcraft, "and if Rebellion be such a Sin, 'tis not the pretences of Defending Liberty and Property, of Destroying Popery & Arbitrary Government, that can make it not a Sin." Vesey was condemning the core of Whig ideology, and he may have been thinking of radical republicans such as Robert West and Nathaniel Wade when he advised his audience to leave the modelling of government to their superiors. "If the preaching of Peace was ever a Duty, it is now, by reason of the Divisions among us."[127]

The harsher climate toward dissent that followed the Rye House disclosures again prompted Presbyterians to seek relief from the government. The Tyrone presbytery argued unsuccessfully to send one or two commissioners to England in the fall of 1683 to beseech Whitehall to respond favorably to a petition for relief. That winter the Down presbytery asked its sister meeting in Antrim if ministers serving in inconspicuous places in each presbytery should test the waters by resuming services in meetinghouses, but after pondering the question for three months Antrim decided in May that this was a matter for the general committee. So too, it opined, was the celebration of the Lord's supper "in the most prudent way considering our present circumstances."[128] The Down meeting then began pressing for a joint address to the lord lieutenant seeking religious liberty, which Antrim agreed to draft at Tyrone's suggestion. The Antrim clergy also concurred with Tyrone's proposal that ministers who had begun returning to their meetinghouses should cease until Ormond had come back to Ireland inasmuch as he might "have greater liberty if any imprudence obstruct not." This was a politic suggestion, particularly because the duke's wrath against nonconformists had cooled by the time he returned from England. Discussions about the wisdom of resuming services in the meetinghouses dragged on in the presbyteries until December 1686, at which time Antrim learned that the clergy in Down had quietly returned to their churches without official action in the presbytery.[129]

By the time Ormond returned to Ireland in 1684 the country was calm. For the most part, neither side sought a confrontation, though there were exceptions. Sir Robert Colvill warned that disorders would "hardly be prevented unless the roote be plucked up, for tender dealing will never gaine upon people of such perverse principles." But Francis Marsh, archbishop of Dublin, reported to Ormond that dissenters in the capital were still not meeting in early February 1685.[130]

The government continued to keep a wary eye on links between

Presbyterians in Scotland and Ireland. Radical Covenanter activity was apparently slight at this time, although in October 1683 the militant Scottish Cameronians, condemning the indulgence policy as Satan's work, sought an alliance with Presbyterians in Dublin. Radical Covenanters in Ireland, such as the Belfast bookbinder James Caldwell, thought their counterparts in Scotland were "in the right" and circulated a document calling on Presbyterians to oppose both Church of Ireland clergy and moderate dissenters who prayed for the king. The statement also exhorted them to assist Scottish fugitives. Once again the post between Edinburgh and Dublin had lapsed, prompting Ormond to call for its re-establishment in November in the face of restlessness among Ulster Scots. When the government in London received reports of an alleged Covenanter rebellion planned for Ulster in December 1684, it ordered the arrest of dissidents travelling to Ireland.[131]

From the lay perspective, particularly that of officials at all levels, security was the overriding concern in dealing with Protestant nonconformists. There were obviously exceptions, such as Wetenhall among the clerics and Rawdon among the prominent laity, but for the most part ecclesiastical and lay leaders viewed nonconformists through different lenses. The Galloway and Bothwell Bridge rebellions in Scotland heightened security concerns because of the frequent movement of ministers and others across the North Channel, and the bitterness of the succession struggle and the intense conservative reaction following the disclosure of the Rye House plotting exacerbated tension, resulting in a crackdown on large outdoor conventicles as well as unauthorized services in Dublin. Yet even in these dark years at the end of Charles's reign, Irish nonconformists could gather in small groups, keeping their cause alive without unbearable suffering. Had it not been for the provocative actions of extremists, lay leaders might well have implemented a relatively broad-based policy of toleration, the objections of most prominent clerics notwithstanding. Had that happened, leading clergymen in time would probably have felt less threatened by the nonconformists and embraced a *modus vivendi*, thereby considerably reducing the level of religious tension in Ireland and perhaps promoting a measure of ecumenical cooperation.

Toleration, Survival, and Resurgence: Nonconformists from the Reign of James II to the Eve of the Penal Laws

THE LAST DECADE and a half of the seventeenth century was a period of sharply differing fortunes for nonconformists in Ireland. For the benefit of his fellow Catholics, James II embraced a policy of toleration for virtually all who were outside the pale of the established church, but only after suppressing the Argyll rebellion in Scotland and the Monmouth uprising in England, both of which posed more considerable threats to the security of the realms than would appear in the aftermath of their collapse. Under James, nonconformists received not only a substantial degree of religious freedom but also the ability to participate more fully in corporations and to serve as magistrates. Yet had Richard Talbot, earl of Tyrconnell, governed Ireland long enough for James, the impact would probably have been disastrous for Protestants of all stripes, given the earl's resolve to establish Catholic control over the army and civil administration, revise the land settlement on terms favorable to Catholics, and liberate Ireland from English rule.[1] This is much more apparent to modern historians than it was to contemporaries outside Tyrconnell's circle, hence it is not surprising that nonconformist reaction to the revolution of 1688–1689 was mixed. The ensuing time of troubles was hard on nonconformists, as the detailed accounts of Quaker losses (discussed in Chapter 8) reveal. The long shadow of persecution in these years was particularly trying, but the organizations that Scottish Presbyterians and Friends had established in the previous decades were so well grounded that both groups weathered the storm, emerging in the mid-1690s in relatively favorable conditions that enabled them to regain their strength and commence a period of expansion as emerging denominations at century's end.

The Return of Indulgence and Renewed
Fears of Catholic Rebellion

James's accession provoked almost no negative reaction in Ireland. In Belfast an apprentice who was the son of a Presbyterian minister (perhaps Henry Livingstone's son) was reportedly responsible for tearing down a proclamation announcing the new king. At Downpatrick a Mr. Dixon, who was probably a Presbyterian, spoke treasonably on hearing news of James's accession, though he pleaded he had been inebriated. Taking no chances, Ormond wanted him prosecuted to the utmost at the assizes. The king received information that Robert Maxwell, a minister in county Down, had uttered seditious words against him and promoted faction; this was probably Thomas Maxwell, minister at Drumcaw, county Down.[2]

The decision to replace Ormond antedated Charles's death, and the duke left Ireland in February 1685. From that point until James named his brother-in-law, Henry Hyde, earl of Clarendon, to assume the lord lieutenancy, the administration of the realm rested in the hands of Granard and Michael Boyle, archbishop of Armagh. During the late winter and spring of 1685 the government continued to be concerned with fugitives seeking refuge in Ireland. Movement in the opposite direction became a problem in April when approximately 100 disaffected persons, some of whom were Scottish rebels, traveled from Island Magee to Scotland. James responded by reminding the Irish lords justices to maintain regular correspondence with the Scottish Privy Council, and the justices dispatched a troop of horse to the coast to curtail further movements of this nature.[3] When Argyll prepared to invade Scotland, James ordered troops to northern Ireland under Granard's command with instructions that some soldiers be transported to Scotland if required. The government also sent a frigate to patrol the North Channel.[4] By the end of May two more frigates had been sent, and twelve troops of horse and six companies of foot guarded the northeastern Irish coast.[5] With more than 4,000 soldiers in the north at the end of June, reports of restless dissidents were understandably few, though one of Sir Arthur Rawdon's correspondents described the "fanatics [as] tumultuous." Government agents believed they uncovered a plot in

Tipperary in June, though Archbishop Boyle later described it as no more than a disorderly meeting of fanatics at Borrisokane.[6] Taking no chances, Granard's troops confiscated the weapons of persons thought to be disaffected to the government.[7]

The failure of the Argyll and Monmouth insurrections undoubtedly persuaded the more militant dissenters in Ireland to remain quiet, and moderates were probably never enthusiastic about the rebels. In mid-June John Pinney, whose son fought for Monmouth, wrote from Dublin to his daughter Sarah: "I see nothing but trouble & misery comming on these kingdoms," and at the end of July he confided that he could no longer study because of the disquiet and sense of imminent danger. The latter stemmed not only from fear of arrest as the government tightened security but also from Gaelic Irish allegations that Englishmen in Tipperary and Ulster were plotting against the government; in the latter case the fear was not of conspiracy but of being falsely accused of intriguing or being massacred in another Catholic uprising.[8] Colonel Henry Owen, a suspect in the Rye House plotting, was arrested. While Granard was in Ulster someone gave him "a Rebellious, mad, enthusiastick paper" indicating dissidents in the region purportedly "intended all possible confusions both in church & state, while they pretended nothing but religion."[9] In fact, Ireland was generally calm, and Archbishop Boyle informed Ormond in late August that few conventicles met in Munster, Leinster, and Connaught. At Kilmallock, county Limerick, someone—probably a dissenter—assaulted a Church of Ireland minister while he was reading the burial service, but this was an isolated incident. A far more common reaction was to consider emigrating to America. "All Sober people here," wrote Pinney to his daughter Rachel in December, "are inclined & pr[e]p[ar]ing to go to West Gursey."[10]

The Argyll and Monmouth rebellions did not produce a common view of nonconformists among prominent lay and ecclesiastical leaders. Sometime after the announcement in August 1685 that Clarendon would be the new lord lieutenant and his arrival in Ireland early the following year, Lord Guildford urged him to repress the Presbyterians because their Calvinist tenets endangered the realm.[11] The future dean of St. Patrick's, William King, espoused a much more modest view when he came to the defense of the bishops of Cork and Kilmore, who had been attacked by Peter Manby, dean of Derry, for preaching against Catholicism during the Argyll and Monmouth rebellions. (The sermons had actually been delivered in March.) Manby castigated conformists who arranged marriages with "Whiggish" rather than Catholic families, particularly because Robert Sanderson, bishop of Lincoln, had argued that Rome was a true church from which Anglicans derived their own priestly succession. In contrast, Sanderson and other learned men contended that "the Fanatics [were] no Church at all." To the latter assertion King retorted that "the Order of Episcopacy [was] in as much danger from the Papists as the Fanatics, both equally designing the subversion of it as it stands established by the Law of the Land." Catholicism, in fact, he considered more dangerous because of its doctrines, including papal supremacy, whereas Protestant nonconformists intended only "to prey upon the Land & the Revenues of the Church." If some conformists preferred to marry dissenters rather than Catholics, King argued, they had good reason, for Presbyterians differed from Anglicans in no "material point" of theology apart from their espousal of lawful resistance, a doctrine not unique to them. Disagreements between conformists and Presbyterians over discipline, he contended, were "no sufficient cause to them of Division, either in affection or Church-Communion," but substantive theological differences between conformists and Catholics prevented intercommunion.[12]

When Manby, whose wife was Catholic, converted to Catholicism, King wrote *An Answer to the Considerations Which Obliged Peter Manby . . . to Embrace . . . the Catholick Religion* (1687), a work in which he continued to view adherents of Rome more harshly than Protestant nonconformists. "Neither all Protestants are Catholick members of the Church, nor are Protestants only; those among Protestants, that embrace the Catholick Faith, and make no Separation from their lawful Governors, and that live in unity of Faith and charity with their neighbour Churches are Catholick members, and have that Unity, which is essential to the Catholick Church." Because Presbyterians, Congregationalists, Baptists, Fifth Monarchists, and Quakers had separated from their "lawful Governours," they were not part of this church, yet their "Crime" was less serious than Manby's. Nonconformists were rebels, but Manby had united with a foreign power that intended to enslave his country. King had some advice for the nonconformists: Presbyters should not preach against the constitution of the church of which they were members but seek reform by applying to those with the power to implement it. Nor could presbyters who are censured or suspended continue to discharge their offices or instigate a schism to regain them. This, he asserted, the Church of Ireland argued "against the Presbyterians and other Sects amongst us, that either have no Ordination or Appointment to their Offices from the Church of England and Ireland, or else abuse the Power against her, which was once given them by her, and from which they are again legally suspended."[13] King was thus content to declaim against the nonconformists' right to preach without calling for the forcible repression of their services.

Throughout Clarendon's administration the nonconformists quietly observed their religious practices while avoiding confrontations with the government. Bishop Wetenhall noted this with obvious relief: "Those, who are not of us, at least hereabouts, are not yet so insolent as to disturb us." He fretted, however, that the nonconformists enervated Protestant security by their separation from the established church. Clarendon was more sanguine, at least with respect to those of English ancestry in Ireland; of the Scots, he told James, he knew too little to make a judgment. Some, he said, thought most of the English in Ireland were "fanaticks, of Cromwell's brood" and descendants of the parliamentary rebels, but this, he assured the king, was untrue. Most—perhaps six-sevenths—were members of the Church of Ireland and loyal to the government. Clarendon sought to ease people's minds as the precondition to economic prosperity. "My business," he explained to Sir William Trumbull, "is to convince them that neither their religion nor estates are in danger."[14]

Although a committed Anglican, Clarendon offered a scathing critique of the Church of Ireland. The clergy in general were prone to absenteeism, the most conspicuous offender being Thomas Hacket, bishop of Down and Connor, who had not visited his diocese for six years. Many of Hacket's absentee clergy reportedly placed the care of their livings in the hands of "mean and ignorant curates." John Vesey stayed away from his archdiocese of Tuam for three years, but unlike Hacket went back in 1686. Clarendon rejected most requests from clerics who had gone to England to renew their licenses, threatening those who refused to return with forfeiture of their livings. Pluralism continued to be a problem, with some clergymen holding a half dozen or more cures and enjoying incomes as high as £900 *per annum*, of which the curates collectively received a mere £150; for this, he complained, the incumbents preached only once a year. Though the clergy in Dublin were generally worthy, he deemed the lesser clerics in other areas unruly and loath to take advice. Anthony Dopping, bishop of Meath, was in Clarendon's judgment a dull preacher who meddled in politics in his sermons, an offense for which the earl suspended two clerics of lesser status in November 1686. He claimed never to have met a man of worse character than Dean Manby. Nor was Clarendon content with the physical condition of the churches, whose "ruinous state [was] . . . very melancholly." Given these conditions, he concluded, many people flocked to Catholic priests and nonconformist preachers.[15] The king himself contributed to the problem by leaving the archbishopric of Cashel and the sees of Clonfert and Elphin vacant.[16]

Ireland remained quiet through the spring of 1686 at least in part because the government treated Catholics and nonconformists with relative leniency. In Dublin the latter could meet for worship, though not in their churches. Catholics built a Capuchin friary and a Franciscan church and hoped to acquire a building in Kilmainham, west of the city, for Jesuit use. In late June James ordered the admission of Catholics to corporations without requiring them to take the oath of supremacy.[17] A dissident named William Baird was incarcerated and fined £500 at the Derry assizes for seditious speech, but allegations of this nature against James's critics while he was still duke of York became so commonplace that Clarendon issued a proclamation in July banning further prosecutions for such offenses prior to the death of Charles II.[18] Allegations of plotting connected with the Monmouth rebellion by the Kinsale merchant Robert Clarke were probably spurious, but the government took no chances and imprisoned the accused.[19] Clarendon had instructions to apprehend David Montgomery of Langshaw, a Scottish radical and Argyll rebel who had also been involved in planning an insurrection in his homeland in connection with the proposed Monmouth-Shaftesbury uprising in England; Langshaw had a small estate in Ireland. The unsuccessful search for Montgomery was part of a larger surveillance of the North Channel to apprehend Scottish rebels.[20] Clarendon also attempted to keep the realm peaceful by prohibiting the publication and importing of unlicensed material, including newsletters.[21]

With a Catholic on the throne and expansive Catholic activity in Dublin, rumors of another Catholic uprising were perhaps inevitable. Such stories became increasingly common in the latter half of 1686, well before the announcement in January 1687 that Tyrconnell would succeed Clarendon (but with the title of lord deputy). Rumors of plundering by Gaelic Irish in the autumn heightened the tension, purportedly forcing some in counties Waterford and Cork to hide in the fields. Prosecutions of those who spread the rumors brought some calm to this region, but Westmeath and Longford in particular were plagued by the same problem.[22] An exasperated Clarendon told his brother, the earl of Rochester: "If I am left alone, I will undertake every thing should be quiet; but if there be not a vigorous course taken to put a stop to these reports, there will not want oaths to prove every body on horseback, armed, and caballing about the Lord knows what, when they are all in their beds." As early as the spring of 1686 Protestants had begun sending money to America with a view to emigrating because of the potential Catholic threat, and by the summer one observer noted that an "abundance of families" was leaving for England, Scotland, and the plantations.[23]

With the coming of Tyrconnell the nonconformists enjoyed greater toleration. In early March 1687 dissenting clergy began holding services in their meetinghouses, though many nonconformists continued to emigrate. Thousands of houses stood vacant in Dublin, according to Pinney. Nathaniel Mather opted to stay in Ireland, for he believed Protestants could live under wise and just Catholic rulers.[24] Indulgence was already the policy in Ireland when James issued a declaration bestowing it on England in April. The Irish government formally reissued the declaration on 11 April. When the king sought public support from Irish nonconformists for his policy, Tyrconnell persuaded some, including Presbyterians in Ulster and Dublin, Congregationalists in Dublin, Quakers throughout the country, and unspecified dissenters in Munster, to submit addresses. In theirs the Dublin Presbyterians acknowledged the king's "influence surprising our jealous Minds with Security, by Your Royal Word, and enforcing due Loyalty by making Mens Conditions easie."[25]

Tyrconnell did not trust the nonconformists, particularly the Ulster Scots, whom he suspected of conspiring and engaging in seditious correspondence with dissidents in Scotland. The earl of Sunderland found his arguments unpersuasive, primarily because dissenters in Scotland and England were quiescent, and ordered Tyrconnell not to provoke distrust among the Ulster Scots "without great occasion." Nevertheless, in September 1687 troops were quartered in Ulster "to keep the Scotch Protestants in awe," and Tyrconnell continued to disarm Protestants.[26] Under his administration the Church of Ireland remained Protestant, though key vacancies, including the deanry of St. Patrick's, were not filled and the chapel of Dublin Castle became Catholic. As early as February 1687 Wetenhall had expressed his disquietude, remarking that "now at length none of us think our mountains fast." In these circumstances the flow of emigrants from the country continued; "multitudes" of Protestants, remarked Nathaniel Mather, fled to England in the summer of 1687.[27]

The policy of indulgence opened the way for the participation of nonconformists in corporations. The Presbyterian merchant Thomas Pottinger negotiated a new charter for Belfast and became the town's first "sovereign." Two other Presbyterians, William Lockhart and William Craford, were elected burgesses at Belfast in 1687. At Derry in the years before the siege, four Presbyterians served as aldermen, nine (of 24) as burgesses, and two as sheriffs.[28]

At the government's request, the Quakers agreed in the fall of 1687 to submit a list of persons qualified to serve as magistrates and appointed a committee of ten, including the Dublin merchants Anthony Sharp and Samuel Clarridge, to prepare it. When Dublin received a new charter in November, Sharp and Clarridge were among the 24 aldermen. Friends served in other corporations as well, including those at Cork and Limerick. Such involvement in the political arena concerned some Quakers, hence the half-yearly meeting commissioned John Burnyeat and John Watson to prepare a statement "of tender advice to friends who are so concerned to keep to the truth in every thing, that the honour thereof may be cheifly in their eye & that no Just offence may be given by them." Burnyeat and Watson recommended that Quaker officeholders "keep low, tender and watchfull in all things" and wait for the counsel of the Spirit before acting. They were also to forbear using "such words, Customs, Gestures & Garbs as are not agreeable to the simplicity of the truth, nor doth answer the plainness of our holy Profession."[29] Fox too offered counsel to Quakers in office, reminding them not to take oaths, wear formal gowns, or participate in feasts with other magistrates, and to sit with their hats on in the presence of other officials. They must preserve every person's rights and property, disturbing no one in his or her "divine right or liberty, for the good, Just, holy and Righteous law of God preserves all both In their divine right and Liberty and in their Natural Liberty and property." Fox exhorted Quaker magistrates to work for the removal of mandatory tithes; if Friends were summoned to their courts, Quaker magistrates were not to pronounce judgment against them for refusing to pay tithes.[30] Under Tyrconnell, in fact, many Friends were exempt from paying tithes. William King would later reflect bitterly on this episode, complaining that the government rendered the established clergy's jurisdiction insignificant "by encouraging the most Obstinate and Perverse Sectaries, and by shewing them Favour according as they were most opposite and refractory to all Ecclesiastical Discipline, and paying their Dues to the Clergy." He was thinking especially of the Quakers who had been allowed to serve as burgesses and aldermen.[31] At no time in their previous history had circumstances been better for the Friends than they were on the eve of the revolution, but such toleration as they enjoyed was only a temporary expedient to help James and Tyrconnell restore the realm to Catholicism.

The Revolution and the Time of Troubles

James's Catholic policies coupled with Tyrconnell's distrust of the non-conformists made it improbable that dissenters would provide substantive support for the government in the crisis of 1688, but the policy of indulgence and the inclusion of nonconformists in the magistracy gave them slight pause before some of them embraced Prince William. During the summer of 1688 a messenger from Scotland reported to William Carstares, one of William's agents, that dissenters in Scotland were devoted to the prince and princess, and that Ireland "if taken notice of is not in so bad a posture as many think" because Ulster Presbyterians "did keep a correspondence and were resolved to stand by one another in case of any attempt" against them. Their motive was primarily fear of another Catholic uprising, not fidelity to a political cause. Because the Scottish Presbyterians had utilized the indulgence to reinvigorate their ecclesiastical organization, they were effectively positioned to endorse William when he invaded England in November. Presented by Patrick Adair and John Abernethy, their message extolled his glorious deliverance of the kingdoms from Catholicism, urged him to preserve Protestantism in Ireland, and pledged the Presbyterians' support.[32]

The Presbyterian apologist James Kirkpatrick claimed a major role for his fellow believers in helping William achieve his triumph: "In Ireland the Presbyterians Exerted themselves with the utmost Vigor, Zeal and Activity for Accomplishing and Maintaining the late Happy Revolution." The Presbyterian ministers, he averred, were "early in Countenancing that Glorious Work," meeting frequently in 1688 with some of the nobles and gentry in the Church of Ireland and helping to defend Ireland against James's supporters. The Anglican apologist William Tisdall made a similar claim of Protestant unity in the early stages of the revolution, but noted that it failed to last.[33]

Kirkpatrick and Tisdall are only partially correct. Information about the activities and movements of most Presbyterian ministers is unknown, but some fifty of them are known to have fled Ireland during the revolution and its immediate aftermath. In the summer of 1688 many Presbyterians ceased going to church in the belief that many of their ministers had left, prompting the Antrim presbytery to insist that the clergy were still fulfilling their responsibilities. Nevertheless, the Down and Antrim presbyteries established a committee to consider ways "to avert or present the hint of a growing schism breaking out in this country by some wild persons," a reference to their concern that Presbyterian extremists associated with the United Societies in Scotland would take advantage of the flight of Presbyterian clerics to broaden their base.[34]

Two documents from these zealots manifested their unwillingness to compromise and their prophetic zeal. In the first, they accused traditional Presbyterian ministers in county Down in January 1689 of breaking their covenant vows: "Yow most unfaithfully have flinched from and yeelded up not only the royalties and prerogatives of our lord but also the just liberties and priviledgs of these Lands into the hands of these antichristian powers." Instead of following the colors of an avenging Lord, the traditional Presbyterian ministers had fled to Antichrist. By repudiating the Galloway and Bothwell Bridge rebels instead of engaging in their cause, the clergy had "given it under [their] hands and seals that the sheding of al the blood of the saints one scaffolds is good service." By embracing the "present hel hatcht libe[r]ty"—a reference to the *de facto* policy of toleration—the Presbyterian clergy endorsed the government that had executed the rebels. In the second document, a letter to Ireland dated 9 April 1689, the zealots issued a prophetic warning against imminent judgment and held out hope for a faithful remnant: "Many a warning yow have goten O covenanted lands and many a warning hast thow gotten O irland but before it be long god shal give you one for all for what ever sinful pease may be pretended."[35] Faced with a choice of William or James, some of these partisans, whose leader was David Houston, supported the prince.[36]

In the meantime the mainline Presbyterians became increasingly active. At Letterkenny Presbyterian women forced the conformist Nathaniel Cooper from his pulpit so the Scottish Presbyterian William Liston could preach, but when the latter learned of their actions he spoke elsewhere. If meetinghouses were ruined or in disrepair, Liston, like some of his colleagues, did not hesitate to preach in parish churches. In July 1690 the synod of Ulster chastised such ministers because their actions were illegal and offensive to the government. In the diocese of Derry Presbyterians reportedly pulled a cleric from his pulpit and confiscated his gun. Throughout Ulster many nonconformists allegedly refused to pay tithes, and dissenters on the earl of Donegall's estate at Six Mile Water, armed with pitchforks and half-pikes, reportedly declined to pay their rents and wounded some of Donegall's men.[37] At the popular level the scene was hardly one of Protestant unity in many places, though Protestants later joined forces in the siege of Derry, when conformists and Presbyterians shared the cathedral. The Scottish Presbyterian ministers Thomas Boyd, David Brown, William Crooks (Cruix), William Gilchrist, James Gordon, John Hamilton, John Mackenzie, John Rowatt, and John Wilson served the beleaguered city, with Brown, Gilchrist, Hamilton, and Wilson perishing during the siege. Eighteen conformist clergymen were also there.[38]

A sense of crisis pervaded the country as reports of William's landing in England spread, provoking considerable speculation that Irish Catholics would rebel. On 8 December Francis Marsh, archbishop of Dublin, told Dr. William King how he had attended Tyrconnell "upon occasion of that generall terrour hee is informed has like an infection seared most of the People." The lord deputy insisted his government harbored no ill intentions toward anyone in Dublin, whatever her or his religious persuasions, but he would not permit rebellious acts to go unpunished. Marsh's mission was to persuade the populace to conduct themselves properly and not provoke the government "by any rude aggressions, tumultuary assemblies or appearing in armes."[39]

Tyrconnell and the Council issued a proclamation on 25 January 1689 branding riotous assemblies and the seizure of fortified places, weapons, and ammunition as treasonable; those responsible were ordered to withdraw in return for pardons or face prosecution. Amid rampant rumors of a Catholic rebellion, Protestants were fleeing the island or, in the north, banding together in armed associations. The Sligo association called for a free Parliament and unity with England. The earl of Mount-Alexander agreed to defend the Ulster Protestants against Catholics, but Tyrconnell was not to be counted out. Short of money to pay his troops, he nevertheless had 40,000 soldiers and sufficient control to confiscate the weapons of Protestants in Dublin.[40] He and the Council ordered the "treasonable" associations of Protestants in Ulster and Sligo to disband, and on 7 March he offered a full pardon to all except Mount-Alexander, Massereene, and eight others if they obeyed. A week later Lieutenant-General Richard Hamilton's troops overwhelmed Mount-Alexander's men, causing their organization in eastern Ulster to collapse and the earl to flee to the Isle of Man. On the 25th James issued a proclamation affirming the free exercise of religion in Ireland and ordered all Irish subjects in England or Scotland to return within forty days. As tolerant as this appeared, the king probably would have ousted the nonconformists from the magistracy had he established lasting control over Ireland. "The Presbyterians," he told the earl of Balcarres, "are not good masters in any government"; he was referring primarily to Scotland, but the situation in Ulster cannot have escaped him. The Anglo-Irish in Dublin shared his view.[41]

James's proclamation of religious liberty brought an address of gratitude from the Friends, who pledged their loyalty, requested an opportunity to respond to negative comments about themselves, and asked for royal protection in light of the despoilment they were experiencing. In August James expressed his satisfaction with the Friends' loyalty to the government and formally took the Quakers, their lands, and their possessions into royal protection. Moreover he exempted Friends from all previous proclamations dealing with disaffected Protestants and from all forfeitures or penalties incurred thereby. Neither magistrates nor the military were to disturb or restrain them, "it being our Royal Intention that no differences should be made betweene such part of our Said Protestant Subjects & any other in actuall obedience to us."[42] James was not only rewarding the Friends but also sending a message to other nonconformists that they too could enjoy similar treatment if they returned to obedience. Two weeks later Burnyeat informed Charles Marshall in London that the Quakers were sustaining heavy losses at the hands of both armies though their meetings were not disrupted by magistrates. Meetings in Leinster and Munster, in fact, were large. A year later Quakers in Limerick suffered such severe depredations that the Leinster provincial meeting appointed Edmundson and Burnyeat to draft a petition to James seeking relief. After delivering it Gershon Boate and Thomas Winslow reported that the king accepted it, "spoke mildly . . . and promised to do for the safety of friends in Lymerick what hee could."[43]

In the same month James extended royal protection to the Friends, Adair, Abernethy, and Colonel Arthur Upton petitioned William for favors, citing the Presbyterians' sufferings, their loyalty to his cause, and their early declaration of support. They asked that henceforth no penalties be imposed on nonconformists; that the king, acting as "a Nursing-Father," encourage "the Purity of the Gospel in Worship and Discipline, till there be a legal Establishment of both"; that needy Presbyterian clergy, some of whom had been in besieged Derry, receive a share of "the Public Charitable Collections"; and that those ministers who had been forced to flee be encouraged to return to their pastorates by the promise of royal financial support until such a time as the people could maintain them. The petitioners did not request the abolition of episcopacy in northern Ireland. The duke of Shrewsbury conveyed William's favorable response to Abernethy and Adair on 28 September. William promised to pay the *regium donum* at a rate of £800 *per annum*, and in a letter to the duke of Schomberg he extended them royal protection.[44]

Thus nonconformists were divided in 1689, with the Friends tied to James and the Presbyterians to William. Circumstances were conducive for Anglicans and Presbyterians to explore the latter's accommodation in the established church. Writing at the time, the historian and recorder of Kinsale, Richard Cox, commented that the differences between "Episcopalians" and dissenters (by which he meant Presbyterians and possibly Congregationalists) were little noticed in Ireland "because they really do manage this Affair more prudently than some other more celebrated Nations, and sacrifice these petty Fewds to the common Interest of opposing Popery."[45]

Indeed, William King made a significant contribution toward comprehension in "The Present State of the Church." Proposing a compromise on the crucial issue of ordination, he suggested future ordinands must have the approval of the bishops and a majority of their presbytery. Reordination of Presbyterian clergy would neither invalidate nor diminish previous ministerial acts but make the original ordination "more unexceptionable" to the entire church. King was even willing to connive at the inclusion of Presbyterian ministers who refused reordination if they conformed in all other respects, a position at odds with that espoused in the Church of Ireland after the restoration. King was prepared to accept changes in the liturgy as long as all parties agreed on a "form of prayer," and he was agreeable as well to curtailing the number of holy days and the use of the organ and the surplice, terminating readings from the Apocrypha, limiting the use of the Book of Common Prayer, and preparing a new edition of psalms for singing. He was also prepared to modify the baptismal service by removing the direct responsibility of godparents, cease requiring the Book of Common Prayer at funerals, permit standing or kneeling at communion, and make the sign of the cross in baptism optional. Anthony Carpenter has cogently argued that "The Present State of the Church" was an emergency proposal that could not have won widespread support among either conformists or Presbyterians.[46] It would be hard to argue with his conclusion, the brilliance and fairness of the proposed compromises notwithstanding.

In the same month Presbyterians and Quakers petitioned William and James respectively, the prince, on the heels of the Jacobites' lifting of the siege of Derry and their defeat at Enniskillen, dispatched a new army to Ireland under the command of the duke of Schomberg. His troops quickly captured Carrickfergus but did little else before disease and illness sapped their strength. With 15,000 troops William himself came to Ireland in June 1690, defeated James at the Boyne on 1 July, and occupied Dublin. When the Irish made their stand at the Shannon, William besieged Limerick, only to run out of ammunition before he could capture the city. After William had returned to England, Baron van Ginkel renewed the assault on Limerick in August 1691 and forced the defenders to negotiate an end to the fighting in the so-called Treaty of Limerick (October 1691).

The time of troubles imposed considerable hardships on the nonconformists, even in Dublin, which had to house refugees and provide financial assistance to stricken believers throughout the country. The scale of Quaker material losses (discussed in Chapter 8) was staggering. Warring armies inflicted much of the damage, but Gaelic Irish plunderers, or rapparees (from "rapaire," a half-pike), caused considerable losses. In areas under Gaelic Irish control, as the Quaker Joseph Pike of Cork recounted, Protestants "were often abused and confined; two or three could hardly meet or speak together without danger." Both the presbyteries in Ulster and the Friends' six-months meeting in Dublin continued to function despite trying conditions. Meetings sometimes had to be moved and churches with vacant pulpits could not always be supplied, but the amount and regularity of the business that did transpire is surprising. Friends traveling to London for the half-yearly meeting faced considerable danger, primarily from the rapparees. It was difficult to find lodging in towns en route because soldiers had commandeered virtually all available rooms. In November 1690 only two Friends from Cork could attend the national meeting, and the peril was so great that none could go to either session the following year.[47]

The Presbyterians achieved one significant gain during the war. After William landed near Carrickfergus on 14 June 1690, a Presbyterian delegation that included Archibald Hamilton and Patrick and William Adair called on William as he moved through Belfast. They reminded him of their pledge of support after he invaded England and of his promise to renew the *regium donum*, which James had suspended, at the rate of £800 *per annum*. Lieutenant-General James Douglas persuaded William not only to grant the request but also to increase the stipend to £1,200. According to Sir Robert Southwell, Douglas believed "that as King James works by his priests, so these men will do like service to his

Majesty by uniting the people unto him, and making a good report of things in Scotland." According to the king's instructions to the collector of the port of Belfast, from whose customs the money was to be taken, the funds were to be paid quarterly, with the first payment on 24 June 1690. Southwell correctly estimated that the money would be enough to give each minister £15 *per annum*. Between 1691 and 1693 the payments were irregular, but the government paid the arrears in March 1694 and made regular disbursements for the remainder of the reign.[48]

The Growth of Nonconformity
and the Anglican Triumph

In a 1702 tract vindicating Presbyterian marriage John MacBride, referring to the attitude of conformists toward Presbyterians, distinguished sharply between Anglican clerics of "intemperate Zeal" as well as those for whom "the love of Money hath engag'd to be thus unseasonably vexatious" on the one hand and the civil authorities, who "have been, and continue to be just and kind to us," and lay conformists "with whom we have a substantial Agreement, and charitable Conversation" on the other.[49] Although overdrawn and only partially correct with respect to the motivations of Anglican clergy, MacBride's thesis had much truth in it. In the dozen years following the conclusion of the time of troubles the conformists and Presbyterians, some of whom who only a few years earlier had entertained thoughts of comprehension, fought bitterly over toleration for dissenters and the validity of Presbyterian marriages, with some attention as well to nonconformist education. Each side had capable apologists, chiefly William King, Samuel Foley, and Tobias Pullein for the Anglicans and Robert Craghead and Joseph Boyse for the Presbyterians.

Although historic liturgical and theological issues coupled with differences in polity were very much a part of this multifaceted dispute, a crucial factor was the enemic state of the Church of Ireland after years of neglect under James followed by the war's depredations. One of the church's apologists, William Tisdall, painted a dismal portrait of conditions in the north. Numerous Scots, he averred, were moving into northern Ireland, displacing conformist tenants ruined during the war. Within a few years of the troubles, he noted, the majority of aldermen and burgesses in the principal corporations of Ulster were dissenters, yet he also insisted the Church of Ireland still had "considerable

Congregations" in most northern towns and large numbers of country parishes.[50]

The visitations of 1693–1694 confirmed what the ecclesiastical dignitaries essentially knew, namely that much of the established church, especially in the west, was in serious financial and physical straits. Perhaps it would have been wiser to accommodate the Presbyterians in the Church of Ireland and thereby incorporate not only their numbers but also their assets, yet the prelates instead viewed them as competitors at a time when all available resources were required to preserve the church. Of the 85 parishes in the diocese of Cork, 23 had no church and the edifices were in ruins in 28 other parishes. Forty-four parishes in the diocese of Cloyne had no church, and many others had sustained damages in the rebellion of the 1640s or in the recent war. Because many livings in this diocese were so poor, a minister reputedly needed four or five to have "a very ordinary subsistence." Yet Bishop William Palliser reported that most of his clergy were deserving and resident, "almost as regular as can be well expected under our present disadvantageous circumstances." More than half the churches in the diocese of Clogher required repairs, and in the diocese of Killala the cathedral at Achonry was in ruins though its counterpart at Killala was in good shape. Henry Ryder, bishop of Killaloe, painted a dismal picture of his diocese: "The Country is Generally wast, most of the liveings worth little, some nothing, and the best scarce[ly] A Competency." Agents of the earl of Thomond (who was only five years old at this point) controlled most of the rectories and impropriations, hence "the generality of the Clergy must be in a mean Condition." Ryder's cathedral was in disrepair though the abbey church was in decent condition, but of the other 127 churches whose condition Ryder reported, an appalling 92 were in disrepair; work was underway on some of the others.[51]

Bishop Anthony Dopping had 55 clergy, fifteen of whom were nonresident, to serve the 197 parish churches and 106 chapels of ease in the diocese of Meath. Before the outbreak of the war only 48 churches and chapels were in decent condition, the rest having been ruined in the 1640s, though their walls still stood. Another five churches had been wrecked in the time of troubles. A number of parishes were devoid of Protestants, among them Ballymagarvey, Rathfeigh, Milltown (in the barony of Ratoath), Rathbeggan, Athlumney, Kilmessan, Drakestown, and Donaghpatrick. Dopping attributed the appalling conditions to a variety of factors in addition to damages sustained in the upheavals of the 1640s and the time of troubles. The parishioners, he charged, were negligent in paying church rates, nor had the impropriators and clergy been conscientious in repairing the churches. He also blamed weak ecclesiastical authority, which was restricted to presentments, censures, and expensive proceedings in church courts to prosecute offenders.[52]

In the diocese of Down and Connor the visitors complained that divine service, hospitality, and poor relief were neglected because of the prevalence of nonconformists and the shortage of manses and glebe, causing many clerics to be nonresident. The incumbents of some churches opted not to seek the recovery of their glebe and other rights lest they be deemed litigious "& disoblige their patrons & great parishioners, or hazard their own mony." Because most inhabitants were dissenters who refused to serve as churchwardens, the churches were in disrepair. Problems existed with some of the clergy, such as the minister at Ballymoney, whose bad eyesight and poor health prevented him from conducting services, or the incumbent at Ardclinis, who was admonished to live "a more sober life." The mostly absentee vicar of Donegore refused to pay the salary of his curate, reducing the latter to such misery that he committed suicide.[53]

Somewhat surprisingly King's report of his visitation of the diocese of Derry was generally optimistic. In a letter of 11 May 1694 to Dopping he reflected: "I perceive almost from every place that the congregations do increase, & I hope that tru devotion doth encrease as well as the outward appearance of it & many of the dissenters, do submitt to penance for their crimes." His principal problems were poor people who fled their habitations when cited to an ecclesiastical tribunal and itinerant schoolmasters who undermined regular schools. Sixteen days later he was somewhat less optimistic as he reflected "that much more is to [be] don than I even expected both as to reformation of the clergy & laiety, & the uniting dissenters to the church."[54] In physical terms the picture must have been bleak, for when Bishop William Nicolson visited the same diocese in 1718 he reported that many of the parish churches were demolished; he called them "Non-Cures," adding that some clerics held as many as seven of such livings while residing in Dublin.[55]

The debate over toleration must be seen against this background of an established church shorn of numerous landed possessions and with many of its churches in disrepair or utter ruin. Beleagured by these conditions, the prelates were in no mood to accommodate spiritual rivals. They were influenced by other factors as well, including the example of Scotland, where triumphant Presbyterians gained control of the established church after the revolution, forcing some episcopalian clerics to search for new livings.[56] Whereas the bishops and their supporters were relatively tolerant of Quakers and nonconforming Huguenots, neither of whom had a territorial base, represented a political threat, or enjoyed influential backing at the English court, they saw the Presbyterians in the north as a danger. Many in the Irish House of Commons would have been cognizant of the likely challenge to their power had Presbyterians been permitted to sit in their midst, and they may have been concerned as well about postwar economic developments in the north, where the linen industry was replacing the woolen. According to Tisdall, "the Failure of our Woolen Manufactory sunk the Church Interest of Ireland in the same Proportion, that the Encouragement of the Linnen Manufactory did raise the Interest of Presbytery." The woolen weavers, who returned to England or emigrated to the Low Countries when their industry declined, were generally conformists, he argued, whereas most of the linen workers were Scottish Presbyterians who had moved to Ireland after the revolution. " 'Tis evident," Tisdall observed, "the Dissenters seem at present to be almost in full Possession of our Trade." In fact this development occurred over the space of a decade, with a key event being the passage in 1699 of an English statute prohibiting Irish exports of woolen cloth. The relative lateness of this development diminishes the likelihood that it had a substantial impact on the toleration debate in the mid-1690s. Tisdall's thesis must also be revised to take into account the fact that some key leaders who transformed the Irish linen industry were Quakers in the Lurgan area, among them Thomas Turner and Robert Hoope. Moreover, the economic changes were less religious than regional, for Catholic tenants raised much of the flax and conformists in Armagh profited from the linen industry. Gaelic Irish weavers suffered the most from the decline in the woolen manufactory.[57]

As the war drew to a conclusion King anticipated a toleration bill akin to the 1689 English statute. To the bishop of Meath he indicated he would not oppose such a bill, but he put forth five clauses he thought an Irish bill should include: First, no dissenters should have meetinghouses in garrison towns. Secondly, everyone who worships in a dissenting church should pay something to support the poor of her or his parish, even if the amount is only 6d. *per annum.* Thirdly, every nonconformist meetinghouse must pay a fee to the Exchequer. Fourthly, no former conformist should be permitted to attend a dissenting church without first consulting his or her parish minister, and finally, no criminal or excommunicate from the Church of Ireland should be accepted as a member of a dissenting congregation without first rendering satisfaction to the established church for his or her offense.[58]

Nonconformists in Ireland were among the beneficiaries of an English statute (3 William and Mary, cap. 2) passed in 1691 that provided an alternative affirmation to the traditional oath of supremacy (2 Elizabeth I, cap. 2). Even some Friends found it possible to take the affirmation (see Chapter 8). By taking the new oath or affirmation, nonconformists could qualify for public office. "There is a Gap set open for dissenters," complained William Smyth. Nevertheless, nonconformists were still subject to the 1559 and 1666 acts of uniformity, the first of which (2 Elizabeth I, cap. 2) required attendance at a parish church but was rarely enforced. The second (17 & 18 Charles II, cap. 6) imposed a fine of £100 on any minister without episcopalian ordination who administered the Lord's supper and it required schoolmasters to be licensed by a bishop's ordinary.[59]

Dissatisfied with this situation Irish nonconformists wanted something akin to England's Act of Toleration. This view was shared by the English court, at whose instigation the lords justices drafted a toleration bill in the summer of 1692. As the Quaker merchant Anthony Sharp had predicted in December 1691, the Irish Parliament included opponents of toleration, and these men were powerful enough to block any bill that excluded a sacramental test. Such a test would have been anathema to all Friends and most other nonconformists. After Viscount Sydney, the new lord lieutenant, apprised the English court of these circumstances the bill was dropped in November. At the time of the next English Parliament in 1695, Irish Presbyterians renewed their campaign for a toleration act with the support of James Johnston, the Scottish secretary, and Henry Lord Capel, the Irish lord deputy. Again the effort to pass a toleration act failed because the Irish Privy Council refused to send a draft bill to England without provision for a sacramental test. Nor could Capel get a bill through either house in the Irish Parliament, thanks primarily, claimed King, to prelatical opposition.[60]

Despite the lack of a toleration act in Ireland the Presbyterians in the north were generally left alone owing to the favor they enjoyed from the English court and their degree of political entrenchment and economic power. King eschewed a policy of coercion in the diocese of Derry, preferring persuasion and urging his clergy to hold conferences with the dissenters. King talked to nonconformists on his visitations, persuading some to conform. When dissenters were elected churchwardens he permitted them to serve through deputies, and those who refused even to do this did not face punishment.[61] His concern about appointing a new bishop of Down and Connor following Samuel Foley's death in May 1695 provides an insight into his view of the problems facing the established church in the north. "That country is full of factions, & if any person concerned in them or that will encourage them be promoted" to the diocese, he confided to Dopping, "the consequence will be in all probability very fatall, & put all in a flame." The appointment of "a right good & prudent man" would help to check the growth of dissent and then break its neck. Since coming to the diocese in 1691 he had seen the number of conformists increase in many parishes, and on his recent visitation he confirmed 103 former dissenters. Congregations numbering as many as 100 or 200 had formed in places where none had existed. "This gives me hopes," he wrote, "that If du[e] methods be taken our work is not impossible & the whole of it depends on naming good men for Bishops."[62] Another of Dopping's correspondents, Ezekiel Burridge, voiced similar concerns about the vacancy at Down and Connor because of "the temper of people here & what mischiefe the church labours under." Capel selected Foley's successor, Edward Walkington, because of his reputation as a moderate with a firsthand knowledge of Presbyterians. He soon discovered that the Presbyterians were not inclined to compromise.[63]

In the meantime apologists for both sides dueled through the printed word. King suggested dissenters were magnifying their differences with conformists. "To abstain from a thing confessed to be lawful in the Service of God, meerly because observed by us, is surely very far from a Spirit of Meekness and Moderation: And therefore I may hope that you will not Indulge Your People in such affected distances, that can serve to no other purpose, but to make Parties irreconcilable." He held out hope for compliance in seven areas, the first of which was a simple plea for dissenters to use the Lord's prayer, the implication of such usage being the lawfulness of set prayers. He asked dissenters to kneel during public prayers inasmuch as sitting neither expressed reverence nor had scriptural sanction. He called for the frequent celebration of communion and urged Presbyterians to adhere to that portion of their own Directory which called for the reading of a chapter from each testament in every church service. "I know the People are fonder of Sermons and Lectures of Humane Composure, than of the pure Word of God in its Naked Simplicity; but you know this to be a carnal and sinful Humour in them." King further argued that although the most learned nonconformists accepted occasional communion with the Church of Ireland or England, thousands in Ulster neither attended church nor had their children baptized because they had no Presbyterian minister, and he wanted such persons to worship with conformists. Moreover, he exhorted Presbyterian ministers to warn their followers of the dangers of congregational polity because it failed to recognize provincial and national churches. Finally, he urged nonconformists to help Anglicans combat such offenses as adultery and blasphemy, and not to admit persons excommunicated by ecclesiastical courts to communion.[64] Turning to the laity, King asked: "How is it possible that any Man that has a Zeal for the Purity of God's Worship, should not have his Spirit moved within him, to see a well-meaning People so strangely mis-led, as to content themselves to meet together, perhaps for some Years, with a design to Worship God, and yet hardly ever see or hear any thing of God's immediate Appointment in their Meetings?" He was referring to formal prayers, nonmetrical psalms, the reading of chapters from both testaments, and kneeling during prayer and communion.[65]

In their replies to King, Boyse and Craghead demonstrated that many of the bishop's assertions were erroneous. Presbyterians did not denounce all set prayers, impose a total ban on kneeling, eschew the psalms in prose, neglect readings from either testament, prohibit recitation of the Lord's prayer, or, by their own standards, resort infrequently to the sacraments unless forced to abstain by persecution. King must have known this, which suggests that his attack was intended either as propaganda or as an appeal to casual dissenters who knew or understood little of the Presbyterians' tenets. King may also have been using negative psychology to force Presbyterians to recognize how much common ground existed between themselves and Anglicans. Craghead seems to have sensed this, for he disputed the idea that the only difference between the two groups involved "some harmless Ceremonies." Some conformist practices, he insisted, lacked biblical warrant and others entailed worship of creatures, which Presbyterians adamantly repudiated.[66]

Education was another arena in which conformists, Scottish Presbyterians, and Friends contested, their schools functioning as evolving denominational agencies. Under the terms of the 1666 Act of Uniformity schoolmasters had to obtain a license from an ordinary and conform to the Church of Ireland. Until 1698 the prelates made little effort to enforce this law in the north. After completing his diocesan visitation in 1694 King told Dopping that he had a school in each parish and had ordered the local minister to oversee it and examine the children on the catechism. "That there may be no exception taken, I desire the School-masters to teach & the ministers to examine the westminster catechism where people will not suffer their children to learn the church's," an-other striking indication of his quest to build bridges between conform-ists and dissenters. He was more troubled by "little fellows" who set up schools, lured pupils from regular schools, taught three or four months, and then moved to another location and started again. Because of them, he charged, "the regular schools are broken & the masters not able to live."[67]

As bishop of Down and Connor, Samuel Foley published a tract on education in 1695 entitled *An Exhortation to the Inhabitants of Down and Connor, Concerning the Religious Education of Their Children*. Noting the prior neglect of education, he stressed the parental role, particularly before confirmation. The greatest part of humanity, he contended, were miscarrying as adults because they had been inadequately educated as young people. In his view parents have a fourfold duty to educate their children in the articles of the Christian faith, through exemplary family behavior, by correcting their faults, and by training them in lawful call-ings or "in some Arts and Sciences" whereby "they may become ser-viceable both to themselves and to the publick." Nonconformists would not have quibbled with these aims, though the educational content of the first point (the articles of the Christian faith) would have occasioned dispute. In his tract Foley took pains to urge cordial relations with dissenters. Young people, he insisted, must not learn "little scoffs or by-words against any persons way of worshipping God, who differs from that way in which they are brought up." His rationale was sound: "If you teach your Children to take up prejudices against people, because of their different Opinions in Religion, this will by degrees beget an aversion towards them also upon other accounts."[68]

In 1698 King attempted to crack down on dissenting schoolmasters who maintained grammar schools by having them cited before eccle-siastical tribunals. This was a clerical rather than a governmental initia-tive, as indicated by the synod of Ulster's advice to affected school-masters to seek redress from Clotworthy Upton, a justice of the peace. King's efforts were only temporarily effective and were restricted to his own diocese. The Scottish Presbyterians' "Philosophy School" at Killy-leagh, county Down, continued to operate.[69]

While King was attempting to curtail the growth of dissent in his diocese, Walkington was no less concerned about the same problem in Down and Connor. In September he petitioned the lords justices, noting the "great dissatisfaction" in his diocese stemming from "the unreasonable libertie taken by the dissenting ministers and there elders . . . under colour of that connivance which they have from the Government for the free and undisturbed exercise of their religion." They were not content to assemble in their meetinghouses, he complained, but exercised jurisdiction "openly and with a high hand over those of there owne persuasion." He registered disapproval as well with the Scottish Presbyterians' celebration of the Lord's supper in the fields in formidable groups comprised of worshippers from a dozen or more parishes. Walkington was troubled as well by the Presbyterians' sessions and presbyteries, their philosophy school at Killyleagh, and their performance of marriages. Such actions, he contended, discouraged conformist clergy and undermined their arguments for the necessity of submitting to human as well as divine laws. Walkington petitioned the lords justices "to undeceave these forward men by putting such a stop to the liberties that they assume as your Lordships thinks most convenient for the good of the kingdome and the saftie and honour of the established religion."[70] Instead of going directly to the Irish lords justices, Walkington sent his petition to the bishops of Derry, Kildare, and Dromore in England in the hope of obtaining the support of the English lords justices. The latter referred it back to their counterparts in Ireland and nothing seems to have come of it.[71]

Walkington's concern may have resulted in part from an incident involving John MacBride, the Presbyterian minister at Belfast. On 1 June MacBride had preached on Acts 15:23–26 to the synod of Ulster at Antrim town. Without his knowledge several of his colleagues had the sermon printed with the title, *A Sermon Preached Before the Provincial Synod at Antrim*, and with his position listed as "minister of Belfast," implying he was the only true clergyman in the city. Because of this implication as well as the blatant assertion of independent ecclesiastical jurisdiction, MacBride was summoned to Dublin to appear before a commission that included the lord chancellor, the lord chief baron, the lord chief justice, Walkington, and four other bishops. MacBride admitted he had preached the sermon but disavowed responsibility for the title-page. He answered questions as well concerning his previous mastership of the Presbyterians' philosophy school at Killyleagh, where he denied having taught "disunity." He was soon released with an admonition that he and his colleagues "Cary respectably towardes the established church."[72]

MacBride would shortly contribute a tract to the Anglican-Presbyterian controversy over the validity of Presbyterian marriages. No statute prohibited dissenting clergy from performing marriages, and the Quakers wed without the participation of ordained clergy, but all who married in either of these ways could be prosecuted for fornication in an ecclesiastical court. Dissenting ministers could themselves be punished for having violated civil and ecclesiastical law. The issue appears to have been joined in Ireland as the result of Walkington's petition of September 1698 to the lords justices in which he complained that dissenters "Generally every where celebrate the office of matrimony by which means the seatlements made upon such mariages and the titles of children to there inheritances who are born of persons who are so joined together are rendred desputable at Law."[73] The phrasing suggests that the courts were already handling cases of persons whose parents had been married by dissenting clergy and were therefore adjudged bastards. If this were so to any extent, we could expect to see protests from nonconformists, but we do not. The following July the Ulster synod resolved to send a congratulatory address to the government inclusive of a supplication for the continuance of "our Liberty & Exemption from Molestation on Account of Marrying." MacBride had the responsibility of convening a committee of eight to draft the address. The issue had been raised when the government informed Presbyterians that the bishops opposed their marriages. A synodal committee recommended "that when any of our People desires to be married by a Minister of our Perswausion, none to whom they come shall refuse to marry them, in an orderly way . . . nor scruple to give their Judgement concerning the Forms & Modes of Joining People in Marriage, shewing which are Sinfull, which not, when desir'd by their People so to do."[74]

Attacking Presbyterians by repudiating the validity of their marriages was a potent strategy because it involved the laity as well as the clergy and raised troubling questions about the security of legacies. Sensing this, King began prosecuting Presbyterians on this issue by early 1699, and in the autumn of the same year St. George Ashe, bishop of Clogher, urged the lords justices to support such prosecutions. While agreeing that the bishops' view of Presbyterian marriages was correct, one of the justices, Henry de Massue, earl of Galway, suggested moderation as a politically expedient course. Ashe's campaign yielded results in January 1700, when the lords justices agreed to take appropriate action. Shortly thereafter dissenting clergymen in his diocese began sending people to Anglican clerics to be married. Presbyterian ministers in other areas seem not to have yielded, for in June 1701 the synod of Ulster affirmed and tightened procedures for Presbyterian marriages.

(See Chapter 4.) When Ashe continued to press the government for a proclamation against dissenting marriages, the Presbyterians took their case to the English court and eventually to William, thereby checking the prelatical offensive. The result was a stalemate.[75]

As in virtually every other controversy of note, the marriage dispute produced a pamphlet war. The principal dissenting contribution was MacBride's *A Vindication of Marriage, as Solemnized by Presbyterians in the North of Ireland* (1702). In an ecumenical spirit MacBride appealed to the common interests shared by Protestants in an overwhelmingly Catholic land:

Are not the Breaches amongst us wide enough already, but some Men must be inventing new Engines to drive us further asunder? . . . Is this a Season for these who ought to be uniting against the common Adversary of the Protestant Interest in Ireland, to be combining against peaceable Men for private Interest? Sure we are, none of her Majesty's Subjects are under greater Obligations to stand by one another than the Brittish Protestants in Ireland; who are neither too many nor too strong to maintain themselves against the common Enemy of our Religion and Civil Interest, which are here inseparably linked together.[76]

Two points should be stressed, the first of which was MacBride's endeavor to link the conformist campaign against Presbyterian marriages to private interests, thereby inculcating suspicion that attempts to alter inheritances were the real reason for the Anglican attack. Secondly, the appeal to Protestant unity proved ineffectual because Anglican leaders recognized that, as in 1688–1691, the nonconformists, except possibly the Quakers, had no alternative but to join them if the Catholics revolted.

Developments early in Anne's reign pushed the marriage issue off center stage. In 1703 the Irish government sent a bill to prevent the further growth of Catholicism to London for approval. Reversing its earlier opposition to a sacramental test, someone in the English government—probably Daniel Finch, earl of Nottingham—added a clause requiring a sacramental test of every civil or military officeholder under the crown. Such persons had to swear the customary oaths, make the declaration against transubstantiation, and take communion in the Church of Ireland within three months of entering office. The decision to introduce a sacramental test in Ireland was possibly intended to placate Emperor Leopold I and Prince Eugene of Savoy, neither of whom would have been pleased with the crackdown on Irish Catholics, but it was also a victory for the high church.[77]

When the sacramental test came into force in 1704 many nonconformists were disqualified from serving in municipal corporations and effectively removed as a power in local government. In the ensuing years the test probably enticed some ambitious moderates to cast their lot with the Church of Ireland rather than the Presbyterians. Speaking of Derry city in the dozen or so years before the implementation of the sacramental test, Kirkpatrick observed that "there was scarce A Conformist to be had capable" to hold office. By 1718 Bishop William Nicolson could report that a quarter of Derry's 1,200 families were Anglican; a like number were Catholic and at least half were Presbyterian. This made Derry, in his judgment, one of the most conformable areas in Ulster, for in some parishes the Presbyterians outnumbered conformists forty to one. Although Nicolson had approximately fifty divines in his diocese, all of whom possessed at least an M.A. degree (nine were doctors of divinity) and "generally very valuable Preferments," most resided in Dublin, in effect leaving the spiritual care of their parishioners to Catholic priests. The majority of the population in his diocese, he thought, were Catholics living in dire poverty; "a Ridge or two of Potatoes is all the poor Tenant has for the Support of himself, a wife, and (commonly) ten or twelve bare-leg'd Children."[78]

Legally and politically the Church of Ireland had triumphed over nonconformity, both Protestant and Catholic in the postwar years, but it failed to provide a sense of security notwithstanding the protestations of Presbyterian apologists and loyalists such as James Kirkpatrick that dissenters were political loyalists. "Should the Government withdraw its Protection & the Test Act," reflected Nicolson, "I know not (or rather every man must know and see) what would become of us."[79] The Anglican triumph was hollow. By their refusal to reach an ecumenical accommodation, the Church of Ireland, the Presbyterians, and the Congregationalists ensured the continuation of their preoccupation with internecine Protestant rivalry. In the broader context, religion remained a divisive force in the political and social arena instead of fulfilling its potential for healing and reconciling. Liturgy, theology, and polity were banners to rally competing communities, not bridges for dialogue and enhanced understanding. The effectiveness of their organizational structures had enabled the Scottish Presbyterians and the Quakers to withstand persecution but they also impeded the potential for future unity, especially on the part of the Presbyterians. The tenets, worship, and polity of the Friends, of course, were so distinctive that any prospect for their organic unity with other communities was virtually nil.

CHAPTER 4

The Presbyterians: A Polity for Survival

THE PRESBYTERIANS lost their battle for control of the Church of Ireland in 1660. Excluded from accommodation in the established church by the architects of its episcopalian revival, the Presbyterians found themselves in the position of an illegal sect, notwithstanding the government's normal preference to accord them *de facto* toleration. During periods of persecution, as in the aftermath of the Dublin conspiracy, the Presbyterians struggled to maintain worship services and discipline when some of their ministers were incarcerated and the others had to be circumspect in their pastoral work. As time passed, the Presbyterians also had to cope with the problem of replacing ill, elderly, and deceased ministers.

Survival required the establishment of an effective ecclesiological structure that could sustain Presbyterian communities, particularly during periods of repression. The structure the Scottish Presbyterians developed, as this chapter will argue, was effectively an alternative to the established Church of Ireland. Because of the relative paucity of records for the English Presbyterians, this chapter will focus on the Scottish Presbyterians, commencing with their resuscitation of presbyteries in 1669 or 1670, a general committee no later than 1671, and a synod in 1690. By the turn of the century the Scottish Presbyterians had a well-crafted ecclesiological structure that can properly be described as a denominational church governed by a truly presbyterian polity, something the Presbyterians in England failed to achieve and the Presbyterians in Scotland attained only in the aftermath of the revolution. To supply the clergy to serve this church the Scottish Presbyterians in

Ireland made provisions to train, ordain, and call ministers. As in Scotland, this was no easy task, for they encountered major problems in providing enough ministers to serve their congregations, not least because of their inability to pay adequate stipends. Relegation to *de facto* sectarian status in 1660 also left the Presbyterians in Ireland, as in England and—for those who rejected the various indulgences—in Scotland, with the problem of finding suitable places to gather for worship. Of necessity these were at first informal—homes, fields, and hills—but with the revival of presbyteries the Presbyterians began constructing proper meetinghouses, another contributing factor to the Scottish Presbyterians' evolution into a permanent alternative church in Ireland.

As the Presbyterians adjusted to the altered religious and political conditions of the restoration period, they adopted a range of views with respect to their dealings with other Protestants. The main body of Scottish Presbyterians in Ireland, while gradually establishing the characteristics of a denominational church, cooperated with English Presbyterians in the south and evinced a desire to establish a *modus vivendi* with the Church of Ireland. The English Presbyterians, it will be argued, were more ecumenically minded as manifested by their unity with Congregationalists in various churches. The English Presbyterians, as Raymond Gillespie has averred, were better able to relate to other Protestants because they did not see themselves as "an established type church" in the manner of the Scots but as part of a comprehensive church that recognized other Protestants as "true" churches.[1] At the other end of the Presbyterian spectrum, a dissident group of Scottish Presbyterians that was adamantly opposed to the established church broke with the main body of Presbyterians and survived as a tiny if sometimes nettlesome sect, as did its parent body in Scotland.

Presbyterian Communities

The distinction between Scottish and English Presbyterians in Ireland, or even between Presbyterians and Congregationalists, is less precise than the employment of such terminology suggests. For the most part the Scottish Presbyterians are readily discernible, thanks to the minutes of the Lagan and Antrim presbyteries, the records of the synod of Ulster, and a list of congregations and their ministers sent by Presbyterian clergy in Ireland to the General Assembly at Edinburgh in May 1689. The list identifies 78 congregations in five presbyteries: Down (17), Antrim (24), Lagan (13), Route (9), and Tyrone (15). Alexander Osborne, the minister at Newmarket, Dublin, is included in the Tyrone group, but seven other clergymen (and two probationers) appear at the end of the list as pastors who served in and about Dublin. In fact, they represented two additional Dublin congregations (Bull Alley and Capel Street) and churches at Clonmel, Waterford, Ross, and Enniscorthy. Scottish Presbyterians had recently been or were still ministering at Wexford, Wicklow, Sligo, and Killala, possibly to English as well as Scottish Presbyterians. By 1689, then, Ireland had approximately 88 Scottish Presbyterian congregations with perhaps 22,000 members (roughly 22 percent more than Phil Kilroy's estimate, which assumes an average of 250 members per session, but considerably fewer than Petty's grossly exaggerated estimate of 100,000). Scottish Presbyterians thus comprised roughly 1 percent of the population of Ireland; by way of contrast, Presbyterians in England in the early eighteenth century constituted approximately 3.3 percent of the population.[2]

English Presbyterian numbers in Ireland are much more difficult to estimate owing to the lack of presbytery records and the tendency of English Presbyterians to intermingle with Scottish Presbyterians and Congregationalists. Kilroy identifies five presbyteries—Dublin, Athlone, Galway, Munster, and Drogheda—but her source, Clarke Irwin's Victorian history, does not support this claim. The Athlone and Galway presbyteries were founded in 1841, prior to which their churches were affiliated with the Dublin presbytery.[3] There were, then, three English presbyteries in this period, but we know virtually nothing about their activities. In fact, they corresponded less to presbyteries such as those in Down, Antrim, and Lagan than to Samuel Winter's earlier Dublin and Leinster Association. In other words, they were primarily concerned with common ministerial goals and theological tenets rather than issues of polity. English Presbyterians and Congregationalists freely mixed, and especially in central and southern Ireland they cooperated with Scottish Presbyterians as well.

A number of churches identified by historians as Presbyterian or Congregational probably included adherents of both persuasions. This is certainly true, for example, of Samuel Mather's congregation in Winetavern Street, Dublin, as Henry Newcome noted (see Chapter 6). During the ministry of the Congregationalist Thomas Harrison at Cooke Street, the church's new home commencing in 1673, the worshippers included such prominent Presbyterians as Massereene and the countess of Donegall. Indeed, Massereene's chaplain, the eminent John Howe, preached there, as did his successor Elias Travers, whom the Dublin presbytery ordained at Cooke Street.[4]

This mixed membership explains the apparent ease with which some congregations accepted ministers of differing ecclesiological persuasions. The relative shortage of clergy and the preeminence accorded to pastoral and theological qualifications as opposed to issues of polity were also factors in their moderately ecumenical outlook. In Dublin the Wood Street congregation was for a time under the joint pastorate of the Congregationalist Samuel Marsden and the Presbyterian Danial Williams, and the latter had previously served a combined Presbyterian-Congregational church at Drogheda (see Chapter 6). The churches at Dundalk and Carlow began the restoration with Congregational pastors and ended with Presbyterians. Congregants of both persuasions probably worshipped together at such places as Limerick, Wexford, and Tipperary.[5] At Cork a group of (mostly?) English Presbyterians not only sought the assistance of the Lagan presbytery in finding a minister in 1675 but also ordained a new pastor in 1679 with the help of at least one Congregational minister.[6] By the early eighteenth century English Presbyterians also had churches at Summerhill in county Meath, Kinsale, Youghal, Mallow, Galway, Bandon, Portarlington, Mountrath, and Edenderry. The English Presbyterians probably numbered no more than 4,500 (0.2 percent of the population) at the turn of the century, including the Congregationalists in their mixed churches.

Rebuilding a Structural Framework

The meetings or presbyteries—the terms were used interchangeably in the restoration period—began convening again in late 1669 or 1670 after Robartes had become lord lieutenant and implemented a more tolerant policy. The earliest extant register, that of Antrim, commences in this period on 4 July 1671; Lagan's starts on 21 August 1672.[7] Because the original presbytery of Ulster could no longer convene following the restoration of episcopal authority, the meetings became full-fledged presbyteries. Each of them elected a moderator, whose term varied from three to six months; a moderator could be reelected. Each meeting also appointed a clerk to keep the records, a task for which the presbytery compensated him.[8] The presbyteries required ministers to attend their meetings, and those whose absences did not have prior approval had to provide legitimate reasons or face censure. Inclement weather, illness, compelling business, and trips to Scotland were routinely accepted as excuses, though in 1679 the Lagan presbytery rejected Samuel Halliday's plea that he had been "taking . . . physic." Arriving at the meeting late or departing before its conclusion was subject to the same rules as absences.[9] Excessive absenteeism could force the rescheduling of a meeting, as occurred at Lagan in February 1692; two months later the synod of Ulster complained that some ministers in this presbytery frequently missed its gatherings. Absentees were also a problem because they could not keep abreast of the presbyteries' policies and actions. In March 1678 the Lagan meeting, "considering severall misconstructions of their proceedings & other inconveniencies do follow upon some brethrens pleading exemption from the keeping of the ordinary Meetings or some dyets[,] thereof resolve to bring this to a hearing at the next dyet." When they returned to the subject in April, they contented themselves with insisting that an absent member submit a letter of excuse for the presbytery to judge and that no one leave a meeting early without permission.[10]

The role of elders in the presbyteries seems to have varied from one meeting to another. The Antrim records do not mention elders in attendance until October 1687, but elders participated in the Lagan presbytery throughout the period from August 1672 to July 1681 (at which point there is a gap in the minutes until December 1690). No more than one elder per congregation went to the presbyterial meetings, but almost always some of the churches had no elder present, and specially called meetings rarely included elders.[11] The elders' involvement with the presbytery was especially significant because of the responsibilities they exercised as key points of organizational contact. When the presbytery conducted a visitation, the elders answered questions about the life and performance of their minister. Elders accounted to the presbytery for the maintenance of their pastor and conveyed messages from the meeting to the church pertinent to clerical finances, including admonitions to pay arrears. Elders could negotiate with the presbytery concerning a minister, as when a Derry elder requested Lagan's assistance in 1674 to impose a bond on Robert Rule requiring him to return from a visit to Scotland, or when a Raphoe elder asked the same meeting in 1676 to support its claim to Halliday's services. When elders at Letterkenny could not persuade the congregation to provide requisite clerical maintenance, the Lagan presbytery dispatched representatives to assist them.[12]

The elders' ability to fulfil their responsibilities as links between the congregations and the presbyteries was obviously enhanced if they attended meetings of the latter. Recognizing this, in May 1679 the Lagan meeting asked the general committee to direct all presbyteries to have elders present when they met. Following the return of indulgence in 1687, the Antrim presbytery wanted the committee to discuss the issue again, and at Antrim's October gathering eight elders were present. In December the same presbytery instructed ministers supplying vacant pulpits to select elders to attend the meetings and thus be available to answer questions about common concerns. In June 1691 the Lagan presbytery directed each minister to bring an elder to its gatherings, but in 1695 it ruled that elders from "desolat congregations" be excluded from meetings of the presbytery.[13] Two years later the synod of Ulster issued a regulation similar to that of Lagan's in 1691, noting that having elders in attendance accorded with the Church of Scotland's practice and helped "aqaint Elders with our Discipline." Indeed, 49 elders representing seven presbyteries attended the synod in June 1698. Rule even took an elder with him when the Lagan meeting sent him as a correspondent to the Route presbytery in 1681.[14]

The presbyteries met approximately once a month, though this was subject to various factors, especially political and military conditions. The Antrim presbytery did not convene between 5 March and 4 September 1689 because of "the confusion of the times." In September it scheduled a sequel for October, but on the appointed date it had "an occasional meeting" with its colleagues in Down, thus postponing the next regular gathering to November. The same presbytery's meeting in April 1683 had been devoted solely to a morning of prayer followed by a brief exhortation before adjourning to May. In September 1694 the Lagan presbytery, operating in a stabler environment, enacted that future meetings be held the last Tuesday of each month with the exception of November through February, when sessions every other month would suffice because of winter weather. Meetings could be postponed owing to special circumstances, such as a fair at St. Johnston in April 1674.[15]

More common than postponements or missed meetings were special sessions, or meetings *pro re nata*, which designated members of the presbytery had the authority to call. Such sessions were convoked for a wide variety of reasons and their deliberations required the approval of the delegates at those sessions or subsequent regular meetings. The Lagan presbytery held one in July 1675 when the minister George Keith, who would shortly become a Quaker, did not assume the Ardstraw pastorate as expected; owing to "the present straits" of Presbyterians in Scotland John Hart and Robert Campbell called a special session, judging "it needfull to doe something speedily, in order to getting some

Ministers out of Scotland."[16] After James Tailzour was arrested and fined £5 for not possessing an ordination certificate, the Lagan presbytery had a meeting *pro re nata* in April 1679 to determine a course of action; it decided to discuss the matter at the next session of the general committee and in the meantime to mail Tailzour a certificate. The same presbytery held special meetings in April 1691 in connection with a general fast; in February 1694 to advise Donaghedy, county Tyrone, on obtaining a minister; and in January 1698 with respect to William Holmes's suspension.[17]

The Lagan and Antrim minutes provide a cornucopia of information about the subjects under discussion but relatively little about procedures. At Antrim no one could speak except to the moderator while the session was underway or leave the session table without the moderator's acquiescence on penalty of a six-pence fine (raised to two shillings in October 1688). Single sessions were limited to three hours, and the minutes had to be read and approved prior to the meeting's dismissal; anyone who left early was deemed absent for the entire session. Commencing in June 1675 any minister receiving a stipend had to pay his share of the meeting's expenses unless he was ill or out of the country with the presbytery's approval.[18] Lagan required its moderator to "speak fully & only the Meetings concluded mind" when reporting its business. All presbyteries appointed delegates to the general committee and later the synod, kept and revised records of their activities, and acted on proposals submitted by those bodies. No later than August 1690 at Antrim and May 1694 at Lagan the meetings began with a "Presbyterian exercise," namely exegetical and expository sermons by two ministers.[19]

As Scottish Presbyterian numbers grew, the Down meeting called for the creation of a new presbytery in the summer of 1687 to be carved out of Down, Tyrone, and Antrim and centered at Lisburn. Antrim was agreeable if the process was orderly and no church was separated from its present affiliation without its consent, but Tyrone objected for unrecorded reasons. With the synod of Ulster's approval the Lagan meeting split into the presbyteries of Derry and Strabane in September 1697, but the division lasted only until the following July owing to "Inconveniencies in divideing." Another new presbytery, centered at Belfast, also made its appearance in 1697 when the synod decided that the number of churches in each presbytery should be as equal as possible. This gave Down thirteen congregations, Belfast sixteen, Connor (formerly Antrim) thirteen, Derry (lower Lagan) eleven, and Strabane (upper Lagan) nine; Tyrone would retain its existing churches and add Lurgan, while Route would remain unchanged.[20]

In their relations with local churches one of the presbyteries' most significant responsibilities was visitations. These fell into two categories: "Presbyterial Visitations" conducted by the presbytery in conjunction with one of its gatherings, and much more modest visits in which one or two ministerial agents of the presbytery inquired about such matters as clerical maintenance and the congregation's relationship with its pastor.[21] When Thomas Gowan's visit to Drummaul in 1674 discovered differences between Richard Wilson and some of his elders, the Antrim presbytery dispatched four agents to undertake a fuller visitation. After a sermon by Gowan, he and his colleagues had instructions "to perform the worke of visiteres; if they can heal differences well, if not they are to try matteres of fact and prepar thinges for the meeting; particularlie they are to signifie to any that are at distance with their minister that either they must carry encouragin[g]ly to their minister so as to strengthen his hands in the ministrie or give in a subscribed libell against him or otherwise themselves are to be proceeded against as scandelous persones." The visitors resolved the differences.[22]

The fullest description of a presbyterial visitation is for one that occurred at Donaghmore, county Donegal, in April 1697. It got underway with a sermon on 1 Thessalonians 5:18 by the local minister, Joshua Fisher, whose doctrine the presbytery approved. Fisher answered interrogatories about the session's performance of its duties, including visitation of the sick, but admitted the session book was not current because the church had no clerk. After Fisher was excused, the presbytery called in the session and inquired if it had any criticism of his theology, diligence, and conversation. Session members responded positively when asked "if they kept meettings for prayer & Christian conference for their mutuall Edification," and negatively when queried if they resorted to "privey censures" in the session. The session was then dismissed and heads of families called before the presbytery to indicate if they had anything to object against their minister or session. The presbytery summoned Fisher again, this time to receive the presbytery's recommendations, namely to find a clerk, to update the session book, and to use private censures in the session. The visitation concluded with an examination of the accounts for Fisher's maintenance, which indicated arrears of £19 15s. 2d., prompting a rebuke and admonition from the presbytery to make up the deficit and take measures to prevent this problem in the future.[23]

In addition to visiting churches, the presbyteries dealt with contentious relations between pastors and their flocks, such as that involving John Douglass and the church at Braid, where he had been ordained in 1655. Suspected of involvement in the Dublin plot, he had been imprisoned and required to leave Ireland under bond not to come back without a license. When he returned (by 1671) his congregation suspected he had misappropriated funds. In November 1671 he expressed a willingness to submit to whatever the Antrim meeting thought should be done for the people's good as long as he received a satisfactory "testimoniall" from the presbytery. Prepared in December, the recommendation was considerably less than an unqualified endorsement with its reference to the scandal and the inability to resolve it by formal judicial proceedings. Insisting on his innocence, Douglass rejected the testimonial and demanded a trial. While preparations were underway, Gowan and James Shaw received instructions "to see if he may be brought to ane acknowledgment off his miscarriages and to a serious ingenious confessione."[24]

As the impasse continued, 68 families at Braid complained to the presbytery in April 1672, insisting they were unable to accept Douglass's ministry and petitioning for someone else to baptize their children. As a temporary expedient the meeting asked neighboring clergy to perform the baptismal rites. In June Douglass's detractors submitted a formal statement setting forth their complaints while his backers provided a list of families who supported him as well as a request that the presbytery resolve the dispute. Unable to reach a decision the presbytery took the matter up again in July, at which time Douglass submitted a "satisfying confessione." To this the presbytery responded by "desiring him to studye such a carriage as would evidence the reality of that confessione, and that he would endeavour to gain the people that had been dissatisfied with him." Although the presbytery did not think Douglass had completely repented, it exhorted his congregation to converse with him. When he reiterated his confession at the August meeting the presbytery was satisfied as were representatives of both factions in the church. At their request the presbytery dispatched a representative to Braid to register its approval, and the people pronounced themselves "in some measure satisfied."[25]

The contention did not end here, for by September 1672 Douglass was complaining that Braid lacked a suitable place of worship. Moreover, the congregation, pleading preoccupation with the harvest, failed to provide adequate maintenance for him. After further intervention by the presbytery the issue seemed to be resolved by April 1673, but seven months later Douglass was still not receiving full financial support. Once again the presbytery became involved, this time apparently with more success, for matters remained quiet at Braid through June 1675, when the Antrim minutes abruptly terminate.[26]

By the time the records resume in January 1683, trouble had again erupted at Braid and Douglass had resigned. The church owed him at least £40, an amount less than he claimed. Nor did he leave the parish, where he commanded the support of a plurality of the people and petitioned the presbytery in May to retract his resignation. The meeting not only denied his request but refused to approve a new pastor until the issue of maintenance was resolved. In the meantime it ordered the elders to give testimonials to parents free of scandal who wanted to have their children baptized by Douglass or neighboring clergy. Douglass's supporters petitioned the presbytery in December to permit him to resume his ministry in Braid, and three months later both his opponents and the session asked the meeting to dispatch a delegation to resolve the dispute. Both factions delegated people to collect the arrears, adding to the rancor and confusion. Finally, in June 1684 the exasperated presbytery rendered its judgment that Douglass "hence forth forbear all administrations in Braid, except what the meet[ing] shall hereafter think fitt, & that . . . the whole congregation be seriously admonished to lay themselves forth to the utmost to gratify Mr Duglas for his by past pains among them."[27]

At the presbytery's request, Fulk White supplied Braid in the ensuing weeks, and by the next meeting, in July 1684, one faction in the church petitioned the presbytery for assistance in formulating a call for him to be their regular pastor. At the August meeting Douglass's backers countered with a proposal to call him as their minister, prompting the presbytery to observe that the "flame in the parish is like to continue" given the "stiffness of both parties." For the time being it permitted each faction to have recourse to the minister it favored. Reluctantly the presbytery resumed "the tryal of the Lybel" against Douglass, seeking the advice of other meetings as necessary. When Antrim proposed to send the other presbyteries an account of the affair, Douglass successfully pleaded for a letter stating simply that "he had been imploy'd in the exercise of his ministry among the Br[ethren] here." The presbytery acquiesced on condition that he instruct his followers to resume worshipping with the rest of the congregation under the direction of supply clergy. In return the presbytery directed the church to give him £10 *per annum*.[28]

Once again the resolution of the controversy was only apparent, for in January 1685 Douglass complained to the presbytery that one of his critics had averred "he would rather be in hell than hear Mr Douglas preach in the pulpit of Braid." This struck a responsive chord among Douglass's fellow clerics, for they gave him permission to return to his former pulpit and to baptize children as long as the presbytery authorized this arrangement each month. Sometime after the summer of 1685 Douglass left Braid, but he was back and preaching there by August 1686. Most of the parishioners came to hear him, which seemed "wholly to obstruct their planting" with another pastor. In October the anti-Douglass faction petitioned the presbytery to bar him from preaching in Braid. This time the presbytery wondered "how much the work of the Gospell is obstructed in that place through Mr. Duglas residing & preaching among them," and it complained that he had violated the conditions under which it had allowed him to resume preaching, that he had gone elsewhere "to looke for a settlement," and that he had preached without authorization after his return to Braid. The presbytery ordered Douglass to cease obstructing the gospel by preaching at Braid, but he ignored a summons to appear at the November meeting. He was present the following month when the presbytery learned that 180 heads of families had pledged £18 *per annum* to support another minister until Douglass's backers would "lay aside all animositys & joyn with the rest." They also agreed to provide financial assistance to Douglass as a gesture of peace. The next month Douglass's adherents agreed to contribute an additional £12 and a supply of oats for another minister as long as Douglass received a third of the total stipend until he had a new parish.[29]

Fulk White was ordained at Braid in July 1687, but only after further opposition from Douglass's faction. White accepted the call on the condition that he could resign if he met with excessive discouragement, and this he sought to do in April 1688, apparently because the congregation was remiss in fulfilling its obligations (as was still the case with Douglass). Douglass thereafter either supplied or expressed an interest in supplying Ballymena, county Antrim, but this too was a congregation with problems of arrears, and in October 1688 the Antrim presbytery told Douglass the church could not be supplied until it paid its debts.[30] Extending over two decades, the story of Douglass and the

Braid church provides a striking example of the extent to which a presbytery would go in trying to resolve an acrimonious situation. The episode is no less significant as an indication of the relative degree of toleration enjoyed by Antrim Presbyterians, for the length and intensity of this controversy, which ultimately revolved around the personality of one contentious, stubborn clergyman, would have been highly improbable in a time of substantive persecution.

A second enigmatic case involved Presbyterians in Dublin and their relationship with other Protestants as well as the presbyteries. The first notice of trouble appears in a reference in the Antrim minutes in November 1671 to the absence of four men who had gone to Dublin "to studie a healing of the evils in that congregatione" at Bull Alley, the minister of which was William Jacque. The general committee became involved no later than early 1672, for William Temple, one of its commissioners, wrote two letters from Dublin on 5 and 15 March referring to difficulties. The first of these suggests that the problem may have arisen in connection with an unidentified person who "walks so scandalously" that the Presbyterians were considering taking depositions on oath, an illegal act. In his second letter Temple noted that much of his work in Dublin was aimed at preventing a breach in the Bull Alley church until the general committee found a solution. Jacque, its minister, "and all concerned in these differences" pressed the committee "to determine what shall be the issue of this sad breach."[31] The Antrim minutes for April 1672 cite a request by the general committee that members of the congregation dissatisfied with Jacque submit their grievances to the presbyteries; the latter were then asked to send their judgments to the general committee. The Antrim meeting accordingly received a report from the elders and others at Bull Alley, but Jacque and his supporters submitted nothing in their defense. The presbytery recommended that Jacque share the pastorate with a colleague and warned him to take "a more gaining way with the people" and submit to whatever presbytery the congregation would thereafter be annexed; if not, he faced removal. Jacque, however, petitioned to be affiliated with Antrim instead of Tyrone. Whatever the cause of the dispute, it ruptured the Bull Alley church, and Jacque and his followers established a separate congregation at Capel Street. By June the Antrim presbytery was considering candidates for the Bull Alley pastorate, and in June it sent William Keyes to supply the church. In the meantime the Tyrone meeting, with which Jacque was affiliated, found the Dublin situation "verye troublesome" and wanted to terminate its relationship with him. The general committee considered establishing a new presbytery in Dublin involving "such ministers as are there that shall be willing to join with the rest of the Sinod, and to subject themselves to there bretheren," but decided against this until the controversy surrounding Jacque was resolved.[32]

Jacque not only established another church but also administered the Lord's supper and baptism without consulting the presbytery of Tyrone, and for this Antrim censured him and requested that the general committee administer the reproof. Lagan, however, questioned whether Jacque would submit to censure and proposed instead that he first give a written pledge to submit to the judgment of the committee or the various meetings. His submission finally came in May 1673 in a written statement professing regret for having offended other Presbyterians and requesting that he and his congregation at Capel Street be annexed to the Antrim meeting. Although the latter had previously suggested that Jacque and his church affiliate with Down, it acquiesced to Jacque's request because of the principle that the congregation should decide. Lagan and Route were of the same judgment, but Tyrone disagreed. Relations between Jacque and the Tyrone presbytery remained tense, for in the spring of 1675 the latter successfully appealed to Antrim to admonish Jacque to have "a more prudent carriage" toward Tyrone.[33]

Jacque and Keyes, now the regular minister at Bull Alley, developed a decent working relationship and in November 1676 proposed the establishment of a committee of Presbyterian ministers in the Dublin area to be affiliated with some of the presbyteries in northern Ireland. Antrim agreed if William Liston of Waterford and William Cocks of Clonmel did not object. Sensitive to the need for greater cooperation among Presbyterians, Liston and Cocks would concur only if the English Presbyterian ministers in southern Ireland joined. The plan apparently died, but in April 1681 Keyes and Jacque requested approval from Lagan for any of its ministers residing in the south to join clergymen in the same region affiliated with the Antrim and Tyrone presbyteries to try and then to ordain Gideon Jacque for the church at Wexford. Lagan authorized Cocks to do so, and similar approval came from Antrim and Tyrone. In an ecumenical spirit, Lagan also requested the participation of English Presbyterians in Dublin as well as Congregationalists who had been ordained by "a consistory of Presbyters."[34]

By January 1683 a committee had been organized in Dublin, but the circumstances cannot be known because of crucial gaps in the Lagan and Antrim minutes. New trouble was brewing by May 1683 when

Antrim received a request from various members of Jacque's Capel Street congregation to persuade John Hutcheson to accept a call to be his copastor. Jacque, however, had "no clearness" to accept Hutcheson as a colleague, hence the presbytery refused to present the call to Hutcheson. The meeting worried as well whether settling Hutcheson in Dublin might endanger the Presbyterians' liberty, perhaps an implicit reminder of the controversy that plagued Braid. Yet the presbytery reconsidered in June and asked Jacque to accept Hutcheson as his colleague; he refused. In the meantime Hutcheson's adherents sought the other presbyteries' advice, and one of his followers wrote to the Antrim meeting accusing Jacque of unspecified "irregularities" which "might seem to render him unfit for the Ministry at least in Dublin." Although the presbytery was dubious of such charges and admitted it "would have been glad if no such motion had been started, yet being far from palliating any brothers enormitys or conniving at known faults, [it] cannot prohibit him the presenting of what he has proposed, unless by mutual condescention between parties concerned, matters might be so carry'd as there might be no further noise about it."[35]

By December the situation at Capel Street had degenerated to the point that Hutcheson's supporters petitioned the presbytery to be constituted as a new congregation if Hutcheson could not be Jacque's copastor. Letters followed from both factions as well as Jacque's brother Gideon and the Dublin committee. After pondering this material the presbytery concluded in March 1684 that the parties were irreconcilable and ordered William Jacque and his backers to permit the dissenting group to establish their own congregation under Hutcheson or another minister of their choosing. Following the breach "a considerable number" of people who had hitherto associated with no congregation joined the group that had split from Jacque and established a church at Newmarket.[36]

Understandably, the Antrim meeting petitioned the general committee to be relieved of all responsibility for churches in the Dublin area, but the request failed. Almost immediately the controversy flared up again when Thomas Boyd, a leader of the Newmarket group, libeled William Jacque. The latter, no longer willing to trust the Antrim presbytery, virtually repudiated its authority to adjudicate the case, whereupon it responded by threatening to censure him. Jacque countered by appealing to the synod, though offering to accept a hearing in Dublin as long as it was conducted on his terms.[37] In the meantime Hutcheson sagely rejected the call from the Newmarket church, which thereupon sought the services of Dr. Gilbert Rule. The latter was "discourag'd on the account of his being discountenanced & lookt down upon by Mr Jacque, the Ministers of Dublin & sev[eral] professors therein, & particularly that separation of theirs without & before the meetings allowance" as well as by Boyd's libel against Jacque and Boyd's suit in Chancery against him. Desirous of persuading Rule to accept the Newmarket pastorate, Antrim urged the congregation to confess its separation in an unlawful manner and retract the libel and Chancery suit. With the aid of a mediator the respective parties agreed to these terms in June 1686 on condition that Boyd's written charges against Jacque, which had been sent to the Antrim meeting, be destroyed. Internal peace slowly settled on Dublin's Presbyterians in the ensuing years, but not until the Antrim presbytery had once again demonstrated extraordinary patience in dealing with fractious members more preoccupied by internal rivalries than the daunting challenge of winning converts in southern Ireland or establishing closer relations with other Protestants.[38]

The Bull Alley-Capel Street-Newmarket saga demonstrated the extent to which presbyteries communicated with one another on common concerns. Much of this dialogue occurred through correspondents dispatched from one meeting to another on an as-needed basis. On many occasions one presbytery took the initiative by asking another meeting to send a representative, as when Route sought a correspondent from Antrim in the summer of 1671 "in regard of some businesses of concernement." Intermeeting relations were seldom controversial, though matters of dispute sometimes arose, especially over competition between churches seeking to hold or recruit ministers.[39] The presbyteries were sensitive to independent action by one of them "in things of common concernment." Tyrone was incensed in 1679 when Down presented a formal statement to the government, apparently professing its loyalty, without the concurrence of the other meetings. The same presbytery was apparently holding communion services on its own and some of its members were reputedly taking the oath of supremacy. On all these issues, and on the observance of fasts or thanksgiving days "upon publike accounts," Tyrone insisted that the meetings act in concert. In its anger Tyrone not only called a meeting of the general committee without proper authorization but also "encroach[ed] upon the power & liberty of other Meetings in sending three of their number to that late Committee, & pleading for & assuming a vote to each of the three."[40] Such breakdowns in relations were rare, owing at least in part to the ability to resolve serious issues in the general committee and subsequently the synod of Ulster.

By the time the earliest presbytery records commence in this period

(July 1671), the general committee was operating. Its early sessions were apparently irregular, undoubtedly called as needed, for in 1674 both the Lagan and Antrim presbyteries supported the idea of annual meetings, with sessions *pro re nata* if essential. At first, authority to summon the latter apparently rested with the moderator of the previous meeting, but in 1679 Lagan proposed that Down and Antrim share this power.[41] For most of the pre-revolutionary period each meeting sent two delegates to the general committee, though as early as 1674 the latter proposed that each presbytery send five ministers and one or two elders; given the political circumstances in which they were operating, Lagan objected and the number of delegates was held at two. In 1687 Antrim sent three.[42]

According to Adair the original intent of the general committee was "to consult . . . for the welfare of the whole, and to recommend to the various meetings such steps as their present exigencies demanded." Delegates typically carried instructions for the committee to discuss, and on their return brought a copy of the committee's minutes for presentation at the next meeting of the presbytery. A designated clerk maintained a record of the committee's transactions, for which he received fees paid by each minister in attendance (9s. each *per annum* from the Lagan clergy in 1676 compared to 3s. apiece from ministers from other meetings). Because the committee had no power over the presbyteries, delegates often carried back "overtures" for the meetings to approve or reject, and by the mid-1670s each minister was supposed to receive his own copy of these proposals. In 1680 Lagan proposed that overtures rejected by the meetings be expunged from the register (which apparently has not survived). The general committee considered a plan in 1672 and 1679 to give it authority over the presbyteries, but the latter refused to enact it, nor did they approve a 1672 proposal to permit individuals or churches to address the committee directly instead of going first to a presbytery. Thus the committee was a convenient vehicle for the exchange of views and the formulation of possible courses of action but it had no legislative or disciplinary powers. It was therefore feasible in May 1683 for Antrim to suggest the termination of regular annual meetings for the committee and the increase of direct correspondence between presbyteries.[43] But the usefulness of regular meetings was such that they continued to convene.

The general committee proposed the establishment of a synod in May 1687, but the presbyteries determined it was inexpedient at that time. When the general committee subsequently appointed William

Adair a commissioner to meet with the government in Dublin, the Down and Antrim meetings in September 1687 wanted him to inquire if a synod could convene. Nothing came of this, but in the spring of 1688 the general committee again asked the presbyteries if it would be expedient to have either a synod or "a meet[ing] of delegate Brethren with power" to replace the committee. Again the presbyteries demurred, but in March 1689 the committee proposed that a synod convene in April; Antrim wanted this delayed until the commissioners conferring with the government in London had reported. Antrim did name four representatives to meet in Belfast with delegates from Down as soon as a synod could be convoked. The first synod met at Belfast in September 1690. Almost nothing about this synod survives, and it may have been only a delegated (district) synod unlike the provincial synod of Ulster that convened at Antrim in September 1691.[44] The latter marks the culmination of the restoration of full-fledged presbyterian polity, a task that had taken two decades to accomplish.

Some of the synod's procedures were borrowed from the general committee. Presbyteries paid fees to support a clerk who took minutes, copies of which were then submitted to the presbyteries. The clerk took roll, absentees had to provide legitimate excuses or be censured, and unauthorized early departures from synod meetings were condemned. The synod elected a moderator to preside over its deliberations, the substance of which was provided in the form of overtures or instructions from presbyteries to their delegates. The latter comprised a minister and an elder from each church, though some were occasionally absent.[45]

Because the number of delegates to the synod of Ulster was so large compared to the intimate size of the general committee—32 ministers and 21 elders in 1691, 55 and 44 in 1697, compared to 10 ministers on the general committee—the synod had to institute a system of committees. It created the first of these—the committee of overtures—in 1694 to draft proposals for the full synod to consider on such matters as the presence of elders at meetings of the presbyteries, communion regulations, and education. The synod of 1697 added two more committees, the first on bills, which dealt with the transfer of clergy, and the second to supervise revision of the presbyteries' registers. A year later the synod appointed a committee to evaluate excuses from absentees, and in 1699 a steering committee "for considering & expedeing such things as shall come orderly before this Synod" made its appearance.[46] Membership on the committees was limited to the clergy, whose dominance was further underscored commencing in 1697 when they met as a block termed an *interloquitor*.[47]

The synod of Ulster convened once a year at Antrim, usually in June. As with the presbyteries and the general committee, it could meet in exceptional circumstances *pro re nata*. It did so in February 1696, for example, to deal with the contested transfer of Francis Tredeall from Armagh to Donegore. When the synod engaged in the previously noted reorganizational effort in June 1697 that expanded the number of presbyteries from five to seven, it proposed that two delegated (district) synods meet biannually: Dromore (Belfast, Down, and Tyrone) in May and November, and Coleraine (Antrim, Derry, Route, and Strabane) in February and August. The general synod would continue to meet annually. This arrangement lasted only a year, for the Belfast synod successfully spearheaded a proposal that limited the district synods to one meeting a year (Coleraine in March and Dromore in October). Another major reorganization occurred in June 1702, when the number of presbyteries increased to nine and the number of district synods to three, namely Belfast (Antrim, Belfast, and Down), Lagan (Coleraine, Convoy, and Derry), and Monaghan (Armagh, Kirktown, and Stonebridge).[48] By this time the Scottish Presbyterians had established a denominational church with an ecclesiological structure that had enabled it to survive periods of persecution as well as internal feuding. Such internecine strife, especially in the Dublin region, mitigated against efforts to establish greater unity with English Presbyterians and Congregationalists, though a fair amount of cooperation nevertheless existed.

Clerical Preparation and Ordination

The Presbyterians faced a daunting task in finding sufficient qualified ministers to serve their congregations. To meet their needs they had to develop a system to educate and ordain recruits and to call and sustain pastors. Again, organization was the key to the modest success they enjoyed. During the period from the restoration to the mid-1690s at least 169 Presbyterian ministers served in Ireland. Biographical data for many of them is scant, but a prosopographical portrait can be constructed. Of the 138 whose country of origin is known, the preponderance—105 (76%)—were born in Scotland compared to a mere 24 (17.5%) in Ireland and nine (6.5%) in England. The year of birth is known for only 48 of the 169: fifteen were born in the 1610s and 1620s and were thus young men when the Bishops' Wars erupted; twelve were born in the 1630s and would have known something about the Cromwellian occupation of Scotland and at least indirectly of the post-rebellion decade in Ireland. Those born in the 1640s (9) were probably cognizant of the restoration of the traditional order, whereas those born in the 1650s (10) and 1660s (2) knew little or nothing firsthand of the revolutionary era.[49]

As a group the 169 clergymen had an impressive educational background. No less than 113 (67%) had Scottish M.A. degrees, 58 (51%) of which were from Glasgow, 44 (39%) from Edinburgh, six from St. Andrews (5.5%), and five (4.5%) from King's College, Aberdeen. Another seventeen (10%) are known to have studied at Glasgow (11), Aberdeen (3), Edinburgh (1), St. Andrews (1), or Trinity College, Dublin (1), and Gilbert Rule graduated M.D. from Leiden in 1665. Most of those with Scottish M.A. degrees received them in the revolutionary decades (25 in the 1640s, 36 in the 1650s), compared to one (Hugh Peebles) in the 1620s and nine in the 1630s.[50] After the restoration Scottish universities continued to graduate respectable numbers of young men who subsequently spent at least part of their careers in Ireland (19 in the 1660s, 20 in the 1670s, two in the early 1680s). Two English Presbyterians graduated B.A. from Oxford and one from Cambridge, whereas a fourth studied at Oxford. In September 1691 the synod of Ulster formally enacted that henceforth no one be admitted to the ministry without a university degree, and in 1702 it required prospective candidates to complete the standard philosophy curriculum followed by four years of theological studies. At least 22 ministers were sons of clergymen, and the group of 169 ministers included ten pairs of brothers.[51] For their services in Ireland during the Protectorate at least thirty of these Presbyterians received government salaries. Half of the 169 clergy shared the experience of ejection at the restoration: 65 in Ireland, fifteen in Scotland, and five in England. More than forty others were too young to have had a position from which to be ejected. Another trial awaited many of the ministers, at least fifty of whom fled Ireland in the troubles sparked by the revolution. At least 33 ministers were imprisoned in Ireland at some point in this period, and the actual number is almost certainly higher. Thus the Presbyterian clergy who ministered in Scotland in the restoration era were largely Scottish-born, well-educated men who shared the personal strains of ejection, imprisonment, or flight from civil war.

Whether a university graduate or not, a candidate for the Presbyterian ministry had to undergo a rigorous examining process prior to ordination. The experience of David Cunningham (M.A., Glasgow, 1667) provides a useful example. In August 1671 the Antrim meeting, satisfied with recommendations from Presbyterians in Scotland, admitted Cunningham to "tryells" as an expectant with a view to "licentiating." In fifteen days he was instructed to preach at Templepatrick on Colossians 3:1, subsequent to which he had to demonstrate his exegetical ability to the next presbytery by explicating a thesis *de perseverantia sanctorum*. His homily was acceptable and he successfully "sustained [his] disputes" on the perseverance of the saints. The presbytery then instructed him to "have popular Doctrine" on Romans 8:1, to demonstrate his knowledge of biblical languages, to explain Psalm 12 in Hebrew, and to answer "Chronologicall" (historical) and catechetical questions at the October meeting. In the meantime he had "to goe and reasone with the brethrene of Downe, against this meetting may have ther judgment of his licentiating as ane expectant."[52]

Armed with a letter of approval from the Down presbytery, Cunningham completed his initial trials on 3 October and received a license to preach "as ane expectant ore probationer for the Minis[try] wherever he should have a first Call." By the time of the December meeting he had preached at Connor, county Antrim, several Sundays and the congregation had petitioned the Antrim presbytery to permit him to continue doing so until the latter convened the following month. The presbytery recommended that the minister of a neighboring church send an elder to Connor to ascertain if the people were satisfied with Cunningham, and again the response was positive. In January, as Cunningham prepared to travel to Scotland, the presbytery, wanting his trials completed before he left, directed him "to exercise and add" Philippians 3:1 "that the people may then signifie ther myndes more fully anent him."[53] Exercising, often referred to as "making" or occasionally as the "doctor's part," involved the scholarly exposition of the text, whereas "adding"—the "pastor's part"—entailed the practical application of the theme(s) of the text.[54]

By the time the presbytery convened in February, the church at Connor had issued a call to Cunningham. Richard Wilson and John Haltridge simultaneously received calls from the congregations at Drummaul and Island Magee respectively, and the presbytery invited the three expectants to "speak ther myndes" about the calls. Although the expectants voiced "some scruples," these were resolved and the candidates submitted to the will of the presbytery, "whereupon the meetting resolved to enter them one tryalls in reference too ordination for the said paroches." To expedite the process, the presbytery scheduled an interim session in a fortnight "onlie for receiving off tryalls, and then the ordinations meetting att the ordinarie tyme for other Comon busienesse, and even then to receive tryalls also." In February Cunningham "exercised and added" Philippians 3:1–2, after which the presbytery instructed him "to have popular doctrine" on James 3:10 at the next meeting as well as copies of his thesis on another common head, *de judice controversiarum.* At the March meeting Cunningham defended his thesis after providing exegesis of it in Latin, demonstrated his knowledge of foreign languages by expounding the thirteenth psalm in Hebrew and selections from the Greek New Testament, and answered historical and theological questions. Only now was he ready for ordination, which, under less than favorable political conditions, had to be held inconspicuously on a Wednesday night, 27 March, in the church at Carncastle. Adair preached the ordination sermon on Isaiah 6:8, after which he gave Cunningham his charge, posed a final set of doctrinal questions, and listened as the expectant "engaged to fidelitye in the Ministry and particularly in that charge of Conyer together with submission to his brethrene in the Lord." With prayer and the imposition of hands, Adair thereupon ordained Cunningham. Seven months had elapsed since the Antrim meeting first considered him, a testimony to the care and rigor of the process, even at a time when ministers were in short supply.[55]

In early 1672, after several presbyteries decided to proceed with ordinations, the general committee drafted extensive regulations governing trials and ordination and submitted them to the presbyteries for approval. The rules were intended to result in "the more harmonious and secrett way" of ordaining men. Until the regulations were approved, the presbyteries were to ordain candidates as they had been doing. Under the proposed regulations, to be admitted to trials a candidate first had to provide testimonials from ministers where he had resided that addressed not only his integrity and suitability for the ministry "according to Scripture rules" but also his piety, peacefulness, prudence, "and other degrees of fittnesse as may peculiarlye capacitate him for such a charge as he may be called too." No less important was an assessment of him by the ministers of the presbytery with which he would be affiliated, hence he had to "converse for some space off tyme with the brethrene amongst whom he is to officiate, during which tyme he may be imployed to preach not onlye in vacant congregationes butt with Ministers, in ther congregationes and in ther hearing." The general committee urged that this assessment be done as inconspicuously as possible, "whereof the designe of tryall should be as litle discovered to the partye as may be." The time allotted to this assessment was left to the discretion of each presbytery, though with a caveat not to forget the apostolic rule to "lay handes suddenlye one no man."[56]

Furthermore the general committee urged that no one be considered unless there was a good probability that he would prove satisfactory. "It will be dangerous for the persone to be engaged once and then reported for insufficiencye," and perilous for the presbytery inasmuch as a rejected candidate might become a government spy. To prevent premature consideration no minister was to discuss a potential candidate publicly until he had privately consulted other clergymen who knew the person. When these requirements had been met, a call could be issued to the candidate with the presbytery's concurrence by the elders of a congregation and "such off the people as desire him, who are to engadge under ther hand to subject themselves to his Ministrye, to give him encouragement competent to his worke." Given the political climate, the committee underscored the importance of secrecy, and to this end it proposed that "no more should be mad[e] knowne unto the people butt that he is to preach among them (the purpose of his ordinatione being concealled) with all signifying to them, thate ordained or not ordained ther call oblidgeth them to subject themselves to the worde in his mouth and foundeth such a relatione betwixt him and them as they may not cast him off att ther pleasure, nor he remove from them." The intent was not to terminate the requirement for congregational approval basic to presbyterian polity but to restrict it to those who were "lovers off the truth and really willing to subjectt themselves to the ordinances of Chryst and the Government of His Church." The Lagan meeting, however, objected to the provision enjoining a congregation from severing its link to an expectant, "it being not clear that a person not ordained can have such a relation to a people as afterward."[57]

The general committee insisted that the trials be rigorous and thorough, including exercises (paired sermons involving exegesis and application, or "making" and "adding"), popular sermons, common heads, disputations, "questionarye tryalls in the sence of Scripture seeminglye contradictorye," and examination in foreign languages, history, and theology. Although as much secrecy as possible was to be observed, "yett that all may have satisfactione in a matter wherein all are concerned," the presbytery or presbyteries with which the candidate was formerly associated had to send representatives to assist in the trials. (The Antrim meeting agreed to this provision only when it could conveniently be implemented.) Moreover, because a formal proclamation of the trials and proposed ordination could not be made in the current political circumstances, the general committee proposed that the appropriate presbytery send representatives to the congregation to which the expectant was ministering to inquire of his life and theology and whether the church was willing to accept him as its pastor. The Antrim presbytery deemed even this procedure too perilous and suggested instead that a neighboring minister make the requisite inquiries and report to the meeting.[58]

With respect to the ordination service the general committee again stressed the need for secrecy, proposing that attendance be limited to ministers and elders of the meeting (or a majority of them in the case of large presbyteries), representatives from neighboring meetings, and select members of the ordinand's congregation, preferably its elders. Following a sermon on the nature and necessity of the ministry, the ordinand had to answer interrogatories satisfactorily, demonstrating the soundness of his faith, his adherence to Reformed tenets, and his opposition to Catholicism, Arminianism, prelacy, Erastianism, "independencye, and whatsoever else is contrarye to sound doctrine, and the power of Godlinesse." He also had to profess fidelity to the Covenant and a commitment to "peaceablenesse and subjectione to his brethrene in the Lord." Then ensued the act of ordination, entailing the imposition of hands with fasting and prayer, and the extension of the right hand of fellowship. To all this the Antrim presbytery agreed with a single exception, namely the inclusion of representatives from other meetings and parishioners; for the sake of secrecy Antrim wanted to limit attendance to the ministers of the meeting.[59]

The proposed regulations concluded with provisions governing the activities of the newly ordained clergyman. Initially he was to spend time in Scotland or within the boundaries of another presbytery practicing his ministerial duties, "sparinglye, and by degrees." When he returned to his own church he was to perform his duties prior to attending a meeting of the presbytery. On the latter occasion the other clergymen were to welcome him and members of his congregation were to receive him as their minister. With the modifications noted above, the Antrim presbytery endorsed the new regulations. The Lagan meeting too had no substantive objections.[60]

Meeting records shed further light on the Presbyterian practice of trials and ordination. Because Presbyterians took the procedures very seriously, a candidate could not assume approval. In July 1671 the Antrim meeting, having received a request from the Down presbytery to give its judgment concerning the expectant William Bell, recommended that Down investigate allegations of inappropriate behavior before licensing him to preach. The Lagan presbytery insisted in January 1673 that Robert Kennedy obtain fuller testimonials from Scotland before he could be admitted to trials. Inadequate education could also be a barrier; in 1697 William Gray sagely decided to study at a university before attempting his trials. Insufficient preparation probably accounted for John Lee's dilatory progress during his trials in 1688; the exasperated Antrim meeting appointed one of its members to inform him it resented his slowness as well as his failure to honor the presbytery's schedule.[61]

During Robert Simpson's trials in 1676 the Lagan presbytery approved his discourse on Acts 5:31 but nevertheless asked him to explicate another text (Galatians 2:20) to demonstrate "his gift & faculty of raising doctrines & observations & application." On his second attempt he failed to "answer the design & expectation of the brethren," though they allowed him to present his exegesis on election in Latin and his common head on the same subject in English. The moderator reproved him for his offensive conversation. Simpson eventually completed his trials and received a call from the congregation at Faughanvale, but he refused to accept it, notwithstanding the efforts of Robert Rule and Robert Craghead to persuade him to do so.[62]

The common heads assigned to expectants by presbyteries focused on theological tenets dear to Calvinists. Freedom of the will, the subject and causes of election, the efficacy of grace, the certitude of salvation, the saints' perseverance, and the extent of the atonement were among such themes. Expectants distributed theses to members of the presbytery at the meeting preceding the one in which they were to defend their views. The minutes regularly record the subjects but rarely cite the theses. An exception was the thesis defended by William Holmes on the subject of universal redemption before the Lagan presbytery in October 1692: *Christus pro omnibus et solis electis mortuus est.*[63] Some topics were Protestant mainstays, such as justification *sola fidei*, the role of good works, and the completeness of Christ's satisfaction,[64] whereas others reflected such "denominational" interests as presbyterian polity, Presbyterian origins, the institution of the office of ruling elders, and the election of ministers.[65] Some topics virtually mandated that the expectants attack the Presbyterians' religious rivals. Catholics were targeted in themes dealing with the mass, Antichrist, human ceremonies in divine worship, and the keys to the kingdom, while sectaries were the focal point of common heads on separation and enthusiasm.[66] Other themes ranged from sabbath institution and observance, the church's power, and heaven to the perfection of Scripture, the magistrate's power in religious affairs, the evangelical ministry, and wisdom.[67]

For the most part, ordinations proceeded without controversy from the early 1670s to the end of the century. On rare occasions practical exigencies required a modification of the usual procedures. When the Lagan presbytery was preparing to ordain William Henry in March 1674, for example, it received Antrim's approval but decided not to wait for reports from the other presbyteries because of "the great necessity & desolation" of the people in the Donegal-Ballyshannon area. In the summer of 1675 the Tyrone presbytery sought Lagan's advice as to the wisdom of ordaining ministers for churches unlikely to provide sufficient maintenance; Lagan urged Tyrone to proceed, knowing that the affected clergy could be transferred if financial support proved inadequate.[68]

The three decades commencing in the early 1670s were a time when Scottish Presbyterians in Ireland regularized ordination practices, another manifestation of institutionalization. The regulations drafted by the general committee are the most obvious example, but the trend continued in subsequent years. In 1680 the committee requested that presbyteries submit the names of newly ordained ministers and licentiates. The committee's records are not extant, but this information first appears in the minutes of the synod of Ulster in June 1694. The synod was also interested in formalizing the questions proposed to ordinands, but it had to wait years for a draft owing to Alexander Hutcheson's dilatoriness. In June 1702 it enacted that an ordination be celebrated as a fast day by both the ministers and the congregation where the ceremony occurred, a fitting observation of an event so critical to the ongoing life of the Presbyterian church.[69] The incorporation of fasting heightened the sense of congregational participation, thereby reinforcing the sense of distinctive community. The ordination ceremony set apart not only the candidate for his pastoral duties but also the congregants from those around them who were adherents of other religious groups. Ordination, then, was a rite of communal identity as well as the approbation of a candidate for the ministry.

Pastoral Calls, the Clerical Shortage, and Ministerial Stipends

If ordinations were straightforward, calls often were more complex because of the crucial importance of finding a compatible match between pastors and congregations and because of competition between churches for pastors. One major difficulty was a requirement that a congregation's call be virtually unanimous, though this was normally attainable.[70] Lack of consensus in calling Archibald Young to Glenavy in 1673 may have been a factor in his decision to go to Downpatrick instead, but the Antrim presbytery also considered the wishes of the Down meeting and "the considerableness" of Downpatrick, "which hath so great need to be planted." At Glenavy "some few persones in repute for piety" were reluctant to accept Young. Sixteen years later the same church had problems when only two-thirds of its members supported a call to David Airth; the remainder apparently withheld financial support, for a year later, in 1690, Airth asked to be transferred because of insufficient maintenance.[71] Sometimes the dissenting members were few in number, as the six at Ballymena who objected to John Darroch in 1688, but fewer than a third of the members of the long-troubled church at Braid (Broughshane) supported a call to Fulk White in 1684, prompting the Antrim meeting to deny their request. At Drummaul two years later, approximately 120 of 320 congregants resiled from a call to John Wilson, upon which the Antrim meeting expressed its resentment at the congregation's slackness in having the gospel preached and insisted that the dissenters either provide solid reasons for their stance or approve another godly man recommended by the presbytery. When the church remained divided, Wilson rejected the call and the presbytery threatened to leave it unsupplied "for some time." In fact, visiting clergy supplied Drummaul while the church paid arrears to Wilson and the previous pastor's widow. Finally, in November 1687, those who had objected to Wilson (with one exception) agreed with his supporters to reissue his call, and he was finally ordained there in May 1688.[72] The Antrim meeting also acted resolutely with Donegore in 1687, insisting that it unanimously call someone or accept the presbytery's nomination unless it was prepared to forgo a minister.[73]

The divisions in the cases hitherto noted probably stemmed from personality differences or preaching styles, but in 1687 four dissenters at Lisburn objected to a call to Alexander McCracken on theological grounds. The records of the Antrim meeting provide no particulars, but its investigation found neither unsound nor heterodox doctrine. Consulted in the matter, Tyrone and Down advised against McCracken's taking the Lisburn pastorate. Antrim considered their recommendation, using as its excuse the fact that the Lisburn church had issued its call without first consulting the presbytery, but it was afraid "of breaking that congregation." When the four dissidents agreed to accept Mc-Cracken, the presbytery tendered the call, and he was ordained in July 1688.[74]

Throughout most of the late seventeenth century some churches issued calls and then sought the presbytery's blessing (as in the Lisburn case) whereas others first requested the meeting's acquiesence as well as its assistance in persuading a minister to accept a call. Not until 1695 did the Lagan meeting stipulate that henceforth no congregation extend a call without the presbytery's approval; the Antrim meeting had regarded this as the norm by 1687.[75] Whichever procedure was employed, a presbytery could block a call for various reasons, especially a congregation's procrastination in fulfilling its financial obligations, reticence to provide adequate maintenance, or inability to reach agreement on the location of an edifice. In August 1687 the Antrim presbytery refused a request from the Lisburn church to call John Munro, partly because Munro was disinclined to accept, partly owing to the meeting's belief that it would be difficult to replace him at Carnmoney. The meetings seem not to have abused this power, even when approving a call meant losing a clergyman to another presbytery, though Route refused to approve Derry's call to Thomas Fulton in 1672. In April 1691, in contrast, the same meeting permitted Peter Orr to accept a call from Glenarm in the meeting of Antrim "upon discovery that he can't comfortably stay where he is, or in some other place of their meeting."[76] Lagan withheld its approval of Enniskillen's call to William Holmes in 1692 until the synod determined whether the church was in the Lagan presbytery, indicating a sensitivity to intermeeting relations.[77]

Calls involving the movement of ministers between Scotland and Ireland sometimes required diplomacy, though cooperation was common. In 1675 the Ardstraw church sought Lagan's assistance in obtaining Gilbert Rule's help to find a minister in Scotland. Rule's brother Robert was already the minister at Derry, and later the same year that church wanted to call Gilbert to be Robert's co-pastor, a proposal approved by the Lagan presbytery, though nothing came of it.[78] In 1680, when the church at Stirling called Robert to be its minister, Lagan protested, urging the other presbyteries to submit their views on the matter to the general committee. Robert remained at Derry, a testimony to the effectiveness of Lagan's campaign to keep him.[79]

Ministers had the right to refuse a call, and a number of them did so. This carried the risk of pressure from a presbytery if it thought the call should be accepted. In 1686, when McCracken was reluctant to accept a call from Duneane and Grange, the Antrim presbytery asked him to supply the church as frequently as possible or "if he be positive to refuse their Call, that he declare so much expressly to them both for the meetings vindication & the people put from any expectation of our condescension to their desire." He still rejected the call.[80] Ministers who received calls from other churches took them seriously, sometimes agonizing over whether to accept or reject the offers and typically seeking their meeting's advice. When Carnmoney called Patrick Shaw in 1673, he expressed to the Antrim presbytery "the sense he had of his owne insufficiencye for any place," but he submitted to the meeting's judgment and accepted the charge.[81] In July 1675 the same meeting heard Carrickfergus tender a unanimous call to Archibald Hamilton, but when he professed not to be "clear as yet to declare himself either to the meeting or people of Carrickfergus, but [desired] to have some further time for adviseing and dealing with God in so weighty ane affaire," the presbytery, "fearing lest delayes occasion inconveniencies," asked him to continue preaching every Sunday at Carrickfergus until he made up his mind. This he agreed to do, but within a month he followed the recommendation of the Tyrone meeting to accept the pastorate at Armagh.[82] When James Gordon, who had fled to Scotland during the time of troubles, refused to return to Glendermott, it called John Harvey of New Abbey, Dumfries; he agreed to consider the call on the condition that if he remained in Scotland the congregation would not "reflect upon him as having disappointed them."[83]

If anything, the soul searching was more intense when a minister had to consider two or more calls simultaneously. When Archibald Young received calls from Glenavy and Downpatrick in 1673 he turned to the Antrim meeting for guidance, and as we have seen, his colleagues sent him to the latter, in part because of pleas from the Down presbytery. Later the same year the Antrim meeting rejected Tyrone's recommendation that Robert Henry be sent to Glasleck, county Down, preferring that he accept Carrickfergus's call instead. The tables were turned in 1684 when the Tyrone meeting refused to permit John Abernethy to consider a unanimous call from the church in Antrim because he was pondering an invitation from Moneymore, county Derry, and there should not be "competition of Calls"; Abernethy went to Moneymore.[84]

A more complex case arose in the fall of 1688 when several congregations vied for the services of John Darroch of Argyll, not least because he could preach in Gaelic. After Glenarm called him, Layd and Cushendall, also in county Antrim, issued an invitation, seeking his services

every fourth Sunday in return for supplying a quarter of his maintenance, and a representative from the Route meeting suggested that if he
accepted this call, Layd and Cushendall could probably be annexed to
Glenarm. Ballymena also called Darroch, who in any event could not
accept any invitation without the Church of Scotland's authorization.
Because Glenarm had been the first to call him, the Antrim meeting
instructed Darroch to supply it, Layd, and Cushendall on an interim
basis. The Church of Scotland's conditional approval arrived before the
January 1689 session, but that Church and the presbytery of Kintyre
reserved the right to recall Darroch "when Providence opens up a door
for his return." He seems to have served Glenarm only briefly, for he
fled at the revolution and apparently never returned. By April 1690
Glenarm was looking for a new pastor and considering Neal Gray,
another minister in Scotland.[85]

The Lagan presbytery dealt with a number of ministers who wrestled with multiple calls. James Tailzour (Taylor) received invitations
in 1675 from Letterkenny, Urney, and three parishes in Fermanagh—
Monea, Enniskillen, and Derryvullan—that pooled their resources.
Asked for his preference, Tailzour left the decision to the presbytery
"because he knowes not how to doe it." According to the minutes, "the
Meeting, after seeking light & counsell from the Lord in this particular,
& after much deliberation & reasoning about it, doe unanimously conclude & declare that they think his going to & settling of Fermanagh will
be most for the Glory of God, & the advancement of the Gospell of
Christ."[86] When Ardstraw, Strabane, and Termonmaguirk issued calls
to Robert Wilson in 1677, he decided he was "unclear" to accept any of
them. In 1680 Tailzour was again the recipient of multiple calls, this time
from Glendermott and Killigarvan, county Donegal. Claiming he was
"in the dark about this matter & knowes not what to choose," he asked
the Lagan meeting to decide, but it refused, insisting he make up his
own mind. While pondering his options he received a call from Muff in
county Donegal, and his Fermanagh congregations asked him to continue serving them, though they were unable to support him financially.
When the presbytery finally suggested that Tailzour go to Glendermott,
he complied.[87]

The synod of Ulster occasionally involved itself in matters pertaining
to calling. It heard a particularly controversial case in July 1699 which
pitted the parish of Antrim against the Belfast presbytery. The latter had
refused to approve Antrim's call to James Kirkpatrick because he had
not preached before the Antrim presbytery and did not have the unan-

imous approval of the Antrim church; moreover the Belfast presbytery had previously recommended that he accept Templepatrick's call. The synod decided in Belfast's favor and then approved a regulation that no call be tendered to a minister or an expectant unless the presbytery of the congregation issuing the invitation had appointed one of its members to formulate the call. The intent was to ensure that a presbytery was cognizant that one of its churches was issuing an invitation. A proposal to permit a young man to receive only one call at a time was defeated, but the following year the synod enacted "that Plurality of Calls may be recommended" to a minister or expectant only by his own presbytery, by his synod if the invitations came from several presbyteries, or by the general synod if the calls came from churches in more than one regional synod.[88] Thus the freedom of churches to compete for clergy and of ministers to consider offers was preserved.

This freedom did not permit a minister to relinquish a pastoral charge without his presbytery's authorization. The presbyteries were normally willing to grant a minister's request for dismission, though if the reason was the congregation's slackness in rendering financial support, a meeting typically delayed action to see if it could prod congregants to pay arrears.[89] The grounds for dismission were normally a desire to accept another call, a church's inability or unwillingness to provide adequate maintenance, or a minister's ill health. In 1687, however, the Antrim meeting refused David Cunningham's request for dismission on grounds of ill health but permitted him to go to Scotland to recuperate. A more difficult problem arose in early 1688 when the Route presbytery asked the general committee "whether or not, when a brother is like to be oppressed with discouraging apprehensions upon the account of personal danger in this country, the meet[ing] shall press him to stay." In the judgment of the Antrim meeting, each case had to be tried on its merits by the appropriate presbytery.[90]

Throughout the period, but especially during the time of troubles, a shortage of clergy was an incentive for churches without pastors to call those ministering elsewhere. Raymond Gillespie has calculated that the ratio of Presbyterian clergy to families in 1660 ranged from 1 to 31 in the Route to 1 to 201 in the presbytery of Antrim. The region served by the Lagan presbytery had a ratio of one Presbyterian minister to 130 families compared to a conformist ratio of 1 to 31 and a Catholic ratio of 1 to 105 or 120 in the roughly equivalent diocese of Derry.[91] Scotland was an obvious source of recruiting more ministers, but in the post-revolutionary years that country too lacked sufficient numbers of Presbyterian clergy. As a result, churches and presbyteries in both countries competed for preachers.[92]

Movement from one Presbyterian congregation to another could be particularly attractive if one's congregation lagged in its maintenance, but "transportation," as the Presbyterians referred to a ministerial move, was only possible with a presbytery's consent. Presbyterians regularly used the threat of declaring a minister transportable, that is, free to accept another call, to prod recalcitrant congregations into paying arrears, not always successfully. Such was the case at Raloo, county Antrim, in 1674, when the people were convinced of their "utter incapacity" to support a minister and accepted the Antrim meeting's decision to grant Robert Kelso "ane act of transportability."[93] When conditions deteriorated in early 1688 several presbyteries declared some of their clergy transportable, enabling them to move to Scotland. This alarmed Antrim, which protested that work might be found for these clerics in Ireland if the meetings communicated with each other more regularly. Prompted by Antrim, the general committee resolved in April 1688 that a meeting which declared a minister transportable must inform the other presbyteries in Ireland, and that no clergyman had the right to leave the country without his meeting's authorization. The other presbyteries would have two months to seek his services before his presbytery could issue a "testimoniall" permitting him to depart Ireland.[94]

Given the shortage of clergy, transportation was sometimes a complex and even contentious process. Two cases will illustrate this, the first of which involved a call from Belfast to Adair in 1674 accompanied by a request to the Antrim meeting to transport him from Carncastle. The presbytery invited representatives from both churches to appear before it and asked Adair to state his views, but when their presence failed to resolve the issue the meeting sought the advice of the other presbyteries, each of which received statements from Belfast, Carncastle, and Adair. Down, Lagan, and Tyrone favored Adair's transfer to Belfast whereas Route was opposed. The Antrim presbytery accordingly debated, prayed, and ultimately concluded that "in consideration of the greater good of the Church in the north of Ireland, & the considerable unanimity of the rest of the meetings for the said transportation, they judge[d] Mr. Pat. Adaire now called by the providence of God to serve" at Belfast.[95]

Whereas Adair's case was complex but harmonious, the second was contentious. In 1696 the general committee transferred Francis Iredell from Donegore to Armagh on the condition that if he found "insupportable Grievances" there, he could apply to the synod of Ulster for relief. During the first seven months he was supposed to have ministered at Armagh, he was there only four Sundays, excusing himself because of illness, pressing affairs, and inclement weather. "His Transportation thither," he insisted, "was most Gravanimous and crushing to him, both in Body and Spirit, & would (if not prevented) render him unfit for Work there or any other new Place, that Congregation being very numerous & spacious; beside which, his going thither would much prejudise his Secular Affairs, & tend to break Dunnagore." The synod thereupon repealed his transportation but rebuked him "according to the Nature of his Crime" for defying the committee.[96]

Inadequate numbers of clergy meant that the presbyteries regularly concerned themselves with supplying vacant pulpits and that ministers typically were responsible to meet the spiritual needs of churches in addition to their own. This imposed heavier burdens on the clergy, not least because of the travel involved. To address the problem, in the autumn of 1672 the general committee proposed the use of young men to supply "desolate congregations," to which the Lagan meeting concurred only if "such young men as are strangers" first report to the presbytery responsible for the vacant churches; if not the meeting insisted that it be exempt from the responsibility of supervising them. This was a classic example of Presbyterian reluctance to yield significant authority to a central entity.[97]

Rarely did the need to supply vacant pulpits cause controversy, though ministers missed or postponed assignments rather often owing to inclement weather, ill health, or pressing concerns. When this happened the presbyteries were understanding and rescheduled the visits. The meetings accorded special attention to supplying congregations in the principal towns. In the fall of 1672 the general committee considered a request from the congregation at Bull Alley, Dublin, to have ministers supply it for three-month stints, but Lagan and Antrim demurred on the grounds that no pastor could be away from his congregation for more than eight weeks. Churches whose ministers were absent for extended periods themselves became candidates for supply. Normally, therefore, presbyteries assigned ministers to supply a vacant pulpit for a week at a time, occasionally as part of a rotation over an extended period. When Robert Rule left Derry to visit Scotland in 1675, the Lagan meeting sought assistance from Route and in the meantime established a rotating schedule commencing with the eldest minister and extending through the youngest, but with William Hampton preaching every third sabbath.[98]

The intertwined demands of Belfast and Carrickfergus indicate the problems involved in supplying churches. Commencing in 1668 William Keyes, the Belfast pastor, supplied Carrickfergus on alternate Sundays, but in November 1671 the latter church, citing the inconvenience of this arrangement, petitioned the Antrim meeting to have Keyes assigned to Carrickfergus exclusively. At the same time the Belfast congregants wanted Anthony Shaw to become their co-pastor along with Keyes, but when nothing came of this they offered Keyes the substantial sum of £60 *per annum* if he would be their full-time pastor. Consequently the presbytery had to make provisions to supply Carrickfergus commencing in February 1672 and continuing until Robert Hendry accepted the church's call and was ordained in April 1674. During this period the church failed to find a new minister in Scotland, unsuccessfully called Alexander Hamilton of Benburb, county Tyrone, and finally obtained Hendry only when Antrim persuaded Hendry's congregation at Glasleck to acquiesce in his transfer, the objections of the Tyrone meeting notwithstanding.[99]

In the meantime, when it was the Antrim presbytery's turn to supply Bull Alley, Dublin, it dispatched Keyes in July 1672 and made provisions to fill his Belfast pulpit. Although Antrim and Lagan objected to having one of their clergy minister at Bull Alley more than eight weeks, the former permitted Keyes to serve there much longer because of his success in increasing the congregation's size. When Bull Alley invited Keyes to be its permanent pastor, the Belfast congregation protested. Although Keyes wanted to return to Belfast, he acknowledged that the Bull Alley congregation would disintegrate without a regular pastor. Antrim referred the case to the general committee, which transferred Keyes to Dublin in the spring of 1673. Thus the Antrim presbytery had to supply Belfast, which in January 1674 persuaded the presbytery to send representatives to seek permission from the earl and countess of Donegall for the Belfast congregation to select a minister, with the meeting's approval, "according to principles owned by us." If they refused, "the brethren aforesaid [were] to leave the obstruction of the planting of that place at their door." When the earl and countess concurred, the congregation successfully called Adair from Carncastle with Antrim's assistance in October 1674. More than two years had elapsed since Keyes had been loaned to Bull Alley—a long time for a church to rely on visiting clergy.[100]

The Presbyterians employed various expedients to deal with the clerical shortage, among them the sharing of ministers. Drumragh, Termonmaguirk, Donacavey, and eventually Longfield shared the services of John Rowatt in the mid-1670s, though not without arguing over how much of his time each would receive and taking their quarrel to the Lagan meeting. About the same time William Hampton ministered to Burt, Inch, and Elagh; in 1691 Burt added an aisle to accommodate congregants from Fahan. Lagan left the division of labors to Hampton. After moving to Lifford in 1682, Rowatt subsequently ministered as well to Strabane and Donaghedy during the time of troubles, provoking complaints from his Lifford congregants. Discussions in 1693 aimed at sharing Samuel Halliday's labors among Omagh, Ardstraw, and Urney proved fruitless. More often than not, sharing caused friction.[101]

An alternative was the unification of parishes, as at Drumragh and Longfield, which combined in 1677. A decade later the church at Glenavy feared disintegration unless it could unite with Magheragall, Maghaberry, and Ballinderry in county Antrim. Proposals for union were just as likely to be rejected, not least because of the potential travel distances for some parishioners and perhaps as well over fears of diminution of power. Grange and Duneane balked at uniting in 1688 until they reached agreement over the location of two meetinghouses, and Elagh, Coshquin, and Ballynagalliagh objected to a merger with Derry in 1696. In 1688 the general committee proposed that any parish unable or unwilling to support a minister should unite with an adjacent vacant congregation, but the Antrim presbytery would accept this only if the minister and people concurred, thus preserving congregational authority. The synod of Ulster, however, succeeded in 1697 in reorganizing the churches at Ballee, Drumee, and Down into two congregations.[102]

Merging parishes and sharing pastors reflected not only a ministerial shortage but also inadequate financial resources in many parishes. Presbytery minutes are replete with references to clerical maintenance and arrears in the payment of stipends. Indeed, ministerial maintenance rivals supply as the most discussed subject in the presbyteries. "Competent" maintenance included an adequate stipend, a manse, and often a stipulated amount of grain. Peat and the use of land for tillage or pasturage were sometimes offered, and in a few cases so was labor to work the land, as at Cappy in 1680, Donaghmore in 1691, Clogher in the same year, and Enniskillen in 1697. The people of Enniskillen also offered to build "office houses" and fence the land, and those at Clogher, county Tyrone, to lay turf. The people at Donaghedy, county Tyrone, proffered a house, peat, a garden, an acre of meadow, two acres of grain, enough additional grain for a horse and two or three cows, and as much more land as the minister wanted to use.[103] The presbyteries monitored maintenance, periodically expressing concern, as Antrim phrased it in 1673, that some clergymen were "much neglected by their congregations," hence it resolved "to lay out themselves in their serious indeavours to get the same remedied so far as they shall be able." A year and a half later, in early 1675, Down expressed its concern to Antrim "that the brethren are all under great straites for want of maintainance, and that the Gospel Ministry in Ireland is like to cease upon the accompt that there is no way for the maintainance thereof."[104]

According to the Antrim meeting the "ordinary allowance" for a Presbyterian minister in Ireland in January 1674 was £30 *per annum*, substantially less than most Ulster Presbyterians had received in the 1650s. The figure of £30 was an accurate estimate, for the stipends offered by 24 churches mentioned in the Antrim and Lagan records in the period 1672 to 1680 averaged £28 11s. 3d. *per annum*. When the two extremes—£60 at Dublin and £12 at Killybegs—are removed, the average was £27 17s. 9d. Judging from stipends paid by eight churches in the Antrim meeting in the period 1686 to 1688, clerical income dropped nearly eight percent, to £25 15s. *per annum*. Stipends rose in the 1690s: 27 churches mentioned in the Antrim and Lagan records and the synod of Ulster minutes offered stipends averaging £33 9s. 3d., or £32 2s. 10d. with the two extremes—£80 at Dublin and £20 at Ballyclogh—removed. These figures must be used with caution, for most churches provided a manse or an additional contribution toward housing, and some, as we have seen, offered grain, fuel, or the use of land. Grain amounts are often stipulated whereas the amount of acreage is not. When Derryloran attempted to keep John McKenzie in 1691, it could offer a stipend of only £14, but it calculated the value of the farmland at £8 to £9 *per annum*.[105]

A no less compelling reason for caution in assessing clerical stipends was the endemic problem of churches that failed to make timely payments or found it impossible to raise the sums that had been pledged to lure ministers. In 1675 the Fermanagh parishes of Enniskillen, Monea, and Derryvullan offered £30 to obtain James Tailzour, upped the bid to £40, and then could provide only £26 after he accepted the post, of which only half had been paid by October 1676. Presbyterians in the Lurgan-Magheralin area hoped to pay a stipend of £40 in 1691 but had to scale it back to £30. The ability to honor the offers undoubtedly fluctuated with changing economic conditions and the number of people in a congregation able and willing to provide financial support. At Strabane in 1675 ten men paid most of the £25 stipend, yet at Braid, long plagued by controversy, 180 families provided a mere £18 in 1686.[106]

Ascertaining the extent of the arrears problem is complicated by the fact that the recorder of the revised version of the Antrim minutes excluded much of the material about grievances concerning clerical maintenance. By the time he made this decision, in May 1674, eight churches had been cited in the minutes between September 1673 and April 1674 as being in arrears, and Glenavy was added to the list in September 1674. Indeed, Carncastle had been in arrears for four successive years concluding at All Saints, 1672, and the ensuing year had not yet been calculated.[107] The minutes begin recording arrears again for a brief period between October and December 1683, when three churches are mentioned. In the nearly six years commencing in January 1686 fifteen congregations were cited for being in arrears, among them Ahoghill, county Antrim, which owed the extraordinary sum of £177 in 1691.[108] Elsewhere, during a span of nearly two years, from July 1673 to April 1675, seventeen congregations affiliated with the Lagan presbytery were late in paying their pastors, though some only modestly so, and between January 1692 and April 1695 eight churches were similarly remiss.[109] Apart from admonitions to churches to fulfill their responsibilities, the presbyteries had little recourse other than to threaten to transfer ministers from congregations that made no serious efforts to deal with their arrears.[110] Commencing in 1696 the Lagan meeting imposed financial obligations on churches without clergy in return for supply by visiting ministers.[111] Given the financial constraints under which many congregations operated, the problem of supplying ministers would have been much worse had it not been for the suasive endeavors of the presbyteries. Organization was thus the key to providing many Presbyterian churches with pastors in the late seventeenth century. Without those clergymen the Scottish Presbyterians over time would probably have experienced a crippling decline in their numbers until they, like the English Presbyterians, the Congregationalists, and the Baptists, were virtually a spent force in Ireland.

Meetinghouses

During the 1660s Presbyterian worship services were of necessity confined mostly to conventicles in secular settings, but this was increasingly less so in the 1670s, the decade when the Scottish Presbyterians commenced the evolutionary process that resulted in their becoming a denominational church by century's end.[112] Not until early in the 1670s did a less restrictive government policy make possible a concerted Presbyterian program to build or repair meetinghouses. Some congregations apparently had no reasonable alternative other than to construct new buildings, as at Donaghadee, county Down (by August 1672) and Antrim (in the summer and fall of 1672).[113] In some cases a congregation rented temporary quarters until a new meetinghouse was completed or in lieu of constructing its own building, as at Kirkdonald.[114] A number of congregations had no suitable place to worship, a fact duly noted by official visitors dispatched by one or another of the presbyteries. Such was the case at Braid (Broughshane) and Ballyclare, and in the region of Donegal town, Ballyshannon, and Belleek, where the Lagan meeting wanted a church "erected conveniently in the midst of their bounds."[115] As congregations increased, whether by population growth, the impact of toleration, or the incorporation of neighboring groups, some meetinghouses had to be enlarged. In August 1672 the Lagan meeting recommended that Presbyterians at Drumragh, county Tyrone, who shared John Rowatt with the congregation at Termonmaguirk and often went there to hear him preach, add an aisle to the latter church to solve the problem of overcrowding. The same presbytery made a similar recommendation to Burt in 1691, partly as a condition for the appointment of a minister; by 1698 its edifice could accommodate more than 800 worshippers. More drastic expansion was necessary at Donaghmore, county Donegal, by early 1695 when the meetinghouse could hold barely a third of the congregation, prompting the Lagan presbytery to order its enlargement "with all convenient speed."[116] The scattered congregation in the southern region of county Donegal, which had meetinghouses at Mountcharles and Ballintra, planned to construct a new edifice in the spring of 1699 in or near Donegal town spacious enough to hold all its members.[117]

Presbyterian congregations were sometimes reticent to build meetinghouses, in part because of the expense but probably also owing to concern about the possibility of renewed persecution and the loss of their buildings. The Antrim and Lagan meetings occasionally promised to appoint clergy to vacant congregations only if the latter provided appropriate edifices. Presbyterians at Glenavy, county Antrim, accepted these terms in November 1673 and within two months had a place to worship. When the small congregation at Termonmaguirk requested a greater share of John Rowatt's ministerial services in 1676, the Lagan presbytery insisted that it provide a convenient church prior to the next meeting a month later.[118] Given the limited time, the presbytery presumably expected the people to rent or borrow a suitable structure.

The presbyteries periodically pressured congregations not to procrastinate in building or repairing houses of worship. In 1687–1688 Glenavy was one of the more difficult congregations, forcing the Antrim meeting to threaten to transfer its minister unless the people erected a new church in a central location. At Donaghmore in 1695, Presbyterians cut timber for a new meetinghouse but could not decide where to build it, prompting the Lagan presbytery to urge them to erect the building near the old edifice as long as it was not on land owned by the Church of Ireland.[119] Instead they rebuilt their existing church; the results were unsatisfactory, probably because of faulty construction or weather damage, for in 1697 the presbytery had to press them to repair the building. Likewise in 1697 the same presbytery instructed Presbyterians at Moyne and Sligo "to putt their meetting house in better care."[120]

For many congregations no issue was more contentious than the sites on which to build their churches. Essex's policy of toleration was barely in place before Presbyterians at Burt, Inch, and Elagh were arguing about where to locate their meetinghouse; in September 1672 the Lagan meeting dispatched John Hart and Robert Campbell to instruct them to select a place "where the body of the people may most conveniently meett." Hart was unable to make the journey, but he submitted written advice, and Campbell and Thomas Drummond viewed the possible sites, conferred with the congregants, and ultimately selected a location.[121]

Five years later, in 1676, the Lagan presbytery mediated another dispute over the site of a proposed meetinghouse, this time involving the people of Urney, county Tyrone. When initial efforts to resolve the argument failed, the meeting sent Campbell and John Hamilton with "full power & commission to take away that difference . . . by whatsoever means they could find most expedient."[122] After two years of contention and the mediation of various ministers, including Robert Rule, the congregation finally agreed to build the church on land owned by a Mr. Babington if Rule could obtain the bishop of Derry's permission. When that approval was forthcoming, Babington changed his mind. An exasperated presbytery thereupon dispatched William Trail to "represent to the people of Urney the power of Ministers & Elders to determine the conveniency of places of Worship, & to shew them that it is the M[eeting]s mind, that both ends of the parish should promise a submission of this their controversy to the Meeting." At first the Urney Presbyterians refused to comply, but in October 1679 delegates from both factions appeared before the presbytery. After deliberation the meeting ruled that the new church would be built on a site selected by a committee consisting of ministers and ruling elders appointed by the meeting along with three representatives from each of the two disputing parties. By September 1680 the church had at last been constructed at Tullymoan, but division continued, forcing the presbytery to send Robert Wilson, Robert Craghead, and Campbell to Urney to attempt to heal the breach. They seem to have been successful, though the controversy flared up again in 1697.[123]

The Antrim presbytery dealt with several disputes concerning the location of meetinghouses. One involved the refusal of Presbyterians at Duneane to relocate their church in 1674 to accommodate worshippers from Grange. Four years later, by which time the latter people had their own building, the presbytery could not persuade them to agree on a location central to both places despite the fact that attendance for sermons at Grange was poor. After Massereene himself concluded that hope of uniting the two congregations was futile, they consented to build meetinghouses as close to each other as feasible to share the same minister.[124]

The Antrim meeting also became embroiled in the affairs of Drummaul when its congregation pondered the construction of a new church, opting at first to locate it three-quarters of a mile outside the town. When church members reconsidered, in part to contemplate building two houses of worship, the meeting pressed them to erect their edifice at the agreed-on site. Divided among themselves, the congregation balked, finally prompting the exasperated minister, John Wilson, to request release from his charge. The breach widened after a group appointed to select an appropriate site announced its decision, only to have a disgruntled faction offer to pay £1 10s. if the meetinghouse was constructed where they desired. This group ultimately conceded defeat, leaving the congregation at last agreed on the location of the new building. Wilson remained their pastor despite substantial arrears in his salary.[125]

Perhaps the most unique dispute involved the Letterkenny congregation. In October 1678 the Lagan presbytery deputed Campbell to visit the congregation "to deal with that people about their Meeting-house." More than a year later, in April 1680, the congregation asked the meeting to send John Hamilton "to help them to order their affairs" concerning the church, but another seven months passed before Hamilton presented the presbytery with a proposed resolution of the (still unspecified) dispute. At least part of the dissension centered on the location of the pulpit, for the presbytery found it necessary, after hearing Hamilton's report, to dispatch Robert Rule and William Hampton to Letterkenny. They reported to the next meeting, in December 1680, where delegates instructed them to send a written statement of their proposed solution to the congregation.[126] The minutes provide no details about the dispute, but it was probably over whether the pulpit or the communion table should be centrally situated.

Judging from the minutes of the Lagan meeting, seating first posed a serious problem in 1697 at Donaghmore. The presbytery found it necessary to appoint five men to resolve the dispute. The same year it instructed Presbyterians at Ardstraw, county Tyrone, to see "that their seats be setled according to the payments of particullar heads of families," an indication of the extent to which Presbyterians had adjusted to the settled conditions of a new era.[127]

All of these disputes underscore the extent to which the Scottish Presbyterians were caught up in the problems of space allocation and building characteristic of most institutions. Neither private houses nor other informal settings were deemed suitable, yet a number of congregations lacked or were reticent to commit the financial resources necessary to provide meetinghouses. Cooperative ventures involving several congregations typically sparked disputes over where to build a meetinghouse. Once again, the presbyteries provided an institutional framework in which to resolve these problems.

Presbyterians in the Wider Christian Community

As the Scottish Presbyterians developed the institutional structure that contributed to their evolution into a denominational church in Ireland, all but an extreme fringe maintained cooperative relations with virtually all other Protestants except Friends. Despite the often hostile rhetoric from Anglican clerics, the periodic repression of conventicles, conformist attempts to require the Book of Common Prayer for marriages and funerals,[128] and intermittent incarceration,[129] fines, excommunication, and pressure to serve as churchwardens,[130] Presbyterian relations with the Church of Ireland were sometimes cordial. Dealings with the various bishops of Derry were often tense or even confrontational,[131] but in 1679 Wild authorized the Presbyterians to construct a meetinghouse; the landowner, however, refused permission. At the same time the Route meeting complained that Wild was presenting nonconformists for excommunication and imprisoning them, prompting Lagan to advise its members to submit similar complaints to Robert Henry in Dublin for presentation to the court.[132]

On several occasions the Antrim meeting referred to Presbyterian clergy as ministers of the Church of Ireland, suggesting that they did not see their differences with conformists as marking a permanent rupture in the established church.[133] The most intriguing case of Anglican-Presbyterian cooperation occurred in the late 1660s and early 1670s at Antrim owing to Massereene's influence. In February 1668 he came to the defense of Presbyterians in Antrim who faced excommunication for failure to pay fees previously levied by officials of Bishop Jeremy Taylor. The new bishop, Roger Boyle, claimed to know nothing of the dispute after he had been approached by Dr. Colvill at Massereene's instigation. Massereene thereupon instructed James Cunningham, the Presbyterian minister in Antrim, that he and his people were to obey no orders other than those issued by Boyle or Colvill. Of the ecclesiastical officials who threatened the Antrim Presbyterians Massereene blustered: "I will (if I live) in a shorte tyme make all those abominable fals Apparators and Informeing Raskalls that abuse the people and destroye the Countrye wearye of Lyveing in or aboute our partes, I shall find them out, and I hope to have them severely punished." Massereene counseled the Presbyterians not to act rashly, promising he would "trye what the law will doe and remove the Causes and persones to dublin and bring them that have a hand herein to plead the Grounds of this proceeding whether legall or not."[134]

Because the Presbyterians (whose congregation included both English and Scots) had no meetinghouse in Antrim, Massereene arranged for them to use the parish church. After John Howe arrived in the spring of 1671 to serve as Massereene's chaplain he preached there on Sunday afternoons. When Gowan went to Antrim following Cunningham's death, he too received an invitation to preach in the parish church immediately following the traditional service. In March 1673 he asked the Antrim meeting if he should accept this invitation as long as his Presbyterian listeners were "not ensnared to countenance the liturgye nor profane the sabbath by attending att the Church Doore when it is reading, and, withall, so that a considerable number of the people doe not absent themselves from the publick ordnances in the congregatione" because they objected to this accommodation. The presbytery approved this arrangement. Some Antrim Presbyterians—undoubtedly the stricter Scots—found this objectionable, however, and Gowan, undecided about accepting the call, turned again to the meeting for advice. This time it proposed that Massereene's assistance be sought to reconcile the disagreements. The presbytery deputed Adair, Thomas Hall, and Robert Cunningham to confer with him and members of the Antrim congregation.[135]

After Adair, Hall, and Cunningham reported to the presbytery in July, a long debate ensued in which Gowan and Howe unsuccessfully pressed the meeting to declare whether preaching in the church following the liturgy was a sin; the delegates took refuge in insisting that other presbyteries must be consulted, though they affirmed their willingness for Gowan to continue preaching in the parish church. Reflecting the problems he was having with some members of the congregation, Gowan then asked the presbytery if it would enjoin the absentees to be present at the Presbyterian ordinances as long as he "preserved [the people] from profaneing the Sabbath and from being inveigled in the matter of hearing the Comon Prayer booke." The presbytery refused to respond until it had ascertained whether or not his conditions had been implemented, nor would it consent to Gowan's request that he be allowed to treat absentees as disorderly and scandalous, thereby denying them "church privileges." The meeting also indicated it would have recommended that he cease using the parish church had it not been for their respect for Massereene. Not surprisingly, Gowan considered leaving Antrim, prompting the presbytery to seek Massereene's assistance in persuading him to stay, a task in which Massereene was successful.[136] Although the Presbyterians were not of one mind concerning the sharing of parish churches, they were seemingly united in their hostility to hearing the liturgy. The Antrim meeting's approval of the Presbyterians' sharing of the Antrim parish church is ample evidence that this was not an issue that clearly demarcated English and Scottish Presbyterians.[137]

Little information survives about Presbyterian relations with other Protestant nonconformists in Ireland before the late 1690s. In April 1681 the Lagan meeting asked Presbyterians in the Dublin area to invite English Presbyterians and "such Ministers of the Congregational way & judgment as have been ordained by a consistory of Presbyters" to participate in the ordination of Gideon Jacque at Wexford. This tantalizing glimpse into Presbyterian-Congregational relations suggests that a cooperative spirit sometimes prevailed, yet eight years earlier, when Wil-

liam Cocks and William Liston were preparing for ordination, the Antrim presbytery took a narrower approach, insisting that each ordinand
embrace the Westminster Confession; view ordination as conveying "a
primary relation to the Church ministeriall and onely a secondary to the
place in which hee is . . . to labour"; endorse the work of reformation
against Catholicism, prelacy, and erastianism; subordinate himself to
presbyterian polity; and subscribe to the Act of Bangor. Antrim ministers were concerned that some nonconformists in the Dublin area were
not committed to all of these principles.[138]

Differences within the nonconformist community were also evident
in 1667 because of a controversy over occasional communion. The problem was set forth in a letter dated 8 July to eight English nonconformists—Richard Baxter, Lazarus Seaman, Thomas Manton, Thomas Ja-
comb, William Bates, William Jenkins, Matthew Poole, and Samuel
Rolls. The authors were four nonconformist clergy in Dublin, Daniel
Rolls (Samuel's son); Thomas Parson, who had served at St. Mary's,
Limerick, in 1660; John Hooke, a minister at Drogheda during most of
the 1650s; and the earl of Donegall's chaplain, Noah Bryan. They described the existence of two dissenting churches in Dublin in 1667, one
of them—Winter's former church—Congregational "and so organized
as that they exercise the power of the Keys in highest censures," and the
other Presbyterian, "gathered all over the city" by a stranger (probably
a Scot) and "somewhat like the former." The unnamed Presbyterian
minister, his elders and deacons, and his congregation did not believe
they were properly constituted to exercise the disciplinary power of
censure and thus celebrate communion, but they contended that they
could partake of the Lord's supper with godly people in other churches.
This practice, however, offended the Congregational ministers, many of
whose congregants, the writers claimed, were actually Presbyterian in
outlook. Some of these people insisted they had the liberty to take
communion with other ministers and Christian laity. Other godly persons in Dublin, unaffiliated with either of the two churches, desired to
join in communion services administered by the writers, as did many
members of the Congregational and Presbyterian churches.[139]

Rolls, Parson, Hooke, and Bryan—classic examples of "mere nonconformists" who placed godly fellowship and worship above polity—
posed questions to their mostly Presbyterian colleagues in England:
Could a gospel preacher administer the Lord's supper to a body lacking
the power of excommunication? Would this profane the ordinance and
thus violate Presbyterian principles? Could persons occasionally be

admitted to communion if they customarily worshipped in another church and thus had no role in selecting the officers of the congregation with which they wanted to share communion? Could Congregationalists take communion with them? Could four or five "Preaching Presbyters" unite to administer the Lord's supper, and could they engage in the related acts of admonition, suspension, and excommunication? "May they not at least in these matters act with as much clearenes, and confidence before the lord & men as one Minister (in this [city] with us) cald Presbyterian, not yet quitted as to his relation to a people and Presbytery in the country."[140]

Pleading physical infirmity as well as isolation from the other addressees, Baxter replied without consulting the others. In his judgment a minister was a schismatic if he thought his congregants were disorderly or violated their duty to him if they occasionally partook of the Lord's supper with other Christians "whom the united Churches have not declared unfitt for Christian Communion or their notorious scandals made unfit." Moreover, it was essential to the ministerial office to exercise the power of the keys, namely admitting by baptism, excluding by excommunication, and restoring by absolution. If a group of godly people asked a minister to officiate even for an hour, they were "*pro tempore* an organized body" for whom the power of the keys could be exercised if "there shall be just occasion." Occasional communion, averred Baxter, should be permitted to all Christians who professed themselves members of the universal church, were not excommunicated, and had not forfeited their right by scandalous living. However, such communion must not be so frequent as to signify a forsaking of one's regular pastor and a separation from one's own congregation. As an officer of the universal church any minister could "guide occasionall assemblies" of Christians unable to unite with regular congregations, and he could occasionally administer communion to a settled church if it temporarily had no minister or if it wanted to demonstrate its catholicity by communing with him. Baxter concluded with a parting shot at the offending Presbyterian and Congregational churches in Dublin: "If there be any that hold schismaticall principles, & confine their communion to a party, sect or particular church, & are offended with such as do not as themselves, you are guilty of scandall if you seem to comply with them, & do not disowne their way, though you offend them."[141] Baxter's plea for ecumenical worship was appropriate for churches struggling to survive, and indeed it seemed to reflect the views of a majority of lay dissenters in Dublin.

The willingness of Scottish Presbyterians to cooperate with other Protestants was also manifest in their work in southern Ireland. When Archibald Hamilton preached in the south in 1672 at the behest of the general committee, he was so successful that Colonel Jerome Sankey (who had been and probably still was a Baptist) and others wanted him to settle in the area. Members of the Antrim presbytery who conferred with Hamilton believed that "a faire doore [had] opened for the worke of the Gospell there," but the meeting responded cautiously, insisting that all the presbyteries first "be ripe in ther thoughts about the expediencye" of Hamilton settling in the region. Hamilton remained in the north, but the Antrim meeting expressed a willingness to join with other presbyteries to supply the south if the people there so desired. In 1673 William Cocks and William Liston took up pastorates at Clonmel and Waterford respectively, probably ministering to English and Scottish Presbyterians alike.[142] The following year, Cocks asked the Lagan presbytery to commission John Hart to visit the south, but although recognizing "the need which that part of the Lords vineyard hath of a visit," it believed the time was not ripe. The same year, in response to a request from people in Cork city (where the Independent Edmund Weld had ministered in the late 1650s), the Antrim presbytery dispatched William Jacque and Matthew Haltridge to preach, but they found little encouragement on their sojourn. Nevertheless in 1675 a Mr. Barclay settled in Cork, prompting Lagan "to encourage him . . . in the work of the Lord there, & to desire that as he is in his judgment a Presbyterian, so he would really show himself to be such, by testifying his submission unto the advice of his brethren & subordination unto the Courts & Judicatories of Jesus Christ established amongst us." A Presbyterian congregation was still meeting in the Cork area in 1679. In the meantime contacts continued between the presbyteries on the one hand and Clonmel and Waterford on the other. By the beginning of 1675 Liston was having problems at Waterford and asked to be transported; the Lagan presbytery approved in October 1676. By that time Presbyterians were also active in Tipperary, Longford, and Sligo.[143]

Interest in the south continued in the 1680s. Bandon (where Weld had ministered in 1655–1656) had a Presbyterian church by 1680 and Gideon Jacque was ordained at Wexford in 1681. In the spring of 1687 the general committee considered "if any method of opening a door for planting the South of Ireland with the Gospell may be thought on," particularly because several people, such as Robert Kelso, were deemed "fitt for that purpose." In response to a request from the south, Antrim sent John Wilson to preach later that year, but the onset of revolution and war apparently checked any major new activity in southern Ireland.[144]

After the war, interest in the expansion of nonconformist activities in southern Ireland resumed, but this time all five dissenting churches in Dublin took the lead. As in the case of the Common Fund in England, which Presbyterians and Congregationalists had established in 1690, Ireland's General Fund was also an ecumenical endeavor. Initially proposed in 1696, it was finally established in 1710 with support from the Congregationalists as well as the Scottish and the English Presbyterians. Each of the five Presbyterian and Congregational churches in Dublin sent its two ministers and two laymen to sit on the board of trustees; joining them were seven other donors who had contributed £100 or more to the fund. Its goals were to foster liberty of conscience, encourage clergy to assume pastorates among the poorer rural congregations, establish new churches, and support ministerial students. Unlike England's Common Fund, which broke up in 1695 owing to theological conflict between the Presbyterians and the Congregationalists, Ireland's General Fund continued to thrive as an example of constructive ecumenical endeavor.[145]

Relations with the Friends, whom the Presbyterians seemed only interested in refuting, were anything but ecumenical. At some point prior to September 1673 the Lagan meeting commissioned Hart to write a document attacking the Quakers, and this he was to circulate among some of his clerical colleagues for criticism. In November he read a draft to the presbytery, which found it acceptable and encouraged him to continue. The following January the minutes record that he read "a paper about Revelations against the Quakers," but nothing more is known about this work. Also in 1673 the Presbyterian minister James Burges accused the Friends of rejecting the doctrines of the Trinity and predestination, worshipping in a manner that contravened Scripture, and glorying in their wealth. For the Quakers James Parke denied all such allegations in *The Way of God and Them That Walk in It, Vindicated* (1673).[146]

About the same time that Hart commenced his manuscript, the Antrim meeting commissioned Gowan and Howe to compose a refutation of the Friends. The inspiration for this decision and probably that of the Lagan presbytery came in a gathering of ministers from several meetings at Ahoghill, county Antrim, "about some businesse off publick concernment" prior to 5 February 1673. Tyrone and Down subsequently approved Gowan's and Howe's commission. Howe apparently lost interest or lacked sufficient time to contribute, for in June 1675 the minutes record a request from Gowan alone that nothing regarding his anti-Quaker polemic be mentioned in the register "which shall . . . retard his diligence in the work." A draft was ready by the summer of 1680 when Antrim seems to have sought the approval of the other presbyteries prior to publication (this falls in a gap in the minutes). Lagan insisted on seeing the manuscript prior to authorizing it and offered to have it copied or to reimburse Antrim for the fees of an amanuensis. Gowan sent part of his work—"some of his Treatises"—which the Lagan ministers promised to review, but the outcome is lost because of a gap in the records.[147]

The Lagan clergy may have suggested substantive revisions, for in May 1683 the Antrim records note that Gowan was preparing "a compendious treatise" against the Friends and would be exhibiting his theses. When the work remained uncompleted at Gowan's death the Route presbytery asked Antrim to commission a qualified person to complete what was now depicted only as a "litle treatise" against the Friends. Thomas Hall received the appointment in August 1684, and the following April the meeting asked the general committee for instructions concerning the manuscript. The project apparently collapsed in May 1686 when Hall admitted he had not started work on it.[148]

Nothing seems to have survived of this polemical project that extended over thirteen years. Although the Presbyterian clergy unquestionably shouldered onerous ministerial burdens and thus had little time for scholarly pursuits, the inability of Howe, Gowan, and finally Hall to bring the project to fruition may also suggest that Presbyterians did not consider Friends a major threat. Moreover, by this time the Scottish Presbyterians were more concerned with a schism in their own ranks that led to the creation of a breakaway sect affiliated with the United Societies in Scotland.

The Birth of a Sect: The Radical Covenanter Alternative

Unlike the large majority of Presbyterians in Ireland, who cooperated in varying degrees with the Congregationalists and gradually established a *modus vivendi* with the Church of Ireland (though not without periodic tensions), a relatively small number of Presbyterians, fired by their fidelity to the Covenant, opted for a path of religious exclusivity and confrontation. Their leader was David Houston (1633–1696), whose convictions finally led him to break with the Scottish Presbyterians in Ireland. Born near Paisley in Scotland, he earned an M.A. degree at the University of Glasgow in 1654. He was in Ireland by 1661, at which time he supplied vacant pulpits in the Antrim towns of Ballymoney and Glenarm. With ministers such as Michael Bruce and John Crookshanks, he was probably involved in successful efforts in 1668 to persuade people in the baronies of Dunluce, Kilconway, Glenarm, and Cary to take the Covenant. Charged with engaging in ministerial activities without the consent of a presbytery as well as offensive conduct, he appeared before the Antrim meeting in August 1671 and was advised to return to Scotland. He agreed on condition that he receive a testimonial, but this the presbytery refused, given his (unspecified) scandalous conduct at Glenarm. It did, however, offer to provide him with "a lyne . . . bearing as favourable a representation of his case as they could *salva veritate*," which he accepted. By September he was attempting to satisfy the Route presbytery for his offenses and had publicly acknowledged his "irregular carriage" at Ballymoney. On this basis he appealed to the Antrim meeting to retract its advice that he return to Scotland, but this it refused to do without the other presbyteries' consent.[149]

Houston's offense was in part the attention he was receiving from the magistrates, who were preparing to arrest him in March 1672. With this in mind Captain William Houston sought to convince David of his "Irregulare & sinfull cariage [and] shewed him that he was represented to the civill magistrat as a very turbulent man & disquyeter of the peace." The captain subsequently reported to the deprived minister John Shaw that Houston seemed to be sensible of his misdeeds, blaming the unnamed persons who had "putt him upe & advysed him to these offensive wayes." He indicated a willingness to submit to the presbyteries, accept their censure, cease preaching if ordered to do so, and leave the country if required. The Antrim meeting was wary inasmuch as Houston had previously indicated remorse only to lapse into unacceptable behavior. Nevertheless, as Adair reported, the presbyteries could not reject his repentance, though Antrim advised Route to "let him declare & solemnly ingadge his submission to your determinatione in his present case, & to the directione of the brethren of other meetings as the cause s[h]all require." Houston subsequently presented a written confession to the general committee which the presbyteries found adequate, but his "penitentiall sermon" in the spring of 1673 did not satisfy Route. Its painstaking concern with Houston was grounded at least partly in the fear that his undisciplined preaching could endanger the indulgence enjoyed by Presbyterians. "I look upon that Howstons carriage," Alexander Hutcheson told Thomas Wylie of Coleraine, "as a necessary ballast to your liberty." Houston finally satisfied Route and received permission to return to the pulpit in July 1673, but Antrim advised Route not to give him a testimonial until he had preached "in such places as themselves shall thinke fit both for trying of his after carriage and for repaireing his reputation."[150]

Houston seems to have caused no problems in Ireland in the ensuing decade despite continuing Covenanter activity. As we saw in Chapter 2, Robert Hendry and Samuel Halliday attracted the government's attention in early 1677, at which point Covenanter documents were seized. About the same time the militant Richard Cameron was preaching in Ireland, for in November 1678 the Scottish presbytery of Dunscore accused him, among many other things, of having preached a sermon at Strabane in which he likened indulged ministers and their followers to Cain, called them idolators and persecutors, and declared them "guilty of all the blood shed since Abel," especially that of the Galloway rebels. He also reportedly accused the indulged clergy of never having profited a soul.[151] During the Bothwell Bridge rebellion Cameron and his brother Michael were in the Netherlands attempting to buy weapons. After the insurrection failed, Cameron became the leader of a band of zealots that included Donald Cargill and the assassin David Hackston and held large outdoor conventicles in Scotland. On 22 June 1680 this group issued a manifesto at Sanquhar, Dumfries, in which they denounced Charles II as a tyrant and the duke of York as a Catholic. Government forces defeated the Cameronians at Aird's Moss, near Muirkirk, Ayrshire, killing the Cameron brothers in the process. Cargill escaped, subsequently preached to more conventicles, discussed the assassination of Charles and James, and was at last captured and hanged in July 1681.[152]

Despite the loss of their leaders the Cameronians reorganized themselves as the United Societies in December 1681. Together they comprised approximately eighty local societies with a membership estimated by one contemporary of some 6,000 or 7,000 persons in Scotland. In January 1682 members of the group issued another radical manifesto denouncing Charles and his government and distributed copies at Lanark. An inevitable crackdown on dissidents ensued, but the United Societies survived. Desperately in need of ministers, they sent three young men to study at the University of Groningen and turned as well to five Presbyterian clergymen, three of whom—Michael Bruce and the

Galloway rebels Samuel Arnot and Alexander Peden—were in Ireland. The calls to these men cited three motives:

First, becaus ther is so much Ignorance in the cuntrey Anent the very fundamentalls of religione, 2ly. becaus ther is none now in Scotland to hold up the fallen banner of our Lord by the preaching of the Gospell. 3. becaus ther is so much need of baptisme to Infants & so many like to be putt hard to it, what by reproach from pretended frinds, and persecutione from enimies, becaus their Infants are not baptized.

All five rejected the invitation, probably because of the Societies' commitment to tyrannicide.[153]

In the summer of 1683 James Renwick, one of the students sent to Groningen by the United Societies, was returning home when he refused to toast the king's health, was forced to take a different ship, and disembarked in Ireland. In Dublin he won converts to the militant cause of which he was a part. On 24 August he wrote:

All the people of this place were following men who did not follow the Lord, and thought they were right enough. Yet now, some of them are saying, we have been misled; we never knew before this, that we were standing betwixt the Lord's camp and His adversary's.

These people, who belonged to William Jacque's Capel Street congregation, pressed Renwick to remain in Ireland, citing a greater need than existed in Scotland, but he declined. With the approval of his disciples he accepted Jacque's invitation to meet on two occasions. Jacque wanted to know why Renwick enticed members of his congregation to leave and how he could preach in Dublin without a call or ordination. Renwick retorted that he was drawing people from sin, not a true church, and that he could not accept a call to preach from Jacque because the latter was not a faithful minister of Christ. Moreover Renwick asserted that he would be ordained only by true ministers. He questioned Jacque, demanding to "be satisfied anent his entry to that congregation, the exercise of his ministry during his continuance therein, and now his yielding it up at the enemy's command—all which had to be reconciled with the work of God, our engagements, and the duty of a minister."[154] As reflected in this exchange, the gulf between the traditional Presbyterians and the United Societies was considerably wider than that between the former and the Congregationalists.

Renwick's return to Scotland did not terminate contact between the United Societies and like-minded Presbyterians in Ireland. On 3 October 1683 the Societies wrote to the people with whom Renwick had associated in Dublin, averring that the indulgence and indemnities were Satan's work "whereby Christs Crown was established upon a mans head, which some men, Loveing worldlie ease, more then Truth, embracing, they betrayed the Cause of God."[155]

While he was in Dublin Renwick was probably responsible for the circulation of a paper urging Presbyterians not to support clerics of the state church or moderate dissenters who prayed for Charles. "The Paper Imported that they should stand for all those that have or would fly for Religion from Scotland and for their Bretherne that were under affliction there and that they were to assist them to the utmost of their indeavours." Three Belfast men, the bookbinder James Caldwell and the coopers James Coborn and John Robinson, were among those responsible for enlisting sympathizers to sign the document, after which they were to send it to Glasgow. Unable to obtain enough signatures, the men burned the document. The government learned of it only in November 1684, when Adair, who was among the clergy Caldwell deemed unfit to hear, informed the authorities. Unpersuaded that the document was only a petition, Ormond's secretary concluded that it was a list of persons who intended to participate in a Covenanter insurrection. Caldwell may have alluded to such a plan when he confessed that the Covenanters were "in the right and upon occac[i]on he would Joyne with them against all others."[156]

The government in fact received reports of a purported Covenanter insurrection scheduled for 1 December 1684 in northern Ireland from Alexander Finiston, a Downpatrick carpenter, and Robert Camlin, a Loughinisland carpenter. Recruiters had allegedly told them Lieutenant Gawen Hamilton would be one of the commanders and that "all the Presbyterians in Killelea and elsewhere in the County of Downe were to Rise up in Arms and to goe on with Fire and Sword." The insurgents would allegedly obtain weapons on the day of the uprising at the Killyleagh fair, and one of their objectives was supposedly to cut Sir Robert Maxwell, a local magistrate, in quarters. Ormond concluded that Caldwell was probably a recruiter for this proposed rebellion: "I cannot but looke upon it as one damnable conspiracy," he told Sunderland. In fact, the alleged conspiracy was probably baseless.[157]

No later than 1686, Covenanters in Ireland wrote to the United Societies, condemning those in their country who had supplicated their enemies for liberty to preach and craved union with them. This group wanted no unity unless it was based on holiness, and they castigated Presbyterian moderates for rarely mentioning the covenants and never denouncing prelacy. They justified their split with moderates thusly: "We could not be clear to give over hearin[g] of them till the Lord sent your suplications and declarations our way & untill the Lord opened our eyes to sie the wrongs thei have woefully done against our Lord & his laws & Intrest; therfor we think it our duty" no longer "to hear them or Joyn with them or own them as faithfull ministers." No one, they believed, could condemn them for disowning the moderate Presbyterian clergy because the latter had supplicated the enemies of God and opposed the party of truth. "We declair if we had known them as well as we doe now we should not have hard them or owned them in thei[r] evile cawese." The zealots concluded by requesting the United Societies to write to them as soon as possible.[158]

When the United Societies again sought a minister in June 1686, they dispatched representatives to England to speak with Anthony Slie and to Ireland to talk to Houston. The resulting report about Houston was sufficiently encouraging to persuade the Societies to invite him to Scotland for further discussions, but they told him they had obtained unspecified information "whereof you would Do well to clear yourselfe."[159] Houston was in fact in trouble with the Route, Down, and Antrim presbyteries because of his "disorderly, schismatical & dangerous proceedings." According to the Antrim presbytery "multitudes" were following him "in those extravagant courses with a sighting & reflecting upon the Ministers & exposing his dangerous heterodox opinions & divisive expression in his sermons & otherwise." Antrim therefore dispatched two representatives to consult with Down about "supressing the growing schism & flame." Summoned to answer the charges, Houston responded in writing, repudiating the presbytery's authority and appealing to the General Assembly in Scotland. Route suspended Houston and Antrim demanded his deposition, a copy of which was to be sent to Scotland. With the consent of the other presbyteries, Route deposed him from the ministry in February 1687. His "tenacious" followers were to be treated as scandalous persons and denied participation in the sacraments. By July 1687 about two dozen of Houston's supporters at Ballymoney, Ballycastle, Ahoghill, Finvoy, and Drummaul issued a testimonial on his behalf, to which the Antrim presbytery responded by requesting Route to publish a manifesto detailing his immorality and miscarriages since he first came to Ireland.[160] Six of those who signed Houston's testimonial appeared before the Route presbytery, where they stood accused of condemning all the ministers of Christ in Ireland as false. To this the six retorted: "We are not to be your judges, whether you be Ministers of Jesus Christ, or not; for Ministers may be Ministers of Christ, and yet they may be such, as some Christians cannot have communion and fellowship with in several things." The subscribers defended Houston, charging the ministers of the presbytery with failing to preach covenant obligations.[161]

In the meantime the United Societies had dispatched an agent to Ireland to investigate the accusations against Houston; he concluded they were calumnies. Houston accepted an invitation to visit Scotland, where he and a supporter attended a gathering of the United Societies in December. They read to him portions of an apologetic statement "wherein are sumarily comprehended some signall steps of our Churchs defection, & a brief Declaration of our present testimony." Concurring with their principles, Houston showed the group his license to preach, a statement he had composed to Presbyterian ministers in Ireland explaining why he refused to subordinate himself to them, and generally favorable testimonies from persons to whom he had ministered. Asked about the terms on which he had once ministered in a meetinghouse in Ireland, he responded that "the termes of his holding were not sinfull for he was setled by the ministers upon the call of the people: And whensoever he knew of any transaction of the Ministers with the (so called) Magistrats That he forsooke his meeting house, & refused subordination to these ministers." Satisfied, the United Societies permitted him to preach in Scotland but he turned down a formal call and returned to Ireland in early 1687.[162]

Contacts between the United Societies and their Irish sympathizers continued. The former treated the latter as equals and brethren "under the same indissoluble bond of our holy Covenants." In March 1687 the United Societies requested more frequent contact between the two groups and urged the Irish to "deall freely in admonishing us, wherein you thinke wee err, or goe beyond, or come short of our dutey." Houston returned to Scotland in late spring after preaching to "considerable numbers." In July the "sundry Societies" in Ireland invited Renwick to visit them, and Houston went back to the island later in 1687.[163]

In April 1688 the "Generall Corespondant Mitting" of the Irish zealots issued a formal statement expressing their position. They would not engage in religious fellowship with any who accepted the Declaration of Indulgence or who "owneth or pleadeth, or payeth, or acteth in, or for, defection, or acts scandlous, or owneth any usurpation in Church or Steat" contrary to "the suorn Reformation of the true Protestant Presbrtirian Church of God in Brittan and Irland." They resolved to maintain the church's testimony, expecting in return to be preserved in "the hour of temptation." All who were not obstinantly scandalous or malignant were welcome to attend their services. Their polity was virtually identical with that of the moderate Presbyterians they condemned, though their numbers were vastly smaller. Each congregation or "Societie" selected a representative to attend a county meeting (or presbytery), and those representatives or commissioners also attended the general correspondents' meeting (in effect a synod).[164]

The Irish societies presumably adhered to the relatively detailed entrance requirements set forth by Renwick. Those seeking membership had to state their reasons for doing so and explain why they were separating from those with whom they had formerly worshipped. Strangers had to provide a certificate from the church to which they had belonged or inquiries had to be made concerning the soundness of their beliefs and lives. Persons holding false principles or living scandalous lives could not become members. Specifically, prospective members had to state their views of the covenants; "the late work of reformation"; the prophetic, kingly, and priestly offices of Christ; ecclesistical polity and prelacy; hearing clergy of the established church; Erastianism "& Joyning with the indulged" ministers; clergy who ceased the public exercise of the ministry because of penal laws; the suffering of the "late martyrs" in Scotland, that is, the Galloway and Bothwell Bridge rebels; and those who entered into bonds not to disobey the penal laws. Moreover a prospective member had to pledge not to divulge "matters reasoned or concluded in the society but in soe far as the society doth allow to be done with general consent." If a candidate made it this far and answered "other proper questions," he or she then had to assent to the society's articles.[165]

As enunciated by Renwick, those articles commenced with a statement that effectively captured the mindset which characterized the societies in both countries:

Taking into our serious consideration the lords late manifestation of his wonderful loving kindnes, tender mercy & great love to these lands together with the great ingratitude, the sinfull & shamefull defections, the present obstinancy & impenitency of this generation, the luke warmnes, newtrality & sinful complyanc of temperizing profesors, the many spiritwal & temporal Judgments & plagues that has already overtaken us, together with the dreadful plagues & woes & fearful Judgments that ar now hanging above our heads & threatned to be powred out in a signall maner to our astonishment, rwin & destruction . . . we doe Judge it our duty to search & try our ways & turn again to the lord.

The societies accepted Scripture as the sole standard of doctrine and living, held preaching and sacraments in high esteem as long as the ministers were faithful, and deemed it their duty to decry temporizers and backsliders. They claimed the right to repudiate members who embraced doctrinal errors or were "seduced to any sinfull course," but only to the point of exhorting them to reform, not disowning them. To prevent schism they agreed to lay aside matters that proved too difficult to resolve until such time as godly brethren elsewhere could be consulted.[166]

Sometime prior to 6 June 1688 Houston was arrested and taken to Scotland under guard, but agents of the United Societies rescued him before the party reached Edinburgh. In the meantime, on behalf of the Irish societies John Moor had written on 6 June to their fellow believers in Scotland requesting an ordained minister and in the interim the services of Alexander Shields. The tone of the request, in which Moor referred to their "lowe Case & Condition," indicated that the Irish societies were in trouble. The Irish societies wrote again on 26 December, citing their sad condition, comparing themselves to a handful of sheep without a shepherd, and expressing concern about the sword of the enemy that was at their door. They appealed to the Scots to "come over and help" them as participants in a common cause. The word of the Lord, they claimed, was being trampled not only by their avowed enemies but also by "pretended frinds to the Causse." Above all they cried out for a pastor, especially to administer baptism.[167]

Houston returned to Ireland by early 1689 and settled in or near Newtownards, county Down. Early in the time of troubles he entered into a bond with Mount-Alexander, pledging to work for peace and, if needed, to provide troops on condition that the Covenanters could appoint their own officers. In September 1690 the synod of Ulster summoned him to appear before the Antrim presbytery in November to answer for his conduct, but he defiantly ignored this and numerous subsequent summons, though some of his followers attended sessions of the Antrim presbytery in 1691 and were "tenderly discoursed with." In September Antrim reported to the synod of Ulster that it had received no information against Houston from anyone, including Hugh Wilson, who had been making inquiries in Scotland, hence it dropped proceedings against Houston. The synod, however, commissioned Peter Orr to draft a declaration against Houston and asked Adair and Wilson to edit it. The declaration was to set forth "his irregular and immoral practices whereupon he was formerly depos'd, notwithstanding he continues in the same course." From this point he was adjudged "none of our Communion," and Presbyterians were ordered not to join him in worship on pain of being considered scandalous. The synod ordered that copies of the declaration be sent to the presbyteries and read in the churches as the meetings deemed appropriate.[168] When Houston died in 1696 his principal legacy was the seemingly permanent separation of radical Covenanters from the main body of Irish Presbyterians.[169]

The last decades of the seventeenth century were thus critical in the history of Irish Presbyterians. Ousted from the established church in 1660, periodically persecuted by a government understandably concerned about security, and forced into *de facto* sectarian status in the 1660s, the Scottish Presbyterians around 1670 commenced the task of rebuilding an effective ecclesiastical structure, recruiting and training ministers, raising funds to support their pastors, and providing meetinghouses. Two decades later, in 1690, they crowned their ecclesiological work by summoning a synod. Careful attention to organization was thus a critical component in their survival and development as a fledging denominational church. Although their strength was manifestly in the north, they cooperated with English Presbyterians and Congregationalists in Dublin and elsewhere to expand the nonconformist cause. Their willingness to live in peace with the Church of Ireland, the ideological attacks of many of its leaders notwithstanding, was unacceptable to David Houston and like-minded Covenanters, whose long history of troubled relations with moderate Presbyterians finally led to the establishment of an extremist Presbyterian sect.

CHAPTER 5

The Presbyterian Way: Worship, Discipline, and Social Responsibility

AS CRUCIAL AS ECCLESIOLOGICAL organization was for the survival and emerging denominational character of Scottish Presbyterianism in Ireland in the late seventeenth century, religious life infused that organization with the spiritual vigor without which it could not have prospered. This chapter will therefore turn from matters of polity, ministerial supply, the construction and repair of meetinghouses, and intra-Protestant relations to those aspects of religious life that were vital to the Presbyterian experience: preaching, catechizing, the sacraments, fasting, marriage rites, discipline, and the exercise of social responsibility. Historians have long recognized the primacy of preaching in Presbyterian worship, not least as a means to proclaim the gospel, guide the faithful in Christian living, and reinforce their commitment to the community's ideals. But the significance of fasts and sacraments has not always received the attention they merit as instillers of a powerful sense of both individual and communal renewal, particularly at the emotional level. The sacraments and fasting were the religious community's means of expressing and renewing its solidarity and distinctive identity, especially in the face of persecution. Far more than the sermon, sacraments and fasts provided believers with that unique point of contact in which they were simultaneously communing with God and their fellow Christians. Particularly in the great festal communions that became a feature of Presbyterian worship in Scotland and northern Ireland, believers would have experienced a profound sense of union, both physical (with their fellow worshippers) and spiritual (with both the latter and God). If baptism was the rite of initiation, the Lord's supper and fasting were rituals of spiritual and communal renewal, the reaffirmation of loyalty to a community often in tension with the traditional society of which the Presbyterians were also members. In that sense, the sacraments and fasting sustained the tension between earthly and heavenly communities that was fundamental to the Christian life.

In the face of this tension, most believers must have been tempted to reduce the conflicting demands to conform to worldly ways on the one hand and to adhere to the higher standards of their religious community on the other. Discipline was therefore critical as a means to see that the standards of living espoused in biblically based sermons were practiced in daily living. In practice, discipline entailed the imposition of the group's standards on those who had succumbed to the less rigorous ways of the world. Although concerned at one level with the recalcitrant and the wayward, discipline in a broader sense was intended to inculcate the notion that all believers should live an orderly life, manifesting their faith in outward actions that reflected the higher standards embraced by their religious community. For Irish Presbyterians in the late seventeenth century this included the provision of charitable relief and education. These two concerns, it will be argued, were the primary foci of social responsibility—the practical embodiment of godly ideals in daily living.

The Primacy of the Word: Preaching and Catechizing

For Presbyterians the heart of the worship service was the sermon. The appropriate model was a sermon characterized by biblical doctrine, clarity of expression, and simplicity of language. As the synod of Ulster expressed the standard in 1697, preachers must "use a sound Form of Words in Preaching, abstaining from all romantick Expressions & hard Words, which the vulgar do not understand, as also from all Sordid Words & Phrases."[1]

A sense of the content of Presbyterian homilies can be gleaned from a manuscript collection of sermons preached in the latter half of 1681 by John McKenzie, a native of county Down who had earned his M.A. degree at Edinburgh University in 1669. Four years later he was ordained at Derryloran (Kirktown), county Tyrone.[2] He preached these sermons throughout the north. His texts came primarily from the New Testament, especially the epistles attributed to Paul and Peter, though he also preached from the Psalms and the Song of Solomon.

Three themes stand out in McKenzie's sermons, the first of which is a practical, largely noncontentious assertion of Reformed Protestant tenets. For McKenzie justification by faith was the "fundamentall principle of the Christian religion." He embraced a doctrine of election, according to which Christ offered grace and mercy to all, though few could accept because most lacked the requisite faith. McKenzie warned his hearers of the perils of heresy, especially as espoused by Arminians, Socinians, Pelagians, and Friends. Churches founded in keeping with the pure principles of New Testament polity were a magnet to attract such heretics: "It hath been a very usuall thing and is so that wherever the Lord plants the Gospell and gathers a church for himself priviledged with the purity of ordination and administrations according to his own institution, there Satan hath his agents to foment heresies to subvert and darken the true doctrine of Christ that he may obtain his own ends viz. the destruction and ruine of souls."[3]

Like heresy, human traditions were a major target of McKenzie's attack. Jesus, he argued, provided precepts to regulate the church just as he gave believers "excellent promises and offers for their encouragment." In ecclesiological terms such offers were embodied in the ordinances, more narrowly conceived as the sacraments, more broadly as including prayer and preaching. Rightly observed, these ordinances were the source of "an assurance of an interest in God . . . which bears up the soul in all troubles and prompts the soul to study the preservation of its interest." Proof of election could be found in the care with which one sought God in the ordinances, the source of communion and fellowship with the divine. Given the importance attached to ordinances, the antipathy of McKenzie and his fellow Presbyterians to human traditions—the reputed corruptors of ordinances—is understandable.[4]

McKenzie's third theme—the one accorded most attention—was the duty of holy living, particularly perseverence through persecution. McKenzie viewed his age in largely negative terms as an era of egregious sins and little spiritual contrition, and thus a time of trials for the godly. Tribulation was the gateway to the kingdom of God, a trial of spiritual endurance but not a cause of despair. He held up Christ's sufferings as a source of strength for struggling believers, who were exhorted to fulfill their duties as the means of perseverence. "As there is nothing the soul ought to be more sure of than to be informed in and fixed upon true principles, so their care is to be how they may walk sutable to those principles when fixed upon them." Right doctrine, in other words, must be reflected in holy living, the pattern for which is Jesus himself. The holy life is a regulated one, a life governed by the principles of the covenant: "Our Lord will have his people under bands, they must not walke at randome as Libertines without anything to bound them but their own will, they must be under his yoke [and] give obedience to all his comands." In practice this meant suppressing passion; eschewing excess in food, drink, and apparel; and, as necessary, forsaking worldly preferment, estates, honor, and even family and life. Viewed in positive terms, averred McKenzie, "there is nothing [that] can more in any consideration contribute to evidence our sincere study of holinesse, than to converse with the aw[e] of God upon our souls with true fear of offending him; and entertaining the true sense of our pilgrimage state as being but sojourners here."[5]

Militant Covenanter sermons could have a very different tone. A sermon preached in 1687 by an unidentified Covenanter was a classic jeremiad. His initial remarks were delivered to a group of ministers and possibly ruling elders assembled in a church while the people gathered outside for communion. He began with a general warning of imminent judgment: "Prepare to meet thy god O irland," for the Lord is coming to punish the earth's inhabitants for their sins and to scatter his people throughout the kingdoms of the world. The preacher not only condemned James II for shedding the blood of the godly in Scotland but forecast a dreadful fate for the people of Ireland, who would perish in "grivous deaths," being neither lamented nor buried, "but their carcases shal be for meate for the fouls of the heaven and the beasts of the earth." He had scathing words for the clergy: "What wil yow doe who are the watchmen when the inhabitants of the land shal die in their iniquity and their blood wil be required at your hand?" They had neither sought the lost nor repaired the broken. When the magistrates were remiss in checking James II, the ministers failed to testify against them, "but in stead thereof you went in and out of your houses at his command." Thus in northern Ireland neither sacrifices nor offerings would keep them from being cast from God's presence owing to their iniquity. In their place God would raise up the unlearned "and set them up in the service of the San[c]tury."[6]

After he excoriated the clergy this Covenanter went outside to speak to the people, again in somber, judgmental, and prophetic tones. This would be one of their last communions before "the judgments come on: many a time have you trampled upon the blood of the son of god by your abuseing of your communion tables and soe you are more guilty then the people of irland that have shed the blood of the saints." He denounced magistrates among the prospective communicants for failing to use their authority in God's cause, hence the Lord would take the sword from their hands and give it to their enemies. Casting the net of blame more broadly, he castigated hypocrites, accusing them of having "goten something of a name to be a cloak to cover your hypocrisie with, but the lord is com in out of his place to strip you bare of that name and to bring you forth in your blacks and your whites and let it be seen in the sight of the world how deceitfully you have dealt with him; therfor fly fly fly in to your chambers, fly in to your strong holds, fly in to the rock of ages to hide your selves."[7] Clearly, the tone and even the content of the sermons of moderate Presbyterians and militant Covenanters could be strikingly different, the former pastoral and attuned to the spiritual needs of a people undergoing periodic tribulation, the latter admonitory, judgmental, and sometimes strident.

Instruction in the tenets of the faith and Christian living was also available through lectures and catechizing. References to a weekly lecture are rare, probably reflecting the shortage of clergy and their need to supply a host of vacant pulpits. In February 1688 the church at Lisburn entreated the Antrim meeting to expedite the trials and ordination of Alexander McCracken and in the meantime to permit him to visit the sick and give a weekly lecture, but this was apparently only a temporary expedient until he was ordained (July 1688) and could preach there on a regular basis.[8] References to catechizing are also scarce, probably because it was an expected duty and not controversial. In February 1694 the Lagan meeting received a request from Presbyterians at Moyne, county Donegal, for the usual supply of a visiting minister, with an appeal that he spend a day or two catechizing the people. When John Mairs, minister at Loughbrickland, county Down, supplied the church at Longford (Corboy) for eleven Sundays before he was transferred there in June 1697, he catechized the congregation only once, perhaps an indication that catechizing was often irregular. Infrequent instruction might explain why only a quarter of Derry's congregation could recite the catechism in 1696.[9]

Most catechizing presumably utilized the Westminster Assembly's *Confession of Faith and the Larger and Shorter Catechism*, many editions of which were published in Scotland beginning in 1648, subsequent to which copies undoubtedly crossed the North Channel. The first known Irish edition did not appear until 1758. By that time a number of catechisms by English authors based on the Shorter Catechism had been issued in Ireland: Thomas Lye, *A Plain and Familiar Method of Instructing the Younger Sort According to the Lesser Catechism* (London, 1662; Dublin,

1683); John Wallis, *A Brief and Easie Explanation of the Shorter Catechism* (London, 1648; Dublin, 1683); Joseph Alleine, *A Most Familiar Explanation of the Assemblies Shorter Catechism* (London, 1672; Belfast, 1700); and Thomas Vincent, *An Explicatry Catechism: or an Explanation of the Assemblies Shorter Catechism* (London, 1673; Edinburgh, 1675; Glasgow, 1697; Belfast, 1700). The Shorter Catechism itself was printed at Belfast in 1694.[10]

Only one Presbyterian in Ireland in the pre-revolutionary period—Robert Chambers, a probable associate of Thomas Blood's in the Dublin plot—is known to have written a catechism. Licensed in England as a Presbyterian in 1672, he returned to Ireland shortly thereafter,[11] and eight years later, when he was living in Dublin, wrote "An Explanation of the Shorter Catechism of the Reverend Assembly of Divines." Given his likely complicity in the Dublin plot in the early 1660s, Chambers's exposition of the fifth commandment is worth noting. Subjects must obey the "wholsom laws" of magistrates, rendering tribute and reverence to them and not traducing their authority "upon Every sleight occasion to prejudice their subjects against them." Magistrates in turn have a responsibility to make "holy & just Laws for the Maintenance of piety & justice," and above all to promote "the interest of religion." Chambers insisted that magistrates have no authority over people's consciences when they command things repugnant to the word of God, but subjects, he said, must not contemn their superiors. Turning to the eighth commandment Chambers explicated a minister's duty as preaching the word of God and administering the other ordinances to those from whom he received maintenance. A lawyer, he opined, must seek equity more than profit and must neither engage in a bad cause nor delay a law suit.[12] Thus catechizing could extend well beyond theological tenets and spiritual duties to embrace such subjects as the responsibilities of magistrates and subjects on the one hand and vocational duties and ethics on the other.

All catechisms underscored the importance of properly observing the sabbath, but this seems not to have been a significant problem judging from the surviving minutes. In June 1698, by which time the Presbyterians enjoyed considerable freedom of worship, the synod of Ulster found it necessary to recommend that its constituent presbyteries diligently suppress breaches of the sabbath. The hunger for preaching throughout the period gave Sundays a positive focus. The church at Burt was probably typical in having both morning and afternoon sermons on the sabbath.[13] The Presbyterians' pronounced attachment to the spoken word was a key ingredient in developing and sustaining their spiritual life, but so too were such rituals as the sacraments and fasting, wherein they made the proclamation of the gospel visual and concrete.

Sacraments, the Festal Tradition, Fasting, and Marriage

Baptism was an element of worship the Presbyterians took very seriously. Congregations without ministers requested the presbyteries to supply them with qualified men who could not only preach but also baptize.[14] In 1692 when the church at Maghera wanted to call John Thomb as its minister, the synod of Ulster recommended that Thomb, who had to go to Scotland for the conferring of his degree, exchange pulpits with James Scott of Duneane for one Sunday to enable the latter to baptize several children at Maghera; in theological terms, baptism was not necessary for salvation, but the Maghera episode clearly manifested an unwillingness to delay baptism while Thomb traveled to and from Scotland.[15] A high view of baptism is also suggested by the Antrim presbytery's decision in 1683 to permit the Antrim church, which at that time had no minister, to invite neighboring clergymen to baptize its children privately.[16] In 1686 the Carnmoney session, troubled by "the irregularity of many in this parish in coming to get the ordinance of baptism without absorbing the end and order," insisted that parents be prohibited from having their child baptized until they had brought their elder or his "token" to the minister and provided the session clerk with the child's name for insertion in the register. Another manifestation of baptism's importance was the Lagan meeting's concern in 1678 about a young man in Letterkenny who had not been baptized; Robert Campbell was instructed to confer with him and to baptize him if he was satisfied with the candidate's profession of faith.[17]

Baptism could be withheld from children whose parents had engaged in scandalous behavior for which they remained unrepentant. Several of these cases appear in the records of the Antrim meeting. In 1685 the Tyrone presbytery lodged a complaint with Antrim against Joseph Hamilton for allegedly baptizing the child of a man "who was formerly under scandall not yet remov'd"; the Antrim meeting acquitted Hamilton. The Donegore session brought a complex case before the meeting in June 1688 involving David Rippet, who eventually confessed that he had married his niece; his case had initially been presented with this query: In the event of "a child brot forth in fornication to a person now deserting the country [could a church] take satisfaction from the woman & baptize the child?" When Antrim sought the advice of the Down and Tyrone meetings, the former averred that a guilty person who had rendered satisfaction by submitting to censure could have his or her child baptized. Inasmuch as Rippet was now deceased, the presbytery deputed a representative "to deal with his incestuous relict by censure." Widow Rippet had to confess her incest before the session twice and the meeting once, but when she appeared before the latter she was "seemingly little sensible of her sin," hence the meeting referred her back to the session. There, according to the presbytery's instructions, she had to confess before the congregation, after which her child could be baptized even though she had not been absolved of her offense.[18] In a final case worthy of note, in early 1691 the Antrim presbytery pondered the matter of William Galt of Braid, who steadfastly denied allegations of adultery. Unable to determine the validity of the charge, the meeting ordered his wife to present their infant for baptism, thus according more weight to the value of baptism for the child than the possible sexual misconduct of the father.[19]

The dramatic role of the Lord's supper in the worship of Irish Presbyterians was established well before the restoration era, and in fact extended back to the 1620s and the revival movement. Parts of Scotland too experienced this revival, but festal communions diminished to some degree after 1645 when the General Assembly endorsed the Westminster Directory. In contrast to the practice of the large festal communions, the Assembly approved only one service of preparation, permitted a maximum of three ministers to officiate, recommended greater frequency of communion (thus undermining its special nature), and made no mention of a concluding post-communion service on Monday. The Assembly did not ban outdoor meetings, but these could not take place while a service was underway in a church. Festal communions revived in Scotland as part of the conventicling movement that emerged in the early 1660s, and this was probably true of Ireland as well, though details of what transpired at Presbyterian conventicles in the 1660s are scarce.[20] In March 1669 hundreds of Presbyterians in Dublin celebrated communion, commencing with a public fast on Thursday and two preparatory sermons on Saturday, and concluding with two sermons on Monday. Presumably a similar pattern characterized communion services at outdoor conventicles such as that in the Carrickfergus area in late May or early June 1670 when William Keyes and six other preachers ministered to 3,000 or 4,000 persons.[21]

During the period from the restoration to the revolution, three variations of the celebration of the Lord's supper could be found among Scottish Presbyterians in Ireland. The first involved a single congregation, such as that at Templepatrick on 16 June 1660, when preparations were elaborate and the collection totaled £6 4s., £2 15s. of which paid for wine and 17s. for bread.[22] If the Lord's supper was observed at many small conventicles, especially in the 1660s, presumably this was the type of service. Single-congregation observations in which a minister and elders officiated were probably what most concerned the Lagan presbytery in October 1672 when it determined that "the seasons of celebrating the sacrament . . . [must] be left free to every minister as shall see it convenient for the place of his charge."[23] The celebration of communion at Templepatrick in June 1670 appears to have been a grand version of this type. The 19th was designated a sabbath of preparation, and the following day prospective communicants received their tokens. Worshippers heard a preparatory sermon on Saturday and another on Sunday morning, after which the minister, thirteen elders, and six assistants administered the bread and wine. (The use of assistants to help distribute the elements was characteristic of Scottish but not English Presbyterians.) Various members were responsible to bring the elements, the table, four flagons, and napkins. Others received donations on Saturday, Sunday, and Monday at each door and from those who could not crowd into the church.[24]

The second type of celebration involved several clergymen and typically hundreds or thousands of worshippers representing several congregations, and continued the festal tradition dating from the 1620s. Such was the case at Burt, where the congregation hosted the celebration on an annual basis. In October 1678, for instance, the Wednesday preceding communion was set aside for a fast, with sermons by John Hart and Burt's own minister, William Hampton. William Trail preached on Saturday, the day of preparation, and both Hampton and David Brown preached on Sunday, leaving the closing sermon on Monday to Robert Rule. The observance varied the following year when services were held at Carnamaddy, county Antrim; a baptism as well as a sermon were featured in the Monday service. So many communicants were present for the communion rite in July 1681 that Hampton preached to those in the church and James Gordon of Comber and Robert Craghead to those without. By 1694 the session had to invite five ministers to help celebrate the Lord's supper. One member went to Belfast to obtain 36 pottles (eighteen gallons) of wine, and twelve others brought such items as flaggons, cups, linen, and ground wheat for the bread. The church paid £6 7s. 10d. for this communion, £4 17s. 6d. of which was for wine, 12s. for its transportation, 8s. for wheat, and 3s. 6d. for tickets.[25] Such quantities were probably not unique, for the observance of the Lord's supper at Templepatrick in August 1693 required fourteen gallons of wine and 48 loaves of bread.[26]

The third form of celebrating the Lord's supper involved itinerant Covenanting preachers who typically moved between Scotland and northern Ireland. Their services were emotional, their sermons often condemnatory of Stuart rule and Anglican worship, and at least in some cases worshippers had to subscribe to the Covenant before partaking of the elements. Among the preachers who presided over these services was Michael Bruce, "a fierce & pernicious Zealott," as one conformist described him. Those loyal to the Church of Ireland typically lumped the latter two forms of observing the sacrament together inasmuch as both tended to draw large crowds and often met entirely or partly outdoors. Such services incited fear in the hearts of some conformists. "In this Corner of Ulster [near Coleraine] our Presbyterian Communions are very numerous and terrible," wrote an Anglican in June 1679, citing crowds of between 3,000 and 4,000 near Coleraine and at Castlefinn, 3,000 at Ballykelly, and 2,000 outside Derry's walls. Many worshippers, according to this hostile observer, were "as malicious and bloody enemys of the Church of England as any Jesuits in the world."[27]

In the calmer conditions of the mid- and late 1690s the zeal to attend communions ebbed, underscoring the extent to which the festal communions had been both encouraged by the persecutorial conditions of the restoration period and contributors to Presbyterian survival owing to their important role in sustaining a pronounced sense of religious community. At Derry, where the congregation numbered some 2,400, only 984, some of whom were undoubtedly from other churches, received communion. Presumably, however, numerous others were present to hear the sermons.[28]

Scheduling and administering the Lord's supper sometimes posed problems. In May 1675 the Lagan presbytery had to postpone its meeting because of a communion service at Donaghmore, and three months later it scheduled its meeting at Taughboyne for the Monday following the administration of the sacrament in that congregation. During periods of government pressure some churches had to suspend communion, at least publicly. In May 1677, for instance, Robert Campbell inquired of the Lagan meeting if he could "freely & safely set about the giving of the Communion in the parish of Reigh [Ray], county Donegal, in as publick a manner as before." In this case the presbytery recommended that he proceed and gave him the latitude to delay the celebration until after the harvest.[29] In May 1684, amid the lingering effects of the Rye House investigations, the Antrim meeting asked the general committee not only if the congregations of the presbytery could return to their meetinghouses but also "about the celebrating of the Lords Supper in the most prudent way considering our present circumstances."[30]

Over time the presbyteries developed rules governing communion. The Antrim meeting seems to have taken the initiative. Although its minutes are silent for the year in question, the Lagan records for July 1678 refer to a paper from Antrim containing proposals concerning "the externall order of Communions," but no details are provided. The Down meeting formulated its own communion regulations without obtaining the concurrence of the other presbyteries, prompting the Tyrone meeting in August 1679 to ask the Antrim, Lagan, and Route presbyteries to join it in appointing "an Authoritative Committee to prevent separate actings" and to request that the Down meeting cease making rules on its own.[31] In the spring of 1684 Down asked Antrim to support its proposal for the general committee to formulate rules regulating communion, and three years later the Antrim meeting itself called for "former rules about communion [to] be observ'd to prevent numerous confluences." Clearly there was a need to regulate communion celebrations to maintain a sense of order.[32]

Another problem resulted from having a number of ministers preach and officiate at communion. The usual number was two or three, but sometimes more were involved. When the Lagan meeting arranged a communion for Ramelton in August 1677, it appointed Robert Craghead to preach on Saturday, William Hampton on Sunday morning, John Hart "if there be need of a lecture," William Trail on Sunday afternoon, and Hart on Monday. A decade later the Antrim presbytery declined an invitation to send two representatives to the Down meeting because so many of its ministers were tied up with celebrations of the Lord's supper and pulpit supply. Finally, in May 1684 the Antrim meeting limited the number of ministers at a communion service to three, with a provision excluding neighboring clergymen from participation, apparently to encourage nearby congregations to worship in their own churches. The presbytery also prohibited outdoor preaching on Sundays and Mondays "except in time of tables." The synod of Ulster similarly restricted the number of preachers to three in June 1697, though permitting neighboring ministers to preach on Saturdays and Mondays as part of the communion season. At the same time it stipulated that the ministers convene following the communion services to assess one another's doctrine and conduct "during that Work," another indication of the significance accorded to festal communions.[33]

The frequency of celebration varied owing partly to changing degrees of persecution and toleration, partly to the ability and willingness of people to travel to congregations where festal communions were held, and partly to differences between English and Scottish Presbyterians. The English celebrated the Lord's supper frequently, usually monthly or every six weeks, though some observed communion weekly or at two-month intervals. The typical Scottish congregation observed the sacrament once or twice a year, though some congregations, especially during the time of troubles, had communion once or twice, if at all, over a four-year period. Some Scottish celebrations drew communicants from widespread areas, suggesting that such worshippers may have partaken of the Lord's supper as often as eight or ten times a year late in the century. If a minister was available, the session determined the frequency of celebration. Between December 1687 and January 1689 Alexander Sinclair administered the Lord's supper five times at Waterford and four times in a nearby church that had no minister, but when the war commenced he fled to Bristol.[34] In 1698 Craghead implied that Presbyterians had not been celebrating the Lord's supper often enough. Scripture admittedly said nothing about how often the sacrament should be celebrated, but he urged that celebration should be frequent as long as communicants had sufficient time to prepare themselves spiritually. In a barbed attack on conformists he contended it was "vain to glory in the multitude and frequency of Communions, where it's known that persons of gross Ignorance, and Immoralities for licentious living, are not only admitted to the Lord's Table, but threatened, if they will not partake, however unprepared." Communion, in other words, could never be a test of politico-religious loyalty to the regime.[35]

As in Scotland and England, Irish Presbyterians exercised care with respect to those admitted to the sacrament. Craghead stipulated two prerequisites for participation: "Competent knowledge of the greatest Gospel truths" and an affirmation of belief in those principles. In practice, sessions were no less interested in the conduct of prospective communicants. At Carnmoney in April 1686, the session, preparing to celebrate communion after a lengthy period of "desolation" without a minister, instructed all elders to inquire "concerning scandalous persons and delinquents in their several quarters that they may be brought to the session to give satisfaction . . . and likewise that they enquire concerning each as not testified for from the places they came last from," that is, that they produce testimonials from their previous churches attesting to their good behavior. Prospective communicants who passed the examination received lead tokens typically made by each church from its own mold. Visitors from other congregations who intended to partake of the elements procured tokens from their ministers or elders who were present or brought certificates indicating their fitness to commune. Sessions took their responsibilities seriously. At Burt in July 1694, Joanna Stinson received a token only after she promised to give satisfaction before the congregation for her "uncleanness."[36] The Lagan meeting demanded an inquiry in 1679 when it received reports that a reputed convert from Catholicism had been admitted to the Lord's supper by Presbyterians in both Down and Antrim before he had publicly renounced his adherence to Rome. In 1700 both the Belfast presbytery and the synod of Ulster had to mediate a dispute between Alexander McCracken and his session at Lisburn on the one hand and Robert Stewart and his father on the other after the session excluded the Stewarts from communion for allegedly casting aspersions on McCracken. In this case tokens had become weapons, inducing the synod to demand that the parties "bury all their Differences in Oblivion, and abstain from all Imitating Reflections & Cavills hereafter, otherwise they shold be look'd upon as disorderly, & dealt with accordingly."[37] In some cases worshippers without tokens could attend the services despite being excluded from communion, but they had to position themselves so as not to hinder communicants moving to and from the table. In other cases, as at Templepatrick, those without tokens could not enter the church.[38]

Like the larger festal communions, Presbyterian fasts caused periodic consternation for magistrates, partly because they defied royal proscription, partly because thousands of Presbyterians in a particular region, such as the Lagan, observed a fast simultaneously. Had the authorities succeeded in seizing the Lagan meeting's records in 1681,[39] their fears about fasts would probably have been substantially assuaged. Both public and private fasts were intensely spiritual occasions, sometimes focusing on humiliation, sometimes on thanksgiving. Presbyterians were sensitive to the government's concern about fasts and apparently restricted their observance to private fasting in the period preceding the *de facto* indulgence. The general committee that met in the spring or summer of 1672 asked the meetings to appoint private fasts, each of which would be observed by three or four ministers. In August the Lagan presbytery accordingly divided its clergymen into three groups for this purpose, and private fasts were observed twice in the ensuing months.[40] The Presbyterians restored public fasts only after careful deliberation. After the general committee asked each presbytery in the fall of 1672 to submit its views on the resumption of public fasting, the Lagan meeting, "considering the difficulties of the way of managing of it at this juncture of time," delegated Hart to write to Dublin to seek Semple's advice. By November Semple had reported that Presbyterians "in other places" were observing public fasts without hindrance from the magistrates. Indeed, on 1 October the Antrim presbytery had appointed a public fast; the preceding month the fast had been private.[41]

Presbyterians remained sensitive to the government's position regarding fasts. On the occasion of the discovery of the alleged Popish plot the Lagan meeting resolved to hold a fast on 28 November, but if a magistrate designated any preceding day for a fast, the latter would have precedence. Moreover, if a magistrate subsequently appointed a fast or day of thanksgiving because of the discovery, it too would be observed. When William and Mary ordered a weekly fast on Fridays in September 1690, the Lagan presbytery complied. With a view to the expected sitting of Parliament the same presbytery urged the synod to appoint a public fast in 1697, and the synod concurred unless the government itself designated one before the first Wednesday in July. Again in June 1702 the synod recommended that its ministers observe a fast as soon as the government announced one.[42] What had originally been a source of tension between the Presbyterians and the authorities became a mutually observed ritual with political and patriotic overtones under William and Mary.

Presbyterians observed fasts for a variety of reasons ranging from sacramental preparation to repentance for sins, though bad weather and hope for conditions conducive to planting and harvesting were the most common.[43] Inclement weather was sometimes linked to sinful behavior, as in August 1673 when the Antrim meeting called for a fast, "taking to their serious consideration the sad and dreadfull evidences of Godes wrath appearing in the unseasonablenes of the weather and withall the manifold sinnes wee stand under the guilt of and the danger that the Church and worke of God in these landes is under."[44] In May 1674 the Lagan meeting proclaimed a day of public humiliation because of a famine which it blamed on "the crying sins of the Land." On several occasions presbytery records attribute subsequent improvements in the weather to fasts, but normally the purported effects, if any, are not mentioned.[45] Fasts were observed during the time of troubles, when Parliament met in 1693 and 1697, and to seek divine intervention on behalf of persecuted Protestants on the continent in 1698 and 1700.[46] The difficulties of propagating Protestantism in Ireland sometimes occasioned fasting, as in the Antrim meeting in November 1673: "The brethren taking to their serious consideration the very great hasard the worke of God in these landes is in and with all how unworthie wee have walked and yet doe walk of our mercies and priviledges and particularlie our litle fruitfullnes under and suitablenes to the Gospell, and taking to heart the other manifold greivous sinnes that every where abound, and particularlie within our own boundes, doe appoint Wednesday the 19th. instant to be set apart for solemne publicke fasting, prayer and humiliation."[47]

An undated manuscript entitled "Some Considerations About Fasting" by a Presbyterian in Ireland or Scotland contends that the reasons for a public fast should be clearly articulated, "for if one party shall fast taking the causes to their sense and an other taking them to their [different sense] it is a scorning of that holy exercise of fasting."[48] Public fasting entailed a pronounced sense of communal purpose—a spiritual direction or goal in which all shared. Typically the fasts appointed in the minutes of the Lagan and Antrim presbyteries and the synod of Ulster identify the reasons for their observance. Sometimes these relate to specific local problems, such as a spirit's reputed appearance in James Shaw's family at Carnmoney in September 1672, supposedly causing distemper in Shaw's body and confusion in the parish, or "the greatest outbreaking of prophanity" at Raphoe and Letterkenny in or before January 1680.[49] Occasionally the reasons for a fast were very general, as in November 1689, when the Antrim presbytery cited "the many evidences of God's wrath against us," perhaps referring to the political upheaval, or in December 1674, when the Lagan meeting called for a fast because of "the desolations which the Lord hath lately made among us."[50]

Several times the reasons for a fast were multiple in nature and precisely laid out. Such was the case in July 1673 when the Lagan meeting cited four causes for a fast: heavy rains which threatened to destroy the crops; the propagation of the gospel in the world; "the calling of the Jewes & fulness of the Gentiles, & the ruine of the Turk, & Antichrist the

Pope of Rome, & particularly the purging of these Kingdomes of Popery & Superstition"; and prayer for God to "pour out much of his Spirit" on the king and lesser magistrates. This fast neatly combined natural phenomena, global awareness, millenarianism, and concern for government at all levels. Much later, in June 1698, the synod of Ulster appointed a fast with an eye to inclement weather in recent years at planting and harvest time, famine in Scotland, the persecution of the Huguenots in France, and the prevalence of sin among Irish Presbyterians.[51]

The fullest exposition occurred in February 1681 when the Lagan meeting prepared for a fast that prompted the Privy Council to command Ormond to suppress similar observances in the future as violations of royal authority. The presbytery divided the "Causes of Humiliation" into three categories—sins, judgments, and petitions. Included in the sweeping catalogue of sins were atheism, blasphemy, apostasy, perjury, the slighting and breaking of covenants, defection from the work of reformation, "Unparallelled Profanity," sabbath-breaking, sexual infidelity, inebriety, covetousness, and "Our Stupidity under all the threatenings of wo[e] & desolation imminent." This was a typical list of failings denounced by religious moralists, particularly those in the Puritan tradition; only the reference to broken "solemn & personal Engagements, Covenants, & Vows," with its evocation of the Solemn League and Covenant, could have concerned magistrates. The judgments targeted Catholicism, a particularly sensitive subject on an island the majority of whose inhabitants were Gaelic Irish. The meeting denounced "the Mystery of Iniquity & Hellish Popery," warned of the imminent threat of another "bloody Massacre," and lamented the plight of Protestants throughout Europe, especially in Britain, France, and Ireland. The inclusion of Britain was significant in view of the struggle in England over the presumed succession of the Catholic duke of York. Lagan Presbyterians concluded with a fivefold petition for God to grant repentance and pardon to people for these abominations; to stop the inundation of popery; to revive the work of reformation in the hearts of the people; to preserve the king and his subjects from the Catholic conspiracies; and to "continue pure Gospell-Ordinances amongst us." [52]

The frequency of fasts varied considerably. The Lagan meeting called for six public fasts between August 1673 and February 1681 and another nine between April 1691 and August 1697. In addition a number of private fasts were held in conjunction with meetings of the presbytery during the first period and fasts were observed by local churches in both periods.[53] Between September 1688 and March 1691, an obviously critical time, the Antrim meeting observed fourteen fasts, an average of nearly one every two months. Presbyterians in Antrim appear to have been more inclined to fast than their compatriots in the Lagan. In April 1675 the Antrim presbytery called for "the praying people of each congregation (five or six meetings together in severall quarters of the parish)" to keep private fasts biweekly for at least several months. A decade later the meeting instructed each minister to remind the "praying people" of his parish to fulfill their duty to fast and pray, "which is now resolv'd on to be a continu'd practice." Amid the turmoil of the revolution Antrim Presbyterians resolved that every minister should observe a fast once a week, and in June 1691, against a backdrop of war, the presbytery directed that a fast be observed the first Friday of every month "during the Campaign." [54]

The anonymous document "Some Considerations About Fasting" stipulated that a public fast could be appointed by either the church or the civil magistrate but reserved the right to ignore a magisterially designated fast if it were for inappropriate causes such as an unjustifiable war or "the preservation of an unlawfull conqurse." Presbyterians in Ulster refused to observe a fast day in the spring of 1679. In practice, both presbyteries and synods (including their predecessor, the general committee) had the authority to designate fasts in Ireland, and in February 1692 the Lagan meeting authorized each minister to determine whether or not to observe one.[55] A presbytery's right to do this without the concurrence of the other meetings, however, was disputed. Whereas the Lagan meeting insisted on every presbytery's ability to appoint fasts within its jurisdiction, the Tyrone meeting argued to the contrary. Sixteen months later, in December 1680, the Lagan meeting was sensitive to Tyrone's position in seeking the concurrence of the other presbyteries to approve a public fast; in the meantime it called for private fasts among its own congregations.[56] Ironically, by the time Lagan heard from the Tyrone and Route meetings in February 1681, each had already observed a public fast. Moreover both the Tyrone and Down presbyteries had concluded that each meeting should appoint its own fast, for "as matters now stand its not fit to have our Fast all in one day throughout the five Meetings." After the Coleraine synod held a fast on its own authority, the synod of Belfast advised in June 1700 that henceforth no fast be designated without its concurrence. The principle of cooperation was not new, for fasts had been jointly proclaimed by the meetings of Tyrone and Antrim in 1675 and by Down and Antrim in 1689.[57]

Little information survives concerning details of fast observance, though the core was preaching, prayer, and abstinence from food and daily toil. When the Lagan meeting called in November 1676 for more frequent fasts at the congregational level it recommended that each minister seek the assistance of one or two neighboring clergymen. The following February the presbytery deputed Hart and Craghead to help Thomas Drummond at Ramelton. When possible, therefore, fast days would have featured multiple sermons, as at Ardstraw in early 1678; the Lagan meeting appointed Craghead to preach in the morning and John Rowatt in the afternoon on a day of humiliation "for their long desolation & severall dissappoyntments."[58] As with most Presbyterian worship, the spoken word was the focal point of fasting, but the communal aspect of the rite was no less important because of its enhancement of group identity.

The sermon was also part of the marriage ceremony, at least from the early 1670s onward. Prior to the commencement of *de facto* toleration Presbyterian marriages presumably occurred in conventicles or perhaps at small family gatherings. By 1673 the bishops, unwilling to recognize Presbyterian nuptials, were prosecuting nonconformists for fornication. To counter this the Lagan meeting in November 1673 asked its moderator, Robert Rule, to inquire if the other presbyteries were solemnizing marriages publicly and proclaiming them not only among fellow Presbyterians but also "with the Curats." By January the meetings of Route, Antrim, and Tyrone had reported that nearly everyone was publicly performing marriages, hence Lagan followed suit.[59] With the resumption of persecution in the early 1680s public proclamation again ceased, at least among the congregations of the Antrim presbytery, which sought the general committee's advice in May 1687. Six months later the presbytery resumed the practice of publicly proclaiming the intention of people to wed, but only after consulting the meetings of Down and Tyrone. In the absence of objections to public proclamation, the Antrim presbytery permitted "every one to do therein as conveniency will allow," presumably a recognition that in some locations private celebrations were still necessary.[60]

The session was responsible to ensure that marriage was properly contracted. At Burt the session not only required one man to make a public confession of "the sinfull and scandelous way of his mariag" but also rebuked the parents of both bride and groom "for ther scandalous Cariag therein." Two years later the session examined another man about his marriage. The precise nature of the offense in these cases is not stated, though it might have involved prenuptial pregnancy, handfasting, or marriage in the Church of Ireland. A member of the Carnmoney church confessed the latter offense in 1691. In another Burt case a father asked the session to prohibit his son from marrying a particular woman; although the session concurred with the father's judgment, it referred the case to the presbytery, but the couple eventually had a curate marry them.[61]

Between 1699 and 1701 the synod of Ulster standardized marriage practices, another indication that the Scottish Presbyterians had evolved into a denominational church. Henceforth "when any of our People desires to be married by a Minister of our Perswausion, none to whom they come shall refuse to marry them, in an orderly way, as has been done by us formerly, nor scruple to give their Judgement concer[n]ing the Forms & Modes of Joining People in Marraige, shewing which are Sinfull, which not, when desir'd by their People so to do." The need for this resolution indicates that at least some Presbyterian ministers had been sending couples to conformist clergy to be married. All Presbyterian clerics were now to explain the differences between Anglican and Presbyterian marriages when asked to do so. The synod also insisted that no couple be married until they had been proclaimed on three successive sabbaths, and that a minister who violated this regulation be rebuked and suspended at the discretion of his presbytery. A couple belonging to a church without a minister had to seek the requisite proclamations in a neighboring parish. A year later, in June 1702, the synod admonished four clergymen for violating this rule.[62] Thus the Scottish Presbyterians, confident of their institutional identity, entered the eighteenth century firmly resolved to uphold their rights to perform marriages, and to do so in a public setting befitting the status of a full-fledged church. Marriage, the sacraments, and fasting were spiritual rites that bound the Scottish Presbyterians in a distinctive religious community, the behavioral standards of which were maintained by the imposition of discipline.

Discipline: Governing the Wayward

Because the Church of Ireland regarded the imposition of discipline as its province, its exercise by the Presbyterians contributed to Anglican disaffection toward nonconformists. Perhaps most magistrates were more tolerant of nonconformists in part because the latter held their members to a high standard of conduct, punishing such offenses as sexual license and inebriety. With respect to their social behavior and assistance to the needy the overwhelming majority of nonconformists must have been model citizens. Nor can the government have missed the point that their subordination to this discipline was voluntary, with social pressure and religious conviction the only forces inducing compliance. Adherence to nonconformity was not a license to libertine behavior.

Much of the effectiveness of Presbyterian discipline depended on its public administration, but this could be imprudent for a group reliant on the government for *de facto* toleration. In August 1672, for instance, the Antrim presbytery referred the case of an adulteress in the Antrim congregation back to the session, "the tyme being such that the brethrene could not call such persones so frequently before them as usually." This was in keeping with a proposal from the general committee, which was chary of antagonizing the government. A year later the same presbytery summoned a Braid man accused of incest with his aunt; hitherto it had only been possible to admonish the couple privately. Public punishment was still feasible in 1674, when the Antrim meeting instructed the Braid session to deal further with an adulterer the presbytery itself had already rebuked.[63] What the Lagan meeting called the "full rigor" of discipline had not yet been restored by the summer of 1675 when it asked the general committee to ascertain the judgment of the other presbyteries as to whether this could now be done. The following May Lagan concluded that each minister should restore the exercise of discipline gradually, "as he can win to it, in his congregation with conveniency: & that there shall be a mutuall forbearance of judging one another in this matter." The period when public discipline was injudicious had created a situation in which at least some congregations were reluctant to see its revival. Restoration came slowly, for eight months later, in January 1677, the Lagan meeting exhorted its ministers to proceed with this work, suggesting, however, that before any pastor "bring any Scandalous person to the publike, he is to take advice of the Meeting about it."[64]

In the mid-1680s the public exercise of discipline again became imprudent, though in May 1687 the general committee concluded that discipline could be revived where this could be done without "palpable inconveniency." Public notice of impending discipline was to be made only in the local congregation, and the presbytery was to be consulted first in difficult cases. Caution was the order of the day, but by November the Antrim meeting saw no impediments to "the laudable custom of censuring scandalous persons, in publick." Antrim informed its fellow presbyteries of Down and Tyrone of its action. In April 1688 the general committee approved the public exercise of discipline as long as ministers consulted their sessions in advance.[65]

The surviving records say relatively little about the standards of conduct to which Presbyterians held themselves. Sexual relations were limited to marriage, with fornication, adultery, and incest prohibited. The synod of Ulster set standards of apparel for the clergy and their families, insisting that it be "grave & decent" rather than gaudy, vain, or "sordid," and that "powderings, vain Cravats, Half Shirts, & the like" be avoided. For the laity moderation and simplicity were the ideals, but the sessions, judging from the few records that remain, seem not to have dealt with this problem. Inebriety was of course condemned, and the clergy were exhorted to shun sumptuous meals on communion Mondays and ordination days, when the clerical temptation to celebrate must have been substantial. In speech, slander and profanity were unacceptable. So too were such offenses as failure to pay debts, commercial dealings on a fast day, desertion of a spouse, abortion, and disruptive behavior in a congregation.[66]

The overwhelming number of disciplinary cases involved sexual offenses, especially fornication and adultery. During the space of a month and a half in late April and May 1686, the Carnmoney session dealt with ten female and six male fornicators. Fornication offenses also dominate the records of the Burt session. The sessions handled most such cases, whereas the presbyteries manifested a pronounced interest in adultery, probably because it was not simply a sexual offense but a defilement of marriage. Between August 1672 and May 1675 the Antrim meeting dealt with fourteen alleged adulterers but no fornicators, and in the period from May 1683 to June 1691 the respective numbers were 33 and seven. Lagan considered the cases of nine adulterers and two fornicators between November 1673 and April 1681, and the numbers for the period from January 1694 to July 1698 were 21 and eleven respectively.[67] The number of accused adulterers and fornicators for Antrim and Lagan may have been greater, for some cases are described only as scandals.[68] During the periods noted, Antrim discussed three cases of incest and Lagan one.[69]

The punishment of fornication and adultery varied. In most instances the offender had to confess to the session and three times to the congregation, but in some cases an acknowledgment to the session on three separate occasions was sufficient. At Carnmoney a guilty person had to repent before the session, undergo counseling with an elder, and then appear before the session.[70] Punishment could be less onerous, as when George Boyle of Carnmoney was absolved after only two appearances before the session because his fornication was an old scandal. Similarly, when a woman in the Taughboyne church confessed she had committed adultery four years previously, the Lagan meeting advised her to confess only before the session "lest the scandall might arise of new," but if rumors spread she would have to make a public statement to the congregation. Some offenders received harsher treatment than the norm. The Lagan meeting insisted that a Ballindrait man confess his adultery to the congregation by voluntarily rising in the church rather than waiting to be called. Someone who committed a sexual offense with a person in another parish had to confess publicly in each place; Margaret Nily, who was guilty of fornication with men in Taughboyne and Burt, had to confess before each congregation one time.[71]

Only the more serious cases, especially those involving adultery, went to the presbyteries. They typically rebuked and exhorted an offender before referring a case back to the minister and session for the requisite public acknowledgement and absolution.[72] In a few cases a presbytery insisted on an offender's reappearance before it or a report of a session's action prior to absolution. The meetings sometimes found professions of repentance inadequate and demanded further evidence of remorse, as in the case of a Braid couple who were not "sufficientlye sensible off their fall."[73] Not surprisingly, some offenders were slow to appear before the sessions, but the latter were normally accommodating in providing additional opportunities for repentance. When two Donegore men refused "to give satisfaction for fornication," the Antrim meeting ordered the minister and session to deal further with them, and if the two remained recalcitrant "their names & scandal [were to] be published openly in the congregation."[74] Shaming was the core of Presbyterian punishment, but where an unbaptised child was involved, refusal to perform the rite without adequate parental remorse was probably a greater penalty as well as an inducement to repent.[75]

A minority of the accused professed innocence, and sometimes a session or a presbytery permitted these people to attempt to clear themselves by compurgation. Some, such as a Carnmoney man in 1692, successfully pled that they were victims of unjust slander. The issue was sometimes complicated because of paternity questions. Presbyteries referred certain cases back to the sessions for resolution, probably because of easier recourse to witnesses. In an unusual variation of this procedure, Lagan referred an adultery case to the Ardstraw session in 1697 at the request of a man who wanted an investigation to clear his name.[76] In August 1688 Antrim pondered one of the more difficult cases: On her deathbed a Braid woman had accused James Cathcart of having fathered her child out of wedlock, but child support was not a factor because the infant had also died. Cathcart swore his innocence in a civil court and now sought to do the same in a Presbyterian tribunal, claiming to have a witness. The presbytery remanded the case to the Braid session and asked to be informed of the outcome.[77] Compurgation did not guarantee acquittal. In 1691 the Antrim presbytery considered allegations against William Campbell, "he seeming to be stupid," and Janet Gardner. When Campbell insisted on his innocence the presbytery ordered that he purge himself by taking an oath in the presence of the Carnmoney congregation "with certification." The call for witnesses must have been sobering, for the couple confessed their guilt and submitted to censure. Another couple professed their innocence of adultery, with the husband contending he had only kissed another man's wife in his presence and spent time alone with her; the Antrim meeting referred the case to the session of Larne and Carnmoney.[78]

Although premarital sex among couples intending to marry was common in early modern Europe, Presbyterians refused to sanction the practice. If caught, couples who had sexual relations and subsequently married were punished for fornication; some prevaricated in unsuccessful attempts to claim their marriages had predated copulation. Young ladies who made love to men promising marriage were undoubtedly common.[79]

Several unusual cases merit comment. The Ballymena session required Antrim's assistance in a case involving Andrew Boyd, who had allegedly committed adultery with Marian McQuistine, impregnated her, and subsequently gave her six pence with which to purchase a drug to induce abortion. Because Boyd had a good reputation, the presbytery suggested he be permitted to attempt to clear himself by compurgation before the session. In another case, at Burt in 1695 Janet Surgen admitted to having borne a child sired by a man to whom she was not married, but she insisted the sexual encounter had not been "a voluntarie act but a rapture [i.e., rape]." In return for permission to have the infant baptized, she and the father had to pledge to educate the child, and she also had to promise to repent if the session proved she had voluntarily engaged in sex rather than being raped.[80] The records include several cases of adultery between Presbyterians and Gaelic Irish, presumably

Catholics. The most mysterious case involved Isabell Hill of Ballyeaston, county Antrim, who confessed an adulterous relationship "together with other most heinous aggrevating sins, accompan[y]ing the said adultery"—offenses deemed too horrific to record. Whatever the crimes, forgiveness was possible because she appeared "somewhat broke[n]," hence the Antrim meeting rebuked her and remitted her case to the Ballyeaston session. There was forgiveness too for a Killead woman who relapsed into adultery. The problem of deserting spouses probably accounted for a case at Burt in 1694 in which a man faced charges of unlawful cohabitation with a woman whose husband was thought to be alive.[81]

The most celebrated adultery case involved the Ballyeaston minister Stafford Pettigrew, who reportedly had an adulterous relationship before he was licensed to preach. The case went all the way to the synod of Ulster, which investigated in July 1699. Interrogated by a committee appointed by the synod, Pettigrew professed his innocence, "unless sporting & rumaging, as he term'd it were judged scandalous." Summoned before the full synod, he listened as the moderator, Hugh Kirkpatrick, set forth "the Crime alledg'd against Him, the Damning Nature of it, the Danger of covering it by Dissimulation, the Necessity of Repentance, and of Glorifying God by a free & True Confession." When Pettigrew would confess nothing more, the synod adjudged him guilty of "leavity with the Woman," rebuked him, and appointed another committee to investigate further under the auspices of the Antrim presbytery. When the synod convened in June 1700 it heard the committee's report, found Pettigrew innocent of adultery, and instructed Fulk White to preach a sermon at Ballyeaston in which he conveyed the synod's verdict to the congregation.[82]

Non-sexual disciplinary cases covered a wide range of behavior as suggested by the records of the Carnmoney session in the early 1690s. Inebriety seems not to have been a major problem. The session absolved a member of the church who became inebriated at a fair in 1692 after he confessed and promised to behave. Another case involved a man who got drunk on a fast day in 1690, the same year three other members of the same church traded with soldiers on a fast day, subsequently confessed, promised to be more watchful in the future, and were absolved. The session meted out the same disciplinary treatment to a man who bought stolen goods from the Danes, whereas a man who confessed to a long absence from the public ordinances had only to promise to attend more frequently.[83] An adequate expression of repentance coupled with recognition of sessional authority was nearly always enough to satisfy session members, whereas obstinate refusal to yield to a session was in itself a separate offense.[84]

One slander case attracted considerable notoriety. In 1694 William Liston, minister at Letterkenny, filed formal charges in the Lagan presbytery against John Semple for allegedly libeling him. Semple had reputedly called Liston a common drunkard, a babbling fool, and a base cur; accepted bribes from rich offenders who wanted to avoid shaming; preached such railing sermons that people were incapacitated from serving God; called the elders rogues, liars, and knaves; defamed his predecessor and abused his widow; robbed orphans of their inheritance; and failed to undertake pastoral visits. Semple had even allegedly threatened to write a biography of Liston aimed at disgracing him. Summoned to defend himself, Semple denied only that he had called Liston a common drunkard, though Semple's witnesses testified to the contrary. After hearing witnesses on both sides and weighing the evidence, the presbytery pronounced Semple guilty of gross slander, reproved him sharply, and ordered him to acknowledge his guilt before the Letterkenny congregation. Semple refused to make this confession, repeatedly ignored the presbytery's summons to reappear before it, and ceased attending Presbyterian services. He tried to make peace in November 1695, by which point Liston was dead, but the presbytery demanded a more explicit acknowledgment of guilt than he was willing to make.[85]

Other disciplinary offenses concerned marriage. For marrying in the Church of Ireland—which undermined the community's distinctive character and called into question one of its basic rites—one could be haled before a Presbyterian session, but the validity of the marriage was not questioned and a manifestation of repentance was sufficient to obtain forgiveness. Citations in the minutes for disorderly conduct in marriage could refer to Anglican nuptials or domestic discord; the records are sometimes imprecise.[86] The Lagan meeting considered a single case of desertion in this period. The circumstances are murky, but one Daniel Carmichael left his wife and family in Scotland and came to Ireland. Replying to appeals from ministers in the Church of Scotland, the Lagan presbytery asked him to explain his action, in response to which he promised to send for his wife. When Scottish clergy forwarded additional charges, Lagan requested that he reappear, but this he apparently never did.[87]

Ministers and sessions were also responsible for maintaining harmony in their churches. Antrim succinctly enunciated the governing principle: "For people of divisive principles let Min[iste]rs be carefull cautelously to refute such by instilling sound knowledge of the contrary principles by diligence in doctrine & holy conversation to recomend the truth upon hearts, & if any prove wild rather respight than tamper with them."[88] At the local level the session appointed a small number of members to mediate disputes on a case by case basis, a method similar to that employed by Friends. Refusal to subject oneself to the session could result in a citation to appear before the presbytery,[89] and on occasion the meetings therefore found it necessary to deal with divisions that threatened congregational harmony.[90]

Ministers subjected themselves to appropriate standards of conduct through a process known as private censure, which occurred from time to time at gatherings of a presbytery. On these occasions each clergyman left the room while his colleagues assessed his conduct and doctrine and then decided whether to approve them. The process concluded with words of exhortation, admonition, and encouragement to the ministers. The practice apparently varied from presbytery to presbytery; indeed the Antrim minutes do not mention private censures. Not until June 1701 was the practice regularized when the synod of Ulster approved a proposal from the synod of Coleraine that presbyteries conduct private censures biannually and sessions at least once a year.[91] Private censure was a manifestation of the importance of discipline as well as a means of upholding fidelity to theological purity as defined by the Westminster Confession of Faith. Its regularization in 1701 was another manifestation of the emergence of the Scottish Presbyterians as a denominational church.

The shortage of clergy did not result in decreased standards for ministerial candidates or a failure to discipline the few clerics who strayed. When the people in the Sligo area, having no pastor, petitioned Lagan in 1672 to ordain William Patterson, it asked "that meekenes may be used towards him." But the presbytery judged Patterson's practices scandalous, sinful, and dangerous because he was preaching and baptizing without having undergone trials and ordination. Lagan therefore instructed the Sligo group to regard him as an intruder rather than a lawful minister. Even with a Catholic on the throne and Protestantism's future uncertain, the general committee in May 1687 asked the presbyteries to warn sessions and congregations of "vagrant pretended ministers," a classic example of institutional control over the pastorate.[92]

One of the more serious cases involved William Forsayth, whom the synod of Ulster prohibited from preaching in 1696. Nevertheless he continued to do so in the presbytery of Tyrone and was publicly cited in the pulpit at Monaghan to appear before the synod in June 1697. He had previously been condemned by the synod of Glasgow, whose declaration was now read to the Ulster synod. In lieu of appearing Forsayth sent "a railing letter," which was read to the synod. The latter, deeming it essential "to secure the Country from his wicked Way," ordered a proclamation read in every congregation he visited instructing people not to "own, entertain, or hear him." He was again cited to appear before the next synod, but he denied its authority as well as that of the Tyrone presbytery. In June 1698 the synod demanded that Presbyterians disown him as "an obstinate, scandalous Person, . . . to be looked upon as none of ours, nor to partake of sealing Ordinances amongst us, much less to be looked upon as a Preacher of the Gospel, being never licens'd so to do."[93]

In a less severe case, the Lagan presbytery suspended William Holmes in 1697 because of his dealings with a Mrs. Rowatt and her daughter. Accused of "scandalous carriage" in their house, he was cited before a joint meeting of the presbyteries of Derry and Strabane, where he confessed and manifested sufficient repentance to have the suspension lifted. This was done by a representative of the presbyteries in a sermon in Holmes's church at Urney.[94] Holmes's offense was probably a sexual indiscretion for which his penitence was adjudged sufficient in contrast to the much more heinous act of unauthorized preaching of which Patterson and Forsayth were guilty. In addition Forsayth flagrantly defied presbyterian authority, for which he was condemned at the highest level and publicly disowned. These cases manifest the importance Irish Presbyterians accorded to the legitimate, authorized preaching of the word on the one hand and the maintenance of discipline and authority on the other. The former involved the heart of their mission in society, the latter the structure that enabled them to fulfill that mission in keeping with what they perceived to be the dictates of the gospel.

Social Responsibility

The Presbyterians' sense of social responsibility involved not only their self-imposed disciplinary system to monitor behavior according to standards more rigorous than those of society in general, but also the regular provision of charitable relief and, where possible, educational opportunities. Administering charity was primarily the local congregation's responsibility, but the presbyteries considered the more serious cases, and once the synod of Ulster began meeting, it was occasionally involved in matters of relief. In June 1697 it pronounced itself satisfied with the charitable work of the presbyteries after they reported they were diligently collecting and expanding funds for "pious uses."[95]

A sense of giving patterns at the local level can be ascertained in the session records of Templepatrick, Kirkdonald (Dundonald), and Burt. At Templepatrick in the period from 28 March to 4 December 1660 charitable gifts were made on 22 occasions to 38 recipients; some of the latter undoubtedly obtained assistance on more than one occasion, hence the number of people who received help was presumably fewer than 38. The average gift was nearly 3s., with the largest being 10s. and the smallest 3d. The donations totaled £5 10s. 4d., with the average per collection being slightly more than 5s. (These figures exclude a grant of £2 5s. to a student at St. Andrews University.) At Kirkdonald the average collection in the period from 7 January to 22 April 1682 was only 3s. 6d., and this dropped in the early months of 1683 (6 January to 16 March) to a mere 1s. per collection, probably reflecting the crackdown on dissent. During the seventeen months terminating on 13 May 1680 the Burt congregation gave £7 13s. 4d. to 34 recipients; again the number of people who received help was undoubtedly smaller. The average gift was 4s. 6d., with 3s. the smallest and 6s. the largest. In 1691 the same church gave slightly less than 4s. per collection, and this barely increased in 1694.

At Burt men were more often recipients of aid than women: in the seventeen months ending 13 May 1680 help went to men nineteen times, women thirteen times, and children on three occasions. Yet at the communion service on 28 July 1695, of the 21 recipients of charity fourteen were women, five of them widows. Among those helped by the congregation were a man who lost his possessions in a fire, the ill and blind, an elderly lame man, and two fathers (probably widowers) who received money to pay for nursing their children. A few people, such as Martha Arnot, received weekly pensions (5d. in April 1683); when she died the church contributed 3s. for her funeral. Others received help with funeral expenses as well. The church gave one man 6d. for spectacles and provided charity to a boy whose tongue had been cut out by Gaelic Irish bandits, or Tories. Most relief apparently went to needy Presbyterians, but a poor boy from England and a stranger from Newtown Limavady, county Derry, were among the outsiders who benefited.

The Kirkdonald church similarly bestowed funds on widows and other women, the elderly victims of Tory violence (including a Gaelic Irish man), the victim of a fire, and the mentally and physically ill, including a boy "diseased in his feet." Help was also extended to a poor member who had to bury his wife, to disbanded soldiers and a poor seaman, and to a "poor distressed man who had suffered shipwrack of all he had." There was assistance too for a man whose goods had been distrained because of his nonconformity, for a man unable to pay his hearth tax, and to a "Grecian priest socald." Church members responded positively to outsiders who carried letters of commendation from such magistrates as Granard and the mayors of Carrickfergus and Derry; Derry's mayor, for instance, had written on behalf of a needy Huguenot.[96]

The cases the presbyteries took up were more serious than those handled by the sessions and therefore required greater expenditure of funds. On various occasions each minister received instructions to bring a specific amount of money, typically a shilling or more, to his presbytery to assist a designated person. The amount could be greater, such as the 5s. required of the Antrim clergy to aid one Andrew Jackson in 1683, or the 6s. assessed the Lagan clergy to compensate a Coleraine man who had paid legal fees to defend a poor man "from that officiall [church?] court."[97] Compared to the modest sums dispensed by sessions, those provided by presbyteries could therefore be fairly substantial. The Antrim meeting doled out £2 to a handful of needy people between 1687 and 1691 and an ill Belfast woman received £1 10s. in 1683, though most gifts were smaller.[98] A major exception was the ongoing assistance provided to orphans, particularly those whose fathers had been ministers. This was a special situation, closely related to a church's obligation to support a clergyman's widow. When many churches had difficulty raising funds to pay their ministers, the added burden of assisting widows and orphans of deceased clergy inevitably led to numerous cases of late payment and the need for intervention by the presbyteries.[99]

The demand for such monies limited support for other needy people, whose level of assistance and priority were secondary to those of ministerial widows and orphans. The best documented case is that of Francis Simpson, whose father Gilbert had been ordained at Ballyclare in 1655 and continued to minister following his ejection in 1661. After the latter's death around 1670 the Lagan meeting supported Francis, "a very hopefull boy" who was "prudent & sober & diligent in his studies," while other presbyteries assisted his sibling. When the general committee asked the presbyteries in 1674 to expand the number of orphans they supported, Lagan objected "because of the great difficulty we finde already in maintaining these we have on hand." Moreover it instructed its commissioners to the next general committee to demonstrate that it could not continue to supply Francis without assistance from other meetings in the amount of £2. To support Francis at Strabane required £5 *per annum*, hence Lagan asked its churches to contribute 4s. 6d.[100] To reduce this burden the presbytery considered placing him in the family of a Mistress Stewart, who would receive a £3 *per annum* subsidy, but nothing seems to have come of this, and in July 1675 Lagan asked the general committee to have the other presbyteries assume responsibility for Francis on the grounds that he was "more theirs than ours." This too came to naught, for the following May Lagan complained that each of its ministers had contributed 9s. *per annum* for the past four years while members of other presbyteries had donated only 3s. for Francis's sibling.[101]

Discussing the needs of the poor was a time-consuming business for the presbyteries. In April 1674 the Antrim presbytery, complaining that discussions of poor relief diverted attention from other business, instructed ministers to cease bringing the needy to the meetings and instead to provide assistance at the parish level. This action may have eliminated the attendance of the poor at the presbytery's meetings but it did not obviate consideration of the plight of the needy. The gap in the Antrim minutes between July 1675 and December 1682 prevents us from knowing if further reform measures were introduced in this period, but in May 1683 the presbytery attempted to solve the nagging problem of churches that were remiss in submitting their contributions by directing each clergyman to bring 1s. to each meeting "to be put in a stock purse for relief of objects of charity."[102] The common fund undoubtedly proved to be useful but it did not cure the problem of negligent churches and ministers, for in June 1688 the presbytery proclaimed that clergy who did not attend meetings and contribute to collections were to be censured. The problems inherent in relieving the needy had prompted Antrim the previous spring to ask the general committee whether individual ministers could recommend persons for relief "without their bounds." Reflecting the trend for more centralization, the Tyrone meeting replied that presbyteries but not ministers should make such recommendations.[103] Indeed, Lagan had begun to curtail the ability of individual clergy to provide relief as early as October 1678 when it enacted that no minister could donate funds from "the poors box" to strangers without the presbytery's authorization even if those strangers carried commendations.[104]

The demand for poor relief necessitated cooperation among the presbyteries and therefore contributed to the evolution toward a denominational church. Despite the eventual complaints by the Lagan meeting, the shared responsibility for Gilbert Simpson's children was a major example of cooperation. On several occasions Tyrone recommended indigent persons to Antrim for assistance, and the latter informed Down, Route, and Lagan of Andrew Jackson's plight in 1684. A decade earlier Antrim had recommended another man's case to the other presbyteries. In 1678 Tyrone and Lagan combined to help a man victimized by fire. Given the fact that money was involved, misunderstandings were perhaps inevitable. Route and Antrim were at odds over aid to two needy youths in 1683 when the latter presbytery insisted it had promised only to commend the young men to other meetings, not to send funds.[105]

The Antrim and Lagan minutes often provide no details about the recipients of aid other than that they were needy. Apart from the degree of their need their cases echoed those of the sessions. Some must have been utterly destitute: In 1674 Antrim assigned a dozen congregations to help Charles McAlmont and seven churches to assist Margaret Wilson of Braid.[106] Orphans, widows, victims of fire, the ill, and the deformed appear in the registers, as do a handful of prisoners, probably incarcerated for nonconformity or debt; at least one prisoner had been excommunicated for refusing to serve as a churchwarden, and another was the minister John Greg.[107] Presbyterians provided financial assistance as well to prisoners in foreign lands, especially those incarcerated by the Muslims.[108] On several occasions the Lagan meeting responded positively to strangers in need, including a merchant who had recommendations from the lord lieutenant himself, once again demonstrating that Presbyterians did not confine charity to their own group.[109]

Charity and education overlapped in the Presbyterians' commitment to assist financially needy students. Such assistance, in the words of the Lagan meeting, was "a necessary duty." Lagan formally supported a bursar. In 1691, for example, Samuel Henry received £3 3s. Lagan and Antrim both aided deserving students on a less formal basis. In response to a deathbed request from the Urney minister James Wallace in 1674, Lagan pledged that each parish would give John Semple at least 6s. *per annum* to support his studies. At Thomas Gowan's suggestion, each church in the Antrim meeting in 1672 agreed to provide a needy student with 3s. *per annum*, and three years later the same presbytery pledged half that amount per church to "a pious and hopefull youth . . . who has gone through a great part of his course of Philosophie at Antrim Schoole, and now will be necessitated to loose the present opportunity if he be not supplyed." In 1685, however, Antrim terminated aid to a student who did not "prosecute his learning."[110]

Gowan, whom the author of a government report called "a severe Nonconformist," founded his school at Antrim in 1666 or early 1667, offering young men a philosophy curriculum with the presbyteries' blessing. In December 1674 the Antrim meeting complained that the establishment of similar schools in Ulster endangered his enterprise. Yet a report on Ulster schools by a conformist in August 1673 had averred that of the province's sixteen schools, only one—that at Strabane—was taught by "a Fanaticke person." William Leggat, a Glasgow-educated Scot, had a seminary at Dromore in the early 1670s; some of his six divinity students already had the M.A. degree. Students attended classes in Leggat's home twice a week, debated theological questions in public, and permitted auditors to propose topics for disputation. Leggat supported Gowan's school, urging at least one of Gowan's alumni to assist the school financially. John Hutcheson's philosophy school at Newtownards, which was operating by decade's end, may have been one of those to which the Antrim meeting objected in 1674.[111]

To ensure the continued success of Gowan's school the Antrim presbytery recommended that it be the only "philosophic schoole" in the province; that ministers in Ulster support it by advising parents and guardians "of such as intend to follow that kinde of learning" to send their children there; that one presbytery oversee the school, including its curriculum, pedagogy, polity, and discipline; that the school remain in Antrim; and that Gowan continue as its overseer. Lagan supported the continuation of the school at Antrim under Gowan but proposed that two or three of the closest presbyteries appoint visitors to monitor it. Lagan also urged the school's masters and overseers to replace laureation with a certificate declaring that a graduate was qualified to teach liberal arts.[112]

When Tyrone called for the establishment of a divinity school in 1675, Antrim concurred on the condition that it be in Antrim, with Gowan and John Howe as its overseers, and that students compensate their masters liberally.[113] The school lapsed when Gowan died in 1683, and Fulk White's attempt to revive it in 1685 failed for lack of students. By November 1687 John Binning obtained the government's approval to establish a philosophy school at Comber, county Down, and a year later

Archibald Pettigrew opened a school in Belfast.[114] Because James McAlpine's philosophy school at Killyleagh, county Down, "flourisheth well during the Time of its Standing," the synod of Ulster gave the school its blessing in 1697. Yet as late as 1698 the synod complained to the government that in many places Presbyterian children could not be taught by schoolmasters of their own persuasion.[115]

Closely related to the educational task was the Presbyterians' decision in 1672 to commission John Drysdale to write their history. This was another sign of the early stages of the transition to a denominational church, for the Scottish Presbyterians clearly thought of themselves as a distinct entity possessing traditions worth recording, both for instructional purposes and as a guide by which to shape the future. The Antrim presbytery asked Thomas Hall and Patrick Adair to submit their collections of relevant material to Drysdale, and Adair at least complied, but only after procrastinating ten months. Meanwhile Lagan requested Thomas Drummond to relate what he could remember about the Presbyterians before the wars of the 1640s, while William Semple and James Wallace were asked to do the same for the postwar period. Indeed, the presbytery urged each minister to "note what he has observed." By July 1675 progress had apparently been minimal, for Lagan urged "that the business of the longed-for History be vigorously carryed on & promoted by the brethren of Down & Antrim, as best they can," and it promised them whatever papers in its possession they desired. True to its word, Lagan searched for and found various documents which it offered to Adair in June 1676. Not until the following year did Adair officially assume responsibility for writing the history. By the time of his death around 1695 Adair had completed the history of the Presbyterians in Ireland to 1670. For arranging to have a copy made his son William received £2 from the synod of Ulster in June 1697. The synod commissioned Archibald Hamilton and Alexander Hutcheson to "revise the said Collections" of Adair, including the history, and give their judgment.[116] Although not without faults and a Presbyterian bias, Adair's work remains an indispensible source for any history of Protestantism in Ireland in the half century terminating in 1670.

It is instructive that the Scottish Presbyterians' decision to commission their history should have been made shortly after the revival of presbyteries in 1669 or 1670. The Presbyterians manifestly had a sense both of what they wanted to accomplish and of the significance of their past as a guide by which to chart their future. If the ecclesiological structure they fashioned was the engine that drove their cause, the vigorous religious life analyzed in this chapter was the fuel that fired the engine. One without the other would have been powerless. Yet to the extent that religious life shaped the Presbyterians' identity in opposition not only to Catholicism but also to the Church of Ireland, it was a force that mitigated against Christian union. Its success was predicated on the perpetuation of a fractured Christendom, not on the possibility of building bridges to achieve intercommunity reconciliation. The price of survival as a distinctive ecclesiological entity was the hardening of those characteristics that set the Presbyterians apart from other religious communities.

CHAPTER 6

Declining Sects: Congregationalists and Baptists

WHEN THE RADICAL cause began to collapse in Ireland in late 1659, the Independents and the Baptists lost their political support, exposing the shallow roots of both movements. Congregationalists and Baptists alike survived the restoration of royal authority and the established church, but neither enjoyed an effective base of support nor did either develop an organizational structure that could serve as the foundation of future expansion. Of the two groups the Congregationalists were the stronger owing at least in part to talented ministers such as Samuel Mather and Thomas Harrison, yet their willingness to cooperate closely with the Presbyterians in Dublin and the south diminished their sense of distinctive polity. Theologically they were also fundamentally of one mind until the Presbyterian Thomas Emlin embraced Socinian tenets around the turn of the century, but even then the rest of the Presbyterians remained loyal to their Reformed principles. Moreover, the Congregationalists' union with the Presbyterians in southern Ireland was made easier because English Presbyterians of necessity employed a polity that hardly differed in practice from that of the Congregationalists. The Baptists, the efforts of Richard Lawrence and Jerome Sankey notwithstanding, seem almost to have vanished by 1700, but this is largely an illusion stemming from the paucity of surviving evidence. Nevertheless, unlike the Baptists in England, especially the General Baptists, they did not develop a national or regional organization and clearly remained a sect as they entered the eighteenth century.

Critics of "a Linsey-woolsey Religion": The Congregationalists

Two undated documents in the Carte Manuscripts record conventicles that met in Dublin in the early 1660s. Sixteen are mentioned, though some of these may have involved congregations that gathered in different homes and were thus enumerated more than once. Of the eight that can be identified by religious preference, two were Presbyterian (the congregations of William Jacque and Dr. Daniel Rolls), two Congregational (the churches of Samuel Mather and Edward Baines), and three Particular Baptist (the groups identified with Christopher Blackwood, Colonel Richard Lawrence, and Colonel Jerome Sankey). The eighth was either a Presbyterian congregation ministered to by Francis Roberts or a Baptist church linked to Edward Roberts. Most of the other conventicles are identified only by the names of the inhabitants in whose houses they met, such as the clothiers William Walker and Nicholas Taylor, the butcher John Green, the carpenter E. Gilbert, the cooper Mr. Funbank, and a William Haddock, a Captain Sands, and a Colonel Parker. Mather preached twice on Sundays (from 8:00 A.M. to noon and from 2:00 to 5:00 P.M.) as well as on Thursday (from 2:00 to 5:00).[1]

As we have seen, Congregationalists were implicated in the Dublin conspiracy. Baines and Stephen Charnock were probably in the circle of plotters, and a congregation in Dublin—probably that of Baines—supported it. In the period of repression following the plot's disclosure, the Congregationalists Zephaniah Smith of Clonmel and Timothy Taylor of Carrickfergus went to prison. The following year Mather was briefly incarcerated in September for preaching at a conventicle. Several months later the Congregationalists sustained another blow when Edward Wale, the minister at Waterford, died. Among his beneficiaries were two Congregational ministers, John Millard, "sometyme preacher of the Gospell," and Joshua Hubberd (Hobart), an "impoverished" clergyman.[2] The adjectives used to describe the two men poignantly reflected the plight of many Congregationalists in Ireland after 1660.

Undaunted by his imprisonment Mather continued to be a conspicuous leader of Congregationalists in Dublin. Around 1666 or 1667 he preached a sermon on Genesis 4:26 in which he justified the right of the godly to withdraw from "the wicked party," a stinging rebuke to the Church of Ireland. Because this group had now become dominant in the established church, excluding them was not feasible and separation was therefore justifiable. Reflecting the popular fear of Catholicism among many Protestants, he told his congregation in the late summer of 1667 that Christ's curse would fall on those who attempted to restore popery "and raise up the Ruines that [Christ] hath brought upon it." The following May he borrowed an analogy from the clothing industry to sustain his attack on conformists: "Our late Innovators . . . are for a Linsey-woolsey Religion, a mixture of sound and wholsome Doctrine, with Antichristian popish worship." Mather continued this theme in a September 1668 sermon in which he warned that those who departed from the strict rule of Scripture and entered "a way of Superstition" would never know when to stop and thus would multiply their idols and increase their idolatries. Those who wore a surplice for the sake of peace might as well use the sign of the cross in baptism or bow to altars. For Mather compromise with the Church of Ireland was out of the question.[3]

Uncompromising but not militant, Mather was highly critical of the Fifth Monarchist Jeremiah Marsden, who preached to a conventicle at Mather's house in 1669. Marsden had not only refused to pray for the king but had also likened him to the rulers of Sodom and Gomorrah. "If you had only preached against the ceremonies," Mather told him, "I could have gone cheerfully to prison with you, yea I could have gone . . . singing, and tryumphing even to the gibbet, and to the gallows with you in that cause: but not for preaching down Magistracie and preaching up the 5th Anarchy." Attacking monarchs and civil government, he contended, contravened the spirit of the gospel, the teachings of the Westminster Assembly, and the Savoy Confession. "What is Antichrist but a minister intruding into the worke of a Majestrate: A minister first abusing the power of the Keys, and then invading and usurping the power of the sword." By the time the authorities learned of Marsden's sermon he had traveled to York, but they ordered Mather to cease holding conventicles, threatened to incarcerate him, and reportedly informed both Charles and the archbishop of Canterbury of the incident.[4]

Because of Mather's reputation for scholarship, an unidentified Protestant asked him to refute an earlier Catholic work to which Richard Baxter, in *A Key for Catholicks* (1659), and John Owen, in *Animadversions on a Treatise Intituled Fiat Lux* (1662) and *A Vindication of the Animadversions on Fiat Lux* (1664), had already responded. Someone had sent a manuscript copy of the Catholic treatise to "a person of Honour" in Ireland challenging Protestant divines to reply. The unidentified recipient asked Mather to prepare an answer, which the latter completed in July 1670, but not without professing his sense of inadequacy: "As I have reason to acknowledge the great respect and value you are pleased to put upon me, so withall I must needs own my own unworthiness and insufficiency for this, or any other good word or work." Probably owing to the political climate, publication was delayed until 1672 and the commencement of Essex's more tolerant policy. The work was entitled *A Defence of the Protestant Christian Religion Against Popery: In Answer to a Discourse of a Roman Catholick*. In it Mather warned that even the true visible church could "fall away," but he directed most of his attention to attacking what he called the apostate church of Rome, whose claim to biblical authority he roundly denounced. "That Apostate Church, and the Head thereof, that is Babylon, and Antichrist, hath no right to any one promise in the Book of God, but stands directly under all the Threatnings and Curses written therein." The Catholic church, he contended, was a major purveyor of heresy and schism, the latter both within itself and between itself and other churches. Using Scripture, Mather sought to refute Rome's claim to be free of error before embarking on a comparative analysis of selected authors who had written for or against Catholicism. At the suggestion of an unidentified reviewer of the work while it was still in manuscript, Mather appended a concluding chapter discussing the advice Catholics had given to their popes.[5]

Another of Mather's posthumously published works, *Irenicum: or an Essay for Union* (1680), promoted closer relations between Congregationalists, Presbyterians, and Particular Baptists. Convinced that most of their disagreements were rooted in misunderstandings, he explored how close these groups could "come together, supposing each party to remain unconvinced of any error in their way." He identified three areas of basic agreement, the first of which entailed concurrence on doctrinal fundamentals as reflected in the Westminster Confession of Faith, the Savoy Confession, and a Baptist confession of 1650. The latter must have been the third edition of the Particular Baptists' *Confession of Faith*, published in 1651, rather than the General Baptists' *Faith and Practise of Thirty Congregations, Gathered According to the Primitive Pattern*, issued the same year. The three groups agreed too, argued Mather, on the duties of charity and Christian love, especially toward fellow believers. Finally they concurred on the basic acts of worship, namely prayer, preaching, and sabbath observance as reflected by the fact that they customarily attended one another's services in Dublin.[6] The latter is a significant observation about the extent of ecumenical activity among Protestant dissenters in the capital and calls to mind the practice of occasional communion discussed in Chapter 4.

Mather recognized that differences existed among Congregational-ists, Baptists, and Presbyterians with respect to "matters of Institution and Church-Worship, in the Second Commandment," but even here he underscored four uniting principles, including adherence to the Bible as the rule in faith, life, and worship, and the belief that ministers were divinely appointed to preach, administer the sacraments, and impose censure. The groups concurred that the Lord's supper should not be administered "promiscuously unto all" and that "the Ceremonies and other Episcopal Inventions in the worship of God are sinful and unlaw-ful." Some differences between Congregationalists and Presbyterians, in Mather's view, were superficial, such as the speculative relationship between visible and invisible churches, the insistence of some Presbyte-rians that ministers could be ordained only to specific congregations rather than to the ministry at large, and disagreements over political issues. The fundamental differences between Congregationalists and Presbyterians involved polity, the disciplinary power of the keys, and "the extent as to the external dispensation of the Covenant of Grace sealed by [baptism]." On the last point Presbyterians averred that all who professed Protestantism as well as their children were part of the covenant, whereas Congregationalists limited it to those who not only declared themselves Protestant but also "walk[ed] without offence" and their children. The Baptists differed by excluding children. Be-cause none of these points was incontrovertibly a fundamental error, Mather contended that dissenters should "bear with one another" in these disagreements.[7]

Given the congruence in so many crucial areas, Mather advocated "a mutual owning and giving the right hand of Fellowship to each other as true Churches and Ministers of Jesus Christ, in whom something of his grace and presence doth appear." He urged that members of the groups involve themselves in one another's affairs, giving mutual advice and assistance, and that "Approved Members" be permitted to take com-munion occasionally in other congregations. Because they agreed on the basics, they were all visible Christians and thus had a duty to unite as much as possible, seeking peace and suffering together for the sake of their consciences. Given the importance of conscience, Mather recog-nized the right of each group to retain those practices unique to it, though he hoped that increased contact would resolve some disagree-ments. The times, he concluded, made greater unity seasonable.[8]

Mather continued to be much less charitable to the Church of Ireland, though he offered an olive branch to those who had demonstrated sensitivity to persons with tender consciences. Dissenters, he argued, owe such people esteem and Christian love, and they should be ready to unite with them. Union was impossible with those "whose way of Worship doth exclude the Scripture and the Ministry, and who make promiscuous administrations and Superstitious Ceremonies, the condition of their Communion." God, he averred, had departed from their "dead and blasted forms," and those who continued to cling to them must be shown the error of their ways.[9]

In the absence of church books, informers' reports provide valuable if rare glimpses into Congregational activities. In September 1668 Mather was reportedly preaching every Sunday morning at 7:00 A.M. in a house on Ormond Green in Dublin, and Mather, Edward Baines, or Timothy Taylor of Carrickfergus preached there at 5:00 P.M. Sometimes two men preached at each service. Samuel Cox was also active, preaching in a malthouse in Thomas Street in August, and so too was the Presbyterian Daniel Rolls. Complaining to Ormond in June 1669 of the growth in the number of conventicles in Dublin, Archbishop Margetson observed: "I can finde very few of that gang in & about this citty that are considerable enough for there quallityes to be taken notice of, but there Numbers are constituted of merchants, & tradesmen, inferior persons, who usually are lead in matters of relligion rather by the lunges then by the reason of there teachers, and therefore are the sooner subjected by them to the temptations of disobedience."[10] Margetson confirms the middling social status of dissenters, but his allusion to the power of nonconformist pulpit rhetoric smacks of envy, particularly considering contemporary complaints about inferior Anglican preaching. In any event, although death stilled the powerful pen of Samuel Mather in October 1671, his brother Nathaniel succeeded him as pastor of the New Row congregation.[11]

Following Baines's death in 1670 his congregation, reflecting Mather's ecumenical interests, called the Presbyterian Henry Newcome of Manchester to be its pastor. Newcome agonized over the call, which the congregation formally extended on 25 July 1670. He found the proffered maintenance adequate, the opportunity to serve precious, the likelihood of continuing religious liberty appealing, and the friendship of the lord mayor-elect a welcome bonus. Against this weighed the "great divisions" among Irish nonconformists, the congregation's being "generally leavened with Independency, and practising separation"; mistrust of an assistant identified as "Mr. C."; and Thomas Harrison's desire for the position and his being "so much fitter for it." When Newcome's letter requesting an extension of time for him to consider the call miscarried, the congregation selected Harrison. The church was then worshipping in Winetavern Street but in 1673 moved to a new meeting-house in Cooke Street.[12]

Like the Presbyterians, the Congregationalists showed only limited interest in refuting the Friends. In 1670 Timothy Taylor contributed an epistle to Thomas Jenner's *Quakerism Anatomiz'd and Confuted.* Jenner, who had been at Christ's College, Cambridge, before serving as a minister at Horstead and Coltishall, Norfolk, had retired to Carlow. In an epistle dedicatory to the earl and countess of Donegall, Jenner explained that he wrote his book out of "a sense of the danger that the Church of God is in, by reason of the spreading Gangrene of Quakerism in the Kingdom." In the body of his book Jenner contended that the Friends were instrumental in the growth of Catholicism because they rejected Reformed ministers, espoused a doctrine of justification by works, asserted that believers could keep the law perfectly, denied the imputed righteousness of Christ for justification, averred that the Bible was carnal and not the supreme rule for faith and life, and pretended to receive revelations and perform miracles.[13]

The intent of Taylor's epistle, dated at his study in Smithfield, Dublin, was to convince the Friends "that there is an Antichrist without, as well as within; and that they themselves are made use of to retrieve the cause of the man of sin (a dangerous and prevailing interest) in these Nations." Like a number of other authors, including Richard Baxter, Taylor erroneously argued that Quakers and Jesuits were linked. Not one Friend in a hundred, he thought, was "a dogmatical formal Papist," but many Jesuits were Quakers, "stalking under them, and plowing with their Heifer." From another perspective the Friends were like the 200 men who ignorantly followed Absalom. Although Taylor dismissed most Quaker doctrines as abominable lies, he reserved his heavy ammunition for the Jesuits, whose master design reputedly aimed to lure as many of the godly as possible and to "lay the axe to the root of the Tree, that those which should not close with their new Gospel might be hewed down by them." Because Quakers repudiated the gospel ministry, the ordinances, and ecclesiastical polity, they reportedly served the Jesuits' design by striking at the very foundation of faith. Taylor not only wrote his epistle for Jenner but also saw the book through the press when Jenner was hobbled by gout.[14]

For the decade 1677–1687 the Mather correspondence provides valuable insight into Congregational activity in Ireland. In January 1677

Increase Mather, John Eliot, and others thanked the dissenting congregations in Dublin for contributions to relieve the suffering caused by
fighting with the Amerindians. Apart from Quakers in Ireland, no other
European Protestants had sent assistance. In contrast to the repression
to which some nonconformists were subjected in England at this time,
Nathaniel Mather reported on several occasions in 1678 that Irish dissenters were enjoying religious liberty, "a wonder of power & mercy."
Yet he also confided to his brother Increase that until he saw "some
course taken for the free course of the preaching of the Gospell & for a
more effectuall reformacion, [he] expect[ed] not that the Lord's controversy with these nacions should bee at an end." Mather monitored
developments not only in England and America but also in Scotland,
where the repressive acts of the Highland Host in the southwest dismayed him, and the European continent, where he worried about the
persecution of the Huguenots as well as Calvinists in Austria and Hun-
gary.[15] The difficult times confronting dissenters in the early 1680s are
reflected in the Mather correspondence. In March 1681 Nathaniel sent a
letter to Increase by Archibald Maclaine, a Scot who had moved from
Dublin to Belfast, where he taught school until prosecution for nonconformity in a bishop's court forced him to flee. Another correspondent,
the Congregationalist minister John Bailey, formerly of Chester and
now at Limerick, wrote mournfully to Increase in May 1682 that "the
wofull, sinfull & sinking condition of these nations would be too large
for me to tell you." Despite his recent success in organizing a congregation in Limerick, he predicted that the three kingdoms faced desolation
unless God intervened, apparently referring to the intense politico-
religious struggles being waged between Tories and Whigs. Yet few, he
said, thought of fleeing except his followers in Limerick, who remained
with him only "as an act of love & self denyall."[16] In a letter to Cotton
Mather dated 6 June 1683 Thomas Bailey reiterated the mounting dangers to the godly in England and Scotland, but noted that dissenters in
Ireland still enjoyed their liberty. This did not cheer Bailey, for he attributed the dissenters' toleration to the government's determination to
permit Catholics to enjoy religious freedom, recognizing that it would
have been almost impossible to tolerate Catholics while repressing Protestants. He made the Church of Ireland shoulder much of the blame
for this: "How blind & mad, deceived & deluded are our conforming
clergy; all for the duke of York, all against Dissenters."[17] Before the
storm was over, John Bailey surmised, the godly would receive greater
light to understand the book of Revelation.[18]

The Baileys' dire missives are not the only evidence for the growing problems facing Congregationalists in the early 1680s. Harrison died in September 1682, but shortly before his demise his congregation in Cooke Street, Dublin, invited John Pinney to be his successor. In November of the same year Nathaniel Mather reported to Increase that his financial support had declined substantially, with further reductions likely. No less disconcerting was the appearance of dissension within his congregation, possibly owing to external political pressures but more probably to a disagreement over whether to appoint Nathaniel Weld as a teacher in the congregation. "Hee increaseth & shineth more & more," but some members opposed the appointment because Weld was only twenty-two years old. Even before the Rye House disclosures the archdeacon of Dublin had begun prosecuting nonconformists, the earliest victims being General Baptists, but Nathaniel Mather heard reports that he too was a target. Although he still enjoyed his freedom in late June, he wondered how long such liberty would last.[19]

Toleration temporarily ended in July 1683 when the government prohibited conventicles, forcing dissenters to meet quietly in private houses if at all. Pinney contemplated returning to England despite the fact that dissenters there suffered similarly, but he continued to preach in Dublin. The following March Nathaniel informed Increase that dissenters still had to meet in homes, but with the connivance of magistrates who were content to keep the meetinghouses closed. Mather's congregation, including visitors, was too large to gather in a single house, hence it met in two places simultaneously, with Mather responsible for one service in the morning and Weld the other; the two men then switched places for the afternoon service and repeated their morning sermons. Congregationalists and Presbyterians were still meeting in private homes in May 1684 with the magistrates' knowledge. By December, however, Nathaniel could tell Increase that "our libertys in the Gospell are through the Lords good hand to us still continued as formerly."[20]

The repression of 1683–1684 forced John Bailey, who had been banned from preaching in Limerick, to emigrate to New England, where he became Samuel Willard's assistant at the Old South Church in Boston. His departure gave Nathaniel Mather an occasion to reflect on Bailey's earlier visits to Dublin. On such occasions the sites where he preached had been crowded "as no other place was at any time."[21]

Throughout this period the Congregationalists in Ireland made a sustained effort to publish Samuel Mather's works as well as to obtain books. When John Bailey thanked Increase Mather for sending copies of the latter's publications, he apologized for not being able to reciprocate, "being cast in the end of the kingdome, at a great distance From Books, especially new ones." In 1679 John Eliot sent Nathaniel Mather a copy of one of his works, probably *The Harmony of the Gospels* (1678), but Nathaniel relied on Increase for most of his books, including the latter's *Diatriba de Signo* (1682); sermons on prayer, the sacraments, and sleeping during sermons; his treatise on comets; and his *Essay for the Recording of Illustrious Providences* (1684). Increase also shipped Nathaniel a copy of Urian Oakes's sermon on Ecclesiastes and assorted catechisms by New England divines, including those by John Norton and James Fitch.[22] In turn Nathaniel sent Increase manuscript copies of some of his sermons with the caveat that they could be published only with a statement stipulating they had not been composed with publication in mind. Nathaniel insisted he had no time to revise them. The sermons were on Zachariah 3, Psalm 25:6–7, Acts 3:25, Luke 7:38, Galatians 5:17, and Hebrews 6:2; he deemed those on Luke and Acts ready for publication, those on Zachariah and Hebrews in need of revision, and those on Psalms "so broken & imperfect that you cannot make them out." Some, he confessed, did not deal with the subjects that most interested him, and he did want not his name or city printed on the Zachariah sermon which had been preached at an ordination service in a private house. The bishops, he feared, would be sensitive to this challenge to what they believed to be their exclusive right to ordain.[23]

The project to print some of Samuel Mather's works was underway by February 1678, when Nathaniel persuaded the officers of his congregation to bestow their approval. At that point he anticipated the printing would have to be undertaken in the Netherlands, hence it "cannot be effected suddenly." By early 1683 the manuscript had been shipped instead to London, but the intended printer insisted that subscribers in Ireland would first have to raise at least half the printing costs. The work was projected to be a folio volume selling for approximately 10s. with an epistle by Nathaniel and possibly a second by John Owen. Nathaniel was initially optimistic that the necessary subscribers could be found in Ireland, but in May 1683 he reported to Increase that the volume would probably have to be secretly printed in Dublin. By that point subscribers had pledged approximately £35, "they beeing to have 5 books at the rate that 4 are sold by the bookseller." The printing was underway in Dublin in August, but at a rate of not more than two sheets a week, probably to avoid attracting the magistrates' attention.

Nathaniel, who did the proofreading, expected the book to run to seventy or eighty sheets. In March 1684 the work had progressed to the point that Nathaniel could send a sample to Increase, and the finished product was finally shipped, unbound, in December. In the end, subscribers paid 7s. per unbound copy, with a fifth copy free for every four they purchased.[24]

Congregationalists continued to enjoy a measure of toleration in James II's reign, though at first they still could not worship in their meetinghouses in Dublin. Nathaniel Mather's letters from this period reflect the mounting concern of all Protestants as Catholics received civil and military offices and worshipped openly in the capital. By the late summer of 1686 some ministers were preparing to leave the country and at least one had already returned to England. Fears of a repetition of the 1641 bloodshed weighed heavily on the minds of some, but Mather stayed. Dissenters were subject to a recusancy fine of 9d. per sabbath, but talk of using the Act of Uniformity to repress conventicles led nowhere once Tyrconnell announced an indulgence in February 1687. Because of this some dissenting ministers in Dublin began holding services in their "convenienct & capacious" meetinghouses, though others left for England. Mather remained, convinced "that it is as good for Protestants that are cordially so, to live under wise & just Popish Governors as such Protestants as wee have had many." The following year he left Dublin to accept the pastorate of the Congregational church in Paved Alley, Lime Street, London.[25]

Congregationalists in Ireland survived the restoration in greater strength than most historians have assumed, though obviously still only a pale shadow of themselves in the 1650s. James Anthony Froude's observation of their post-1660 status is far too gloomy: "The few families of Independents which remained were condemned to spiritual isolation" and in the absence of schools and chapels they could not perpetuate their faith to their children, who embraced Catholicism.[26] In fact, Congregationalists survived in Dublin to the turn of the century and beyond, sharing their spiritual life with Baptists and English Presbyterians. The New Row congregation alone baptized 418 persons between 1662 and 1700, and another 94 in the first five years of the eighteenth century. Phil Kilroy plausibly suggests that at its height this church may have had approximately a thousand baptized members. Yet the Congregationalists' inability to replace Thomas Harrison, John Pinney, and especially Nathaniel Mather was a critical blow to their ability to prosper, as was their failure to establish a broad-based organization. As we have seen, some Congregationalists merged with the Presbyterians, a fate that presumably would not have dismayed Mather. The combined Independent-Presbyterian congregation at Drogheda to which the Congregationalist Thomas Jenner had ministered in the 1650s was under the care of the Presbyterian Daniel Williams from around 1664 until his departure for Wood Street, Dublin in 1667. At the latter church Williams served with the Congregationalist Samuel Marsden and later with the Presbyterians Gilbert Rule (from 1682 to 1687) and Joseph Boyse (from 1683).[27] The church remained Presbyterian. Apparently most of the other mixed congregations similarly ended up in the Presbyterian camp, probably because Presbyterian polity maintained stronger links between churches.

Keeping the Candle Burning: Resolute Baptists

Because of their radical religious views and political affiliations the Baptists were marked people at the restoration, in Ireland as in England. The saddler George Pressick, whose *Case of Conscience* pleaded his right as an innocent party to remarry after divorce, tried to curry favor with Broghill, Coote, and Sir Theophilus Jones by pointing out that he had attacked Thomas Patient's treatise on baptism.[28] Far more serious was the assault on the Baptist church at St. Dunstan's Hill, near Thomas Street, Dublin, on the night of Sunday, 4 May 1660. The mob tore down the pulpit, ripped up the seats, and committed "other insolencies." Although some perpetrators were arrested, various conservatives used the incident to fan apprehensions among the Baptists that they faced imminent persecution and could expect no relief from the king's pledge of liberty to tender consciences. "Already," one of Ormond's correspondents noted, "their free exercise [of religion] begins to be hindered." Some moderates suggested that Charles condemn the attack, but this he seems not to have done, perhaps because no one told him of it.[29]

In June 1660 Sir Edward Nicholas received an intelligence report listing "dangerous persons" who had recently left Ireland for England, among them the Baptists Adjutant-General William Allen, Quartermaster-General John Vernon, Colonel Jerome Sankey, Colonel Richard Lawrence, Colonel Robert Barrow, Major Peter Wallis, Major John Godfrey, Captain Thomas Walcott, Captain Joseph Deane, and Edward Roberts of Waterford. Of these men only Sankey, Lawrence, Walcott, and possibly Roberts are known to have subsequently returned to Ireland.[30] Christopher Blackwood also went to England at the restoration but came back to Ireland in 1662 and remained there until his death in 1670, whereas Patient returned to England and stayed there. Daniel Axtell had gone to England to help suppress Booth's rebellion in 1659; he was executed as a regicide in October 1660.[31] Having depended so heavily on military officers to lead them in the 1650s, the Baptists thus lost most of their leaders at the restoration.

While in England, two Baptists who would later return to Ireland had an opportunity to pledge their loyalty to the Stuart regime. Following the Fifth Monarchist rebellion of Thomas Venner and his supporters in January 1661 a group of Baptists drafted a Humble Apology denouncing the rebels for "pretending to introduce a Civil and Temporal Reign and Government of Jesus Christ by their Swords, and to subvert all Civil Government and Authority." They further denied all knowledge of the conspiracy. Among the thirty signatories were Blackwood, Sankey, and Roberts.[32]

The government won a propaganda victory in July 1662 when an unidentified Baptist and former major in the Cromwellian forces made his peace with the Church of Ireland. The ex-officer, who claimed never to have been rebaptized as an adult, applied to Michael Boyle, bishop of Cork, to have his eight children baptized. Boyle demanded a public confession and recantation in the presence of the congregation and a signed confession in the church register as well as an examination of his children. When the major consented, Boyle asked the dean of Cloyne and others to attend the public ceremony so "that it may be performed with the greater solemnity and gravity." As Boyle explained to Bramhall, the major's conversion was "the first example of this nature that I have mett with" since the revolutionary upheavals. He recognized that "the practise of the Ancient church was very severe uppon the like occasions, but the condition of the times being such as they are, it may [be] thought more providentiall to win the people by fayre persuasions & easy punishments then to prosecute them with the severity of a stricter discipline." Bramhall approved the moderate approach, the wisdom of which was underscored the same month when another conversion transpired. An elated Boyle reported to the archbishop that "this moderate & yet honorable way of righting the church will conduce much to bring in those who I am very confident would not otherwise have adventured to looke towards us."[33]

The Baptists won something of a propaganda victory of their own in the spring of 1674 when George Crichton, a Dublin barrister, left William Jacque's Presbyterian congregation, joined a Baptist church, "&

was dipped." The Presbyterians, however, claimed that Crichton left only after he had been convicted of "diverse scandalls." Because of his affiliation with the Baptists the session suspended him and the Antrim presbytery subsequently resolved that "his suspension & scandalous carriage . . . be publickly intimated."[34] Whether Crichton was guilty of misconduct or was merely the victim of propagandistic retaliation is impossible to ascertain.

Reports of dissident activity in the early and mid-1660s provide scattered glimpses of Baptists. In September 1662 Edward Worth, bishop of Killaloe, complained to Ormond that Edward Hutchinson, "the Arch-Anabaptist in these parts" and formerly the chaplain of Colonel Daniel Abbott's regiment, and others were spreading rumors and inciting discontent. Among them was the assertion that Gaelic Irish would soon replace the English in the Irish army. Hutchinson claimed to have obtained his information from letters posted from England. Justices of the peace issued a warrant for his arrest but he went into hiding.[35]

In the crackdown following the initial disclosures of the Dublin conspiracy Orrery arrested an unnamed Baptist preacher as well as a Presbyterian minister for spreading reports that the English would soon lose their lands "& that we should this summer be in Blood." He also secured Colonel Henry Pretty, a Baptist and former governor of Carlow, and required him to post a £1,000 bond to appear when summoned. About the time the plot was discovered in early 1663 Pretty went to Dublin and Leinster prior to preparing to sail on an armed vessel from the Limerick area to Brazil. He had told Dungannon, however, that he intended to travel to Smyrna. Orrery suspected Pretty and others intended to use the ship to escape if the plot failed. The source of the earl's information was the Baptist Thomas Jackson, "a Quick Rationall Fellow," who went to prison for allowing Pretty to flee. Orrery also arrested Walcott, who had returned to Ireland about the time of the plot, examined him, and sent him to Dublin. As part of his security arrangements Orrery forced some "Phanatticks," possibly including Baptists, to leave Limerick and Waterford, though he permitted others to stay because they were important for the economy. Later, in 1667, Orrery informed Ormond that most of Limerick's merchants were Baptists who took the oaths of allegiance and supremacy.[36]

In May 1663 James Butler reported to a government official, possibly Ormond, about a meeting of "fanaticks" at Clough in county Wexford. Among them were Lieutenant-Colonel Nicholas Kempson (or Kempston), Edward Ludlow's brother-in-law; Lieutenant-Colonel Solomon

Richards; and Captain Samuel Shere. The religious views of these men are unknown, but they were reportedly corresponding with Quartermaster Swan, a former servant of Ludlow's, and Mr. Lamb, "the Grand minister of the Anabaptists in this County." This may have been the General Baptist Thomas Lamb, soapboiler and chandler, who had helped Pretty expel the minister at Devizes, Wiltshire, in 1646, and had also signed the Humble Apology in 1661. More likely, however, it was William Lamb, who later preached in Dublin in the mid-1670s. Kempson's group, members of which had been arrested at a private meeting in November 1662, were acting suspiciously and believed to be linked to the plotting in Dublin.[37] From Nenagh, county Tipperary, came a report the same spring that Edward Hutchinson, "a Grand Preacher of the Anabaptists," and Robert Clarke and Paul Gremball, "two great Anabaptists," had been arrested, undoubtedly in connection with the crackdown stemming from the discovery of the Dublin plotting. Indeed, one of the conspirators, Lieutenant-Colonel William More, owned an estate in the country and himself was incarcerated at Clonmel. Hutchinson was arraigned at Clonmel in 1664.[38]

Ormond's papers include a list of suspected dangerous Baptists in the barony of Rathdown, south of Dublin, in December 1663. All but one are obscure: Major Henry Jones and another person of the same surname of Stillorgan; Thomas Taylor and Daniel Morris of Leopardstown; Dr. John Harding, formerly a Baptist minister in Cork, "and the townsmen" of Kilgobbin; and Mr. Harding and Sergeant Baillie of Jamestown. By this time the government also had a report that Christopher Blackwood's Particular Baptist congregation was meeting at Major William Lowe's house in Abbey Green on Sundays for sermons at 7:00 A.M., 10:00 A.M., and 2:00 P.M. The congregants also gathered on Thursdays from 10:00 A.M. to 5:00 P.M. Lawrence's church worshipped on Sundays from 7:00 to 10:30 A.M., and Sankey's on Sundays and Fridays at 4:00 P.M. If the Roberts on this list is Edward rather than the Presbyterian Francis, a conventicle "sometimes" met at his home in the Inns.[39]

Additional glimpses of the Baptists in this period resulted from their contacts with Quakers and from the letters of Oliver Plunkett, Catholic archbishop of Armagh. Colonel Richard Lawrence and Major Henry Jones debated "moral religion and water baptism" with William Penn at his house in Dublin in November 1669 after Penn and four others had visited Lawrence at his home in the village of Chapelizod earlier the same day. In the spring of 1670 the Quakers Margaret and S. Mitchell visited the Baptist church at Youghal and reportedly converted several of its members to their cause. At Galway in August 1672 "a Jangling [contentious] Baptist" made a similar attempt to recruit converts at a Quaker meeting. In the early 1670s Plunkett complained about the presence of Baptists as well as Friends, Presbyterians, and conformists in his province, especially in the dioceses of Raphoe, Derry, and Clogher. Like other Protestants the Baptists, he claimed, were obtaining leases for lands seized from Catholics.[40]

Some sense of what Baptist sermons were like can be found in manuscripts of sermons preached by Sankey and William Lamb in 1674 and 1675. In general Lamb's sermons stressed repentance, by which he meant "a true repentance & not a legall repentance: . . . repentance given of god . . . brings us out of our miserable state and brings us home unto god." He also preached on hope and deliverance in times of trouble, particularly those of a spiritual nature: "Hee will heare thy Cry and will come and delliver." Comfort, the certainty of divine promises, and holy living were other important themes in his sermons, as was the power of God in creation and his role in governing the world. Convinced that holiness "becomes the house of god," Lamb castigated barren fruits, notably "dead" preaching, "dead" prayers, and "dead" works. Either Lamb or Sankey preached a potent sermon on spiritual warfare, that is, "a continuall warr against the old man" using spiritual weapons. The real enemy was not a repressive state but corrupt human nature. In a sermon on Romans 3:20, Sankey stressed the theme of justification by faith. "Works kills and makes dead and dull," but by the imputed righteousness of Christ believers are "in as good Condition as the very angells of heaven." Nothing in these sermons of Lamb and Sankey was subversive other than the implied criticism of the Church of Ireland and the deadness of its sermons and ritual.[41]

The most dramatic success story among the Irish Baptists in the restoration period was that of Richard Lawrence, who had amassed a substantial estate in the 1650s. Having served the Protectorate in part as a member of a committee to survey forfeited Irish lands, he knew a great deal about the country. Seeking payment of his arrears he had petitioned Cromwell and the Council of State in 1657 for £500 or £600 worth of land in counties Dublin, Cork, and Kildare. He would later claim he had lost an estate worth £5,000 *per annum* under the Act of Settlement, but this was probably as exaggerated as his insistence that he had supported the restoration. In any event he became a successful upholsterer in the 1660s—so prosperous that he increased the value of his stock from £1,500 to £5,500 in seven years, attracting Ormond's attention.[42] By the spring of 1668 Lawrence was helping Ormond establish a new linen manufactory at Chapelizod, west of Dublin on the river Liffey. In May Lawrence dispatched an agent to England and the Netherlands to obtain economic information and artisans, and also to consult with Ormond, who was then in England. If Ormond found the agent unsatisfactory, Lawrence promised to terminate his own business in Dublin and devote himself exclusively to the Chapelizod endeavor. As he told Sir George Lane, however, he did not expect the manufactory to be profitable for two or three years. Lawrence took the occasion of his letter to Lane to defend his fellow nonconformists: "For the generallity of the protestant Nonconformists of all Opinions whoe makes Gods word theire ground of faith & Rule of Life, I knowingly affirme it and if it were Convenient Could gett Thowsands to Subscribe That they Esteeme his Graces Governement over them under his Majestie as one of the greatest Temporall blessings they Enjoy in this World."[43]

Despite his commercial acumen, Lawrence was in financial straits by 1679. Even before his involvement in the linen works he had helped to establish the town of "Brachingyerd" (Brackenstown, county Dublin?) without compensation. Around 1679 Lawrence claimed that Ormond had not honored his agreement with him on the Chapelizod project and that he had sustained losses in excess of £500 *per annum*. He also noted he had served on the Council of Trade for thirteen years and because of his cumulative public service was now in debt. He therefore petitioned for the right to provide clothing and cloth to the army. In 1682 Lawrence published a new edition of *The Interest of Ireland in Its Trade and Wealth Stated*, in which he ranged from the negative impact of tenuous land tenure on prosperity to poor reform, stricter enforcement of vagrancy laws, and schemes to increase employment.[44]

During the exclusion and succession crisis the government monitored Lawrence's activities because of his radical background and Baptist convictions. Sir John Davis, one of Arran's correspondents, suspected Lawrence was a supporter of Monmouth and Shaftesbury. Davis knew Lawrence was corresponding with Edmund Murphy, a potential Irish witness in whom Shaftesbury was interested in connection with prosecuting the Popish plot. Government agents monitored Lawrence's mail in 1680, discovering in the process that he was communicating with a Mr. Roberts, almost certainly the Baptist Edward Roberts.[45] In the spring of 1683 the government's increasing pressure on nonconformists affected several Baptists. Nathaniel Mather reported to Increase in April that a General Baptist preacher, "a joyner, but a man of good knowledg

& better spirit & savor than would bee expected, considering his principles," had been excommunicated and another unidentified Baptist
cited by an ecclesiastical court. Following the disclosure of the Rye
House plotting, the government, trying to ascertain possible Irish involvement, interrogated Lawrence about Walcott. Lawrence admitted
he had known Walcott many years but deemed him a troublesome man
who was "against all governments" except a commonwealth. He also
acknowledged having met the Rye House conspirator Richard Rum-
bold on his last trip to England, and knowing Colonel Henry Owen,
John's brother, though he insisted the colonel had never attended Baptist services. Lawrence apparently did not go to prison, but he died the
following year and was interred at St. Werburgh's in Dublin. Although
dissenters were restricted in holding services during his last years, in
May 1684 Nathaniel Mather reported that a small group of General
Baptists was "not restreyned," probably, he surmized, because of its
"inconsiderablenes." As a result of the crackdown following the disclosure of the Rye House plotting, a small number of Baptists from
Tipperary, Kilkenny, and Cork emigrated to Pennsylvania and New
Jersey.[46]

Before leaving the Baptists, the congregation at Cork founded by
Major Edward Riggs in 1651 should be revisited. John Coleman, who
had been briefly preceded by Thomas or William Lamb, became the
pastor around 1653 and continued in that position until his death in approximately 1680. Among the members of the small congregation were
the children of schoolmaster Woods, one of Riggs's earliest associates, a
son named George who served as a deacon and a daughter named
Lucia. Around 1677 Riggs married Ann Allen of Lower Ormond, both
of whose parents were Baptists. Aged approximately 25, some 35 years
younger than her husband, she was his third wife. She was responsible
for reviving the church after it nearly ceased to exist for two decades
following Coleman's death. By that point the congregation numbered
five women and perhaps a handful of men, at least some of whom were
on the point of joining another dissenting congregation because they
had no pastor. At the same time a small group of Baptists in Clonmel,
unable to support a minister on its own, cooperated with Cork to call
Joseph Pettit as their joint pastor.

Ann Riggs played a crucial role in persuading Pettit to come to Cork
and not only paid for the construction of a meetinghouse but also purchased a cemetery so Baptists would no longer be subject to harrass-
ment when they buried deceased members. The English-born Pettit,

who had once worked as a shopkeeper for a Dublin alderman, was persuaded to study for the ministry by John Edward, a pastor in Dublin. Thanks to Edward's support, Pettit obtained financial support to study divinity and biblical languages, and subsequently preached in Dublin before accepting the invitations from Cork and Clonmel. Major Riggs pledged £30 *per annum* for Pettit's services. Riggs died in 1707, leaving an estate worth approximately £1,200 *per annum*, and his widow lived until 1741. Pettit died at Cork in June 1729, aged 55. The crucial support provided to Baptists in Cork by Ann and Edward Riggs undoubtedly prevented that church from suffering the fate of the Baptist congregation in Cloghkeating, to which James North ministered. By the early eighteenth century many of its members had "gon off to a different Profession and are now so blended as scarce to be distinguished."[47]

Baptists and Congregationalists thus survived the loss of their political support in 1660 and continued to exist throughout the restoration era, perhaps in more places than we realize because of the paucity of records.[48] The forty years after 1660 are a story of survival, no matter how tenuous and imperfectly understood, not obliteration. Both groups, especially the Congregationalists, had several influential leaders, hence it would be erroneous to aver that either sect suffered significantly owing to leadership problems. The emphasis in both traditions on local autonomy mitigated against the formation of a strong regional or national organization, but this might have been overcome to some degree had they established associations of the kind the Baptists had in the 1650s and the General Baptists continued to have in England in succeeding decades. Kevin Herlihy has argued that government repression made it impossible for the Baptists to found such an organization,[49] but all of the other Protestant nonconformists managed to do so. (The Congregationalists, of course, did so only in conjunction with the Presbyterians.) The Irish Baptists apparently shunned their own broad-based organization because of several factors, including their small numbers and a sense of the need to promote cooperation among Protestants. Moreover, the Congregationalists failed to create a sense of distinctive identity, preferring instead to work closely or even merge with the English Presbyterians, whose theology they shared and whose polity differences in Dublin and southern Ireland were minimal in practice. A spirit of ecumenicity, however limited, helps to explain why the Irish Congregationalists did not become a denominational church by the turn of the century. To a lesser degree the Baptists too cooperated with the English

Presbyterians in southern Ireland.[50] Indeed, Lawrence in 1682 even proposed "a right understanding and charitable Union" between nonconformists (excluding Quakers and Muggletonians) and godly members of the Church of Ireland, that is, all those who "agree with the Religion established by Law in all its Fundamentals, nay in all its Substantials."[51] Such cooperation was encouraged to a considerable degree, especially among the smaller nonconformist groups, by a sense of Protestant community in the face of a much larger Catholic population.

CHAPTER 7

The Society of Friends and Its Work

LIKE THE BAPTISTS, the Friends had been a sect in the 1650s and remained so during the early years of the restoration period. More so than any other Protestant community they were victims of persecution throughout most of the period under review, as the survey of their history in Ireland in the reigns of Charles II and James II manifests. (The nature and extent of their suffering will be examined more fully in Chapter 8.) As in the case of the Scottish Presbyterians, the Friends' survival depended heavily on their ability to establish a viable organization, which they began to do in 1668, shortly before the Presbyterians revived their meetings. Just as the Scottish Presbyterians needed a functioning ecclesiastical structure to cope with David Houston and the extremist Covenanters, so the Friends had to rely on their organization to deal with the fissure instigated by John Story and John Wilkinson.

This chapter will analyze the development and nature of Quaker polity in Ireland, which was not identical to that in England, and it will underscore the effectiveness of their ecclesiological structure in governing the movement. It will also examine the wide variety of institutional devices the Quakers employed to govern their affairs, such as certificates for public Friends (ministers), marriage, relocation, and financial assistance; epistles, published works, and censorship; and procedures for the construction and maintenance of meetinghouses and burial grounds. By the end of the seventeenth century Irish Friends were more organized than any other Protestant group with the exception of the Church of Ireland, particularly if one considers the Quakers' structured system to control the publication and distribution of books and pamphlets, their maintenance of separate burial grounds (as did some Baptists), and their network of traveling public Friends. Operating in the shadow of persecution, the Friends, like the Scottish Presbyterians, developed an ecclesiological structure that not only enabled them to survive but also transformed them from a sect to a denominational church.

Historical Overview

The history of the Friends in Ireland from 1660 to 1700 is one of impressive growth despite recurring periods of persecution, usually of a financial nature but sometimes involving incarceration. From thirty local meetings in 1660 the movement expanded until it numbered 53 in 1701. Of these 24 were in Leinster, eighteen in Ulster, and eleven in Munster. Altogether they had perhaps 3,000 members, less than a tenth the number of Quakers in England.[1] In the early stages the Irish Friends were concentrated in four areas: the major port towns, namely Dublin, Cork, Waterford, and Limerick; the Ulster meetings at Grange, Ballyhagan, Lurgan, and Lisburn; the more fertile agricultural regions of central Leinster such as Mountmellick, Edenderry, Moate, Newgarden, Athy, and the Mullingar area; and such small eastern towns as Wicklow, Carlow, and New Ross. The Quakers of southern Ireland came primarily from northern England (Cumberland, Westmorland, northern Lancashire, Northumberland, and northern Yorkshire), with most of the rest migrating from southwestern England. Unlike their Presbyterian neighbors the Friends of Ulster also originated in northern England rather than Scotland. As Richard Vann and David Eversley have indicated, the Quakers in northern Ireland engaged largely in commerce and industry rather than agriculture, lived for the most part in townlands amid a rural environment, and were relatively prosperous. Elsewhere Irish Quakers were generally involved in agriculture and to a lesser degree in trade, especially in linen. Few were common laborers or persons of substantial wealth.[2] The largest Quaker community was in Dublin, the country's leading port. In Cork, Ireland's second most important port, Quaker numbers were not extensive though many of the city's leading merchants, including the Newenham family, were Friends; the single meetinghouse in Cork, constructed in 1678, could seat 200. Ireland's third and fourth largest ports in the third quarter of the century, Waterford and Limerick, were also centers of Quaker activity, but in the fifth port, Galway, the garrison commander expelled Friends in April 1660 after first incarcerating six of them. Quakers maintained a presence there into the 1670s, by which point their members drifted away, and the last Friend in Galway was reportedly preparing to move to Pennsylvania in 1683.[3]

The crackdown at Galway, where John Burnyeat and Robert Lodge had been active, was part of a fresh wave of persecution following the relatively mild years of the late 1650s. In the words of William Edmundson,

> now was King Charles coming in, and these Nations were in Heaps of Confusion, and ran upon us, as if they would have destroyed us at once, or swallowed us up, breaking up our Meetings, taking us up in Highways, and haling us to Prison; so that it was a general Imprisonment of Friends in this Nation.[4]

Edmundson himself was one of 124 Friends incarcerated in 1660, a substantial increase over the single Quaker jailed the previous year and nearly as high as the 135 imprisoned in 1661. Miles Gray was beaten and jailed at Carrickfergus and Coleraine in 1660 before going to Downpatrick, where he spent more than a year in jail. For exhorting members of the parish church at Newtown, county Fermanagh, to repent, John Edwards was incarcerated for six months and fined £100. When Margaret Blanch urged those attending a funeral of one of her relatives at Waterford to repent, she went to prison for six months and was also excommunicated; her husband was jailed for more than a year at Tipperary. Others, including the Dutch-born Abraham Fuller, measured their imprisonment in weeks or even days, as happened to Friends at Cavan. Because she testified against "will-worship" in a parish church at Waterford, Eleanor Tatlock and her husband were banished from the town, and others suffered distraint of their goods.[5]

The crackdown, which was neither uniform in its enforcement nor unvarying in its severity, strengthened the Friends' resolve. Edward Burrough, who had sailed from Bristol to Cork in June 1660 on his second visit to Ireland, informed Friends in London that the "little flock" of Irish Quakers, their "seed sown in weakness," had nevertheless been "preserved in its beauty" despite the afflictions to which they were subjected. In an undated letter from Cork apparently written about this time and intended for the population at large, he reiterated the prophetic themes so characteristic of the Friends' message in the 1650s:

> The day of the lord is approachinge, & the day of account Drawes neare upon yow ye Inhabitants of the earth, the time of your Covenant is expired. . . . This is the Day of your visitation. . . . The sword of the lord is Drawen against yow, & the whirlwind of his wrath is gone forth.

Before Burrough returned to England in February 1661 he traveled some 2,000 miles throughout Ireland, bolstering the faith of earlier converts and winning new adherents. Throughout his journey he enjoyed, by his own account, "very free passage in the principal cities and towns."[6]

In a letter to George Fox dated 17 August 1660 Thomas Loe confirmed the sporadic nature of the persecution. Writing from northern Ireland he reported that the situation there was "prettee Coole." Meetings "inlargeth dayly" and "all is quiate," yet at Cork, Bandon, Limerick, and other places in the west which he had just visited, persecution was substantial since the restoration of the traditional government. Friends in that region suffered imprisonment, physical beatings, the disruption of their meetings, and banishment from the towns.

Whole meetings have been carried to prisons in severall places, & at Limrick they have kept freinds neare 4 weekes together, & at Dublin the greatest part of a quarter of A yeare, & at Corke they have severall times don the same. I was there a littell while since, at a monthly meeting & neare the End of our meeting Thay Came with a gaurd of souldiers & Caried away all the men freinds to prison, & soe about waterford thay have don the same & allmost in all parts of the nation.

Yet he insisted to Fox that matters were "generally well" among the Friends, whose meetings were "fresh & liveing," and whose converts were increasing. Perhaps more surprisingly he told Fox he knew of no Quaker in prison at the time he wrote apart from some who had refused to pay tithes. Loe himself had been jailed several times, but only for short periods.[7]

From his prison cell in Rome John Perrot sent encouragement to Friends in Ireland in an epistle dated 3 July 1660. Intended to be copied and distributed to meetings throughout the country, it exhorted Quakers to attend their meetings faithfully, letting their zeal "burne in the house of god" so that minds would "be melted, & the drose Cast back, & god increased in the furnace." The allusion was to the ordeal of Shadrach, Meshach, and Abednego in the fiery furnace (Daniel 3). In a companion epistle to Irish Friends probably composed about the same time, Perrot exhorted them to be faithful in their battles and patient in their tribulation, promising them ultimate victory. He then switched to garden imagery befitting the island's beauty: "Oh Ireland the thoughts of my fathers Seed, & Lambes & tender plantes, among thy Briers & Thornes, you the thoughts of the Lillyes & Roses & Greene Bowes, & fruitefull Branches, to part from the young Ones, the vertue of my Life reaching them all, I am Even broken & Melted, aboundantly, into Waters; All stand to finish a Testimony for God." Perrot would return to Ireland with John Browne for several months in early 1662.[8]

In the year prior to Perrot's return, persecution of the Friends intensified. In April 1661 Edmundson informed Margaret Fell that numerous Quakers had been incarcerated at Cork, Waterford, and Limerick and that many had been fined substantial sums for meeting illegally, but he also noted that Friends in Ulster still enjoyed considerable liberty. Burrough probably wrote his undated appeal to Irish magistrates about the same time, and almost certainly prior to 4 May. He urged the magistrates to act moderately in "the breaking up of seperated meetings" despite pressures from higher authorities, appealing to their consciences that rigorous repression violated divine law. "God never made you judges over mens consciences in spirituall matters, but onely in outward thinges." Magistrates must permit "sectaries" freedom to worship according to their consciences, just as they would demand such liberty for themselves if the Catholics attempted to force them to attend mass. "But now you will say, you have good occasion to breake the seperated meetings, because they will rebell against the Goverment as it hath hapned at London," referring to the abortive Fifth Monarchist rebellion of Thomas Venner in January 1661, "to which I say I hope you will not condemn all for some." The Friends, he insisted, were not a rebellious people but patient sufferers.[9]

Responding to the king's initial attempt to implement a policy of indulgence rather than to Burrough's appeal, on 4 May the lords justices ordered the release of 42 Friends at Cork as well as unnamed others at Waterford, Limerick, Youghal, Maryborough (Portlaoise), and Cashel as long as they had been jailed solely for religious offenses. Moreover, they instructed those affected to appear before a chief magistrate to profess their loyalty to the king and to promise not to engage in any activity that would breach the peace; they were also commanded to pay any fees owed to their jailors. The lords justices warned the Quakers that any meetings outside the home for worship except the services of the Church of Ireland were still illegal and that offenders would be punished. In short, the directive amounted to amnesty for past religious infractions, not indulgence for the future.[10]

The prisoners at Cork responded with a statement of their principles, which they described as their "second Adresse," thus indicating they had previously submitted a statement that had probably enunciated their beliefs and petitioned for their release. Insisting their incarceration had been wrongful, they protested the "hard Conditions" of their release which required them to accept responsibility for their suffering but offered them no security from future persecution unless they foreswore their meetings and thereby broke their covenant with God. This they refused to do. Even pledging loyalty to the monarch was unacceptable because it implied their previous behavior had not been peaceful and innocent. The Friends were troubled as well because they did "not know how farr the words (dutifully) & (loyally), may be Construed & extended to obleidge & bind [them] & whether it be not meant to limmit & restraine [them] from gods spirituall worship." Nor would they pay jailors' fees, they insisted, because they had been unlawfully imprisoned. Their chief grievance was the lords justices' refusal to recognize their meetings as proper services of worship, "to which wee testifie & solemnly affirm"—in terms almost tantamount to an oath—"that our meetings were Instituted & Continued according to the will of god, & the doctrine of Christ & his disciples," and are devoted to worship, prayer, edification, and "working out our owne salvation with feare & trembling."[11]

Although these Friends refused to cease meeting, they offered a pledge to assure the lords justices, Parliament, and people of Ireland of their peaceful intentions:

Wee doe owne Charles the second . . . to be the Chife & supreame Magistrate & Ruller under god, in these kingdomes & dominions.

2ly That (saveing & Reserving Inviolable our obedience, faith & duties to Almighty god) wee doe (next under him) acknowledge, owne, & truely shall performe, our duty & obedience to the king, & unto all his righteous & Just Commands. . . .

3ly That if the king require ought of us, which is Contrary to our faith, & which for Conscience sake wee Cannot freely doe; or leave undone, wee shall rather Chuse, patiently to suffer, then to sinn. And shall not rise up with Carnell weapons to resist him, or worke our owne deliverance (hereby utterly renounceing the use of all such Instruments whereby to draw the bloud of any man, or break the publique peace). . . .

4ly That wee doe utterly Renounce all plotting, Conspiring & atempting violence, against the king, his goverment, or any insubordinate [sic] authority under him; but doe declare it to be our principall, & is & shalbe our Constant practice (if we are in health & able) forthwith to apeare before any person or persons in Lawfull authority over us . . . according to due & Lawfull Summons given us for that purpose.

In keeping with these principles the Friends pledged "to exersize [themselves] in active or passive obedience to the king," in return for which they sought not only their release but also freedom to meet peacefully in keeping with Charles's pledge of liberty to tender consciences in the Declaration of Breda.[12]

Edmundson subsequently claimed credit for having gone to Dublin and persuaded the lords justices to sign the order to release imprisoned Quakers, copies of which were dispatched to the appropriate sheriffs. In the ensuing month and a half Edmundson traveled around the country to determine whether or not Friends had in fact been released, often finding that they were still incarcerated. Informed that Quakers in Maryborough were yet in prison for refusal to pay the jailor's fees, he obtained a certificate from the justices indicating this and took it to Dublin. After first persuading the lord mayor to liberate Burnyeat and Lodge, who had been jailed a day earlier for attending an illegal meeting, he prevailed on the earl of Mountrath to obtain an order from the Council to free imprisoned Friends. Issued on 17 August, it had the desired effect in most places, for by late November Quakers were in jail only at Cork, and they expected imminent release. Yet Friends were not free of trouble, for at least some bishops and their officials summoned them to their tribunals for such offenses as not having had their children baptized, working on holy days, or recusancy.[13]

The number of Friends imprisoned in 1662 dropped to 47, a reflection of the growing realization among secular officials that Quakers posed no security threat nor did incarceration persuade them to embrace the established church. In the aftermath of the Dublin conspiracy in 1663, Ormond was determined to make Quakers obey the law, but they resolved to remain in prison until the magistrates wearied of keeping them there. In August the conformist minister George Clapham reported to the bishop of Kildare from Mountmellick, where Edmundson and Gershon Boate, whose father had been Charles I's physician, were active, that Quakers in this area were "as high as ever," having received their freedom at the last quarter sessions owing to Ormond's proclamation. Although Quaker meetings were still illegal, magistrates in the Mountmellick-Rosenallis area were ignoring them.[14] From the same region John Thompson, an ally of Ormond's, informed the duke that the Friends were dispatching "ther number one after another abroad where they know Any Confused people; they Compass sea and Land to make one prosylite." They sent some of these traveling ministers to Ulster, where by year's end Thompson learned their numbers were increasing, "And As they Multiply in Number soe likways doe they in Turbulency And keeps there Conventions A little More publiquelie." Around

Mountmellick too he noticed the Quakers' greater boldness, though by year's end a few of them had conformed to the Church of Ireland.[15] On 16 January 1664 Fox and other Quaker leaders could report to Friends in general that in Ireland, as in Barbados, New England, Maryland, Virginia, and Scotland, "truth is of good savour and the power is stirring." A frustrated Thompson reflected the Quakers' confidence a month and a half later when he told Ormond that Friends in his area believed their persecution was over, "from which supposition they take so much Confidence that ther is no liveing by them in qu[i]etnesse."[16]

The abatement of persecution notwithstanding, some Friends still went to prison in the mid-1660s. Abraham Fuller and Thomas Holme recorded only eleven cases in 1663, two in 1664, thirteen in 1665, two in 1666, and 37 in both 1667 and 1668, but these figures were incomplete. In February 1664, for instance, a group of Dublin Friends meeting in a private home refused the command of four constables to disperse, whereupon approximately twenty of them, including the bishop of Killaloe's wife, were jailed. Perhaps about the same time Edmundson and others were imprisoned "several Times," but the magistrates finally decided not to incarcerate Edmundson because "they had too many in Prison already, who were kept from their Labours and Families."[17] Some officials locked up only the leaders, as in the case of Ralph Sharply, deemed the "cheife of the Quakers" at Carrickfergus, who went to jail in 1666 after refusing to plead to several indictments and allegedly uttering seditious words in court. The intercession of an unidentified "noble Lady" on his behalf was of no avail. Orrery confined Thomas Loe, "who had got together a great Number of his Tribe," the following year.[18] The mayor of Cork, Christopher Rye, was primarily responsible for sparking a new wave of persecution. In 1667 he sent William Penn and eighteen others to prison for illegally meeting on 3 November; for the same offense he imprisoned seven Friends on 24 November and nine on 8 December, and he continued to arrest them the following year.[19]

Thus persecution was on the upswing by the time Fox landed at Dublin on 10 May 1669 in the company of James Lancaster, Robert Lodge, John Stubbs, and Thomas Briggs. Fox was well aware of this, as reflected in his critical reference to the smell in the air, possibly an allusion to smoke from peat fires and certainly a metaphorical reference to the smell of evil: "When wee came on shore, the Earth and the very aire, smelt with the corruption of the Nation, and gave Another smell then England to mee, with the corruption & the blood, and the Massacres, & the foulenesse that Asscended." His three-month sojourn in

Ireland was primarily significant because of the impetus he gave to organizing (discussed below), but he also bolstered the spirits of Irish Friends and, unintentionally, the government's efforts to crackdown on Quakers. Fox was a marked man when he arrived in Ireland, and a number of magistrates were reportedly frustrated by their inability to find and arrest him. Cognizant of the peril, Fox cloaked parts of his tour, especially in the north, in relative secrecy, even to the point of asking Friends in England not to write to him while he was in Ireland lest they reveal his location to the authorities.[20]

Some magistrates appear to have been less than diligent in seeking Fox's apprehension. When he and his party arrived in Dublin they spent hours inquiring where they could find local Friends, and they subsequently spent several days in the capital attending weekly, provincial, and men's meetings, none of which were secret. Fox openly baited Catholics, especially in southern Ireland, at various times offering to pay a priest two pence if he would say a mass for Fox's horse: "The candles had A Mass, & the Lambs had A Mass, why might not his horse have A Mass?" At Bandon Fox converted the mayor's wife, and for her sake, her husband claimed, he did not apprehend Fox. By the time Fox reached Cork four warrants for his arrest were outstanding, yet he brazenly rode past Mayor Rye's door en route to the city marketplace and so close to the town prison that jailed Quakers saw him. While he was near Limerick several Friends told Fox the magistrates had a description of him, and he was henceforth more guarded in his movements, though still attending provincial, men's, and general meetings and challenging Catholics. After moving through Ulster he returned to Dublin, where his presence worried more timid Friends, yet he not only stayed but also attended the six-months meeting as well as men's and women's meetings. Prior to returning to England Fox devoted a week to answering papers from monks, friars, and "protestant Preists." Accompanied by nearly a hundred Quakers to the ship that would take him back to England, Fox could hardly have been missed by the magistrates. Lancaster, Briggs, Lodge, Holme, and an unidentified Dublin Friend returned to England with him.[21]

Other Friends visited Ireland in 1669, among them Penn, John Wilkinson, John Banks, and Solomon Eccles. Some were women, notably Katherine Cooper, Hester Lund, and two visitors from Virginia, Alice (Ambrose?) and Mary (Tomkins?).[22] At Galway the music teacher Eccles, naked from the waist up and with a pan of coals on his head, went with Randal Cousins, Nicholas Gribble, and Henry Bloodsworth to a

Catholic service outside the town and exhorted the people to repent. The group then came into the town and delivered the same message, subsequent to which all four were jailed. Altogether, according to Fuller and Holme, 141 Quakers went to prison in 1669, the highest total for any year between 1660 and 1700. Under Rye and his successor, Matthew Deane, Cork continued its dubious achievement of being a leading center of Quaker persecution. Deane not only arrested most of the male Friends in Cork but also refused to permit those who were artisans to continue their trade in prison to support their families. Moreover he issued multiple indictments against Quakers arrested for attending more than one illegal meeting.[23]

Persecution abated again in the 1670s when imprisonments averaged twenty *per annum* according to the figures of Fuller and Holme, with the high of 37 occurring in 1678 following Ormond's return as lord lieutenant. The polemicist Thomas Jenner, whose *Quakerism Anatomiz'd and Confuted* was published in 1670 in the hope of winning back converts, referred to the movement's growing numbers and reported a recent meeting, probably in Dublin, attended by some 500 Friends. "Quakerism," he contended, was "but the opening of the vast and horrid sink of the dead Sea of Old Heresies."[24] The Friends' mood was reflected in a tract written by the Dublin merchant Anthony Sharp the following year. In it he chided those who "pretended to a Gospel Ministry" for persecuting Christians who merely followed their consciences. Urging repentance while there was still time, he warned persecutors that any blood they shed would be on their own heads. "Consider it you that have this plenty and doe not you read wherefore the Lord [punished] by sword and plauge, by hail and by fire against the nations of the heathens?"[25]

Visiting Friends continued to crisscross Ireland in the 1670s. Among them were Lodge and Burnyeat, both of whom made their third and fourth visits; John Banks, who went to Ireland six times between 1671 and 1682; and Oliver Sansom, who reckoned that he traveled some 950 miles on a four-month journey in 1676 that took him as far afield as Lurgan and Antrim in the north, Limerick in the west, and Cork and Youghal in the south. Women such as Alice Leak, Mary Worrell, and Katherine Norton as well as two unidentified women from Lancashire also traveled through Ireland in the 1670s. Norton (née McLaughlin) had been born in Ireland of Gaelic Irish parents and educated at Derry, after which she emigrated to Barbados, where she married and was later converted by Fox. Traveling with Thomas Trafford in 1678, she visited most of the meetings in the north, where she found the Friends "as Innocent a plain people as I have been amongst." Thomas Curtis of Reading visited meetings at such places as Limerick, Tipperary, Rosenallis, Abbeyleix, and nearby Ballinakill in Queen's county (Laois). Accompanying Curtis for part of this trip was Anthony Sharp, who offered advice on which places to visit.[26] The itinerary of the former Congregationalist James Parke took him from Dublin to Rosenallis and then to Moate in county Westmeath, where he attended a "considerable" meeting. From there he traveled to Cavan, Armagh, Lurgan, and Drogheda before returning to Dublin. In contrast Humphrey Norton followed a southern circuit that took him to Dublin, the Wexford area, Waterford, Youghal, Cork, Kinsale, Bandon, Limerick, and Galway. The most ambitious journey was probably that of Burnyeat, who had previously been to Ireland in 1659–1660, 1664, and 1669–1670. Between 24 May and 25 December 1673 he visited most of the meetings twice, ranging from Cork and Bandon to counties Armagh and Antrim. For the most part these traveling ministers were left alone by the authorities, but John Stubbs, who did not return with Fox to England in 1669, was subsequently incarcerated at Cork and would have been whipped and banished had it not been for the intervention of Quaker merchants.[27]

Some of the best documented travels are those of John Banks of Cumberland, who first came to the island in 1670 after receiving an invitation from John Tiffin, who himself traveled to Ireland nine times in his career. Arriving at Carrickfergus, he and Tiffin visited meetings in Ulster, where they were "well satisfied of the Truth of [their] Service" before moving to the Dublin area. He returned to Ireland in May 1671 in time to attend the half-yearly meeting in Dublin, "and a Glorious Heavenly Meeting it was, where many Faithful Brethren from all Parts of the Nation were come." He remarked in glowing terms about the unity and fellowship that characterized this meeting, and commented as well on the determination of Irish Friends to journey throughout the country "that the Gathered may be Established, and that they that are not yet Gathered may be Gathered." At Edmundson's suggestion, he went to Wicklow, where one or two Quakers lived but where no meeting existed. With "several Friends and Friendly people" he met in a carpenter's shop, but the tiny group was soon disrupted by troops dispatched in response to a local minister's complaint. When Banks questioned a serjeant's authority, he was arrested and taken to the governor's house, where he denounced the priest as a minister of Antichrist and attempted to address the curious who gathered outside. The governor thereupon had him and two others jailed for violating the Conventicle Act. When an obliging jailor permitted Banks to have visitors, he won more converts. The imprisonment lasted only three days, after which the governor freed Banks despite the latter's refusal to appear at the next assize or quarter sessions or to promise to hold no more meetings.[28]

Banks returned to Dublin and then in the company of George Gregson and two others journeyed to Ulster, where he attended the provincial meeting. His heart, however, was in the south, and he made plans for an ambitious trip that would take him from Wicklow and Wexford to Clonmel, Tallow, Youghal, Cork, and the west, "where the Lord is bringing forth a People." "The Harvest," he wrote to his wife in June 1671, "is very great in this Nation." When Friends in Wicklow requested another visit, he went there in the summer and this time held a meeting without disturbance from the authorities. Shortly thereafter, the parish minister prosecuted and imprisoned Quakers for refusing to pay tithes and other religious offenses. Banks returned to England the same year, perhaps without completing his planned sojourn to the south and west, though he was at Mallow, county Cork, in August. Two years later "the Lord required it of [him] to go and visit Ireland again." Apart from another visit to Wicklow, where he called on fourteen imprisoned Friends, virtually nothing is known of this trip.[29]

When Banks came back to Ireland in 1675 he again went to Wicklow. By this time the minister who had stringently opposed him had died and the town no longer had a garrison. Under these circumstances the Friends were prospering and enjoyed regular meetings. On this trip he "Travelled most of the Nation thro'," including Ulster, where he met at Antrim in defiance of Massereene's order.[30] Returning to Ireland in 1676, he traveled with John Watson, another Cumberland man, to Wicklow, Wexford, Clonmel, Tallow, Youghal, Cork, the west, Charleville, Mallow, and Limerick. After attending the provincial meeting in Dublin, he expressed concern over growing strife within the movement: "Oh! that Friends might live in Love and Unity together; . . . and whatsoever would arise among them, that in its rise in any wise tends to the breaking of their Heavenly Unity, and Brotherly Fellowship, and sowing of Dissention in the Churches of Christ, may be nip'd in the Budd."[31] Banks revisited Ireland in 1682 but almost nothing is known of this trip.[32]

The unity for which Banks longed was severely tested at Dublin in the late 1670s. In the spring of 1677 a sexual liaison between one of the leading members, Samuel Clarridge, and his maid scandalized the meeting, and Clarridge exacerbated the problem by responding defiantly to charges of misconduct. (See Chapter 8.) About the same time the Dublin meeting struggled with the case of John Marshall, against whom a testimony was issued "for his oposeing the power of God in Geo. Gregson." His alleged offense occasioned a lengthy statement at the six-months meeting warning that the spirit of darkness had endeavored to undermine God's work in Dublin by destroying unity through backbiting, false accusations, and the like. For the sake of restoring harmony Marshall submitted, though he subsequently told Sharp in private that he had not done so because he was guilty. Persuaded of his innocence, Sharp denounced the meeting's testimony against Marshall on 10 November. Two days earlier the half-yearly meeting had ruled that those who had signed the testimony and now felt differently could withdraw their names, while those who had not signed were permitted to do so at this late date.[33] The strife troubled visitors to Dublin. From England James Parke wrote to Sharp on 24 November that he was "Sensible of that reproach and Infamy that was brought upon the Truth of God in your city and nation by some that profess it there," and the following April Robert Stepney wrote to Sharp from London about "the Difference" among Friends in Dublin, urging reconciliation. Early the following month Dublin Quakers resolved their disagreements and issued an exhortation "to watch against the enemy that sowes dissention & strife amongst Godes people." Clarridge put forth his own statement expressing sorrow for having offended Friends.[34]

The dissension did not conclude here, for by early 1679 the Story-Wilkinson dispute was causing controversy in Ireland. The debate had erupted in England, primarily over the nature and role of women's meetings, recording papers of condemnation except at the instigation of the guilty party, opposition to mandatory written testimonies against tithes, an insistence on silence while Friends were speaking or praying, and limiting the number of Quakers who attended business meetings. The dispute intensified in May 1675 when the Story-Wilkinson group established its own business meeting, and matters worsened two years later, in June 1677, when the yearly meeting of ministers banned services for worship in the houses of those who had participated in schismatic business meetings. In the course of the controversy Fox met with Story and Wilkinson at Worcester Castle in January 1675, with Thomas Lower present to support Fox, and Thomas and Ann Curtis as backers of Story and Wilkinson.[35]

In March 1679 Thomas Curtis wrote to Sharp and his wife protesting scandalous allegations against Story and Wilkinson circulating in Ireland. He was no less incensed about allegations that he had accused Fox of "setting up popery In england," the source of which was reputedly the Dublin linen draper James Fade. The latter had subsequently claimed this was all a mistake. "A Reconciliation is desired by many friends," Curtis told the Sharps, but if this could not be achieved, "all these differences will be made much higher than ever they were." The following month, as both sides in the dispute claimed the movement's soul, Penn, George Whitehead, William Meade, and nine other Quakers informed Irish Friends that Story had adopted a conciliatory attitude in his meeting with them. Consequently they urged all Quakers to "be exercised towards him, for the Bringing of him nearer to his Brethren who are in the ancient fellowship." At the half-yearly meeting in Dublin in May, Irish Quakers signaled their loyalty to Fox by appointing a committee of six men to receive reports of unsavory words or letters spoken or written by Curtis to anyone in Ireland concerning differences between the majority of the movement and the Story-Wilkinson group.[36]

In May 1680 Sharp wrote to Story, expressing concern that he and his supporters were not in unity with the main body of Friends and urging Story to go to the yearly meeting in London and seek peace by expressing a willingness to take its advice as far as he could with a good conscience. He also recommended that Story encourage his supporters to be there as well "in the same Spirit of forgiveness and peace." If Story felt disinclined to attend the meeting, Sharp asked him to write seeking reconciliation. In a letter to the London yearly meeting on the disunity resulting from the dispute, Sharp appealed for an end to the recriminations that had become so embittered in the aftermath of the denunciation of Story and Wilkinson by the yearly meeting in June 1677. Confusion reigned in some meetings: "In time of prayer, in Publick meetings that some sit with their hats on, and some with their hats of[f] and that by those that are against John Story and John Wilkinson in confusion amongst themselves and not only in time of John Storys prayers but also when others pray publickly that have a kindness for them and mercy, for their restoration into unity again." Neither the offense of Story and Wilkinson nor the ensuing testimony against them, Sharp argued, justified their expulsion from the movement. Like God, he averred, the Friends must blend mercy with judgment.[37]

Irish Quakers emerged from the internal tensions of the late 1670s with their unity intact. In a letter dated 12 May 1682 from the six-months meeting to the yearly meeting in London, Irish Friends reported that for the most part they enjoyed peace and unity among themselves and suffered little at the hands of the authorities apart from "Some Small matter" of tithes. Indeed, Fuller and Holme indicate only fourteen imprisonments in the period 1680 to 1682.[38] At the six-months meeting in November 1683, according to Burnyeat, the Quakers enjoyed "a blessed Season" of peace and love, "and so all was sweet and comfortable." Despite rumors that the laws against nonconformists would shortly be enforced, meetings were "large and full" throughout the country, with some areas reporting a receptivity to the Quaker message among outsiders. Burnyeat visited meetings in the counties of Queen's, Wicklow, and Carlow, and meetings at Edenderry, Moate, Cork, and the Bandon area in 1682.[39] Among the other traveling ministers in the early 1680s were William Bingley of London (accompanied for a time by Sharp and Clarridge), Mary Worrell, Eleanor Starkey, Benjamin Bangs of Norfolk, and the Cumberland men James Dickinson and Thomas Wilson. After traveling with Wilson in Leinster and Munster, Dickinson went north, where he had "several meetings amongst people that professed not with us," winning several converts, presumably Baptists or Congregationalists. At Antrim Bangs attracted an overflow crowd, some of whom pelted his audience with soil and turf while he preached.[40]

Despite continuing problems at Cork and rumors of an impending crackdown, the situation worsened for the Friends only after the disclosure of the Rye House plotting in the late spring of 1683. Even then, according to the figures of Fuller and Holme, the number of Quakers imprisoned in 1683 rose only to eighteen.[41] Not until early August did magistrates move against Friends in Dublin, at which time the latter refused a command to disperse and, unlike other nonconformists, disobeyed an order to cease holding meetings. Quakers elsewhere in Ireland behaved similarly. Incarcerated in the Marshalsea, Burnyeat exhorted imprisoned English Friends in Gloucester to remain steadfast: "Though the Winds do blow, and the Waters swell and toss, and the unestablished be driven to and fro, and so afflicted in their Spirits, yet this Rock abides for a Habitation and Being of Safety unto all them, that keep firm thereunto." Although the earl of Arran expressed sympathy for the Quakers, not until October were Burnyeat and his fellow prisoners released following their written appeal to the lord deputy. He imposed no conditions.[42]

During the remaining months of Charles II's reign the government generally left Irish Friends alone. Fuller and Holme record only eight imprisonments in 1684. Following his liberation Burnyeat visited every meeting in Ulster and reported in early February 1684 that he had "found things in the main very well." By mid-March he had been through most of the south and west, where he observed similar conditions.[43]

When James II succeeded his brother on the throne, magistrates were temporarily uncertain as to how nonconformists should be treated. Fuller and Holme report only two imprisonments in 1685, but Edmundson and several other Friends were briefly jailed in Dublin. For the most part, the pre-revolutionary years were good ones for the Quakers. Traveling ministers continued to crisscross the country, among them Dickinson, Oliver Sansom of Berkshire, Christopher Story of Cumberland, Joan Vokins, and Benjamin Brown and Thomas Musgrave of Yorkshire. Dickinson preached a message that proved to be prophetic as he warned Friends "to be careful that they might have a habitation and settlement in the power of God; for a time of trial would come upon them, that would try all their foundations."[44] Burnyeat continued to report large, peaceful meetings in Dublin and Ulster. Many thought the half-yearly meeting in May 1685 attracted a record number of participants, and Burnyeat observed that "to our publick Meetings [in Dublin] abundance of other People come, even far more than could get into our House," at least in part because other nonconformists were reticent to resume their services. His visit to the meetings of southern Ireland in the summer was uneventful, and on 29 June 1686 he could tell a fellow believer in London that Irish Friends enjoyed "a Degree of that Rest, which the Distresses, that are from below, cannot Reach."[45]

Quaker leaders in England sought to take advantage of the improved climate by deputing George Whitehead to present the earl of Clarendon with a select list of Irish Friends who would apply to him on matters of Quaker concern. When Whitehead gave him the list on 3 November 1685 prior to his departure for Ireland, Clarendon responded favorably. Fox asked that two or three Friends call on the earl after he arrived in Dublin.[46]

The Friends benefited from James's policy of indulgence and responded favorably to Tyrconnell's request to send supportive statements to the king. On behalf of fellow Quakers in Ireland, Edmundson, Sharp, Fuller, Francis Randall, Thomas Trafford, and John Tottenham drafted an address thanking James and expressing their loyalty, but also pointing out that many of them had suffered significant financial losses because of their faith. They asked the king not to listen to accusations against them without giving them an opportunity to defend themselves. Sharp and seven others submitted the petition to Tyrconnell in July 1687.[47] That fall the government announced its intention to include Quakers and other nonconformists in the corporations, a policy with which the Friends complied.[48] (See Chapter 8.)

Even in these good years there were hints of trouble to come. At Youghal in July 1686 the town council discussed the possibility of quartering some of the five companies of foot in Quaker homes on the grounds that the Friends benefited by trading in the town but refused to serve as churchwardens, constables, and similar officials. In the spring of 1687 the government quartered troops at Mountmellick and Rosenallis, two of them in Edmundson's home. When he fed them boiled veal, oat bread, cheese, butter, and milk, they complained vigorously, causing Edmundson to fear for his life. He urged Sharp and Burnyeat to warn Tyrconnell that if the practice continued, many persons would be driven from their occupations.[49] In general, the Friends enjoyed relative quiet until the outbreak of war in 1689.[50] The time of troubles that ensued virtually stopped English Quakers from touring Ireland until 1692, after which visits were commonplace for years.[51] The war inflicted substantial suffering on Friends, but the mid- and late 1690s was a period of recovery and growth notwithstanding the continuation of heavy financial penalties (discussed in Chapter 8.)

Organizing the Society

The organization of the Friends in Ireland was not identical to that in England. Indeed, prior to his visit to Ireland in 1669 Fox appears not to have realized this, for the previous year he encouraged Irish Friends to settle their men's monthly meetings in addition to the "generall Quarterly meetinges" they supposedly had. In fact, Irish Friends had no quarterly meetings *per se* until the late 1690s. The Irish equivalent, the provincial or six-weeks meeting to which Fox was referring, dated from 1668. The first mention of a monthly meeting occurs in Thomas Loe's letter of 17 August 1660, in which he casually refers to his attendance at such a meeting at Cork. The Irish equivalent of the national yearly meeting in England, the half-yearly meeting, first convened in August 1669 at the time of Fox's visit and later in the same year on 5 November at Penn's lodging in Dublin. Women's meetings predated Fox's visit, but Edmundson observed that when Fox was in Ireland "he settled Men and Women's Meetings among Friends throughout the Nation." This was much to Edmundson's liking, for as he told Fox, he had been concerned about organizational matters for several years; "this gave every faithful Friend a Share of the Burthen."[52]

The system was essentially democratic. As a statement in the records of the half-yearly meeting in November 1687 explained, the original "Constitution" called for each provincial meeting to appoint at least six delegates to attend the national meeting in Dublin. These representatives were to be "such as are well qualified and fit to make application to the Government when there is occasion."[53] The intent was never to restrict the number from each province to six but to encourage the attendance of as many suitably qualified men as wanted to participate. As a result some of the monthly men's meetings, including those at Moate, Lisburn, and Lurgan, regularly named two or sometimes three of their members to attend. The Dublin men's meeting appointed delegates but often encouraged all qualified, interested men to participate. Not surprisingly, the biggest delegation at the half-yearly meetings was typically from Leinster, and many times that delegation was larger than the combined strength of its counterparts from Munster and Ulster. Between November 1673 and May 1689 the Leinster delegation averaged fifteen, or roughly twice the size of the Munster and Ulster delegations. Decisions of the national meeting were based on consensus, not voting, but the Leinster delegates' numerical superiority would have given their province considerable weight. In addition to the official delegates, many people apparently attended as observers; in May 1680, 200 to 300 people were present at the national men's and women's meetings.[54]

Several basic problems beset the half-yearly meeting. As members remarked in November 1687, its provisions concerning the appointment of delegates had not been "fully kept to by every Province meeting," an apparent reference to the fact that occasionally fewer than six delegates had represented a particular province. But this was a rare happening and in recent years had only occurred once—in November 1685 when Munster sent four representatives. The complaint was more likely made with reference to the quality of certain delegates. "Our desire," the meeting indicated in November 1687, "is that such as are leading men in each Province may Looke upon themselves [as] concerned in this service." By May 1696 the problem of unqualified attenders had become serious enough to require a formal provision for barring "disorderly unfitt Raw persons." At the commencement of each half-yearly meeting one delegate was chosen from each province and a fourth from Dublin "to take effectuall care dureing the time of the said Meeting of busines to keepe out all such persons as are not approved of by sensible freinds that know them." Hitherto such responsibility apparently rested with a paid doorkeeper. The May 1696 meeting also recommended that men's and women's meetings take the same care to exclude unfit persons from their gatherings, and the Leinster provincial meeting made a point of reporting that it had done so by the following November. Irish Friends were thus somewhat stricter in excluding unfit persons than their colleagues in England.[55]

Another problem was not organizational but pragmatic. Given the fact that so many Friends engaged in trade and manufacturing, the biannual gathering of delegates afforded a ready opportunity to conduct commercial transactions, a practice that rendered Quakers subject to criticism from hostile outsiders. In November 1683, therefore, the delegates decided the conduct of trade during the meeting was "a great inconveniencie . . . both as to the Cumbering of friends minds when they should be Concerned about the Lords business, & it hindereth the service of Truth, & also giveth occasion for some to Judge that Friends are Covetous minded." The admonition not to conduct business during the national meetings had to be repeated again and again. Unable to terminate the practice, the delegates in May 1697 asked provincial meetings to caution Friends not to bring merchandise or cattle to Dublin at the time of the half-yearly meetings. No one, they added, must think such gatherings were "for the mannagement of outward or worldly concernes." When even this step proved ineffectual, the delegates in November 1699 urged members of the Dublin men's meeting to report offenders to their respective men's meetings.[56]

Few regulations existed with respect to the operation of the six-months meetings, the conduct of which was undoubtedly expected to emulate the local and provincial men's meetings. By the mid-1690s the six-months meetings must have become somewhat unruly, for the delegates in May 1696 found it necessary to insist that Friends in attendance "sit downe orderly" and that those with something to bring before the meeting speak audibly and one at a time. Some delegates must have been leaving early, for the Leinster provincial meeting and the Moate men's meeting deemed it necessary to instruct their delegates to remain at the half-yearly meeting until all business had been concluded.[57]

The mandate of the six-months meeting was broad, ranging from matters of worship and service to the recording of sufferings and application to magistrates on behalf of victims of persecution. In Novem-

·ber 1669 the half-yearly meeting examined provincial records of sufferings, returned Ulster's as inadequate, and instructed each provincial
men's meeting "to be more punctual in the registering of all sufferings,
and to transmit them in briefly [sic] to the National Meeting." It also
prepared an address for Penn and William Morris to deliver to the
mayor of Dublin, who treated them harshly and refused to release incarcerated Friends.[58] The six-months meeting also dealt with the more
severe or problematic cases of discipline brought to its attention by
provincial meetings, the articulation and application of Quaker standards of behavior, the publication and distribution of printed materials,
and budgetary oversight of collections and disbursements. The half-
yearly meeting was extensively involved in the construction of meetinghouses in Dublin as well as educational matters, and it served as the
vehicle for official communications with the yearly meeting in England,
notably the annual report commencing in the early 1680s on "the affairs
of Truth" in Ireland.[59] Beginning in the late 1690s it appointed representatives to attend the yearly meeting in London, and it received and often
circulated epistles of note from individual Friends around the world.
The six-months meeting accumulated material for the yearly meeting in
London dealing with the identity of imprisoned Friends; the number
discharged in the past year and how their release was obtained; the
number who died in jail; the deaths of "publick friends"; the number of
meetinghouses constructed and new meetings founded; the progress
of the movement, with special attention to matters of education and
standards of behavior; and the "signall Judgments" that had befallen
persecutors.[60]

Over the years the procedures employed by the half-yearly meeting
became more structured. The best example pertains to the meeting's
interest in maintaining appropriate behavioral standards. In May 1672
the delegates appointed seven men to report in November on how local
meetings were dealing with recent statements from the half-yearly
meeting concerning fashion. In November 1677 the meeting assigned
representatives from the provinces to make inquiries about adherence
to previous testimonies on fashion, household goods, holy days, tithes,
and the manufacture and sale of goods "truth will not allow of." Reports of the investigation were to be made to the provincial meetings,
and if conditions were not "cleare and well," a report was to be submitted to the half-yearly meeting. These investigations subsequently became the basis of a structured system of visitation (see Chapter 8). Then,
in November 1692, the six-months meeting instructed each provincial

meeting not only to appoint Friends to inspect each local meeting to ensure compliance with behavioral standards but also to name one or two Quakers from each local meeting to make inquiries concerning worship, public Friends, and testimonies. In May 1694 the half-yearly meeting directed this select committee of "Friends of the ministry" in each province to meet at least once each quarter with the two Quakers from each local meeting responsible for inquiries concerning worship and testimonies so that "a right understanding may bee had how all things are among Friends, & advice may bee given where needfull." Commencing in 1694 the provincial committees appointed delegates to convene in a select or "chamber" meeting prior to the half-yearly meeting to discuss matters of national concern.[61]

At the provincial level, meetings, which were held at six-week intervals, were especially concerned with discipline but they were no less significant as the intermediary between local meetings and the half-yearly meeting. This was particularly so in the latter part of the period under review as Quakers formalized and expanded procedures to monitor behavioral standards, worship, testimonies, and the ministry of public Friends. Unlike the half-yearly meeting, provincial meetings gathered at various locales in each province, prompting periodic discussion and minor competition among local meetings desirous of serving as host. At the suggestion of the Antrim women's meeting, the Ulster provincial meeting decided in February 1693 to rotate future gatherings between Ballyhagan, Lurgan, and Ballinderry.[62]

The provincial meeting was, of course, responsible to see that at least six qualified people attended the half-yearly meeting and to take a record of the province's sufferings with them. In November 1685 the six-months meeting formally scolded the Munster meeting for not sending sufficient delegates, to which Munster retorted that it had previously relied on volunteers and that it would take steps to ensure the participation of the requisite amount in the future. As in many democratic societies, the right to participate seems to have been taken for granted and was tempered by apathy. In October 1681 the Ulster provincial meeting had found it necessary to chide the Lisburn meeting for sending insufficient representatives.[63] The provincial meetings also wrestled with the problem of barring unfit members from meetings at all levels.

Apparently referring to Samuel Clarridge's reluctance to acknowledge his sexual impropriety to the Dublin men's meeting, Anthony Sharp asked the Leinster provincial meeting in May 1678 if a person who refused to subject himself to his meeting's authority should be permitted to participate in the provincial meeting on business not involving him. To this the provincial representatives responded that such a person would be advised to subordinate himself to his meeting. The problem of unfit members became more pressing as the movement expanded in the relatively peaceful years following the time of troubles. In September 1693 the Ulster provincial meeting had to appoint fourteen men to speak to persons who attended its gatherings but were "not faithfull in their testimonies & of blameles Conversation."[64]

The provincial meetings had a mandate from the half-yearly meeting to prevent "Raw and unfitt persons" as well as those who refused to accept mediation of their disputes or adhere to imposed judgments from attending men's and women's business meetings. The Leinster provincial meeting candidly acknowledged in July 1698 that it had not been successful in barring unfit persons from men's meetings, particularly those who manifested "great Charracters of Covetousnesse and Earthly mindednesse." The following year the same meeting resolved that a person who had been "once enlightened" but subsequently "defile[d] himselfe with a woman," denied the fact, and then confessed (as had Clarridge) should not be permitted to attend meetings "untill the Lord grants Repentance unto amendment of Life" and this was demonstrated to the satisfaction of Friends. Still, the problem continued, for in January 1700 the Leinster provincial meeting, concerned that one or more persons "not Conformable to Gospell Order" were present, reiterated its directions to monthly meetings to prevent such persons from attending sessions, especially at the provincial level. At its gathering in October 1700 the Leinster delegates recommended to the monthly meetings that no members, whether male or female, be permitted to participate in sessions "to adjudge others" unless they were subject to "the Order" of their meeting.[65]

The provincial meeting played an important role in the transmission of material from one body of Friends to another. Most commonly this involved the dissemination of documents from the half-yearly meeting to the monthly meetings, but it also entailed occasional communications pertaining to Friends in London or correspondence with other provincial meetings. The latter also concerned themselves with care of the poor, widows, and orphans as well as marriages.[66]

Because traveling in Munster was often hazardous, meetings in the Tipperary area organized a six-weeks meeting in 1681, the records for which commence in August of that year. Originally it convened at Clonmel, but after 1685 it sometimes met at Kilcommonbeg. Beginning in

1692 the provincial and half-yearly meetings authorized Tipperary Friends to hold a monthly meeting to conduct business at Knockgraffon; in addition to the latter, its component meetings were Cahir, Clonmel, Cashel, Kilcommonbeg, and Waterford (after 20 February 1693). The six-weeks meeting, which remained subordinate to the Munster provincial meeting, rotated between Kilcommonbeg, Clonmel, and Waterford.[67]

The term "monthly" meeting suggests a regularity in gathering that was often not the case; the Dublin meeting, moreover, met biweekly. Monthly meetings conducted a variety of business ranging from discipline, care of the poor, and financial matters to the time[68] and place of worship and business meetings as well as collections. They also dealt with such matters as the construction and maintenance of meeting-houses and burial yards. Monthly meetings were the foundation of the Friends' system of record keeping, for each meeting was responsible to maintain an accurate account of births, marriages, deaths, testimonies, and papers of disownment and condemnation. Papers from half-yearly and provincial meetings were read at monthly meetings, following which appropriate action was taken if necessary, sometimes including a decision to read a paper to local meetings for worship.[69] Although monthly meetings usually had more than enough to keep them busy, sessions with no business to consider were not unknown, particularly at a smaller meeting such as Lurgan.[70]

Monthly meetings concerned themselves with a variety of matters directly relevant to spiritual concerns. The Dublin men's meeting, for instance, appointed special services in the 1690s, particularly for children and servants, to remind them of Quaker principles. These proved beneficial, "the Lord owning the same by affording his divine tendring power." In June 1700 the men's meeting convened a special service for husbands and wives, and in November of the same year for heads of families, both male and female. These gatherings too proved to be useful.[71] In June 1696 the Dublin men's meeting insisted it was "necessary and decent" for men and women to sit separately in the meetinghouse, and it made a special point of conveying this decision to the women's meeting; members of the two sexes had clearly been sitting together in meetings of worship. To ensure an appropriate setting for meetings, the Dublin men's meeting began appointing two of its number in the mid-1690s to prevent Friends' children and servants from playing outside the meetinghouse while sessions were underway.[72]

Much of the monthly meetings' business increasingly involved the implementation of directives from the half-yearly and provincial meetings. Monthly meetings selected delegates for the latter, and some also dispatched representatives to the former. In keeping with instructions from the higher bodies, they attempted to prevent unsuitable men from attending both their own sessions and the provincial and six-months meetings. Reports of action taken in this regard are not common. One such case occurred at Moate in June 1695, when the men's meeting decided John Still was unfit to sit with them until he acknowledged "his evill." Another involved Richard Middleton of Dublin, who learned he was unwelcome to sit in the gallery (normally reserved for public Friends) until he came "into nearer unity" with Quakers.[73] At Lisburn the men's meeting appointed sixteen of its members in April 1697 to determine which persons were qualified to participate in business meetings, and in October it asked those responsible for visiting families to counsel unfit persons not to attend business meetings "untill they be in more unity with frinds and walk more answereable to truth." Some degree of apathy was present at the local level, for the Dublin men's meeting found it necessary in the late 1690s to urge all Friends "approved and thought fitt" to attend its sessions unless they had a sufficient reason for their absence.[74]

Monthly men's meetings in Leinster received instructions from the province in January 1698 to prohibit the "Rash Irreverent Appearances" that had recently disrupted some gatherings. If those in attendance failed to manifest a meek, quiet spirit, the two members in each meeting responsible for the oversight of the ministry and worship were to counsel them. In both the men's and women's meetings Friends were expected to avoid extremes in speaking and debate and to talk one at a time.[75] The need for such a reminder suggests that business meetings sometimes involved heated debate and occasional loss of decorum.

The half-yearly, provincial, and especially the women's meetings periodically issued epistles to Friends, but such missives from men's meetings are relatively rare. The Dublin men's meeting sent one to Friends in its area on 7 October 1673 in which it exhorted believers to use the light of Christ "to see how it is with you in the Inward man whether you are going forward on your Journey towards the everlasting rest of the soul or whether there is a Stand or a stop In any." The meeting beseeched each Friend to wait for the emergence of the same power and life that had arisen in Christians of the past. "Wait to feel that which Quickneth up to everlasting Life." The authors then turned from this characteristic Quaker theme to the practical matter of admonishing members to attend meetings at the appointed times and not to disrupt the work of the Spirit by arriving late.[76]

According to Edmundson, Fox settled men's and women's meetings while in Ireland, though Fox himself says nothing about women's meetings in his account of the trip apart from a reference to his attendance at one in Dublin.[77] Nevertheless there is no good reason to doubt the validity of Edmundson's statement, given the fact that Fox could readily have encouraged women as well as men to organize more effectively. Because executive authority resided in men's meetings, records for the women's meetings in this period are confined to epistles, the earliest of which date from the late 1670s. Almost nothing is known about women's meetings in Ireland prior to this time, though they clearly existed. For defaming them, William White found himself in trouble with the Lurgan men's meeting in the spring of 1675. Banks probably represented a more prevalent view among Friends when, in November 1676, he encouraged women to meet frequently and to establish women's meetings in places which had none. Husbands, he insisted, must not discourage their wives from participating in such gatherings. He highlighted several concerns that occupied women's meetings, particularly the upholding of Quaker standards concerning customs and fashions, care of widows and orphans, and fidelity to plain, honest speech.[78]

In November 1677 the half-yearly meeting may have unintentionally and implicitly raised the idea of a national women's meeting by issuing a formal epistle to women Friends. The delegates instructed them to investigate the condition of widows and young women "as to their manner of living and whether any of them live out of services (of the younger sort) and live by themselves which may give an occasion of liberty and looseness." They were also to reprove busybodies who spread mischievous tales and Quaker midwives who attended baptismal ceremonies or accepted the monetary gifts that were traditional on such occasions. The notion of collective responsibility seems to have suggested to at least some women the desirability of a national meeting to explore how best to deal with these issues. Led by Mary Robinson and Elizabeth Steere, the women's meeting at Cork called for a national women's meeting to convene once or twice a year. They made their plea in a letter to the half-yearly meeting dated 16 April 1678 and signed by 31 other women.[79]

Three weeks later, on 8 and 9 May, the six-months meeting approved the creation of a national women's meeting to be held once a year at the time of the half-yearly meeting in May. The decision to hold only one gathering a year may have constituted a bow to critics of women's meetings. The delegates assigned the provincial women's meetings the responsibility of determining the minimum number of representatives from each province, "leaving all others to their Liberty who are stirred up in their own Spirits to be there also." The three women's provincial meetings subsequently determined that each of them should send at least six envoys to the national meeting.[80]

At the provincial and to some degree at the monthly levels the women's meetings generally assembled at the same time as their male counterparts, though they met separately. The situation varied at the monthly level. At Lurgan the men's meeting decided the previous practice of men and women assembling in different places and at different times was inconvenient, hence it opted to hold future gatherings simultaneously. Because the attempt to impose uniformity in this respect in Ulster proved to be controversial, the provincial meeting decided in August 1679 that each monthly meeting could determine the time of its men's and women's gatherings. At Moate and probably elsewhere, men and women met together before separating for their respective business meetings. At the request of the Dublin women's meeting, it assembled with the men in May 1701 "to good satisfaction," but such a practice may have been virtually unique.[81]

Although women's meetings had no executive authority, they involved themselves in a wide range of matters and the men both sought their advice and respected their decisions. Women's meetings played a major role in determining the suitability of candidates for marriage, not least by conducting investigations into the "clearness" of the potential brides. Women participated extensively in establishing Quaker standards for home furnishings and decoration as well as women's and children's apparel. They were involved in the placement of apprentices and the provision of relief to the indigent, widows, and orphans. Women could take up their own collections, and in September 1688 the Dublin women's meeting pledged £30 toward the cost of the meetinghouse and other buildings in Meath Street. When the number of Friends at Carrickfergus dropped to "but a few" in the fall of 1692, its women's meeting took the initiative in seeking the advice of the Ulster provincial meeting; given the option of remaining independent or joining with Lisburn Quakers, the Carrickfergus Friends opted for the latter.[82]

Like the various men's meetings, the women banned unfit persons from attending their assemblies. Such are those, said the Leinster provincial women's meeting, "whose Conversations manifests them that they are not of us, tho' they may frequent our publick meetings, for such are a Clogg and Burden to our work and service." The diligence of the Newgarden women's meeting in undertaking this responsibility was questioned by the Leinster provincial meeting in May 1699 when it directed Newgarden Friends to determine whether Mary Sparrow was qualified to participate in women's assemblies and "be a writer for friends or otherwise Appeare in Truths businesse or Church affairs." If she proved unfit, the provincial meeting insisted on an explanation of Newgarden's neglect. Because Sparrow was "in a tender frame of spirit" and acknowledged her careless behavior, the Newgarden meeting received permission to decide whether she could attend business meetings, but she was temporarily banned from writing or engaging in church affairs.[83] Thus the surviving records make it abundantly clear that the Friends had a well-structured organization by 1700 capable both of providing a setting for communal worship and of conducting the community's business.

The Friends' Business

Because Quakers eschewed a professional ministry and formal ordination, their ministers—public Friends—operated with relatively few restrictions in comparison, for example, with conformist or Presbyterian clergy. Anyone, of course, could speak in a meeting of worship, but not without the risk of censure, nor was everything that was said presumed to be spiritually inspired. If censure was the exercise of a negative voice to block someone not deemed to speak the truth, the bestowal of certificates was a positive affirmation of a Friend's spiritual gifts and suitability for the ministry. A certificate amounted to a meeting's stamp of approval that the bearer was qualified to be a public Friend. For a public Friend about to embark on "truth's service," the monthly meeting provided a certificate, as the Dublin men did for Anthony Sharp in 1695 and 1699 and for George Rooke in 1698 and 1700.[84] Meetings had an obligation to warn each other if they knew of unsuitable persons who had set out as itinerant ministers. On several occasions in the 1670s the Bristol meeting alerted Irish Friends about Charles Woodward, who "traveled abroad as a preacher to the burthening of some and [is] creeping into the affections of others who hath not knowledge of the wickedness & deceitfullness of his heart."[85] Certificates, then, were an institutional check on those who hoped to represent the Friends, and in this respect they served the same function as ordination in other Protestant communities.

Certificates served various other purposes. To be married with a meeting's approval required a certificate attesting to a couple's "clearness," and a certificate was increasingly necessary when someone moved from one meeting to another owing to the potential for scandal resulting from the unwitting admisssion of persons with unsavory backgrounds. Such was the case of Elizabeth Partridge, who began participating in Quaker meetings in Dublin in 1680. In response to a query for information from Dublin, Friends at Nailsworth, Gloucester, reported that she had attended their meeting "but never In the unity of Friends or in the least accounted one." On the contrary, *because* she went to their gatherings she had become "a reproach to Truth" inasmuch as she engaged in inappropriate conduct with a man other than her husband who supported her child. Because of their conduct, complained Nailsworth Friends, "truth was trampled on by our adversarys." The Dublin men's meeting reported to Liverpool Friends in 1688 that John Peck, who had requested a certificate, had scandalized Dubliners by his flight, leaving a wife, children, and debts.[86] By the 1690s Dublin Friends were increasingly chary about the arrival of people who were seemingly Quakers but had no certificates.[87] For the most part, however, meetings regularly granted certificates indicating good behavior.[88] Certificates for all of these purposes were additional manifestations of institutional control and thus a characteristic of the Friends' evolution into a denominational church.

Another way of dealing with potential problems involving migrants was to require Friends to obtain permission from their monthly meeting prior to relocating. When George Gregson informed the Leinster provincial meeting of Ulster Friends who were emigrating to America, the Leinster delegates responded in March 1674 that Quakers had "long since" agreed that persons intending to leave must notify their meeting and "take their advise, that soe wheither they stay or goe, it may be in the unity of Friends." This stipulation seems to have been difficult to enforce, for the half-yearly meeting had to reiterate it a number of times, including May 1682 when it spelled out the procedures in detail. Friends planning to move to America or elsewhere were first to report to their monthly or provincial men's meeting to obtain a certificate indicating the latter's "Unity or Disunity with their removing." Young or unwed people migrating to America had to take certificates indicating their clearness with respect to marriage, and ample time had to be allowed for meetings to make the usual inquiries. In typical Quaker fashion, the half-yearly meeting stipulated that Friends in Ireland record certificates of removal. When the Ulster provincial meeting reiterated the requirement for a certificate of removal in September 1693 it stressed that the intent was to permit Friends to counsel those desirous of leaving, presumably reflecting a fear that too many might emigrate.[89] Requests for emigration received careful consideration and sometimes resulted in the imposition of conditions. The Lurgan men's meeting authorized William Smith's application to move in 1693 only if he agreed to settle near another Quaker meeting and obtain its approval before he concluded a purchase or rental agreement. Friends were especially chary if the proposed emigrant was in debt. When Joshua Swanson petitioned the Dublin men's meeting for permission to relocate to the north for health reasons in 1699, it assisted him with £2 12s. but also insisted he obtain his creditors' consent. In 1682 the Ulster provincial meeting required the debtor James Atkinson, who sought approval to move to America, to surrender all his possessions to satisfy his creditors, and if that proved insufficient, it ordered him to "give up his body alsoe."[90] After admitting that a Friend had proposed to marry her, Sarah Brogdale could not procure a certificate to emigrate to America in 1683 until the Dublin men's meeting had inquired of the man if he "doth claim any promise of her"; he cleared her. In the same year the Dublin men were wary of issuing a certificate to Philip England to move to America simply because he had recently relocated to Dublin from Moate, hence they ordered an inquiry into his background there.[91] The Dublin meeting was understandably reluctant to approve the request of the wealthy linen merchant Robert Turner, friend of Sharp and Penn, to emigrate to Philadelphia in 1683, and he in turn resented requests to explain his actions in person to the men's meeting; he made the move, taking seventeen indentured servants with him.[92] Friends could be generous in providing financial assistance to needy Quakers emigrating to America, though sometimes with conditions. The Moate men's meeting offered John Ball £4 in 1687, payable only after it learned of his safe arrival in America, and the Leinster provincial meeting was willing to supplement Moate's grant of £4 to John Lock in 1683 with an additional £2 only after Abraham Fuller interviewed him and offered him financial assistance if he stayed in Ireland.[93]

As in the case of emigrants, public Friends who traveled required not only certificates but sometimes financial aid. This was originally provided on an *ad hoc* basis, but beginning in 1679 the Friends implemented procedures to provide assistance in a more orderly manner. In that year the Leinster provincial meeting appointed a committee of four to look into the needs of Friends traveling in the ministry and to report all financial obligations "belonging to a General or Province Charge in that

Accompt." Four years later the same meeting asked this committee to advise the women Quakers in Dublin concerning the provision of Friends in the ministry with clothing and linen and to report the resulting costs and other charges to the meeting. To care for the horses of Friends who traveled in the ministry, the Dublin men's meeting built a stable in 1692 and provided hay for the animals; the cost of keeping such horses amounted to £5 4s. in 1700. The Lisburn monthly meeting decided in 1699 to pay the expenses of public Friends who ministered in areas where Quakers had seldom or never met. All of this suggests that public Friends in Ireland were less likely to have the resources to support themselves than did their English counterparts, but they raised the necessary funds through careful organization.[94]

In the calmer years following the time of troubles the Friends implemented additional, non-monetary procedures for public Friends who traveled on ministerial work. To monitor and modestly control such activities, the Leinster provincial meeting in December 1692 asked public Friends to report their proposed trips to their men's meetings or their elders so that "they may be advised, assisted or helped in their Concerne or Service." About the same time problems were occurring in the meetings for worship when traveling ministers visited because both younger and older members spoke at such length as to preclude the visitors from giving their testimonies. If, as Richard Vann has argued, "speaking in meeting was an awesome matter for the early Friends," this was no longer the case in Ireland by the early 1690s. In November 1693 the half-yearly meeting had to advise newer Quakers to keep "strictly to the power which first opens in them to speak, which teaches not only to keep down in the Cross to the Mans part, but to know when to keep silent." Older Friends, including public ministers, were not to speak so long in their own meetings as to be tedious or "unserviceable." Instead of preserving the best wine for last, the delegates asserted, "a Generall flatness hath come over the Meeting[s]."[95]

Other problems involving traveling ministers demanded attention. One pertained to the custom of having Friends accompany ministers on their journies, presumably for spiritual fellowship, guidance over strange terrain, and safety. In December 1695 the Dublin men's meeting complained about two men who had been away from their businesses for a long period of time while accompanying traveling ministers in Ulster; this, it believed, amounted to "evile service." To deal with such problems, those who wanted to accompany traveling ministers began obtaining certificates by the end of the century, another mark of corporate control. A related problem involved appropriate companions for women who journeyed in the ministry. In 1698 the Leinster meeting directed that a "staid, sober, plaine woman friend" rather than "proud-like unsettled Girles or Lasses" travel with a woman minister, and in 1701 the half-yearly meeting called for a halt to the practice of girls and boys accompanying traveling women ministers.[96] In addition to testifying, commencing in 1701 traveling Friends in Leinster were expected to submit reports about meetings in remote areas to Amos Strettell in Dublin. By that time the Quakers faced a shortage of qualified "preachers" to take advantage of the "great Opennesse and Enclination in & amongst people to hear Truth declared." The provincial and half-yearly meetings thus had to turn their attention to finding qualified Friends to meet the need.[97]

The Quakers seized every opportunity to spread their message through the written word, an aspect of their work to which their meetings, especially at the national and provincial levels, accorded diligent attention. This element of their work involved handwritten epistles as well as printed books and tracts. These epistles were often copied and disseminated to other meetings, thus providing Friends with a personal, inexpensive means of communicating with one another. Understandably Fox's letters were cherished and disseminated widely, not least because they provided the movement's guidelines. His letter of 13 July 1671, read at the half-yearly meeting on 5 November, called on Friends to adhere to "the Ancient Principles of Truth," including sound language and testimonies against priests, tithes, masshouses, church rates, worldly fashions, profanity, oppression, and "the worlds Joyning in Marriage." When the Leinster meeting was seeking precedents against oaths in 1674, it requested a copy of Fox's epistle on this topic to Friends in Munster and Ulster. The respect accorded to his letters is evident from the same meeting's care in 1677 to have copies of his epistle to the women's meetings compared with the original before dissemination to women's meetings in Leinster. The importance attached to his views is also apparent in the Leinster meeting's decision in 1690 to send each of its monthly meetings a copy "of the Papers of the heads upon which George Fox spoak last yearly meeting." As the preeminent member of the Dublin meeting, Sharp had the honor of reading Fox's last epistle to Dublin Friends. Four years after Fox's death, Leinster Friends had one of his epistles copied from his journal and read at the provincial meeting because it was "very suitable to the present Concerne upon friends minds for the preservation of all."[98]

Many epistles other than Fox's were read in meetings. Some came from the hands of such noted Friends as Banks, Penn, Stephen Crisp, James Parke, William Bingley, and Charles Marshall, but the Quakers listened as well to such lesser lights as Gertrude Deriknickson and James Chamberlain whose messages they deemed useful.[99] The Friends heard missives from abroad—from Crisp in Germany, from Katherine Evans and Sarah Cheevers in Malta, from Robert Mallins at Plymouth en route to Barbados, from meetings in London and Cumberland, from Philadelphia warning Friends not to come to Pennsylvania without certitude of their clearness, and from forty women Quakers in Virginia.[100] Most of the letters contained spiritual counsel, such as that offered in May 1661 by Burrough, who urged Irish Friends to "put away all strife" and noted fondly how he was "refreshed in the thoughts of my labour while I was with you, who had a previous day & season of visitation before the dore was shutt."[101] Most letters from women's meetings were markedly spiritual in content, though some contained reports of their proceedings. Letters between all levels of men's meetings in Ireland were routine and typically concerned the Friends' wide range of business. By 1700 the volume of epistles intended to be read in meetings was such that the Leinster provincial meeting appointed a committee to determine whether they were suitable for reading in public services.[102]

To understand Quaker printing in Ireland, it is essential to bear in mind the development of Quaker publications in England. From the outset of the movement the press played a crucial role in asserting Quaker principles, defending Friends from attacks by their numerous adversaries, and stating their case to the authorities. Over the course of his career Fox was a voluminous if undisciplined writer, yet as early as 1656 he had urged his followers not to print materials excessively. A decade later a group of public Friends gathered in London recommended that select Quakers review manuscripts prior to publication, but not until 1672 did the yearly meeting establish a committee of ten to undertake this work. The following year Fox founded the second-day meeting, a principal purpose of which was to approve works for publication. For another half dozen years both groups concerned themselves with the press, and in the meantime the Friends established the meeting for sufferings in 1675. After the collapse of state censorship in 1679, the latter group attained ultimate responsibility for the printing and distribution of Quaker literature, though the second-day meeting continued to determine which manuscripts would be published. In En-

gland the chief means of financing publications were the general collections for the service of truth in 1668, 1672, 1676, and 1679. During
this period the system of distribution altered. Initially Quaker printers
shipped books to Friends in local areas for disposal, but in 1672 the
yearly meeting began setting quotas for books, with each printer guar-
anteed sales of 400 in 1672, 600 in 1673, and 690 in 1674. Recipients of the
books in the counties sold or gave them away, and local meetings reim-
bursed them for unsold copies. After 1679 Quaker printers received
orders for specific amounts from booksellers or meetings.[103]

In the early years of the Quaker movement in Ireland the Friends
relied extensively on England for printed materials, though some items
were apparently published in Ireland and smuggled into England. A
letter from Philip Ford, a Quaker merchant with close ties to Penn,
dated 9 June 1670 at Cork to Edward Man, a colleague of George Whitehead's, refers to his shipment of books to Francis Rogers in Bristol. They
included a work on liberty of conscience—possibly Penn's *The Great
Case of Liberty of Conscience* (1670)—and sufficient quires of sheets to
make perhaps 300 copies of an attack on Catholicism. A government
agent intercepted the letter and sent it to Joseph Williamson, who cryptically noted on it, "seditious books out of Ireland."[104]

The dependency of Irish Friends on English printers is apparent in
1671, when the half-yearly meeting prepared to receive a shipment of
1,000 unbound copies of Penn and Whitehead's *A Serious Apology for the
Principles and Practices of the People Call'd Quakers* (1671). Of these, 400
were intended for the Dublin men's meeting, some of whose copies
were to be given to the lord lieutenant, the Council, and other prominent persons. The intent was to divide the remaining 600 copies equally
among the three provinces for dispersal by the men's meetings, but the
total shipment was approximately 120 books short. Leinster province
ultimately received only 170, of which Newgarden got 48, Wicklow two,
and Wexford, Moate, and Mountmellick forty apiece.[105] This was an
unusual transaction, for most orders in this period were for relatively
small numbers of books. Leinster and Ulster Friends shared 250 copies
of Thomas Forster's *A Guide to the Blind Pointed to* (1671) in 1673, copies
of which were to be sold for 5½d. each.[106]

In May 1674 the half-yearly meeting allocated copies of twenty titles
to the three provinces in roughly equal amounts, though the numbers of
the various titles varied substantially. The largest orders were for 500
copies of James Parke's *The Way of God, and Them That Walk in It* (1673) at
1½d. each, 469 copies of Edmundson's *A Letter of Examination* (1672) at

half a penny each, 150 copies of Elizabeth Hendricks's *An Epistle to Friends in England* (1672) at the same price, and 140 copies of Penn and Whitehead's *A Serious Apology*, the latter to be given to eight men, presumably booksellers. Easily the most expensive volume in this collection was Burrough's *The Memorable Works of a Son of Thunder and Consolation* (1672), nineteen copies of which were distributed at 13s. 8d. Two works of Fox's were included: 98 copies of *Several Papers Given Forth for the Spreading of Truth* (1671) at 4d. and sixteen copies of an unspecified epistle at half a penny each. Penn's "*Holy Truth*," 24 copies of which (at 3d. each) were en route, was probably his *Truth Exalted*, though he also published *Truth Rescued from Imposture* in 1671 and *The Spirit of Truth Vindicated* the following year. The dozen remaining works, which included epistles by Patrick Livingstone and William Smith, averaged nearly 34 copies each, or almost forty if two titles totaling nine copies between them are eliminated. The average cost of eleven of the twelve titles (excluding one for which the price was not cited) was 2½d., making the tracts affordable.[107]

In the spring of 1675 Irish Friends concluded an agreement with their English counterparts that twelve copies of every Quaker publication printed in England be shipped to Ireland, and in May of that year the publication of Quaker works in Ireland received a considerable boost when the half-yearly meeting instructed Friends in Cork to contract with a local printer to issue 1,000 or 1,500 copies of Fox's *A Warning to England, and to All That Profess Themselves Christians*. It was undoubtedly this volume to which the Leinster provincial meeting referred in September 1675 when it allocated 100 copies to the Dublin meeting and forty each to the other meetings. The involvement of the wider Quaker community in the publication process is reflected in the Leinster delegates' order that each meeting "take care to see all corrected before us," a reflection of the Friends' interest in the production of accurate texts. The bill for printing Fox's *Warning* in Cork was £4 3s. 8d., or a penny apiece if the print run was 1,000 copies.[108] In 1676 the half-yearly meeting disbursed funds to print a number of other titles, all of which were unidentified except for an unspecified volume of Edmundson's for which the meeting paid £3 7s., presumably to a Cork printer. Irish Friends continued to obtain some books from London, as in 1676 when they committed to purchase sixty copies of Francis Howgill's works, fifty of which were bound in sheepskin for 11s. 11¼d. each, and ten in leather for 12s. 11¼d.[109] In 1679, when the six-month's meeting wanted 450 to 500 copies each of two of Fox's epistles, it turned again to a Cork printer but only after first approaching a printer in Dublin. These tracts were paid for out of the general account, but booksellers also sold Quaker works. In 1677 the half-yearly meeting was interested in purchasing (out of general funds) some or all of the Quaker publications in James Hammond's stock for distribution to the provincial meetings. In the same year the Ulster provincial meeting laid out £15 4s. 4d. for the purchase of "20 great bookes," presumably an unspecified quantity of twenty titles, including works by Howgill, Smith, William Bayly, Thomas Ellwood, James Parnell, and George Keith.[110]

The first explicit indication of self-imposed censorship among Irish Friends is found at the half-yearly meeting in November 1676, though the meeting's earlier decisions to have works printed implies that it approved their content. At the 1676 gathering the delegates first listened to a paper by Thomas Carleton before instructing Robert Turner to ask the second-day morning meeting to print 400 or 500 copies for Irish Friends. Eighteen months later the half-yearly meeting appointed a committee of twelve to determine if one of Carleton's papers was fit to go abroad, presumably for printing, and seven years later a five-man committee studied Carleton's writings with a view to possible publication, a project his widow agreed to fund. The half-yearly meeting decided to print 1,000 copies of Ellwood's *A Seasonable Disswasive from Persecution* in 1684 only after hearing it read.[111]

The delegates followed a similar procedure on a fairly regular basis. Such was the case with Fox's *The State of the Birth Temporal & Spiritual*, 1,000 copies of which were printed in Ireland in 1683 "for a General service"; an address to the bishops and clergy of England and Wales, 2,000 copies of which were printed in Ireland in 1685; and a paper setting forth the Friends' position on tithes, 500 copies of which were published at Dublin in 1687. The decision to print at least the first two of these works did not amount to censorship in any real sense, for the tracts had already been published in England. In 1688 the national meeting authorized the publication of 1,000 copies each of a testimony from the women's meeting in Yorkshire and a statement of advice to Friends from one of the provincial meetings, but it insisted that Burnyeat and John Watson edit the latter. The Dublin men's meeting exercised minor censorship in September 1683 when it listened to Joseph Sleigh's advice to his children before ordering 500 or 1,000 copies printed locally. Later in the same year the Dublin meeting appointed a committee of three to decide whether to print a testimony to Sleigh; the committee opted to do so.[112] Although a modest degree of censorship existed, it was not controversial throughout the period from 1660 to 1700.

After 1679 most and possibly all printing of Quaker material in Ireland was done at Dublin. Such was the case with the works mentioned in the preceding two paragraphs. A thousand copies of Fox's address to vintners and innkeepers came from a Dublin press in 1682, 400 of them slated for Leinster and the remainder divided equally among Munster and Ulster. The following year 500 copies each of three more of Fox's papers were printed in Dublin at a cost of £4, paid for by the general account and divided equally among the provinces. Cork, however, provided a convenient backup, as suggested by the half-yearly meeting's decision in 1686 to hire a Cork printer if arrangements could not be made in Dublin to print 1,000 copies of Edmundson's paper of May 1680 on marriage.[113]

Another aspect of the half-yearly meeting's publishing interests pertained to the printing of records of Quaker sufferings in Ireland. In November 1681 it decided to publish the data for the previous decade, the earlier records already being in print. If possible the delegates wanted 200 copies printed in Dublin, but they were prepared to use a London printer if necessary. The following May the meeting appointed a committee of eight men, including Sharp and William Stockdale, to prepare the material for the press, and two members of the committee, William Williamson and James Carr, agreed to compare the manuscript with "the General Record" to ensure accuracy. The committee thereupon drafted the format according to which Friends at the provincial level were to compile their data. Essentially the material was to be submitted in two books, one concerning suffering for refusal to pay tithes and the other for declining to swear oaths, pay church rates, or attend services in the Church of Ireland. By May 1683 the manuscript had been prepared and was read to the half-year's meeting. The delegates named a committee of four to edit the preface and the appended testimony, and Williamson had the responsibility of deleting the names of those the delegates thought should not "be exposed to print in the said book." The meeting increased the print run to 500, for which it paid £50, or 2s. apiece, for unbound copies. The binding was done in Dublin before the books were shipped to the provinces.[114]

The time of troubles halted Quaker publishing in Ireland. Partly for this reason and partly because of the need to coordinate their testimonies to Burnyeat, who had died in the autumn of 1690, with those of Friends in England, the Dublin meeting sent its material to the second-day morning meeting, which edited the collected material in 1691 for printing. Dublin Friends received a copy of the edited manuscript for their approval. The half-yearly meeting distributed unidentified books to the provinces in November 1691 with the intent that they be read in monthly and local meetings, but these volumes probably came from England. This was certainly the case with unspecified volumes shipped from Bristol in early 1692 by Barbara Blaugdone, probably copies of her journal, *An Account of the Travels, Sufferings & Persecutions of Barbara Blaugdone* (1691). By July of that year copies of one of William Bingley's works, probably his *Faithful Warning Once More to the Inhabitants of England* (1690), were being distributed; Ulster Friends had 100 to disseminate, with most of them going to Lisburn (24), Lurgan (20), Ballyhagan (18), and Antrim/Grange (13).[115]

Irish Friends resumed their printing in the fall of 1692. In November the half-yearly meeting ordered the printing of 1,000 copies of a work by Thomas Laythes at public charge and invited members to bring books deemed fit for reprinting to the next session. The delegates also paid the cost of printing papers intended for distribution to Parliament out of the general account.[116] Subsequent press runs were impressive: 2,000 copies of Whitehead's *The Christianity of the People Commonly Called Quakers Vindicated* (1690) at the public charge in 1693; 1,000 copies of Penn's *A Key Opening a Way to Every Common Understanding* the same year; 1,500 copies of the testimony given by Richard Manliffe shortly before his death in 1693; 3,000 copies of Paul Moon's paper the same year; 1,000 copies of one of Edmundson's papers in 1694; 1,500 of one by Henry Lamb the same year; 400 copies of Thomas Carleton's works, also in 1694; 1,200 copies of Alexander Pyott's apology in 1697; 1,000 copies of Fox's *An Epistle to the Household of the Seed of Abraham* in 1697; another 500 copies of Whitehead's *The Christianity of the People Commonly Called Quakers Vindicated* in 1698 at a cost of £2 19s. 6d. for the Dublin men's meeting; another 2,500 copies of Penn's *Key* in 1699 (1,062 of which were for Leinster, 750 for Ulster, and 688 for Munster); 1,500 copies of Penn's *A Reply to a Pretended Answer, by a Nameless Author, to William Penn's Key* in the same year (500 of which were to be given away and 425 allocated to Leinster, 300 to Ulster, and 275 to Munster); 2,000 copies of an epistle to Irish Friends by Thomas Wynne in the same year; a further 3,000 copies of Whitehead's *The Christianity of the People Commonly Called Quakers Vindicated*, also in 1699; 3,000 copies of one of Edmundson's papers, probably his epistle on marriage, in 1700; 1,500 copies of Benjamin Lindley's *The Shibboleth of the Priest-hood* (1678) in

1701 at public expense; 1,000 copies of Richard Claridge's *Mercy Covering the Judgment Seat* (1700), also paid out of the general account the same year; and another 2,000 copies of Pyott's apology and a like number of Penn's *Primitive Christianity Revived*, both in 1701.[117] The size of these runs not only reflects an extraordinary commitment to and interest in the printed word but also underscores how much the Friends had changed from the mid-1650s, when Fox had urged his followers to be slow to take up the pen. By century's end the Friends hungered for the written word, but their organization in Ireland was manifestly capable of meeting the demand in most instances.

Their increasing affection for printed matter notwithstanding, some major works were in relatively short supply. In the fall of 1694 the Quakers had only 27 copies of Fox's journal (edited by Ellwood) for distribution to public Friends and meetinghouses, and all or some of them were given out in return only for the cost of their shipment from London (2s. 2d. per copy to Dublin, 2s. 6d. to Lurgan).[118] The collection of Fox's epistles published in 1698 was more common—the Leinster province ordered ninety copies in January 1699, and Friends in the Lisburn men's meeting purchased four at a cost of 14s. 2d. (3s. 6½d. each).[119] Another relatively expensive classic was Robert Barclay's *An Apology for the True Christian Divinity*, which Irish and English Friends wanted to reprint in 1700. After considerable discussion, the former decided to have the work done by Joseph Ray in Dublin, with a run of 1,500 copies in large octavo at a cost of 3s. 8d. apiece. But the printing could not be done in Dublin because suitable paper was unavailable, hence Irish Friends contracted with Tace Sowle of London for 2,000 unbound copies at 2s. 2d. each, 500 of which had arrived by November 1701. The cost apparently deterred some potential purchasers, for as late as April 1706 the Leinster provincial meeting decided that the unsold copies in its possession should be dispensed to the monthly meetings, each of which was asked to take 25 percent more copies than it had originally subscribed for.[120]

From at least the late 1670s and probably much earlier the men's meetings acquired and loaned copies of Quaker literature. The libraries appear to have been relatively small and the procedures informal; in some cases a record of borrowers appears at the end of a volume of minutes, the names crossed out to indicate the books were returned. The minutes record appeals to Friends to return books which belong to the meeting. In 1677 the Lurgan men's meeting owned eight volumes: three copies of Howgill's *The Dawnings of the Gospel-Day* (1676) and single copies of Burrough's *The Memorable Works of a Son of Thunder and Consolation* (1673), Parnell's *A Collection of the Several Writings Given Forth from the Spirit of the Lord* (1675), Keith's *Immediate Revelation* (1668), Penn and Whitehead's *The Christian Quaker and His Divine Testimony*, and an unspecified work by Isaac Penington. The library of the Moate men's meeting consisted of only three books in the mid-1680s: Penn and Whitehead's *The Christian Quaker*, Penn's *Reason Against Railing*, and William Smith's *Balm from Gilead* (1675). The larger and wealthier Dublin men's meeting owned Ellwood's *Truth Prevailing and Detecting Error* (1676), Keith's *Immediate Revelation*, Fox's journal, and unspecified works by Burrough and Ellwood.[121]

The Friends' concern with the written word was closely related to their desire to preserve a record of their past. This was especially pronounced at the end of the century when conditions of peace provided ample opportunity to reflect on the movement's early history, but the founder's death in 1691 would have been no less important. As in the case of the Scottish Presbyterians in Ireland, the Quakers' decision to record their history marked their respect for the past, the importance of their traditions in the shaping of future thought and action, and their maturation as a community resolved to perpetuate its sense of distinctive identity. Unlike the Scottish Presbyterians in Ireland, the Friends contributed to the creation of histories that were international in scope. Irish Friends assisted in the movement-wide search to catalogue Fox's letters, books, and manuscripts in 1697, and the following year the half-yearly meeting launched a search for Thomas Loe's writings.[122] The same session called for each monthly meeting to gather information about the rise and progress of truth, including data about who first introduced the Quaker message in the area, the earliest converts, the sufferings that ensued, the identity of both moderate and persecuting magistrates, the judgments that befell the latter, "what friends in the particular meetings the Lord brought forth in a publique Testimony and when," and "what faithfull men there were and good Examples that had not a publique Testimony that served in their Generation according to Truth." The resulting material was compiled in 1700, reviewed by Edmundson, and cast in final form by Thomas Wight of Cork as *A History of the Rise and Progress of the People Called Quakers in Ireland*. In 1699 Irish Friends also responded positively to a request to provide historical material to Willem Sewel for what became *The History of the Rise, Increase and Progress of the Christian People Called Quakers* (1st Dutch edition, 1717; 1st English edition, 1722).[123]

In addition to their concern with handwritten epistles and a wide range of printed materials, meetings at all levels had to deal with meeting sites. As late as 1701 nearly half the meetings in Ireland—26 of 53— gathered in private homes. Of Leinster's 24 meetings, fourteen had meetinghouses, of which three had been built by "particular" (local) Friends. Ulster had seven meetinghouses, four of them constructed by local Friends, and eleven meetings in private homes, whereas six of Munster's eleven meetings had their own buildings, none of which were apparently built by local Quakers alone. Meetings such as Edenderry in King's County (Offaly) which assembled in private homes were able to move from one house to another as needs dictated, but this was feasible only as long as their numbers were relatively small. When Friends wanted to establish a meeting at Blessington, county Wicklow, in 1699, no suitable building could be found to rent, forcing them to commence plans to build.[124]

The monthly meeting at Newgarden (later Carlow) confronted a variety of problems concerning meeting sites. After plans to use Margaret Heritage's house in Newgarden fell through in 1672 when she opted not to relocate, the Leinster provincial meeting urged Friends at nearby Athy to construct a meetinghouse. This apparently proved unnecessary, for another building was donated to them, though it required expansion in 1674. Local Friends arranged for the construction of a new meetinghouse at Athy in 1704, the cost of which—£50—was ultimately borne by the provincial meeting, with Dublin (£15 12s. 6d.) and Mountmellick (£10 12s. 6d.) paying the largest share.[125] At Castledermot, another of Newgarden's constituent meetings, a three-man committee received a commission from the provincial meeting in 1674 to find a suitable house or land on which to construct a meetinghouse, the specifications of which included space for six or seven couples, a fireplace, and a partition. After fourteen months they decided to build and insisted that the new meetinghouse be completed in twelve weeks, replete with seats. The resulting structure was spacious enough to add a gallery five years later that extended from door to door and was three steps high. By 1702 the meetinghouse needed repairs and expansion, but the walls and timber had rotted so extensively that it was necessary to construct a new building at a cost of £140, the greatest portion of which was borne by Dublin (£45 10s.), Mountmellick (£30 6s. 8d.), Newgarden (£23 6s. 8d.), and Wexford (£17 10s.).[126]

In Ulster the meetings also coped with assorted problems. Plans to build a meetinghouse near Carrickfergus in the early 1680s had to be scrapped when some members engaged in scandalous conduct; the land leased for the proposed building, which never materialized, was used for a burial ground. Friends at Glenavy and Belfast rented meeting places, the latter at a cost of £1 16s. *per annum*; for years Glenavy Quakers engaged in a running battle with a smith over the rent. As the time of troubles came to an end and the movement expanded, Lurgan Friends found it necessary to enlarge their meetinghouse.[127]

Meetinghouse concerns are best documented for Dublin, where the spatial needs were greatest because the city was the home of the country's largest meeting and the site of the half-yearly assemblies. In the early 1670s the meeting appointed two men each year to keep the meetinghouse clean and in good repair. By the fall of 1677 the old meetinghouse at Bride's Alley was inadequate and a search got underway to find either land on which to build or a suitable structure to lease. The Friends soon opted to lease a house in New Row, adjacent to Sharp's house, from a Dublin alderman, but Dublin Friends made it clear they alone would not support its upkeep. In May 1682 the half-yearly meeting therefore allocated each province a share of the maintenance at New Row, namely 37.5 percent to Leinster, 35 percent to Munster, and 27.5 percent to Ulster.[128]

By 1683 the Bride's Alley and New Row buildings were no longer sufficient to meet the Quakers' needs, and the half-yearly meeting consequently considered property in Brabson's Liberties, Meath Street, with the idea of erecting not only a new meetinghouse but also "Conveniencies" that could turn a profit, the total cost of which was estimated at £600. Because such profits would benefit Friends in general and because the new building would house the six-months meeting, members of local meetings received invitations to contribute. The meeting sought a lot at least 50 feet wide and 120 feet deep with a sixty-year lease. As donations were collected, the earl of Meath leased land to the Friends on which several houses already stood; the Quakers subsequently rented these to private parties.[129] Construction had to be delayed because of difficulty raising the necessary funds; nearly £548 had been spent by November 1685. The building had exterior walls sixteen-feet high, gabled ends, a slate roof, two fireplaces, a gallery, wooden floors, and an upper story where the women met.[130]

Upon completion of the new meetinghouse in 1687, the Friends rented the New Row building to a private party for use as a warehouse, and the older Bride's Alley structure, which was adjudged inconvenient, was leased to a local Quaker. The Friends continued to use a

Bride Street building for services until September 1692, when agreement could not be reached with the owner for a new lease. To replace it the Quakers leased a site in Sycamore (Crown) Alley between Damask and Essex Streets. In January 1693 Dublin Friends decided to hold Sunday morning, Tuesday afternoon, and men's meetings at Meath Street and Sunday afternoon and Friday meetings at Sycamore Alley.[131] They added a second structure at the latter location in 1695 to accommodate small groups, and two years later they erected a 28-foot-square house with a gallery adjacent to the Meath Street meetinghouse after the women protested that its upper floor was unsafe for their gatherings. In the meantime one or two rows of seats with backs were added to the two principal meetinghouses, and in 1698 the Friends constructed a gallery on the north side of the Meath Street meetinghouse, thus concluding Quaker construction projects in Dublin in the seventeenth century.[132]

Meetings at all levels, particularly the monthly, were also responsible for burial grounds. Much of the oversight involved routine maintenance, though a few meetings faced special challenges. In Dublin the cemetery near Stephen's Green was full in 1698, requiring Friends to lease new grounds at Dolphin's Barn, southwest of the city center. Like its predecessor near Stephen's Green, the new cemetery was walled, in this case to a height of nine feet. Corpses were interred in orderly rows, as at Lurgan. Drainage occasionally posed problems, especially at Lurgan, where efforts to find alternate property failed. The Friends' insistence on simplicity carried over to their graveyards, even at the expense of practicality. In Ulster some Friends had been erecting boards at gravesites to record the date and time of burial so corpses were not dug up before they had been "sufficiently consumed," but the provincial meeting banned this practice in 1674 on the grounds that such boards might subsequently "tend to superstition and Idollatry [such] as making Crosses or severall other things that may be invented by people of vaine mindes." Separated in many respects in life, Irish Friends, like their English counterparts, were largely segregated in death as well. In 1681 Dublin Quakers insisted that no one be interred in their graveyard without the authorization of a two-man committee responsible for its oversight, and in 1698 the Leinster provincial meeting unanimously agreed that those who had "turned their back on truth in their life time" be excluded from Quaker burial grounds. The latter was an explicit repudiation of backsliders.[133]

Rent, repairs, construction costs, printing, financial assistance to traveling Friends in the ministry, aid to the poor, and assorted other financial needs were met by contributions. These were less voluntary than the term suggests, for national, provincial, and monthly meetings periodically assessed constituent members specified sums and normally expected to receive payment. Legally enforceable remittances such as tithes and church rates were, of course, intolerable to Friends, hence the collection of funds—even specifically assessed amounts—was a matter of spiritual suasion, yet the Irish Quakers almost always managed to raise the money they required, even if this occasionally took longer than desired. One of the most striking testimonies to the vitality of the Quaker movement in Ireland is the success with which it raised significant sums of money without recourse to legal means.

The disbursements of the half-yearly meeting provide a useful indication of the flow of Friends' expenditures throughout this period. The annual expenses rose from £36 4s. 8d. in 1675 to an average of £62 18s. 4½d. in 1677–1678 before dropping back to the more normal level of £39 7s. 2d. *per annum* between 1681 and 1687. The unusually high total for 1677 stemmed from the allocation of £38 6s. 2d. for sixty copies of Howgill's books, the cost to be equally divided among the three provinces, and an additional charge of £12 12s. 1d. to Leinster and £4 to Munster for other books.[134] The 1678 disbursements were high because of the expense of the New Row meetinghouse (£42 5s.).[135] The Friends reduced their expenditures drastically during the time of troubles, laying out an average of £4 12s. 7d. *per annum* between May 1689 and May 1692. As conditions improved, disbursements rose to an average of £25 1s. 8d. between 1692 and 1696 before climbing sharply at the end of the century. From £19 12s. in 1697 disbursements increased to £89 14s. 4d. in 1698, £127 13s. 6d. in 1699, and £115 15s. 10d. in 1701. The rise in 1698 was largely owing to a payment of £26 11s. 3d. for books: 1,000 copies of a work by Pyott, 1,000 of a book identified as *Household Faith*, and 100 of George Whitehead's *An Antidote Against the Venome of the Snake in the Grass* (1697).[136] Printing expenses were again substantial in 1699, including £46 9s. for 1,500 copies of Penn's *A Defense of a Paper, Entitled, Gospel Truths, Against the Exceptions of the Bishop of Cork's Testimony* (900 copies of which were bound and the rest only stitched), £22 for 2,500 copies of Penn's *Key*, and £40 for 100 copies of Whitehead's *Antidote* and fifty of Thomas Taylor's works.[137] Of the 1701 disbursements, £89 5s. 10d. was for publishing.[138]

The largest expenses were for printing and the construction of the Dublin meetinghouses. Rent for the New Row lot was £12 *per annum*, and occasional expenses were sometimes substantive, as the payment of £16 14s. for costs associated with assizes in November 1682 and £12 to Friends emigrating to America three years later. Support to public Friends was rare (a total of £4 in November 1676 and May 1677 was unusual), and the half-yearly meeting spent nearly £3 in May 1693 for a petition to the lord lieutenant regarding Friends' refusal to take the oath. Other common payments—for the recorder, the doorman at the national meeting (typically 12s. *per annum*), postage, maintenance, and occasional charity—were typically small.[139] At the end of the period the Friends began receiving substantial income (£27 13s. in May 1701) from the rental of houses left to the meeting by George Gregson, and expenses were occasionally offset to some degree by one-time legacies, such as Robert Wardell's in 1699 (£23 12s.), but most such gifts were earmarked for the poor.[140] The bulk of the money came from donations, and a committee appointed at the half-yearly meeting assigned each provincial meeting its share of the national expenses. At the outset of the period Munster paid the largest amount, but in the late 1670s that obligation went to Leinster, which retained it for the rest of the period. The following table indicates the share of each provincial meeting:

Date	Leinster	Munster	Ulster
May 1672	34.5%	46.8%	18.7%
May 1677	45.2	30.8	24
May 1682	37.5	35	27.5
May 1687	37.5	35	27.5
May 1692	37.5	35	27.5
May 1697	37.5	35	27.5
May 1701	42.5	27.5	30

Because of military movements and fighting in the north, Ulster paid nothing in November 1689.

The provincial meetings in turn allocated their expenses among the monthly meetings. In Ulster, the meetings at Ballyhagan, Lisburn, and Lurgan bore the heaviest share of the expenses (22.4 percent each in 1677), though Ballyhagan was hard hit in the time of troubles; its share dropped to 14.2 percent in 1692 compared to 28.4 percent each for Lisburn and Lurgan.[141] In 1677 Leinster apportioned expenses as follows: Dublin, 30 percent; Mountmellick, 22.5 percent; Moate, 17.5 percent; Wexford, 15 percent; Newgarden, 10 percent; and Wicklow, 5 percent.

The growth of the Dublin meeting is vividly reflected in the figures for 1692: Dublin, 50 percent; Mountmellick, Wexford, and Newgarden, 14.2 percent each; and Wicklow, 7.5 percent.[142]

In addition to paying its share of the national bill, a provincial meeting had additional expenses, including writs and other legal costs, recording sufferings and epistles, postage, occasional grants to monthly meetings for meetinghouses, and charity. The Leinster provincial meeting sometimes ordered additional books for its constituent meetings. Legal costs were rare but could be fairly substantial, as in February 1682 when the Leinster meeting paid £4 12s. 7d. to attorneys for Daniel White, John Watson, and Samuel Watson.[143]

Local meetings had to bear their own expenses but could seek help from their respective provincial meeting if necessary. A local meeting could appeal for a reduction of its share of provincial charges because of a decline in its fortunes, as Moate successfully did in 1686. Unless they used private homes, local meetings required funds to rent meetinghouses or, if they owned their own, for leasing the land. They also needed money for charity, aid to public Friends, and incidental expenses, such as paper to keep their records. At Moate, an average-sized meeting in Leinster judging from its share of the provincial budget, collections averaged slightly more than £5 *per annum* between 1668 and 1670, rose to more than £12 in 1671, and hovered around £13 in the early 1680s. Each family or single adult was apparently expected to contribute a minimum amount to each collection, presumably tailored to one's financial circumstances. Such, at any rate, is suggested by the fact that on occasion the Moate meeting ordered double, triple, or greater collections to meet specific needs. In late 1683, when a typical collection amounted to approximately 14s., a "sixfold collection" in September brought £14 17s. 4d. and a treble collection in January 1687 £2 3s. 9d.[144]

The Friends' ability to raise money consistently and in amounts large enough to meet their needs indicates both substantial discipline and an effective organization. They amassed even the considerable sum of money required for the Meath Street meetinghouse, though not as rapidly as they had hoped and apparently not without tension between Dublin and the provincial meetings. Nevertheless, raising necessary funds always remained subordinate to spiritual principles, as reflected by the numerous occasions on which Dublin Friends refused or returned contributions from people whose lifestyles fell short of strict Quaker standards.[145] The skill with which the Friends organized themselves is no less evident in their use of certificates to regulate public Friends, marriage, relocation, and financial aid. No other dissenting group even attempted to establish its own system to publish and disseminate books and pamphlets or to censor itself, nor did any other community (with the exception of at least some Baptists) make a concerted effort to build and maintain its own burial grounds. For a community that insisted on imposing few organizational restraints on its worship, the Friends demonstrated impressive talent in structuring other aspects of their movement, and therein lies one of the most significant keys to their success.

CHAPTER 8

The Quaker Way and the Friends' Place in Late Stuart Society

IN ECCLESIASTICAL terms the Friends separated themselves more substantially from traditional religion than did Presbyterians, Congregationalists, and Baptists. Their determination to uphold truth—to adhere to the strictest standards of apostolic doctrine and life—manifested itself in the enunciation and application of rigorous yet simple standards of conduct, reinforced positively by testimonies and negatively by the imposition of discipline against those who breached these standards. Although the Friends never sought to live in isolation from the rest of society, much of their existence was separatist in intent. They married in their own unique way, educated themselves as much as possible, distinguished themselves by the plainness of their living, and buried their dead in grounds of their own. Like the Presbyterians the Friends had a keen sense of social responsibility, ranging from distinctive marital procedures to diligent provisions for widows, orphans, the indigent and ill, education, apprenticeships, and Friends held captive in foreign lands. The Friends' careful preservation of records stemmed in part from their experience as a group that suffered periodic persecution and collected such materials to reinforce its communal identity. The records also served to maintain an accurate account of the members, their fidelity to the community's code of conduct, and the measures the group embraced to regulate its affairs and finance its activities. Quaker records contained the regulations and guidelines for their distinctive way of life, and in that respect they played a crucial role in helping to perpetuate the Friends' existence as a unique people; yet the Quakers also developed the basic characteristics of a denominational church by 1700.

As in England, Quaker relations with fellow nonconformists as well as Anglicans were generally tendentious, though increasingly in the last decades of the century the Friends eschewed confrontation unless subjected to persecution. Adamant in their adherence to their principles, they assiduously attended assizes and quarter sessions primarily to help fellow members who were in trouble for such offenses as refusing to take oaths or pay tithes and church rates, but they were also there to monitor the behavior of such Friends when they confronted the majesty of the law. The record of Quaker suffering in the last four decades of the century reinforces the thesis that the movement remained vigorous and committed, underscoring one of the principal themes of this book, namely that vibrant religious life was no less important than effective organization to sustain a nonconformist community through persecution and provide the necessary conditions for its evolution from a sect to a denominational church.

Quaker Conduct

Sensitivity to conscience was hardly unique to Friends, though an impartial observer cannot fail to be struck by the intensity of conscience among many Quakers. Two examples must suffice, both taken from autobiographical statements of essentially unknown men in the Lurgan record book. A recovering victim of a gunshot wound, Robert Wallace, who had lapsed from his Quaker commitments in a fruitless attempt to find spiritual solace elsewhere, bemoaned his prodigal period: "If I had ten worlds I would give them all for a good conscience and the redemption of my soule." Confessing his "disorderly walking," he reflected that he had become sensible of his "Lost Condition, when the dreadfull handwriting upon the wall of gods judgment was against [him], oh then did [he] Cry for healing ballsome for [his] inward wound." Repentance enabled him "to see the sun to arise, & the day star to apeare againe." No less sensitive to his conscience, Hugh Stamper's experience was strikingly different as he neared death after 23 years of unbroken involvement in the Quaker movement:

Truth is as beautifull at this day, as it was at the beginning. . . . There is no weight nor burthen Layes at my doore, I have wronged no man in England nor ireland. . . . Always if there was any difference, I tooke the wrong for peace sake, I have not oppressed any man.

Reviewing his life in terms of the behavioral standards articulated by Irish Friends, he had a clear conscience.[1]

The basic principles on which the Friends' behavioral standards rested were straightforward. Rooted in the deep-seated spiritual conviction that truth must be proclaimed in unadorned simplicity, the fundamental Quaker social tenet was a mandate not to detract from the witness of truth by superfluity. "I would have Friends to stand in that which is plain," advised Burnyeat. The half-yearly meeting was troubled in May 1699 that repeated efforts to implement standards of plainness had fallen short, but the zeal to attain this goal retained the force to move a meeting: "The mighty Bowing power of the Lord seized this meeting in an Extraordinary manner, and a liveing Concerne and Zeal ariseing in many hearts for the bringing downe of such Babylonish adornings, and for the Promotion of the Testimony of Truth which allwayes required and leads into plainness and humility." The world's way, the Friends believed, was to pursue excess, to go to extremes, to be extravagant. The pride at the root of such pursuits darkened the understanding, precluding the sight of God's kingdom and encumbering people with worldly concerns. To be godly was to be simple in every aspect of life. "Live in Peace and Love together amongst your selves," exhorted Burnyeat, "and in a holy, solid Life before all Men, keeping out of the Spirit of the World in all things."[2]

In addition to the spiritual motivation for embracing this standard of truth and simplicity, a practical consideration was also operative owing to the Friends' need to defend themselves against foes who endeavored to tar them with the brush of scandal. One example must suffice. In 1661 a story circulated in London to the effect that the Quaker Humphrey Stone had been cited before the mayor of Dublin on charges of blasphemy and the repudiation of civil law. Supposedly reproved by one of the mayor's aides, he stabbed and killed the latter, for which he was reputedly decapitated and his head impaled. When Stone's mouth opened and shut, according to the story, the mayor ordered the head parboiled and reimpaled. At the Friends' insistence, a city clerk investigated the story, found it mendacious, and issued a signed statement asserting such.[3] The best protection against scandalous accusations was to live blameless lives, thus not tarnishing truth's cause.

Conformity with truth, as the Friends put it, required that at all times conversation be "weighty & solid, not airy & light." Foolish, vain speech did not edify and thus was eschewed. Nor was flattery appropriate: "Daub them [not] with smooth and fained words that Weakens thy Testimony," advised the Dublin men's meeting in 1676. An epistle from Fox read in all meetings admonished Friends to beware of slander, backbiting, and idle jests, remembering that the speech of saints is "seasoned with salt and . . . minister[s] grace to the hearers." In 1684 and 1686 the half-yearly meeting sent an epistle to all men's and women's meetings in Ireland bemoaning what it perceived to be the dishonoring of truth by young people's lax conversation, and urged parents to cease indulging their children. Acceptable speech did not, of course, include the traditional names of the days and months, for these were not scriptural language, but in 1698 Irish Friends banned even the casual use of "pray" (as in "I pray thee") on the grounds that such speech was "more in imitation of a vain Custom than in Reverence to Parents or Masters and Mistresses."[4]

Apart from the repast served on special occasions, very little was said about food until the end of the period. The half-yearly meeting in May 1699 prohibited excessive provision of "Rich and delicious fare," but it decided this was a subject—like apparel and the "ordering" of children—best left to women. The latter responded by issuing an epistle to all local women's meetings in Ireland asking Friends to avoid "making too great provision for Tables &c" because this troubled some Quakers.[5] The Friends did not call for abstinence from alcoholic beverages, though (as will be seen) they did not countenance drinking to excess. This was also their position with respect to the use of tobacco. Warnings to the contrary notwithstanding, by the end of the century Friends were smoking and chewing it in amounts large enough to provoke official concern. In November 1701 the Leinster provincial meeting insisted that "Truths limitts and bounds be observed in the use of this herb, both as to manner, quantity and season, that the service of it may not be abused." This was in keeping with Edmundson's admonition two years earlier to eschew "Excessive Customary, uncomely smoking of Tobacco."[6]

The Friends devoted more time to discussing appropriate standards of dress than any other social theme apart from determining the clearness of people to marry. This was because apparel more than any other factor distinguished Friends from other people in the minds of the latter, thus forcing Quakers to devote considerable attention to the area most scrutinized by outside observers. Over the course of the period under purview, regulations concerning dress became increasingly more detailed as Friends strove to specify which aspects of clothing should be repudiated as manifestations of vanity, superfluity, and a quest to be fashionable. Clothes could not be particularly colorful, for "Gay gould-ring or gay apparel" detracted from God's work. The same criterion generally applied to striped cloth and flowered silk, though this occasioned some debate after the half-yearly meeting spoke out against their use in November 1687. The following May a committee of thirty merchants, clothiers, and tailors agreed on the ideal of plain garb but refused to prohibit the manufacture or sale of patterned, figured, or striped clothing. In 1693, however, the national women's meeting rejected all figured and striped woolen cloth. Nine years later the women reiterated a strict standard, urging Friends not to wear silks and "all those glittering halfe silks which make a great show, and all light Colours in Garments" as well as any expensive array. The delegates also asked Quakers to cease using embroidered linen, "it being a trouble to friends."[7]

The Quakers sought the advice of the tailors among them in setting appropriate standards for clothing. For a time the tailors met together to fulfill this responsibility, but the practice fell into disuse for some years until the half-yearly meeting revived it in 1687. Copies of the tailors' statements about dress prepared on this and later occasions were distributed to the provincial and monthly meetings. Quaker tailors who made only plain clothing were at a competitive disadvantage in the wider market, hence the half-yearly meetings urged Friends to patronize tailors of their own persuasion and not, in the words of the May 1695 delegates, "out of Curiosity Runn to the world for Taylors." That session, in fact, recommended that tailors convene in each province at least every six months, though they altered this at the next session to annual gatherings.[8] Commencing in 1701 Quaker shoemakers assembled to discuss appropriate styles of footware, at which time some of them admitted having made fashionable shoes. In 1693 the national women's meeting had decried cloth shoes, and six years later it declaimed against "very White Shooes with Redd heels"; in 1700 it banned even plain white shoes. No less acceptable was the use of heel blocks to enhance height.[9]

In addition to limiting the fabrics, colors, and patterns appropriate for Quaker apparel, the Friends imposed strictures on style. In 1676 the Dublin men's meeting prohibited padding under the armholes of garments, and a dozen years later the national women's meeting condemned the wearing of gowns or sleeveless, peaked cloaks. The women's meeting reiterated this position in 1693 and additionally condemned mants lined with black or any other "very different" color. The women's meeting in 1696 deliberated whether mants should be worn at all before deciding that even those who could wear them in good conscience should forbear because they offended some Friends; however, if some insisted on wearing them, mants must be plain. The women spoke out in 1693 against lace-draped headdresses known as "cornets," black and white pleated and welted bands, satin girdles, quilted or white fustian petticoats, and painted calico frocks and aprons. They also insisted that "fine stays" not be visible, and six years later they made the same point about bosoms and stomachers (coverings for the chest worn under the lacing of bodices). No less acceptable were white frocks made of fine cloth with broad double hems or fine white aprons. The national men's meeting in the same year took aim at needless buttons and skirts, "long flap sleev'd Coats," and "foolish dresses." Finally, in 1701 the women warned against costly buttons on sleeves and clasps on bands and scarves. These admonitions and exhortations notwithstanding, some Friends continued to wear offensive clothing. In 1701 the Dublin men's meeting expressed concern that some of its members continued to don wide-skirted coats; a few offenders agreed to have them altered as inconsistent with "the plainness of truth." When the Leinster provincial meeting received a complaint the same year that some of its members clad themselves in fashionable garments, especially men's campaign-style military coats, the delegates instructed each meeting to "place judgment" on such vain persons.[10]

Headwear too came in for careful scrutiny. Periwigs were acceptable for those suffering from baldness or relevant infirmities, but only if the wigs were not superfluous in length. "Ruffling Periwiggs" were unacceptable. Quakers with adequate hair were not to cut it off to don wigs. Women could wear plain headdresses and hoods as long as the latter could not be pinned back and were not "New fashioned"; hoods with long flaps and long scarves were controversial and were to be eschewed except for large women. Effective in 1693 the national women's meeting limited hoods to a length of 54 inches and scarves to 72 inches. Handkerchiefs, "a modest dress of themselves," could be worn if they were not too large or displayed "after the New fashion," that is, hanging from pockets. In 1688 the national women's meeting decried tall hairstyles designed to attract attention, a position it reiterated five years later when it also condemned coiffures with double borders of muslin or other fabrics.[11]

The same principles carried over to the decoration and furnishing of homes, where again the key criterion was simplicity. The six-months meeting in 1671 deplored the unnecessary decorating of houses "with those things which in the best doe butt feed the lust of the eye (and therefore Must needs Minister into vanity and soe nott like to adorne the Gospell of Christ Jesus . . .)." In practical terms this entailed the rejection of display shelves for pewter and brass, "Turkey work Chaires of flourishing Colours," large mirrors, white window curtains, polished or fine furniture of all types, and paintings, prints, and sculpture ("Images of Things"). Friends could keep Turkish chairs if they were covered in a plain, single-colored fabric, and pewter and brass could be used in kitchens as necessary. Walls, partitions, and mantles were to be unpainted wherever possible, but if painting were necessary, only a single "civil" color could be applied. The Quakers deemed carved plaster ceilings superfluous and therefore objectionable, and they rejected "the rubbing of Roomes for the Satisfieing a Nice-mind"—polishing floors, walls, and staircases—as needless. Ordinary linen was acceptable, though not table linen and damask. In 1693 the national women's meeting banned the use of children's linen with welts and needlework, long calico window curtains, and bedroom curtains with fringes or ribbons. In 1696 the Leinster provincial meeting considered keeping records of all dealings with members who possessed "the great things of the world," but this proved too controversial to implement.[12]

As in the case of the tailors, the Friends sought advice from joiners, founders, and ships' carpenters in their midst. In 1694 they recommended that chests of drawers be plain and without elaborate detailing. Tables and chairs had to be plain, serviceable, devoid of carving, and not in keeping with the latest fashion. Clockcases and beds should not have elaborate molding, and all furniture as well as wainscoting was to be of a single color. Ship-builders were not to use brass and were to exercise great care in carving images, and founders were not to cast images in brass or make superfluous items. The Friends wanted their saddlers to make only plain saddles and trappings.[13]

Apparently not until 1705 did Irish Friends issue a substantive statement regarding gardens. Concerned that "there is and may be great Superfluity and too great nicety in Gardens," the Leinster provincial meeting exhorted Quakers to plant "in a lowly mind," keeping their gardens plain and utilitarian, "rather admireing the wonderful hand of Providence in causeing such variety of necessary things to grow for the use of men, then to please a curious mind."[14]

The Friends sought simplicity as well in their public occasions. As the Dublin meeting expanded, funerals must have become somewhat disorderly, for in 1679 its men resolved that henceforth Friends would go to funerals three and at most four abreast, the women following the men, with everyone behaving solemnly, neither discussing business nor speaking at all. The meeting appointed two men to supervise funerals. By 1694 the desired decorum had broken down, prompting the men's meeting again to act, this time ordering Friends to walk two abreast in silence. Coffins were to be plain, having neither cloth coverings nor needless folds of cloth. As of 1699, Friends were not to give or receive mourning scarves or gloves at funerals. The Friends usually donated money to the needy at funerals, but by 1701 this had become cumbersome, probably because of the numbers in attendance, hence legacies for the poor were to be distributed at other times. The ideal was that burials should manifest "as much stillness as may bee." The half-yearly meeting complained in 1694 that Friends had "run into Superfluous Excess" at funerals by partaking of wine, brandy, "strong-waters," cake, and tobacco, the use of which was condemned on such occasions. The Dublin men's meeting, however, thought that wine might be served as long as "the Concerned Elders" approved.[15]

Marriages too had to be orderly and simple, that is, conducted in a manner "Suitable to the Solemnity and Solidity of the Occasion." The principal problem was a tendency for the provision of food to turn into a marriage feast, yet those who refused to honor this custom drew criticism from non-Quakers who were present for the marriage. Sensitive to this, in 1695 the six-months meeting recommended that Friends "avoid makeing provisions at such a time as the vaine custome of some is, and not out of niggardliness nor Covetousness nor yeat for want of Affectionatness & civill Respect to our friends or Aquaintance[s]." Perhaps in part because of the number of people present for marriages, the Dublin men's meeting decided in 1700 that cold food alone could be served, and only—like drink—in moderate quantities. A year later the Leinster provincial meeting complained that too much food and liquor were still being consumed at marriages. The national women's meeting banned the giving and receiving of gloves at marriages in 1699.[16]

By the turn of the century the Friends were concerned about superfluity in connection with childbirth. On such occasions, the national women's meeting reflected in 1700, the Friends should "be Bowed under a deep sence of the great mercy and delivering hand of the Lord, and carefull to avoid all superfluities," including excessive speech, unnecessary company, surfeit of food and drink, and the traditional spice-cakes, "all which is Judged to Border so near the worldes way and practice that they are a griefe to the tender hearted, and a dishonour to Truth." Following childbirth, mothers were urged to nurse their infants.

Beginning in 1696, a mother who was unable to do so had to consult the elders of her meeting prior to seeking a wetnurse. Some Quaker women preferred wetnurses, for the national women's meeting condemned those who had the ability but not the inclination to wetnurse as having "a Nice or Curious mind." After the turn of the century the Friends manifested growing concern about the use of nannies, or "dry Nurses," who were thought to enjoy excessive liberty, thus exposing them to great temptations. Quakers were concerned as well that some nannies had previously been guilty of misconduct.[17]

In their daily lives Friends had a duty to engage in occupations "commendable & suitable to truth," and to do so diligently. Rarely did meetings have problems on this account, though Dublin Quakers had to deal with two men in 1681 who made their living operating alehouses in their homes. This, the meeting decided, was inappropriate unless they operated as inns, selling food, providing lodging, and stabling horses. Because of the experience of several Friends who had sustained losses "both as to their service for the Truth and otherwise" as stewards of great men, the half-yearly meeting in 1695 advised Quakers to shun this occupation or to enter it only after consultation with mature Friends. Women no less than men were responsible for their occupational activities.[18]

The Friends enunciated specific behavioral standards for a number of occupations. Merchants must neither buy nor sell superfluous goods, honor their word to all people, and avoid covetousness and oppression. Beginning in 1687 they were supposed to gather annually to discuss their conduct and to determine what goods were unfit for Friends to manufacture or sell, the criterion being anything that dishonored truth. Given the problem of inaccurate or dishonest weights and measures, the Leinster provincial meeting exhorted its members in 1695 to ensure that their measures agreed exactly with the standard ones employed in their market. In the face of dearth in 1698, the Leinster meeting urged Friends "to have a tender Consideration how they hold up the price [of grain], or keep it back from Threshing Expecting great Rates"; instead the delegates asked Quakers to supply needy neighbors with grain and other provisions as necessary. Millers, moreover, were encouraged to exact less than their customary toll for grinding grain during a dearth. Acting on information from the meeting for sufferings in London, the half-year meeting in 1700 cited reports of the damage done to the Quaker movement by young men and factors responsible for cargoes because of their embezzling and "Loose Courses of Life." To prevent this, the delegates directed that Friends who owned or were undertakers for ships bound to foreign ports stock suitable provisions and not overload vessels with goods or passengers. Moreover, Quakers transporting themselves on such ships henceforth had to obtain a certificate from their meeting.[19]

The Friends spoke out as well with respect to the observance of traditional customs associated with occupational activity. When an artisan initially took up employment he or she customarily made a monetary contribution (the "Entring penny"), the proceeds of which paid for celebratory drinking. Such customs included the combers' "Pad-Ale" and the smiths' "Foot-Ale." Masters and journeymen were to eschew such customs, both because they encouraged drinking and because they oppressed those forced to pay. Quaker employers were not to frequent alehouses with their workers, and in general Friends were to avoid conducting business (and smoking tobacco) in such places. Midwives had instructions not to attend baptisms or even dress infants for christening, nor were they to accept the traditional monetary gift from sponsors ("Gossips") at baptisms.[20] Merchants and artisans were to keep their shops open on holy days, including Christmas, as a testimony against "the superstitious Idolatrous observation of times." In the late 1690s the Quakers wrestled, however, with the question of whether or not it was consistent with truth to market items used by others to celebrate holy days.[21]

Friends in Ireland, as elsewhere, regularly reminded themselves of the dangers of indebtedness. Those who fall into this trap, as one of Fox's epistles reminded Quakers everywhere, bring "a scandall upon truth." Borrowing *per se* was not objectionable as long as one had the ability to repay, nor was lending money at interest prohibited as long as the terms were equitable. The Friends warned merchants in particular not to go excessively into debt. As the country plunged into the time of troubles, the Leinster provincial meeting advised Friends to avoid borrowing and to repay their loans, "that in these Callamitous times freinds may only Run the hazard of their owne Substance." Friends resolved in 1692 that Quakers who needed to borrow money should first make their needs known to the elders of their meeting, thereby obtaining funds from other Friends if possible. The purpose was not simply or perhaps even primarily charitable, for the delegates made it clear that this system was intended to curtail those who "privately or willfully runs into Debt to the reproach of truth and Damage of Creditors."[22]

Employers and landlords were the object of various ethical admonitions, the focus of which was the repudiation of oppressive conduct. The Friends asked employers not to pay their workers in goods if possible, but if monetary reimbursement were impractical employees had a right to know precisely what they would receive. In 1696 the Dublin men's meeting acknowledged that some workers preferred payment in goods which they could sell for a profit, and this practice was deemed acceptable. Like generations of social reformers before them, the Friends denounced rackrenting as a form of oppressing the poor and encouraged landlords to be sensitive to "the honour of Truth." The Leinster provincial meeting instructed its constituent members in 1697 to conduct a "narrow Inspection into friends takeing of Lands that neither the Ingrossing nor hard holding up of price, nor [holding] back for selling part to poor friends, and others that may be worthy, give no Just Occasion of offence, nor Complaint." Negotiations, in other words, must be conducted in fairness to all to prevent justifiable aspersions from being cast on Friends.[23] Quakers were not supposed to rent or lease farm or glebe lands held by the bishops or other clergy in their official capacity, but after the time of troubles some Friends did so. In November 1700 the half-yearly meeting recommended that provincial meetings prevent this practice and bar violators from meetings until full satisfaction had been given. Ulster posed a special problem because some northern Quakers lived on episcopal lands leased by their ancestors before they became Friends. This, however, did not justify others taking such leases.[24]

All significant pronouncements concerning amusements and pastimes date from the late 1690s and beyond, suggesting that as Friends found themselves in a more tolerant society and evolved into a denominational church, some members began embracing contemporary customs. The pastimes addressed by meetings from the late 1690s on indicate that some Quakers were tempering their historic sense of being a separated people. As in the case of apparel and home furnishings and decorations, the Friends found it increasingly necessary to articulate more detailed statements about what things were or were not conducive to truth. When the Dublin men's meeting learned in early 1696 that some Quaker children took cocks to school and threw stones at them to make them fight, it insisted that this be stopped. The same meeting admonished three members in 1699 for attending a club, and in 1706 the Leinster provincial meeting asked Quaker combers to cease participating in a club with other combers because of "gr[e]at Abuses." Quaker

combers accordingly met and "in a Zeale for Truth" condemned attendance at the club.[25] In the meantime the Leinster provincial meeting asked its constituent members in 1703 to determine whether any
Friends or their sons kept greyhounds or other hunting dogs or had
guns for hunting and used them "after such a manner or in such Company as may not become Truths Professors." As early as 1695 the Dublin men's meeting had pronounced the use of guns and crossbows by
young people and apprentices dangerous and unseemly, and it banned
all use of the crossbow and told Friends with guns or fowling pieces to
keep them away from children. By 1700 Quaker young people were attending fairs in Dublin despite having no business to transact, sparking
concern about the evil consequences that might result. Other Friends
went to horse races; some even entered a horse, causing a scandal.
Friends, of course, were not supposed to gamble, but the Dublin men's
meeting also denounced horse racing as a form of vanity and oppression. The half-yearly meeting instructed Friends in 1701 not to allow
young people, apprentices, and servants to go to fairs "without real
lawfull business, nor to see vain shews, sports or pastimes nor to walk
abroad on first days because of the inconveniency and danger that
may attend it." Indeed, the Dublin men's meeting had argued in 1684
and thereafter that no Friend should stroll in the fields after Sunday
meetings.[26]

Concern with Sunday pastimes was closely related to the fundamental question of appropriate conduct at Quaker meetings. Friends regularly heard exhortations to attend both Sunday and weekday meetings faithfully, for "a neglect therein," as the national women's meeting
warned in 1690, "causeth much lukewarmness & deadness, so that by
degrees the living sense of Truth comes to be lost." At meetings Quakers
were not to sleep or let their minds wander; those sitting near sleepers
were to awaken them, and if they persisted, to deal with them outside
the meeting, reporting recalcitrant offenders to the men's meeting. In
keeping with Margaret Fell's advice, Friends were supposed to avoid
speaking too much in meetings and were to wait in silence until "the
word be committed to thee to minister," nor were they to "strive for
maistry." Those who rode horses to meetings were advised to refrain
from galloping or riding "after an Airy flirting manner." Business travel
on Sundays was unacceptable, and in general Friends were to prohibit
their children from riding around "to see and be seen."[27]

Like Quakers elsewhere, Irish Friends embraced the standard repudiation of oaths, tithes, and church rates. In the case of oaths, simply

refusing to take them was insufficient; Quakers must not even *seem* to take an oath, the half-yearly meeting insisted in 1677. Strict standards applied with respect to tithes as well, though there were occasional problems with Quakers who permitted relatives or acquaintances to pay their tithes and church rates for them. At Moate in 1680 the men's meeting decided a Friend should not compensate someone with a hive of bees for paying his tithes. Quakers who rented or leased land to sharecroppers were advised to divide the land after sowing to demarcate which portion of the crop belonged to the landowner so that no tithes would be paid from that section. In refusing to pay tithes and church rates Friends were to avoid passionate arguments and confrontations as well as physical resistance. Neither they nor their relatives and acquaintances on their behalf were to purchase goods seized in payment of tithes.[28]

The Quakers' evolution from a sect to a denominational church did not entail the diminution of their confrontational stance with the rest of society over the fundamental issue of mandatory tithing or any abatement, at least in theory, of their objection to superfluous fashions and the ways of the world. Yet the vehemence with which the Quakers asserted these ideals around the turn of the century reflected the fact that some of their members were less punctilious in repudiating the fashionable even as their relations with the wider society became more harmonious. The profession of increasingly precise standards of dress and home decoration was a manifestation of the desire of the more devout Friends to preserve their historic sectarian confrontationalism with prevailing social norms, but the means to enforce stringent Quaker standards were ironically key elements of the Friends' evolution into a denominational church. Without denominational "machinery," any hope of upholding the higher standards would have been remote.

Inculcating and Enforcing Standards of Conduct

To preserve their sense of being a distinctive godly community the Quakers maintained rigorous and sometimes idiosyncratic standards of conduct, apparel, and decoration. During the late seventeenth century the procedures they used to impose this discipline became increasingly more structured. The task of educating and reinforcing Friends in appropriate behavioral standards was primarily accomplished through "testimonies." At one level these entailed formal statements from the national meeting on such topics as apparel, home furnishings and decoration, fidelity to one's word, indebtedness, and trading. The provincial and monthly meetings read and circulated these testimonies, many of which were periodically resurrected and read again, sometimes at quarterly intervals. Such testimonies played a crucial role in reminding mature Friends of and introducing new Quakers to the movement's socio-religious principles.[29] At another level, individual Friends provided testimonies, typically mandatory in the case of tithes and oaths. The intent of obligatory testimonies was ostensibly to provide a record for future generations, but this requirement also afforded a means to monitor behavior. The men's meetings transmitted these testimonies to the provincial and six-months meetings. Those who had paid tithes directly or indirectly since their convincement also had to submit testimonies acknowledging that fact.[30] On a voluntary basis individual Friends could additionally present testimonies of a more personal nature, such as those from persons on their deathbed. After his son died, Abraham Fuller of Dublin wrote a testimony "signifying how the Lord visited him by his power a little before and near his departure."[31] A final type of testimony extolled deceased Friends whose lives and spiritual witness were deemed worthy of reflection. As with so much else involving the Quakers, such testimonies were originally composed only as individual Friends decided to take pen in hand, but in 1695 the half-yearly meeting, reflecting the increasingly institutional nature of the movement, recommended that each province collect records that included not only the date of death but whatever any Quaker wanted to say about the deceased. Individual meetings sometimes made special efforts to prepare testimonies, as at Moate in 1696 after Abraham Fuller died. When Thomas Loe died, so many meetings submitted testimonies that the half-yearly meeting had to prepare a condensed statement for transmission to England.[32]

Home visitations were another means of educating and exhorting Friends, but they were no less a process to monitor behavior and admonish those whose lives were found wanting. With a greater concern for strict discipline than their English counterparts, Irish Friends pioneered home visitations commencing in November 1677 when the half-yearly meeting directed Quakers at the local level to inquire into the conduct of all who professed truth. The following spring the Dublin men's meeting appointed four pairs of men to undertake this responsibility. Women too served as visitors: In May 1679 the national women's meeting asked each local women's meeting to name two members "of an honest life and good report to looke into friends families as to the keeping downe of pride [and] all superfluouse things." In 1681 Dublin Friends expanded their visitation to include shops as well as homes. The results were generally favorable during the period preceding the time of troubles, though women visitors found some things amiss at Cork, Limerick, and Bandon in the early 1680s; reports from women visitors at Newgarden, Wexford, Wicklow, Mountmellick, and Edenderry were more positive. At Dublin the male visitors reported in May 1688 that "where things has not been kept Cleare, there is hopes of Amendment, & that in the Generale things are pretty well." A relatively full report from two male visitors at Limerick a year later reflects a similar blend of concern and cautious optimism. Although they found "an acknowledgment and Submission to the Judgment of Truth and care of friends where things had [been] Done amiss," with Friends apparently remorseful "for What they had done and promised not to do," the visitors also observed that many others had been willing to "confess in Words & Truth but when Oppertunity offers will in works deny it." Since the last visitation, some who had been "Tenderly dealt with and which seemed to take the care of friends kindly have notwithstanding gone from the truth." In its first decade and a half the visitations were thus reasonably successful in bolstering the commitment of the faithful and identifying those who breached the strict Quaker behavioral standards.[33]

As the Friends emerged from the time of troubles the visitations were especially useful as a means of gaining some sense of the movement's strength and renewing the commitment to Quaker standards. The early reports from Dublin were strikingly positive, indicating a willingness to comply with the admonitory assessments of the visitors, and a fresh zealousness to carry on the visitations is apparent in the minutes.[34] As in November 1691 the half-yearly meeting renewed the order for visitation a year later, adding that delegates had experienced "a weighty Concern upon the[ir] Minds & Spirits . . . that Friends might keep out of runing into any Extream & Excess of the world, either in Seeking to get great Farms or runing into Extravagancy of Tradeing or dealing of any kind, and also from Airyness in Deportment, & Multiplicity of Words in bargaining, buying or Selling, or Superfluity in Apparel, Furniture or household stuff."[35] This indicates an early awareness of the temptations enticing Friends in the relatively tolerant circumstances in which they now found themselves. Visitations had to serve as a bulwark against the threat of encroaching secularism.

In keeping with the national meeting's directive, each province appointed visitors to investigate the monthly meetings, and the latter in turn named two men to call on each family. The six-man committee for the province of Leinster received written reports from the monthly meetings in March 1693, whereupon it called for a fresh round of reports before the next provincial meeting in April. Receipt of these reports "much Comforted" the delegates, who decided to continue the visitations, a verdict subsequently endorsed at the national meeting in May. On that occasion the women reported to the women's meetings throughout the country that their visitors—now called overseers—had noted that some had been tempted by vain fashions and worldly customs, hence they issued the detailed strictures on dress and home furnishings discussed earlier in this chapter.[36]

Reports in the ensuing six months that some Friends were stubbornly refusing the visitors' admonitions to reform probably accounted for the national meeting's decision in November 1693 to tighten procedures. At this meeting those who had served as visitors at the provincial level convened separately to assess their work and recommended that the visitations continue. Impressed by the usefulness of this gathering, the meeting ordered that provincial visitors henceforth convene in conjunction with the national meeting.[37] The ensuing reports were encouraging. Visitors called on individuals as well as families (including servants), inquired about spiritual and material conditions, and assessed how well people had responded to previous admonitions to reform. Visitors also examined anything that might cause internal strife or hinder the movement's expansion. In 1694 the Leinster province could report improved attendance at meetings on weekdays as well as Sundays and a receptivity to the Quaker message at such places as Dublin, Edenderry, Birr, Carlow, Arklow, Wicklow, and around Gorey in county Wexford. "As persecutions formerly tryed & proved many," reflected the Leinster meeting in October 1694, "now the Light searches & discovers all."[38]

In the late 1690s, at least in Dublin, the rigor of the visitations abated as the overseers made no attempt to call on all Friends. This relaxation was not the result of heightened compliance with Quaker behavioral standards, for the reports were mixed. The Leinster provincial meeting noted in February 1698 that some Friends believed a "more near Inspection is still awaiting concerning the Circumstances of some that frequent our mens meeting and particularly Guzling drinkers and Company keeping smoakers."[39] Responding to these conditions, the Leinster meeting returned to a "Strict and close discipline" in 1699, and in the same year the Lisburn monthly meeting instructed its overseers to make "a more thorough visit." At the national meeting in May the delegates reinforced the reviving interest in stricter visitations by directing visitors to seek the assistance of the men's or even the provincial meetings if they encountered noncompliance with their admonitions, and they asked the provincial meetings to send eight visitors to each monthly meeting. The Dublin men's meeting returned to a full-scale visitation later in the year and generally found "an openness amongst friends to receive advice given and most promised amendement of those things which were found to be amiss."[40]

The results of this infusion of new vigor into the visitation system were mixed. Some Leinster Friends with substantive landholdings responded to the visitors by donating small tracts to needy persons, yet others were denounced for purchasing goods and cattle whose ownership could not be firmly ascertained. The monthly meetings generally dealt with persons identified by the provincial visitors as requiring reform, but not all of the latter were willing to condemn their offenses in writing.[41] Desirous of giving them sufficient time to amend their lives, Leinster Friends delayed another provincial visitation, possibly owing as well to unspoken concern about the potential power of such a centralized body. At the level of the monthly meeting visitors continued to operate and submit reports to the "preparative" meeting comprised of provincial visitors who met prior to provincial meetings. In late 1700 Dublin visitors were again calling only on those Friends "where it was found needfull or Judged soe," but at year's end the men's meeting asked the women to investigate all Quaker families in the city to determine if they were keeping their children and servants in suitable employments and dress.[42]

Two further developments occurred in the visitation system at the end of the period. In December 1700 the Leinster provincial meeting, seeking an effective means "for Remedy and Removeing of such Nusances as are found more or lesse in most places amongst friends to the griefe of the upright in heart," asked each local meeting to appoint a select committee to conduct a "narrow Inspection" of such matters and report to its monthly meeting; the latter in turn submitted an account to the preparative meeting at the provincial level. The monthly meeting retained the authority to decide when and where to publish the names of refractory persons. The Dublin meeting responded to this directive by convening all male and female visitors as well as public Friends and inviting any other Quakers with information concerning "any thing they know that is like to hurt any particular [meeting] or the progress of truth in the generall" to attend. This group commissioned the visitors to continue their work, seeking the reform of abuses either in the course of formal visits or otherwise as they deemed fit, and to report to the next men's meeting.[43] Then (as noted in the previous chapter), in the spring of 1702 the Leinster provincial meeting terminated the role of the seven provincial visitors who had sat as the preparative meeting, replacing them with two Friends selected by each monthly meeting. The twelve were to attend every provincial and half-yearly meeting, remaining after the conclusion of each to hear complaints regarding the ministry or the management of meetings. The intent of this reform was to "lessen the Bulk and sweldnesse of the preparative meeting which hath of late been uneasie to friends" and to enable the new committee of twelve to convene "upon any occasionall matter of greivance which may offer in Management of the then meeting of worship at times between."[44] This reform not only streamlined the administrative structure but also emphasized local authority.

Recalcitrant Friends risked public condemnation, though Quakers were chary about taking this step rashly. In 1682 the national meeting had to chide Friends for not having reproved in a timely manner all who had acted scandalously,[45] but still the Quakers sometimes demonstrated numbing patience in dealing with errant members. Two examples must suffice. Instead of appearing before the Ulster provincial meeting in February 1685 as requested, Samuel Clarke submitted a written statement concerning his alleged indebtedness, but the delegates found this unsatisfactory and asked him to attend the next meeting. When he again failed to present himself in April, he was told to appear at the next session or explain his absence. After he sent word of his inability to be present at the May meeting, it concluded that his behavior since his first profession of truth had never been acceptable and that for years he had been loose in his conversation and "altogether out of unyty" with the Friends. Clarke was therefore directed to give an account of his "Care of truth in his Conversation since he made profession thereof and shew his reason why freinds have nott sufficient reason and must of necessyty write against him." At last, in July the meeting prepared a paper of condemnation, a copy of which was given to Clarke with a request that he respond to the next meeting. He did so, but this too proved inadequate, hence in September the meeting prepared another paper. Citing illness, Clarke excused himself from the October meeting but promised to attend the next session, whereupon a final decision in his case was postponed. Again he failed to appear in December, but confusion as to whether he had been summoned caused a further delay. After more than a year of dealing with this case, the provincial meeting prepared a final paper of condemnation in January 1686.[46] The second case, which involved Ralph Sharply of the same province, took nearly the same amount of time despite his willingness to write a paper deploring his actions early on. This time the meeting had doubts "if he may by any meanes be reclaimed from his vaine Conversation." Their caution may have been justified, for despite a show of penitence, Sharply raised more questions by becoming inebriated. To help it make up its mind, the meeting finally appointed one of its members to maintain surveillance of Sharply for twelve weeks.[47]

Not surprisingly some of the Friends' adversaries were not reticent to point out the Quakers' seeming dilatoriness in disowning transgressors. The half-yearly meeting advised Friends in 1697 to seek the repentance of wrongdoers without needless or indulgent delays. At the May 1699 meeting the delegates called on all faithful Quakers to isolate malefactors socially: "Its hereby Recommended to friends in Generall to be very carefull to beare a Testimony in their deportment toward Transgressors, and disorderly persons professing Truth, and have not Cleered Truth, nor given that satisfaction that Truth requires as also such as have been denyed, not to shew that Intimacy nor familiarity in keeping such Company, nor frequenting their houses Neither Entertaining them in friends houses with that freedom as faithful friends, And that friends in the Ministry may be Cautious not to lay hands on such."[48]

The slowness with which Friends sometimes disowned malefactors was a consequence of the seriousness with which they viewed such a step rather than an insensitivity to unacceptable behavior. The gravity with which they viewed the problem of transgressors is apparent as well with respect to their unwillingess to accept papers of condemnation without assurance that the repentance to which they testified was genuine. In Leinster beginning in 1682 no one who had committed "grosse wickedness" and submitted a paper of condemnation was permitted to attend the provincial business meeting until the delegates were unanimously persuaded that "a remarkeable change" of life had transpired. True repentance manifested by godly conversation was the criterion for a repentant offender to be received again into unity with Friends. Richard Vann's suggestion that the public reading or posting of papers of self-condemnation was not designed to humble an offender must be qualified: Condemnation of improper action was indeed the primary objective, but a penitent's spiritual abasement was significant and reflected the established church's practice of shaming.[49]

The offense which most plagued the Friends was excessive indebtedness. Debt was a problem in large measure because failure to repay cast doubt on a Quaker's word, but the issue was undoubtedly colored as well by the fact that so many Friends were involved in the realm of trade and manufacturing, where the ability to obtain a loan at a reasonable rate of interest was crucial. It would not do for Quakers to acquire notoriety for failing to repay their loans. As long as one could repay, borrowing *per se* was not objectionable, and Friends periodically loaned money to those in need, not all of whom repaid promptly.[50] On a number of occasions the Friends acted as a third party to facilitate repayment of debts and to mediate bankruptcy disputes. When George Gregson died, leaving a substantial legacy to the Quakers, the national meeting urged his creditors to use all lawful means to recover debts owed to him.[51] Thus the Friends were accustomed to handling cases of indebtedness. They had to be alert to the relatively common problem of people who fled to avoid creditors. Some of those arriving from England without certificates, they later discovered, had emigrated without paying their debts, but Quakers also fled Ireland or moved around the country to escape creditors, and other meetings had to be warned about them. One of the more notorious was Elizabeth Worrell, who borrowed money to open a shop in Dublin over the objections of the local men's meeting. Unable to succeed, she closed her shop without making arrangements to pay her creditors, leaving "an evill savour behind her." The men's meeting reported her conduct to her father in England and eventually tracked her down in Dublin, where she promised to repay but insisted she owed less than her creditors claimed. Dublin Friends eventually disowned her, citing her for disorderly conduct before and while she had her shop as well as for not satisfying her debts.[52]

In early 1696 a rumor circulated in Dublin that Quakers were at least £2,000 in debt. With a mandate from the Dublin men's meeting the visitors conducted an investigation in which they learned that Quaker debts amounted to less than £700, but the incident indicated why Friends had to be sensitive about maintaining good credit. Some apparently found themselves in financial straits because of bad luck, illness, or poor business sense, and the Friends usually treated such people with understanding. Those whose indebtedness was part of a general pattern of misconduct had to issue a paper of condemnation or face disownment.

Such was the case with Edmund Adlington of the Moate meeting, who failed to keep his promises and enjoyed unsavory company; George Seaton, a Dublin apprentice who was lax in going to work and married a non-Quaker by a priest; Edmund Sleigh of Dublin, who reputedly drank too much and was summoned to court because of a debt for beer; and John Foster of Dublin, who spoke scurrilously of Quakers, whose loan he could not repay.[53]

The Irish Friends made no objection to the moderate imbibing of alcohol, although the records suggest that they preferred to limit drinking to weak or moderate beer. The drunkenness of some, of course, could cast a shadow over all Quakers. As the men's meeting at Moate put it, one of their young members "doth practise to Drinck so much Strong drinck that the treuth is dishonored thereby." Inebriety was typically coupled with other offensive behavior, as in the case of William White of Lurgan, who engaged in "vaine Contendings for the truth" when he was drunk, or Meredith Edwards of Dublin, who imbibed excessively and kept bad company.[54] Friends did not categorically prohibit members from operating alehouses, though such an occupation seems to have been rare among them. The Moate meeting condemned Mary Ball for serving alcohol to men "untill or when they are much out of order with Drinck which causes the truth to suffer and many Evill surmisals of her self," and the Dublin meeting disowned Thomas Willson and his wife for keeping a disorderly house at which excessive drinking occurred at unreasonable hours.[55] The Lurgan record book includes a case in which the meeting was patient with a man who attended services for years but was admonished several times for heavy drinking and keeping unfit company. The Quakers attributed his behavior to "weaknes of faith, for friends have, and allwaies had, a tender regard to the appearance of the seed of god in any particular [person], for which they are not willing (on every occation) to discover the weaknes of any, but rather would first as much as in them lieth strengthen the weake in faith." In this case, not until the offender married outside the movement did the meeting issue a testimony against his iniquity and hypocrisy.[56]

The sexual offenses committed by Friends were essentially confined to adultery and fornication, though a Dublin boy accused of "a very bad unclean Act" in 1694 had probably engaged in homosexual conduct. Fornication seems to have been less common than adultery, though certainly not because Quakers took a tolerant view of the former. The Lurgan meeting disowned a couple accused of fornication and used their offense as the occasion for a public testimony denouncing those who lapsed after professing the truth; "when they came to be tryed [they] have turned aside like a broken bow, and some have turned like the dog to the vomit and like the sow that was washed to the wallowing in the mire againe" (referring to 2 Peter 2:22).[57] Friends dealt with a number of cases involving people who were improperly living together, some of whom had spouses. In one instance a Dublin tailor falsely admitted he had married the woman with whom he was living by a priest rather than confess they were unwed. Another unusual case involved a tailor named Richard Clemmons who had moved to Cork and zealously attended Quaker meetings, but insisted his wife, whom he had apparently left in Wicklow or Wexford, was a harlot because she had been involved in an affair and had given birth to children fathered by her lover. Over the objections of Friends in Cork, Clemmons insisted he was free to remarry, "frequented womens company," and finally fled the town without paying his debts, threatening to stab anyone who tried to stop him. Unlike much of early modern European society the Friends did not sanction premarital sex between persons intending to marry.[58]

A number of other cases dealt with Friends who had impregnated their servants. Joshua Marsh, a widower of Lisneany, county Armagh, persuaded the Lurgan meeting he was not responsible for his servant's child, but only because she and the man she later married denied his involvement. A few weeks after the investigation concluded, Marsh became gravely ill, confessed "in great heaviness & anguish of spirit," and shortly thereafter died, as did the servant. His deathbed confession, which the Lurgan meeting issued as a testimony against iniquity, provided a sober warning: "I must confess to my great shame and trouble, that I have gone to the quakers meetings, and have been refreshed in them, and have felt the power of the lord which doth preserve those that are faithfull to it, and would have preserved mee, but I have slighted it afterwards and have hearkened to that which through my unfaith[ful]ness hath brought me to do so great wickedness."[59] A member of the Moate meeting impregnated his servant and then compounded his offense in Quaker eyes by marrying her without properly repenting.[60] The most notorious case of Quaker sexual infidelity involved Samuel Clarridge, a pillar of the Dublin meeting, who got his servant pregnant and then sent her to England under an alias to have the baby. Clarridge eventually confessed, condemned himself, and went on to lead a productive if sometimes stormy role among Dublin Friends.[61]

The records of the Moate men's meeting include two unusual cases, both in June 1685, involving illicit sexual relations between Quaker men and Gaelic Irish women. John Roe got an Irish woman pregnant but then announced his intention to marry another woman, "hiding his filthynes." When the first woman's pregnancy was visible, the meeting counseled the second not to live with Roe, but he took her into his house "in a disorderly way," prompting the meeting to condemn both of them. In the other case William Wasely engaged in disorderly behavior with a Gaelic Irish woman "upon the Roade" and then compounded his offense by beating a young man in the public market because the latter had written a letter deploring his behavior at the behest of the woman's family.[62]

Disciplinary cases involving violence were rare. In 1682 James Mac-Neese, a member of the Lisburn meeting, had recourse to arms when a tithe monger attempted to seize some of his grain; when MacNeese subsequently refused to condemn his actions the Ulster provincial meeting advised the monthly meeting to "take Care to Cleare the truth" by castigating his unruly behavior. Other Friends became embroiled in the violence that swept much of the country in the time of troubles. At Bandon Edward Collier and his wife both took up arms, and she reportedly shot a pistol at someone. About the same time John Bullough of the Lurgan meeting bore arms "amongst the soldiers," and in 1694 Thomas English gave the Moate meeting a paper condemning his service in the army. The following year well-intentioned Quaker young people in Dublin fought with the "rabble" who attacked the Friends' shops on Christmas day.[63] Other instances of violence resulted from flaring tempers, as when Thomas Harding of the Lurgan meeting struck a man who provoked him, or when Thomas Barton of Dublin hit another Quaker in an argument. Samuel Braithwaite, also of Dublin, struck a boy who later died, but Braithwaite insisted his blow did not cause the lad's death. After Richard Chesterman fought with another man on a market day in Dublin, the men's meeting made him publicly denounce his action on the spot where it had occurred as a violation of the Friends' "peacable principle." Over a space of four decades the Friends did a very commendable job of adhering to this ideal.[64]

Among the other distinctive Quaker principles, the prohibition against taking oaths also received widespread obedience. Some who violated this principle contended that swearing "in a Legall way" did not contravene conscience, but the meetings consistently refused to modify their stance. The Dublin men's meeting informed John Gay in

1687 that as a long-time Quaker he had experienced "heavenly oppor-
tunitys to have his understanding fully opened and to be made Sencible
of the Lords power, So that if he were not convinced of the evill of Taking an oath; it must needs be by reason of his unfaithfullness unto what
was made manifest unto him." When William Stanley of Galway reasoned he had done no more than answer queries with his hand on a Bible, the Leinster provincial meeting issued a statement denouncing not
only oaths but even seeming to swear by placing one's hand on a Bible
or any other book. Oaths were unacceptable even if used to provide
evidence against persons accused of illegal conduct: The Lurgan men's
meeting insisted that truth be cleared after Widow Gilpin swore an oath
before a justice of the peace that resulted in a dozen non-Quakers being
bound over to the assizes.[65]

With respect to two other distinctive Quaker principles, few Quakers
appear to have paid tithes or church rates outright, but the Friends had
considerably more difficulty with members who found ways to make
such payments indirectly. A member of the Moate meeting found himself in trouble because he encouraged his tenants to pay church rates,
and the Lisburn meeting had periodic difficulty with Friends who had
others pay their tithes for them or did not uphold their testimonies
against tithes as rigorously as the meeting desired.[66] Cases of Friends
who rendered "hat honor" were very rare despite political and economic pressures to conform. When reproved by the Dublin men's meeting in 1682 for removing his hat in court and other places, Thomas
Cooke retorted that "he could not help it for he could not carry on his
bussiness unless he did so." The same meeting disowned Robert Bos-
well in 1695 for keeping his hat on during prayer in the manner of the
schismatic John Perrot.[67]

Friends were expected to attend meetings regularly, but absentees
usually faced nothing more than admonitions to attend more faithfully.
Excessive absenteeism could lead to disownment. One of the most interesting cases of absenteeism involved Dublin's Samuel Clarridge,
who told visitors in 1693 that he had missed meetings because they
were "not appointed in places to his mind & likeing."[68] Attending services of the established church could also get one in trouble, but such
cases are rare apart from the frequent instances of Friends who married
non-Quakers in churches.[69]

In numerous instances the meeting records do not stipulate the nature of a disciplinary offense, but many of these may have been what
Friends referred to as "disorderly walking" or miscarriages that under-

cut the testimony of truth. Such persons appear to have been guilty of a general pattern of misbehavior that in its totality brought opprobrium on the meetings.[70] In some cases the accused were persons of ill spirit, including Friends who made aspersions about other Quakers, such as Ann Savage of Dublin, who was "hard and Stif" and "cast . . . dirt" on a delegation that visited her. When John Edwards accused Edmundson and others in the Leinster provincial meeting of usurping authority and wielding unjust influence, the delegates castigated his "wrong, britle & uncertain Spirit" and implored him to testify against himself. Clarridge provoked considerable disaffection among Leinster Quakers by his haughty behavior and seemingly shallow repentance for past miscarriages, hence some openly opposed his participation in business meetings until he had been "broken & humbled." At Edmundson's suggestion, Clarridge was permitted to attend but not participate in business meetings without the members' approval.[71]

A variety of other disciplinary problems surfaced during the period, none of which proved to be pervasive. Servants and young people were sometimes prone to engage in disorderly conduct, but the meetings normally expected parents and masters to reprove them, citing only the most recalcitrant offenders to the monthly meetings. If children or servants persistently refused to reform, parents and masters could be asked to expel them from their homes. Disciplinary cases involving marital discord are uncommon. The Lisburn men's meeting cited one of its members for "feasting" as well as keeping inappropriate company, but complaints regarding excessive food were more likely to appear in connection with marriage suppers. Superfluity of a different kind was the subject of several cases involving Quakers who made or sold clothing that violated the standard of simplicity. Nor were offenses involving gambling or cardplaying common.[72]

Quaker discipline sometimes reached into the workplace to deal with infractions of the Friends' behavioral principles. The Lurgan men's meeting made Thomas Head issue a paper of condemnation against himself for building an altar for Catholics; he also returned his fee of £3, "being the wages of unrighteousnes." Six months later, he was again in trouble for working on a "masshouse" and an altar. Others faced discipline for dishonest trading, selling superfluous merchandise, embezzling, and the purchase of plundered goods.[73] The most complex case involved a financial dispute between George Shoar of Athlone and Philip England, his attorney and agent in Pennsylvania, where England managed Shoar's estate. When Shoar refused to pay a bill submitted by

England on the grounds that it was excessive and would jeopardize his children's inheritance, the Moate meeting recommended that Robert Turner and John Fuller inspect the accounts, sell the estate, pay England, and secure the remainder for Shoar's children. Shoar procrastinated, claiming England had not followed his instructions. The meeting finally disowned Shoar: "He should doe Justly to Another as he would that an other should doe to him; which Good councell and Advice he hath Rejected and also Reviled those friends who Gave him that Good councell whereby he hath Denyed us and our principles; and therefore, wee Doe denye and Disown him."[74]

The Friends developed a procedure to deal with internal disputes. The Shoar-England controversy was remarkable primarily because one of the parties rejected arbitration, but this was rare inasmuch as such a refusal could lead to disownment. Sometimes the half-year meeting involved itself in the resolution of disputes, as in a 1674 argument between Clarridge and Joshua Dawson over £30. Probably because such arbitration could be very time-consuming, in May 1676 the meeting appointed twelve men from Leinster and six each from Munster and Ulster to remain behind after the meeting's conclusion to resolve differneces which the local and provincial meetings had been unable to settle. Under this procedure, at least half the referees had to be present to act, and no one could mediate in a dispute in which he was involved. Most controversies were resolved at the local or provincial level by an *ad hoc* committee of arbitration ranging in size from two to more than a dozen, though the usual size was four or six. In particularly contentious disputes each party had the right to approve an equal number of referees. Not until November 1696 did the national meeting find it necessary to address the procedures again. On that occasion it resolved that Quakers who refused to submit their disputes to arbitration or who repudiated the referees' judgment would be banned from all business meetings until they had "given such satisfaction as in such cases is fitting."[75]

The minutes often do not indicate the subjects of the disputes, but such information as does exist suggests that referees faced a wide range of problems. Among them were contentions involving property, fences, quarrels between family members, deeds, repayment of debts, apprenticeships, legacies, and alleged aspersions.[76] In some instances the disputants had to post bonds stipulating they would accept the referees' verdict.[77] Among the more interesting cases was a dispute between Moses Sykes of the Dublin meeting and John Pearson of Kendal, Westmorland, over the former's debt to Pearson. The disagreement, which had commenced in December 1669, was settled in May 1697 only after the Dublin meeting permitted Sykes to select two non-Quakers to serve as mediators along with two of its own representatives.[78]

A closely related problem required meetings to deal with accusations of improper conduct brought by one member against another. The monthly or provincial men's meeting normally handled such charges rather than assigning them to arbitrators. The nature of the accusations ranged from improper sexual conduct to incorrect doctrine and haughty demeanor. In 1682 the Ulster meeting wrestled with allegations by John Furnare against Margaret Unthanke, whom he charged with indecent behavior and "unseemly Caryage" with William Winter. The investigation did not support his assertions, though it found she had not "walked soe wisely & Circumspectly as she ought to have done," especially by permitting Winter to "have too much liberty in her house." She was therefore told to extrude him from her house and company. Another woman in turn accused Furnare of having "proferred to lye with her two severall times." Unspecified charges against George Gregson the same year stemmed, in the judgment of the Lisburn men's meeting, from the accuser's "root Invie."[79] Two Dublin Friends quarreled in 1677 over the means of conversion: After Robert Lodge described how "the people of God came to him," Stephen Atkinson told him his "Doctrine stinks," but Lodge retorted that Atkinson's way "of running to Life is a new way, that will please all that Love their sins." Friends were indisputably a contentious lot.[80]

Internal conflict resolution was intended not only to curtail strife within the movement but also to resolve disputes that might otherwise have gone to law courts. Although Friends were chary of using the legal system, they did not prohibit recourse to it under appropriate circumstances. Suing or having other Quakers arrested was "a practice contrary to Truth," the half-yearly meeting announced in November 1675, and henceforth must cease. Two years later it repeated this pronouncement, adding that Friends should be cautious about instigating legal action against non-Quakers. The national meeting returned to the subject in May 1687, asserting it was "inconvenient and of bad Consequence for Friends to be forward in going to Law, especially when under sufferings for conscience sake," but if they believed they had been grievously wronged and therefore had "freedom to try the Justice of the Law," they were first to seek the advice of their meeting or of elder Quakers. Such a procedure had been followed at Moate in 1684 when the men's meeting could not resolve a dispute between Elizabeth

Slade and George Shoar over possession of a land deed. Shoar petitioned the meeting for permission "to take his owne Course to gitt what is his due" and the meeting decided it could not deny his liberty to take legal action as long as Slade refused to accept the Friends' verdict.[81]

Using the legal system to defend Friends charged with religious offenses was not prohibited; on the contrary, the Quakers habitually provided assistance to such persons, even assigning competent people to attend assizes and quarter sessions on a regular basis (see below).[82] The threat of a suit could be a useful weapon against oppressive authorities, as in 1671 when Francis Marsh, bishop of Limerick, offered to free one Quaker from prison and another from house arrest on condition they not sue him if he seized their goods; they refused. Anthony Sharp, who had been an apprentice to an attorney, went to court in 1687 to prevent Friends from having to pay ground rent twice. Where possible, however, the Quakers preferred to avoid lawsuits even in legitimate cases. In 1677 the Leinster meeting instructed Sharp and Clarridge to obtain the release of John Goodbody from prison, if possible without going to law, but the means were "left to them; and what they doe, Friends will stand by." When John Ashton of Birr, King's County (Offaly), was incarcerated at Clonmel for refusing to take an oath and kept close prisoner for eleven weeks, Friends from the Mountmellick meeting obtained his release without payment of fees or going to court. Commenting on this case, the half-yearly meeting noted that

An Advantage in Law might have been laid hold off. But friends from the first . . . [were] a people unwilling to goe to Law about matters pertaining to Conscience and Truths testimony, haveing allwayes found a more generall Successe in proceeding on such Occasions by Soliciting innocently, proper persons for Redress, then in Seeking to be Relieved by Law where they had an Oppertunity.

Quakers had, in fact, used the courts in connection with matters of conscience, and this statement reflected the Friends' increasingly less confrontational attitude toward the state in the changed atmosphere of the period after the time of troubles.[83]

Some Irish Friends insisted on going to court in civil suits. Between 1692 and 1698 the Dublin men's meeting dealt with four of its members for such actions. Repeatedly it admonished Patrick Nayland to cease such conduct, but though he repented, he soon became embroiled in fresh controversy.[84] These cases notwithstanding, the Friends were strikingly successful in resolving the vast majority of their controversies with their system of internal conflict resolution. By doing so they contributed to their sense of remaining "a community apart"—a sense of separation from worldly ways far more pronounced than that espoused by other dissenters.

Social Responsibility

Like the Presbyterians, the Quakers manifested the disciplined life in a positive as well as a negative manner. The vigor of their religious commitment suffused them with a sense of social responsibility characterized by the upholding of high standards of conduct. This is readily manifest, for example, in the care with which they approached marriage, family responsibilities, relief for the indigent, and education. Like the rest of their activities, marriage as practiced by Friends had to be orderly. Burnyeat aptly expressed the ideal when he wrote about a large wedding in Dublin, after which "a very great Report of Recommendation [was] abroad through the City concerning our Order and Method, and the Gravity and Solemn Manner of our Accomplishing of it." In Ireland the basic structure to ensure orderly marriages was in place by 1672, when the half-yearly meeting spelled out procedures that were probably already in practice. A couple intending to marry had to state their intentions to the women's and men's meetings, both of which then conducted inquiries to ascertain if the couple were free of obligations to others and, if young people, had parental consent. If these inquiries proved satisfactory and the couple's intention to marry had been announced several times to the meeting or meetings to which they belonged, the couple gave themselves to each other during a meeting. A record of their "being Contracted" was then made in the meeting's register.[85]

During the next three decades and beyond, the basic procedure remained the same although some specifics changed. The national meeting considered the introduction of a uniform marriage certificate in 1682 but decided against this as long as each monthly meeting used a certificate that was "consistent with truth & according to the proceedings of the partys." In this respect Irish Quakers, unlike their English counterparts, retained some degree of autonomy for local meetings. Monthly meetings had discretion with respect to advance notice of a prospective marriage. The Ulster province required a couple desirous of marrying to notify at least two men and two women of their meeting no less than three weeks before the latter was scheduled to meet, but Lisburn insisted that at least six women and six men be informed. Once the local men's meeting had approved the prospective marriage, it had to notify the provincial meeting. Objecting to this requirement, the Dublin men's meeting sought permission in 1678 to make the final determination, a proposal with which the Leinster meeting concurred as long as Fox did not object.[86]

As the movement expanded following the time of troubles, Friends wrestled with the distractions which marriages caused in meetings of worship. In December 1693 the Leinster meeting resolved that marriages should occur and certificates be signed near the beginning or middle of a meeting "with as little Bustle as may be," and it directed each meeting to appoint two members to see that marriages were performed "in that good Order and decency as becomes Truth." When the half-yearly meeting took up the issue the following May, it insisted only that marriages occur in meetings in such a manner as not to be disruptive or preclude their conclusion in quietude; it also called on each meeting to appoint two members to supervise weddings. After trying the new arrangement for less than three months, the Dublin meeting reverted to the older practice of having marriages at the conclusion of meetings; celebrating them earlier, it found, caused more disturbance as well as pressure to cut the rest of the worship short.[87]

Other late changes also resulted from the movement's growth and from the consequent need to tighten procedures. By 1696 the Ulster provincial meeting was devoting so much effort to determining whether couples were clear to marry that insufficient time was available to conduct other business. As a result it delegated authority to monthly meetings to make this determination, asking that they report only qualified couples to the provincial meeting.[88] Beginning in 1693 if a prospective couple came from two different meetings the Ulster province required them to produce a certificate indicating an announcement of the pending marriage had been made in the meeting where the wedding would *not* occur. The following year the Leinster provincial meeting asked its constituent members to stop excusing couples from presenting their intentions to marry in person if they were able to do so. After the turn of the century the Leinster meeting bowed to pressure from those intending to marry without its full approval by agreeing to issue marriage certificates to them, but with phraseology indicating such unions only had their "sufferance."[89]

The Friends gave their blessing exclusively to couples who met specified qualifications, though they recognized the legitimacy of marriages which did not fulfill these conditions. Perhaps no criterion was more important than that Friends should only wed persons of like faith. In his widely circulated paper on marriage, Edmundson argued that Quakers should only marry "amongst their own people" according to the terms of the first covenant, the law of Christ, and apostolic doctrine. Moreover, he asserted that Quaker young people who married non-Friends should lose their inheritance; otherwise, non-Quakers, cognizant that Friends were "a thriving people in their outward Substance," would seek Quaker spouses for their children in the hope of material gain. Edmundson's paper sparked considerable discussion at the national meeting in May 1680, particularly since several young people had recently wed non-Quakers. The meeting resolved that parents who suspected that their children intended to marry outside the faith should tell other Friends so the young people could be counseled. If the children persisted, their portions were to be withheld until the youth were reconciled to the truth. These provisions remained in effect for the rest of the period and beyond, but with only mixed results. When James Fade, a member of the Dublin meeting, called on Friends to counsel his daughter as she contemplated marrying a Presbyterian, they persuaded her to wed only with her father's consent. Others followed their hearts; those who did, according to the Dublin men's meeting, "have Lett themselves at a distance from the body of Sensible friends" and must repent. In September 1699 it cited one man and six women as offenders.[90]

A second criterion was parental consent. During the investigation to determine a young couple's clearness to marry, a meeting routinely asked the parents if they approved.[91] If parents could not be located, a couple could still marry. A young man who spoke to a woman about marriage prior to obtaining her parents' consent faced charges of disorderly conduct and had to condemn his actions.[92] This requirement imposed obligations on parents as well as young people, for the former risked condemnation if their meeting adjudged them lenient in acquiescing to marriages with non-Quakers. Around 1673 James and Mary Hutchinson testified against themselves for not having done everything possible to prevent their daughter's marriage to someone of another faith:

We can not but judge, & give up to Judgment that spirit which wrought in our mindes and drew us from standing in our authority in a faithfull single cleare testimony against that thing of our daughter['s] marriage. . . . And this [testimony] may advise and warne all friends that they neither take nor give theire children in marriage with unbelievers, neither let them countenance nor assent to any such thing least they bring themselves under judgment as wee have done for it is contrary to the law of the first covenant and contrary to the testimony of the gospel.

The Leinster meeting exhorted parents who had given permission to a Friend to propose marriage to their daughter to be circumspect in granting such authorizaton to a second person if their daughter refused the first until the latter's offer had been "orderly Recalled." In 1699 the half-yearly meeting also asked parents to resolve any questions about portions before their children had progressed toward marriage so "that Earthly Ends prevail not to break it." Richard Vann has rightly stressed that this emphasis on parental consent recognized the parents' crucial role in forming their children's character.[93]

Age too was important in determining whether or not a couple could wed with the Friends' blessing. The meetings exhorted Quakers not to marry when they were too young, though a minimum age seems never to have been stipulated. Older Friends were to avoid "Matching themselves unequally and disproportionably both in yeares and otherwise." Asked to clarify the latter term in November 1696, the national meeting said it was not intended to refer to differing degrees of wealth or poverty, but it avoided a specific explanation, noting only that Friends must "have an Eye to the truth, and those better parts which mostly honours it."[94] Early marriages were not a major problem for Irish Friends, though they typically wed earlier than their English counterparts, undoubtedly, as Vann and Eversley suggest, because of ample exploitable resources which made it easier to start families earlier. Vann and Eversley have calculated the mean age of marriage for Irish Friends in the period 1650 to 1699 as 28.22 for men and 23.54 for women; male Quakers in northern Britain married at the same age, whereas those in southern England married later, at 29.77. Female Friends in northern Britain wed at 25.54 and in southern England at 26.15.[95]

Fox insisted that Friends not marry their kin, but not until the end of the period was there serious discussion in Ireland about how far this extended. Irish Friends concurred in 1699 that first and second cousins could not marry, but the proposal of some in the Leinster meeting that third cousins should avoid marrying proved to be controversial. In 1706 the Leinster meeting took up the question of whether a surviving spouse could or should marry the first or second cousin of her or his deceased mate; the meeting unanimously agreed that such marriages were unacceptable.[96]

Freedom to marry included "clearness" from obligations to people other than the intended spouse. Meetings investigating couples intending to wed had to inquire not only in areas where they currently lived but also in places of recent habitation to determine whether other persons claimed a prior commitment.[97] A Friend who had made such a commitment—in effect, an engagement—and had not terminated it properly prior to agreeing to marry another person faced condemnation and disownment if he or she refused to repent; so too did his or her intended spouse. Thus the Lurgan meeting ordered Ann Hoope to condemn herself "for her gieving way and being Conserned with more then one [man], or holding two or three in affections at a time, and not being Cleare of one before she held affection to another." Her paper and that of the man she hoped to marry were read to the meeting while they stood before it, an act not unlike traditional shaming in the established church.[98]

Special rules applied to a person wishing to remarry after the decease of her or his spouse. Inquiries concerning such a person's "clearness" had to satisfy a meeting that the husband or wife had indeed died. After David Jones moved to Barbados, he asked the Dublin men's meeting in 1699 for a certificate of his clearness to remarry, claiming his wife was deceased. The investigation discovered not only that she was still living but also that she was guilty of "verry foule and unseemly behaviour." The following year the same meeting refused to approve John Beck's request to marry because it had no proof his intended wife's previous husband was dead.[99] In keeping with Fox's advice, an appropriate waiting period of at least a year was essential before remarriage could occur.[100] The Friends assiduously required surviving spouses with children to make financial provisions assuring their rights prior to remarriage. Thus the Ulster provincial meeting stipulated in 1682 that a widow with children who intended to remarry must settle her estate "under hand and seale" with respect both to what the father had left the children and to anything else the prospective couple intended to add, and that trustees be appointed to see that the children's rights were maintained.[101]

Given these criteria, clearing a couple to marry could be time consuming, especially if one or both of them had resided overseas or had parents who lived abroad. Quakers in Ireland rarely married Gaelic Irish, but they often found spouses in England.[102] In light of the time it took to make the necessary inquiries, Friends advised prospective couples not to act hastily, for "that which is good the Lord will bring to pass in his time." Because disagreements concerning a prospective marriage were prohibited in light of the importance accorded to unity among Friends, couples could be asked to delay their marriages until concurrence had been achieved.[103] While they waited, a couple could not live together.[104]

With respect to the marriage itself, two rules were operative, the first of which stringently prohibited weddings performed by priests. Edmundson's influential epistle on marriage condemned this practice, citing the story of Isaac and Rebecca's wedding as an example to emulate. Virtually all cases of Quakers being married by priests resulted from their decision to wed non-Friends. Those who took spouses in this fashion could repent, be welcomed back to Quaker fellowship, and continue in their marriages, but failure to do so brought disownment. Parents who were forgiving of unrepentant children after they were married by priests were subject to rebuke.[105] The second rule prohibited marital feasts. This was, of course, in keeping with the importance Friends attached to simplicity; a lavish marriage supper, opined the Leinster meeting in 1681, was "like the worlds manners." In November of that year the national meeting exhorted Friends "to keep out of excess & too great provision at the time of the Celebration of Marriages." The natural tendency for exuberant conviviality on such occasions meant recurring tension over this rule and was a factor in Leinster's decision in 1693 to appoint two persons in each meeting to supervise weddings. Fancy apparel was no less acceptable at weddings.[106]

The Friends' distinctive marriage practices raised the practical question of legal recognition. Because they were not married by ministers of the Church of Ireland, Quakers were liable to prosecution for fornication, though church authorities seem not to have pursued this option, preferring instead the more lucrative route of seizing goods in lieu of tithes. By early 1684 the Privy Council had decided to recognize Catholic marriages, which were to be recorded in the office of the bishops' courts. When Edward Wetenhall, bishop of Cork, decided the same procedure could be implemented for Friends, most members of the Cork meeting concurred and appointed Francis Rogers and John Haman to inform the bishops' registrar when Quakers married. The Cork minutes say nothing more about this until 24 March 1688, by which point Wetenhall had told Rogers his registrar would record Quaker marriages if his fee were paid. The meeting instructed Rogers and Haman to ask the registrar if he would record the certificate "fully as we see fit to draw it (in our own book) and will indorse on the back of the Certificate that the same was examined and recorded and allowed of by him or them, and also whether they will leave friends to have their liberty that in case anyone might not have freedom to have their marriage so entered they shall not be troubled for it nor summoned by apparator, But such as are willing to have the marriage so entered will pay as accustomed for it."[107]

In 1688 the Friends took up another issue with the bishops involving marriage. In May the half-yearly meeting directed each provincial meeting to appoint members to ask the bishop of each diocese or his chancellor to cease granting licenses to Quakers to marry without evidence of parental consent on the grounds that this practice violated the canons of the Church of Ireland. These instructions were repeated in 1693.[108]

Concerning the family, Irish Friends, like those in England, had little to say until late in the century, probably, as Vann suggests, because of the early Quaker emphasis on eschatology and mass conversions, or "convincements." The greater concern with family matters also reflected the Friends' maturation as a movement, with more interest in passing their tenets and traditions from generation to generation rather than winning converts from beyond the pale of the Quaker community. Irish Friends expectedly stressed the need for parents to raise children in the ways of truth, teaching them to be obedient, to adhere to the Quakers' behavioral principles, and to engage in honest labor. "Youths [should] be rather recommended to Learn the fear of the Lord to keep their hearts clean," averred the Leinster provincial meeting in 1701, "then any wayes Encourage or countenance untimely fruits of that sort which commonly happens either to gratify a mind that hastens such things to Catch at Riches, or hastily Runs like an Unbeleiver Shewing forth unmoderation." The Friends took obedience very seriously, even to the point of expecting parents to eject exceedingly disobedient children from their homes, though implicitly only if they had come of age. The Leinster provincial meeting struggled in 1687 with the question of whether a Quaker man could take his granddaughter's child into his home given the fact that the latter's mother was rebellious toward the Friends. The Dublin men's meeting condemned one of its members in 1694 in part because he kept "a Loose Family."[109] A major responsibility of the visitors was to ascertain whether Quaker parents restrained their children and servants from idleness and made them adhere to the standard of plainness.[110]

Quaker parents had an obligation to examine their children and servants after meetings of worship to ascertain what benefit they had received, thereby encouraging young people and servants not only to be educated in Quaker principles but also to be witnesses to the inner life of the spirit. To make this possible, the national meeting advised in 1694, parents and masters must "labour to be in a tender senceable frame of spirit that soe their discourse or advice may be seasoned and so prove more Effectuall." Friends were exhorted to bring their children to meetings for worship on both Sunday and weekdays, but in 1701 the Leinster and national meetings stressed the need to leave unqualified children at home rather than take them to business meetings at any level "where they are Exposed to the hazard of more losse in time." Henceforth they could be present in business meetings only with the approval of its members.[111]

Thanks to the meticulous research of Vann and Eversley we have a demographic portrait of the Irish Quaker family. Irish Friends, as we have seen, married somewhat earlier than their English counterparts and thus had slightly larger numbers of children: 9.27 in the period 1650 to 1699 compared to 8.12 for urban Friends in Britain and 7.43 for other British Quakers. Irish Friends also had lower infant, child, and adult mortality, possibly, as Vann and Eversley suggest, because they numbered fewer paupers and aristocrats (with their unhealthy diets) than their British counterparts. The number of children per family who came of age in Ireland was 5.4 compared to 4.0 in southern England and 5.3 in northern Britain. Among Ulster Quakers the mean family size was 6.6. Irish Friends practiced family limitation, spacing the intervals between pregnancies and in some instances prematurely curtailing their reproductive careers. Yet their average intervals between births were typically shorter than that of Quakers in southern England and northern Britain. Moreover, following marriage Irish Quaker women were more likely to become pregnant sooner than their counterparts in southern England, where Quakers attempted to limit family size, but somewhat later than Quaker women in northern Britain.[112]

When they considered family responsibilities the Friends paid heed to provisions for widows and orphans. Visitors had instructions to see that Friends "bee carefull where Fatherles or Motherles Children be under their care that they Carry an even hand towards them in their Education and usage, so as may Answere Truth, and doing to them as wee would others may do to us or ours."[113] As part of their concern for widows and orphans the Quakers attached substantial importance to wills. Friends may have been chary about recourse to law suits but they were keenly sensitive to the legal import of wills and the need to monitor the distribution of legacies. Of course not all proceeds from wills went to widows and orphans, for meetings and especially the indigent were also beneficiaries. As early as November 1673 the national meeting directed Edmundson and Thomas Holme to request precedents from London concerning wills and gifts (as well as deeds for burial grounds). At the same time it appointed a select committee of seven, including Holme and Sharp, to "mind the Concerns of friends deeds of Gift, or wills, buriall places or the like." Local meetings subsequently established comparable committees to inspect wills and communicate with the overseers or executors who administered orphans' estates. In the case of Friends who died intestate, the committees had to inventory the deceased's property. These committees, which met at least annually, reported to their respective provincial meeting. In November 1684 the half-yearly meeting resolved that monthly men's meetings should record wills and inventories of deceased Friends, and that the material in these documents be kept as private as possible. The Lisburn monthly meeting deemed the keeping of such records sufficiently important to pay a member to do so.[114]

Friends also evinced concern for children in their provisions for education and apprenticeships. Just as they insisted that Friends marry only members of their own faith, so they importuned parents to send their children only to Quaker schoolmasters and schoolmistresses. Judging from recurring complaints the Friends were no more successful in achieving adherence to this principle than they were with endogenous marriage.[115] Perhaps those who were educated by non-Quakers may have been more inclined to find spouses in the wider world, but this cannot be proven either way before 1700.

In November 1675 the half-yearly meeting recognized the need for "an able good friend to teach youth & keep a School in this Nation," and to that end it directed each provincial meeting to determine how many children would attend such a school. In the meantime Francis Rogers and Thomas Holme wrote to England at the meeting's behest to ascertain if a qualified Friend was available to establish a school at or near Castledermot. At Fox's recommendation Laurence Routh arrived in the summer of 1677 and after spending a month at Moate settled at Trade's Hill in King's County (Offaly). He accepted a salary of £10 *per annum* plus diet and lodging, with the Mountmellick meeting agreeing to make up any amount not covered by fees. In fact, the number of students proved to be fewer than hoped, leading to a shortage of £5 19s. 2d. the first year, which the Leinster provincial meeting covered. When Fox recommended Richard Gowith to Irish Friends in 1678, the national meeting decided Cork would be the best place for him to teach and asked Friends in that city to provide a schoolhouse. Dublin launched its school (discussed below) in 1680. After the time of troubles the Leinster provincial meeting took the significant step of recommending that each of its constituent members employ a schoolmaster.[116]

The initiative to establish a school in Dublin apparently originated with Alexander Seaton, who began teaching in a house in Bride Street late in the summer of 1680. For an unexplained reason the Dublin men's meeting was looking for another schoolmaster in the fall of 1682, offering to pay him £5 *per annum* to serve as the meeting's recorder in addition to whatever he could earn in school fees. The meeting also planned that the new master would teach in the meetinghouse. In the meantime it asked Seaton to continue his work. By January 1685 the number of pupils was rising, and the meeting offered to pay the expenses of pupils whose families could not afford the charges. Seaton was still teaching in Dublin in 1688, when the meeting agreed to pay him £7 *per annum* as its recorder. In July of that year the men's meeting resolved that once each quarter a committee of six should remind Dublin Friends to support their Quaker schoolmaster.[117]

The revolution must have forced the school in Dublin to close, for in September 1690 Sharp and Amos Strettell wrote to Seaton to tell him they again needed his services. By that point Seaton was bound for Scotland, but the following spring the men's meeting offered John Archer £10 *per annum* plus whatever fees his students paid. Late in 1692 Seaton recommended Samuel Forbes, an usher at Richard Scoryer's (or Scory's) school at Southwark. Although Forbes demanded £40 *per annum*, the meeting agreed to make up the difference between that amount and fees collected from the students. Forbes took up his duties in the Meath Street meetinghouse in March 1693, charging each student 6s. per quarter. Within six months some parents had removed their children from his tutelage and others refused to send theirs because he had not met expectations, particularly with respect to instruction in writing. The diminished number of students posed a financial burden for the meeting, which had reservations about paying Forbes's salary unless he could attract more pupils. The strained relationship continued, with the meeting deciding in 1695 to pay him £10 in addition to student fees, for which salary he was also expected to serve as its recorder. When he insisted on more, the meeting gave him six months' notice, indicating it had been displeased both with his aspersions on Friends and with his inability to keep accurate accounts. Efforts to hire Henry Molyneux proved unsuccessful, but in mid-1696 the Friends replaced Forbes with John Dobbs and Thomas Banks, who also taught in the Meath Street meetinghouse, for salaries of £13 and £10 *per annum* respectively. By the end of 1696 the number of pupils was very small, prompting the men's meeting to make inquiries as to why some parents were sending their children elsewhere. One such was James Whitehill's son, who was sent with the blessing and financial support of the Dublin meeting to study under Gilbert Thompson in preparation to be a schoolmaster.[118]

When John Chambers, who had formerly lived with Robert Barclay's family in Scotland, came to Ireland to teach in 1697, the Dublin meeting hired him for £10 *per annum* plus half of the tuition paid by students. Chambers replaced Dobbs, who had previously expressed a desire to leave, and Banks stayed on, receiving the other half of the student fees plus £4 *per annum* for serving as recorder. Chambers's arrival brought promises from more parents to send him their children, and in November 1697 the men's meeting contracted with him to assume full charge of the school in return for all the fees plus £10 *per annum*. Banks independently taught "fine writing" and mathematics for a salary of £4 *per annum*, while his wife instructed young children to read using primers. Some Friends continued to place their children in non-Quaker schools, forcing the men's meeting to keep pressuring them to do otherwise.[119]

Irish Friends had relatively little to say about the content of education. In May 1680 the half-yearly meeting directed Francis Rogers to contact Ambrose Rigge, Christopher Taylor, and Richard Richardson to ascertain how Quaker schoolmasters in England were teaching Latin, Greek, and Hebrew as well as what books they were using and where they could be obtained. When the meeting received a response, it determined that Quaker schoolmasters in Ireland should follow the "same Rule" and asked them to attend the annual meeting in May 1681 to implement this. Five schoolmasters—Seaton, Routh, Archer, Patrick Logan, and Henry Rose—were duly present and considered both Taylor's letter and the manuscript of a textbook by Richard Jordan. They criticized "the Shortness of the Rules in these books lately put out by friends [in England], viz. Compendium trium Linguarum," which was largely Taylor's work, and they found Jordan's manuscript, which was intended to teach spelling, unsatisfactory, hence the meeting decided not to publish it.[120] In the meantime, the Leinster provincial meeting objected to Thomas Lye's *The Child's Delight: Together with an English Grammar* (1671) because of its allegedly "unsavery" language and offensive illustrations. A Presbyterian clergyman, Lye had been ejected from Allhallows, Lombard Street, London, in 1662 and subsequently ministered at Clapham. The Leinster and Dublin men's meetings prohibited use of his book to teach Quaker children, and the national meeting followed suit in November 1680.[121]

Because of their strict standards concerning the use of books, including their unwillingness to employ many of the Latin classics, Quaker schoolmasters attracted few non-Quakers to their schools. This made the defection of some Quaker children particularly hurtful, and by late 1687 various Quaker schoolmasters began closing their schools. Alarmed, the six-months meeting ordered them not to do so without the approval of their respective men's meeting. Failing agreement at this level, the request to close a school was to be decided by the appropriate provincial meeting.[122]

The concern for utilitarian training that characterized Puritan and especially sectarian thought at mid-century[123] found echoes among Irish Friends at century's end. Monthly, provincial, and national meetings admonished parents not to keep children in school too long or raise them "above their abilitys." Instead they should set children to physical labor, the crafts, or husbandry, recognizing the "many Snares and dangers that youth are lyable to" by idleness. Moreover, parents who keep their children in school or at home too long put "too heavy a Yoak" on masters when the children at last become apprentices.[124]

The half-yearly meeting's articulation of principles concerning apprenticeships commenced in May 1680 when it urged Friends with children fit to be apprenticed to offer them first to other Quakers. Before Friends apprenticed their children to non-Quakers or accepted non-Quakers as their own apprentices, they were to obtain the advice of their meeting. The need for this admonition indicates that Irish Friends were already engaged in apprenticeships with people of other faiths. Two years later the national meeting directed that children who had been placed as apprentices by men's meetings be returned for examination by the respective meeting at the conclusion of their apprenticeships. Children whose parents died during their apprenticeships were also to be examined by the appropriate men's meeting.[125] The Friends apprenticed girls as well as boys, and women as well as men served as masters.[126]

Friends demonstrated a keen sense of social responsibility in their dealings with apprentices. Where necessary the Quakers paid the expenses of placing apprentices. When Abraham Fuller accepted Rebecca Davis as an apprentice, the Leinster provincial meeting donated more than £6 for linen, wool, and other essentials. George Shoar took an apprentice for nine years, but the Leinster meeting agreed to assume responsibility for the young man if Shoar decided not to keep him after a year. When a father complained that his son had been the victim of severe physical abuse by his master, the Moate men's meeting appointed three men to investigate and promised to convene a special meeting if necessary. The meetings also mediated disputes regarding the terms of apprenticeships and dealt with runaways.[127]

The Friends' ability to assist apprentices, orphans, widows, the indigent, and others depended on charitable contributions. Unfortunately for the historian, Fox recommended in 1671 that Friends not keep documents detailing the bestowal of funds to the needy. The earliest extant accounts come from Dublin and commmence only in 1700. Systematically recreating the pattern of Quaker giving before that date is impossible, though scattered data, particularly at the local and provincial levels, provides an impressionistic picture. The principal exception involves the substantial provision of assistance by Irish Quakers to fellow believers in England in the mid-1680s and the reciprocal help given to Irish Friends in the time of troubles (discussed below).

At the national level a committee comprised of delegates from each province determined the amount to be collected to aid the poor and widows, but I have found no details of its operations in this period. The minutes record occasional gifts to meet specific needs: £6 1s. for Quakers bound to New Jersey (1678); £5 to the widow of George Hall, the meeting's late recorder (1681); £5 to purchase a horse for a man whose mare died (1684); £6 to a Friend sailing to Barbados (1685); £3 16s. 3d. for a family en route to Pennsylvania from northern Ireland (1686).[128]

The minutes of the Ulster provincial meeting provide glimpses of charitable activity, most notably a directive to Friends in 1685 to care for the poor in each meeting; it designated one member of each constituent meeting to oversee this responsibility. The scattered donations noted in the minutes cover a range of cases, including gifts to needy prisoners, indigent persons, and a Scottish traveler.[129] The Leinster records reveal much the same picture, with periodic notations of donations to widows, orphans, a man who needed a horse, the burial of an indigent person, victims of fire, and a man who had to visit the baths for medical reasons.[130]

At the local level the minutes of the Moate men's meeting provide more detail about the purposes for which relief was dispensed. When John Ball and his four children were preparing to go to America in 1687, the meeting donated £2 to purchase two shifts (undergarments) and a suit for each of them, a hat for the father, and linen, and an additional

20s. for their travel to Youghal; the shifts were not to be made until it was certain they were leaving. The meeting laid out £2 8s. to purchase a cow on the condition that the meeting would retain ownership but the milk would go to a needy woman; such a practice was fairly common among Quakers. The Moate meeting owned ten cows in 1692 and 1693 which it leased at 20s. per head *per annum*. Included in the assistance given to Widow Roberts in the 1690s was money to repair her house, dig her garden, graze her cow, pay her rent, and purchase wheat and shoes. Others received donations to shoe horses, purchase or repair boots, replace a lost horse, buy a coffin, and acquire wool to make clothing.[131] The specificity with which such gifts were made indicates that Quakers could obtain assistance only after stipulating in detail how the money would be used. Friends did not distribute charity casually or indiscriminately, nor did they provide it to the able-bodied. Some Quakers sought assistance from more than a single meeting, but this practice terminated in 1691 and those who had done so had to return money obtained from meetings other than their own.[132]

Rarely did Irish Friends provide charity to people of other faiths, a practice in which they differed from their English counterparts. The "total non-sectarianism" which Helen Hatton praises as a characteristic of the Irish Friends' poor relief dated from the early eighteenth century, though the case of James Cunningham foreshadowed this. When he and his son were incarcerated at Naas, county Kildare, in 1683–1684, he appealed to the Dublin men's meeting for assistance, citing his family's needs. Although the meeting refused to "stand by him as a friend," it gave him 20s. The six-months meeting responded to Cunningham's complaint that Quakers were ignoring him by calling him "a Jangling contentious man & of a very scandalous Conversation, so that honest friends could never have unity with him." Yet more than a decade later Cunningham was still seeking and obtaining money from the Dublin men's meeting, which unsuccessfully told him to rely instead on his relatives. About the same time this meeting gave another man 6s. but advised him not to depend on Friends for additional relief because his life and conversation were not "agreeable to trueth." Hearing that John Adamson's family was ill in 1685, the Lurgan meeting dispatched two members to ascertain "how he is satisfied Concerning friends principles, to the Intent if friends see it Convenient something may be given" to assist his family. When the agents found him "of weake capacity and understanding touching principles of religion," the meeting decided that aid would be "of more se[r]viss afterwards, so [it] is thought fitt to be forborne till further conveniensie."[133] Repeatedly, the minutes refer only to relief for needy Friends.

Irish Friends readily assisted Quakers in other lands. Friends in New England received help in 1676, and the following year the half-yearly meeting dispatched Joseph Sleigh and Roger Roberts to New Jersey to see if Quakers there were in need.[134] The principal charitable effort to assist Friends abroad came in 1684 and 1685 when Irish Quakers sent substantial help to English Friends who had been victims of the so-called Tory repression. By July 1684 Quakers in the Leinster province had pledged £400 17s. 6d., of which £130 4s. 6d. was from Mountmellick and £120 9s. from Dublin. By the previous month the Ulster meetings had pledged £189 14s., £55 of which was from Lisburn, £54 from Lurgan, and £35 from Ballyhagan. Munster Friends also contributed. In May 1685 the half-yearly meeting called for an additional collection to aid English Quakers. This time the Leinster province pledged £451 11s. 9½d., of which £154 12s. 6¾d. came from Dublin and £138 2s. 3d. from Mountmellick. In the second round Ulster pledged approximately £182. These extraordinary sums vividly manifest the extent to which Friends came together to aid one another amid crisis and the effectiveness of their organization in raising money.[135]

Irish Friends joined their English counterparts in collecting money to redeem captive Quakers in Algiers. In May 1680 the half-yearly meeting instructed Thomas Cooke to write to London for information about what English Quakers had done in this matter. The intent was to inform provincial meetings so money could be raised. Each local meeting appointed several members to collect the funds, and by November 1680 at least £333 and perhaps nearly £523 had been contributed. When additional funds were required, Irish Friends sent £281 13s. 6d. in 1686.[136]

Individual donors in England occasionally bequeathed money for Quakers in Ireland,[137] but the dramatic rendering of aid came during the time of troubles. Initial amounts were relatively small: £101 11s. to Ulster Friends and a further offer of £50 to needy Irish Quakers in any area in the summer of 1690. At the national meeting in November the Friends considered an offer of £200 from the meeting for sufferings in London but decided they could still meet their own requirements.[138] By May 1691 some two dozen families in Leinster who lived near the battlefront needed approximately £70 in aid, but £50 was available from Gregson's will and Leinster Friends raised an additional £50. Against this background, when English Friends again offered help, local meetings received instructions "to inspect into the necessity of every Individual family that may Be accounted Worthy to Be taken care of with an order to send up account [of] what may be needfull for such and what They can accept." The half-yearly meeting in May 1692 accepted £600 from London, which sent an additional £150 to Ulster. A legacy of £60 from an English Quaker raised the total to £810, of which Ulster received £243, Leinster £297, and Munster £270. Barbados donated £100, and by November an additional £1,060 had arrived from England. Early the following year Irish Friends received a further £3,222 10s. from English Quakers.[139] If, as seems likely, the latter amount does not include the £1,060, the total amount was divided as follows:

	£1,060	+	£3,223	10s.	0d.	=	£4,283	10s.	0d.
Ulster	250		726	3	9		976	3	9
Leinster	460		998	8	9		1,458	8	9
Munster	350		917	17	6		1,267	17	6
Individuals			580	0	0		580	0	0

These figures do not include the unknown value of tracts contributed to the needy by affluent Quaker landowners. In any event, as substantial as these donations were, they covered only a small fraction of the deprivations sustained by Irish Quakers in the time of troubles. These losses may have been as high as £100,000.[140] The Friends' ability to survive in the face of such losses was a testimony to the vigor of their religious life and the potency of their organization. To appreciate the extent of this achievement a more detailed analysis of Quaker sufferings is required, and to that we now turn.

Sufferings

Sensing the extent to which they were a persecuted community, the Friends began keeping records of their sufferings—imprisonments, distraint of goods, fines, excommunications, and so forth—as early as 1653. Over time, procedures for recording sufferings became more structured, as did the movement in general. In May 1672 the half-yearly meeting appointed three men from each province to draw up lists of all imprisoned Friends in their provinces, with details as to when, where, and why they had been jailed. A year later the committee of six received instructions to review the reports and "fitt them to be Recorded," and at the same time the meeting decided that no suffering was to be recorded in a monthly or provincial book until it had been registered at Dublin, "& from thence to be Extracted & sent to the Respective Provinces."

Henceforth Friends meticulously standardized procedures to keep these records, even to the point of insisting on uniform language commencing in 1699. The national meeting in May 1678 stressed the importance of accuracy and uniformity by reminding each men's meeting to record its sufferings, correcting any errors before sending the document to the provincial meeting; the latter was responsible to see that all such material was "perfect" prior to submitting it to the national meeting.[141] In the meantime the meeting for sufferings had been founded in London in June 1676; Penn, James Claypoole, and Samuel Newton had the duty of corresponding with Clarridge concerning sufferings in Ireland. Until 1706, records of the sufferings were read aloud at the national meeting, enabling delegates to monitor persecution, the extent to which Friends remained loyal to their principles, and the identity of Quakers in need of legal or financial assistance. The records were also used when Friends petitioned magistrates for relief.[142]

Many records of sufferings have survived, including national accounts dating from 1665 and Leinster provincial records from 1656. Using this material Abraham Fuller and Thomas Holme published *A Brief Relation of Some Part of the Sufferings of the True Christians, the People of God (in Scorn Called Quakers) in Ireland* in 1672. Eleven years later William Stockdale issued a supplement entitled *The Great Cry of Oppression*, containing records for the period 1671 to 1681. Holme and Samuel Fuller, Abraham's grandson, incorporated this material with newer data in *A Compendious View of Some Extraordinary Sufferings of the People Call'd Quakers, Both in Person and Substance, in the Kingdom of Ireland*, published in 1731. Data now in the Great Book of Sufferings at the Friends' Library in London served as the principal source for Holme, the Fullers, and Stockdale. Each of these publications attests the importance attached to suffering as a hallmark of the Quaker community and the profound sense of shared injustice which bound them together, further helping to solidify their sense of identity and encouraging their development of an institutional structure to preserve their heritage.

The records of sufferings pose several problems for the historian. Of these the most serious is the likelihood of their incompleteness, given the meetings' recurring admonitions to people who had not submitted the required accounts.[143] Most of these individuals presumably experienced no losses and may have been reluctant to produce statements because they paid tithes or rates. A second problem involves probable inaccuracies in assessments of the value of distrained goods; this information came from the owners, who may have overvalued their losses, particularly by not discounting their worth to account for prior usage. Moreover, in many instances the data is incomplete with respect to the amount of tithes or rates owed and the value of distrained goods. A cross-check of the minutes of the Moate men's meeting with the Great Book of Sufferings for prosecutions concerning tithes and church rates in the period 1660–1663 reveals that thirteen of 25 cases recorded in the former are omitted in the latter; moreover none of the 32 prosecutions for conventicling in the Moate records appear in the Great Book. In general, the Great Book's entries for Ireland in the 1660s appear to be the more dramatic cases, whereas in the 1670s the Friends placed more emphasis on inclusiveness. The figures discussed below must be used with caution, though they provide a useful indication of the nature and extent of the Friends' suffering and its ebb and flow during the period under consideration.

In their *Compendious View* Holme and Samuel Fuller published comprehensive figures for the value of goods confiscated from Friends from the Protectorate to the end of George I's reign. These figures indicate an increasingly larger value of distrained goods in each period: £17 6s. 8d. *per annum* during the Protectorate; £109 5s. 2d. in Charles II's reign; £395 18s. 7d. in James II's reign; £1,055 14s. 7d. under William III and Mary II; £1,349 19s. 7d. under Anne; and £1,731 16s. 6d. in George I's reign.[144] When tested against contemporary reckonings the assessment of Holme and Samuel Fuller holds up well. The half-year meeting calculated Quaker losses in 1699 at £1,949 3s.; Holme and Fuller have £1,872 2s. 6d. The comparable figures for 1700 are £2,050 15s. 2d. and £2,008 2s. 9d.[145]

These figures must be adjusted for inflation. Given the overriding importance of agriculture for the Irish economy, total rentals provide a useful yardstick. In 1672 William Petty estimated these to be £900,000, and in 1687 he calculated the figure at £1,200,000; in the 1720s the value rose to between £1,600,000 and £2,000,000.[146] Had the value of distrained goods remained constant, taking inflation into account the figure would have been approximately £298 instead of nearly £396 in James's reign and £866 instead of nearly £1,731 at the end of George's reign. Thus the real value of items seized from the Quakers, using this rough gauge, rose by a third under James and doubled by the mid-1720s.

In reality the impact on Friends was considerably greater because prices did not rise uniformly throughout this period. As in England, prices fell in the late 1680s, as did rents (which declined from 3s. 6d. per acre in the early 1680s to 2s. 6d. in 1687). As prices declined, so too presumably did income, exacerbating the impact of increased distraints on Friends. Land prices and rents were low in the early 1690s but rose sharply late in the decade. A recession in 1702 inaugurated a bad economy that lasted a decade, so that distraints in Anne's reign would have been especially difficult to bear.[147]

During the period 1660–1670, using the partial figures of Holme and Abraham Fuller, in 66 tithing cases the Friends lost possessions valued at £190 6s. 10d., with the heaviest losses sustained in Ulster (£135 16s 6d.) and the lightest in Munster (£13 1s.). The average loss was £2 19s. 8d., with the heaviest assessments again coming in Ulster (£4 4s. 11d.) but the lightest in Leinster (£1 3s. 9d.). In the ensuing four years the average distraint dropped by more than half nationally to £1 6s. 6½d., with the Leinster average the highest at £1 11s. 8d. and Munster's the lowest at 16s. 8d. In these four years alone the Friends sustained losses from tithes cases of £410 2s. 3d., with Ulster losing the most (£244 2s. 6d.) and Munster the least (£26 13s. 2d.). The decline in the average loss may have resulted in part from a more indulgent policy on the government's part, but the more important factor was almost certainly the fuller record keeping in Stockdale's account; during the period 1660–1670 the average number of reported cases is six compared to 77.25 in the years 1671–1674. The principle of deliberate selectivity is borne out in the Moate minutes: the average distraint in the six cases (with specific figures) recorded in the Great Book is £1 15s. 8d., nearly six times higher than the average of 5s. 9d. for the nine cases that were omitted.[148] Incomplete reporting in the period 1660–1670 is probably the principal reason for the idiosyncratic peaks of persecution: 1660 and 1665–1666 in Ulster, 1661–1662 in Leinster, and 1669 in Munster.[149]

Friends suffered for a variety of other offenses. During the period 1660–1670, using the data of Holme and Abraham Fuller, officials seized goods worth £74 16s. 2d. from Quakers, £38 12s. 6d. of which was from Ulster, £22 5s. 8d. from Leinster, and £13 18s. from Munster. The average loss in the 76 cases was 19s. 8d., with Munster Friends experiencing the largest confiscations (£1 10s. 10½d.) and Ulster the smallest (16s. 5d.). Refusal to take an oath brought a fine and usually imprisonment. Holme and Fuller cite only seven cases in the period 1660–1670; fines of £5 each and imprisonment were imposed in one Munster and three Leinster cases, whereas two Ulster offenders were fined £2 and £1 respectively but lost goods valued at £2 5s. and £1 10s. Another Leinster offender went to prison but seems to have escaped a fine. An offender at Moate in 1660 was fined 15s. and jailed. Magistrates levied fines for assorted other offences, such as refusing hat honor, declining to toast the king's health, recusancy (Thomas Baker of county Tyrone was fined £20 for this offense around 1665), disregard of holy days, and a woman's declination to be churched following childbirth. Fees could also be imposed for traditional rites, such as baptism and funerals, even when the services of a Church of Ireland cleric were not used.[150]

For meeting illegally a moderate number of Friends went to prison in the period 1660–1670, though most were there for only weeks or even days, but many also had to pay jailors' fees and sometimes hefty fines. Again using material now found in the incomplete Great Book of Sufferings, Holme and Abraham Fuller record at least 533 imprisonments in this period; the number was probably closer to 600 given the fact that some of their citations refer to "others" who were jailed. Of the 533, 60 percent were jailed in Munster, 32 percent in Leinster, and 8 percent in Ulster. The early years, 1660–1662, when 314 (59 percent) went to prison, and 1669, when 139 (26 percent) were incarcerated, were the worst periods. The most severe times were in Munster in 1661 and 1669, when at least 83 and 130 Friends respectively found themselves in prison.

The war years were devastating for Quakers, but not because of fines and distraints. Holme and Samuel Fuller place the latter losses at £671 7s. 9d. in the years 1689–1691; this compares favorably with both the preceding and succeeding three-year periods, where the respective sums are £1,166 2s. 7d. and £2,126 19s. 2d.[151] War losses were the primary culprit. In May 1691 the six-months meeting reckoned Friends had sustained losses totalling nearly £40,000 to the Gaelic Irish alone, excluding the impact of free quarter and damage inflicted by fleeing supporters of James. Friends in the countryside suffered the most, with many losing everything.[152]

The human face of war is apparent only if one looks at its impact on meetings, families, and individuals. In Ulster, where losses over a four-month period had reached £1,315 17s. (excluding free quarter) by mid-July 1689, the Ballyhagen meeting was particularly hard hit, with damages in excess of £870. Forty-nine families or individuals, six of them women, counted losses ranging from £1 to Thomas Calvert's £95 4s. 6d. In the same four months 53 people or families in Lisburn were deprived of £182 13s. 7d., and 31 at Lurgan lost £148 18s. 10d. By November 1689 war losses in Leinster and Munster surpassed £7,000.[153] Before the war ended, many Ulster Friends suffered as well at the hands of William's army. Among them was John Whitsit of county Tyrone, from whom the Gaelic Irish confiscated £40 worth of goods before burning some of his houses. British troops subsequently confiscated his horses and cows, destroyed his bees, dismantled more of his houses for firewood, and seized his tanned leather, household goods, and £60 worth of other items. Not even a widow was safe: the Irish demolished Elizabeth Francis's house and confiscated wheat, cattle, and other goods, leaving little for British soldiers to take except bedding and inexpensive items; her losses totaled £25 16s.[154]

Virtually from the outset of the depredations the Quakers kept precise records. In May 1689 the half-yearly meeting ordered each provincial meeting to "take Account of all the Spoyles and Roberies Committed on them in these distracted times" and submit a copy to the next national meeting. In two years so many needy were being referred to the provincial meetings that the half-yearly meeting established committees to deal with them in Dublin, Mountmellick, Moate, Wexford, and Wicklow.[155]

Many Friends sustained horrendous deprivation during the time of troubles. So too did countless other victims of warfare who left no record of their travails, but unlike many of these people the Friends had been and would be subject to persecution even in peacetime. Historians have rightly pointed out that such repression was neither uniform nor as severe as was once thought, but the infliction of punishment was sometimes both severe and arbitrary, and no Quaker could have been unaware that he or she could fall victim to it. More so than Presbyterians the Friends lived in the shadow of persecution, whether actual or potential, throughout the period, and this cannot have failed to affect their lives both by sharpening the focus between themselves as a separated people and the rest of society and by emphasizing the need for a trenchant organization to preserve their community and its traditions.

As reports of the suffering circulated, indignation and a resolve to persevere must have been ignited among Quakers as they heard about Thomas Lunn of county Cavan, whom two troopers dragged between their horses for two miles and then assaulted, or Eleanor Totlock of Waterford, who was imprisoned and subsequently expelled from the city with her husband for professing the Quaker message in an Anglican church; her children remained behind. For refusing to pay tithes, John Bennet of county Kildare spent more than four years in "a nasty close Dungeon" at Naas, and while he was there a party of men led by the local minister went to his home, beat the residents, and confiscated some of his possessions. Because he did not pay 10s. in church rates, Edward Kemp of Limerick was not only excommunicated but also had his house, which was valued at £20, seized by Bishop Edward Synge, whose agent expelled Kemp's wife and children and threw out his possessions. For disrupting a service at Cork cathedral in October 1670 Solomon Eccles was jailed for ten days and then whipped with at least 87 lashes from the city's north portal to the south gate.[156]

In a final example, Richard Faile, Thomas Lunn, and William Parker, all of whom had recently been incarcerated at Cavan, were in a meeting at Belturbet when they and others were arrested and jailed. Because they could not pay the jailor's fees, he stripped the clothes from some of them. Still in the same year, 1660, these three men and other Quakers were physically assaulted on a road near Cavan and again imprisoned. At the first assizes the judge refused to release them; at the second he fined each man £20 for meeting illegally and £7 for refusing to remove his hat; at the third he fined each of them another £5 for the latter offense. The jailer then sued them for his fees and seized goods worth £30. At the fourth assize the judge was ready to grant them liberty, but the jailer kept them in prison, claiming each person owed him 15s. in fees. They finally gained their freedom, but only after the jailer distrained an additional £23 8s. 6d. worth of goods, including two horses from Faile worth £4 10s., two horses from Lunn valued at £3 10s., and two cows from Parker worth £2 12s.[157] Accounts similar to these are reiterated throughout the Great Book of Sufferings and related documents. The story they tell does not equal the Marian persecutions or the Albigensian crusade in severity, but it helped to mold and sustain the Quakers' image of themselves as a distinctive people. Quaker apologists and advocates who sought relief from the state also found the data useful. In the words of Stockdale, "Our intent in publishing this Book [*The Great Cry*] partly is to make known to the Rulers and Magestrates, and others, the oppression and great sufferings which we endure: . . . and also that people may see that the Teachers of this age are none of Christs Ministers, who are found walking contrary to the commands of Christ, being called of men Master, and preaching for hire."[158] Suffering understandably honed the Friends' confrontational stance toward the rest of society, somewhat mitigating the otherwise perceptible evolution late in the century of better relations between the Quakers and other Protestants.

Relations with the Wider Community

Notwithstanding their recurring experience of state-supported persecution, in their dealings with the government the Friends generally avoided a hostile tone but did not shrink from challenging authorities on both legal and religious grounds. As the Quakers slowly evolved into a denominational church, the fiery spirit of the 1650s did not completely fade but it was increasingly the exception to the rule. Ralph Sharply, whom one conservative depicted as "the Head and leader of the Quakers" in the northeast, reportedly refused to recognize the king's authority when he was haled before the assizes, nor would he respond to charges levied against him. Because he "contemned and affronted the Bench and called them unjust Judges," the latter fined him and interned him at Carrickfergus. The prevailing tone in dealing with the authorities is reflected in the written response of a group of Friends to the governor and lord mayor of Cork, who had tendered the Quakers a bond to sign for their good behavior. Insisting they were already bonded by a covenant with God, they refused, arguing that signing the bond would demean them as subjects and Christians. Seeking to avoid unnecessary confrontation they added: "We say all subjection we yeld unto the higher power & demeane ourselves thereunto & are subject to every ordinance of man for the Lords sake, & not for wrath. . . . We dare not Contemne the attority nor doe any thing in Contempt of the Lords ministers; but declare against & deny all such things."[159]

Friends based their argument with the state on conscience. When the half-yearly meeting petitioned the lord lieutenant and Council on behalf of suffering Quakers in November 1672 and May 1673, it stressed that Friends sustained incarceration, distraint, excommunication, and financial penalties because of their principles. Although they refused to pay tithes and church rates for conscientious reasons, Quakers in Ireland in the period 1660–1700 apparently never declined to pay taxes. Sharp berated a Dublin alderman in 1680 because the latter had violated the Friends' right of conscience by averring they would not have the benefit of the law if they refused to obey it. "What harm," Sharp asked, "hath our religion for Kingdom or city amongst our neighbours that we are lookt on so obnoxious to the law though some of us are no less helpfull in our places amongst you then our neighbours and chargeable to none of you if we dissent as Protestants from the national church [as] many that is made free do, being we have as much Justly to say as any, It is for conscience Sake." The Catholics, he pointedly contended, did not respect conscience during the reformation, but Quakers expected more from Protestants.[160]

Particularly from the early 1670s onward, the Friends, effectively utilizing their improved organization, repeatedly made their case at every level of government using petitions, delegations, and printed materials.[161] The half-yearly meeting resolved in November 1673 to record all petitions to the king, the lord lieutenant, and the Council as well as all conciliar directives concerning Quakers. The delegates also instructed Friends throughout the realm to keep copies of all applications to magistrates and judges as well as their orders pertaining to Quakers. This material was to be submitted to the national meeting with the records of suffering. At Fox's instruction, a Quaker delegation presented Essex with a copy of *The Case of the People Called Quakers, Relating to Oathes and Swearing* in the spring of 1674.[162] Irish Friends distributed numerous other works to political leaders, and after the time of troubles they regularly dispatched agents to attend parliamentary sessions in Dublin and London to monitor legislation crucial to their interests and to lobby for their cause.[163]

The issue to which they devoted the most attention was rooted in their historic opposition to oaths. The heart of that repudiation rested on the conviction that oaths, in the words of Abraham Fuller and Thomas Holme, were "but Figures of this inward Bond or Covenant, confirmed by the Oath of God in the Seed of Abraham, which the True Christians are of, who witness the Substance and End of all Oaths without, and of Strife, Doubts and Variances that occasioned the Oaths."[164] The oath, however, was the cement that bound much of society together. Oaths were intended to assure the obedience of subjects to rulers and of tenants to landlords. In the judicial context their intent was to guarantee truthfulness. For centuries they had enjoyed an almost magical quality by their endless repetition; in a sense, oaths were to society what ritual was to religion. The Friends' refusal to take oaths not only rendered them subject to fines and imprisonment but also, when the laws were strictly enforced, precluded them from serving on juries or in the government, suing to recover debts, proving wills, or offering evidence in court, even in cases in which they were the accused. Some magistrates and judges turned a blind eye to the legal requirement but most did not. The minutes of the London yearly meeting for June 1688 cryptically note that the baron of the Exchequer in Dublin "indulged Friends the Oath, and took Friends Affirmation As in the presence of God."[165]

The Act of Toleration (1689) released Friends from the obligation of swearing the oaths of supremacy and allegiance; henceforth they could affirm their loyalty to the crown, but oaths remained in force in other areas of society. The English House of Lords passed a bill in 1690 to permit conscientious objectors to oaths to make an affirmation, the heart of which was the sentence, "I call God to witness, and appeal to Him as Judge of the truth of what I shall say." The bill did not pass in the Commons before Parliament adjourned. The Friends' yearly meeting in London discussed the issue in 1692, indicating a willingness to use such phrases as "before God," "in the sight of God," "in the presence of God," or "in the fear of God." In September 1692 the Dublin men's meeting sent Sharp, Clarridge, and John Gay to the lord lieutenant with a petition for liberty of conscience and freedom from oaths, to which he responded that he would do what he could for Quakers. At the six-months meeting in November the delegates, apparently dissatisfied with the results of the yearly meeting's discussion in London, sent a letter to the meeting for sufferings proposing that Parliament accept a declaration of truth from Friends in lieu of an oath; if possible they wanted to use only the "yea" and "nay" favored by Jesus. English and Irish Friends remained in contact as Parliament continued to examine the problem.[166]

Irish Friends obtained some relief when the government permitted them to use a declaration in connection with the poll tax, but the wider issue remained unresolved. Thanks to the efforts of George Whitehead in England, William III lent his support to a parliamentary bill allowing Quakers to make an affirmation: "I, A.B., do declare in the presence of Almighty God, the witness of the truth of what I say." The Affirmation Act became effective in May 1696, but instead of satisfying Friends it intensified internal debate over what constituted an oath. At the half-yearly meeting in May the delegates resolved that they would continue to suffer rather than endorse an affirmation that used "the sacred name of the Lord." Most English Friends were willing to accept the affirmation in the statute, though a minority, especially in Wiltshire, were one with Irish Quakers in holding out for the simple use of "yea" and "nay." In November the six-months meeting informed the yearly meeting in London that it was unanimous in its resolution "to keepe to Christs plaine words in matters of Affirmation and Negation in earthly Affaires."[167]

Irish Friends remained adamantly opposed to the affirmation. In August 1697 the Leinster provincial meeting recommended that each of its constituent members remind Friends not to make the affirmation, and it also gave its agents who were present when the Irish Parliament sat the freedom to inform its members that Quakers could not accept any declaration that used God's name. Each meeting in Ireland was supposed to send two members to attend Parliament. In the meantime, at their yearly meeting in May 1697 English Friends agreed to work with Quakers from other lands to seek further relief, and Irish Friends regularly appointed delegates to go to London. Responding to reports about the English Parliament's consideration of a bill to secure the king's safety, the Leinster meeting commissioned three of its members to write to London urging "that timely endeavours may be used to ease our tender Consciences" with respect to the inclusion of God's name in any declaration. It also directed members of the Dublin meeting to make their concerns known to the lords justices and Council, but one judge warned them not to meddle in this area. Nevertheless, in 1698 the half-yearly meeting appointed a committee to monitor the activities of the Irish Parliament; two or three committee members examined the heads of each bill to determine whether or not it affected Quakers.[168]

Because of their refusal to take the declaration in connection with the poll tax, many Friends had to pay double. The half-yearly meeting therefore decided in November 1698 to submit an address to the Irish Parliament explaining the Quaker position. Signed on behalf of Irish Friends by Edmundson and four others, the address explained that it had always been a Quaker principle to live peacefully under the government God had established. Their refusal to accept the declaration, they said, was not the result of disaffection to the king and government but of "a tender Scruple of Conscience." Although some had heretofore subscribed the declaration, their consciences were troubled, hence Irish Friends were now prepared "to declare Our Selves in as full words as are Contained Either in the Declaration of Fidelity or that against the Pope and his Supremacy under any Penalty you shall think fitt (the Sacred name of God not being therein)." Sharp, Abraham Fuller, and twenty others wrote an epistle to Irish Friends asking them to stand unified behind the statement submitted to Parliament.[169] That statement was duly read in the House of Commons, but to no effect, for Quakers continued to face double charges for the poll tax; refusal to pay these charges resulted in further distraining of their goods. Because of this the annual value of distrained goods soared from £554 11s. 2d. in 1692 to £887 1s. 6d. in 1695, to £1,710 18s. 11½d. in 1698, and to £2,000 2s. 9d. in 1700.[170]

In addition to lobbying the government at all levels, Irish Friends, like their counterparts in England, engaged the state in the legal arena. Generally they did this on an *ad hoc* basis, as in November 1671 when the six-months meeting appointed Clarridge and Robert Turner to investigate fines imposed on Quakers at Armagh and Carrickfergus, or in

May 1672 when it dispatched Clarridge and Gregson to the Prerogative Office for information about initiating legal action on behalf of a Quaker widow against a priest. The half-yearly meeting also instructed John Gay to consult with the commissioners of reducement about remitting fines against Friends. To obtain an accurate record of how many Quakers were in prison and for what offenses, the half-yearly meeting in November 1672 appointed a committee of eight comprised of three representatives each from Leinster and Ulster and two from Munster.[171] The committee did not assume responsibility for assigning Friends to assist members who experienced legal difficulties of a persecutorial nature, for the half-year meeting continued to exercise this function.

For the most part Irish Friends handled their own legal affairs, seldom consulting attorneys, a reluctance increasingly less evident among their compatriots in England. An exception occurred in 1672 when the half-yearly meeting in Dublin sought the advice of a lawyer named Whitfield after a jailer refused to release Francis Robson and others despite their having procured a writ of *habeas corpus*. John Hull of Inishbeg, county Cork, apparently required the services of an attorney in 1686 during a complex tithes case, as did Toby Courtney in Ulster the same year. Five years later the national meeting dispatched Sharp, Gershon Boate, and John Tottenham to consult a lawyer for assistance in obtaining the release of William Sparrow and John Clerk, who had been jailed for refusing to pay tithes. In 1693 the Leinster provincial meeting advocated the use of "any . . . meanes according to Truth" to liberate John Lancaster from the Naas jail where he had been detained for refusing to pay tithes, but four years later the national meeting, referring to the case of two Friends imprisoned at Cork on tithes charges, expressed caution with respect to "takeing any course or proceedure by Law," recommending instead that the Munster meeting seek their relief by interceding with the bishop or archbishop.[172]

Judging from the case of John and Samuel Watson and Daniel White, all of whom had been excommunicated, Quakers did not seek legal assistance without considerable forethought. While prisoners their jailor had allowed them limited freedom to leave the jail, for which the judge at the Carlow assizes had issued decrees against both the Quakers (for escaping) and their keeper. The real issue was the denial of legal rights in civil suits to these men on the grounds that they were excommunicate; such persons could not plead in civil cases unless their real property was involved. At the behest of the national meeting Thomas Starkey and John Bennet spoke to the judge on their behalf, but to no avail, hence in May 1681 the meeting directed Starkey, Sharp, and Turner to seek advice and then petition the lord lieutenant and Council to have the case retried at the next assize. Apparently because of the resulting counsel, the Leinster meeting instructed Abraham Fuller in September to request a copy of a report concerning the case. The three complainants must have attempted to sue for recovery of debts, for Fuller was told to warn the judge that "if a favourable Report be not Returned the Consequences may bee of great damage to many honest men and their families in giveing men liberty to take our goods." Both the Leinster and the national meetings then directed Sharp and Turner to assist the three men in seeking redress from the lord lieutenant and Council, and the national meeting also asked them in November 1681 to accompany John Watson to the lord chief justice.[173]

Whether these appeals proved fruitless or were postponed is not clear, but by May 1682 the three men had retained legal counsel. At that time the half-yearly meeting asked White and John Watson to have their attorney prepare a petition to the lord lieutenant and Council "concerning the Report of the Judges" and give it to Sharp, Turner, and Joseph Sleigh, who would continue to assist them. In September Sharp and Sleigh wrote to the second-day meeting in London to learn whether excommunicated persons had the benefit of the law; the response informed them that in England, as in Ireland, excommunicated defendants could stop legal proceedings by pleading. When the case was still unresolved six months later, the meeting asked Sharp, Sleigh, and Starkey to confer with Burnyeat, Fuller, and Francis Rogers. Because Samuel Watson could not obtain the signed decree issued on his behalf at the Carlow assizes, the Leinster meeting in December instructed Sharp to consult the lawyer who had promised to obtain it. If this attorney continued to procrastinate, Sharp was empowered to consult Whitfield before approaching the judges or to speak with the latter first and then obtain Whitfield's advice if necessary. After a judge signed Watson's decree in early 1683, the Leinster meeting resolved that a further request should be made to the lord deputy and Council to rehear the cases of other Friends who had been denied justice in civil suits as excommunicated persons. The meeting commissioned White to search the records in the bishop's court and report to Sharp "that he may know how to Expresse the matter" in the petition. Prior to its submission, Edmundson, Fuller, Bennet, White, John Watson, and Thomas Carleton reviewed it. Ultimately nothing came of this, for Sharp was still waiting in January 1685 for White to complete his search. Shortly thereafter the Friends opted not to submit a petition.[174]

As in England, in some cases Irish Friends turned for legal advice to other experts or sought answers in legal documents. In 1672 the national meeting asked Edmundson and Clarridge to write to Ellis Hookes, the Quakers' recording clerk in London, for information concerning possible ways to prove wills outside episcopal courts and information about proceedings stemming from definitive sentences. The following year the meeting sent Clarridge and Thomas Sawyer to examine documents in the Exchequer to determine if fines of £20 against Thomas Baker for recusancy and a hundred marks apiece against Margaret Trotter and Blanch Holden for testifying in the Lisburn parish church had been estreated, that is, extracted and returned to the Exchequer for prosecution. In another case the six-months meeting in 1700 directed Sharp and Boate to consult with the proctor in an episcopal court who specialized in tithes from gardens for information to help them obtain the release of William Roberts of Maryborough, Queen's County (Laois).[175]

The Quakers were alert for violations in the legal process that would enable them to achieve legal victories. The clearest case occurred in 1684 when a magistrate apparently recorded Joseph Boardman's name on a writ and a *significavit* (a certificate indicating the offense) as Joseph Moony. From the recorder of Dublin Sharp learned that the sheriff of King's County (Offaly), who had imprisoned Boardman at Philipstown (Daingean), could be sued for false imprisonment. The half-yearly meeting therefore commissioned Sharp and John Gee to obtain a writ of *habeas corpus* for Boardman's release.[176] More often the Friends relied on the good graces of officials to intervene on their behalf. In the spring of 1683 Sharp and James Taylor spoke with the lord chief justice and another judge about the suffering of Quakers in Carlow and found both men sensitive to this "beyond Expectation." The chief justice, in fact, promised to "do all the good he could to friends for the time to come." The half-yearly meeting responded in kind by directing Sharp and Taylor to ask these judges if the two could apply on behalf of suffering Friends in Carlow to the lord lieutenant, his deputy, or the Council, "& as they find them to incline or advise to proceed further in it or let it fall." When Sharp and others interceded with the archbishop of Dublin in 1694 on behalf of Christopher Cheater of county Wicklow, who had been jailed for contempt of the episcopal court, they found him moderate and were sufficiently encouraged to continue their intercession. The

Quakers were also willing to use pressure as necessary and where possible, as in 1682 when they were seeking James Wasly's release; they obtained a supportive letter from the chancellor of the diocese of Meath and sent Fuller to show it to the minister responsible for having him incarcerated at Mullingar.[177]

The Friends demonstrated no reticence to appeal directly to ecclesiastics as well as lay magistrates. In November 1696 the half-yearly meeting resolved that henceforth Quakers who suffered for their refusal to pay tithes should first apply to the relevant minister for redress and only then to the bishop and ultimately to the justices of the quarter sessions or assizes. This may have been common practice prior to this date, but the records do not suggest this. Most recorded appeals were to lay or ecclesiastical dignitaries, a number of whom were prelates. Appeals went to James Margetson, archbishop of Armagh, in 1673, and to Michael Boyle, his successor, in 1694; two years later the half-yearly meeting authorized Sharp and Thomas Ashton to petition Boyle on behalf of Ulster Friends "if they find occasion." Intercession with Richard Boyle, bishop of Leighlin and Ferns, on behalf of Orin Smith in 1674 proved ineffectual, but Narcissus Marsh, bishop of Leighlin and Ferns, and William Smyth, bishop of Raphoe, were more sympathetic in the mid-1680s. Marsh, in fact, was instrumental in releasing Robert Howard and James Knowles. The Friends also appealed to Robert Leslie, bishop of Clogher, in 1674; Ambrose Jones, bishop of Kildare, in 1676 and 1678; and the widow of Patrick Sheridan, late bishop of Cloyne, in 1683.[178] Dealings with chancellors were relatively common; those with deans were not.[179]

Commencing in 1683 Irish Friends established the practice of having at least two Quakers at every assize and quarter session to monitor proceedings and assist fellow believers facing charges. The intent was to have monthly meetings assume responsibility for sending qualified Friends, but especially in Ulster the provincial meeting appointed people. Noting that some Quakers prosecuted for tithes had not had the benefit of assistance, the national meeting in November 1687 again urged the provincial meetings to ask their constituent members to delegate qualified persons to attend sessions and assizes. By the spring of 1699 complaints again surfaced that qualified Friends were not always present. In 1706 the Leinster meeting noted "a Jealousy in the minds of some friends least that needfull concern of Attending Assizes and Sessions be neglected by reason some friends who live in one County belong to Meetings in another." The problem of finding qualified people to attend quarter sessions and assizes was clearly an organizational one and underscored the need for improved coordination between meetings.[180]

Friends looked to the government for protection. This was particularly the case at Christmas, when unruly people stoned Quaker shops because they were not closed in observance of the holy day. From the early 1680s the Dublin men's meeting regularly sent several members to the lord mayor, other magistrates, and in the 1690s the commander of the regiment and the lords justices to request that constables keep order. The crowds nevertheless forced many shopkeepers to close at Christmas 1691, persuading some Friends that "there has been to[o] much an Intimation to aveyd the Cross: & not . . . beare a testymony for truth against those supersticions of popery." The Dublin men's meeting advised Quakers "to be cautious & yet not Raysh to opose the Government." The destructive acts abated somewhat in the mid-1690s but were again vexatious in 1697 and 1699.[181]

Quakers were easy targets of violence because of their distinctive ways, their sense of being a separated group, and possibly their adherence to the peace principle. The theme of the Lamb's war, of course, pervaded the Quaker movement. Fox kept the sense of the struggle alive, as in his 1683 epistle to all Friends in which he denounced "the scurrilous and filthy books of lies & defamations" written against the Quakers and urged the faithful to "stand fast in the liberty wherein Christ Jesus hath made you free." Irish Friends tried to keep the struggle in bounds, in part by tempering the deliberately confrontational stance that had characterized the 1650s and 1660s and in part by the half-yearly meeting's recommendation in 1693 that Quakers should not engage in public disputes concerning religion, either orally or in writing, without first consulting "weighty Friends" in their local meeting. Nor could they publish anything without first showing the manuscript to a monthly or provincial meeting. Freedom of expression was increasingly subject to institutional control as the Friends became a denominational church.[182]

The relatively few Quakers who insisted on testifying in parish churches inevitably provoked hostility. Among them were Thomas Murford at Wexford, Eleanor Tatlock at Waterford, and John Edwards at Newtown, county Fermanagh, in the early 1660s; John Edwards at Ballinakill, Queen's County (Laois) in 1669; and Solomon Eccles at Cork in

1670. Simply for attending a service in the parish church at Bandon, a Friend was "violently pulled and haled . . . and it made such an uproar, that the Friend had like to have bin smother'd."[183] On occasion Friends mounted strident written assaults against conformists. In a paper probably composed in 1660–1661, Edward Cook castigated the "wickedness" of young ministers coming to Ireland from Oxford and Cambridge to be installed in "the old masse-houses," the repair of which was paid for by goods confiscated from the populace. These ministers, Cook declaimed, were pluralists who cobbled together four or five parishes apiece, many with fewer than five Protestant families in each. The tithes each cleric received had formerly supported four or five Catholic priests, he averred, and the Catholics could now see by the lives of these conformist clergy "what devourers they are."[184]

One of the more interesting confrontations occurred in 1688 after Robert Lackey of Staplestown, county Carlow, left the Church of Ireland to become a Quaker. When his former minister, Lawrence Potts, counterattacked by accusing Friends of teaching "vile Doctrines," repudiating tithes and sacraments, and preaching illegally, Burnyeat and John Watson retorted in *The Holy Truth and Its Professors Defended*. Like Cook they drove home the point that conformist clerics demanded tithes from many to whom they never ministered. They also denounced Church of Ireland clerics for their involvement in persecution, accusing them of sometimes employing informers, sometimes "appearing in their own persons."[185]

The evidence suggests that confrontations between Friends and other nonconformists in the period 1660–1700 were relatively few. Some Presbyterians in Ulster in 1683 reportedly spread a rumor by "a wicked girl" that cast Quakers in a bad light; three Presbyterian ministers, including William and Gideon Jacque, had allegedly "blazed [it] abroad," hence the half-year meeting appointed a committee comprising Edmundson, Sharp, Carleton, and two others to draft a response, and it ordered Ulster Friends to prepare a formal statement denouncing the rumor.[186]

Irish Quakers devoted surprisingly little attention to those nonconformists who, like themselves, were separatists and had occupied a good deal of their efforts in the 1650s. An undated letter to the Baptists from John Perrot in the characteristic prophetic mode may be from this period, and other contact between the two groups was noted in Chapter 6. Penn, Sharp, Thomas Story, and George Rooke defended Quakers against a series of tracts (now lost) by John Plimpton, a Dublin Baptist, in 1698. This debate echoed many between Baptists and Friends that had been occurring since the 1650s and had helped to refine each community's sense of theological and ecclesiological distinctiveness. Contact also occurred with the tiny Muggletonian sect. In 1673 the Munster provincial meeting noted the presence of Muggletonians, which brought advice from the six-months meeting to "draw up as Many of Muggletons false Principles" as it deemed appropriate and testify against them. Indeed, Penn had denounced the Muggletonians the previous year in *The New Witnesses Proved Old Heretics.*[187]

Congregationalists demonstrated the most interest in challenging the Friends. Thomas Jenner's *Quakerism Anatomiz'd and Confuted* (1670) was discussed in Chapter 6. Penn and Whitehead responded in *A Serious Apology for the Principles and Practices of the People Call'd Quakers* (1671). Nearly two decades later James Barry, a Congregationalist minister in Dublin, frequently attacked Quakers both in his preaching and in his private conversations. Quakers, he contended, denied the resurrection and salvation by "the Coming of Christ." The Friends offered to debate with him about resurrection, justification, election, reprobation, and "Perfection in Sanctification, as to Degrees attainable." The debate, they said, could be in the Meath Street meetinghouse or a place of Barry's choosing and could be as open to the public as he desired. Apparently fearing a largely Quaker audience, Barry responded in a series of unpublished papers, again attacking Quaker tenets but claiming as well that the Friends stirred up animosity, engaged in serpentine acts, and promoted uncharitableness. Reviving an old canard, he charged that Jesuits had spawned the Quakers just as the devil had given birth to the Jesuits.[188]

Occasional hints suggest that intra-Protestant relations were often less contentious than the polemics suggest. The Friends, after all, could never curtail intermarriage between their members and those of other Protestant groups. Without amiable social relations those marriages would not have transpired. If some magistrates persecuted Quakers, others did their best to mitigate such persecution and turned a blind eye to nonconformist religious activities in general. In the early 1690s the earl of Donegall had a Quaker servant,[189] and we know that Friends served as stewards on some landed estates. Although Friends officially made a concerted effort to maintain their separateness, their children sometimes attended school with non-Quakers and they occasionally apprenticed their children to non-Quakers and themselves served as masters of non-Quaker young people. In the late 1680s they participated not only in corporations but also in the magistracy.

As a minority, both religiously and ethnically, Protestants in Ireland increasingly found more common ground as they lived and worked together. In the end the Friends' strong sense of humanity undercut their historic principle of separateness. Despite their efforts to enact more precise behavioral principles, especially concerning apparel, their success in surviving both state-sponsored persecution and the depredations of the time of troubles made them increasingly more acceptable to other members of society by the turn of the century. After all, by that time they, like the Scottish Presbyterians, had become a denominational church. The parallels between them were striking: Both had developed effective ecclesiological organizations; both held their adherents to high ideals and imposed discipline on the wayward; both built meeting-houses, provided financial assistance to the needy, founded schools, and ransomed captives. The Quakers had no formal ministry nor did they observe festal communions, but they developed a system to approve public Friends and held meetings in which the sense of spiritual power was reportedly no less intense than in Presbyterian fasts and celebrations of the Lord's supper. Having made the trek through the valley of the shadow of persecution together, though experiencing travails of different intensity, it is hardly surprising that by 1700 the Friends and the Scottish Presbyterians began to sense that which they held in common.

Epilogue: Reflections

THE HISTORY OF Christianity is to a large extent the story of internecine conflict over competing theologies, modes of worship, polities, and varieties of religious life, complicated to varying degrees by political, ethnic, cultural, economic, and personality factors. The chapter in Christian history which deals with Protestantism in late seventeenth-century Ireland is no exception. Although Catholics overshadowed Protestants by a ratio of eight to three according to William Petty, Protestants in general made no concerted effort to band together in a comprehensive state church or even in a broad-based association. Indeed, for the Friends such a possibility was totally unacceptable, nor would the Baptists have embraced full union with conformists on the one hand or Quakers on the other. For the most part, the Irish Baptists were a spent force, largely devoid of clerical leadership, though their lay leaders, Richard Lawrence and Jerome Sankey, were men of some talent. Baptist congregations were recruiting grounds for Quakers, and some Baptists drifted to other churches in search of ministerial leadership and Christian communion. English Presbyterians and Congregationalists worked together very closely, but their numbers were small, particularly outside Dublin and a few towns in the south; both groups cooperated to some degree with the Scottish Presbyterians, and some English Presbyterians would have welcomed accommodation in the Church of Ireland. The Presbyterians of a Scottish hue who dominated parts of the north were mostly chary of cooperation with conformists despite the mediating efforts of prominent lay leaders such as Massereene. The willingness of the two groups to share the cathedral of Derry during the siege of the city was an exception, not the norm. So too was the sharing of the parish church in Antrim. Late in the century, as in England, Presbyterians and Congregationalists began cooperating more closely: In 1696 they formed the presbytery of Munster (later known as the Southern Association), and they participated as well at the end of the decade in the Societies for the Reformation of Manners in Dublin, but these societies proved unattractive to the Scottish Presbyterians in Ulster.

From the restoration to the turn of the century and beyond, most nonclerical leaders in Ireland pursued an accommodationist policy toward nonconformists, whereas prominent ecclesiastics in the Church of Ireland typically embraced a hard stance. There were exceptions, such as Edward Wetenhall and William King, whose moderately ecumenical outlook, had it been adopted in the early 1660s, might have provided the basis for a comprehensive church settlement. Although some laymen, such as Rawdon, viewed nonconformity in a harsh light, most lay leaders took a more tolerant position in the belief that moderation was conducive to the maintenance of security. When the government cracked down on nonconformity, it did so in the context of perceived threats to security—the 1663 Dublin conspiracy, the Galloway and Bothwell Bridge rebellions in Scotland, and the Argyll and Monmouth insurrections. Because of the government's generally tolerant policy, Irish nonconformists posed no serious security threat after 1663. The proximity of Ireland to Scotland made the former a ready haven for dissident Scottish fugitives, but Ireland was never a fertile recruiting ground for Scottish rebels. The militant covenanting movement found relatively little support in Ireland, particularly after 1666; David Houston and the United Societies were never more than a fractious, small minority among Presbyterians—a sect that broke from the newly emergent denominational church to maintain its pronounced confrontational stance against the world.

Although nonconformists posed no substantive security threat, they insisted on meeting for services of worship, governing their own affairs, and operating to a surprising degree in the open. From the early 1670s they constructed or rented meetinghouses, sometimes on church land or the property of prominent laity, and they even built a church virtually adjacent to the council chamber in Dublin. For the most part theirs was not an underground movement despite the fact that a minority of its adherents indisputably engaged in activities directed against the government. To the administration's credit it was reasonably effective in distinguishing between the vast majority of quiescent nonconformists and the militant minority that plotted against the state. The Presbyterians, of course, prudently reminded civil officials of their record of loyalty to the Stuarts during the interregnum. Apart from such political and ideological considerations, magistrates must have found nonconformists attractive as constructive citizens because of their disciplinary practices and strong disavowal of such vices as inebriety, sexual promiscuity, and failure to repay debt. Nonconformists also contributed to the economy, not only by their industry and mercantile acumen but also by their system of private charity and their emphasis on education. Indeed, the Irish Parliament recognized the economic benefits of moderate toleration when it enacted legislation in 1662 offering a degree of religious freedom to nonconforming Protestant immigrants. Differences over theology, polity, and worship notwithstanding, the nonconformists were constructive forces in the community and valuable allies in any confrontation with the Gaelic Irish, as the events of the early 1690s demonstrated.

If lay officials had solid reasons for their accommodating outlook, those prominent clerics who saw nonconformists as their enemies were not reacting mindlessly. Apart from the obvious disagreements over theology, polity, and worship, all of which were rooted in principle, Anglicans viewed nonconformists as competitors for both a relatively small Protestant populace and restricted financial resources. Given the extremely small number of ministers of any persuasion with facility in Gaelic, the possibility of winning converts among the Irish—never substantial in any event because of ethnic, cultural, political, and economic considerations—was slight. The expansion of one Protestant group was therefore possible only by winning adherents from another or by attracting immigrants from Scotland or England; gains from immigration, however, were apparently more than offset by losses to emigration. The competition for funds was no less intense. The restoration gave conformists control of the island's cathedrals and parish churches, but many of these required repair, particularly after the depredations of the mid-century revolution. Much of the repair had not been done when fresh damages were sustained in the time of troubles. Some conformists also faced legal struggles to regain leases and other property alienated during the interregnum. For their part, nonconformists had to raise funds not only to support their ministers—or the public Friends in the case of the Quakers—but also to construct, purchase, or rent meetinghouses. They needed money as well to provide charity, educate their children, and, in the time of troubles, relieve victims of the fighting.

For the most part, exclusivity thus won out over ecumenicity, though close cooperation between Presbyterians and Congregationalists was a notable exception, as was periodically the case in England during this period.

Irish nonconformists had a number of things in common. All of them looked across the sea for guidance, support, and sometimes sustenance. The Scottish Presbyterians turned to Scotland and the English Presbyterians and the Friends to England, whereas the Congregationalists, because of the Mather connection, had ties to New England. None of the groups saw a need or took the time to draft substantive doctrinal statements, nor were the last four decades of the century a noteworthy period of literary activity. The meatiest works—by writers such as Joseph Boyse and Robert Craghead—appeared at the end of the period. Scottish Presbyterians and Friends demonstrated an interest in recording their histories, the result of which are the invaluable works of Patrick Adair and Thomas Wight. The commissioning of these histories reflects both communities' awareness of their distinctive identities, the significance of their past, and the need to preserve their records for future generations. Both groups began keeping records of their meetings in the 1670s, a reflection of the major organizational efforts in which Scottish Presbyterians and Friends were engaged. Both communities were also similar in their efforts to construct meetinghouses and establish schools. The Quakers, of course, had no interest in founding an equivalent to the Presbyterians' seminary at Killyleagh, but the extent to which both groups constructed meetinghouses underscores the substantive degree of toleration they normally enjoyed commencing in the early 1670s. In many respects the two movements engaged in comparable efforts to discipline wayward members, normally for the same offenses and usually by imposing some form of public admission of errant behavior. This public or semi-public confession was akin in spirit to the practice of shaming in the Church of Ireland. Each group had its distinctive way of performing marriages, but neither repudiated the validity of marriages solemnized by Church of Ireland clergy.

In other respects significant differences existed between nonconformists, and not simply over the obvious issues of theology, polity, and worship. Alone among Irish nonconformists the Friends adopted a rigid, distinctive code of dress and home furnishing—a code more rigorous and detailed than that of their English counterparts. Irish Quakers were strict moralists, rigid disciplinarians, and staunch adherents of the ideal of simplicity, particularly toward the end of the century when the diminution of persecution, the growth of the movement, and economic and social success seemingly threatened the group's distinctiveness as a separated people. Unlike Presbyterians the Friends controlled what their members published, established firm links with English Friends to import some of their literature, and founded lending libraries in their meetings. The Friends were different too in the efforts they made to circulate epistles, whether from the pens of Fox and Whitehead or lesser lights in the movement. The rigorous trials required of candidates for the Presbyterian ministry made university education almost a *sine qua non*, and for that reason the Presbyterians found themselves chronically short of clergy. No such education was required of public Friends, hence the Quakers had ample numbers of people of both genders who criss-crossed Ireland, seeking converts and reinforcing adherents, until at the turn of the century the number of public Friends was finally insufficient to meet the demand. The financial support necessary to assist public Friends, or at least those unable to support themselves, was considerably less onerous for Quakers than the financial demands faced by Presbyterians and Congregationalists to maintain a professional clergy. Quakers could worship without public Friends; Presbyterians and Congregationalists depended on their clergy for sermons, baptism, and the celebration of the Lord's supper. The Presbyterians' clerical shortage made it very difficult to expand their geographical base, whereas the Quakers' ample supply of public Friends facilitated their ability to spread their message. Perhaps no difference between the Presbyterians and the Quakers was more dramatic than their contrary professions of political loyalty in the revolution, when Quakers looked to James II and Presbyterians to William.

All five Protestant nonconformist communities survived the restoration as well as the revolution and time of troubles, though the English Presbyterians, the Congregationalists, and especially the Baptists did so in a severely weakened state. In large part this was the result of the failure of the Baptists and Congregationalists to establish a significant base beyond the military and the civilian republicans in the 1650s and the Congregationalists' ensuing willingness virtually to merge with English Presbyterians. Scottish Presbyterians, with roots that antedated the revolutionary years, continued to expand among Scottish settlers and enjoyed a virtually ineradicable ethnic, social, economic, and religious base as well as a fair degree of geographical cohesiveness at the restoration. For their part the Friends had established meetings among English settlers in many areas of Ireland, and only in the west did their foothold prove to be too tenuous to last. The Quakers owed their strength in part to their ability to win converts among the middling sort whose prosperity lent the movement stability as well as financial resources. Unlike Congregationalists and Baptists, the Scottish Presbyterians and the Friends prospered because of their highly effective organizations and their pronounced sense of communal solidarity. Religion played a substantial role in maintaining their sense of being distinctive communities, thus helping to sustain their identity in a colonial context. For Presbyterians the Covenant was the cement that held them together, checking individualism and upholding common values, tenets, and loyalties. For Quakers the sense of being a people apart, with their own standardized forms of behavior and unique modes of worship, bound them together, overcoming even the internal fractiousness that periodically plagued the movement. The experience of persecution, though seldom severe, contributed as well to their respective sense of cohesion.

By the end of the century Scottish Presbyterians and Friends in Ireland had evolved from sects into denominational churches, though both would undergo additional significant changes in subsequent centuries. Excluded from the established church at the restoration, the Scottish Presbyterians had become a *de facto* sect, a voluntary association of believers and their children with clearly articulated standards of admission, an insistence on allegiance to their group *vis-a-vis* competing religious bodies, a claim to be the proponents of supernatural truths, and a sense of conscious separation from the rest of society, particularly when they gathered in conventicles, ordained their clergy, or observed festal communions. Unlike the Presbyterians, both English and Scottish, the Friends did not enter the restoration period as a religious body whose historic experience and ideals had been those of an established church. The Quakers had been a sect since their beginnings, a religious minority that had consciously separated itself from the rest of society and had manifested a strong resolve to uphold its distinctive tenets. Even as the Friends slowly evolved into a denominational church they retained their thaumaturgical emphasis—their stress on the experiential activity of the Spirit within. In certain respects they seem to have resisted this evolution, for in addition to preserving their thaumaturgical focus they increasingly enforced strict, legalistic standards of conduct, apparel, and domestic furnishings even as the world around them began to accept them socially and economically.

The Friends, beginning in 1668, and the Scottish Presbyterians, commencing a year or two later, underwent a rationalizing process that entailed the development of institutionalized authority, structured systems of discipline, multiregional networks of spiritual leaders, means to raise funds, schools, and, for the Quakers, agencies to censor, publish, and disseminate religious literature. Both groups wanted their histories written, and both maintained substantive records of their activities, including money-raising, discipline, and worship. Such records reinforced each body's sense of communal identity. Both groups constructed meetinghouses, and the Quakers, as part of their resolve to preserve a sense of separation from traditional society, maintained their own burial grounds as well. All of this was possible largely because both bodies developed ecclesiological structures capable of recruiting and nurturing members as well as governing communal affairs, even in the face of period persecution by the state.

In the late decades of the century both the Scottish Presbyterians and the Friends began to manifest other characteristics of a denominational church, though these were in a very early stage of development as the new century dawned. Without retreating from its views on theology, polity, and worship, each group became somewhat less confrontational in its dealings with other Christians. Some Quakers declined in their rigor, though their leaders pressed hard to maintain the social distinctiveness that had demarcated Friends from the rest of society since the movement's inception. Another indication of declining rigor is the breakaway sect founded by David Houston, which is testimony that most Scottish Presbyterians were not sufficiently zealous in their fidelity to the Covenant in the minds of this group. The cooperation between mainline Presbyterians and Anglicans during the siege of Derry and at Antrim is a practical affirmation that these Presbyterians did not regard their tenets as the unique path to salvation; indeed, they had never done so. In contrast, the Friends clung to their idiosyncratic theological tenets as they entered the eighteenth century, and adherents of other groups generally recognized their uniqueness, though in unfavorable terms. This did not, however, stop some Friends from sending their children to school with non-Quakers, from apprenticing their children to non-Quaker masters, or from taking non-Quaker apprentices. Nor, of course, did it prevent Friends from socializing with and marrying members of other faiths, notwithstanding repeated admonitions to the contrary, nor did it hinder Friends from working for, employing, and engaging in commercial transactions with non-Quakers. Despite their occasional willingness to engage in religious disputations, both Friends and Scottish Presbyterians had achieved a substantial degree of social acceptance in Ireland by the turn of the century.

Scottish Presbyterians and Friends—their organizations intact, their members yoked together in striking cohesiveness—were thus well positioned to take advantage of the more tolerant climate that followed the time of troubles and to withstand the implementation of the penal laws in the next century. Had it not been for emigration, their impact on subsequent Irish history might have been greater, yet larger numbers alone would not have enabled them to make inroads among the Gaelic Irish because of the linguistic and cultural barriers as well as the intense resentment resulting from the widespread ouster of the Irish from their lands. To the extent that they concerned themselves with the Gaelic Irish, nonconformists were far more likely to see them as potential threats to revolt than as objects of missionary endeavor or victims in their own land. In many respects, then, the emergence of denominational churches in late seventeenth-century Ireland institutionalized the differences between the religious communities, making it much more difficult in the future to accentuate common ideals and ecumenical cooperation.

REFERENCE MATTER

Appendix: Comment on Sources

Records for the internal history of the Presbyterians in Ireland from the restoration to 1700 are relatively scarce. Only one session book—from the church at Templepatrick in county Antrim—predates the restoration, and its entries cease after 4 December 1660, resuming again, with a single exception for 26 June 1670, on 15 August 1693. A notation, probably made on 26 June 1670, explains: "This blanke [was] upon the persecution of the prelates."[1] The entries for the mid- and later 1690s deal primarily with financial collections and contain some material on marriages and the celebration of the Lord's supper. Although the records of the Burt session (county Donegal) extend from 1676 to 1719, the entries are not always sequential; gaps were left for unexplained reasons and subsequently filled with later material to avoid waste. The manuscript lacks usable contemporary folio numbers and some leaves are missing. The session book for the church at Kirkdonald (Dundonald), county Down, is virtually contemporaneous, intermittently covering the period from 1678 to 1713, with an emphasis on collections, disbursements, and baptisms. In contrast, the session book for the church at Carnmoney, county Antrim, is concerned largely with discipline and the selection of new elders to replace deceased ones. Entries commence in 1686; the early entries mention only one collection.[2]

Reasonably comprehensive records exist for two meetings (presbyteries) and the synod of Ulster. Those for Antrim cover the periods 1654 to 1658, 1671 to 1675, and 1683 to 1691, whereas the Lagan minutes run from 1672 to 1681, and from December 1690 to the end of the century. Separate records are extant for the period from October 1697 to July 1698 when the Lagan meeting was divided into the presbyteries of Londonderry and Strabane. Records of the synod of Ulster commence in September 1691. Books had been kept for the committee that preceded it,[3] but these apparently have not survived. When the synod appointed a standing committee to revise the presbyteries' records in 1697, it obtained minutes for Route beginning in April 1693, for both Down and Tyrone commencing in June 1695, and for Lagan, though delays in procuring records for Antrim continued into the early years of the next century.[4]

Although far from complete, records for the Society of Friends in Ireland in the late seventeenth century are fairly extensive. Minutes of the half-yearly meeting commence on 5 May 1671 and continue unbroken into modern times. Records of sufferings exist for the period under review in varying degrees of thoroughness. Minutes of the various meetings contain relatively frequent indications that some Quakers were remiss in submitting records of their suffering. For the national women's meeting there are no minutes, but epistles to and from the meeting afford insights into its activities commencing in the 1670s. Minutes of the provincial meetings begin in May 1670 for Leinster, January 1675 for Ulster, and 1694 for Munster. Records are also extant for the Munster women's six-weeks meeting from October 1680 to December 1696. Minutes of local men's meetings are spotty: In the province of Ulster the Lisburn minutes date from April 1675, and Lurgan's commence the same year, though the latter's record book contains slightly older material. A record book from Upper Grange, county Tyrone, dates from 1686. In the province of Munster, men's meeting minutes are extant for Cork (from December 1675), Tipperary (from August 1681), and Charleville (from 1689). The fullest minutes are those for the Dublin men's meeting (from February 1678), although early records also survive from two other men's meetings in Leinster province, namely Newgarden (from November 1678) and Moate (from July 1680). Among the additional documents for this period are the extensive collection of Anthony Sharp manuscripts, testimonies against tithes, testimonials of denial and condemnation, and records of births, marriages, and deaths.[5]

As assiduous as the Friends were in keeping records, a number of documents have been lost. For more than a year in 1691–1692 the crucial first volume of the minutes of the six-months meeting could not be found, and at one point the meeting appointed two men to launch a house-to-house search among Quaker homes in Dublin where the volume was likely to be. At last it was found in Anthony Sharp's home, where a maid had mislaid it. Sharp, normally a diligent record-keeper, lost a document on marriage sent to Dublin from the Leinster provincial meeting in 1678. Whether deliberately or accidentally, someone tore the pages for the period March to September 1675 from the records of the same provincial meeting.[6] In other cases, accounts of the earliest meetings were either lost or never recorded. At provincial and six-months meetings notes were taken and subsequently transcribed after being checked for accuracy. In October 1697, for instance, the Leinster provincial meeting commissioned six Dublin Friends "to view and Correct fitt for transcribing" proceedings from 1679 to 1692. Concern for the preservation of records is also apparent by instructions that they be made on good paper as well as "in a good and plaine way," to quote the Leinster meeting's mandate for a book of records. Similarly, in May 1671 the six-months meeting stipulated that records of sufferings submitted to it "be fairly written, & sowed or fastened together in full sheets."[7]

Abbreviations

Adair	Patrick Adair, *A True Narrative of the Rise and Progress of the Presbyterian Church in Ireland*, ed. W. D. Killen (Belfast: C. Aitchison, 1866)
Add. MSS	Additional Manuscripts, British Library
APL	Armagh Public Library
Barnard	T. C. Barnard, *Cromwellian Ireland: English Government and Reform in Ireland 1649–1660* (Oxford: Oxford University Press, 1975)
BDBR	*Biographical Dictionary of British Radicals in the Seventeenth Century*, ed. Richard L. Greaves and Robert Zaller, 3 vols. (Brighton: Harvester, 1982–84)
BKS	Minutes of the Burt Kirk Session, Gamble Library, Union Theological College
BL	British Library
Bodl.	Bodleian Library, Oxford
Calamy Revised	A. G. Matthews, *Calamy Revised* (Oxford: Clarendon Press, 1934)
CCSP	*Calendar of the Clarendon State Papers Preserved in the Bodleian Library*, vol. 5:1660–1726, ed. F. J. Routledge (Oxford: Clarendon Press, 1970)
CH	Henry E. Huntington Library, San Marino, California
CKS	Minutes of the Carnmoney Kirk Session, Presbyterian Historical Society of Ireland
CMHS	*Collections of the Massachusetts Historical Society*
CSPD	*Calendar of State Papers, Domestic Series, 1603–1714*

CSPI	*Calendar of State Papers, Ireland*
DF	Historical Library of the Society of Friends in Ireland, Dublin
DML	Archbishop Narcissus Marsh's Library, Dublin
DMM	Minutes of the Dublin Men's Meeting, Historical Library of the Society of Friends in Ireland
DMunL	Dublin Municipal Library, Pearse Street
DNB	*Dictionary of National Biography*
DWL	Dr. Williams's Library, London
EUL	Edinburgh University Library
GBS	Great Book of Sufferings, vol. 2, Library of the Society of Friends, London
GL	Gamble Library, Union Theological College, Belfast
Herlihy	Kevin Herlihy, "The Irish Baptists, 1650–1780" (Ph.D. thesis, Trinity College, Dublin, 1992)
HMC	*Historical Manuscripts Commission, Reports*
HYNM	Minutes of the Half-Yearly National Meeting, Historical Library of the Society of Friends in Ireland
JFHS	*Journal of the Friends' Historical Society*
Kilroy	Phil Kilroy, *Protestant Dissent and Controversy in Ireland 1660–1714* (Cork: Cork University Press, 1994)
LF	Library of the Society of Friends, London
LisMM	Minutes of the Lisburn Men's Meeting
LPM	Minutes of the Leinster Province Meeting, Historical Library of the Society of Friends in Ireland
LRB	Lurgan Meeting Record Book
LurMM	Minutes of the Lurgan Men's Meeting
LYM	Minutes of the London Yearly Meeting, Library of the Society of Friends, London
MAM	Minutes of the Antrim Meeting, trans. W. T. Latimer, Public Record Office of Northern Ireland
McConnell, *Fasti*	James McConnell and Samuel G. McConnell, eds., *Fasti of the Irish Presbyterian Church 1613–1840* (Belfast: Presbyterian Historical Society, [1951])
MLM	Minutes of the Lagan Meeting, trans. David Stewart, Public Record Office of Northern Ireland
MMM	Minutes of the Moate Men's Meeting, Historical Library of the Society of Friends in Ireland

NAI	National Archives of Ireland, Dublin
NLI	National Library of Ireland, Dublin
NLS	National Library of Scotland, Edinburgh
NWM	Records of the National Women's Meeting, Historical Library of the Society of Friends in Ireland
PHSI	Presbyterian Historical Society of Ireland, Belfast
Pinney	*Letters of John Pinney 1679–1699*, ed. Geoffrey F. Nuttall (London: Oxford University Press, 1939)
PRONI	Public Record Office of Northern Ireland, Belfast
PRO SP	Public Record Office (London), State Papers
RCBL	Representative Church Body Library, Dublin
RPCS	*The Register of the Privy Council of Scotland*
Seymour	St. John D. Seymour, *The Puritans in Ireland 1647–1661* (Oxford: Clarendon Press, 1921)
Synod	*Records of the General Synod of Ulster, from 1691 to 1820*, 3 vols., vol. 1:1691–1720 (Belfast, 1890)
TCD	Trinity College Library, Dublin
TKS	Minutes of the Templepatrick Kirk Session, Public Record Office of Northern Ireland
UPM	Minutes of the Ulster Province Meeting

Notes

INTRODUCTION

1. Bryan A. Wilson, *The Social Dimensions of Sectarianism: Sects and New Religious Movements in Contemporary Society* (Oxford: Clarendon Press, 1990), p. 47 (quoted); Wilson, "A Typology of Sects," in *Religion and Ideology*, ed. Robert Bocock and Kenneth Thompson (Manchester: Manchester University Press, 1985), pp. 299–303; Wilson, *Religious Sects: A Sociological Study* (London: Weidenfeld and Nicolson, 1970), Chaps. 3–9.

2. Armand L. Mauss and Philip L. Barlow, "Church, Sect, and Scripture: The Protestant Bible and Mormon Sectarian Retrenchment," *Sociological Analysis* 52 (Winter 1991): 398.

3. Wilson, *Social Dimensions*, p. 106.

4. B. R. White posits the rise of denominations in England by 1700. "The Twilight of Puritanism in the Years Before and After 1688," in *From Persecution to Toleration: The Glorious Revolution and Religion in England*, ed. Ole Peter Grell, Jonathan I. Israel, and Nicholas Tyacke (Oxford: Clarendon Press, 1991), pp. 318, 323, 325–26, 328–30. Cf. Roger Thomas, "Parties in Nonconformity," in C. G. Bolam, Jeremy Goring, H. L. Short, and Roger Thomas, *The English Presbyterians from Elizabethan Puritanism to Modern Unitarianism* (London: George Allen and Unwin, 1968), pp. 97, 99, 101. Also writing of England, Michael Watts avers that only the Presbyterians evolved into a denomination by 1730. *The Dissenters: From the Reformation to the French Revolution* (Oxford: Clarendon Press, 1978), pp. 388–91.

5. D. A. Martin, "The Denomination," *British Journal of Sociology* 13 (March 1962): 1–14.

6. David M. Thompson, *Let Sects and Parties Fall: A Short History of the Association of Churches of Christ in Great Britain and Ireland* (Birmingham: Berean Press, 1980), p. 7.

7. Wilson, *Social Dimensions*, pp. 109–10 (quoted), 116, 118–19 (quoted).

8. Mark Chaves, "Denominations as Dual Structures: An Organizational Analysis," *Sociology of Religion* 54 (Summer 1993): 147–51 (149 quoted).

9. Cf. Wilson, *Social Dimensions*, pp. 110, 115; Wilson, *Religious Sects*, pp. 19–20.

10. Kilroy, p. 10.

11. For a pioneering discussion of popular religion among adherents of the Church of Ireland see Raymond Gillespie, "The Religion of Irish Protestants: A View from the Laity, 1580–1700," in *As by Law Established: The Church of Ireland Since the Reformation*, ed. Alan Ford, James McGuire, and Kenneth Milne (Dublin: Lilliput Press, 1995), pp. 89–99.

12. Kilroy, p. 10.

13. Ted L. Underwood, "The Controversy Between the Baptists and the Quakers in England, 1650–1689: A Theological Elucidation" (Ph.D. thesis, University of London, 1965).

14. Watts, *The Dissenters*, p. 509.

15. L. M. Cullen, "Economic Trends 1660–91," in T. W. Moody, F. X. Martin, and F. J. Byrne, eds., *A New History of Ireland*, vol. 3: *Early Modern Ireland 1534–1691* (Oxford: Clarendon Press, 1976), p. 389.

16. Ibid., p. 390; Rosalind Mitchison, "Ireland and Scotland: The Seventeenth-Century Legacies Compared," in T. M. Devine and David Dickson, eds., *Ireland and Scotland 1600–1850: Parallels and Contrasts in Economic and Social Development* (Edinburgh: John Donald, 1983), p. 3; J. G. Simms, *Jacobite Ireland 1685–91* (London: Routledge and Kegan Paul, 1969), p. 12; Simms, "The Restoration, 1660–85," in Moody, Martin, and Byrne, eds., *A New History of Ireland*, pp. 448, 452. Cork had a population of 2,400 in 1659. Liam Irwin, "Politics, Religion and Economy: Cork in the 17th Century," *Journal of the Cork Historical and Archaeological Society* 85 (1980): 7.

17. Simms, "The Restoration, 1660–85," p. 453; Philip S. Robinson, *The Plantation of Ulster: British Settlement in an Irish Landscape, 1600–1670* (Dublin: Gill and Macmillan, 1984), pp. 56, 164, 225–27.

18. W. Macaffee and V. Morgan, "Population in Ulster, 1660–1760," in Peter Roebuck, ed., *Plantation to Partition: Essays in Ulster History in Honour of J. L. McCracken* (Dundonald, Belfast: Blackstaff Press, 1981), pp. 50, 52; J. G. Simms, "Dublin in 1685," *Irish Historical Studies* 14 (March 1965): 216; L. M. Cullen and T. C. Smout, "Economic Growth in Scotland and Ireland," in Cullen and Smout, eds., *Comparative Aspects of Scottish and Irish Economic and Social History 1600–1900* (Edinburgh: John Donald, [1977]), p. 4; Mitchison, "Ireland and Scotland," p. 7. Dietary factors and a rising birth rate among Gaelic Irish contributed to demographic growth. Cullen and Smout, op. cit., p. 4; R. F. Foster, *Modern Ireland 1600–1972* (London: Allen Lane, the Penguin Press, 1988), p. 130.

19. Kerby A. Miller, *Emigrants and Exiles: Ireland and the Irish Exodus to North America* (New York: Oxford University Press, 1985), pp. 22, 137; James Anthony Froude, *The English in Ireland in the Eighteenth Century*, 3 vols. (New York: Charles Scribner's Sons, 1897), 1:156.

20. William Petty, *The Political Anatomy of Ireland* (London, 1691), pp. 7–8; *A Faithful History of the Northern Affairs of Ireland* (London, 1690), p. 6.

21. *The Letters of Saint Oliver Plunkett 1625–1681, Archbishop of Armagh and*

Primate of All Ireland, ed. John Hanly (Dublin: Dolmen Press, 1979), p. 530; Bodl. Carte MSS 36, fol. 511r; BL Stowe MSS 213, fol. 304r.

22. Edward M. Furgol, "The Military and Ministers as Agents of Presbyterian Imperialism in England and Ireland, 1640–1648," in John Dwyer, Roger A. Mason, and Alexander Murdoch, eds., *New Perspectives on the Politics and Culture of Early Modern Scotland* (Edinburgh: John Donald [1982]), p. 103; Robinson, *Plantation of Ulster*, pp. 98, 105, 156, 164, 225–27; *CSPD 1686–87*, p. 239; Karl S. Bottigheimer, *English Money and Irish Land: The 'Adventurers' in the Cromwellian Settlement of Ireland* (Oxford: Clarendon Press, 1971), p. 140. Both William King, bishop of Derry, and the Presbyterian minister Robert Craghead estimated the dissenting population of the diocese of Derry at more than 30,000 at the end of the century. Craghead, *An Answer to the Bishop of Derry['s] Second Admonition to the Dissenting Inhabitants in His Diocess* (1698), p. 11.

23. Barnard, pp. 95–98.

24. Seymour, pp. 206–24.

25. Christopher Hill, "Seventeenth-Century English Radicals and Ireland," in Patrick J. Corish, ed., *Radicals, Rebels & Establishments* (Belfast: Appletree Press, 1985), pp. 39–40, 45.

26. Ralph Jennings, Bodl. Rawlinson MSS A.13, fol. 28r.

27. Barnard, pp. 105–8; *BDBR*, s.vv.

28. Barnard, pp. 122–26, 301–2. Henry Cromwell's broad, centrist Protestantism is reflected in his selection of Stephen Charnock, Thomas Harrison, and Francis Roberts as his chaplains and his patronage of Bishop Griffith Williams. In a sermon preached before Cromwell, Williams castigated sectaries: "As it is not safe, to taste of a poysoned dish, so it is as dangerous, to hear an heretical, schismatical, and impostor Preacher." "A Sermon Preached at Cork-House Before Henry Cromwell," in Griffith Williams, *Four Treatises* (London, 1667), p. 14.

29. Barnard, pp. 117–21, 126–29; BL Lansdowne MSS 823, fol. 79r (quoted).

30. S. J. Connolly, *Religion, Law, and Power: The Making of Protestant Ireland 1660–1700* (Oxford: Clarendon Press, 1992), pp. 5–6, 8–10; *An Account of the Chief Occurrences of Ireland* (22–27 February 1660), p. 10 (quoted); *An Account of the Chief Occurrences of Ireland* (12–19 March 1660), p. 36; W. P., *A Letter from Ireland to an Honourable Citizen of London* [1659]; Barnard, pp. 132–34; George Rust, *A Funeral Sermon, Preached at the Obsequies of the Right Reverend Father in God Jeremy Bishop of Down* (London, 1668), p. 15 (quoted).

31. Peter Brooke, *Ulster Presbyterianism: The Historical Perspective 1610–1970* (New York: St. Martin's Press, 1987), pp. 16–19; Marilyn J. Westerkamp, *Triumph of the Laity: Scots-Irish Piety and the Great Awakening, 1625–1760* (New York: Oxford University Press, 1988), pp. 22–23; John Livingston, *A Brief Historical Relation of the Life of Mr. John Livingston Minister of the Gospel* (Glasgow, 1754), p. 6; John M. Barkley, *A Short History of the Presbyterian Church in Ireland* (Belfast: Publications Board, Presbyterian Church in Ireland, 1959), p. 6. Livingston was ordained in 1630.

32. Brooke, *Ulster Presbyterianism*, pp. 17–19; Westerkamp, *Triumph of the Laity*, pp. 23–28, 35; Livingston, *Brief Historical Relation*, p. 67.

33. Barkley, *Short History*, pp. 5, 7–8.

34. Bramhall, cited in Raymond Gillespie, *Colonial Ulster: The Settlement of East Ulster 1600–1641* (Cork: Cork University Press, 1985), p. 31; Robinson, *Plantation of Ulster*, p. 112; Furgol, "Military and Ministers," p. 103; *CSPI 1633–1647*, p. 203 (quoted); Barkley, *Short History*, pp. 8–9.

35. Furgol, "Military and Ministers," pp. 105, 107–109, 111; Barkley, *Short History*, pp. 10–11; John M. Barkley, *The Eldership in Irish Presbyterianism* ([Belfast]: By the Author, 1963), p. 21; *The Letters and Journals of Robert Baillie*, ed. David Laing, 3 vols. (Edinburgh: Bannatyne Club, 1841–42), 2:48.

36. J. P. Kenyon, ed., *The Stuart Constitution: Documents and Commentary* (Cambridge: Cambridge University Press, 1969), p. 264 (quoted); Barnard, p. 122; Walter Makey, *The Church of the Covenant 1637–1651: Revolution and Social Change in Scotland* (Edinburgh: John Donald, 1979), pp. 81–84.

37. Barkley, *Short History*, p. 14; Barnard, p. 123.

38. Robinson, *Plantation of Ulster*, p. 112; Barkley, *Short History*, p. 14; Adair, p. 214.

39. Seymour, pp. 96–97; Brooke, *Ulster Presbyterianism*, p. 42. Cf. MLM, 1:8; MAM 1671–91, fol. 53.

40. Seymour, pp. 97–101; Adair, pp. 217–18, 228.

41. D. J. Owen, *History of Belfast* (Belfast: W. and G. Baird, 1921), pp. 43–44; George Benn, *A History of the Town of Belfast from the Earliest Times to the Close of the Eighteenth Century* (Belfast: Royal Ulster Works, 1877), pp. 397–98; Seymour, p. 210; Barnard, p. 125.

42. BL Lansdowne MSS 823, fol. 57r–v; PRONI MSS D/1759/2A/5, fols. 112–13.

43. MAM 1654–58, fols. 1–2 (quoted), 120–21, 129, 189.

44. Ibid., fols. 40, 106 (quoted), 197–98 (quoted).

45. Furgol, "Military and Ministers," p. 110. As early as 1656 Livingston noted that between 30 and 36 ministers as well as ruling elders from 60 to 80 parishes attended the great presbytery. Livingston, *Brief Historical Relation*, p. 56.

46. John F. Wilson, *Pulpit in Parliament: Puritanism During the English Civil Wars 1640–1648* (Princeton, N.J.: Princeton University Press, 1969), pp. 248, 270; Seymour, pp. 44, 210, 215–16, 218–19; McConnell, *Fasti*, 2:9, 41–42, 44.

47. Clarke H. Irwin, *A History of Presbyterianism in Dublin and the South and West of Ireland* (London: Hodder and Stoughton, 1890), p. 290; James Seaton Reid, *History of Congregations of the Presbyterian Church in Ireland and Biographical Notices of Eminent Ministers and Laymen*, ed. W. D. Killen (Belfast: James Cleeland, 1886), pp. 177–78; Seymour, pp. 160–65; *The Agreement and Resolution of Severall Associated Ministers in the County of Corke for the Ordaining of Ministers* (Cork, 1657), p. 14; Barnard, pp. 117–21; *The Agreement and Resolution of the Ministers of Christ Associated within the City of Dublin, and Province of Leinster* (Dublin, 1659), pp. 2–6, 9–10. Seymour identified 67 Presbyterians among the 376 men officially employed as preachers in Ireland by the Commonwealth, but he could not attribute denominational affiliation to 215 of them (p. 52).

48. Seymour, pp. 208, 214–15, 217, 219, 221; Barnard, pp. 99–100; Geoffrey F. Nuttall, *Visible Saints: The Congregational Way 1640–1660* (Oxford: Basil Blackwell, 1957), pp. 25–26, 30–31; Irwin, *History of Presbyterianism*, p. 235. Wale (or

Whale) is identified as an Independent by Thomas Morford, *The Baptist and Independent Churches (So Called) Set on Fire* (London, 1660), pp. 1, 11.

49. *Calamy Revised*, s.v. Charnock, Veal; Seymour, pp. 208–9, 222, 224; Irwin, *History of Presbyterianism*, p. 230 (noting that Muckle's church later became Presbyterian and affiliated with the synod of Munster).

50. BL Lansdowne MSS 821, fol. 113r–v; Seymour, pp. 207, 216, 224; *Calamy Revised*, s.v. Marsden; BL Lansdowne MSS 823, fols. 43r (quoted), 47r (quoted).

51. *Calamy Revised*, s.vv. Harrison, I. Mather, S. Mather; Seymour, pp. 213, 217, 223; Morford, *Baptist and Independent Churches*, p. 11.

52. R. B. McDowell and D. A. Webb, *Trinity College Dublin 1592–1952: An Academic History* (Cambridge: Cambridge University Press, 1982), pp. 17, 19; *Calamy Revised*, s.vv. Charnock, Veal.

53. Barnard, pp. 112–17, 132–33; *BDBR*, s.vv. Weaver, Steele. While Winter was provost of Trinity College he preached every third week at Monmouth, some ten miles away, reportedly converting both English and Gaelic Irish. J. W., *The Life and Death, of the Eminently Learned, Pious, and Painful Minister of the Gospel, Dr. Samuel Winter* (London, 1671), pp. 13–14.

54. *BDBR*, s.v. Patient; Colonel John Jones, cited in Charles Firth and Godfrey Davies, *The Regimental History of Cromwell's Army*, 2 vols. (Oxford: Clarendon Press, 1940), p. 88 (quoted); Murray Tolmie, *The Triumph of the Saints: The Separate Churches of London 1616–1649* (Cambridge: Cambridge University Press, 1977), pp. 52, 57–58; Seymour, p. 218; B. R. White, "Thomas Patient in England and Ireland," *Irish Baptist Historical Society Journal* 2 (1969–70): 36–48.

55. W. T. Whitley, "The Plantation of Ireland and the Early Baptist Churches," *Baptist Quarterly* 1 (1922–23): 279–80; Seymour, pp. 207, 209, 224; B. R. White, ed., *Association Records of the Particular Baptists of England, Wales and Ireland to 1660*, 3 vols. (London: Baptist Historical Society, 1971–74), 2:119–20; Barnard, pp. 102–3; Herlihy, p. 45; Morford, *Baptist and Independent Churches*, pp. 9, 12, 24–25, 29–30, 35; Thomas Birch, ed., *A Collection of the State Papers of John Thurloe, Esq.*, 7 vols. (London, 1742), 4:91; *BDBR*, s.v. Vernon; Craig W. Horle, "Quakers and Baptists, 1647–1660," *Baptist Quarterly* 26 (October 1976): 361, note 77.

56. Cork Church Book, fols. 1–2, 18; H. D. Gribbon, "The Cork Church Book," *Irish Baptist Historical Society Journal* 1 (1968–69): 8; L. Irwin, "Politics, Religion and Economy," pp. 16–17; White, ed., *Association Records*, 2:120.

57. BL Lansdowne MSS 822, fol. 86r.

58. B. S. Capp, *The Fifth Monarchy Men: A Study in Seventeenth-Century English Millenarianism* (London: Faber and Faber, 1972), p. 122; *BDBR*, s.vv. Axtell, Allen; PRONI MSS D/1759/2A/5, fol. 108.

59. White, ed., *Association Records*, 2:74. For additional information on Baptists in Ireland in the 1650s see Herlihy, pp. 35–69.

60. "Journal of the Life of William Edmundson," *The Friends' Library* 2 (Philadelphia: Joseph Rakestraw, 1838): 96–98.

61. George Fox, *The Journal of George Fox*, ed. Norman Penney, 2 vols. (Cambridge: Cambridge University Press, 1911), 1:405; 2:470; Joseph Besse, *A Collection of the Sufferings of the People Called Quakers*, 2 vols. (London, 1753), 2:457;

Hugh Barbour, *The Quakers in Puritan England* (New Haven, Conn.: Yale University Press, 1964), p. 61; LF Swarthmore MSS 6/6 (quoted); 6/14 (quoted).

62. *BDBR*, s.vv. Fletcher, Blaugdone; Isabel Grubb, *Quakers in Ireland 1654–1900* (London: Swarthmore Press, 1927), p. 21; John M. Douglas, "Early Quakerism in Ireland," *JFHS* 48 (Spring 1956): 15–16, 23; "Record of Friends Travelling in Ireland, 1656–1765," *JFHS* 10 (July 1913): 158; Hugh Barbour, "Quaker Prophetesses and Mothers in Israel," *Seeking the Light: Essays in Quaker History in Honor of Edwin B. Bonner*, ed. J. William Frost and John M. Moore (Wallingford and Haverford, Penn.: Pendle Hill Publications and Friends Historical Association, 1986), pp. 45–46.

63. Kenneth L. Carroll, "Quakerism in the Cromwellian Army in Ireland," *JFHS* 54 (1978): 135, 137; Barnard, pp. 110–11; LF Swarthmore MSS 6/31; *BDBR*, s.v. Ames; Carroll, "John Perrot: Early Quaker Schismatic," *JFHS*, Supplement 33 (London, 1971), p. 1; Swarthmore MSS 5/2 (quoted); 5/9 (quoted); 5/13 (quoted); 6/30 (quoted). Cf. Swarthmore MSS 5/19, 55.

64. BL Lansdowne MSS 821, fol. 68r (quoted); Lansdowne 822, fol. 17r–v (quoted).

65. BL Lansdowne MSS 821, fol. 127r–v.

66. LF Swarthmore MSS 5/22.

67. Carroll, "Quakerism in the Cromwellian Army," pp. 142, 146–47; LF Swarthmore MSS 5/7 (quoted); 5/8 (quoted).

68. LF Swarthmore MSS 5/54 (quoted); 6/36 (quoted); 6/38 (quoted). For other examples see Swarthmore MSS 5/14, 28, 31; 6/12, 44.

69. LF Swarthmore MSS 6/41 (quoted); 6/46 (quoted); 6/47 (quoted).

70. LF Swarthmore MSS 5/27 (quoted); 5/33 (quoted); 6/49 (quoted); William C. Braithwaite, *The Second Period of Quakerism*, 2nd ed., ed. Henry Cadbury (Cambridge: Cambridge University Press, 1961), pp. 228–38.

71. LF Swarthmore MSS 4/62; 5/10 (quoted).

72. Morford, *Baptist and Independent Churches*, p. 43; LF Swarthmore MSS 5/24 (quoted).

73. White, ed., *Association Records*, 2:73–74; LF Swarthmore MSS 5/34 (quoted).

74. LF Swarthmore MSS 4/77 (quoted); Carroll, "Quakerism in the Cromwellian Army," pp. 152–54; Barnard, pp. 111–12.

75. LF Swarthmore MSS 5/23 (quoted); 6/29 (quoted).

CHAPTER 1

1. Charles Firth and Godfrey Davies, *The Regimental History of Cromwell's Army*, 2 vols. (Oxford: Clarendon Press, 1940), p. 479; *BDBR*, s.vv. Cooper, Lawrence; TCD MSS 808, fol. 16or; J. I. McGuire, "The Dublin Convention, the Protestant Community and the Emergence of an Ecclesiastical Settlement in 1660," in *Parliament & Community*, ed. Art Cosgrove and J. I. McGuire, *Historical Studies*, vol. 14 (Dublin: Appletree Press, 1981), pp. 123–24.

2. TCD MSS 808, fols. 16or–162r.

3. Ibid.; McGuire, "Dublin Convention," p. 115.

4. McGuire, "Dublin Convention," pp. 127–29; *BDBR*, s.vv. Blackwood, Rogers; *A Letter Sent from a Merchant in London* (London, 1659/60).

5. McGuire, "Dublin Convention," pp. 129–30.

6. Samuel Cox, *Two Sermons Preached at Christ-Church in the City of Dublin, Before the General Convention of Ireland* (Dublin, 1660), pp. 8 (quoted), 11–12, 14, 21 (quoted), 23 (quoted), 24–28. Cox again preached to the Convention on 9 March at a public fast, calling for separation from pollution but not the church. Ibid., pp. 31, 41. Although bibliographers sometimes attribute the second sermon in this volume to Stephen Charnock, both were by Cox. The confusion stems from the fact that the Convention ordered the sermons of Cox and Charnock preached on this fast day to be printed.

7. McGuire, "Dublin Convention," p. 130.

8. Bodl. Carte MSS 30, fol. 685r; McGuire, "Dublin Convention," p. 131; John Neville, "The Restoration of the Church of Ireland, 1660–1668" (Ph.D. diss., Vanderbilt University, 1976), pp. 180–81.

9. Adair, pp. 234, 240; McGuire, "Dublin Convention," pp. 131–33.

10. NLI MSS 32, fol. 14r (quoted); McGuire, "Dublin Convention," pp. 131, 133–34; BL Add. MSS 45,850, fol. 20r–v (quoted); Ivan Roots, *Commonwealth and Protectorate: The English Civil War and Its Aftermath* (New York: Schocken, 1966), p. 254.

11. *A Collection of Original Letters and Papers, Concerning the Affairs of England, from the Duke of Ormonde's Papers*, 2 vols., ed. Thomas Carte (London, 1739), 2:345–46.

12. McGuire, "Dublin Convention," pp. 134–35; Adair, p. 232; Seymour, pp. 179–80.

13. McGuire, "Dublin Convention," pp. 133, 136; Adair, pp. 239–40 (quoted); Henry Jones, *A Sermon Preach't at Christ-Church Dublin Before the General Convention of Ireland* (London, 1660), p. 27; RCBL MSS 51/1, fols. 98–101.

14. Bodl. Carte MSS 30, fol. 685r.

15. McGuire, "Dublin Convention," pp. 136–37, 145; TCD MSS 808, fols. 83r–88r, 155r–157r (quoted).

16. McGuire, "Dublin Convention," pp. 137–38.

17. Bodl. Carte MSS 30, fol. 689r; E. B. Fryde, D. E. Greenway, S. Porter, and I. Roy, eds., *Handbook of British Chronology*, 3rd ed. (London: Royal Historical Society, 1986), pp. 378–408; Robert Wodrow, *The History of the Sufferings of the Church of Scotland from the Restoration to the Revolution*, ed. Robert Burns, 4 vols. (Glasgow: Blackie, Fullarton, and Co., 1829), 1:44; McGuire, "Dublin Convention," p. 138.

18. Anthem quoted in R. B. McDowell and D. A. Webb, *Trinity College Dublin 1592–1952: An Academic History* (Cambridge: Cambridge University Press, 1982), p. 22; Richard Mant, *History of the Church of Ireland, from the Reformation to the Revolution* (London: John W. Parker, 1840), pp. 605, 609–10. The character of the restored episcopate is astutely analyzed in James McGuire, "Policy and Patronage: The Appointment of Bishops, 1660–61," in *As by Law Established: The Church of Ireland Since the Reformation*, ed. Alan Ford, James McGuire, and Kenneth Milne (Dublin: Lilliput Press, 1995), pp. 112–19.

19. *Calendar of the Ancient Records of Dublin, in the Possession of the Municipal Corporation of That City,* ed. John T. Gilbert, vol. 4 (Dublin: Joseph Dollard, 1894), p. 186 (quoted); *The Rawdon Papers,* ed. Edward Berwick (London: John Nichols and Son, 1819), p. 127 (quoted).

20. Bodl. Carte MSS 31, fols. 49r (quoted), 56r; Geoffrey F. Nuttall, *Richard Baxter* (London: Thomas Nelson and Sons, 1965), p. 86; *CCSP,* 5:63.

21. *A Collection of the State Letters of the Right Honourable Roger Boyle, the First Earl of Orrery, Lord President of Munster in Ireland* (London: James Bettenham, 1842), p. 15 (quoted); Bodl. Clarendon MSS 74, fol. 52r–v (quoted).

22. PRO SP 63 / 306 / 72. For the rash of reputed Ludlow sightings throughout the islands see Richard L. Greaves, *Deliver Us from Evil: The Radical Underground in Britain, 1660–1663* (New York: Oxford University Press, 1986), pp. 38–39, 65, 101, 112. Ludlow and Wogan were in exile on the continent. *BDBR,* s.vv.

23. Bodl. Carte MSS 49, fol. 92r; CH MS HA 14019; NLI MSS 8643(1) (quoted).

24. Bodl. Carte MSS 49, fol. 137r (quoted), 155r–v (quoted).

25. Bodl. Carte MSS 49, fol. 178r.

26. Bodl. Carte MSS 49, fols. 159r, 161r.

27. Bodl. Carte MSS 49, fol. 147r–v; cf. Carte 32, fol. 66r.

28. James Anthony Froude, *The English in Ireland in the Eighteenth Century,* 3 vols. (New York: Charles Scribner's Sons, 1897), 1:155–56.

29. Griffith Williams, *Four Treatises* (London, 1667), sig. B2r; Henry Jones, *A Sermon at the Funeral of James Margetson, D.D.* (London, 1679), pp. 29–30 (quoted); CH MSS HA 15379 (quoted), 15380, 15383.

30. Daniel Burston, *Christs Last Call to His Glorified Saints* (Dublin, [1666]), pp. 29–30.

31. John Vesey, "Athanasius Hibernicus: or, the Life of the Most Reverend Father in God, John, Lord Archbishop of Ardmagh," in *The Works of the Most Reverend Father in God, John Bramhall D.D.* (Dublin, 1676), sigs. n2v, o1r–v; p. xii; Jeremy Taylor, *A Sermon Preached in Christ-Church, Dublin: At the Funeral of the Most Reverend Father in God, John, Late Lord Archbishop of Armagh, and Primate of All Ireland* (London, 1663), p. 32 (quoted).

32. John Bramhall, *A Fair Warning, for England to Take Heed of the Presbyterian Government of Scotland* [1661], pp. 2 (quoted), 20, 34 (quoted), 39. In 1661 Bramhall had doubts about the suppression of dissenters, at least in England, for Gilbert Sheldon, bishop of London, attempted to assuage his concerns. CH MS HA 15778.

33. Daniel Burston, *The Evangelist Yet Evangelizing* (Dublin, 1662), pp. 1, 3–4 (quoted), 7 (quoted).

34. Bodl. Carte MSS 221, fol. 154r (quoted); Carte 31, fol. 58r (quoted); Carte 45, fol. 38r. Cf. Carte 45, fol. 44r (Taylor to Ormond). "Kings and Bishops are the foundations and the great principles of unity, of peace and Government." Jeremy Taylor, *Via Intelligentiae: A Sermon Preached to the University of Dublin* (London, 1662), p. 59.

35. CH MSS HA 15992, 15993 (quoted).

36. CH MS HA 15993 (quoted); *HMC* 78, *Hastings,* 4:114.

37. CH MS HA 15179 (quoted); Greaves, *Deliver Us from Evil,* pp. 212–15.

38. CH MS HA 15184.

39. CH MSS HA 16015 (quoted); HA 16016; Bodl. Carte MSS 45, fol. 113r. On 16 October Ormond responded favorably to Wild's report of 22 August, promising to secure Derry "by such as shalbe considerable countenance to your Proceedings." Carte MSS 49, fol. 139r.

40. NLI MSS 4908, fols. 3v–4r, 7r–8r, 13v–14v, 17r.

41. [James Kirkpatrick], *An Historical Essay upon the Loyalty of Presbyterians in Great-Britain and Ireland from the Reformation to This Present Year 1713* (1713), p. 310; David W. Miller, *Queen's Rebels: Ulster Loyalism in Historical Perspective* (Dublin: Gilland Macmillan, 1978), p. 21; White Kennet, *An Historical Register and Chronicle of English Affairs* (London, 1744), p. 197.

42. Bodl. Carte MSS 45, fols. 38r (quoted), 43r.

43. PRO SP 63/305/7, 30; Bodl. Carte MSS 221, fol. 150r; Carte 45, fol. 38r (quoted). For Greg, Drysdale, Ramsey, and Hutcheson see McConnell, *Fasti*, s.vv.

44. PRO SP 63/305/7, 30.

45. *Collection of the State Letters of Orrery*, pp. 16–17 (quoted); BL Add. MSS 37,206, fol. 15v.

46. Samuel Mather, *A Testimony from the Scripture Against Idolatry & Superstition, in Two Sermons* [Cambridge, Mass., 1670], pp. 25–29.

47. Ibid., pp. 35–75 (quoted at pp. 73, 75).

48. PRO SP 63/304/29; *Parliamentary Intelligencer* (22–29 October 1660), p. 696; *Mercurius Publicus* 43 (18–25 October 1660), p. 688. Another factor that may have helped Mather escape more severe penalties was his reputation among conformists as "a Scriptural, Logical, Methodical Preacher" who had no equal. Increase Mather, in S. Mather, *A Testimony*, sig. A3r.

49. BL Add. MSS 37,206, fol. 15r (quoted); Add. MSS 46,938, fol. 37v; Adair, pp. 245–46. Cf. Mant, *History*, pp. 607–8.

50. BL Add. MSS 37,206, fol. 15r–v.

51. Adair, pp. 246–47.

52. Bodl. Carte MSS 31, fol. 168r–v (quoted); Bodl. Clarendon MSS 80, fol. 350r–v (quoted); *HMC 78, Hastings*, 4:110; *CCSP*, 5:289–90; CH MSS HA 16017, 16018.

53. PRO SP 63/304/45; CH MS HA 13915; Bodl. Carte MSS 31, fol. 59r; PRONI MSS D/1759/2A/5, fols. 118–19 (quoted). One of the more inventive manifestations of hostility was the circulation of a letter in county Down erroneously claiming Presbyterians had been exempted from episcopal government and were free to baptize and marry in ceremonies of their liking. CH MS HA 13901.

54. Gorges to Lane, NLI MSS 8643(1) (quoted); CH MSS HA 13944, 14017.

55. CH MSS HA 13945, 16001; McConnell, *Fasti*, 2:52.

56. PRONI MSS D/1759/2A/5, fols. 187–88, 190–91, 211, 213, 218.

57. Bodl. Carte MSS 30, fol. 685r; PRONI MSS D/1759/2A/5, fols. 188, 210, 213; Bodl. Clarendon MSS 80, fol. 49v (quoted); *CSPI 1660–62*, pp. 173–76; *Council Book of Youghal*, p. 333 (quoted). For the circumstances surrounding the remonstrance see PRO SP 63/304/71.

58. PRO SP 63/306/1 (quoted); CH MSS HA 15592, 15963 (quoted); PRONI MSS D/1759/2A/5, fols. 200–201, 215–17; MSS D/1759/2A/9, nos. 311, 325, 336, 340.

59. PRONI MSS D/1759/2A/5, fols. 217–18; McConnell, *Fasti*, 2:39–40.

60. CH MSS HA 14009, 14138, 14964, 15996, 15997, 16012, 16014 (quoted), 16017 (quoted).

61. *HMC* 63, *Egmont*, 2:5; CH MS HA 15181.

62. Bodl. Tanner MSS 36, fols. 128r (quoted), 137r, 139r (quoted); BL Add. MSS 15,893, fol. 143r (quoted).

63. *HMC* 36, *Ormonde*, n.s., 6:234 (quoted); Bodl. Tanner MSS 36, fols. 135r (quoted), 202r (quoted); BL Add. MSS 15,893, fol. 144r–v.

64. RCBL MS D.14; RCBL MS 51/1; Bodl. Carte MSS 221, fol. 141r; Thomas Carte, *An History of the Life of James Duke of Ormonde*, 2 vols. (London, 1736), 2:210; CH MS HA 15492.

65. Bodl. Carte MSS 36, fol. 454r; DML MS Z.3.1.4, *passim*; RCBL MS D.14, fol. 114 (quoted); BL Add. MSS 37,823, fols. 64v–66v.

66. Bodl. Carte MSS 49, fol. 20r–v; *CSPI 1660–62*, p. 190.

67. A printed copy of the proclamation is bound in Bodl. Clarendon MSS 74, fols. 92v–93r. For another copy see PRO SP 63/306/20.

68. Bodl. Clarendon MSS 74, fol. 98r–v (quoted); I. M. Green, *The Re-Establishment of the Church of England 1660–1663* (Oxford: Oxford University Press, 1978), p. 34; CH MS HA 15096 (quoted).

69. Bodl. Clarendon MSS 74, fols. 292v, 297r (quoted), 385r–v; CH MS HA 16038; Charles Smith, *The Ancient and Present State of the County and City of Cork*, ed. Robert Day and W. A. Copinger, 3 vols. (Cork: Guy, 1893–94), 2:103.

70. Jeremy Taylor, *A Sermon Preached at the Opening of the Parliament of Ireland, May 8. 1661* (London, 1661), pp. 4, 6, 10–11, 13 (quoted), 16, 21–22, 30. In his epistle to the published sermon Taylor mocked the nonconformists, who "pretend tender Conscience against Ecclesiastical Laws: . . . in the simplicity of their hearts [they] follow Absolom, and in weakness hide their heads in little Conventicles and places of separation for a trifle." Ibid., sig. a1v; cf. sigs. A4v–a1r. Thomas Hacket's sermon to Convocation, delivered on 9 May 1661, stressed in part the necessity of preserving a clear distinction between clergy and laity by repudiating the Presbyterian institution of lay eldership. *A Sermon Preached Before the Convocation of Clergy in Ireland* (London, 1662), pp. 20–24.

71. John Bramhall, *A Sermon Preached at Dublin, upon the 23. of Aprill, 1661, Being the Day Appointed for His Majesties Coronation* (Dublin, 1661), pp. 35, 41–42.

72. TCD MSS 616, fols. 4r, 5r–v; *The Journals of the House of Commons, of the Kingdom of Ireland*, 2nd ed. (Dublin, 1783), 1:604–5 (quoted); CH MS HA 16008 (quoted). Cf. Orrery to Ormond, 15 May 1661, BL Add. MSS 37,206, fol. 23r.

73. TCD MSS 616, fols. 4r, 9v–10r (quoted), 11v–12r, 44r; *Commons' Journals*, 1:623; Samuel McSkimin, *The History and Antiquities of the County of the Town of Carrickfergus from the Earliest Records till 1839*, new ed., rev. E. J. McCrum (Belfast: Mullan and Son, James Cleeland, Davidson and McCormack, 1909), p. 61; TCD MSS 1038, fols. 37r, 48v, 58r, 70r–v.

74. John Parker, *A Sermon Preached at Christ-Church, Dublin, Before Both Houses*

of Parliament, May, the 29th. 1661 (Dublin, 1661), pp. 26–27; TCD MSS 616, fols. 20v, 22r, 30r, 44v; Mant, *History*, pp. 634–35.

75. TCD MSS 616, fols. 19r–v, 99r–100r, 103r; *Commons' Journals*, 2:63 (quoted); TCD MSS 1038, fol. 29r; CH MS HA 14127 (quoted). To some extent Parliament postponed major discussions until after Ormond had arrived in Ireland. On 18 April 1662 the bishop of Raphoe wrote to his cousin, the laird of Guthrie, in Edinburgh: "Nothing of moment will be done till my Lord Lieutenant comes over." Scottish Record Office, Guthry of Guthry MSS, GD 188 / 25 / 1 / 4 (13).

76. Jeremy Taylor, *A Sermon Preached at the Consecration of Two Archbishops and Ten Bishops, in the Cathedral Church of S. Patrick in Dublin, January 27. 1660* (Dublin, 1661), sig. A3r.

77. Thomas Rugg, *The Diurnal of Thomas Rugg 1659–1661*, ed. William L. Sachse, Camden Third Series, vol. 91 (London: Royal Historical Society, 1961), p. 142; Adair, pp. 247–50 (quoted).

78. Charles James Stranks, *The Life and Writings of Jeremy Taylor* (London: SPCK, 1952), p. 238; Jeremy Taylor, *Rules and Advices to the Clergy of the Diocesse of Down and Conner* (Dublin, 1661), pp. 15–16 (quoted).

79. Adair, pp. 250–51; Stranks, *Taylor*, pp. 240–42.

80. Bodl. Carte MSS 45, fol. 63r; T. W. Moody and J. G. Simms, eds., *The Bishopric of Derry and the Irish Society of London, 1602–1705*, 2 vols. (Dublin: Stationery Office for the Irish Manuscripts Commission, 1968, 1983), 1:330–31; NLI MSS 8643(1) (quoted); CH MS HA 16011 (quoted).

81. W. Macafee and W. Morgan, "Population in Ulster, 1660–1760," in *Plantation to Partition: Essays in Ulster History in Honour of J. L. McCracken*, ed. Peter Roebuck (Dundonald, Belfast: Blackstaff, 1981), p. 52; Mant, *History*, pp. 627–28 (who says 59 were deprived).

82. [William Tisdall], *The Conduct of the Dissenters of Ireland, with Respect Both to Church and State* (Dublin, 1712), pp. 10–11; Adair, pp. 251–52; CH MSS HA 13975 (quoted), 15491.

83. Bodl. Carte MSS 31, fol. 3r; TCD MSS 1038, fols. 34v–35v, 38v–41v, 44r.

84. CH MSS HA 15183, 15185 (quoted), 15186 (quoted).

85. CH MSS HA 15993, 15994, 15995.

86. CH MSS HA 13943 (quoted), 13954, 15998 (quoted).

87. CH MSS HA 14139 (quoted), 15999 (quoted).

88. CH MSS HA 13946, 16003, 16004 (quoted).

89. CH MS HA 15187.

90. BL Add. MSS 37,206, fols. 87v–88r (quoted); Bodl. Carte MSS 45, fol. 53v.

91. *Whereas in Expectation of Conformity* (Dublin, 1662).

92. *CCSP*, 5:213. Ian Green's depiction of Orrery's "mood" toward nonconformists in this period seems overstated, though the earl subsequently attempted to ban all dissenters and Catholics from the parish of Rathgoggan, county Cork, the seat of his estate, Charleville House. Green, *Re-Establishment*, p. 204 (cf. p. 18); BL Add. MSS 37,206, fol. 124r.

93. Bodl. Carte MSS 66, fol. 365v.

94. CH MS HA 15556.

95. Adair, pp. 264–66 (quoted); Bodl. Carte MSS 45, fol. 462r (quoted).

96. Adair, pp. 268–69; Bodl. Carte MSS 45, fol. 462v (quoted).

97. TCD MSS 1038, fols. 53v–54r; Bodl. Carte MSS 45, fol. 458r; CH MS HA 15768 (quoted). Anglesey, Bagshaw's patron, enjoyed considerable influence in Irish affairs. Mordaunt had said of him in March 1660, when he was not yet a peer: "Ireland is steered by this Gentleman." Anglesey denied knowledge of the conventicle and professed himself a conformist. *Collection of Original Letters*, ed. Carte, 2:316; NLI MS 8643(2).

98. *Rawdon Papers*, pp. 167–68; Bodl. Carte MSS 45, fol. 113v; Carte 68, fol. 548r; Carte 32, fol. 35r (cf. 2r).

99. Bodl. Carte MSS 45, fols. 460r–461r.

100. TCD MSS 1038, fol. 64r–v.

101. *Tudor and Stuart Proclamations 1485–1714*, ed. Robert Steele, 2 vols. (Oxford: Clarendon Press, 1910), 2:86 (no. 692); *CSPI 1660–62*, p. 615; *Kingdomes Intelligencer* 47 (17–24 November 1662), p. 743; *CCSP*, 5:281; Greaves, *Deliver Us from Evil*, p. 140 (where Aland is cited as Oland, as in the newspaper report).

102. *CCSP*, 5:297–98; Bodl. Carte MSS 45, fol. 131r–v.

103. PRO SP 63/304/36; NLI MS 8643(1) (quoted); *CSPI 1660–62*, pp. 423, 426; CH MSS HA 15034 (cf. 15028, 15033).

104. CH MS HA 15037; TCD MSS 616, fol. 57r; *Kingdomes Intelligencer* 52 (16–23 December 1661), p. 770.

105. *CCSP*, 5:275–76, 281, 296–97; *Council Books of the Corporation of Waterford 1662–1700 Together with Nine Documents of 1580–82*, ed. Séamus Pender (Dublin: Stationery Office, 1964), pp. 7, 41; *Calendar of State Papers, Venetian 1661–64*, p. 191; PRO SP 63/313/33.

106. *Kingdomes Intelligencer* (4–11 March 1661), pp. 156–58; John Nicoll, *A Diary of Public Transactions and Other Occurrences Chiefly in Scotland* (Edinburgh: Bannatyne Club, 1836), p. 323; PRO SP 63/308, fol. 25; *RPCS 1661–64*, p. 42.

107. CH MS HA 14014; *CCSP*, 5:213, 284; *RPCS 1661–64*, pp. 263, 309–10; J. C. Beckett, *Confrontations: Studies in Irish History* (Totowa, N.J.: Rowman and Littlefield, 1972), p. 40.

108. PRO SP 63/308, fol. 65 (quoted); *CSPI 1663–65*, p. 490. For an example of the ease with which a modern historian can dismiss alleged plotting see Alan Marshall, *Intelligence and Espionage in the Reign of Charles II, 1660–1685* (Cambridge: Cambridge University Press, 1994), pp. 125–26. The government could not ignore an alleged plot simply because the number of reputed rebels was grossly overstated.

109. Greaves, *Deliver Us from Evil*, pp. 140–50; TCD MSS 844, fols. 223r–224r; Bodl. Tanner MSS 48, fols. 71/81r–75/83r.

110. PRO SP 63/313/227; Bodl. Carte MSS 33, fols. 319v–320r; *The Tanner Letters*, ed. Charles McNeill (Dublin: Stationery Office, 1943), pp. 402–4. Crookshanks argued that Christian faith was free and could not be compelled by a magistrate, nor did the latter have the right to determine *adiaphora*. Bodl. Rawlinson MSS D.830, fol. 248r.

111. Adair, pp. 271–72, 275, 278–79; PRO SP 63/314/142; Bodl. Carte MSS 70, fol. 244r; Carte 32, fol. 686r; Carte 33, fol. 33r; [Kirkpatrick], *Historical Essay*, pp. 378–82. McCormack allegedly came to Dublin in the spring of 1663 to check on

preparations for the uprising. Hart too had reputedly gone to Dublin in connection with the conspiracy. When he was apprehended he tried to bribe the arresting officer to let him escape, and then asked the bishop of Raphoe for permission to go into exile rather than be imprisoned. He was arrested at approximately the same time as William Semple, Thomas Drummond, and Adam White. Although Bishop Leslie regarded the four men as "the Ringleaders" of the Presbyterians in his diocese, he offered to release them on bond if they promised not to hold conventicles or disobey the law; they refused. PRO SP 63 / 313 / 187; Bodl. Carte MSS 32, fols. 294v, 664r–v; cf. Carte 68, fol. 566r.

112. PRO SP 63 / 313 / 187; 63 / 314 / 142; Bodl. Carte MSS 32, fols. 202r, 686r; *CSPI 1669–70*, pp. 26, 57.

113. PRO SP 63 / 313 / 132 (quoted), 186, 187, 209; 63 / 314 / 142; Bodl. Carte MSS 32, fol. 204v. Cf. Carte 32, fol. 208r; Samuel Parker, *History of His Own Time*, trans. Thomas Newlin (London, 1727), pp. 71–72.

114. Bodl. Carte MSS 32, fols. 202r, 403r (quoted), 556r, 596r; McConnell, *Fasti*, 2:41–42. Cf. Carte 32, fol. 469r (report of the bishop of Raphoe).

115. Bodl. Carte MSS 32, fols. 623r, 701r. Wallace's letter reports that many renounced the Covenant and would be punished by God. Thomson wrote to Jackson again on 23 July, indicating he had heard Hart and Boyd were implicated in the plot, and on 5 August, describing the search for Lieutenant-Colonel William More. Carte MSS 32, fol. 724r; 33, fol. 26r. Carr had reportedly passed through Donegal en route to Connaught in early May 1663; there he conferred with Lieutenant-Colonel Claude Hamilton and a preacher named Ker—possibly James Ker, the ejected minister of Ballymoney. Carte MSS 32, fol. 469r–v; cf. fol. 294v.

116. TCD MSS 844, fols. 223r–224r; NLS Wodrow MSS Folio XXVII, fol. 141r; BL Add. MSS 37,206, fol. 117r; Moody and Simms, eds., *Bishopric of Derry*, 1:358; Bodl. Carte MSS 32, fols. 450r, 594r; PRO SP 63 / 309, fols. 123–25; Carte 49, fol. 206r; Carte 33, fol. 28r. The declaration is reprinted in appendix IX, *Memoirs of Mr. William Veitch, and George Brysson, Written by Themselves*, ed. Thomas McCrie (Edinburgh: William Blackwood, 1825), pp. 508–9.

117. Bodl. Carte MSS 45, fol. 135r; Carte 32, fol. 399r; Bodl. Clarendon MSS 79, fols. 174r–175r; PRO SP 63 / 313 / 246; *CCSP*, 5:310.

118. *A Collection of the State Letters of the Right Honourable Roger Boyle, the First Earl of Orrery, Lord President of Munster in Ireland*, ed. Thomas Morrice, 2 vols. (Dublin, 1743), 1:132; Bodl. Carte MSS 32, fols. 461r (quoted), 527r (quoted), 530r (quoted).

119. HMC 20, *Eleventh Report (Dartmouth)*, Appendix 5, p. 11; Bodl. Carte MSS 32, fols. 652r, 655r–v, 674r; Carte 45, fols. 145r, 465r; Adair, pp. 276–77. The other ministers imprisoned at Carrickfergus were John Douglass, Robert Hamilton, John Colthart, John Shaw, James Shaw, and James Wilson.

120. Bodl. Carte MSS 32, fol. 657r; Carte 33, fol. 28r; Thomas Brown, *Miscellanea Aulica* (London, 1702), pp. 292–93; PRO SP 63 / 312, fol. 145; 63 / 313 / 245; 63 / 314 / 5, 20, 59. Cf. *The Montgomery Manuscripts (1603–1706)*, comp. William Montgomery and ed. George Hill (Belfast: James Cleeland and Thomas Dargan, 1869), pp. 237–40.

121. PRO SP 63/313/168; *RPCS 1661–64*, pp. 371–72; *The Diary of Samuel Pepys*, ed. Robert Latham and William Matthews, 11 vols. (Berkeley: University of California Press, 1970–1983), 4:168–69; Bodl. Carte MSS 32, fol. 551r; Carte 70, fol. 521r (quoted); Brown, *Miscellanea Aulica*, p. 297.

CHAPTER 2

1. CH MSS HA 14393, 14394, 14399, 14411, 15936; TCD MSS 844, fol. 227v.

2. Bodl. Carte MSS 45, fol. 141r.

3. Bodl. Carte MSS 144, fols. 39v–40r; Carte 45, fols. 463r, 465r; Adair, pp. 280–81. According to Adair, Ramsey and Drysdale also went to Scotland. Adair says Crawford went too, but a contemporary source indicates he received a license to stay in Ireland. Carte MSS 45, fol. 465r.

4. Bodl. Carte MSS 45, fol. 149r (quoted), 429r; Carte 33, fol. 271r; T. W. Moody and J. G. Simms, *The Bishopric of Derry and the Irish Society of London, 1602–1705*, 2 vols. (Dublin: Stationery Office for the Irish Manuscripts Commission, 1968, 1983), 1:362; NLI MSS 4908, fol. 13v.

5. *CSPI 1663–65*, pp. 324, 360–61; Bodl. Carte MSS 32, fol. 637r; Carte 33, fols. 274r, 303r; CH MS HA 14388.

6. *CSPI 1663–65*, pp. 359–60; Bodl. Carte MSS 33, fols. 274r (quoted), 303r (quoted); CH MS HA 14398; Moody and Simms, *Bishopric of Derry*, 1:373.

7. Bodl. Carte MSS 33, fol. 475r (quoted); Moody and Simms, *Bishopric of Derry*, 1:387–88.

8. CH MSS HA 14396, 14397, 14399, 14400; *The Lauderdale Papers*, ed. Osmund Airy, 2 vols., Camden Society, n.s., nos. 34 and 36 (1884–85), 2:iv; Bodl. Carte MSS 47, fol. 193r; McConnell, *Fasti*, 2:39–40; *CSPI 1669–70*, pp. 194, 649.

9. BL Add. MSS 37,206, fol. 135r–v; PRO SP 29/109/93.

10. Bodl. Carte MSS 33, fol. 750v; Carte 45, fol. 173r–v; Richard Bagwell, *Ireland Under the Stuarts and During the Interregnum*, 3 vols. (London: Longmans, Green, 1909–16), 3:325.

11. *A Collection of the State Letters of the Right Honourable Roger Boyle, the First Earl of Orrery, Lord President of Munster in Ireland*, ed. Thomas Morrice, 2 vols. (Dublin, 1743), 1:252–53, 267; Bodl. Carte MSS 46, fols. 321v, 357r–v, 383r, 392v; Carte 35, fols. 50r–v, 52r–v, 54r, 61r–v, 128r; Thomas Brown, *Miscellanea Aulica* (London, 1702), p. 414 (quoted); BL Add. MSS 37,207, fols. 36r, 114r–v; *CSPI 1666–69*, p. 214.

12. Richard L. Greaves, *Enemies Under His Feet: Radicals and Nonconformists in Britain, 1664–1677* (Stanford: Stanford University Press, 1990), pp. 103–9.

13. CH MS HA 14420; *Collection of the Letters of Orrery*, ed. Morrice, 2:47, 51; *CCSP*, 5:503, 545; *CSPI 1663–65*, p. 644; *CSPI 1666–69*, pp. 8, 104–5; BL Add. MSS 37,207, fols. 10v (quoted), 13r, 42v–43r.

14. Bodl. Carte MSS 34, fol. 628r; Carte 35, fol. 140r–v; *HMC 36, Ormonde*, n.s., 3:226; TCD MSS 616, fols. 233v, 235r, 239v; *The Journals of the House of Commons, of the Kingdom of Ireland*, 2nd ed. (Dublin, 1783), 2:408, 495, 497–98, 505.

15. Bodl. Carte MSS 46, fols. 402v, 404r; Carte 47, fol. 466r; *CSPD 1660–85 Addenda*, p. 165; *Lauderdale Papers*, 1:250; 2:xl–xli; John Cosin, *The Correspondence*

of John Cosin D.D., Lord Bishop of Durham: Together with Other Papers Illustrative of His Life and Times, Surtees Society, vol. 55 (Durham: Andrews, 1872), pp. 158–60; NLS Wodrow MSS Folio XXXI, fol. 233r; BL Harleian MSS 4631, vol. 1, fol. 146r–v; BL Add. MSS 23,125, fol. 185v. Cf. Greaves, *Enemies Under His Feet*, pp. 64–76. In January 1667 Ormond learned that Crookshanks had reportedly been in county Donegal prior to the rebellion to recruit men. Carte MSS 35, fol. 248r.

16. Gilbert Burnet, *History of His Own Time*, new ed. (London: William Smith, 1838), p. 160; Bodl. Carte MSS 46, fol. 410r; Carte 45, fol. 202r; Carte 35, fol. 335r; *CSPI 1666–69*, pp. 251, 278; *Letters from Archibald, Earl of Argyll, to John, Duke of Lauderdale* (Edinburgh: Bannatyne Club, 1829), pp. 42–43.

17. Bodl. Carte MSS 35, fol. 113r; *CSPI 1666–69*, pp. 138, 474; *Collection of the Letters of Orrery*, ed. Morrice, 2:132–33. Dungannon had complained in January 1665 of inadequate provisions for defense, especially in Ulster. Carte 34, fol. 24r.

18. *RPCS 1661–64*, pp. 461–62, 551, 587–88; *Lauderdale Papers*, 1:235; 2:appendix, pp. iv, xix; *HMC 21, Hamilton*, supplement, p. 82; NLS MSS 2512, fol. 82; *RPCS 1665–69*, pp. 285–86, 387.

19. PRO SP 29/239/211; Julia Buckroyd, *Church and State in Scotland 1660–1681* (Edinburgh: John Donaldson, 1980), p. 102; BL Harleian MSS 4631, vol. 1, fol. 163v; *RPCS 1665–69*, pp. 459–60; Robert Wodrow, *The History of the Sufferings of the Church of Scotland from the Restoration to the Revolution*, ed. Robert Burns, 4 vols. (Glasgow: Blackie, Fullarton, 1829), 2:111–12.

20. BL Add. MSS 23,131, fol. 103r–v, 111v, 123r–v; EUL MSS La.III.354, no. 53.

21. BL Add. MSS 37,207, fols. 159r–160r, 165r; Bodl. Carte MSS 45, fol. 201r.

22. Bodl. Carte MSS 35, fol. 138r. Following Wild's death on 29 December 1665 Ormond wrote to Arlington stressing the need to find a replacement quickly, adding that the see of Derry was one in which "a Bishop is more necessary than he will be welcome, and though it be one of the best Bishoprics in the kingdom, yet most of our clergy had rather have a worse with more quiet than [one] that with the trouble that will attend it." Mossom was nominated on 11 January 1666, one week after Ormond wrote this letter. *CSPI 1666–69*, p. 1.

23. CH MSS HA 14448, 14452 (quoted). Cf. HA 14471.

24. Bodl. Carte MSS 45, fols. 449r–450r.

25. Bodl. Carte MSS 45, fols. 456r–457r; cf. fols. 435r–436r.

26. Henry Jones, *A Sermon Preached at the Consecration of . . . Ambrose Lord Bishop of Kildare in Christ-Church, Dublin, June 29. 1667* (Dublin, 1667), sigs. A3v–C1r, pp. 29, 36 (quoted).

27. BL Add. MSS 4763, fol. 508v; Moody and Simms, *Bishopric of Derry*, 1:407–8, 422–26; Bodl. Carte MSS 35, fols. 506r–v, 508r, 510r–v (quoted), 609r, 617r–v, 636r; Carte 36, fols. 59r (quoted), 355r. In Limerick, Foxen, the mayor in 1667, attempted to add nonconformists to the corporation. For a while after the restoration the town clerk was a Presbyterian. BL Add. MSS 37,208, fols. 149v–151v, 154r–v; Bodl. Carte MSS 35, fol. 710r.

28. PRONI MS DIO 4/5/3 (10); Bodl. Carte MSS 35, fol. 756r (quoted).

29. Bodl. Carte MSS 36, fols. 203r–v (quoted), 206r.

30. Bodl. Carte MSS 36, fol. 208r. Taylor had administered Dromore as well as Down and Connor, but following his death on 13 August 1667 Margetson in-

sisted that the sees be divided because they were "disorderly & disaffected." Carte 45, fol. 220r. Most of the period referred to in the investigation discussed above occurred at the end of Taylor's administration. Roger Boyle succeeded Taylor in Down and Connor, and George Rust in Dromore.

31. Bodl. Carte MSS 36, fols. 466v, 493v (quoted), 513r; Carte 49, fols. 608r, 632r, 671r; Carte 37, fols. 18r–v, 78r.

32. CH MS HA 15770; NLS MSS 3473, fol. 49; NLS MSS 7033, fol. 70r; *CSPI 1666–69*, pp. 484, 703; Bodl. Carte MSS 36, fols. 511r, 513v, 607r–v (quoted).

33. Bodl. Carte MSS 49, fols. 445v, 632r (quoted), 671r; Carte 36, fols. 488r (quoted), 490r, 493r (quoted), 537r–v, 607r; *CSPI 1666–69*, p. 585; CH MS 6786.

34. Bodl. Carte MSS 37, fol. 99r–v.

35. Bodl. Carte MSS 49, fol. 667r; Carte 37, fols. 3r, 18r–v, 62r–v (quoted).

36. J. C. Beckett, "The Irish Viceroyalty in the Restoration Period," *Transactions of the Royal Historical Society*, 5th series, 20 (1970): 61–62; Maurice Lee, Jr., *The Cabal* (Urbana: University of Illinois Press, 1965), p. 12; J. I. McGuire, "Why Was Ormond Dismissed in 1669?" *Irish Historical Studies* 18 (March 1973): 295–312; Ronald Hutton, "The Making of the Secret Treaty of Dover, 1668–1670," *Historical Journal* 29 (June 1986): 309–10 (note 62), 315; Hutton, *Charles the Second, King of England, Scotland and Ireland* (Oxford: Clarendon Press, 1989), pp. 260–61. For Charles's statement of the Scottish policy see NLS MSS 578, fol. 102r.

37. Bodl. Rawlinson MSS A.255, fol. 244. PRO SP 63/303/82, tentatively dated July 1660, should be July 1669.

38. Adair, pp. 290–91.

39. *CSPI 1666–69*, p. 771 (quoted); *CSPI 1669–70*, p. 22 (quoted); Hutton, *Charles the Second*, pp. 261–62.

40. Ezekiel Hopkins, *A Sermon Preached at Christ's Church in Dublin, Jan. 31 1669* (Dublin, 1671), pp. 4 (quoted), 8, 11, 25–28; Joseph Teate, *A Sermon Preached at the Cathedral Church of St. Canice[,] Kilkenny, Feb. 27. 1669* (Dublin, 1670), p. 34.

41. *CSPI 1669–70*, pp. 78–79; Bodl. Rawlinson MSS A.255, fol. 292.

42. Adair, pp. 286, 296–98. Bruce was born in Ireland and educated at Edinburgh University.

43. Adair, pp. 286, 298–301; *CSPI 1669–70*, pp. 194, 226–27, 649.

44. Adair, pp. 299–300 (quoted), 301; PRO SP 63/330/232; James Seaton Reid, *History of the Presbyterian Church in Ireland*, new ed., 3 vols. (Belfast: William Mullan, 1867), 2:313, note 21; J. C. Beckett, *Confrontations: Studies in Irish History* (Totowa, N.J.: Rowman and Littlefield, 1972), pp. 36–37; *CSPI 1669–70*, pp. 147–48, 226–27.

45. PRO SP 63/331/34; BL Add. MSS 28,085, fol. 17r–v (quoted; a longer version is recorded on fol. 19r–v).

46. Hutton, *Charles the Second*, pp. 281–82, 284–85. Essex's ability to deal with Catholics may have been facilitated by one of his chaplains, Andrew Sall, formerly a Jesuit; a professor of divinity at Pamplona, Palencia, and Tudela; and a professor of moral theology at Salamanca. Sall, *A Sermon Preached at Christ-Church in Dublin, Before the Lord Lieutenant and Council, the Fifth Day of July, 1674* (Dublin, 1674), title-page.

47. Bodl. Carte MSS 37, fol. 707v; BL Stowe MSS 213, fols. 34v–35r; Stowe 200, fol. 127r; CH MS HA 14515.

48. PRO SP 63/331/130, 130.1; BL Stowe MSS 213, fols. 11v–12r; Stowe 200, fols. 184v–185r, 195r–v.

49. PRO SP 63/331/168 (quoted), 168.1; 63/331/175, 175.1 (quoted); BL Stowe MSS 200, fol. 235r.

50. CH MS HA 14514; BL Stowe MSS 200, fols. 287r (quoted), 301r, 326v; Stowe 213, fol. 57v (quoted).

51. MLM, 1:15–16 (quoted).

52. MLM, 1:18, 45.

53. *HMC 1, Second Report*, p. 212; [James Kirkpatrick], *An Historical Essay upon the Loyalty of Presbyterians in Great-Britain and Ireland from the Reformation to This Present Year 1713* (1713), pp. 383–85; BL Add. MSS 23,135, fol. 213r (quoted); Clement E. Pike, "The Origin of the *Regium Donum*," *Transactions of the Royal Historical Society*, 3rd series, 3 (1909): 255, 268–69. The *regium donum* was paid at least in 1672 and 1676. Bodl. Carte MSS 66, fols. 350v, 356v; CH MS HA 15053.

54. BL Stowe MSS 213, fol. 56r–v (quoted); Stowe 200, fol. 326v (quoted).

55. CH MS HA 14517; BL Stowe MSS 200, fol. 334r–v (quoted); Stowe 214, fol. 301r.

56. B[enjamin] P[arry], *More Than Conqueror: A Sermon Preach't on the Martyrdom of King Charles the I. Jan. 30 at Christ-Church, Dublin* (Dublin, 1673), pp. 14–15 (quoted), 22, 35–36 (quoted). In a sermon on the epiphany at Christ Church, Dublin, the previous year, Richard Berry included a brief attack against those, presumably including nonconformists, who questioned the church's authority: "What strikes deeper at the root of Religion, is, the vile reasonings of reprobate minds against Christian Obedience." Berry, *A Sermon upon the Epiphany, Preach't at Christ-Church, in the City of Dublin, 1672* (Dublin, 1672), p. 27.

57. John Vesey, epistle to *The Works of the Most Reverend Father in God, John Bramhall D.D.* (Dublin, 1676), sigs. A3r–A4v.

58. Beckett, *Confrontations*, p. 37; BL Stowe MSS 213, fol. 338v (quoted); CH MSS HA 14518, 14529, 14549; NLS MSS 3830, fol. 72r–v.

59. NAI MSS M2449, fols. 258–60; Richard Baxter, *Reliquiae Baxterianae*, ed. Matthew Sylvester (London, 1696), III, §256; III, §287 (cf. III, pp. 109–40 for the relevant documents); appendix viii, p. 121.

60. *Selections from the Correspondence of Arthur Capel Earl of Essex 1675–1677*, ed. Osmund Airy and Clement Edwards Pike, Camden Society, 3rd series, 2 vols. (London: Royal Historical Society, 1890, 1913), 1:124–25.

61. *Correspondence of Essex*, 1:125; BL Stowe MSS 213, fols. 179v–180r (quoted), 358r; Stowe 201, fol. 349r; Stowe 204, fols. 209r, 313v, 347r; Stowe 216, fols. 63r–v, 68r–69v, 93r–v; Stowe 217, fols. 34v, 39r–v; NLI Ormonde MSS 2358, fol. 169.

62. BL Stowe MSS 213, fol. 354v; Stowe 208, fol. 398r; Stowe 214, fols. 223r, 235r, 239v (quoted), 278v, 289v, 303r; Stowe 205, fol. 346r; Stowe 207, fol. 251r–v; BL Add. MSS 23,136, fol. 194r–v; *Correspondence of Essex*, 1:242–43, 247, 274; *HMC 1, Second Report*, p. 203.

63. BL Stowe MSS 210, fols. 194r (quoted), 197r–v; Stowe 216, fols. 148r–v, 163r.

64. BL Stowe MSS 211, fols. 45r–v (quoted), 114r; NLI Ormonde MSS 2488, fols. 21–22; Stowe 217, fols. 31v–34r.

65. BL Stowe MSS 211, fols. 45r–v, 238v; *HMC 36, Ormonde,* n.s., 4:19–20 (quoted).

66. BL Stowe MSS 217, fols. 75v, 76v, 78r; McConnell, *Fasti,* 3:64.

67. Beckett, "Irish Viceroyalty," pp. 68, 75–80; CH MS HA 14550; Hutton, *Charles the Second,* pp. 338–40.

68. Bodl. Carte MSS 38, fols. 380r–383r; BL Add. MSS 32,095, fols. 32r–33v.

69. *HMC 36, Ormonde,* n.s., 4:26 (quoted).

70. *HMC 36, Ormonde,* n.s., 4:62, 72; Richard L. Greaves, *Secrets of the Kingdom: British Radicals from the Popish Plot to the Revolution of 1688–1689* (Stanford: Stanford University Press, 1992), pp. 53–55; *CSPD 1676–77,* pp. 548–49; *CSPD 1673–78,* pp. 323, 375.

71. Bodl. Carte MSS 45, fols. 469r–470v; *HMC 36, Ormonde,* n.s., 1:21–22; 4:61–63, 73–74, 80; *HMC 29, Portland,* 2:47; NLS MSS 597, fols. 270r–271r; PRO SP 63/338/108, 135, 140; SP 29/398/133; BL Add. MSS 23,138, fol. 71v; *RPCS 1676–78,* pp. 297–98.

72. *RPCS 1676–78,* pp. 285–87; *HMC 36, Ormonde,* n.s., 4:74–75, 147; PRO SP 63/338/125; CH MS HA 14152.

73. PRO SP 63/338/104; SP 29/398/124; *HMC 78, Hastings,* 2:386–87; *HMC 36, Ormonde,* n.s., 4:69.

74. *HMC 36, Ormonde,* n.s., 4:77, 147–48; PRO SP 63/338/132 (quoted), 143; *HMC 78, Hastings,* 2:387.

75. *HMC 36, Ormonde,* n.s., 4:85.

76. *HMC 36, Ormonde,* n.s., 4:75–76 (quoted); CH MSS HA 15672, 15673; *DNB,* s.v.; *Calamy Revised,* s.v.

77. PRO SP 63/338/131, 132, 134, 135, 141, 142, 143; CH MS HA 15672; *HMC 78, Hastings,* 2:387; *HMC 36, Ormonde,* n.s., 4:88–89, 93–94 (quoted), 99 (quoted), 101–2, 106, 111. Cf. BL Add. MSS 25,124, fols. 157r, 158r.

78. Greaves, *Secrets of the Kingdom,* pp. 10, 19, 25, 156; John Kenyon, *The Popish Plot* (New York: Penguin, 1972), pp. 216–17.

79. *HMC 36, Ormonde,* 2:254–58, 278 (quoted); n.s., 4:15–20; 6:33; Bodl. Carte MSS 38, fol. 676r–v; London *Gazette* 1368 (26–30 December 1678); Greaves, *Enemies Under His Feet,* pp. 204–9.

80. PRO SP 29/366, fol. 595; SP 44/43, fol. 223; *RPCS 1676–78,* pp. 390, 397–98, 404–5, 579–80; *HMC 29, Portland,* 2:47–48; *HMC 36, Ormonde,* n.s., 4:147–48, 201, 206; Greaves, *Secrets of the Kingdom,* pp. 55–58.

81. Bodl. Carte MSS 45, fols. 482r, 486r–v (quoted); *HMC 36, Ormonde,* n.s., 5:112–14.

82. Bodl. Carte MSS 221, fols. 378r, 396r–v, 407r; Carte 45, fols. 504r (quoted), 524r. One of the publications circulating among Covenanters in Ireland was *Naphtali, or the Wrestlings of the Church of Scotland for the Kingdom of Christ* (1667) by James Stewart and James Stirling. Carte MSS 45, fol. 504r; Greaves, *Enemies Under His Feet,* p. 186.

83. *HMC 51, Popham,* p. 244; *HMC 36, Ormonde,* n.s., 5:112–13.

84. *RPCS 1678–80,* p. 219; *HMC 36, Ormonde,* 1:102 (quoted); n.s., 5:87, 126,

128–29, 143–44; PRO SP 29/411/150.1; 29/339, no. 20; 29/339, no. 24; Bodl. Carte MSS 45, fols. 506r, 543r; Carte 70, fol. 488r (quoted); BL Althorp (Halifax) MSS H2 (Coventry to Halifax, 16 June 1679); *Calendar of the Orrery Papers*, ed. Edward MacLysaght (Dublin: Stationery Office, 1941), p. 212; BL Stowe MSS 212, fol. 357r–v; NLI MSS 2491, fol. 175.

85. Bodl. Carte MSS 45, fols. 516r, 518r; Carte 70, fol. 488r; *CSPD 1679–80*, p. 229; *Tudor and Stuart Proclamations 1485–1714*, ed. Robert Steele, 2 vols. (Oxford: Clarendon Press, 1910), 2:115 (no. 906); *Domestick Intelligence* 2 (10 July 1679); *RPCS 1678–80*, pp. 294–96, 412–13.

86. *HMC 36, Ormonde*, n.s., 4:207; 5:189 (quoted), 209; *Calendar of Orrery Papers*, p. 212; Bodl. Carte MSS 221, fol. 415r (quoted).

87. Beckett, *Confrontations*, p. 44; Bodl. Carte MSS 45, fol. 531r–v (quoted).

88. Bodl. Carte MSS 45, fol. 530r (quoted); *RPCS 1678–80*, pp. 655–57. Cf. NLS Wodrow MSS Folio LIX, fols. 271r–272r.

89. Bodl. Carte MSS 45, fol. 531v.

90. Bodl. Carte MSS 45, fol. 533r–v; PRO SP 63/339/39 (quoted); 39.1 (quoted); *HMC 79, Lindsey*, p. 31. Another copy of the declaration is in MLM, 2:24–26. For the address submitted by Adair see MLM, 2:30–32.

91. Bodl. Carte MSS 221, fol. 429r (quoted); David W. Miller, *Queen's Rebels: Ulster Loyalism in Historical Perspective* (Dublin: Gilland Macmillan, 1978), pp. 170–71; *HMC 36, Ormonde*, n.s., 5:209 (quoted). Ironically, Rule was subject to criticism from some members of his congregation at this time for being too moderate. One of Ormond's allies called Rule "a better man than any that I know of his kind." Carte MSS 45, fol. 545r.

92. NLS Wodrow MSS Folio LIX, fols. 271r–273r.

93. Bodl. Carte MSS 45, fol. 488r; Carte 221, fol. 392r–v; *HMC 36, Ormonde*, n.s., 5:125; [William Tisdall], *The Conduct of the Dissenters of Ireland, with Respect Both to Church and State* (Dublin, 1712), p. 14.

94. Bodl. Carte MSS 45, fols. 549r, 553v, 555r; *CSPD 1679–80*, p. 609; PRO SP 63/339/113 (quoted); EUL MSS Dc.1.16, no. 22; *RPCS 1678–80*, p. 481; Greaves, *Secrets of the Kingdom*, pp. 70–71.

95. PRO SP 63/342/25, 35, 44; *HMC 36, Ormonde*, n.s., 6:34–35 (quoted), 65; *CSPD 1680–81*, p. 307.

96. PRO SP 63/342/15, 15.1, 29; *HMC 36, Ormonde*, n.s., 5:615; Bodl. Carte MSS 221, fols. 231r (quoted), 448r, 450r, 452r–v (quoted); Carte 45, fol. 559r; MLM, 2:86–88, 91.

97. Bodl. Carte MSS 45, fols. 567r, 571r (quoted); Carte 222, fol. 448r; PRO SP 63/342/35 (quoted); *HMC 36, Ormonde*, n.s., 6:100.

98. Bodl. Carte MSS 45, fols. 563r (quoted), 569v; Carte 221, fol. 452v.

99. Edward Wetenhall, *The Protestant Peace-Maker* (London, 1682), pp. 9–10, 22 (quoted), 23, 29, 32–33 (quoted).

100. Samuel Foley, *Two Sermons, the First, Preached in Christ-Church, Dublin: Feb. 19. 1681 . . . The Other, Preached in the Cathedral Church of St. Patrick . . . Apr. 24. 1682* (London, 1683), p. 35.

101. Foley, *A Sermon Preached at the Primary Visitation of His Grace Francis Lord Arch-Bishop of Dublin* (London, 1683), pp. 28–29, 30 (quoted), 32, 33 (quoted).

Shortly before Foley's sermon one of King's correspondents, Charles Holcroft, reiterated the polemical comparison of Presbyterian resistance theory to that of the Jesuits and certain scholastics. TCD MSS 1995–2008/8.

102. Cf. Massereene's fear of Catholics serving in the military. Bodl. Carte MSS 219, fols. 210r–v, 212r–v, 214r. Cf. Wetenhall, *Peace-Maker*, p. 29.

103. Robert Ware, epistle to [John Nalson], *Foxes and Firebrands*, 2nd ed. (Dublin, 1682), sigs. A4r–A5r; Ware, *The Hunting of the Romish Fox, and the Quenching of Sectarian Fire-Brands* (Dublin, 1683), sigs. A5r–v (quoted), A6v (quoted).

104. PRO SP 29/415/8 (quoted); *Impartial Protestant Mercury* 92 (7–10 March 1682); *True Protestant Mercury* 117 (15–18 February 1682); HMC 63, *Egmont*, 2:111–12 (quoted); *Calendar of the Ancient Records of Dublin, in the Possession of the Municipal Corporation of That City*, ed. John T. Gilbert, vol. 5 (Dublin: Joseph Dollard, 1895), p. 233.

105. HMC 36, *Ormonde*, 6:509, 519–21 (cf. 1:57–58). In the spring of 1679 Coventry received word from the Netherlands that 4,000 weapons had been shipped to Ireland from Rotterdam by the radical James Washington. Coventry wanted to know if Ormond had ordered them. HMC 36, *Ormonde*, n.s., 5:83.

106. HMC 36, *Ormonde*, n.s., 6:495–96, 500–501, 504–5; McDonnell, *Fasti*, 2:15–16; 3:63.

107. HMC 36, *Ormonde*, n.s., 6:507–8, 509 (quoted), 513, 517, 525–27, 535; 7:48; McConnell, *Fasti*, 2:15–16; 3:63; MAM 1671–91, p. 240. In February 1683 Arran told his father he was confident no weapons had been imported except forty cases of pistols seized from a Scottish peddler in Cork. HMC 36, *Ormonde*, n.s., 6:535. In June 1683 Ormond told Arran he thought there was "a mixture of knavery & frency" in Gordon. Gordon subsequently returned to the Presbyterians, participated in the siege of Derry in 1689, fled to Scotland, and later refused requests from Glendermott to resume his pastorate. Bodl. Carte MSS 219, fol. 464r (quoted); McConnell, *Fasti*, 3:63; MLM, 2:96, 340–42, 359–60; *Synod*, p. 5.

108. Greaves, *Secrets of the Kingdom*, chaps. 3–5.

109. Ibid., p. 155.

110. Ibid., pp. 103, 113–18 *passim*, 125–55 *passim*, 159, 172–74, 178–84 *passim*.

111. Richard L. Greaves, "The Rye House Plotting, Nonconformist Clergy, and Calvin's Resistance Theory," in *Later Calvinism: International Perspectives*, vol. 22, Sixteenth Century Essays and Studies (1994), p. 520; Greaves, *Secrets of the Kingdom*, pp. 190–91; PRO SP 29/343/164.1; Bodl. Carte MSS 169, fols. 26–27, 30.

112. Greaves, *Secrets of the Kingdom*, p. 191; PRO SP 29/427/119; 29/428/94.

113. NLI MSS 4909, nos. 37 (quoted), 38 (quoted), 66; Bodl. Carte MSS 169, fol. 28. As early as September 1663 a man had been committed at the Clonmel assizes for seditious speech because he called James a rogue and the queen a whore. NLI MSS 4908, fol. 17v.

114. NLI MSS 2491, fols. 325–38; Bodl. Carte MSS 45, fol. 10r (cf. fol. 9r).

115. Bodl. Carte MSS 168, fol. 132 (quoted) (cf. fol. 136); HMC 36, *Ormonde*, n.s., 7:59; Bodl. Carte MSS 40, fols. 55r, 57r, 63r; Carte 218, fol. 475v; PRO SP 63/343/139; CH MS HA 15690.

116. *HMC 36, Ormonde,* 1:57–58; n.s., 7:60, 71; PRO SP 63/343/125; Bodl. Carte 168, fol. 144.

117. Bodl. Carte MSS 168, fol. 153. Ormond did not believe the accusation against Granard. *HMC 36, Ormonde,* n.s., 7:102. Walcott had met secretly in London with the earl of Argyll after the latter's escape from Scotland. Greaves, *Secrets of the Kingdom,* pp. 102–3; Carte MSS 168, fol. 146; Carte 219, fols. 482r, 504r; DMunL Gilbert MSS 109, fols. 43–44; *HMC 36, Ormonde,* n.s., 7:374; *HMC 1, Second Report,* Appendix, p. 214; William Veitch, in *Memoirs of Mr. William Veitch, and George Brysson, Written by Themselves,* ed. Thomas McCrie (Edinburgh: William Blackwood, 1825), pp. 142–43.

118. Bodl. Carte MSS 168, fols. 146–47; *HMC 5, Sixth Report,* Appendix, pp. 746–47.

119. Bodl. Carte MSS 168, fols. 9–10, 153, 160, 162; Carte 169, fols. 13, 21; Carte 219, fol. 518r; *HMC 36, Ormonde,* n.s., 7:90–91, 110, 156–57.

120. Bodl. Carte MSS 168, fols. 146, 157–58 (quoted), 159; CH MS HA 14739; *HMC 36, Ormonde,* n.s., 1:57–58; 7:89–90, 96–97. Cf. APL Dopping Correspondence, vol. 1, nos. 35, 36.

121. *HMC 36, Ormonde,* n.s., 7:89–90.

122. Bodl. Carte MSS 50, fol. 287r.

123. Bodl. Carte MSS 219, fols. 480r, 488r–v, 490r (quoted); Carte 218, fol. 473r. Ormond also advised Arran to dissuade Catholics from pressing for greater freedom at a time when Protestant dissenters were being suppressed. *HMC 36, Ormonde,* n.s., 7:152.

124. *HMC 36, Ormonde,* n.s., 7:82 (quoted), 124; Bodl. Carte MSS 219, fol. 506r (quoted).

125. Bodl. Carte MSS 169, fol. 47; Carte 168, fols. 151, 155, 159, 161; Carte 219, fol. 506r (quoted); Carte 218, fol. 490r; *HMC 36, Ormonde,* n.s., 7:95–97, 107–9, 181, 314–16; Pinney, p. 15; PRO SP 63/343/142; Nottingham University Library MSS PwV95, fol. 306.

126. *HMC 36, Ormonde,* n.s., 7:95, 121; Bodl. Carte MSS 168, fols. 152–53, 161.

127. John Vesey, *A Sermon Preached at Clonmell, on Sunday the Sixteenth of September, 1683* (Dublin, 1683), pp. 12 (quoted), 14–15, 20–22 (quoted). Cf. Ware, *Hunting,* sig. A6r.

128. MAM 1671–91, fols. 221, 227, 241 (quoted).

129. MAM 1671–91, fols. 246, 254–55 (quoted), 257, 269, 286–87, 289, 292, 304, 308.

130. *The Correspondence of Henry Hyde, Earl of Clarendon and of His Brother Lawrence Hyde, Earl of Rochester,* ed. Samuel Weller Singer, 2 vols. (London: Henry Colburn, 1828), 1:99; PRO SP 63/343/162.5 (quoted); *HMC 36, Ormonde,* n.s., 7:314–16.

131. EUL MSS La.III.350, fol. 79r; PRO SP 63/340, fols. 36–38; *CSPD 1684–85,* pp. 104–5; *HMC 44, Drumlanrig,* 2:30, 180, 199; BL Lansdowne MSS 1152A, fols. 153r, 154r, 156r, 176r, 177r, 182r, 183r; *RPCS 1684,* pp. 348, 381; *RPCS 1684–85,* pp. 610–11; Bodl. Carte MSS 50, fol. 341r–v; PRO SP 63/343/162, 162.1–6, 165, 166; *HMC 36, Ormonde,* n.s., 7:292; TCD MSS 1178, nos. 16 and 17. For more on radical Covenanter ideology see Chapter 4.

CHAPTER 3

1. John Miller, "The Earl of Tyrconnel and James II's Irish Policy, 1685–1688," *Historical Journal* 20 (December 1977): 817–22.

2. TCD MSS 1178, nos. 18, 20; PRO SP 63/340, fol. 78; McConnell, *Fasti*, 3:78.

3. PRO SP 63/340, fols. 63, 75; BL Add. MSS 41,803, fol. 231r–v; BL Lansdowne MSS 1152, fol. 329r; *HMC* 44, *Drumlanrig*, 2:47, 50, 61.

4. *HMC* 44, *Drumlanrig*, 2:57, 64, 220; *RPCS 1685–86*, p. 29; PRO SP 63/340, fols. 79, 83–85; SP 63/351, fols. 11r, 14r; BL Lansdowne MSS 1152A, fols. 340v–341r, 342r, 344r, 347r–v.

5. PRO SP 63/351, fol. 16r; SP 63/340, fols. 81, 87–88; *HMC* 44, *Drumlanrig*, 2:72–73; BL Lansdowne MSS 1152A, fol. 338r.

6. *HMC* 78, *Hastings*, 2:395; *CSPD 1685*, p. 236; PRO SP 63/340, fols. 102–3; SP 63/351, fol. 38r–v.

7. PRO SP 63/340, fols. 83–84, 88–91; BL Lansdowne MSS 1152A, fols. 340v–341r, 350r–v, 378r–v.

8. Pinney, pp. xv, 19 (quoted), 20–21, 23; *Letters of Eminent Men, Addressed to Roger Thoresby, F.R.S.*, 2 vols. (London: Henry Colburn and Richard Bentley, 1832), 1:70; *HMC* 36, *Ormonde*, n.s., 8:344; *The Correspondence of Henry Hyde, Earl of Clarendon and of His Brother Lawrence Hyde, Earl of Rochester*, ed. Samuel Weller Singer, 2 vols. (London: Henry Colburn, 1828), 1:189. In Cork the mayor removed a sign depicting Monmouth's head and had it solemnly burned. Charles Smith, *The Ancient and Present State of the County and City of Cork*, ed. Robert Day and W. A. Copinger, 3 vols. (Cork: Guy, 1893–94), 2:112.

9. *CSPD 1685*, p. 296; BL Lansdowne MSS 1152A, fols. 174r, 374r; PRO SP 63/351, fols. 63v–64r (quoted).

10. *HMC* 36, *Ormonde*, n.s., 7:346, 354; DMunL Gilbert MSS 109, fol. 60; Pinney, p. 36 (quoted).

11. BL Add. MSS 15,892, fol. 199v.

12. TCD MSS 1995–2008, fols. 1r–v, 2v.

13. William King, *An Answer to the Considerations Which Obliged Peter Manby, Late Dean of London-Derry in Ireland . . . to Embrace . . . the Catholick Religion* (Dublin, 1687), pp. 6, 27. For an excellent discussion of Joseph Boyse's reply in *Vindicae Calvinisticae, or Some Impartial Reflections* (Dublin, 1687), see Kilroy, pp. 172–75.

14. Edward Wetenhall, *The Way to Peace and Publick Safety* (Dublin, 1686), pp. 19–20 (quoted); *The State Letters of Henry Earl of Clarendon*, 2 vols. (Oxford: Clarendon Press, 1763), 1:412–13 (quoted); *HMC* 75, *Downshire*, 1:149 (quoted).

15. *State Letters of Clarendon*, 1:93, 96–98, 245–46, 250–51 (quoted); 2:82–83; Bodl. Tanner MSS 30, fols. 42r–42Br; "Sir Paul Rycaut's Memoranda and Letters from Ireland, 1686–1687," *Analecta Hibernica*, no. 27 (Dublin: Irish University Press for the Irish Manuscripts Commission, 1972), pp. 143–44. In March 1686 James had ordered preachers not to meddle in politics. *To the Most Reverend Father in God, William Lord Archbishop of Canterbury, . . . and John Lord Archbishop of York* (Dublin, 1686), pp. 8–9.

16. D. E. Greenway, S. Porter, and I. Roy, eds., *Handbook of British Chronology*, 3rd ed. (London: Royal Historical Society, 1986), pp. 381, 383, 392.

17. HMC 75, *Downshire*, 1:134; HMC 36, *Ormonde*, n.s., 7:315; *Correspondence of Clarendon and Rochester*, 1:335; *CMHS*, 8:62–64; "Rycaut's Memoranda," p. 153.

18. *State Letters of Clarendon*, 1:139–40; *Correspondence of Clarendon and Rochester*, 1:225–27, 268–69; BL Add. MSS 15,893, fols. 47r, 55r–v, 56v; 15,894, fols. 77r–78r.

19. PRO SP 63/351, fols. 135r–138r, 151r–154r; BL Add. MSS 15,893, fols. 41r, 49r, 50r; *CCSP*, 5:661–62. For spreading rumors that a rebellion had erupted, a resident of Cruicetown, county Meath, faced arrest. APL Dopping Correspondence, vol. 1, no. 53.

20. BL Add. MSS 15,893, fols. 117v–118r; *State Letters of Clarendon*, 1:82; Richard L. Greaves, *Secrets of the Kingdom: British Radicals from the Popish Plot to the Revolution of 1688–1689* (Stanford: Stanford University Press, 1992), pp. 164–65.

21. *State Letters of Clarendon*, 1:109–10, 121; PRO SP 63/351, fols. 171r–172r; BL Add. MSS 15,893, fol. 165r–v; *CSPD 1686–87*, p. 95. The government was still disarming dissident Protestants in May 1686. *CSPD 1686–87*, p. 139.

22. BL Add. MSS 15,894, fols. 48r, 50r–53r; *Correspondence of Clarendon and Rochester*, 1:498, 563–64, 569; 2:89–90, 92–93, 115; PRO SP 63/351, fols. 274r–275r; "Rycaut's Memoranda," pp. 155, 157, 175; HMC 36, *Ormonde*, n.s., 8:346; Smith, *Cork*, 2:113.

23. *Correspondence of Clarendon and Rochester*, 2:78–79 (quoted); HMC 13, *Tenth Report*, Appendix 4, p. 397; HMC 75, *Downshire*, 1:195 (quoted); *CCSP*, 5:671; "Rycaut's Memoranda," pp. 157, 169. Cf. W. Macaffee and V. Morgan, "Population in Ulster, 1660–1760," in *Plantation to Partition: Essays in Ulster History in Honour of J. L. McCracken*, ed. Peter Roebuck (Dundonald, Belfast: Blackstaff, 1981), pp. 56–57.

24. Pinney, p. 53; *CMHS*, 8:65–66.

25. London *Gazette* 2253 (20–23 June 1687) (quoted); 2262 (21–25 July 1687); DMM, 2:115, 117–18; *Tudor and Stuart Proclamations 1485–1714*, ed. Robert Steele, 2 vols. (Oxford: Clarendon Press, 1910), 2, no. 973. An undated document in the Carte manuscripts setting forth reasons why indulged Protestants would not disrupt the kingdom probably dates from this time. Bodl. Carte MSS 45, fols. 451r–452v.

26. PRO SP 63/340, fol. 235; HMC 29, *Portland*, 3:402 (quoted); DWL Roger Morrice, "Entr'ing Book, Being an Historical Register of Occurrences from April, Anno 1677 to April 1691," 2:231; Miller, "Earl of Tyrconnel," pp. 816–17.

27. J. G. Simms, *Jacobite Ireland 1685–91* (London: Routledge and Kegan Paul, 1969), p. 42; Bodl. Tanner MSS 30, fol. 183r (quoted); *CMHS*, 8:67. Cf. Pinney, p. 54.

28. Simms, *Jacobite Ireland*, pp. 35–36; [James Kirkpatrick], *An Historical Essay upon the Loyalty of Presbyterians in Great-Britain and Ireland from the Reformation to the Present Year 1713* (1713), pp. 421–22, 425–26. Cf. T. C. Barnard, "Crises of Identity Among Irish Protestants 1641–1685," *Past & Present* 127 (May 1990): 82.

29. DMM, 2:131, 134; Olive M. Goodbody, "Anthony Sharp: A Quaker Merchant of the Liberties," *Dublin Historical Record* 14 (1955): 17; HYNM, 1:103 (quoted), 105 (quoted).

30. DF Sharp MSS S6, fols. 30r–34v; HYNM, 1:107.

31. [William King], *The State of the Protestants of Ireland Under the Late King James's Government*, 4th ed. (London, 1682), p. 230.

32. PRO SP 8/2, pt. 2, fol. 112Ar (quoted); Morrice, "Entr'ing Book," 2:362; [William Tisdall], *The Conduct of the Dissenters of Ireland, with Respect Both to Church and State* (Dublin, 1712), p. 15; James Seaton Reid, *History of the Presbyterian Church in Ireland*, new ed., 3 vols. (Belfast: William Mullan, 1867), 2:343–55; J. C. Beckett, *Protestant Dissent in Ireland, 1687–1780* (London: Faber and Faber, 1948), pp. 25–26.

33. [Kirkpatrick], *Historical Essay*, p. 395 (quoted); [Tisdall], *Conduct*, p. 15.

34. MAM 1671–91, pp. 429, 435 (quoted). Conformist clerics—at least eighteen in 1689—also fled. TCD MSS 847.

35. EUL MSS La.II.27.1, fols. 105–16, 142–45.

36. *The Montgomery Manuscripts (1603–1706)*, comp. William Montgomery and ed. George Hill (Belfast: James Cleeland and Thomas Dargan, 1869), p. 274.

37. [Kirkpatrick], *Historical Essay*, pp. 413–14; [Tisdall], *Conduct*, pp. 15–16. In April 1689 French and Gaelic Irish Catholics sacked the parish church at Passage, near Waterford, and three French soldiers subsequently attempted to break into Waterford cathedral, then threw stones at its windows and threatened to murder the sexton. Five months later the government ordered Dopping to close the churches and not ring the bells on 15 September because a large number of soldiers would be in the city. APL Dopping Correspondence, vol. 1, nos. 92, 106.

38. McConnell, *Fasti*, s.vv.; *A Great Archbishop of Dublin: William King, D.D., 1650–1729: His Autobiography, Family, and a Selection from His Correspondence*, ed. Sir Charles Simeon (New York: Longmans, Green, and Co., 1906), p. 291. The Presbyterian minister Daniel Williams estimated that at the time of the siege Presbyterians outnumbered conformists in Derry ten to one. According to one of his correspondents, a dissenting minister in the city, the Presbyterians lost six-sevenths of the men in their congregations. Williams, *The Protestants Deliverance from the Irish Rebellion, Begun October 23. 1641* (London, 1690), pp. 32–33.

39. TCD MSS 1995–2008/61.

40. *Tudor and Stuart Proclamations*, ed. Steele, 2:128 (no. 1009); *Montgomery Manuscripts*, p. 273; Simms, *Jacobite Ireland*, pp. 48–56.

41. *Tudor and Stuart Proclamations*, 2:129 (no. 1020), 129–30 (no. 1029); HMC 45, *Buccleuch*, 2:39 (quoted); W. H. Crawford, "Ulster as a Mirror of the Two Societies," in *Ireland and Scotland 1600–1850: Parallels and Contrasts in Economic and Social Development*, ed. T. M. Devine and David Dickson (Edinburgh: John Donald, 1983), p. 61.

42. HYNM, 2:3–4; TCD MSS 2203 (quoted).

43. Joseph Besse, *A Collection of the Sufferings of the People Called Quakers*, 2 vols. (London, 1753), 2:484–85; LPM, fol. 223 (quoted).

44. [Kirkpatrick], *Historical Essay*, pp. 405–8; Reid, *History*, 2:397–98.

45. Richard Cox, *Hibernia Anglicana*, pt. 1 (London, 1689), sig. c2v (quoted). Cf. [Kirkpatrick], *Historical Essay*, pp. 409–10; *Montgomery Manuscripts*, pp. 273–74.

46. Anthony Carpenter, "William King and the Threats to the Church of

Ireland During the Reign of James II," *Irish Historical Studies* 18 (March 1972): 25–28. The conformists' support of William provoked some bitter reactions. Cf. these lines from an anonymous poem addressed to Samuel Dopping:

> For Thee [William] the Prelate will his church betray
> . . .
> Rebells like witches when they have signed the Rolls
> Must serve their Masters tho they dam[n] their souls.

PRONI MS DIO 4 / 13 / 2 / 1. James McGuire explains why most conformist clerics in Ireland supported William in "The Church of Ireland and the 'Glorious Revolution' of 1688," *Studies in Irish History: Presented to R. Dudley Edwards*, ed. Art Cosgrove and Donal McCartney (Dublin: University College, 1979), pp. 137–49.

47. Joseph Pike, *Some Account of the Life of Joseph Pike of Cork, in Ireland* (London: Darton and Harvey, 1837), pp. 48–49, 50 (quoted); MAM, 1671–91, fols. 458, 460, 474, 498, 544–45; MLM, 2:112.

48. [Kirkpatrick], *Historical Essay*, p. 397; HMC 71, *Finch*, 2:301 (quoted); Beckett, *Protestant Dissent*, pp. 106–7. In 1695–1696 funds from the *regium donum* were used to send Presbyterian commissioners to Scotland and to call on William. MLM, 2:299, 422.

49. [John MacBride], *A Vindication of Marriage, as Solemnized by Presbyterians in the North of Ireland* ([Belfast?], 1702), sig. A2r–v.

50. [Tisdall], *Conduct*, pp. 19–27.

51. PRONI MSS 4 / 4 / 4 (1); 4 / 4 / 4 (2); 4 / 4 / 4 / (3) (quoted); 4 / 4 / 4 / (5) (quoted); 4 / 4 / 4 / (6); APL Dopping Correspondence, vol. 2, no. 232 (quoted). S.J. Connolly sagely cautions against relying overmuch on contemporary depictions of the Church of Ireland's financial state. Undoubtedly the financial picture was significantly better 25 to 50 years following the end of the war, as Connolly contends, but in the mid-1690s the physical impression of devastation would have been potent. *Religion, Law, and Power: The Making of Protestant Ireland 1660–1760* (Oxford: Clarendon Press, 1992), pp. 181–82.

52. DML MSS Z.3.1.4, fols. 142–62. To meet some of Meath's needs, Henry Compton, bishop of London, urged Dopping to use episcopalian clergy driven from Scotland after the revolution. APL Dopping Correspondence, vol. 2, nos. 227 and 234. The number of parish churches in decent repair in 1693 was only 25. See the analysis by Philippe Loupès, "Bishop Dopping's Visitation of the Diocese of Meath 1693," *Studia Hibernia* 24 (1988–1989): 127–51.

53. PRONI MSS DIO 4 / 5 / 3 (23) (quoted); RCBL MSS 31 / 5, fols. 297–301.

54. APL Dopping Correspondence, vol. 3, nos. 256 (quoted), 289 (quoted).

55. DMunL Gilbert MSS 27, fols. 177 / 167–178 / 168.

56. APL Dopping Correspondence, vol. 2, nos. 227, 234.

57. Beckett, *Protestant Dissent*, pp. 35–38; [Tisdall], *Conduct*, pp. 17–18 (quoted); L. M. Cullen, *An Economic History of Ireland Since 1660* (London: B. T. Batsford, 1972), p. 35; W. H. Crawford, "Drapers and Bleachers in the Early Ulster Linen Industry," *Négoce et Industrie en France et en Irlande aux XVIIIe et*

XIXe Siècles, ed. L. M. Cullen and P. Butel (Paris: Centre National de la Recherche Scientifique, 1980), pp. 113–14, 116–17; David Dickson, *New Foundations: Ireland 1660–1800* (Dublin: Helicon, 1987), p. 49.

58. APL Dopping Correspondence, vol. 2, no. 197.

59. APL Dopping Correspondence, vol. 2, no. 205; Beckett, *Protestant Dissent*, p. 29.

60. DF Sharp MSS S7, fol. 32r; Beckett, *Protestant Dissent*, pp. 31–34.

61. *Great Archbishop*, ed. Simeon, p. 35; J. C. Beckett, "William King's Administration of the Diocese of Derry, 1691–1703," *Irish Historical Studies* 4 (September 1944): 171–72.

62. APL Dopping Correspondence, vol. 3, no. 289.

63. APL Dopping Correspondence, vol. 3, no. 287 (quoted); Beckett, *Protestant Dissent*, p. 37.

64. William King, *A Discourse Concerning the Inventions of Men in the Worship of God*, 2nd ed. (London, 1694), pp. 170–78. See also Kilroy, pp. 175–78. Oliver Plunkett had previously attacked the Presbyterians for repudiating set prayers, including the Lord's prayer. *The Letters of Saint Oliver Plunkett 1625–1681, Archbishop of Armagh and Primate of All Ireland*, ed. John Hanly (Dublin: Dolmen Press, 1979), p. 443.

65. King, *Discourse*, pp. 187–88.

66. J[oseph] Boyse, *Remarks on a Late Discourse of William Lord Bishop of Derry: Concerning the Inventions of Men in the Worship of God* (London, 1694), *passim*; Robert Craghead, *An Answer to the Bishop of Derry['s] Second Admonition to the Dissenting Inhabitants in His Diocess* (1698), *passim*; *Great Archbishop*, ed. Simeon, pp. 37–38. King responded to Boyse in *An Admonition to the Dissenting Inhabitants of the Diocese of Derry* (Dublin, 1694) and *A Second Admonition* (Dublin, 1695). Craghead's *Answer* responded to the latter and was composed at the request of the Presbyterian James Lennox, mayor of Derry. See the thoughtful discussion of this debate in Kilroy, pp. 178–87.

67. APL Dopping Correspondence, vol. 3, no. 256.

68. Samuel Foley, *An Exhortation to the Inhabitants of Down and Connor, Concerning the Religious Education of Their Children* (Dublin, 1695), fol. A2r–v, pp. 1–2, 4, 7–8, 14–15 (quoted), 25–27.

69. Beckett, *Protestant Dissent*, pp. 40–41; *Synod*, pp. 32–33.

70. NLS Wodrow MSS Quarto XXVIII, fol. 107r.

71. NLS Wodrow MSS Quarto XXVIII, fol. 107v.

72. *Synod*, p. 26; NLS Wodrow MSS Quarto XXVIII, fol. 107v.

73. NLS Wodrow MSS Quarto XXVIII, fol. 107r; Reid, *History*, 2:484ff.

74. *Synod*, p. 39; Clarke H. Irwin, *A History of Presbyterianism in Dublin and the South and West of Ireland* (London: Hodder and Stoughton, 1890), p. 15, note 1.

75. *CSPD 1699–1700*, p. 241; Beckett, *Protestant Dissent*, pp. 117–18; *Synod*, pp. 53, 61. At the same time the bishop of Raphoe was prosecuting nonconformists for refusing to use the Book of Common Prayer at funerals. *CSPD 1699–1700*, p. 241.

76. [MacBride], *Vindication*, sig. A2v. For replies to this work see Ralph Lam-

bert, *An Answer to a Late Pamphlet* (Dublin, 1704) and Edward Synge, *A Defence of the Establish'd Church and Laws* (Dublin, 1705). See also Kilroy, pp. 195–98.

77. J. G. Simms, "The Making of a Penal Law," *Irish Historical Studies* 12 (1960–61): 105–18; Beckett, *Protestant Dissent*, pp. 43–45.

78. Connolly, *Religion, Law, and Power*, p. 163; [Kirkpatrick], *Historical Essay*, pp. 427 (quoted), 451; DMunL Gilbert MSS 27, fols. 177–78 / 167–68, 179 / 169 (quoted), 181 / 171, 189 / 179. For other comments on the prevalence of nonconformists in the north see [Tisdall], *Conduct*, p. 18; [MacBride], *Vindication*, sig. A2r; DMunL Gilbert MSS 189, fol. 127. In 1694 Nathaniel Foy, bishop of Waterford, attributed the conformists' failure to reduce Catholics and nonconformists to obedience by "salutary discipline" to the obstructionist common law courts. APL Dopping Correspondence, vol. 3, no. 257.

79. DMunL Gilbert MSS 27, fol. 186 / 176.

CHAPTER 4

1. Raymond Gillespie, "Dissenters and Nonconformists, 1661–1700" (unpublished manuscript [1994]).

2. NLS Wodrow MSS Octavo XII, fols. 1r–4v; James Seaton Reid, *History of the Presbyterian Church in Ireland*, ed. W. D. Killen, 2 vols. (Belfast: William Mullan, 1867), 2:589–91; Kilroy, p. 25; Michael R. Watts, *The Dissenters: From the Reformation to the French Revolution* (Oxford: Clarendon Press, 1978), p. 509.

3. Kilroy, p. 42; Clarke H. Irwin, *A History of Presbyterianism in Dublin and the South and West of Ireland* (London: Hodder and Stoughton, 1890), pp. 165, 237.

4. Alexander Gordon and G. K. Smith, *Historic Memorials of the First Presbyterian Church of Belfast* (Belfast: Marcus Ward, 1887), p. 10; James Armstrong, "History of the Presbyterian Churches in the City of Dublin," appendix to *Ordination Service* (London: Hunter; Dublin: Burnside, 1829), pp. 85–86.

5. Irwin, *History of Presbyterianism*, pp. 230, 281, 290, 299, 307–8; Kilroy, pp. 45, 71–72, 75. The Congregationalists and Presbyterians at Dundalk, county Louth, united in the 1690s to form a single (Presbyterian) church. Raymond Gillespie, "The Transformation of the Borderlands, 1600–1700," in *The Borderlands: Essays on the History of the Ulster-Leinster Border*, ed. Gillespie and Harold O'Sullivan (Belfast: Institute of Irish Studies, Queen's University of Belfast, 1989), p. 78.

6. MLM, 1:162–63, 328.

7. Adair, p. 291. For the interchangeability of "meeting" and "presbytery" see MLM, 1:135, 137–39, 141.

8. MAM 1671–91, fols. 16, 141, 156, 176, 335; MLM, 1:140, 164, 201–2, 229, 249, 266; 2:74, 158, 411. Commencing in January 1672 the Antrim meeting asked each church to contribute half a crown for the clerk's stipend (fol. 16).

9. MLM, 1:112, 198–99, 299, 301; 2:33, 41, 430B; MAM 1671–91, fols. 121–22.

10. MLM, 1:294 (quoted), 298–99, 301; 2:133, 361–62; *Synod*, p. 7.

11. The thirteen gatherings of the Lagan presbytery between August 1672 and November 1673 averaged 3.3 elders, and this doubled to 6.4 in the period from January 1674 to July 1681. Twice—in August 1679 and May 1680—twelve

elders were present, and eleven elders were in attendance five times. The average number of elders at the Antrim meeting between October 1687 and February 1689 was 11.25, but this dropped to 4.2 in the tense period from March 1689 to September 1690 before rising to an average of 10.8 between November 1690 and December 1691, the latter stages of the war notwithstanding. Gatherings of the Lagan presbytery between December 1690 and October 1691 averaged 3.3 elders, or a mere 2.6 if the last month (when 8 attended) is omitted. Between January 1692 and April 1695, as the country returned to normal, the average number of elders attending the Lagan presbytery rose to 4.8. Some elders in this presbytery, of course, would have found it more difficult to participate in meetings than would their counterparts in the Antrim presbytery because of the greater distances to travel. These averages include special meetings, some of which had multiple sessions; elders' attendance fluctuated from session to session. The averages cited here reflect only the initial sessions.

12. MLM, 1:88, 101–3, 120, 137, 141, 167; 2:20, 34, 213, 269, 466–67.

13. MLM, 1:333; 2:113, 288; MAM 1671–91, fols. 331, 336, 345, 353, 374.

14. *Synod*, pp. 22 (quoted), 26–28; MLM, 2:90.

15. MAM 1671–91, fols. 209, 460–61; MLM, 1:104–5; 2:250.

16. MLM, 1:37, 63, 72, 184 (quoted); 2:194, 460–61.

17. MLM, 1:331; 2:110, 222, 490.

18. MAM 1671–91, fols. 194, 204, 368, 438.

19. MLM, 1:186, 294; 2:225, 231, 439–40; MAM 1671–91, fols. 239, 241, 270, 484.

20. MAM 1671–91, fols. 339, 344, 352; MLM, 2:473, 519; *Synod*, pp. 23–24, 26–28, 30 (quoted).

21. For examples of the latter type of visitation see MAM 1671–91, fols. 123, 128, 428; MLM, 1:42, 93; 2:207, 218. Cf. Kilroy, pp. 19–20.

22. MAM 1671–91, fols. 128, 139, 155 (quoted).

23. MLM, 2:437–39. For other examples see MLM, 2:92–93, 405–6, 411–12; MAM 1671–91, fols. 280, 322, 380–81, 502–4.

24. MAM 1671–91, fols. 7, 9–10, 13, 20–21, 25 (quoted).

25. MAM 1671–91, fols. 29, 39–40, 43–44, 46, 50–51 (quoted), 52–53, 57 (quoted).

26. MAM 1671–91, fols. 57, 64, 84, 87, 127, 133, 153.

27. MAM 1671–91, fols. 206–7, 209–11, 215, 220, 222, 231–33, 238, 242–43 (quoted).

28. MAM 1671–91, fols. 248, 251–52 (quoted), 256.

29. MAM 1671–91, fols. 262 (quoted), 264–65, 267, 270–71, 295 (quoted), 297–98 (quoted), 302, 306–7 (quoted), 311–12.

30. MAM 1671–91, fols. 314–15, 320, 324–25, 329, 333, 340, 394, 398, 402, 409, 418, 439.

31. MAM 1671–91, fol. 8 (quoted); NLS Wodrow MSS Folio XXVI, fols. 217r, 221r (quoted).

32. MAM 1671–91, fols. 30–32 (quoted), 43–44, 48–50, 54; MLM, 1:7–8 (quoted). Kilroy (p. 120) implausibly attributes the division to contention involving the Covenanters because the Lagan presbytery also discussed the Act of

Bangor. MLM, 1:8. The juxtaposition of the two issues in the minutes, however, does not prove linkage, particularly since neither Jacque nor Keyes was a militant Covenanter.

33. MAM 1671–91, fols. 66, 75, 94–95, 119–21, 193 (quoted); MLM, 1:28, 53, 57.

34. MLM, 1:242, 246; 2:93–94.

35. MAM 1671–91, fols. 213–14, 217–18 (quoted).

36. MAM 1671–91, fols. 223–24, 226, 229–30, 234–35.

37. MAM 1671–91, fols. 241, 246–47, 250, 252–55, 257, 259–60, 262–63, 265, 279.

38. MAM 1671–91, fols. 266, 281–83 (quoted), 288–89, 291; Kilroy, pp. 129–30.

39. MAM 1671–91, fols. 2 (quoted), 153–54, 171–72, 372–73, 408, 539; MLM, 1:26; 2:195–96, 198, 217–18.

40. MLM, 2:17–19 (quoted), 22, 27–28 (quoted).

41. MAM 1671–91, fols. 2–3, 164; MLM, 1:7, 114, 335–36; 2:14, 21, 27.

42. MAM 1671–91, fols. 2, 16, 325; MLM, 1:41, 62, 121, 174.

43. Adair, p. 293 (quoted); MAM 1671–91, fols. 3, 44, 60–61, 66–67, 120, 163–64, 213, 216, 240, 286–87; MLM, 1:41, 114, 181–83, 218–21, 333–34; 2:59, 64, 304–5.

44. MAM 1671–91, fols. 335, 350, 413 (quoted), 459–60, 494; *Synod*, p. 1. The Lagan presbytery had objected to holding the 1692 synod in Belfast. MLM, 2:108–9. The Lagan minutes for August 1672 refer to Presbyterians in Ulster as a synod, an explicit recognition of their unity even if a formal synod could not sit. MLM, 1:7.

45. MAM 1671–91, fol. 519; MLM, 2:125, 157, 367; *Synod*, pp. 22, 26, 28–29.

46. *Synod*, pp. 1, 13, 16–18, 20–22, 24, 28–29, 35; MLM, 2:456–59.

47. *Synod*, pp. 25, 30, 33, 36–45 *passim*.

48. MLM, 2:139, 391–97; *Synod*, pp. 23–24, 32, 57–58.

49. Data from McConnell, *Fasti*; Hew Scott, *Fasti Ecclesiae Scoticanae: The Succession of Ministers in the Church of Scotland from the Reformation*, rev. ed., 7 vols. (Edinburgh: Oliver and Boyd, 1915–1928); *Calamy Revised*; MLM, preface; Bodl. Carte MSS 45, fol. 446r; Carte 36, fol. 511r–v; HMC 36, *Ormonde*, n.s., 5:125. I have excluded seven Presbyterian ministers—Mungo Bennett, William Brown, William Caldwell, Donald Richmond, Andrew Rowan, Robert Rowan, and George Wallace—who conformed by 1661. James Fleming, who was ejected in 1661 and conformed approximately a year later, is included. English clergy such as Lancelot Smith, Henry Staples, and Robert Wood, who were ejected in England and subsequently went to Ireland but apparently did not serve as ministers, are omitted. So too is John Pinney; though he was licensed as a Presbyterian in England in 1672, he served a Congregationalist church in Dublin as Thomas Harrison's successor for a decade. I have included four English ministers who served as chaplains in Ireland: Edward Bagshaw (to Anglesey, though in Ireland only from July to September 1662), Noah Bryan (to Donegall), John Howe (to Massereene), and James Small (also to Massereene).

50. McConnell does not provide the date when James Pitcairn received his M.A. degree from St. Andrews. *Fasti*, 3:79.

51. *Synod*, pp. 6, 57. Of the 619 Presbyterians who ministered in Ireland in the eighteenth century, 71 percent were sons of farmers, 20 percent sons of clergy, 4

percent sons of merchants (mostly late in the century), 4 percent unknown, and one percent other. John M. Barkley, "The Presbyterian Minister in Eighteenth Century Ireland," in *Challenge and Conflict: Essays in Irish Presbyterian History and Doctrine*, ed. J. L. M. Haire (Antrim: W. and G. Baird, 1981), p. 49.

52. MAM 1671–91, fols. 3, 5 (quoted).

53. MAM 1671–91, fols. 6–7 (quoted), 11, 15 (quoted).

54. Cf. MLM, 1:289; 2:366, 368; MAM 1671–91, fol. 442.

55. MAM 1671–91, fols. 19 (quoted), 21–24, 26 (quoted).

56. MAM 1671–91, fols. 18–19 (quoted), 25, 32–33 (quoted). With respect to the role of the presbytery in assessing a candidate, the Antrim meeting qualified its acceptance, insisting this requirement "shall not extend to those who are new and has stayed long in the countrye." Ibid., fol. 37.

57. MAM 1671–91, fols. 34–35 (quoted); MLM, 1:24 (quoted).

58. MAM 1671–91, fols. 35–36 (quoted), 37–38. In lieu of heavily theological common heads, the Lagan meeting preferred cases of conscience, but it seems not to have pushed the issue. MLM, 1:24.

59. MAM 1671–91, fols. 36, 38.

60. MAM 1671–91, fols. 37–38; MLM, 1:24. In 1671 the earl of Tweeddale suspected that Presbyterians in western Scotland were preparing to send expectants to England and Ireland for trial and ordination. NLS MSS 7025, fol. 9r–v.

61. MAM 1671–91, fols. 2, 434; MLM, 1:38; 2:471. In June 1698 the synod of Ulster insisted that expectants and probationers be subject to the meetings in whose districts they resided and that they not go to another presbytery without adequate testimonials. *Synod*, p. 33.

62. MLM, 1:221, 225, 227–30, 251, 254, 256–57.

63. MAM 1671–91, fols. 5, 20, 27, 102, 107, 383, 389, 396, 398–99; MLM, 1:86, 95, 181, 198, 221, 240; 2:160 (quoted), 280, 282, 373–74, 416, 418, 503–4, 530, 533.

64. MAM 1671–91, fols. 21, 320, 326, 340; MLM, 1:4–5.

65. MAM 1671–91, fols. 72, 248, 253, 340–41, 347, 448, 450.

66. MAM 1671–91, fols. 21, 27, 41, 47, 72, 74, 89, 100, 186, 238, 244, 248, 298, 302, 317, 398, 402, 409; MLM, 1:54.

67. MAM 1671–91, fols. 85, 95, 101; MLM, 2:283–84, 318, 416, 426, 428.

68. MLM, 1:101–2, 182.

69. MLM, 2:60; *Synod*, pp. 13–14, 20, 29, 38, 43, 48, 55, 57.

70. Cf. e.g. MLM, 1:222, 236, 240, 281, 286; MAM 1671–91, fols. 107, 126–27, 242, 271, 274, 283. At least some of these calls were signed. MAM 1671–91, fols. 106–7, 457.

71. MAM 1671–91, fols. 91, 98, 457, 462, 469, 472, 475.

72. MAM 1671–91, fols. 259, 304–5, 318, 323, 331–32, 341, 354, 365, 371, 377, 385–86, 396–97, 403, 437–38.

73. MAM 1671–91, fol. 356.

74. MAM 1671–91, fols. 363–65, 372–73, 419.

75. MLM, 1:4, 30, 85–86, 170, 216, 249; 2:292; MAM 1671–91, fol. 2.

76. MLM, 1:12–13, 126; MAM 1671–91, fols. 283, 287, 294, 341, 514 (quoted).

77. NLS Wodrow MSS Folio XXVI, fol. 212r; MLM, 2:371.

78. MLM, 1:185, 190–91.

79. MLM, 2:51–52.

80. MLM, 1:97, 295, 306 (quoted), 311; 2:505.

81. MAM 1671–91, fols. 86 (quoted), 141.

82. MAM 1671–91, fols. 107 (quoted), 113.

83. MLM, 2:138–39, 144, 209 (quoted).

84. MAM 1671–91, fols. 91, 137, 253 (quoted), 257.

85. MAM 1671–91, fols. 437–38, 452–53 (quoted), 462, 465, 467–69, 475.

86. MLM, 1:188, 192–93 (quoted).

87. MLM, 1:253, 259 (quoted); 2:58–59 (quoted), 65–66, 69–70. See also the cases of William Holmes, MLM, 2:137–38, 141–45 *passim*, 150; Samuel Halliday, ibid., 2:169; and others, 2:263, 265, 300, 369, 371–72, 374, 386–87.

88. *Synod*, pp. 36–37, 41–42.

89. MLM, 1:269–70, 284, 303, 310; 2:37, 124, 157–58, 359–60; MAM 1671–91, fols. 158, 177; *Synod*, pp. 10, 18.

90. MAM 1671–91, fols. 319, 343, 390–91, 413 (quoted); MLM, 1:27, 284. Ministers who stayed away from their parishes too long received orders from the presbyteries or synod to return. MLM, 2:340, 349, 360; *Synod*, pp. 9, 14.

91. MAM 1671–91, fols. 141, 334–35, 389; MLM, 1:1, 29, 35, 94, 169, 193; MLM, 2:81, 168; *Synod*, p. 2; Raymond Gillespie, "The Presbyterian Revolution in Ulster, 1660–1690," *The Churches, Ireland and the Irish*, ed. W. J. Sheils and Diana Wood (Oxford: Basil Blackwell for the Ecclesiastical History Society, 1989), p. 166.

92. NLS Wodrow MSS Quarto LXXIII, fols. 48r, 60r, 91r–v; Folio XXXIV, fol. 83r; J. C. Beckett, "William King's Administration of the Diocese of Derry, 1691–1703," *Irish Historical Studies* 4 (September 1944): 167; Pinney, p. 86. Cf. the undated plea (probably written in 1689) from the session at Glasgow seeking the services of Craghead and Thomas Kennedy: "We must still hope that you will be so tender of our desolat case & many sad circumstances." Wodrow MSS Quarto XXVIII, fol. 77r.

93. MAM 1671–91, fols. 148–49; MLM, 1:27, 158–59, 230–31; 2:47, 69–70, 113–14, 494. Cf. MAM 1671–91, fols. 417, 426, 447–48.

94. MAM 1671–91, fols. 382, 387, 390, 412.

95. MAM 1671–91, fols. 166–67, 169, 171–72, 174–75 (quoted).

96. *Synod*, pp. 20–21 (quoted), 23.

97. MLM, 1:25.

98. MLM, 1:26, 170, 172–73; MAM 1671–91, fol. 60. Cf. MLM, 1:180, 190–91, 195, 197, 210, 212, 216, 224, 227.

99. McConnell, *Fasti*, 2:44; MAM 1671–91, fols. 9, 11–12, 14, 18, 24, 28, 39, 43, 52, 56, 62, 67–70, 73, 76, 81, 86, 97, 101, 106–7, 113, 117, 122, 126–27, 131, 137, 153–54, 159.

100. MAM 1671–91, fols. 50, 56, 62, 68, 70–73, 76–77, 81, 83–84, 87–88, 97, 104, 112, 116, 122–23, 126, 130, 134–35 (quoted), 136–37, 143–44, 147–48, 157, 161, 166–67, 169, 171–72, 174–75.

101. MLM, 1:52, 55–56, 60–61, 75–76, 92, 153, 217, 253, 255–56, 260, 268–69, 333; 2:42–43, 55–56, 67–68, 126, 128, 195, 201, 206, 210–11, 238, 346–47, 433, 444–45, 487.

102. MLM, 1:257, 278; 2:423–24, 491; MAM 1671–91, fols. 342, 404, 411–12; *Synod*, pp. 22, 30, 37. Cf. MLM, 2:466, 471, 509; *Synod*, pp. 3, 29.

103. MAM 1671–91, fols. 137, 397, 452, 456, 533; MLM, 1:121, 153, 165, 268; 2:62, 67, 135, 169–70, 212, 223, 276, 314, 327, 430A, 459, 514, 517, 540; *Synod*, pp. 2, 4; BKS, entry for 30 April 1678.

104. MAM 1671–91, fols. 124 (quoted), 182 (quoted).

105. MAM 1671–91, fols. 18, 132; *Synod*, pp. 6, 10–11; MLM, 1:220.

106. MLM, 1:168, 192, 198, 235; MAM 1671–91, fols. 306, 528–29, 533, 537.

107. MAM 1671–91, fols. 117–18, 144–45, 149, 151–52, 160–61, 170–71.

108. MAM 1671–91, fols. 219, 221–22, 276–532 *passim*; for Ahoghill see fol. 503.

109. MLM, 1:55–166 *passim*; 2:132–276 *passim*.

110. Cf. e.g. MLM, 1:142–43, 159.

111. MLM, 2:426, 441.

112. See e.g. Bodl. Carte MSS 36, fol. 511r–v; Carte 45, fol. 446r. Gillespie overstates the use of secular settings in the 1670s. "Presbyterian Revolution," p. 163.

113. MLM, 1:6; MAM 1671–91, fol. 58. According to John Stevenson the meetinghouses in county Down were thatched structures with a t-shaped groundplan. *Two Centuries of Life in Down 1600–1800* (Belfast: McCaw, Stevenson and Orr, 1920), p. 141.

114. MAM 1671–91, fol. 105; Kirkdonald Session Book, entries for 15 February 1685; 8 March 1686; August 1686; 30 November 1686; 28 November 1687. The Kirkdonald Session Book is blank from 1688 to 1693, subsequent to which rents are not mentioned for the rest of the century.

115. MAM 1671–91, fols. 57, 93; MLM, 1:61, 85 (quoted).

116. MLM, 1:4; 2:115, 267 (quoted), 347. The aisle built at Termonmaguirk by the people of Drumragh may have been intended in part to enable them to sit together. In 1647 the Templepatrick church asked its members south of the river dividing the parish to sit on the south side of the church; those living north of the river were to sit on the north side. W. T. Latimer, "The Old Session-Book of Templepatrick Church," *Journal of the Royal Society of Antiquaries of Ireland* 31 (1901): 264.

117. MLM, 2:516–17.

118. MAM 1671–91, fols. 127, 132; MLM, 1:217.

119. MAM 1671–91, fols. 381, 388–89, 398, 404, 410, 427; MLM, 2:277, 290, 296, 303, 316.

120. MLM, 2:302, 447 (quoted), 449, 485.

121. MLM, 1:13 (quoted), 20. The site is identified as Carnamadie, which is not to be confused with Carnamaddy, county Antrim. William Hampton often preached at the former. BKS, *passim*.

122. MLM, 1:267, 273, 279 (quoted), 286, 314, 316.

123. MLM, 1:321, 335; 2:13 (quoted), 16, 36–37, 76, 450.

124. MAM 1671–91, fols. 138, 163, 379, 387, 399, 404, 411.

125. MAM 1671–91, fols. 378, 385, 396, 428, 434, 440, 445, 449, 493, 513, 527, 536, 542. In 1698 the church at Down, unable to reach an agreement with Presby-

terians at Ballee concerning the location of a meetinghouse, requested mediation by the synod of Ulster, but the latter referred the dispute to the presbytery of Down. *Synod*, p. 31.

126. MLM, 1:316–17 (quoted); 2:52 (quoted), 77, 79–80, 82.

127. MLM, 2:439, 467, 472, 485 (quoted).

128. *Synod*, p. 33.

129. E.g. MLM, 1:73, 132, 296–317 *passim*, 331.

130. *Synod*, p. 33; MLM, 1:317.

131. MLM, 1:15–16.

132. MLM, 1:335; 2:13; *Synod*, p. 25.

133. MAM 1671–91, fols. 336, 381–82.

134. Bodl. Carte MSS 36, fol. 205r. Previously imprisoned on suspicion of complicity in the Dublin plot, Cunningham had been released because of Massereene's intervention. In 1675 the Lagan meeting sought Massereene's intervention with the bishop of Raphoe on behalf of a Letterkenny man. McConnell, *Fasti*, 2:11; MLM, 1:188.

135. [James Seaton Reid], *History of Congregations of the Presbyterian Church in Ireland and Biographical Notices of Eminent Presbyterian Ministers and Laymen*, ed. W. D. Killen (Belfast: James Cleeland, 1886), pp. 15–16; *DNB*, s.v. John Howe; MAM 1671–91, fols. 82–83 (quoted), 88–89, 102–3; Bodl. Carte MSS 36, fol. 511r.

136. MAM 1671–91, fols. 108–11 (quoted), 114, 117. Antrim Presbyterians subsequently sought Lord and Lady Massereene's assistance in matters involving Gowan's arrears and a replacement following his death. The presbytery also sought their help in resolving a dispute over the possible merger of Duneane and Grange. MAM 1671–91, fols. 222, 249–50, 404–5.

137. MAM 1671–91, fols. 225, 234, 241, 244, 286.

138. MLM, 2:93–94; MAM 1671–91, fols. 99, 104–5. The author of *An Apology for, or Vindication of the Oppressed Persecuted Ministers & Professors of the Presbyterian Reformed Religion, in the Church of Scotland* ([Edinburgh], 1677)—Alexander Jamieson or Hugh Smith—expressed an ecumenical view concerning Presbyterians and Congregationalists, between whom, he averred, the differences were slight and could be resolved "if there were a healing condescending temper" (p. 22). For cooperation between dissenters around the turn of the century see Kilroy, pp. 44–47, 73.

139. DWL Baxter MSS, 3:76r.

140. DWL Baxter MSS, 3:76r–v.

141. DWL Baxter MSS, 3:78r–v.

142. MLM, 1:7, 76–78; MAM 1671–91, fols. 70 (quoted), 77, 82.

143. MAM 1671–91, fol. 164; MLM, 1:122 (quoted), 133, 158, 162–63 (quoted), 168–69, 194–95, 208, 213–14, 218, 225, 237, 244, 328.

144. Liam Irwin, "Politics, Religion and Economy: Cork in the 17th Century," *Journal of the Cork Historical and Archaeological Society* 85 (1980): 20; MLM, 2:93; MAM 1671–91, fols. 330 (quoted), 337–38. Recurring shortages in financial support and clergy dampened but did not still a missionary impulse among Scottish Presbyterians in Ireland. The most obvious field—the Gaelic Irish—was geographically at hand but culturally remote owing to the language barrier that

only the rarest minister could bridge. John Darroch was one such, as were John Simpson, Patrick Simpson, and Archibald McClean. In 1699, when Dublin Presbyterians wanted to visit Ulster on a preaching tour, they asked the synod of Ulster to provide one or two ministers who could preach to the Gaelic Irish while they addressed the British; the synod appointed McClean to provide this service. *Synod*, p. 38; Gillespie, "The Transformation of the Borderlands," p. 78. Further afield the Americas beckoned. In 1678 Captain Archibald Johnston wrote to members of the Lagan meeting requesting the service of a minister for Barbados. Johnston's agent, William Denniston, told the presbytery that such an effort would enjoy both liberty and encouragement, but the meeting declined to approve the mission without knowing what support would be forthcoming. When Lagan received a request from Maryland for a minister in early 1680 it sought the advice of the other presbyteries. Tyrone and Down thought the time was not right but they sought further information, and the following year Lagan ordained Francis Mackemie, who left for Virginia. The minutes indicate only minimal contact between Irish Presbyterians and New England; the minister William Holmes was welcomed back from the latter in 1691 by the Lagan meeting. MLM, 1:312–13; 2:82–83, 85–86, 119, 349–50; McConnell, *Fasti*, 3:77; MAM 1671–91, fol. 263. The Lagan presbytery invited Josias McKee to join it if he decided to leave Virginia. MLM, 2:228.

145. Irwin, *History of Presbyterianism*, pp. 32–35; B. R. White, "The Twilight of Puritanism in the Years Before and After 1688," in *From Persecution to Toleration: The Glorious Revolution in England*, ed. Ole Peter Grell, Jonathan I. Israel, and Nicholas Tyacke (Oxford: Clarendon Press, 1991), pp. 325–28.

146. MLM, 1:64, 68, 73, 88; Kilroy, pp. 145–46.

147. MAM 1671–91, fols. 77–78 (quoted), 82, 206 (quoted); MLM, 2:64, 79, 82, 85. The "treatise against error" which the general committee requested and the Antrim meeting commissioned Gowan and Howe to write may have been the proposed refutation of the Quakers. MAM 1671–91, fol. 120.

148. MAM 1671–91, fols. 212, 254–55, 257, 259, 268, 286.

149. Bodl. Carte MSS 36, fol. 490r; MAM 1671–91, fols. 3–4 (quoted), 5–6; McConnell, *Fasti*, 3:68.

150. NLS Wodrow MSS Folio XXVI, fols. 218r, 219r (quoted), 222r (quoted), 224r, 225r, 227r (quoted); MAM 1671–91, fols. 25–26, 53–54, 58–59, 64, 78–79, 83, 90–91, 97, 106 (quoted), 140–41; MLM, 1:7, 23.

151. NLS Wodrow MSS Folio LIX, fol. 203r.

152. *A True Account of a New and Strange Sect* (London, 1681); Richard L. Greaves, *Secrets of the Kingdom: British Radicals from the Popish Plot to the Revolution of 1688–1689* (Stanford: Stanford University Press, 1992), pp. 62, 69–75.

153. Greaves, *Secrets of the Kingdom*, pp. 81–86; EUL MSS La.III.344.2, no. 64 (quoted); Michael Shields, *Faithful Contendings Displayed* (Glasgow: John Bryce, 1780), pp. 50–51.

154. W. H. Carslaw, *The Life and Letters of James Renwick the Last Scottish Martyr* (Edinburgh: Oliphant, Anderson and Ferrier, 1893), pp. 65–66 (quoted), 68–69 (quoted).

155. EUL MSS La.III.350, fol. 79r.

156. PRO SP 63 / 343 / 162.1 (quoted), 162.2, 162.3 (quoted), 162.4, 162.6.

157. PRO SP 63 / 343 / 162 (quoted), 162.3, 162.5 (quoted), 165, 166.

158. EUL MSS La.III.350, no. 177.

159. EUL MSS La.III.344.1, entries for 24 June and 22 September 1686; MSS La.III.350, no. 209 (1) and (2).

160. MAM 1671–91, fols. 299–300, 302–3, 307, 312–13, 315–16, 321–22, 331, 336, 339, 351–52, 358–59, 379, 386–87, 396, 426.

161. EUL MSS La.III.350, no. 216.

162. EUL MSS La.III.344.1, entry for 22 December 1686; MSS La.III.350, no. 209 (2) (quoted).

163. EUL MSS La.III.344.2, no. 210 (quoted); MSS La.III.344.1, entry for 1 June 1687; Carslaw, *Life and Letters of Renwick*, pp. 231, 246–47.

164. EUL MSS La.III.350, no. 231.

165. NLS MSS 5408, fol. 50r–v.

166. NLS MSS 5408, fols. 50v–54r.

167. EUL MSS La.III.344.1, entry for June 1688; Ian B. Cowan, *The Scottish Covenanters 1660–1688* (London: Victor Gollancz, 1976), p. 132; EUL MSS La.III.350, nos. 232 (quoted) and 240 (quoted).

168. MAM 1671–91, fols. 494–95, 505, 509–10 (quoted), 515; *Synod*, pp. 5–6 (quoted), 11; *The Montgomery Manuscripts (1603–1706)*, comp. William Montgomery and ed. George Hill (Belfast: James Cleeland and Thomas Dargan, 1869), p. 274; Adam Loughridge, *The Covenanters in Ireland: A History of the Reformed Presbyterian Church of Ireland* (Belfast: Cameron Press, 1984), p. 13. Cf. *Synod*, p. 32. In 1694 Houston reportedly preached to a congregation of 500 at Armey, county Antrim. Kilroy, p. 116.

169. John Macmillan came from Scotland to minister to the small bands of radical Covenanters in Ireland in 1707 and 1715. Kilroy, p. 133.

CHAPTER 5

1. *Synod*, p. 25.

2. McConnell, *Fasti*, 3:77.

3. PHSI MS Sermons of John McKenzie on Romans 8:32 (28 August 1681; quoted); 2 Peter 2:7 (17 July 1681); Colossians 2:6 [14 or 21 August 1681] (quoted).

4. PHSI MS Sermons of McKenzie on Colossians 2:6 [14 or 21 August 1681]; Matthew 11:28 (24 July 1681); Psalm 27:4 (7 August 1681).

5. PHSI MS Sermons of McKenzie on Psalm 51:7 (11 September 1681); 1 Peter 5:8 (11 December 1681); 2 Peter 2:7 (17 July 1681); 1 Peter 3:19 (November 1681); Song of Solomon 1:4 (4 September 1681); 1 Peter 3:18 [October or November 1681] (quoted); Matthew 11:29 (31 July 1681; quoted); Psalm 27:4 (7 August 1681); Romans 8:32 (28 August 1681); 1 Peter 1:17 (25 December 1681).

6. EUL MSS La.II.27.1, fols. 80–83. Cf. the similar tone of Alexander Peden (though he preached this sermon in Scotland): *Sermons Delivered in Times of Persecution in Scotland, by Sufferers for the Royal Prerogatives of Jesus Christ*, ed. John Howie (Edinburgh: Johnstone, Hunter, 1880), p. 559.

7. EUL MSS La.II.27.1, fols. 84–85.

8. MAM 1671–91, fol. 386; McConnell, *Fasti*, 3:77.

9. MLM, 2:220; *Synod*, p. 21; Raymond Gillespie, "The Presbyterian Revolution in Ulster, 1660–1690," in *The Churches, Ireland and the Irish*, ed. W. J. Sheils and Diana Wood (Oxford: Basil Blackwell for the Ecclesiastical History Society, 1989), p. 164.

10. I am indebted to Dr. Ian Green for this data.

11. *Calamy Revised*, s.v.

12. GL, Robert Chambers, "An Explanation of the Shorter Catechism of the Reverend Assembly of Divines," fols. 368–69, 372–74, 410. Thomas Hall, minister at Larne, county Antrim, wrote *A Plain and Easy Explication of the Assembly's Shorter Catechism*, which was published at Edinburgh in 1697.

13. *Synod*, p. 333; BKS, *passim*.   14. MLM, 1:252; 2:148, 151, 442.

15. *Synod*, p. 8.   16. MAM 1671–91, fols. 219–20.

17. Quoted in John M. Barkley, *The Eldership in Irish Presbyterianism* ([Belfast]: By the Author, 1963), p. 40; MLM, 1:309.

18. MAM 1671–91, fols. 273 (quoted), 408 (quoted), 411, 419–20 (quoted), 422–23, 431.

19. MAM 1671–91, fols. 505, 509.

20. Marilyn J. Westerkamp, *Triumph of the Laity: Scots-Irish Piety and the Great Awakening, 1625–1760* (New York: Oxford University Press, 1988), pp. 28–34, 59–60; Leigh Eric Schmidt, *Holy Fairs: Scottish Communions and American Revivals in the Early Modern Period* (Princeton, N.J.: Princeton University Press, 1989), pp. 34–35; Richard L. Greaves, *Enemies Under His Feet: Radicals and Nonconformists in Britain, 1664–1677* (Stanford: Stanford University Press, 1990), pp. 52–53, 60–64, 86–96.

21. NLS Wodrow MSS Folio XXVI, fol. 211r–v; *CSPI 1669–70*, pp. 147–48.

22. TKS, fols. 162–63.

23. MLM, 1:27.

24. TKS, fol. 169.

25. BKS, entries for 9, 12–14 October 1678; 8, 11–13 October 1679; 27, 30, 31 July 1681; 1 August 1681; 9, 12–14 August 1682; 25 June 1694.

26. TKS, fol. 171. Cf. Kilroy, pp. 20–21.

27. Westerkamp, *Triumph*, p. 68; BL Stowe MSS 216, fol. 143r; Stowe 214, fol. 232r (quoted); Bodl. Carte MSS 36, fol. 488r; Carte 45, fol. 433r (quoted).

28. Gillespie, "Presbyterian Revolution," p. 164.

29. MLM, 1:170, 186, 262 (quoted).

30. MAM 1671–91, fol. 241; cf. fols. 245–46, 269.

31. MLM, 1:303; 2:18 (quoted), 22; cf. 1:310.

32. MAM 1671–91, fols. 235, 331, 336 (quoted); BL Stowe MSS 214, fol. 232r.

33. MLM, 1:276; 2:420, 462–63, 466, 510; MAM 1671–91, fols. 241 (quoted), 342; *Synod*, pp. 22, 25 (quoted). Cf. MLM, 2:440.

34. John M. Barkley, "The Evidence of Old Irish Session-Books on the Sacrament of the Lord's Supper," *Church Service Society Annual* no. 22 (May 1952): 26–27; MLM, 2:102B-D. Communion at Carnmoney was delayed for a time in 1672 because of "confusiones" in the parish apparently stemming from a member's reputed dealings with a spirit. MAM 1671–91, fols. 54–55.

35. Robert Craghead, *An Answer to the Bishop of Derry['s] Second Admonition to the Dissenting Inhabitants in His Diocess* (1698), pp. 21, 24–25 (quoted).

36. Craghead, *Answer*, p. 23 (quoted); Barkley, "Session-Books," pp. 28, 31; BKS, entry for 5 July 1694; NLS Wodrow MSS Folio XXVIII, fol. 149r (Synod of Glasgow, 1694); [James Kirkpatrick], *An Historical Essay upon the Loyalty of Presbyterians in Great-Britain and Ireland from the Reformation to This Present Year 1713* (1713), pp. 559–60.

37. MLM, 1:334; *Synod*, 1:44–45 (quoted).

38. NLS Wodrow MSS Folio XXVIII, fol. 149r; Barkley, "Session-Books," p. 28.

39. Bodl. Carte MSS 45, fol. 559r.

40. MLM, 1:9, 13–14, 19, 22, 24, 31.

41. MLM, 1:25, 32; MAM 1671–91, fols. 60, 65–66.

42. MLM, 1:322, 326; 2:459; MAM 1671–91, fol. 488; *Synod*, pp. 26, 61–62.

43. MAM 1671–91, fols. 65–66, 146, 172, 435; MLM, 1:58–59, 122; 2:52, 73, 176, 350, 352, 399; *Synod*, p. 31.

44. MAM 1671–91, fol. 115; cf. fol. 146.

45. MLM, 1:114 (quoted); 2:52, 73, 77.

46. MAM 1671–91, fols. 457, 472; MLM, 2:176, 459; *Synod*, pp. 31, 43.

47. MAM 1671–91, fol. 129; cf. fol. 146.

48. NLS Wodrow MSS Folio XXXI, fol. 281r.

49. MAM 1671–91, fols. 59, 66; MLM, 2:43.

50. MAM 1671–91, fol. 462; MLM, 1:151; cf. MLM, 1:287.

51. MLM, 1:58–59; *Synod*, p. 31.

52. MLM, 2:86–88. For a copy in the government's possession see PRO SP 63/342/15.1. In September 1689 the synod of Glasgow called for a fast, in part because of Ireland's distress and "the prevailing of ane anti christian party there." The following January the synod again appointed a fast, in part because of the problems of Protestants in Ireland and France. NLS Wodrow MSS Quarto XXVIII, fols. 78r, 79r.

53. MLM, 1:58–59, 61, 114, 120, 127, 132, 151, 159, 207, 242–43, 250, 287, 289, 322, 326; 2:43, 46, 52, 73, 77, 83, 86–88, 91, 112–13, 119–20, 140, 176, 179, 224, 235, 299, 343–45, 350, 392, 399, 401, 442, 446, 451, 465.

54. MAM 1671–91, fols. 193 (quoted), 266, 268 (quoted), 435, 439–40, 453–54, 456–57, 459–62, 465, 472, 475, 485, 488, 491, 496, 499, 505, 509, 525 (quoted).

55. MAM 1671–91, fols. 411–12, 420; MLM, 2:110, 136, 343–45, 459; *Synod*, pp. 6, 20, 26, 31, 53, 61; *HMC 36, Ormonde*, n.s., 5:125.

56. NLS Wodrow MSS Folio XXXI, fol. 281r; MLM, 1:220; 2:17, 83.

57. MLM, 2:86 (quoted); *Synod*, p. 43; MAM 1671–91, fols. 187, 192, 453–54, 456.

58. MLM, 1:242–43, 250, 286–87 (quoted), 289; Bodl. Carte MSS 221, fol. 452r–v.

59. BKS, entry for 9 December 1680; MLM, 1:73, 86. Like marriages, funerals could also pose problems when burials were prohibited unless they were conducted according to the rites in the Book of Common Prayer. *Synod*, p. 33.

60. MAM 1671–91, fols. 330, 366, 380.

61. BKS, entries for 10 March 1678, 28 March 1680, 2 August 1691; CKS, entry

for 20 May 1691. The Carnmoney session also dealt with two cases of disorderly conduct in marriage in 1692. Entries for 21 June 1692.

62. *Synod*, pp. 39 (quoted), 53, 61.

63. MAM 1671–91, fols. 52 (quoted), 108, 135.

64. MLM, 1:183, 208, 214, 222–23 (quoted), 247 (quoted). Cf. Kilroy, pp. 22–23.

65. MAM 1671–91, fols. 335–36 (quoted), 366 (quoted), 371, 380, 414.

66. *Synod*, pp. 25, 33, 46; MLM, 2:240, 246–49, 254, 267; MAM 1671–91, fols. 189, 194, 223; CKS, entry for 25 May 1690.

67. CKS, entries for 12 April 1686 to 26 May 1686 *passim*; MAM 1671–91, fols. 52–201 *passim*, 211–534 *passim*; MLM, 1:79–333 *passim*; 2:95–96, 214–521 *passim*. Cf. Kilroy, p. 22.

68. MAM 1671–91, fols. 355, 380, 506, 525, 539–40; MLM, 1:17, 95, 101, 131; 2:228, 232, 237, 257, 262, 267, 273, 278, 290, 297, 303, 315, 324, 454–55, 507, 518, 523.

69. MAM 1671–91, fols. 108, 195, 422, 431; MLM, 1:79.

70. BKS, entries for 15 and 29 December 1678, 12 January 1679, 23 August 1691, 18 April 1695; CKS, entries for 12, 19, and 26 May 1686.

71. CKS, entry for August 1689; MLM, 1:239, 270 (quoted); 2:96, 115–16, 347.

72. MAM 1671–91, fols. 52, 60, 135, 145, 180, 185, 192, 211; MLM, 1:273, 333; 2:214, 502.

73. MLM, 1:244; 2:219, 396; MAM 1671–91, fols. 64–65 (quoted), 482.

74. CKS, entries for 21 April 1686; 6, 12, and 19 May 1686; 21 June 1692; BKS, entries for 11 September 1692, 22 September 1695; MAM 1671–91, fols. 493–94 (quoted); MLM, 2:317.

75. BKS, entries for 6 February 1681, 26 March 1681, 10 May 1694, 21 October 1684, 18 April 1695, 8 September 1695.

76. CKS, entry for 21 June 1692; MLM, 1:247; 2:424, 440, 449, 454, 463, 487; MAM 1671–91, fols. 479, 481, 497–98, 516, 529, 534; BKS, entries for 26 May 1695, 22 September 1695, 30 January 1696.

77. MAM 1671–91, fols. 428–29.

78. MAM 1671–91, fols. 357, 365, 512 (quoted), 517 (quoted), 521. Cf. CKS, entry for 24 October 1690.

79. Kirkdonald Session Book, fol. 2; BKS, entries for 24 July 1691, 9 August 1691; MLM, 1:213; CKS, entry for 10 August 1690.

80. MAM 1671–91, fols. 189–90, 194; BKS, entries for 10 May 1694, 7 February 1695.

81. MLM, 2:215, 310–11; MAM 1671–91, fols. 357 (quoted), 486; BKS, entry for 18 January 1694.

82. *Synod*, pp. 39–40 (quoted), 42.

83. CKS, entries for 25 May 1690, 22 June 1690, 10 August 1690, 24 October 1690, 15 June 1692.

84. BKS, entry for 2 December 1694; MAM 1671–91, fol. 507.

85. MLM, 2:240–44, 246–49, 254, 267–68, 273, 278, 290, 315, 324–25.

86. CKS, entries for 20 May 1691, 21 June 1692.

87. MLM, 1:37–38, 41, 45, 48, 51, 56.

88. MAM 1671–91, fol. 240.

89. BKS, entries for 24 July 1691, 28 August 1693, 5 July 1694, 25 February 1696. Cf. NLS Wodrow MSS Folio XXVI, fols. 215r–216r.

90. MAM 1671–91, fol. 315; MLM, 1:17, 173–74, 185; 2:76.

91. MLM, 1:28, 42, 65, 114–15, 199, 262, 302; 2:73–74, 77, 486; *Synod*, pp. 49, 56.

92. MLM, 1:2–3 (quoted); MAM 1671–91, fol. 337 (quoted).

93. *Synod*, pp. 19 (quoted), 29 (quoted).

94. MLM, 2:472–73, 482–83, 487–88, 490–92.

95. *Synod*, p. 19.

96. For quoted passages see Kirkdonald Session Book, entries for July 1679, November 1679, 6 January 1681.

97. MAM 1671–91, fols. 107, 119, 135, 142, 190, 203, 209; MLM, 1:177–78; 2:159–60 (quoted), 166, 207, 212, 218, 224.

98. MAM 1671–91, fols. 206, 326, 374, 504.

99. E.g. MAM 1671–91, fols. 73, 77, 107, 119, 124, 134, 139, 163, 180, 276, 283, 285, 347, 354, 381, 401, 422, 439, 481; MLM, 1:24–25, 31, 47–48, 51, 68, 75, 109, 143, 146, 153–54, 164–65, 169, 188; 2:145, 147–49, 154, 156, 373, 375, 377, 383, 451–52.

100. McConnell, *Fasti*, 2:49; MLM, 1:5, 24–25, 31, 47–48, 51, 68, 75, 80, 83–84, 109, 111–12 (quoted), 119, 127, 143–44 (quoted).

101. MLM, 1:149–50, 160, 163, 177 (quoted), 219.

102. MAM 1671–91, fols. 155, 212 (quoted), 219, 402, 407.

103. MAM 1671–91, fols. 216, 231, 330 (quoted), 352, 414.

104. MLM, 1:316.

105. MLM, 1:292, 306; MAM 1671–91, fols. 164, 197, 205, 246, 254.

106. MAM 1671–91, fol. 154.

107. MLM, 1:17–18, 44, 64, 115, 119–20, 132, 239, 284, 292, 317, 322; 2:148, 188, 263, 270, 445–46; MAM 1671–91, fols. 93–94, 97, 235, 459; HMC 78, *Hastings*, 2:366.

108. Kirkdonald Session Book, entries for September 1679, 31 May 1685; MLM, 2:85; MAM 1671–91, fols. 191, 205, 211, 219, 221, 227, 234, 244, 254, 260–61, 269–70, 276, 286, 293, 295, 301, 307–8, 374, 387, 389, 394; *Synod*, pp. 11, 20, 49, 60.

109. MLM, 1:39, 76; [James Kirkpatrick], *An Historical Essay upon the Loyalty of Presbyterians in Great-Britain and Ireland from the Reformation to This Present Year 1713* (1713), pp. 440–49. Cf. MAM 1671–91, fol. 445.

110. MLM, 1:36, 68, 95, 138, 143, 150, 157, 161, 166, 176–77, 196; 2:117, 155, 258–59, 308, 315, 321, 349, 352, 381, 477, 538, 542–44; MAM 1671–91, fols. 65, 156, 168–69, 172, 183, 191 (quoted), 266 (quoted).

111. Bodl. Carte MSS 36, fol. 511r (quoted); MAM 1671–91, fol. 178; BL Stowe MSS 202, fols. 330r–331r; Bodl. Carte MSS 221, fol. 375r; McConnell, *Fasti*, 3:68; [Kirkpatrick], *Historical Essay*, p. 505. See the biographical sketch of Gowan in Thomas Witherow, *Historical and Literary Memorials of Presbyterianism in Ireland (1623–1731)* (Belfast: William Mullar, 1879), pp. 53–59.

112. MAM 1671–91, fols. 178–79, 182, 185, 191, 196, 202; MLM, 1:157, 182–83.

113. MAM 1671–91, fols. 188, 203; Kilroy, p. 28.

114. MAM 1671–91, fols. 273, 277, 287, 363, 443. George Fleming's daughter taught at Benburb, county Armagh, around 1670, and Archibald Maclaine maintained a school at Belfast in the late 1670s. Kilroy, p. 34.

115. *Synod*, pp. 22, 32–33; [Kirkpatrick], *Historical Essay*, p. 506.

116. MAM 1671–91, fols. 32, 75; MLM, 1:26–27 (quoted), 182 (quoted), 191, 198, 201, 203, 225, 227, 264; *Synod*, p. 25.

CHAPTER 6

1. Bodl. Carte MSS 45, fol. 437r; Carte 221, fol. 373r.

2. *DNB*, s.v. Samuel Mather; NAI MSS 4/206/1 (Prerogative Will Book, 1664–84), fols. 130v–133v. Wale's son-in-law, Josiah Marsden, was the brother of the Fifth Monarchist and Congregational minister Jeremiah Marsden, a correspondent of Samuel Mather's. *BDBR*, s.v. Jeremiah Marsden. Following Charnock's death in July 1680, John Johnson described him as "a powerful Preacher, a good Casuist, a judicious Divine, a Doctor, yea, Professor in Divinity." John Johnson, *The Shining Forth of the Righteous: A Sermon Preached Partly upon the Death of . . . Stephen Charnock* (London, 1680), p. 40.

3. Samuel Mather, *The Figures or Types of the Old Testament* ([Dublin], 1683), pp. 31 (quoted), 129 (quoted), 203 (quoted), 352 (quoted).

4. Bodl. Rawlinson MSS D.1347, fols. 25r–31r. Cf. Kilroy, pp. 66–68.

5. Mather, *A Defence of the Protestant Christian Religion Against Popery: In Answer to a Discourse of a Roman Catholick* (1672), sig. A3r (quoted), p. 39 (quoted).

6. Samuel Mather, *Irenicum: or an Essay for Union* (London, 1680), pp. 2–4. For the Baptist confessions see William L. Lumpkin, *Baptist Confessions of Faith* (Philadelphia: Judson Press, 1959), pp. 153–71, 174–88.

7. Mather, *Irenicum*, pp. 4–6 (quoted), 8–15 (quoted).

8. Ibid., pp. 17–19.

9. Ibid., pp. 6–7.

10. Bodl. Carte MSS 36, fol. 468r; Carte 37, fol. 78r (quoted).

11. R. H. Murray errs in suggesting that Congregationalist and Baptist ministers had disappeared in Ireland by 1670. "The Church of the Restoration," in *History of the Church of Ireland from the Earliest Times to the Present Day*, ed. Walter Alison Phillips, 3 vols. (London: Oxford University Press, 1933–34), 3:130.

12. *The Autobiography of Henry Newcome, M.A.*, ed. Richard Parkinson, 2 vols. (Manchester: Chetham Society, 1852), 2:185–92 (quoted at pp. 189–90); *Calamy Revised*, s.v. Thomas Harrison; Kilroy, pp. 40–41.

13. Thomas Jenner, *Quakerism Anatomiz'd and Confuted* (1670), sigs. A2r–A4v, pp. 164–65.

14. Timothy Taylor, epistle to ibid., sigs. a1r–b6v; William M. Lamont, *Richard Baxter and the Millennium: Protestant Imperialism and the English Revolution* (London: Croom Helm, 1979), pp. 47–48, 127. Another literary contribution was the epistle by Harrison and Daniel Rolls to the pseudonymous *Lemmata Meditationum* (Dublin, 1672), a collection of pious soliloquies.

15. *CMHS*, 8:9 (quoted), 11, 13–14, 15 (quoted), 56 (note 691).

16. Ibid., 8:29, 486–87 (quoted).

17. Ibid., 8:489–91.

18. Ibid., 8:492–93.

19. Introduction to Pinney, pp. xi-xii; *The Twenty-Sixth Report of the Deputy Keeper of the Public Records and Keeper of the State Papers in Ireland* (Dublin: Her Majesty's Stationery Office, 1894), p. 392; *CMHS*, 8:41 (quoted), 44, 46.

20. *CMHS*, 8:47–48 (erroneously dated 1682), 54, 56, 60 (quoted); Pinney, pp. 15–16.

21. *CMHS*, 8:56; Kilroy, pp. 71–72.

22. Ibid., 8:21, 44–45, 55, 493 (quoted).

23. Ibid., 8:50–51, 53–54 (quoted), 60.

24. Ibid., 8:12, 43–44, 45 (quoted), 50–51, 54, 60.

25. Ibid., 8:62–64, 65–66 (quoted); *DNB*, s.v. Nathaniel Mather.

26. James Anthony Froude, *The English in Ireland in the Eighteenth Century*, 3 vols. (New York: Charles Scribner's Sons, 1897), 1:156–57.

27. Clarke H. Irwin, *A History of Presbyterianism in Dublin and the South and West of Ireland* (London: Hodder and Stoughton, 1890), p. 235; Kilroy, p. 69; James Armstrong, "History of the Presbyterian Churches in the City of Dublin," in *Ordination Service: Sermon; Discourse on Presbyterian Ordination; Address of the Young Minister; Prayer on Ordaining; and Charge* (London: Hunter, 1829), pp. 68–69; *DNB*, s.v. Daniel Williams. Williams had come to Ireland as chaplain to the countess of Meath. At least one Congregationalist minister, Claudius Gilbert, conformed after the restoration. George Benn, *A History of the Town of Belfast from the Earliest Times to the Close of the Eighteenth Century* (London: Marcus Ward, 1877), pp. 374–75.

28. George Pressick, *A Case of Conscience Propounded to a Great Bishop in Ireland* (1661), sig. A2r. There is no evidence for Kilroy's supposition that Pressick was a Church of Ireland minister (p. 162). For popular hostility to Baptists in England see Henry Jessey, *The Lords Loud Call to England* (1660).

29. *A Collection of Original Letters and Papers Concerning the Affairs of England, from the Duke of Ormonde's Papers*, ed. Thomas Carte, 2 vols. (London: James Bettenham, 1739), 2:326–27.

30. BL Egerton MSS 2542, fol. 370r–v. For Allen, Vernon, Sankey, Lawrence, and Walcott see *BDBR*, s.vv. For Deane, Wallis, and Godfrey see Charles Firth and Godfrey Davies, *The Regimental History of Cromwell's Army*, 2 vols. (Oxford: Clarendon Press, 1940), pp. 591–92, 613–15. See also "Dangerous Persons Come Lately out of Ireland, 1660," *Transactions of the Baptist Historical Society* (1912–13), 3:251–56.

31. For these men see *BDBR*, s.vv.

32. Thomas Grantham, *Christianismus Primitivus* (London, 1678), pt. 3, pp. 7–9. For Venner's rebellion see Richard L. Greaves, *Deliver Us from Evil: The Radical Underground in Britain, 1660–1663* (New York: Oxford University Press, 1986), pp. 50–57.

33. CH MSS HA 13,994 (quoted); 13,995 (quoted).

34. MAM 1671–91, fol. 162.

35. Bodl. Carte MSS 31, fol. 612r.

36. Bodl. Clarendon MSS 79, fols. 181r–184r; PRO SP 63/313/76, 164; BL Add. MSS 37,208, fol. 150v.

37. Bodl. Carte MSS 32, fol. 481r; *BDBR*, s.v. Thomas Lamb; Firth and Davies, *Regimental History*, p. 117; *Kingdomes Intelligencer* 47 (17–24 November 1662), pp. 743–44.

38. Bodl. Carte MSS 32, fol. 538r; Frank Bate, *The Declaration of Indulgence 1672: A Study in the Rise of Organised Dissent* (London: University Press of Liverpool by Archibald Constable, 1908), p. xxiii. A Baptist congregation was also worshipping at Lower Ormond in Tipperary; among its members was Captain Stephen Allen. Herlihy, p. 76.

39. Bodl. Carte MSS 33, fol. 254r; Carte 45, fol. 437r; Liam Irwin, "Politics, Religion and Economy: Cork in the 17th Century," *Journal of the Cork Historical and Archaeological Society* 85 (1980): 16–17.

40. William Penn, *My Irish Journal, 1669–1670*, ed. Isabel Grubb (London: Longmans, Green, 1952), p. 22; *CSPI 1669–70*, pp. 151–52; DF Sharp MSS S4, fol. 25; *The Letters of Saint Oliver Plunkett 1625–1681: Archbishop of Armagh and Primate of All Ireland*, ed. John Hanly (Dublin: Dolmen Press, 1979), pp. 373, 394, 443, 454–55. Plunkett did not mention Baptists when he discussed Protestants in Down and Connor (p. 144). For Jones see Greaves, *Deliver Us from Evil*, p. 254, note 39; Firth and Davies, *Regimental History*, p. 411.

41. TCD MSS 151, fols. 2r–11r (quoted at 8r), 12r–17r (quoted at 13r, 17r), 20r–22r (quoted at 22r), 27r (quoted), 33r–36r, 41r–55r (quoted at 44r).

42. *BDBR*, s.v. Richard Lawrence; Bodl. Carte MSS 66, fol. 303r.

43. Bodl. Carte MSS 36, fol. 330r–v (quoted); Carte 49, fol. 645r. Cf. Carte 36, fols. 503r, 521r–v, 523r–524r, 609r; Carte 49, fol. 643r; Carte 50, fol. 38r. On several occasions in the 1670s Lawrence entertained Archbishop Michael Boyle in his home. Herlihy, p. 89.

44. Bodl. Carte 66, fols. 303r–v, 323r–v; T. C. Barnard, "Crises of Identity Among Irish Protestants 1641–1685," *Past & Present* 127 (May 1990): 77–78.

45. Bodl. Carte MSS 39, fol. 186r, 210r; Richard L. Greaves, *Secrets of the Kingdom: British Radicals from the Popish Plot to the Revolution of 1688–1689* (Stanford: Stanford University Press, 1992), pp. 34–35.

46. *CMHS*, 8:44, 56–57 (quoted); Bodl. Carte MSS 168, fols. 141–42; *BDBR*, s.v. Lawrence; Herlihy, pp. 78–79.

47. Cork Church Book, fols. 1–6, 17–19 (quoted at fol. 3).

48. Around 1800 the number of Baptists in Ireland was approximately 500; they met in five congregations in the south and east. H. D. Gribbon, "Irish Baptists in the Nineteenth Century: Economic and Social Background," *Irish Baptist Historical Society Journal* 16 (1983–84): 4–5.

49. Herlihy, p. 207.

50. Ibid., pp. 93–94.

51. Richard Lawrence, *The Interest of Ireland in Its Trade and Wealth Stated* (Dublin, 1682), sigs. ff3r (quoted), ff4v.

CHAPTER 7

1. HYNM, 2:305; Kilroy, p. 90; Helen E. Hatton, *The Largest Amount of Good: Quaker Relief in Ireland 1654–1921* (Kingston and Montreal: McGill-Queen's Uni-

versity Press, 1993), p. 34. John Stephenson Rowntree suggested that the number of meetings at the end of the century was virtually the same as that in Yorkshire, which had 84. *Quakerism, Past and Present: Being an Inquiry into the Causes of Its Decline in Great Britain and Ireland* (London: Smith, Elder, 1859), p. 77. Kilroy (p. 90) estimates the total number of Friends in Ireland between 1660 and 1714 to have been between 5,500 and 6,500.

2. Richard T. Vann and David Eversley, *Friends in Life and Death: The British and Irish Quakers in the Demographic Transition, 1650–1900* (Cambridge: Cambridge University Press, 1992), pp. 36, 47–48, 59–60, 63. Frederick B. Tolles estimates that Quakers numbered 600 to 700 families in the provinces of Leinster and Munster by 1700. *Meeting House and Counting House: The Quaker Merchants of Colonial Philadelphia 1682–1763* (Chapel Hill: University of North Carolina Press, 1948), p. 30.

3. HMC 36, *Ormonde*, n.s., 7:116, 121; J. G. Simms, *Jacobite Ireland 1685–91* (London: Routledge and Kegan Paul, 1969), p. 13; Vann and Eversley, *Friends*, p. 50; D. Dickson, "The Cork Merchant Community in the Eighteenth Century: A Regional Perspective," *Négoce et Industrie en France et en Irlande aux XVIIIe et XIXe Siècles*, ed. L. M. Cullen and P. Butel (Paris: National de la Recherche Scientifique, 1980), p. 47; Richard S. Harrison, *Cork City Quakers: A Brief History, 1655–1939* ([Cork]: By the Author, 1991), p. 4; Kenneth L. Carroll, "Quakerism in Connaught, 1656–1978," JFHS 54 (1979): 188, 191.

4. Carroll, "Quakerism in Connaught," p. 188; William Edmundson, *A Journal of the Life, Travels, Sufferings and Labour of Love in the Work of the Ministry*, 2nd ed. (London, 1774), p. 45.

5. Abraham Fuller and Thomas Holme, *A Compendious View of Some Extraordinary Sufferings of the People Call'd Quakers* (Dublin, 1731), p. 126; Joseph Besse, *A Collection of the Sufferings of the People Called Quakers*, 2 vols. (London, 1743), 2:464–67.

6. Elisabeth Brockbank, *Edward Burrough: A Wrestler for Truth 1634–1662* (London: Bannisdale Press, 1949), pp. 129–30 (quoted); LF Swarthmore MSS 6/4 (quoted); "A Memoir of the Life and Religious Labours of . . . Edward Burrough," *The Friends' Library* 14 (Philadelphia: Joseph Rakestraw, 1850): 483 (quoted).

7. LF Swarthmore MSS 4/238.

8. LF Swarthmore MSS 5/20 (quoted); Swarthmore 5/39 (quoted); Kenneth L. Carroll, *John Perrot: Early Quaker Schismatic*, JFHS, Supplement No. 33 (London, 1971), pp. 49–50.

9. LF Swarthmore MSS 4/78; 5/5 (quoted).

10. LF Swarthmore MSS 5/91.

11. LF Swarthmore MSS 5/92.

12. Ibid.

13. Edmundson, *Journal*, pp. 45–47; Besse, *Collection*, 2:469–70.

14. Fuller and Holme, *Compendious View*, p. 126; Bodl. Carte MSS 32, fol. 619r; Carte 33, fol. 148r (quoted).

15. Bodl. Carte MSS 33, fols. 146r (quoted), 225r, 269r.

16. LF Portfolio 16, no. 7; Bodl. Carte MSS 33, fol. 332r (quoted).

17. Fuller and Holme, *Compendious View*, p. 126; *HMC 63*, *Egmont*, 2:8; Edmundson, *Journal*, p. 48 (quoted).

18. Bodl. Carte MSS 45, fols. 187r (quoted), 467r (quoted); BL Add. MSS 37,208, fol. 46r (quoted).

19. GBS, vol. 2, Munster Province, Cork, 1667, 1668; Besse, *Collection*, 2:475.

20. *The Journal of George Fox*, ed. Norman Penney, 2 vols. (Cambridge: Cambridge University Press, 1911), 2:136–37 (quoted); H. Larry Ingle, *First Among Friends: George Fox and the Creation of Quakerism* (New York: Oxford University Press, 1994), p. 225.

21. Fox, *Journal*, 2:138 (quoted), 139.

22. Penn, *Journal*; "Record of Friends Travelling in Ireland, 1656–1765," *JFHS* 10 (July 1913): 158–59. Between September 1669 and August 1670 Penn traveled extensively in southern and central Ireland using Cork as his base. Among the places he visited were Dublin, Mountmellick, Rosenallis, Carlow, Cashel, Youghal, Kinsale, Skibbereen, Bandon, Tallow, and Baltimore.

23. GBS, vol. 2, Connaught Province, Galway, 1669, and Munster Province, Cork, 1669; Fuller and Holme, *Compendious View*, p. 126.

24. Fuller and Holme, *Compendious View*, p. 126; Thomas Jenner, *Quakerism Anatomiz'd and Confuted* (1670), pp. 172–73, 175 (quoted), 217–18.

25. DF Sharp MSS S1, fols. 33, 43, 46.

26. "Record of Friends Travelling in Ireland," p. 159; John Burnyeat, *The Truth Exalted in the Writings of That Eminent and Faithful Servant of Christ John Burnyeat* (London, 1691), pp. 37–38, 61–62; John Banks, *A Journal of the Life, Labours, Travels, and Sufferings* (London, 1712), pp. 34–90 *passim*; "The Life of Oliver Sansom," *The Friends' Library* 14 (Philadelphia: Joseph Rakestraw, 1850): 71–79; DF Sharp MSS S4, fols. 95–97; S5, fols. 4, 15–16 (quoted), 17–18; S8, fol. 13r–v; John M. Douglas, "Early Quakerism in Ireland," *JFHS* 48 (Spring 1956): 22.

27. DF Sharp MSS S4, fol. 93; LF Swarthmore MSS 6 / 22; LF Portfolio 16, no. 58; Burnyeat, *Truth*, pp. 26–29, 32–33, 37–38, 61–62.

28. William C. Braithwaite, *The Second Period of Quakerism*, 2nd ed., rev. Henry J. Cadbury (York: William Sessions, 1979), p. 302, note 1; Banks, *Journal*, pp. 34–35 (quoted), 37–38 (quoted), 39–44.

29. Banks, *Journal*, pp. 44, 45–46 (quoted), 50, 173.

30. Ibid., pp. 50 (quoted), 51–52.

31. Ibid., pp. 62–64.

32. Ibid., pp. 90, 95. He made a final visit in 1694. Ibid., pp. 135–37.

33. HYNM, 1:36–38, 44; DF Sharp MSS S1, fols. 188–89 (quoted).

34. DF Sharp MSS S4, fol. 98 (quoted); S5, fol. 1; DMM, fols. 13–14 (quoted); HYNM, 1:52–53.

35. Braithwaite, *Second Period*, pp. 294–323.

36. DF Sharp MSS S5, fols. 21–24 (quoted), 26–27 (quoted); HYNM, 1:57.

37. DF Sharp MSS S8, fols. 18r–19v (quoted), 20r–21v (quoted).

38. LYM, 1:133 (quoted); cf. ibid., fol. 121; Holme and Fuller, *Compendious View*, p. 126.

39. Burnyeat, *Truth*, pp. 75, 160, 169; LF Swarthmore MSS 6 / 66.

40. DF Sharp MSS S5, fols. 65v–66r, 67r, 71r–v; "Record of Friends Travelling

in Ireland," p. 160; James Dickinson, "A Journal of the Life, Travels, and Labours of Love," *The Friends' Library* 12 (Philadelphia: Joseph Rakestraw, 1848): 372 (quoted); Benjamin Bangs, "Memoirs of the Life and Convincement of Benjamin Bangs," *The Friends' Library* 4 (Philadelphia: Joseph Rakestraw, 1840): 228.

41. Fuller and Holme, *Compendious View*, p. 126; DF Sharp MSS S5, fol. 74v; Burnyeat, *Truth*, pp. 75–76; LYM, 1:144.

42. Burnyeat, *Truth*, pp. 77–79, 81, 170 (quoted); Bangs, "Memoirs," p. 229. Cf. Bodl. Carte MSS 169, fol. 17. In a period of approximately one year commencing in September 1682, Bangs traveled some 1,750 miles and held 180 meetings outside Dublin. "Memoirs," p. 229.

43. Fuller and Holme, *Compendious View*, p. 130; Burnyeat, *Truth*, pp. 81–82 (quoted). Cf. NWM, fol. 65; LYM, 1:154.

44. Fuller and Holme, *Compendious View*, p. 130; Edmundson, *Journal*, p. 129; Christopher Story, "A Brief Account of the Life of Christopher Story," *The Friends' Library* 1 (Philadelphia: Joseph Rakestraw, 1837): 154; "Record of Friends Travelling in Ireland," pp. 160–61; Dickinson, "Journal," pp. 373–74 (quoted).

45. Burnyeat, *Truth*, pp. 86–91 (quoted at pp. 87 and 90). Cf. John Banks, *An Exhortation to Friends, to Keep in Remembrance* (London, 1687), p. 6. Fuller and Holme report three imprisoned Quakers in 1686 and none in 1687 and 1688. *Compendious View*, p. 130.

46. "George Fox to Friends in Ireland, 1685," *JFHS* 7 (December 1910): 181.

47. LF Sharp MSS S9, fol. 10r–v; LF Portfolio 16, no. 25.

48. DMM, 2:131, 134; LF Sharp MSS S6, fols. 30r–31r, 34r–v; HYNM, 1:103, 105.

49. *The Council Book of the Corporation of Youghal, from 1610 to 1659, from 1666 to 1687, and from 1690 to 1800*, ed. Richard Caulfield (Guildford, Surrey: J. Billing and Sons, 1878), p. 371; DF Sharp MSS S6, fols. 28r–29r.

50. NWM, fol. 81; LYM, 1:195.

51. "Record of Friends Travelling in Ireland," pp. 161–67.

52. Fox, *Journal*, 2:126; LF Swarthmore MSS 4/238; Penn, *Journal*, p. 21; Edmundson, *Journal*, pp. 58–59 (quoted). Cf. Isabel Grubb, "The Settlement of Church Discipline Among Irish Friends," *JFHS* 45 (Autumn 1953): 75–77.

53. HYNM, 1:102.

54. HYNM, 1:66–67.

55. HYNM, 1:102; 2:80 (quoted), 101; Richard T. Vann, *The Social Development of English Quakerism 1655–1755* (Cambridge, Mass.: Harvard University Press, 1969), pp. 108–14. In May 1697 the six-months meeting doubled the number of Dublin representatives assigned to this task. Ibid., 2:110.

56. HYNM, 1:83–84 (quoted); 2:42, 80, 110 (quoted), 210–11; DMM, 3:238v.

57. HYNM, 2:80; LPM, fols. 25, 49; MMM, fol. 33v.

58. HYNM, 2: preliminary folio; Penn, *Journal*, p. 21 (quoted).

59. HYNM, 1:87 (quoted), 91, 108.

60. LYM, 1:121; HYNM, 2:273–74. An eighth query was added in 1703 concerning the extent to which the advice of the six-months meeting had been followed.

61. HYNM, 1:8, 43 (quoted); 2:39 (quoted); LF Swarthmore MSS 5/115, fol. 12; LPM, fol. 255.

62. UPM, fol. 151. Cf. LPM, fols. 174, 202, 206, 209; MMM, fol. 45v; LisMM, entry for 2 March 1693.

63. LPM, fol. 35; HYNM, 1:92–94; UPM, fol. 45.

64. LPM, fol. 62; UPM, fols. 161 (quoted), 166.

65. HYNM, 2:118, 154, 169; LPM, fol. 408 (quoted), 440 (quoted), 446, 468; DMM, 3:224v.

66. UPM, fols. 39, 42, 52, 83, 84, 86, 90, 113, 119; Thomas Wight, *A History of the Rise and Progress of the People Called Quakers, in Ireland, from the Year 1653 to 1670,* rev. John Rutty (London: William Phillips, 1811), pp. 115–16.

67. Goodbody, *Guide,* pp. 3, 47–48.

68. Meeting times for services of worship were not standard. Commencing in August 1690, for example, Dublin Friends met on Tuesdays at 2:00 P.M. and Saturdays between 9:00 and 10:00 A.M. In May 1700 they began holding afternoon meetings on Sunday. At Moate in October 1685 the men's meeting asked that Sunday meetings not extend beyond 11:00 A.M. and that Wednesday meetings end by noon. Because of the brevity of winter days, the Lurgan men's meeting decided in November 1694 that its meetings for worship terminate by 10:00 A.M. DMM, 2:231; 3:240v; MMM, fol. 29v; LurMM, fol. 58.

69. Cf. LisMM, entry for 6 Dec. 1682; LurMM, fols. 30–31, 40–41.

70. LurMM, fols. 4–5, 9, 13–14, 17, 22, 25, 45; MMM, fol. 42v.

71. DMM, 3:61v–62r, 128v–129r, 159v–160r, 244v–245r (quoted), 261v–262r.

72. DMM, 3:129v, 151v, 269v.

73. LisMM, entry for 1 Feb. 1694; DMM, 3:139v, 243v–244r (quoted); MMM, fol. 69r (quoted).

74. LisMM, entries for 22 April 1697; 7 Oct. 1697 (quoted); DMM, 3:161v, 255v.

75. LPM, fols. 275–76, 390–91 (quoted); LurMM, fols. 55, 57.

76. DF Sharp MSS S4, fols. 37–38.

77. Edmundson, *Journal,* pp. 58–59; Fox, *Journal,* 2:147.

78. LurMM, fol. 3; Banks, *Journal,* pp. 185–90. The first folio of NWM contains an undated list of seventeen women's meetings in Ireland. Of these, eight were in Ulster province (Cavan, Charlemont, Ballyhagan, Lurgan, Lisnagarvy [Lisburn], Carrickfergus, Ballymoney, and Antrim-Grange), six in Leinster (Dublin, Moate, Mountmellick, Newgarden, Lambstown [Wexford], and Ballycane [Wicklow]), and three in Munster (Cork, Limerick, and Waterford). NWM, fol. 1. For the development of women's meetings in England see Arnold Lloyd, *Quaker Social History 1669–1738* (London: Longmans, Green, 1950), Chap. 8.

79. NWM, fol. 37; HYNM, 1:53.

80. HYNM, 1:51, 54 (quoted); NWM, preliminary folio.

81. UPM, fols. 26, 33 (cf. 65–66, 133); LisMM, entries for 23 May 1678 and 17 April 1679; LPM, fol. 209; LurMM, fol. 10; MMM, fol. 7v (cf. 11v); DMM, 3:274v–275r.

82. DMM, 2:177; LisMM, entry for 3 Jan. 1695; UPM, fols. 137, 143.

83. NWM, fol. 96 (quoted); LPM, fols. 432 (quoted), 434 (quoted).

84. DMM, 3:101v–102r, 200v, 202v, 207v–208r, 247v. Cf. Vann, *Social Development,* pp. 99–100.

85. *Minute Book of the Men's Meeting of the Society of Friends in Bristol 1686–*

1704, ed. Russell Mortimer, Bristol Record Society, vol. 30 (1977), pp. 75, 127, 140 (quoted). Woodward went to Ireland in 1678.

86. DF Sharp MSS S5, fols. 44r–45r; DMM, 2:176.

87. DMM, 3:191v–192r, 227v; LPM, fol. 285.

88. See e.g. MMM, fols. 10v, 15v, 49v; UPM, fols. 50, 52.

89. LPM, fol. 23; HYNM, 1:63, 76–77 (quoted); UPM, fols. 161, 163 (cf. fol. 52); LisMM, entry for May 1701. At the outset of the period of resettlement following the time of troubles, the half-yearly meeting was concerned that Friends not locate in remote areas where they were precluded from attending meetings. HYNM, 2:15. The oldest register of certificates of removal—that from Dublin—dates from 1682.

90. LurMM, fol. 53; DMM, 3:219v–220r; UPM, fol. 53 (quoted).

91. DMM, 1:205, 209, 223–24 (quoted). In 1682 the Ulster provincial meeting asserted that emigrants who were clear to marry have this noted on their certificates. UPM, fol. 50.

92. DMM, 1:205–6, 219–20; Audrey Lockhart, "The Quakers and Emigration from Ireland to the North American Colonies," *Quaker History* 77 (Fall 1988): 67, 76–77. According to Raymond Gillespie, 39 Friends left Ireland for Pennsylvania in the 1680s, three in the 1690s, and 26 in the first decade of the eighteenth century. "Explorers, Exploiters and Entrepreneurs: Early Modern Ireland and Its Context, 1500–1700," in *An Historiographical Geography of Ireland*, ed. B. J. Graham and L. J. Proudfoot (London: Academic Press, 1993), p. 144.

93. MMM, fol. 37; LPM, fols. 127–28. Cf. DMM, 3:219v; MMM, fol. 13v.

94. LPM, fols. 80 (quoted), 132; DMM, 1:50; 3:26v, 247v, 253v; LisMM, entry for 23 February 1699; Vann, *Social Development*, pp. 98–99, 118. Cf. DF Sharp MSS S6, fol. 16r.

95. Vann, *Social Development*, p. 96 (quoted); LPM, fol. 256 (quoted); HYNM, 2:35–36 (quoted).

96. DMM, 3:113v (quoted); LPM, fols. 366, 412 (quoted); HYNM, 2:314.

97. LPM, fols. 485, 487 (quoted).

98. HYNM, 1:3 (quoted); LPM, fols. 23, 48, 222 (quoted), 315 (quoted); DMM, 2:255. See also NWM, fols. 3–6; UPM, fols. 22, 70, 88, 98; LPM, fols. 105, 141, 180, 199, 227; DMM, 2:115; HYNM, 1:62.

99. UPM, fols. 70, 82, 127; MMM, fol. 35v; DMM, 2:115–16; HYNM, 1:35, 93; LPM, fols. 228, 421; NWM, fols. 37–42.

100. LPM, fols. 162, 180; LF Swarthmore MSS 6/20; 6/61; DMM, 1:229; 2:255; NWM, fols. 47–48.

101. LF Swarthmore MSS 6/57.

102. LPM, fol. 464.

103. This paragraph is based on Thomas O'Malley, "'Defying the Powers and Tempering the Spirit,' A Review of Quaker Control over Their Publications 1672–1689," *Journal of Ecclesiastical History* 33 (January 1982): 72–88.

104. *CSPI 1669–70*, p. 152.   105. HYNM, 1:3; LPM, fol. 11.

106. HYNM, 1:15; LPM, fol. 16.   107. HYNM, 1:26–27.

108. HYNM, 1:29–30, 33; LPM, fol. 34.

109. HYNM, 1:32–33, 35–36.

110. HYNM, 1:38, 58; DMM, 1:45; UPM, fols. 19, 21.

111. HYNM, 1:35, 52, 83, 86, 89, 91; DMM, 2:5.

112. HYNM, 1:103, 108; DMM, 1:233–34.

113. HYNM, 1:76, 78, 82, 95, 98; DMM, 1:205–6, 209, 213–15 (cf. 1:135). In 1686 the Dublin men's meeting paid £2 for 1,000 copies of two testimonies of advice to young people from London Friends; 500 copies would have cost 30s. DMM, 2:54, 56–57.

114. HYNM, 1:74, 76–78, 80, 82–83, 85, 88, 90; DMM, 2:25.

115. DF Sharp MSS S7, fol. 37r–v; LPM, fols. 236, 242; HYNM, 2:20; UPM, fol. 129. Irish Friends obtained books from England at other times as well. Among them were William Tomlinson's *An Awakening Voice to the Papists* in 1683, Whitehead's *An Antidote to the Book Called The Snake in the Grass* in 1697, and other refutations of anti-Quaker attacks in 1700–1701. DMM, 1:213–14; HYNM, 2:126, 258.

116. HYNM, 2:24.

117. HYNM, 2:29, 34, 40, 52, 127, 167, 185, 213, 257, 283, 314–15; LPM, fols. 268, 301, 303, 320, 429; DMM, 3:178v–179r, 211v–212r.

118. HYNM, 2:53; LPM, fols. 304, 306; DMM, 3:90v; LurMM, fol. 57; LisMM, entry for 20 June 1695.

119. LPM, fol. 425; LisMM, entry for 29 June 1699.

120. DMM, 3:232v, 235v, 238v, 244v–245r, 267v–268r; HYNM, 2:230, 255, 313; LPM, fols. 572, 576.

121. LurMM, fol. 7; MMM, fols. 20r, 21r, 22v, 25v; DMM, 1:63, 123, 280; 2:278; 3:284v. For calls to return borrowed books see LurMM, fol. 27; LisMM, entry for 28 January 1697; DMM, 3:130v, 131v, 148v.

122. HYNM, 1:126, 146; LisMM, entry for 26 August 1697.

123. HYNM, 2:147 (quoted), 228, 254–55, 283–87; LPM, fols. 457, 461; DMM, 3:226v, 227v, 243v–244r, 260v, 267v–268r.

124. HYNM, 2:305; LPM, fol. 57; DMM, 3:206v–207r.

125. LPM, fols. 15, 26, 555, 557, 559, 561, 563, 567, 570.

126. LPM, fols. 26, 34, 90, 496, 501, 515. For galleries in England see Vann, *Social Development*, p. 100.

127. Samuel McSkimin, *The History and Antiquities of the County of the Town of Carrickfergus from the Earliest Records till 1839*, new ed., ed. E. J. McCrum (Belfast: Mullan and Son, James Cleeland, Davidson and McCormack, 1909), p. 61, note 2; LisMM, entries for 23 March 1681, 29 July 1685, 27 October 1686, 15 December 1686, 24 August 1687, 6 September 1688, 16 October 1693; UPM, fol. 81; LurMM, fol. 49.

128. HYNM, 1:8, 16, 43–44, 78; DF Sharp MSS S5, fol. 8; DMM, 1:15–17, 91, 95.

129. HYNM, 1:84, 88–89, 91; UPM, fols. 60–61; MMM, fol. 32v.

130. HYNM, 1:91–93, 95–96; LPM, fols. 173–74. The Leinster province alone had subscribed £445 13s. 6d. by December 1683. LPM, fol. 141.

131. HYNM, 1:99; DMM, 2:103–4; 3:17, 26v–28r, 32v, 35v, 36v, 44v.

132. DMM, 3:73v, 93v–94r, 95v, 128v–129r, 145v, 244v; HYNM, 2:82, 96; LPM, fol. 356.

133. DMM, 1:53, 137, 221; 3:141v, 168v, 170v, 172v–173r, 184v; LPM, fol. 409;

LurMM, fols. 11, 14, 16 (quoted), 18, 28, 31–32; Vann, *Social Development*, pp. 127–28.

134. HYNM, 1:38, 41.
135. HYNM, 1:55.
136. HYNM, 2:148–49.
137. HYNM, 2:184–85, 214–15.
138. HYNM, 2:289, 316.
139. HYNM, 1:38, 79–80, 93; 2:30–31.
140. HYNM, 2:214–15, 289.
141. UPM, fols. 23, 131.
142. LPM, fols. 49, 239.
143. LPM, fol. 110.
144. LPM, fols. 52, 169–70, 178; DMM, 2:64.
145. See. e.g. DMM, 1:269–70; 2:205–6; 3:146v–147r.

CHAPTER 8

1. LRB, no. 1, fols. 20–21 (quoted), 36 (quoted).

2. John Burnyeat, *The Truth Exalted in the Writings of That Eminent and Faithful Servant of Christ John Burnyeat* (London, 1691), pp. 89 (quoted), 175 (quoted); LF Swarthmore MSS 5 / 115, fol. 12; HYNM, 2:82–83, 181 (quoted).

3. DF Sharp MSS S4, fol. 1. Cf. Richard T. Vann, *The Social Development of English Quakerism 1655–1755* (Cambridge, Mass.: Harvard University Press, 1969), pp. 140–41.

4. HYNM, 2:32–33 (quoted), 96–97, 238; DF Sharp MSS S4, fol. 49 (quoted); S5, fols. 32–33; NWM, fols. 5, 103, 105; LPM, fol. 324; LF Swarthmore MSS 5 / 115, fols. 8, 17–18; DMM, 3:177v.

5. HYNM, 2:181; NWM, fol. 111.

6. LPM, fols. 490–91; William Edmundson, *An Epistle to Friends Given Forth from Leinster-Province Meeting in Ireland* (1699), p. 27.

7. HYNM, 1:5–6 (quoted), 102, 106–7 (quoted); DF Sharp MSS S4, fol. 48; NWM, fols. 90, 127 (quoted). Cf. Vann, *Social Development*, pp. 192–96. Joseph Pike ruefully noted that Quaker wives in the early 1690s wore expensive clothing, including silk, though of a plain color. *Some Account of the Life of Joseph Pike of Cork* (London: Darton and Harvey, 1837), pp. 65–66.

8. HYNM, 1:100–1, 106–8; 2:70, 282–83; UPM, fol. 87; LF Swarthmore MSS 5 / 115, fol. 17 (quoted); DMM, 3:103v–104r.

9. HYNM, 2:282–83; NWM, fols. 90, 111 (quoted), 121.

10. DF Sharp MSS S4, fols. 48–49; NWM, fols. 82, 89–90, 98–99, 123; HYNM, 2:206; DMM, 3:273v–274r (quoted); LPM, fol. 487 (quoted). Margaret Fox warned against overemphasizing external simplicity. Arnold Lloyd, *Quaker Social History 1669–1738* (London: Longmans, Green, 1950), p. 73; Bonnelyn Kunze, *Margaret Fell and the Rise of Quakerism* (Stanford, Cal.: Stanford University Press, 1994), p. 25. Cf. Vann, *Social Development*, p. 195.

11. LF Swarthmore MSS 5 / 115, fol. 8; HYNM, 2:206; NWM, fols. 82, 89–90, 94–95, 102–3, 111; LisMM, entry for 24 August 1701.

12. HYNM, 1:5–6 (quoted); 2:40–41, 86 (quoted), 166–67, 206; LPM, fol. 179; DMM, 2:129, 131; NWM, fols. 90–92, 94–95 (quoted), 104–5, 111, 121, 123. Pike noted that in the early 1690s many Friends had fine furniture, including veneered chests of drawers, stands, cabinets, and desks made of varnished walnut

and olive wood. Some had finely carved chairs, large mirrors with elaborate tops, fringed curtains, multi-colored hangings, and large moldings and cornices. *Account*, pp. 65–66.

13. HYNM, 2:41.

14. LPM, fol. 568.

15. DMM, 1:51; 3:77v (quoted); HYNM, 2:40 (quoted), 41, 313–14 (quoted); NWM, fol. 111; LPM, fol. 407.

16. LPM, fol. 487 (quoted); HYNM, 2:59; LF Swarthmore MSS 5/115, fol. 17 (quoted); DMM, 3:238v; NWM, fol. 111.

17. LPM, fols. 453, 584; NWM, fols. 96 (quoted), 98–99, 103, 120 (quoted).

18. HYNM, 1:43 (quoted); 2:58; DMM, 1:107–10.

19. UPM, fols. 26, 38–39; HYNM, 1:102; 2:230–31; DMM, 3:197v, 202v–203r; LPM, fols. 316, 404 (quoted), 415. In 1697 the Dublin men's meeting stipulated that Friends must not "have the Custom of any goods in Exportation or importation." DMM, 3:174v.

20. DMM, 3:105v; LPM, fols. 324–25 (quoted); HYNM, 2:70; NWM, fols. 54, 58, 64, 100–101.

21. HYNM, 2:81 (quoted), 86; LPM, fol. 335.

22. NWM, fol. 3 (quoted); HYNM, 1:98; NLI MSS 94, fol. 41 (quoted); UPM, fols. 45, 69, 145 (quoted); DMM, 3:15.

23. HYNM, 1:55–56; 2:70; DMM, 1:138v; LF Swarthmore MSS 5/115, fol. 18; LPM, fols. 341 (quoted), 365 (quoted).

24. HYNM, 2:14, 257–58.

25. DMM, 3:120v–121r, 213v–214r; LPM, fol. 581 (quoted).

26. LPM, fol. 521 (quoted); DMM, 3:54v, 116v, 248v, 249v, 251v–252r; HYNM, 2:275 (quoted). For gambling see NWM, fol. 3.

27. HYNM, 1:98; 2:32–33, 207 (quoted), 314 (quoted); NWM, fols. 83–84 (quoted); DMM, 3:254r; LRB, no. 1, fol. 32 (quoted); LPM, fol. 435.

28. HYNM, 1:36, 100, 102–3; 2:32, 258–59, 274–75; MMM, fol. 6v; LPM, fols. 286, 466–67, 487.

29. LF Swarthmore MSS 5/115, fol. 6; HYNM, 1:70, 90; 2:166–67; UPM, fol. 38; LPM, fols. 96, 159.

30. LPM, fols. 91, 94; DMM, 1:81; HYNM, 1:70–71; UPM, fols. 35, 40, 75, 77; LurMM, fol. 14.

31. HYNM, 1:16, 69; DMM, 2:109 (quoted).

32. HYNM, 2:58–59, 81, 166; MMM, fols. 71v, 73v; DMM, 3:129v, 131v.

33. DMM, 1:7, 101; 2:159 (quoted); NWM, fols. 44–45 (quoted), 62, 64; MMM, fol. 32v; DF Sharp MSS S6, fol. 54r–v (quoted); HYNM, 1:101.

34. NLI MSS 94, fol. 41; HYNM, 2:15; UPM, fols. 118–19; NWM, fols. 85–86; DMM, 3:3, 12.

35. HYNM, 2:22.

36. LPM, fols. 254–55, 262, 264, 266; MMM, fol. 47v; DMM, 3:47v; HYNM, 2:27; NWM, fols. 89–90. Cf. UPM, fol. 155. Leinster added a seventh visitor in August 1693 to help in Dublin. LPM, fol. 275.

37. LPM, fols. 272–73, 283–84; HYNM, 2:31–33.

38. DMM, 3:74r, 102v–103r, 139r, 151v–152r; HYNM, 2:46–47, 51, 55–56 (quoted), 62; NWM, fols. 92–94.

39. DMM, 3:160r, 167r, 200r; HYNM, 2:132–33; LPM. fol. 392 (quoted); NWM, fols. 104–5.

40. HYNM, 2:180, 199–200, 222; LisMM, entries for 12 January 1699, 23 February 1699; DMM, 3:214v–215r (quoted).

41. HYNM, 2:222–23; LPM, fol. 447. Cf. NWM, fols. 113–14.

42. HYNM, 2:244; DMM, 3:224v, 237v–238r, 246v, 253v–254r, 255v, 262v–263v (quoted), 275v–276r.

43. LPM, fols. 472–73 (quoted); DMM, 3:265v (quoted), 267v (quoted), 268v–269r.

44. LPM, fols. 501–2 (quoted), 504.

45. HYNM, 1:79.

46. UPM, fols. 67–73, 75.

47. UPM, fols. 75, 77, 80–84.

48. HYNM, 2:127, 183 (quoted).

49. LPM, fols. 115 (quoted), 117, 270; LF Swarthmore MSS 5/115, fol. 12; Vann, *Social Development*, p. 138.

50. LurMM, fols. 27–28, 30, 38, 40, 44, 55; MMM, fol. 40v; DMM, 3:15, 128v–129r, 146v–147r, 198v–199r, 241v–242r, 257v–258r; UPM, fols. 94, 96–97; LPM, fol. 29.

51. LisMM, entries for 18 May 1682, 28 March 1688, 29 May 1690, 6 July 1693, 28 May 1695, 16 January 1696; DMM, 3:57v, 58v, 60v, 65r, 69v, 79v, 89v–90r, 98v; LurMM, fol. 37; LPM, fol. 44; UPM, fol. 28A; HYNM, 2:20.

52. UPM, fol. 46; DMM, 1:155, 243–44, 269–70; 2:7, 13, 31–32, 70–73, 79–80, 182–84, 187–88; 3:73r–76r, 88v–89r, 115v–116r, 171v–172r, 182v.

53. DMM, 2:144–47; 3:29v–30r, 118v–119r, 131v, 132v, 138r; MMM, fol. 10v. See also LurMM, fols. 31–34, 37; LPM, fols. 13, 84; DMM, 1:191; 2:107–8, 111–12, 227; 3:102v–103r, 112v, 113v–114r, 133v–134r, 135v, 165v–166r, 194v, 241v–242r; UPM, fols. 36, 79.

54. MMM, fol. 11v (quoted); LRB, no. 1, fol. 24 (quoted); DF Sharp MSS S5, fol. 6. Cf. DMM, 3:59v, 62v, 63v; UPM, fol. 27; LisMM, entry for 12 June 1701.

55. MMM, fols. 30v–31r, 35v; DMM, 3:212v–215v.

56. LRB, no. 1, fol. 23. For other cases of inebriety see MMM, fols. 31v, 36v; LisMM, entries for 29 November 1688, 9 April 1696; LurMM, fols. 13, 18, 49–50; DMM, 3:149v–151r.

57. DMM, 3:70v–71r (quoted); LRB, no. 1, fol. 22 (quoted). Cf. LRB, no. 1, fol. 52; UPM, fol. 52; DMM, 3:72v; LisMM, entry for 15 July 1697.

58. DMM, 1:7; 3:175v, 181v, 182v–183r, 252v–253r; DF Sharp MSS S4, fols. 42–44; LPM, fol. 55.

59. LRB, no. 1, fols. 19–20; LurMM, fols. 55–57.

60. MMM, fol. 11v. For other cases see MMM, fol. 31v; DMM, 3:145v–147r.

61. HYNM, 1:39–42, 44; DMM, 1:5, 11; DF Sharp MSS S1, fols. 175–82.

62. MMM, fol. 27v.

63. UPM, fols. 54–55; HYNM, 2:2; LurMM, fols. 41–42 (quoted); MMM, fol. 66v; DMM, 3:90v.

64. LRB, no. 1, fol. 25; LurMM, fols. 29–30; DMM, 3:74v–75r, 76v–77r, 79r,

213v–214r. At Cork in 1669 the Quakers reportedly met illegally in arms. Joseph Besse, *A Collection of the Sufferings of the People Called Quakers*, 2 vols. (London, 1753), 2:476.

65. DMM, 2:111–12 (quoted); LPM, fols. 48, 58–59, 61, 64–65, 67–68, 71–72, 74; HYNM, 1:44; LurMM, fol. 28. For other cases see LPM, fol. 43; LurMM, fol. 16; LisMM, entry for 28 December 1687; DMM, 2:213; UPM, fol. 34.

66. MMM, fol. 68v; LisMM, entries for 2 December 1685, 6 September 1688, 20 November 1701; LurMM, fols. 8–9.

67. DMM, 1:161–62 (quoted), 164–65; 3:99v–100r.

68. DMM, 3:48v, 49v, 52r (quoted); LisMM, entries for 15 June 1677, September 1685, 2 June 1696; HYNM, 2:31, 38; LurMM, fols. 8, 12, 19–20, 23, 56.

69. DMM, 1:183–84.

70. LurMM, fols. 5, 9–11, 13, 16, 18, 23, 52, 59; MMM, fols. 24v, 27v, 29v; LisMM, entries for 9 March 1687, 13 July 1687, 24 August 1687, 28 December 1687, 5 February 1691, 17 August 1693; HYNM, 1:15; LPM, fol. 63; DMM, 3:119v.

71. DF Sharp MSS S5, fols. 9–10 (quoted); LPM, fols. 70, 73, 120, 125–27; HYNM, 1:197–200. Cf. UPM, fol. 87.

72. LurMM, fols. 6, 20, 37, 41–42; LisMM, entries for 27 March 1681, 2 March 1693, 28 March 1695; DMM, 1:27–28, 181–82, 187; 3:70v–71r, 177v–179r; HYNM, 1:75; LPM, fols. 105, 287–88.

73. LRB, no. 1, fol. 19 (quoted); HYNM, 1:29, 31; 2:232–33, 267–70; LurMM, fols. 26–27; LisMM, entry for 16 October 1693; DMM, 2:247, 249; 3:181v–182v, 183v–184r; LPM, fol. 259; UPM, fols. 84, 102.

74. MMM, fols. 38v–41v.

75. HYNM, 1:27–28, 32–34; 2:94 (quoted).

76. See e.g. LurMM, fols. 9, 15, 45–46; MMM, fols. 16v, 20v, 22v, 24r, 28v, 46v, 50v; UPM, fols. 66, 99–100, 103; LisMM, entries for 11 February 1685, 19 January 1693, 21 September 1699.

77. E.g. UPM, fols. 63, 95.

78. DMM, 3:151v–152v, 154v–155r, 156v–157v. For other cases see LPM, fols. 38–39, 42, 60, 66; HYNM, 1:52, 58, 62; LurMM, fols. 3, 5, 26, 36–38, 43; UPM, fols. 39, 49, 94, 96, 99, 108–11, 125, 147, 149, 151, 159, 161; LisMM, entries for 28 February 1683, April 1690, 5 February 1691, 11 June 1691, 7 January 1692, 19 May 1692, 15 September 1692, 15 June 1698, 18 May 1699.

79. UPM, fols. 46–47 (quoted), 49; LisMM, entries for 18 May 1682, 21 June 1682.

80. DF Sharp MSS S4, fols. 101–4. See also HYNM, 1:59–60, 95–96.

81. HYNM, 1:32 (quoted), 43, 100 (quoted); MMM, fol. 21v (quoted).

82. Cf. UPM, fols. 82–84, 86–87.

83. DF Sharp MSS S4, fol. 17; LPM, fols. 47–48 (quoted), 188; HYNM, 2:311–12 (quoted).

84. DMM, 3:23, 132v, 133v, 165v–166r, 167v, 168v–169r, 192v–193r.

85. Burnyeat, *Truth*, p. 82 (quoted); HYNM, 1:12–13 (quoted). Cf. DF MSS 9D MM VIII B2 (Minutes of the Women's Six-Weeks Meeting, Cork, 1680–1696), *passim*. The standard account of Quaker marriage practices is Vann, *Social Development*, pp. 181–88.

86. HYNM, 1:80 (quoted); UPM, fols. 26, 46; LisMM, entry for 21 February 1678; DMM, 1:20; LPM, fol. 64; Lloyd, *Quaker Social History*, p. 60.

87. LPM, fol. 288 (quoted); HYNM, 2:38; DMM, 3:78v, 85v.

88. HYNM, 2:82; LisMM, entry for 2 June 1696.

89. UPM, fol. 157; LPM, fols. 296, 567, 571.

90. HYNM, 1:63–67, 72; DF Sharp MSS S1, fols. 83–84; S5, fol. 34; UPM, fols. 49, 52; LPM, fols. 163, 270; DMM, 2:97–101; 3:116v–117v, 220v, 249v; LurMM, fols. 50, 54. Cf. Lloyd, *Quaker Social History*, pp. 57–58.

91. UPM, fols. 54, 57, 65, 77, 83–84, 90, 92, 133; LPM, fols. 13, 15; MMM, fol. 8v; LurMM, fols. 31, 51.

92. UPM, fols. 42, 143; DMM, 1:153–54; 3:95v; HYNM, 1:22–23; LPM, fols. 269, 277; MMM, fol. 50v; LisMM, entries for 3 June 1697, 26 December 1700.

93. LRB, no. 1, fol. 18 (quoted); LPM, fols. 24, 322; LurMM, fol. 38; DMM, 3:116v–117v; HYNM, 2:207 (quoted); Vann, *Social Development*, pp. 187–88.

94. HYNM, 2:82 (quoted), 97 (quoted).

95. Richard T. Vann and David Eversley, *Friends in Life and Death: The British and Irish Quakers in the Demographic Transition, 1650–1900* (Cambridge: Cambridge University Press, 1992), pp. 94, 96–97, 105; LPM, fol. 482.

96. LRB, no. 1, fol. 30; LPM, fols. 426, 581; NWM, fols. 108–9; HYNM, 2:180. Cf. Lloyd, *Quaker Social History*, pp. 58–59.

97. UPM, fols. 26, 66, 72, 110; LPM, fol. 44.

98. LurMM, fols. 33–34 (quoted); DF Sharp MSS S4, fols. 9–10; LPM, fols. 41, 69, 72; MMM, fols. 12v, 14v–15v, 18r–v; LisMM, entries for 6 December 1682, 22 June 1692; UPM, fols. 135, 137.

99. DMM, 3:213r–214v (quoted), 249v; UPM, fol. 99; MMM, fol. 8v.

100. LPM, fol. 229; DMM, 2:203–4; DF Sharp MSS S6, fol. 27r.

101. UPM, fols. 49, 62, 67–68, 81, 107, 166; LPM, fols. 41, 44–45, 231, 261; DMM, 1:245–46; MMM, fols. 26v, 35v, 50v.

102. Vann and Eversley, *Friends*, p. 51. Cf. *Minute Book of the Men's Meeting of the Society of Friends in Bristol 1667–1686*, ed. Russell Mortimer (Bristol: Bristol Record Society, 1971), pp. 31–32, 99–100, 119, 154, 213; LurMM, fols. 55–56; R. S. Mortimer, "Early Irish Friends in the Records of Bristol Meeting," *JFHS* 48 (Autumn 1956): 75–76.

103. LPM, fols. 28 (quoted), 44; LisMM, entries for 30 June 1686, 11 August 1686.

104. LPM, fol. 55; cf. fol. 399.

105. HYNM, 1:64–65; LPM, fols. 4, 11–12, 270; LRB, no. 1, fols. 17–18; LurMM, fols. 5, 41, 44, 49–53, 56; MMM, fol. 6v; UPM, fols. 44–45; *Bristol Minute Book*, p. 167; DMM, 2:101; 3:228v; LisMM, entries for 17 February 1692, 17 August 1693, 19 July 1694, 29 August 1694, 22 November 1694, 20 March 1701.

106. LPM, fols. 105, 287–88; HYNM, 1:75; 2:38.

107. Olive C. Goodbody, "Seventeenth-Century Quaker Marriages in Ireland," *JFHS* 50 (1964): 248–49.

108. HYNM, 1:107; LPM, fols. 202–3, 270, 283; MMM, fol. 53v.

109. Vann, *Social Development*, pp. 167–68; LPM, fols. 182, 283, 465, 470–71, 482 (quoted); HYNM, 2:33; NWM, fols. 54, 99; LurMM, fols. 14, 49; DMM, 3:68v (quoted).

110. LPM, fols. 279–80; DMM, 3:263v; HYNM, 2:277–78. Cf. LisMM, entry for 11 January 1697.

111. LF Swarthmore MSS 5 / 115, fol. 15 (quoted); LPM, fols. 372, 486 (quoted); HYNM, 2:314.

112. Vann and Eversley, *Friends*, pp. 53, 134, 158–61, 240, 243, 246, 248–49.

113. HYNM, 2:97.

114. HYNM, 1:23–24 (quoted), 89, 91; LPM, fols. 153, 156–58, 264; DMM, 2:113–14; UPM, fol. 69; MMM, fols. 40v, 46v; LisMM, entry for 19 April 1694.

115. HYNM, 1:104; 2:11, 57, 277–78; LPM, fol. 321.

116. HYNM, 1:31–32, 54; LPM, fols. 53–54, 75, 271. The Lisburn meeting raised money in 1700 to hire a schoolmaster. LisMM, entry for 22 August 1700.

117. DMM, 1:83, 97–98, 179; 2:21, 23, 164, 166.

118. DMM, 2:233–34, 265; 3:40v, 48v, 59v, 62r–v, 95v–96v, 107v, 109v–110r, 119v, 122v, 127v–128r, 139v, 142v–143r, 150v.

119. DMM, 3:147v, 154v, 155v–156r, 157v, 170v, 172v, 174v, 187r, 226v, 242v, 246v–247r. A Quaker school was in operation in Cork by 1702. Kilroy, p. 106. The demand for primers provides some indication of the extent of Quaker education at the lower level. The national meeting ordered 2,000 copies in 1672 and 1,000 in 1695. HYNM, 1:7; 2:59.

120. HYNM, 1:64, 69, 71–72; LPM, fol. 95. Cf. Lloyd, *Quaker Social History*, pp. 169–70.

121. LPM, fols. 92, 94, 96; DMM, 1:89, 93, 95–96; HYNM, 1:69; *Calamy Revised*, s.v. Thomas Lye.

122. HYNM, 1:104.

123. Richard L. Greaves, *The Puritan Revolution and Educational Thought: Background for Reform* (New Brunswick, N.J.: Rutgers University Press, 1969), *passim*.

124. DMM, 3:263v (quoted); LPM, fol. 478 (quoted), 482 (quoted); HYNM, 2:278–80.

125. HYNM, 1:63–64, 78. Cf. Lloyd, *Quaker Social History*, pp. 170–72.

126. E.g. LPM, fols. 33, 54, 56; DMM, 3:91v–92r, 145v–146r, 211v; MMM, fol. 68v.

127. LisMM, entry for 13 June 1688; LPM, fols. 54, 56; UPM, fols. 104, 121, 163; DMM, 1:199–201, 217; 2:253; 3:85v–86r, 91v–92r, 141v–142v, 144v, 158v–159r; LurMM, fol. 45; MMM, fol. 18v.

128. HYNM, 1:52, 73, 75, 89, 93.

129. UPM, fols. 22, 43–44, 53, 74, 83, 91–92, 129.

130. LPM, fols. 33–38 *passim*, 45–46, 49, 51, 65, 69, 97, 218, 239.

131. MMM, fols. 2r, 3r, 9r, 18v, 19v, 22v, 29r, 37v, 45v, 48v, 49v, 66r–v, 68r, 70r–v.

132. LisMM, entries for 31 October 1689; 19 August 1693; DMM, 2:261–62. For other examples of such specificity see DMM, 1:243, 243A–244A; 2:259; 3:5, 13, 49v–50r, 99v, 110v–111r, 115v–116r, 117v, 122v, 218v, 222v, 234v–235r; LurMM, fols. 11, 17, 26–27, 31, 37, 42–43, 46, 51; LisMM, entries for 29 May 1690, 26 March 1691, 26 November 1691, 22 June 1692, 15 March 1694, 3 June 1697, 18 November 1697.

133. DMM, 1:239–40 (quoted); 2:97–98; 3:125v, 127v–128r (quoted), 138v; HYNM, 1:87–88 (quoted); LurMM, fol. 26 (quoted); Lloyd, *Quaker Social History*,

p. 42; Helen E. Hatton, *The Largest Amount of Good: Quaker Relief in Ireland 1654–1921* (Kingston and Montreal: McGill-Queen's University Press, 1993), pp. 5, 28; Vann, *Social Development*, pp. 144–48.

134. *CMHS*, 8:56, note; HYNM, 1:45. When Irish Friends learned in 1699 that Scottish Quakers suffered because of a dearth of grain, they offered assistance. HYNM, 2:214.

135. HYNM, 1:86, 90–91; LPM, fols. 147, 149–50, 159, 161; UPM, fols. 63, 69–70.

136. HYNM, 1:63, 69, 90, 92, 94–95, 98; LYM, 1:88; LPM, fols. 91–92, 164, 169; DMM, 1:81; 2:52, 54; MMM, fols. 7v–8r; UPM, fols. 74–75, 77. See Kenneth L. Carroll, "Quaker Slaves in Algeria, 1679–88," *JFHS* 54 (1982): 301–11. For the English background see Lloyd, *Quaker Social History*, pp. 38–40.

137. E.g. HYNM, 1:92; 2:19, 39, 95; UPM, fols. 74, 141; MMM, fol. 30v.

138. UPM, fol. 106; DF Sharp MSS S7, fol. 14r–v; LPM, fol. 223; HYNM, 2:7–9.

139. DF Sharp MSS S7, fols. 32v–33r; LPM, fols. 237, 245, 248–49, 257, 260; HYNM, 2:11–12, 19–20, 23, 30; UPM, fol. 141.

140. LPM, fol. 408; William Braithwaite, *The Second Period of Quakerism*, 2nd ed., rev. Henry J. Cadbury (York: William Sessions, 1979), p. 628.

141. HYNM, 1:7, 14–15, 16 (quoted), 51; 2:182; cf. 1:30, 33, 62, 80.

142. *Letters, &c., of Early Friends; Illustrative of the History of the Society*, ed. A. R. Barclay (London: Harvey and Darton, 1841), pp. 346–53; *The Short Journal and Itinerary Journals of George Fox*, ed. Norman Penney (Cambridge: Cambridge University Press, 1925), p. 296, note; HYNM, 1:69. Claypoole was Oliver Cromwell's son-in-law.

143. E.g. LurMM, fols. 10, 17, 22, 31; MMM, fol. 72v; UPM, fols. 107, 151; LPM, fols. 224, 349; LF Swarthmore MSS 5 / 115, fol. 11; HYNM, 2:57.

144. Abraham Fuller and Thomas Holme, *A Compendious View of Some Extraordinary Sufferings of the People Call'd Quakers* (Dublin, 1731), p. 135.

145. HYNM, 2:309; Fuller and Holme, *Compendious View*, p. 131.

146. L. M. Cullen, *An Economic History of Ireland Since 1660* (London: B. T. Batsford, 1972), pp. 20, 44–45.

147. Ibid., pp. 20, 25, 32–33, 40–44.

148. Five of the nine cases do not stipulate a value for confiscated lambs. From other sources I have assigned a value of 1s. 6d. to one lamb.

149. The English figures for this period were also markedly incomplete. Craig W. Horle, *The Quakers and the English Legal System 1660–1688* (Philadelphia: University of Pennsylvania Press, 1988), pp. 281–84. The figures in Thomas Holme and Abraham Fuller, *A Brief Relation of Some Part of the Sufferings of the True Christians, the People of God (in Scorn Called Quakers) in Ireland* (1672), differ only slightly from those in the Great Book of Sufferings.

150. See e.g. MMM, fols. 56r, 57r, 64r; HYNM, 1:19; Holme and Fuller, *Brief Relation*, pp. 47–49; Besse, *Collection*, 2:472–73; GBS, vol. 2, Leinster Province, co. Wexford, 1662; Ulster Province, co. Armagh, 1670; Leinster Province, Queen's co., 1669; Munster Province, Waterford, 1666; Munster Province, Cork, 1661, 1667; Ulster Province, co. Cavan, 1670.

151. Fuller and Holme, *Compendious View*, pp. 130–31.

152. HYNM, 2:13.

153. PRONI MS D / 2224 / 1; HYNM, 2:5. Leinster losses stood at more than £900 in May 1689. HYNM, 2:1.

154. PRONI MS D / 2224 / 5; cf. D / 2224 / 2, 3.

155. HYNM, 2:2 (quoted), 4–5, 10–11; LPM, fols. 211, 213; UPM, fols. 102, 107; LurMM, fol. 41; LisMM, entry for 27 June 1689.

156. GBS, vol. 2, Ulster Province, co. Cavan, 1660; Munster Province, Waterford, 1660; Leinster Province, co. Kildare, 1670 (quoted); Munster Province, Limerick, 1663; Munster Province, Cork, 1670.

157. GBS, vol. 2, Ulster Province, co. Cavan, 1660.

158. William Stockdale, *The Great Cry of Oppression* (1683), sig. B4r.

159. Bodl. Carte MSS 221, fol. 215r (quoted); LF Swarthmore MSS 5 / 94 (quoted).

160. HYNM, 1:10–12, 16–20; DF Sharp MSS S1, fols. 22–25; S9, fol. 23r–v (quoted).

161. See e.g. HYNM, 1:14–15, 24–25, 30, 88, 100; 2:1–2, 5, 22, 24; DMM, 2:189; 3:37v; LPM, fol. 215; DF Sharp MSS S1, fols. 22–25; S8, fols. 14r–15r.

162. HYNM, 1:24, 27; *Letters*, ed. Barclay, pp. 195–96.

163. LPM, fol. 250; UPM, fols. 133, 153; HYNM, 2:124, 126, 128, 259–60.

164. Holme and Fuller, *Brief Relation*, p. 75.

165. LYM, 1:201; Vann, *Social Development*, p. 141.

166. DMM, 3:32v–33r; HYNM, 2:25; LPM, fol. 254; Braithwaite, *Second Period*, pp. 180–83.

167. DMM, 3:116v–117r; Braithwaite, *Second Period*, pp. 183–87; HYNM, 2:81, 96, 103–5 (quoted).

168. LPM, fols. 380–81, 395 (quoted); HYNM, 2:146, 202, 276; DMM, 3:179v–180r.

169. HYNM, 2:146, 166, 434–36 (quoted); LPM, fols. 404, 408.

170. LPM, fol. 419; HYNM, 2:200, 202; Fuller and Holme, *Compendious View*, p. 131. The controversy continued until 1722. See Braithwaite, *Second Period*, pp. 188–204.

171. HYNM, 1:3, 7, 9.

172. HYNM, 1:7; 2:14, 125; DF Sharp MSS S6, fols. 18r–21r, 23r–v; LPM, fols. 285, 287 (quoted); UPM, fol. 81; Horle, *Quakers*, p. 172.

173. HYNM, 1:57, 71–72, 74–75; LPM, fol. 105 (quoted).

174. HYNM, 1:74–75, 76 (quoted), 79–80; LPM, fols. 108, 119, 123–24, 127 (quoted), 155. The half-yearly meeting also ordered that a lawyer be consulted in the similar case of Thomas Calvert in 1687. HYNM, 1:102–4.

175. HYNM, 1:8, 14; 2:259, 298–99; Horle, *Quakers*, pp. 187–88, 192–95.

176. HYNM, 1:85–86.

177. HYNM, 1:81 (quoted); 2:52–53; LPM, fols. 112, 118, 132. See also HYNM, 1:87; LPM, fol. 296.

178. HYNM, 1:23, 27, 34–35, 43, 81, 83, 85, 87, 92; 2:37–38, 81 (quoted), 97; LPM, fols. 24, 42–43, 60, 178; LisMM, entry for 31 December 1684. Cf. LPM, fol. 307.

179. For deans see LPM, fols. 333, 371; for chancellors see HYNM, 1:9, 23, 27, 29.

180. LPM, fols. 124, 150, 176, 276, 336, 573 (quoted); MMM, fols. 15v, 50v, 66v, 67v, 69v, 70v, 73v; UPM, fols. 57–58, 60, 63–64, 80; LurMM, fols. 31–32; HYNM, 1:102; LisMM, entries for 15 July 1697, 26 August 1697, 28 July 1698, 7 April 1699, 3 July 1700.

181. DMM, 2:17–20, 243–44 (quoted); 3:7, 66v–67r, 89v–90r, 114v–115r, 141v–142r, 174v–175r, 262v–263r. Cf. CH MSS HA 14499.

182. LRB, no. 1, fols. 28–29; HYNM, 2:34.

183. Holme and Fuller, *Brief Relation*, pp. 41–44 (quoted at p. 43).

184. LF Swarthmore MSS 6/8 (quoted).

185. John Burnyeat and John Watson, *The Holy Truth and Its Professors Defended* ([Dublin], 1688), pp. 7, 11, 22 *et passim*. See also Kilroy, pp. 206–8. In 1693 Sharp wrote a retort to two sermons preached by a cleric at Wicklow, and he also disputed with a Catholic. DMM, 3:66v–67r; DF Sharp MSS S1, fols. 116–29. For the debate between Penn and Wetenhall in 1698–99 see Kilroy, pp. 208–11.

186. HYNM, 1:83.

187. LF Swarthmore MSS 5/32; HYNM, 1:15, 20–22; Kilroy, pp. 87–89, 208.

188. John Burnyeat and Amos Strettell, *The Innocency of the Christian Quakers Manifested, ad. cal.* Burnyeat, *Truth*, pp. 187–93, 201–2. Cf. Kilroy, pp. 151–57. Barry finally published his critique of the Quakers in 1715 under the title *The Doctrine of Particular Election Asserted and Approved*.

189. UPM, fol. 127.

APPENDIX

1. TKS, fol. 168.

2. The following session books also survive; the dates indicate when entries commence: Antrim (1674), Connor (1693), Larne and Kilwanghter (1699), Drumlanrig (1699), and Aghadowey (1702). Cf. John M. Barkley, *The Eldership in Irish Presbyterianism* ([Belfast]: By the Author, 1963), p. 22.

3. MLM, 2:59.

4. *Synod*, pp. 17–19, 24, 30, 38, 42, 47, 55.

5. See Olive C. Goodbody, *Guide to Irish Quaker Records 1654–1860* (Dublin: Stationery Office for the Irish Manuscripts Commission, 1967).

6. HYNM, 2:13, 19; DMM, 1:15; LPM, fol. 33.

7. LPM, fols. 92, 267 (quoted), 382 (quoted); HYNM, 1:1.

Manuscripts

Armagh Public Library: MSS G.II.22–24 (correspondence of Bishop Anthony Dopping, 1680–99, 3 vols.).

Bodleian Library: Carte MSS, 30, 31, 32, 33, 34, 35, 36, 37, 38, 39, 45, 46, 47, 49, 66, 68, 70, 79, 144, 219, 221; Clarendon MSS 74, 79, 80; Rawlinson MSS A.13, A.255, D.830, D.1347; Tanner MSS 30, 36, 48.

British Library: Add. MSS 4,763; 15,892–15,894 (Hyde Papers); 23,125 (Lauderdale Correspondence); 23,131 (Lauderdale Correspondence); 23,136 (Lauderdale Correspondence); 23,138 (Lauderdale Correspondence); 25,124; 28,085; 32,095; 37,206–37,208 (Orrery-Ormond Correspondence, 1660–68); 37,823 (Nicholas Papers: Instructions to Irish Officials, 1661–62); 41,803 (Middleton Papers); 45,850; 46,938; Althorp (Halifax) MSS H2; Egerton MSS 2542; Harleian MSS 4631; Lansdowne MSS 821–23 (correspondence to Henry Cromwell), 1152 (examinations of Monmouth rebels); Stowe MSS 200, 201, 204, 205, 207, 208, 210, 211, 212, 213, 214, 216, 217 (Essex Papers).

Dr. Williams's Library: Baxter Manuscripts; Roger Morrice, "Entr'ing Book, Being an Historical Register of Occurrences from April, Anno 1677 to April 1691," 3 vols.

Dublin Municipal Library, Pearse Street: Gilbert MSS 27; 109 (Granard MSS: Mountjoy's "Narrative"); 189 (John Dunton's "Tour of Ireland").

Edinburgh University Library: MSS La.II.27 (papers concerning Donald Cargill *et al.*); La.III.344, 1, 2 (documents concerning Cameronians); La.III.350 (Covenanter documents); La.III.354 (letters to Lauderdale, 1661–80).

Gamble Library, Union Theological College: Minutes of the Burt Kirk Session, 1676–1719; Robert Chambers, "An Explanation of the Shorter Catechism."

Henry E. Huntington Library: MSS HA 13901, 13915, 13943, 13944, 13945, 13946, 13954, 13975, 13994, 13995, 14009, 14014, 14017, 14019, 14127, 14138, 14139, 14152, 14388, 14393, 14394, 14396, 14397, 14398, 14399, 14400, 14411, 14420, 14448, 14452, 14471, 14499, 14514, 14515, 14517, 14518, 14529, 14549, 14550, 14739, 14964, 15028, 15033, 15034, 15037, 15053, 15096, 15179, 15181, 15183,

15184, 15185, 15186, 15187, 15379, 15380, 15383, 15492, 15556, 15570, 15592, 15690, 15963, 15672, 15673, 15768, 15936, 15992, 15993, 15994, 15995, 15996, 15997, 15998, 15999, 16001, 16003, 16004, 16008, 16011, 16012, 16014, 16015, 16016, 16017, 16038 (Hastings Manuscripts).

Historical Library of the Society of Friends in Ireland: Minutes of the Dublin Men's Meeting, 1677–84, 1684–91, 1691–1701, 1701–10; Minutes of the Half-Yearly Meeting, 1671–88, 1689–1706; Minutes of the Leinster Province Meeting, 1670–1706; Minutes of the Moate Men's Meeting, 1680–1731; Minutes of the Women's Six Weeks Meeting, Cork, 1680–96; Records of the National Women's Meeting, 1676–1776; Sharp MSS.

Irish Baptist Historical Society: Cork Church Book (microfilm).

Library of the Society of Friends, London: Great Book of Sufferings, vol. 2; Minutes of the London Yearly Meeting; Portfolio 16; Swarthmore MSS, vols. 4, 5, 6.

Marsh's Library: MSS Z.3.1.4 (Bishop Anthony Dopping's Visitation of the Diocese of Meath, 1693).

National Archives of Ireland: MSS M2449, fols. 167–272 (Thomas Morrice, "Memoirs of the Most Remarkable Passages in the Life and Death of the Right Honourable Roger Earl of Orrery"); MSS 4/206/1 (Prerogative Will Book, 1664–84).

National Library of Ireland: MSS 32 (Orrery Correspondence); 94 (minutes of the Half-Yearly Meeting, Dublin); 2358 (Ormonde Manuscripts); 2488, 2491 (undated Ormonde manuscripts); 4908, 4909 (Clonmel Assize Records); 8643 (1), 8643 (2) (Lane Manuscripts).

National Library of Scotland: Wodrow MSS Folios XXVI, XXVII, XXVIII, XXXI, XXXIV, LIX; Octavo XII; Quarto XXVIII, XXIX; MSS 578; 597 (Lauderdale Papers); 2512 (Lauderdale Papers); 3473 (autobiography of Gabriel Semple); 3830 (Miscellaneous Papers); 5408 (Covenanter documents); 7025; 7033.

Nottingham University Library: MSS PwV95 (Portland Manuscripts).

Presbyterian Historical Society of Ireland: Minutes of the Carnmoney Kirk Session; Minutes of the Kirkdonald Kirk Session, 1678–1713; Sermons of John McKenzie, 1681.

Public Record Office, London: SP8/2; SP44 (entry books); SP29 (state papers, Charles II); SP63 (state papers, Ireland).

Public Record Office of Northern Ireland: MSS CR4/12B/1 (Minutes of the Templepatrick Kirk Session, vol. 1); D/1759/1A/1, 2 (Minutes of the Antrim Meeting, trans. W. T. Latimer; the Gamble Library has a copy); D/1759/1E/1, 2 (Minutes of the Lagan Meeting, trans. David Stewart); D1759/2A/5 (notes abstracted by St. John D. Seymour from documents in the Public Record Office, Dublin, since destroyed); D1759/2A/9 (list of royal presentations to benefices, 1535–1665); D2224/1–6 (documents relating to the suffering of Quaker families in Ulster, 1689–91); DIO 4/4/4 (visitations of the dioceses of Killala and Achonry, Clogher, Killaloe, Ossory, Limerick, Cloyne, Cork, Ross, and Down, 1693); DIO 4/5/3 (miscellaneous documents pertaining to the Church of Ireland); DIO 4/13/2 (letters to Bishop Anthony Dopping and his son Samuel, 1685–96); LGM 5/1 (Lurgan Record Book); MIC 16/1A (Minutes of the Ulster Province Meeting); Q/5/LBM 1/1–3 (Minutes of the

Lisburn Monthly Meeting, 1675–1735); Q/5/LBM 1/1–3 (Minutes of the Lisburn Monthly Meeting); LGM 1/1 (Minutes of the Lurgan Men's Meeting, 1675–1710).

Representative Church Body Library: MSS D.14 (Dr. Edward Worth's survey, diocese of Killaloe, 1661); 31/5 (visitation records, diocese of Connor, 1693); 51/1 (copy of account book of Henry Jones, bishop of Meath, 1661–81).

Scottish Record Office: MSS GD 188/25/1/1–12 (Guthry of Guthry Manuscripts).

Trinity College, Dublin: MSS 151 (sermons of W. Lamb and H. Sankey); 616 (Journal of the House of Lords, 1661–66); 808; 844; 1038 (proceedings of the Upper House of Convocation, 1661–66); 1178 (letters to Sir Robert Southwell); 1995–2008 (King Correspondence); 2203 (proclamation, 2 August 1689).

Index

The religious affiliation of nonconformists is indicated by the following abbreviations: P = Presbyterian; C = Congregationalist (Independent); B = Baptist; Q = Quaker. Clerical conformists are designated CC; prelatical appointments are generally indicated only when relevant to dicussions in the text. In this index an "f" after a number indicates a separate reference on the next page, and an "ff" indicates separate references on the next two pages. *Passim* is used for a cluster of references in close but not consecutive sequence.

Library of Congress Cataloging-in-Publication Data

Greaves, Richard L.

   God's other children: Protestant nonconformists and
the emergence of denominational churches in Ireland,
1660–1700 / Richard L. Greaves.

      p. cm.

   Includes bibliographical references and index.

   ISBN 0-8047-2821-6 (cloth : alk. paper)

   1. Dissenters, Religious—Ireland—History—17th
century.   2. Presbyterian Church—Ireland—History—
17th century.   3. Ireland—Church history—17th
century.   4. Church and state—Ireland.   [1. Society of
Friends—Ireland—History—17th century.]   I. Title.

BX5203.2G74 1997

280.4'0941509032—dc21   96-50486

                                                              CIP

∞   This book is printed on acid-free, recycled paper.

Original printing 1997

Last figure below indicates year of this printing:
06   05   04   03   02   01   00   99   98   97